Mastering

British Politics

Fourth edition

F.N. Forman
and
N.D.J. Baldwin

First edition 1985 reprinted four times
Second edition 1991 reprinted four times
Third edition 1996
Fourth edition 1999

Published by
MACMILLAN PRESS LTD
Houndmills, Basingstoke, Hampshire RG21 6XS
and London
Companies and representatives
throughout the world

ISBN 0–333–76548–6

A catalogue record for this book is available
from the British Library.

10   9   8   7   6   5   4   3   2   1
08   07   06   05   04   03   02   01   00   99

Printed in Great Britain by
Creative Print & Design (Wales), Ebbw Vale

To the memory of
J.F.R.F. and D.A.M.B.

Contents

List of Figures

Preface

This book is a general introduction to the British system of Government and politics. It is an attempt to convey clear information about every significant aspect of the subject and to facilitate an understanding of the British political system and contemporary British politics.

Since the third edition of this book was published in 1996, a great deal of consequence has happened in British politics. Most noticeably, the Conservative Party finally met its Waterloo and was swept out of office at the 1997 General Election by a bored and contemptuous electorate. It was replaced by a new Labour Government led by Tony Blair with the largest Parliamentary majority ever achieved in the history of the Labour Party. Combined with the psychological effects of the looming millennium, this seems to have had a substantial impact upon the public mood and possibly on British political culture, long considered to be one of the most stable and admirable aspects of British society.

The new public mood appears more than ready to give Tony Blair and his colleagues a considerable amount of latitude within which to take forward their project of 'modernisation' – a long word which can evidently be stretched to encompass everything from turning the Labour Party into a highly professional election winning machine with the minimum of ideological baggage to reforming Britain's age-old Parliamentary institutions and, in due course perhaps, even its electoral system. At the same time the Nationalist parties in Scotland, Wales and Northern Ireland have all benefited from the willingness of 'New Labour' to make some timely and historic concessions to the Nationalist pressures emanating from all parts of the Celtic fringe; and the Liberal Democrats enjoyed New Labour's willingness to explore, albeit rather tentatively, various ways of narrowing the gap between the two parties of the centre-Left in Britain – a gap which became a chasm in the early years of this century when labour gradually replaced the fragmented and increasingly marginalised Liberals as the principal opponent of the Tories.

Another large theme which is evident in British politics at the turn of the century is the accelerating erosion of the nation state and all its works; such that its political institutions are challenged from above and below, its jurisdiction is challenged from within and without, and its traditional competences are challenged by new power centres principally to be found in the global media and financial markets. Both the process of political competition and the substance of political culture are inevitably affected by these formidable forces which owe their allegiance to no particular territory, jurisdiction or state. The result is that it is becoming harder to speak of 'British politics' as an authentic and recognisably distinct area of study or social experience; and people living in these islands, as elsewhere, are increasingly seeing themselves as individuals rooted essentially in their immediate localities but identifying also with the wider communities of Europe and the world.

For this edition of the book the practical consequences are that we have felt it necessary to emphasise: the considerable changes in Britain's evolving constitution (Chapter 2); the sea-change in voting behaviour which was reflected in the result of the 1997 General Election (Chapter 4); the transformation of all the institutions of Parliament to a greater or lesser extent (Chapters 9–11); the shrinking role and capacities of the nation state (Chapter 15); the changing structures of sub-national government (Chapter 16); and the softer, fuzzier nature of governance in Blairite Britain. Of course, not everything has changed in a few years. Britain and its political system will be as recognisable to students and practitioners of politics in the early years of the twenty-first century as they are at the tail end of the twentieth century. Nevertheless we hope it will be apparent to those who read this book, whether they are already familiar with the subject or come new to it, that British politics are an endlessly fascinating subject which repays close study by experts and laymen alike.

As in previous editions, many people have helped in the preparation and development of the text. We would particularly like to thank Sheila Tofts and Amanda Mabbitt for their typing skills (and endless patience), Suzannah Tipple and her colleagues at Macmillan for their encouragement and support, and Sally Vince for her editorial assistance. We must record our gratitude to those who have over the years helped with the content through general discussion or through reading and commenting upon various draft chapters: Charles Anson, Mary Baber, Sir Robin Butler, Lord Lawson, Lord Merlyn-Rees, Richard Mottram, Sir Patrick Nairne, Professor Lord Norton of Louth, Chris Pond, Professor Rod Rhodes, Peter Riddell, Michael Welsh and David Willetts. Our thanks are also due to all those individuals – in Government Departments, Agencies, public bodies and other groups – who provided us with information.

Any insights achieved in this edition – and indeed in earlier editions – owe a great deal to these individuals. Any errors of fact or opinion are, of course, entirely our responsibility.

London and Wroxton
February 1999

F.N. Forman
N.D.J. Baldwin

Acknowledgements

The authors and publishers wish to thank the following for permission to use copyright material: Philip Allan Publishers Ltd for **Fig. 4.1** from article by J. Garland and M. Rowe, *Politics Review*, 7:1 (September 1997); Tim O'Donovan for data in **Fig. 9.1** from his letter to *The Times*, 2.1.98; Guardian News Service Ltd for data in **Fig. 3.2** from *The Guardian*. 18.11.97 Copyright © The Guardian; The Controller of Her Majesty's Stationery Office for crown copyright material in **Figs. 5.2, 13.2, 14.1, 14.3, 16.8, 16.9**, from the Civil Service Code, CM 4014 1998, CM4057 5th rpt Committee on Standards in Public Life, DETR data, and *Civil Service Yearbook*; MORI for data in **Fig. 4.3**; Vacher Dod Publishing Ltd for material in **Figs. 12.2, 14.4** from *Vacher's Parliamentary Companion*, 1998 Newspaper Publishers Association for data in **Fig. 7.1**.

Every effort has been made to trace the copyright-holders, but if any have been inadvertently overlooked the publishers will be pleased to make the necessary arrangement at the first opportunity.

Acknowledgement

PART 1

The Political and Electoral Context

1 British political culture

Any book on British politics has to begin with a chapter on British political culture, since this is the context within which British politics take place. The term 'political culture' is taken to mean the historical, cultural and attitudinal setting within which British political institutions have to function.[1] It is not easy to generalise about British political culture, but it is possible to identify some key characteristics which influence both the process and the outcome of politics in Britain.

1.1 Key characteristics

The key characteristics of British political culture can be stated quite simply, but they need to be qualified and refined if they are to be useful to students of British politics. It has often been said that politics in Britain are influenced by the notable continuity of Britain's national history, the unitary nature of the state, the underlying cohesion of the society, and the degree of political agreement on fundamental issues. Traditionally, there has been considerable moderation in the policies pursued by successive Governments of all parties and this has been matched by a considerable degree of public detachment from the process of politics, except, of course, at election times and on other occasions when political crises or scandals heighten media and public interest.

General statements of this kind have often been made and sometimes in a rather complacent tone. Yet it would be unwise to accept them at face value and it would be well to examine the extent to which they now accord with the evidence available today.

Historical continuity

There has been notable continuity in Britain's national history and the country is one of the oldest nation states in Europe. Such continuity is symbolised by some of its national institutions, such as the Monarchy and the two Houses of Parliament, which date back at least to medieval times (see Chapters 9, 10 and 11 for further details).

Although there have also been some notable discontinuities in Britain's national history, such as the Civil War and the interregnum in the mid-seventeenth century, the country has not been invaded successfully against the popular will since 1066, and the only successful revolution since the Civil War was the political coup of 1688 when James II fled the throne and William and Mary were invited by Parliament from Holland to take his place. This continuity applies to a greater or lesser extent to all parts of the United Kingdom.

In the case of *Wales*, the Welsh have been living in the same kingdom as the English since the fourteenth-century English conquests. The link was later reinforced and personified by the victory of Henry Tudor (a Welshman) at the battle of Bosworth Field in 1485, and subsequently ratified by Act of Parliament in 1536 at the behest of his son Henry VIII.

In the case of *Scotland*, the constitutional bond between the Scots and the English was first established in 1603 when James VI of Scotland succeeded Elizabeth I of England and so became James I of England. The bond was later sealed by the Act of Union in 1707, although what was by then the Hanoverian succession (from Germany) to the throne of the United Kingdom was not secure until the defeat of the Young (Stuart) Pretender in 1745.

In the case of *Ireland*, the troubled relationship between the Irish and the English can be traced back at least to the Anglo-Norman invasion of Ireland in 1169–71. The Act of Union in 1800, which marked the unification of the two countries in one kingdom, was later ruptured by the 1916 Irish national uprising. This led to the partition of Ireland in 1921 and the creation of the six counties of Northern Ireland in 1922 as the last remaining part of the United Kingdom on the island of Ireland.

The result of this long and chequered history is that the British people now live in what is known officially as the United Kingdom of Great Britain and Northern Ireland. However, it will be more convenient in the rest of this book to use the colloquial term 'Britain' to describe the country as a whole. Figure 1.1 is a map of the British Isles showing the boundaries of England, Wales, Scotland and Northern Ireland; as well as the location of some of the principal cities.

Unitary state

One important consequence of Britain's national history is that the people now live in a unitary state. This means essentially that the laws passed by Parliament at Westminster apply normally to the entire country and that in nearly all important matters it is correct to speak of the country being governed from London. However, this observation has to be increasingly qualified to take account of Britain's membership of the European Union, the process of devolution to Scotland and Wales and the changes in the Government of Northern Ireland associated with the peace process, all of which have in practice diluted the doctrine of Parliamentary supremacy and the dominance of London. In addition, there is also a well-established structure of local government in Britain which can claim a degree of legitimacy, since local Councillors are directly elected by the people in their localities. Yet (as we shall see in Chapter 16) the powers and functions of local government are determined by Parliament at Westminster and were substantially reduced by successive Conservative Administrations in the period 1979–97.

Figure 1.1   Map of the British Isles

Unlike the situation in the United States or Germany, where there are codified constitutions which define the legal rights and duties of the various levels of government, in the United Kingdom it is Parliament which is legally and constitutionally supreme (except in those matters where European law now prevails) and its writ runs throughout the United Kingdom. Of course (as we shall see in Chapters 17 and 18), the law of the land in certain areas can be interpreted and sometimes modified by judicial decisions in the Courts and, increasingly, by the European Court of Justice as well. Yet in Britain it is still a basic principle that traditionally no institution has been considered on a par with Parliament and it is this which has given force to the idea that Britain is a Parliamentary democracy in a unitary state.

Cultural cohesion

For a long time there has been considerable cultural cohesion in Britain which has been reinforced by the fact that about four-fifths of the total population are English and about four-fifths live in urban or suburban areas. This means that in many respects the great majority of the British people live similar lives and hold a range of common attitudes based upon broadly common experience. They purchase goods manufactured for a mass market, they use common public services, they earn their living in a number of recognisably standard ways, they spend their leisure time in a range of common pursuits, and they share broadly similar aspirations for themselves and their families. Above all, they are subjected every day to the same influences of the mass media which (especially in the case of television) now do more than anything else to create a sense of shared national experience.

On the other hand, there are some significant cultural variations which derive from a wide range of economic, social, geographical and ethnic factors. For example, the traditional industrial structure in the midlands and the north of the country has been significantly different (until recent times) from the more modern service structure in the south and the east of the country, at any rate outside parts of London. Yet this pattern too has been changing as old industries have declined and sometimes disappeared altogether, while a new and predominantly service economy has grown up to a greater or lesser extent in all parts of the country under the spreading influence of new information technology.

Equally, while in the nation as a whole ethnic minorities make up no more than about 5.5 per cent of the entire population, there are some parts of the large cities – for example, London, Birmingham or Leicester – where people from ethnic minorities account for more than 20 per cent and sometimes as much as 35 per cent of the local population.[2] In recent times these demographic developments have led some from within the Moslem community, for example, to call for the establishment of legal and constitutional arrangements designed to give them special status and a real degree of cultural and religious autonomy within the United Kingdom.

In all parts of the country British society still divides on class lines, although many of the traditional class distinctions based upon the occupation of the male head of household have been rendered increasingly meaningless by changes in the labour market and in the balance of economic power and responsibilities within families.[3] From one point of view it seems that, as people in all classes become more similar in their ways of life and material aspirations, the tendency towards social uniformity could increase. Yet from another point of view this looks less likely, because of the widening disparities of income and wealth between the poorest and the richest sections of society.[4] Indeed, current social developments in Britain and elsewhere suggest that there is a growing gulf between the experience and prospects of the well-off and skilled majority who are in well-rewarded and relatively secure economic positions and the disadvantaged and relatively unskilled minority who are either employed in peripheral, part-time and low paid work or are not economically active at all, at any rate in the formal economy.

In future, much will depend on the extent to which common economic and social aspirations are fulfilled or thwarted by the distribution of the available opportunities between different individuals, different social groups and different parts of the country. It will also depend on the extent to which nationalist or racist impulses are stoked up or dampened down, especially for those living in outlying or ethnically distinct parts of the country.

With regard to the various sub-national identities, a small minority of the Welsh are Welsh speaking and attracted by the cause of *Plaid Cymru*, the Welsh Nationalist party, and their number could grow if the process of devolution enhances the sense of Welsh identity throughout the principality.

A somewhat larger minority of Scots identify with the cause of the *Scottish National Party* (SNP), which aspires to full Scottish independence within the European Union. Although in 1998 opinion poll support for the SNP stood at 44 per cent, opinion north of the border has traditionally seemed more disposed towards the idea of devolution to a Scottish Parliament. This was perhaps evident from the success of the referendum campaign on this issue in September 1997.[5]

In *Northern Ireland*, political circumstances are even more peculiar in that opinion is divided on religious and constitutional lines according to the contrasting attitudes of the Protestant/Unionist and Catholic/Nationalist communities towards the idea of eventual Irish reunification. The hard-line Protestant/Unionists wrap themselves in the Union Jack, but might prefer to have self-government for their part of Ireland free from Westminster control as they did from 1922 to 1972, when they governed themselves from Stormont Castle in Belfast. The hard-line Catholic/Nationalists, who support *Sinn Féin* (the political wing of the Irish Republican movement in the north), have been prepared to use both the bomb and the ballot in their struggle for reunification with the rest of Ireland. Since the end of 1993 the British and Irish Governments have been working together in a positive effort to advance what has been described as 'the peace process' in Northern Ireland. This initiative by the two Governments was originally prompted by exploratory talks between John Hume, leader of the Social Democratic and Labour Party, and Gerry Adams, leader of Sinn Féin. It was formalised in the Downing Street Declaration signed by John Major and Albert Reynolds on 15 December 1993. It was subsequently carried forward by ceasefires announced by both the Irish Republican Army (IRA) and the Unionist paramilitaries in August and September 1994. Although the IRA ceasefire was brought to an end with London's Canary Wharf bomb in 1996, it was reinstated in July 1997, and the whole 'peace process' culminated in the Belfast Agreement on Easter Friday 1998.[6]

Due allowance must, therefore, be made for all these nationalist and centrifugal forces in the United Kingdom. We should also take account of the growing cultural diversity in British society, which can result, for example, in the existence of primary school classes in such places as Tower Hamlets in London or Handsworth in Birmingham in which white, Anglo-Saxon pupils are in a tiny minority and English is not the first language for the vast majority of these children when they are at home.

Deference and its decline

Tradition speaks of the British as a particularly deferential people, inclined not merely to be law-abiding and with a tendency to defer to authority in general, but to accept – even prefer – to be governed by those 'born to rule'. Low levels of crime, the comparative absence of politically motivated violence, an (essentially) unarmed police force and the continued existence of – indeed respect for – the Monarchy were all said to be indications of this deference.

However, during and as a result of the 1960s British society itself changed, with significant consequences for this traditional deference. One particular example illustrates this: the appearance of the television programme *That Was The Week That Was* and the satirical magazine *Private Eye* in the early 1960s undermined ingrained habits of deference – in this particular regard, deference to politicians and to the so-called Establishment which ruled the country – with breathtaking speed. As has been pointed out: 'the sheer daring with which politicians were pilloried ... the venal, the corrupt and the simply pompous and self-serving were regularly exposed ... [meant that] politicians were no longer allowed to inhabit some lofty moral empyrean in which their judgments were not to be questioned by the yahoos over whom they ruled.'[7] It had a profound impact on British consciousness, which, in terms of the decline of deference, it has been impossible to reverse. Since that time the public perception of politics and the standing of politicians among the public have never been quite the same.

Party politics

Party is the overwhelmingly dominant factor in British politics. British Government is party government – government by and through political parties. Indeed, one cannot begin to understand British Government and politics without understanding the significance played by organised, centralised, disciplined political parties. More than this, the traditional view is that Britain in fact has a two-party system – originally the Whigs and the Tories; subsequently the Liberals and the Conservatives; from the early years of the twentieth century, essentially the Labour Party and the Conservative Party. Such a view may be based on a rather selective analysis of British political history – and a somewhat English-orientated perspective at that, but it has nonetheless underpinned much of our understanding of the British political system over the years.

A part of this – indeed, growing from it – was the belief that everyone could be described as being either 'on the Left' or 'on the Right'. The Left/Right dichotomy evolved into a linear approach to the political spectrum, namely one where it was possible to place everyone somewhere on a Left–Right line – a line that stretched from the extreme-Left through the hard-Left to the far-Left through the mainstream Left to the Left-of-centre into the centre-Left to the Right-of-centre to the centre-Right through the mainstream Right to the far-Right ending in the extreme-Right – and even this would not be a definitive listing. Such an approach was always an over-simplification; today it is extremely misleading. Contemporary research has redefined the British political spectrum into a two-dimensional matrix with a Centrist position in the middle, and with belief or rejection of economic freedom on the vertical axis and belief or rejection of personal freedom on the horizontal axis.[8] This is shown in Figure 1.2.

In such an approach, on the one hand a Conservative believes in 'market forces' as opposed to Government intervention as the best way to resolve economic matters, but also believes in Government intervention in personal matters – such as the criminalisation of drug-use, the regulation of consensual sex between adults and abortion. On the other hand, a Socialist believes the exact opposite, namely that Government intervention in the economy is better than leaving things to market forces and that there should be limited Government involvement in personal matters. An Authoritarian is distrustful of all forces in society except that of the Government and demands Government intervention in all matters, economic and personal, while a Libertarian favours a 'hands-off' or *laissez-faire* approach by Government; in essence

Figure 1.2 The British political spectrum

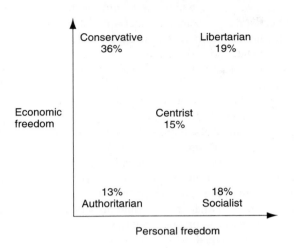

Note:
The percentage figures represent the cross-currents of political opinion based on replies to 21 questions received from 1700 individuals questioned by MORI during the 1997 General Election campaign. See note 8 at the end of the chapter.

no Government intervention in either economic or personal matters. This is the contextual matrix within which party politics needs to be viewed in contemporary Britain.

Political consensus

There is an underlying political consensus in Britain, but it needs to be carefully defined if we are not to get the wrong ideas about it. A clear distinction has to be drawn between consensus on matters of policy and consensus on matters of procedure. We shall therefore deal briefly with each in turn.

Consensus on matters of policy was most marked during the Second World War, when there was a strong national commitment to a united war effort both at home and abroad. In the spheres of economic and social policy this was reflected in the general support given to the goals of the 1942 Beveridge Report, which foreshadowed the principal elements in the postwar Welfare State and the 1944 Keynesian White Paper on Employment, which established the postwar objective of full employment. Such an approach was adhered to in broad terms by successive Governments, whether Labour or Conservative, for 25 years or so after the war. However, in the later 1960s this consensus began to be called into question during the period of the second Wilson Administration (1966–70) and it was all but abandoned in the early 1970s during the first two years (1970–72) of the Heath Administration.

From the late 1970s until the downfall of Margaret Thatcher in 1990, policy consensus was out of fashion and party politics were polarised, at any rate between the dominant elements in the two main parties. However, under the more pragmatic leadership of first John Major (1990–97) and then William Hague (1997–), and with the emergence of Tony Blair as the elected leader of the 'new' Labour Party in 1994, and the subsequent victory of New Labour at the polls in 1997, there have been some signs that British politics have assumed a more consensual pattern once again, one based upon those Thatcherite ideas which have come to be broadly accepted, namely a greater sense of economic realism, a respect for market forces, lower direct taxes, the diminished political role of the trade unions, the preference for home ownership, and the shrinking of the state industrial sector.

Some have sought to describe this new consensus as 'capitalism with a human face', as 'Thatcherism with a social conscience', or as 'Socialism harnessed to economic realism'. Others have spoken of a 'Third Way',[9] a course between the politics of the 'old Left' – state control, centralised planning and what critics would describe as enforced equality leading to the oppression of individualism and limits on individual freedoms – and the 'new Right' – *laissez-faire*, reliance on the markets and what critics would describe as rampant individualism leading to social indifference. It is also a way forward between the two traditional types of leftist approaches, namely between an idealogically pure approach (what critics would disparage as 'doctrinaire') and a pragmatic approach (what critics would disparage as 'unprincipled), in short an attempt to harness principle to practical politics, a way to take the traditional values of the Left – social justice, equality, solidarity, internationalism – and recast them for contemporary circumstances and conditions. It is an inclusive as opposed to an exclusive approach to politics, a way to adapt the nation state to the global realities of today.

As far as policies are concerned, this approach is reflected in a recognition of the implications of economic globalisation and the necessity for prudent financial policies. Consequently the role of government is to ensure that individuals and businesses are equipped to survive and compete in this global market. Part of this is an understanding that education and skills are the basis of modern employability and a recognition of the impact and role of modern technology. There is also an awareness of a need to reform welfare provision to encourage individuals off benefit and into work. In short, we have seen the concept emerging of the state as enabler and regulator – rather than the state as provider – and of the state as investor in human and social capital.

The Third Way has perhaps taken two of the twin – though often contradictory – principles of revolutionary change, namely liberty and equality, and sought to balance them with the third and least remembered, namely fraternity – or in contemporary language, community or civic spirit – and apply this to sub-national and supra-national levels of political activity as well as the national level.

Having said this, however, there are nonetheless areas of policy and policy issues which are actually or potentially very divisive not only between the parties but also within the parties. Issues such as European Economic and Monetary Union, indeed Britain's whole position in and relationship with the European Union, the future nature and scope of the welfare state, and constitutional reform all fall into such a category. On the subject of constitutional reform it is interesting to note that it has often been said that such reform should only be introduced if supported by a widespread and general consensus. However, a survey of constitutional change over the years – from the 1832 Reform Act through the 1911 Parliament Act and the 1972 European Communities Act to the 1993 ratification of the Maastricht Treaty – does not support such an argument. Indeed, it shows that far-reaching constitutional reform is usually only implemented in the face of considerable opposition, even hostility, from at least some elements in the political class of the time. For example, despite opposition from the Conservative Party the Labour Government elected in 1997 made progress in a variety of ways towards its objective of overhauling and modernising the British constitution, changes which moved the country towards a more federal – certainly a less unitary – more written, codified constitution. Indeed, it is this, perhaps, that will be seen as the basis of the 'Blair Revolution'; that the period at the end of the twentieth century and into the twenty-first century will probably be seen as a period of significant institutional change in Britain, a time of political empowerment for some of those previously excluded from real influence and an incremental 'revolution' in the political values and methods of governing the country.

By contrast, the 1960s in Britain were a period of social reform which was reflected in the following landmark developments:

- the considerable expansion of higher education in the wake of the Robbins Report (1963);
- the abolition of capital punishment (1965);
- reform of the laws on homosexuality (1967);
- the legalisation of abortion (1967);
- the wide availability of the contraceptive pill (late 1960s);
- the abolition of the system of theatrical censorship (1968);
- the noticeable relaxation of cinema censorship;
- a less deferential media (both print and electronic);
- reform of the divorce laws (1969);
- the lowering of the age of maturity from 21 to 18 (1969).

Put all this together and it is clear that British society changed considerably as a result of the 1960s. Nonetheless, it was change within the social sphere, change which neither directly challenged the economic consensus which had grown up since the 1945 Attlee Government, nor the political consensus which – certainly in the mainstream of the two main parties – saw no need for fundamental constitutional reform. Indeed, there are those who have argued that the social empowerment of the 1960s had no immediate political implications in Britain, unlike the upheavals which took place during the same period in France, West Germany and the United States.

As far as economics is concerned, it was the 1945–51 Labour Government of Clement Attlee which established the postwar consensus under which the country was governed for more than a quarter of a century, a consensus centred around a belief in activist, interventionist Government, a belief that it was the responsibility of Government to find solutions to problems whenever and wherever they arose. Although this consensus was either modified or extended by successive Conservative and Labour Governments, there was no substantial or sustained challenge to it until the three successive Administrations of Margaret Thatcher between 1979 and 1990. During this period the commitment to full employment was abandoned, the battle for 'sound money' was given priority, the role and responsibilities of the state were deliberately reduced and the powers of trade unions were curbed. In the process, public attitudes and perceptions changed, leading to a greater sense of economic realism, more awareness of and respect for market forces and greater acceptance that people should not look to Government for solutions to every problem. In short the economic empowerment created by the 'Thatcher Revolution' effectively demolished much of the postwar economic order and established a new 'common ground', one with which the then Government's political opponents were obliged to come to terms as a necessary precondition for their own return to power.

Following the election of the Labour Government led by Tony Blair in 1997, we have seen a third stage of change within Britain, namely institutional reform and political empowerment. Within 18 months of taking office – following referenda – power was being devolved to a Scottish Parliament, a Welsh Assembly and a London Mayor and Assembly, while a new Northern Ireland Assembly and a Council of the Isles came into being as part of the attempts to bring the Northern Ireland peace process to a successful conclusion. Proportional representation was introduced for elections to the Scottish Parliament, the Welsh Assembly and the European Parliament, while a commission under Lord Jenkins gave advice on proportional representation for Westminster elections. The European Convention on Human Rights was incorporated into UK domestic law; freedom of information legislation was being prepared; proposals for the modernisation of the procedures of the House of Commons were being considered and reform of the House of Lords was also in the pipeline. The Government signed the Council of Europe's 'Charter of Local Self-Government', designed to guarantee the freedom of local Councils from central Government interference, and was apparently intent on moving power selectively from Whitehall to the regions of England – a policy which may lead to the creation of elected regional Assemblies where there is local demand for it. Other matters – such as the decision to make the Bank of England responsible for setting interest rates, and the declaration that there were no constitutional objections to Britain joining the single European currency when the economic conditions were right (and after securing public approval for such a move in a referendum) – could be seen as part of the package also. In short, the Government unleashed some of the most sweeping constitutional changes since the Great Reform Act (1832), which serves to indicate that far-reaching reforms can be introduced without complete policy consensus covering all the practices.

Consensus on matters of procedure, on the other hand, seems to have survived intact in its traditional form for a much longer period. Ever since the successive extensions of the franchise in the nineteenth and early twentieth centuries (see Chapter 3), this kind of consensus has been signified by widespread agreement on the desirability of using Parliamentary channels for the implementation and ratification of political change. However, certain powerful pressure groups and minority sections of public opinion have occasionally challenged this view – for example, those who backed or took part in the campaigns for non-payment of the 'Poll Tax' in the late 1980s. It has included widespread acceptance of the view that General Election results should be regarded as decisive, provided, of course, the popular ballot produces for the victorious party a clear majority in the House of Commons. It has also included broad agreement on the undesirability of making extensive constitutional changes unless backed by overwhelming all-party support.[10] Nevertheless, this last assumption did not seem to inhibit the Thatcher Government's sustained assault on the alleged overspending and other shortcomings of local government, and has not deterred the Labour Government of Tony Blair from introducing wide-scale constitutional reform, including a Scottish Parliament in Edinburgh and a Welsh Assembly in Cardiff.

It should be noted that all such examples of procedural consensus and periodic departures from it need to be seen against the background of the recurrent constitutional controversies which arise in Britain from time to time, especially when national institutions feel threatened by their counterparts at sub-national and supra-national level. Since the mid-1970s there has been a long-running argument about the merits or otherwise of devolution to Scotland and Wales, reform of the House of Lords, the use of referenda in a Parliamentary constitution, the possible introduction of proportional representation in the name of achieving a 'fairer' electoral system, reform of the official secrecy law and the desirability of a Freedom of Information Act and the need for a Bill of Rights. Between 1992 and 1997 the Conservative Parliamentary Party was split, and the Conservative Government ultimately defeated, at least in part, by the bitter dispute over the extent of Britain's commitment to the process of European integration. For these and other reasons it is now harder than it used to be to argue that there is a secure procedural consensus in British politics.

1.2 Other significant features

There are a number of other significant features in British political culture which are worth mentioning at this stage. Some are more associated with the period from 1945 to 1979. Others arise from the growing diversity of British society in recent times, which has served to reduce its traditional cultural and political cohesion.

Moderation of Governments

It has been traditional to argue that a significant feature of British political culture is the moderation and restraint shown by all Governments.[11] This has been reflected in the fact that, whereas all modern British Governments with a working majority in the House of Commons have had almost unfettered powers of legislation and political decision, they have usually exercised such power in a rather moderate and restrained way. Of course, such an assertion always seems more credible to the supporters than the opponents of any Government. Nevertheless there are some compelling reasons why it has often been borne out in practice, notwithstanding the noticeably more ideological tone and actions of central Government in the 1970s and 1980s.

Such moderation should not be confused with what were identified as middle-of-the-road policies of the kind pursued with conviction and continuity by Labour and Conservative Governments in the first 25 years or so after the Second World War. Rather, it should be defined as a clear recognition by nearly all politicians in office that the vast majority of the British people greatly prefer an atmosphere of willing co-operation to unwelcome conflict and are more than likely to cast their votes at elections under the influence of such a preference. An even more fundamental reason for such moderation and restraint is that the economic and political realities of the modern world impose such cautious behaviour upon all Governments, no matter how abrasive or exhilarating the rhetoric may be. In the complex conditions of the interdependent world in which we live and with the growing realisation of our common ecological as well as economic predicament, every Government soon discovers that it can wield relatively little creative power, except on the surface or in the margin of events. Both at home and abroad there are many other influential participants in the political process who can prevent any Government from being able to achieve much more than that. It is in this sense of impaired capacity for taking truly independent and effective action that any modern Government simply has to be moderate and restrained in what it attempts to do.

Public detachment from politics

It has also been said of British political culture that the British people are relatively detached from the process of party politics, put a high value on the maintenance of political stability, and are not usually keen to face up to the need for radical change, especially if it would affect them directly.[12] This view is reflected in the typically low turn-out at local elections; and the strength of parochial opposition to any larger developments which may be in the wider public interest, but which threaten to disturb 'my back yard'. It is also reflected in the widespread public preference for the quiet life and for 'cultivating one's garden' which finds expression in various social institutions from pubs to fishing clubs that absorb so much of the time and energy of the British people. In these circumstances the idea of active or continuous participation in the process of party politics appeals to no more than small and unusual minorities in the population, although the willingness to defend particular interests or advance particular causes is now a defining characteristic of the modern, media-influenced democracy in Britain.

The British people join a myriad of voluntary organisations according to taste and experience. Indeed, the British are some of the foremost 'joiners' in all the advanced industrial countries. Whether individual citizens are members of the National Trust or the Consumers' Association, the MCC or the RSPCA, they find themselves involved in the process of politics from time to time, even if only in connection with a single issue at a particular time (see Chapter 6). The point is that most ordinary citizens are not very sanguine about the role or capacity of Government – hence the familiar joke, 'I'm from the Government and I'm here to help you'. The result is that many people have concluded that it is not very sensible to hold high expectations of Government or other public agencies and this has led them to be especially wary of the promises made by politicians at election time. Yet paradoxically such scepticism and even mistrust of Government does not prevent many of the same people, notably those employed in the public sector or competing for positional goods in the political marketplace, from looking to Government and other public agencies for material advantage or redress of grievances.

As Paul Barker has written, there has been 'an undoubted retreat into the shell of self (or perhaps self plus family)'.[13] Concern with relative advantage or deprivation within narrowly defined reference groups and a determination to protect one's local environment have been more evident than general interest (except when artificially prompted by opinion pollsters) in the competitive performance of the economy or the transcendent issues of war and peace, ecological survival or disaster. The struggle for material satisfaction, or in some cases day-to-day survival, is so all absorbing for most people that few have either the time or the inclination to involve themselves directly in the formal process of party politics. In these circumstances the idea of a conscious political culture has meaning and resonance only for practising politicians, pressure group activists and media or academic pundits. Having said that, however, it is as well to notice that these atypical people seem to have grown in number and influence in recent times, especially the so-called spin doctors.

Social fragmentation

It can be argued that in recent times British society has become more fragmented than it was during the period from 1945 to 1979. There is a good deal of evidence for this, both systematic and anecdotal. In terms of hard economic facts, the gap has widened since 1979 between the richest 10 per cent and the poorest 10 per cent of the population.[14] The labour market has become significantly more stratified as a result of technological development, more flexible patterns of employment and greater self-confidence among senior managers. This has led to a growing proportion of casual and insecure workers within the labour force, the imposition of many more short-term contracts, a dramatic growth of part-time work (especially for women), and a secular trend towards self-employment as more and more firms have shed labour and staff. Even the declining (though preponderant) proportion of core workers still enjoying the full panoply of acquired rights and privileges feel more insecure than they used to in the modern labour market.

In terms of political attitudes, the most resonant observation of the 1980s was Margaret Thatcher's assertion that 'there is no such thing as society'.[15] This summed up in a single phrase the rampant individualism of those years which created a new layer in the property-owning democracy, a temporary and unsustainable property boom and a number of new millionaires. In the long recession which followed and in the more sober and cautious 1990s, the prevailing social attitudes are rather different and have become markedly more communitarian. However, the legacy of personal insecurity and social division has remained, nowhere more obviously than in the starkly different career prospects of the minority which has marketable skills, training or tertiary education, and the majority of people in all generations (but especially those over 50) who missed the opportunity to enhance their intellectual capital. In short, there are many who argue – especially, although not exclusively, on the left of British politics – that Britain became a dramatically more unequal society in the period 1979–97 and that this was too high a price to pay for the new opportunities which have been enjoyed by some people.[16]

1.3 The European context

Although Britain joined the European Community (as it then was called) back in 1973 (see Chapter 18), it has only been comparatively recently that Britain's membership of what is now called the European Union has begun really to influence not only how things are done, but what can (and cannot) be done in British politics. The 1972 Treaty of Accession allowed Britain a transition period of five years in most cases within which to adapt its laws and practices to the European model in those areas of policy where European law was applicable. It did not take Harold Wilson and the then Labour Opposition very long to decide that the terms of membership were not good enough and would consequently have to be renegotiated by a future Labour Government. This is precisely what happened when Labour came to power in 1974 and soon after Britain's membership on the basis of Labour's 'renegotiated terms' was approved by a two to one majority in the 1975 Referendum.

By the time that Margaret Thatcher and the Conservatives returned to power in 1979, it had become clear that Britain's net financial contribution to the European Community budget was unacceptably large. Consequently, she and the then Foreign Secretary, Lord Carrington, set out to negotiate special rebate arrangements designed to limit Britain's net contributions in future years. This was an objective which they achieved and for a few years thereafter the British political class seemed to be relatively content (apart from a few die-hard anti-Europeans in both main parties) with the terms and conditions of Britain's membership.

However, the evangelists for the European idea on the Continent (and to a limited extent in Britain) continued to work towards their ultimate goal – the evolution of an ever closer union of European peoples. In the minds of the Founding Fathers and their disciples this has always implied a process of European nation-building which one day would reach fruition with the creation of a European state to complement the constituent states of the European Union. The momentum in this direction was resumed in the 1986 Single European Act which made legislative provision for the creation of a Single Market throughout the European Community. This was a project which appealed to Margaret Thatcher and her senior Conservative colleagues, because it was a tangible expression of market economics on a European scale. Yet it necessarily entailed a pooling of sovereignty by all the member states to an extent which had not been attempted successfully since the 1950 Coal and Steel Community from which Britain stood aside. Thus both the depth and the breadth of European integration, to which Britain committed itself, were very significantly extended at that time.

More recently, Britain's European partners, in what has now become a European Community of 15 member states, were keen to complement the liberal economics of the Single Market with other measures of common policy in the social and political spheres. At the end of the 1980s they therefore set in motion a programme of further integration which eventually culminated in the 1992 Treaty of Maastricht. At the heart of this new twist in the spiral of European integration was the idea of progress by stages towards Economic and Monetary Union and a single European currency (euro). This further degree of European integration alarmed John Major and Douglas Hurd, then British Prime Minister and Foreign Secretary respectively. They therefore insisted upon Britain's right to defer a decision on such a step, unless and until a future British Government and a future British Parliament decided to take it. They also negotiated for Britain an opt out from all the provisions in the so-called Social Chapter of the Treaty – notably those concerning the right of workers to be consulted by their employers through Works Councils and other measures designed to mitigate the social consequences of market forces.

For the Conservative Government during the period 1992 to 1997 the issue of Europe came to be the most disruptive on the political scene. For much of the time the Prime Minister, John Major, sought to hold back the mounting pressures within the party in favour of ruling out altogether British membership of a single European currency, and by 1997 the Government was sounding more sceptical than ever, not simply on the issue of monetary union but on European matters generally.

There were changes of both substance and tone with the return of the Labour Government under Tony Blair in 1997, in that Ministers immediately signed up to the European Social Chapter, declared that there were no constitutional objections to Britain joining the single European currency when the economic conditions were right (after securing public approval for such a move in a referendum), and generally sought to strike a more positive tone about future British involvement in all matters European.

The reason for dwelling upon these developments is to emphasise the extent to which Britain's membership of the European Union has influenced, is influencing and will continue to influence the development of British political culture over the years. In recent times the attitudes of many in the British political class (especially in the Conservative Party) have become more querulous and defensive towards the European project. Yet the reality is that Britain is most unlikely ever to quit the European Union, and there is no provision in the European Treaties for the expulsion of a member state – however troublesome or uncooperative it may become. On the other hand, the process of ever closer European integration is driven by private sector interests as well as by leading politicians, and there is evidence that business people, tourists, young people and many others take the existence and the opportunities of the European Union very much for granted. Thus in the longer run the correlation of forces does not favour the more cautious and sceptical approach adopted by many Tories and people of the older generation in Britain.

1.4 Conclusion

When we consider British political culture, the main need is to distinguish between the cluster of dated myths and stereotypes which still appears in some accounts and the changing political and social realities which must qualify such traditional notions. If we wish to have an up-to-date understanding, it is necessary to realise that many of the traditional values and assumptions of British politics have been called into question by recent developments. For example, when the British economy grew strongly during most of the 1980s, there was little evidence of the values of civic culture which had been identified and admired by American academics visiting Britain in the 1950s and 1960s. A spirit of tolerance and a disposition to compromise were hardly the hallmarks of the Thatcher era and both main parties polarised significantly. In many ways British society became coarser in the 1980s as the British economy grew rapidly and a large number of people began to rise or fall by their own efforts.

Yet British political culture in the 1990s appears to have developed in rather different directions. At first this was partly due to the obvious differences between Margaret Thatcher 'the warrior' and her immediate successor, John Major 'the healer'. It is also partly due to the influence of the so-called 'modernisers' in the Labour Party, who supported first Neil Kinnock, then John Smith and then Tony Blair in their efforts to convince the electorate that the modern Labour Party no longer threatened the interests of the middle class – or indeed anyone else for that matter.

The most significant explanation, however, may be that after the boom and bust economic cycle of the late 1980s and early 1990s, great swathes of British society (especially those living in London and the South East) have become markedly more debt-averse and risk-averse. The result is that the public mood for the rest of the 1990s and on into the new millennium seems likely to be more cautious and sober than before. If sustained, this is likely to affect many aspects of economic, social and political behaviour; notably by encouraging more people to veer towards co-operation rather than conflict when they have a choice. The quest for equality had its heyday in the immediate postwar period. The quest for liberty reached its apotheosis during the later Thatcher period. It may be that at the turn of the century the hour of fraternity or community has arrived. If this is indeed so, it seems likely to be true in several different senses, including the growing realisation that people in Britain are living as much in a European and global context as in a British political culture. Furthermore, the extensive and far-reaching constitutional changes initiated by the Labour Government of Tony Blair following their 1997 electoral triumph cumulatively point the way towards a profound transformation of the British system of Government and, consequently, of British political culture.

Suggested questions

1 What are the key characteristics of British political culture and how have these been influenced by Britain's membership of the European Union?
2 Is the nature of British society conducive to the practice of democratic politics?
3 How has the growing heterogeneity of British society affected British political culture?

Notes

1. See D. Kavanagh: 'Political culture in Great Britain, the decline of the civic culture'; in G. Almond and S. Verba (eds), *The Civic Culture Revisited* (Boston: Little, Brown, 1980), pp. 136–62.
2. For example, in 1997 Asian votes accounted for 36.1 per cent of all voters in Ealing Southall, 31.7 per cent in both Birmingham Ladywood and Birmingham Sparkbrook & Smallheath, and 31.5 per cent in Leicester East. See 'The Asian Vote', *The Times*, 12 April 1997 (from information supplied by Zee TV).
3. For example, many more women now go out to work than in former times and in some households women are now the principal or sole earners.
4. In 1995 a report from the Joseph Rowntree foundation ('Inquiry into Income and Wealth', February 1995) chronicled the widening of the gap between rich and poor during the 1980s to the point where, by 1992–93, one in four people was living on income below half the national average. In 1996 a report entitled 'Poverty: The Facts' published by the Child Poverty Action Group claimed that poverty was widespread and had grown alarmingly since 1979, explaining that by 1992 24 per cent of the population (13.7 million) were on or below the level of income support – while in 1979 the proportion had been 14 per cent; and that by 1992–93 25 per cent of the population (14.1 million) were on incomes less than half the average after allowing for housing costs – in 1979 the proportion had been just 9 per cent. Having said this, however, a study by Alissa Goodman and Steven Webb for the Institute for Fiscal Studies, entitled 'For Richer, For Poorer; The Changing Distribution of Income in the United Kingdom, 1961–91' (IFS Commentary No. 42, June 1994), showed that the increase in income inequality during the 1980s dwarfed the fluctuations in inequality seen in previous decades. The income share of the poorest tenth of the population fell back from 4.2 per cent in 1961 to 3 per cent in 1991 with most of this fall occurring during the 1980s. By contrast the share of the richest tenth of the population rose from 22 per cent to 25 per cent over the three decades.
5. On 11 September 1997, on a turnout of 60.16 per cent, 74.29 per cent of the Scottish electorate voted in favour of there being a Scottish Parliament, and 63.48 per cent agreed that such a Parliament should have tax-varying powers.

6. At the basis of this agreement was the principle of consent, namely that Northern Ireland was to remain a part of the United Kingdom for as long as the majority of the people of Northern Ireland wished this to be the case. Because of this the Government of the Irish Republic was to amend Articles II and III of its Constitution removing its territorial claim on the North. Similarly, however, the British Government was to repeal the Government of Ireland Act, 1920, and pass legislation allowing for a referendum on the status of Northern Ireland to be held every seven years. See 'The Belfast Agreement: An Agreement Reached at the Multi-Party Talks on Northern Ireland, April 1998', CM 3883.
7. Obituary of William Rushton, *The Times*, 12 December 1996.
8. See J. Blundell and B. Gosschalk, *Beyond Left and Right: The New Politics of Britain* (London: Institute of Economic Affairs, 1997).
9. See A. Giddens, 'After the Left's Paralysis', *New Statesman*, 1 May 1998.
10. See 'Delivering Constitutional Reform' published by The Constitution Unit in 1996.
11. See R.M. Punnett, *British Government and Politics*; 6th edn (London: Heinemann, 1994).
12. See A.H. Birch, *The British System of Government*; 9th edn (London: Allen & Unwin, 1993).
13. *New Society*, 29 November 1979.
14. See IFS Commentary No. 42.
15. See Margaret Thatcher's long interview with *Woman's Own*, 31 October 1987.
16. See W. Hutton, *The State We're In* (London: Jonathan Cape, 1995), pp. 169–192.

Further reading

Alford, B.W.E., *Britain in the World Economy Since 1880* (London: Longman, 1996).
Almond, G.A. and Verba, S. (eds), *The Civic Culture Revisited* (Boston: Little, Brown, 1980).
Blundell, J. and Gosschalk, B., *Beyond Left and Right: The New Politics of Britain* (London: Institute of Economic Affairs, 1997).
Brittan, S., *Left or Right: The Bogus Dilemma* (London: Secker & Warburg, 1968).
Catterall, P. (ed.), *Contemporary Britain, An Annual Review* (Oxford: Blackwell, 1998).
Clark, P., *Hope and Glory: Britain 1900–1990* (London: Allen Lane, 1996).
Dahrendorf, R., *On Britain* (London: BBC, 1982).
Harrison, B., *The Transformation of British Politics 1860–1995* (Oxford: University Press, 1996).
HMSO, *Social Trends 27* (London: The Stationery Office, 1997).
HMSO, *Britain 1999, An Official Handbook* (London: The Stationery Office, 1999).
Marquand, D. and Seldon, A., *The Ideas that Shaped Post-War Britain* (London: Fontana Press, 1996).
Marr, A., *Ruling Britannia: the Failure and Future of British Democracy* (London: Michael Joseph, 1995).
Marwick, A., *The Sixties. Cultural Revolution in Britain, France, Italy and the United States* (Oxford: University Press, 1998).
Morgan, K.O., *The People's Peace, British History 1945–89* (Oxford: OUP, 1990).
Paxman, J., *Friends in High Places: Who Runs Britain?* (London: Michael Joseph, 1990).
Robbins, K., *Great Britain: Identities, Institutions and the Idea of Britishness* (London: Longman, 1998).
Rubinstein, W., *Capitalism, Culture and Decline in Britain, 1750–1990* (London: Routledge, 1993).
Sampson, A., *The Essential Anatomy of Britain* (London: Hodder & Stoughton, 1992).
Tiratsoo, N. (ed.), *From Blitz to Blair* (London: Weidenfeld & Nicolson, 1997).

Websites

Office for National Statistics   http://www.ons.gov.uk

⬡2 The evolving constitution

A constitution is usually defined as a body of fundamental principles, rules and conventions according to which a state or other organisation is governed. According to such a definition, Britain has a constitution. Yet, as we shall see, it is notably different from the constitutions of most other democratic countries, principally because it has been uncodified and has traditionally relied upon the idea of Parliamentary supremacy.

2.1 Key characteristics

Although the key characteristics of the British constitution can be stated quite simply, they contain some powerful paradoxes and internal contradictions. This is mainly because it is an evolving constitution which is changing and developing all the time. At one time some characteristics may be particularly significant, at another time others, and so on. This makes it an interesting subject to study, but one which is hard to describe in a definitive way.

No codification

The British constitution is unusual in that it has been uncodified and has not been assembled at any time into a single consolidated document. This makes it very different not only from the American constitution and those found on the Continent of Europe, but also from those of many Commonwealth countries which were granted their constitutional independence by Britain. Indeed, of all the democratic countries in the world, only Israel is comparable to Britain in having no single consolidated document codifying the way in which its political institutions are supposed to function and setting out the basic rights and duties of its citizens.[1]

Yet in the absence of a single, basic constitutional text, it should not be assumed that Britain has no constitutional documents from which guidance can be derived where there is a need to elucidate the laws and conventions which govern British politics. For example, *Magna Carta*, which was signed by King John at the behest of the barons in 1215, is perhaps Britain's best-known constitutional document. It provided in 61 clauses a clear statement of feudal laws and customs. Many other documents of equal or greater constitutional significance have been drawn up since then.

The Bill of Rights in 1689 put the stamp of Parliamentary approval on the succession of William and Mary to the throne deserted by James II and extended the powers of Parliament at the expense of the Crown. *The Act of Settlement* in 1701 was described in its preamble as 'an Act for the further limitation of the Crown and the better securing of the rights and liberties of the subject'. *The Act of Union with Scotland* in 1707 declared in Article 3 that 'the United Kingdom of Great Britain be represented by one and the same Parliament to be styled the Parliament of Great Britain'. *The Act of Union with Ireland* in 1800 brought about the formation of the United Kingdom of Great Britain and Ireland, later to be amended to 'Northern Ireland' following Irish partition in 1921.

The Reform Act in 1832 was the first of a series of statutes over the period from then until modern times which were designed to extend the franchise at Parliamentary elections. *The Ballot Act* in 1872 introduced secret ballots for all elections to Parliament and all contested municipal elections. *The Local Government Act* in 1888 established elected County Councils for the first time in new administrative counties. *The Parliament Act* in 1911 regulated the relations between the two Houses of Parliament and confirmed the legislative supremacy of the House of Commons, while reducing the maximum span of a Parliament from seven to five years. *The Redistribution of Seats Act* in 1944 established independent Parliamentary Boundary Commissions to demarcate the constituencies on a fair and regular basis. *The Representation of the People Act* in 1969 lowered the voting age from 21 to 18. *The European Parliamentary Elections Act* in 1978 provided for direct elections every five years to the European Parliament. *The Human Rights Act* in 1998 incorporated the European Convention on Human Rights into United Kingdom law, thereby giving people opportunities to enforce their rights under the Convention in British courts rather than having to incur the cost and delay of taking a case to the European Human Rights Commission and Court in Strasbourg. It is worth noting that, with the exception of Magna Carta and the Bill of Rights, all the examples given are drawn from statute law – in other words, Acts of Parliament. This emphasises the overriding importance of Parliament in Britain's traditionally uncodified constitution.

There are, however, many other documentary sources, including judicial proceedings, which clarify Britain's constitution by setting out the rights and duties which subsequently the people have come to take for granted. For example, in *Bushell's Case* of 1670, Lord Chief Justice Vaughan established the independence of juries. In *Sommersett's Case* of 1772, Lord Mansfield recognised the freedom of a former slave from the American colonies on the grounds of his residence in England and argued that slavery was 'so odious that nothing can be suffered to support it but positive law'. In *Beatty v. Gillbanks* of 1882, Justice Field established the principle that a man may not be convicted for a lawful act, even if he knows that it may cause another to commit an unlawful act.

Other sources of guidance on Britain's traditionally uncodified constitution include *Erskine May*, the classic and constantly up-dated reference book written by successive Clerks of the Commons on the procedures and privileges of the lower House; and certain learned works written by eminent constitutional authorities down the ages, such as Blackstone and Bagehot.[2]

Considerable flexibility

Another key characteristic of the British constitution is its considerable flexibility. This has derived partly from the absence of neat constitutional formulae consolidated into a single, authoritative document – in contrast, for example, with the codified constitution of the French Fifth Republic. However, it is essentially because no Parliament can bind its successors and any Parliament can undo the legislation of its predecessors that it is difficult to achieve formal methods of constitutional limitation in Britain. Since Britain joined the European Community in 1973 the fabled flexibility of British constitutional arrangements has begun to be eroded by the gradual impact of European law. Increasingly the rulings of the European Court of Justice determine and codify sections of British law in those areas covered by the various European Treaties to which Britain is a party. In the process British constitutional and legal arrangements are beginning to resemble those on the Continent of Europe and even more so following the Human Rights Act 1998.

It is, therefore, apparent from even a cursory study of British history that the traditional flexibility of Britain's constitution has stemmed from the way in which the theoretically absolute and unlimited power of Parliament (in effect the governing majority in the House of Commons) has been severely modified and limited in practice by the weight of political tradition and precedent, the influence of constitutional conventions, and the well-established commitment to the rule of law. All these traditional and practical constraints upon the theoretical supremacy of Parliament are now joined by the invasive influence of European law as a function of Britain's membership of the European Union. Together they qualify the traditional precepts and represent the latest stage in the evolution of the British constitution.

Importance of conventions

Another key characteristic of the British constitution is the importance of conventions – in other words, established custom and practice. The conventions which have been so powerful in their influence upon constitutional developments in Britain are the product of organic growth over the centuries. They include, for example, the convention that the Monarch should send first for the leader of the largest single party in the House of Commons when it is necessary to form a new Government following a General Election or the fall of a Prime Minister in office; and the convention that Ministers are responsible and can be held to account by Parliament for what does or does not happen in their Departments.

This helps to explain why certain principles not declared in law – such as the Royal prerogative or Ministerial responsibility – have developed so fully over the years. It is also one of the reasons why there have been such formidable obstacles to the achievement of deliberate constitutional reform in Britain. Another reason validated by long experience is that it is usually necessary to secure all-party agreement for such changes, and yet this precondition has rarely been fulfilled. Hence there is a paradoxical quality in Britain's constitutional arrangements which can best be understood only after close study of the way in which its political institutions have evolved over the centuries rather than by reference to any basic constitutional document. This is why we refer to Britain's evolving constitution which reflects the more general development of British politics and society over the centuries.

2.2 Views of the constitution

For schematic purposes we can say that there are really three different views of the constitution in Britain. There is the *classic liberal view*, which is based on nostalgia for the period when the House of Commons really did hold sway over the Executive. There is the *governmental view,* which is based on the assumption that the Executive is answerable not so much to Parliament as to the electorate every four or five years at General Elections. There is the *empirical view*, which seeks to take account both of the weakness of Parliament in relation to the Executive and of the Government of the day in relation to all the other limiting forces in the real world both within Britain and abroad.

Classic liberal view

Of the various interpretations of the British constitution which have been put forward over the years, perhaps the most traditional is the classic liberal view which is associated with the writings of Bagehot and Dicey in the nineteenth century.[3] This view holds that the House of Commons is the supreme political institution with the power to make and unmake Governments, pass any laws and resolve the great political issues of the day. The classic liberal view is shown in diagrammatic form in Figure 2.1.

It accords only subsidiary constitutional significance to the Monarchy and the House of Lords. It takes little account of the political parties, pressure groups, the Civil Service, the media or public opinion. As R.H.S. Crossman pointed out, such a view could only have been valid for the period before any significant extension of the franchise, before the establishment of disciplined political parties with national organisations, and before the development of an impartial meritocratic Civil Service.[4]

This classic liberal view applied only during a brief era, 1832–67, when the House of Commons really was supreme. During that atypical period no fewer than ten Administrations fell because the House of Commons withdrew its support. By about 1885 the main principles propounded by Bagehot and Dicey were already being eroded or overtaken by new political realities which became steadily more apparent during the last quarter of the nineteenth century. For example, the legislative supremacy of Parliament was gradually overcome by the growing power of the political parties as they sought to appeal to a wider electorate which was extended in successive Reform Bills. The rule of law, which Dicey had identified as a fundamental principle of the constitution, was not necessarily the paramount consideration for all participants in the political process, at any rate for the disadvantaged sections of the community which often appealed to superior notions of natural justice. The importance of conventions meant little to all those who were outside the charmed circle of Parliamentary politics.

In modern conditions students of the British constitution need to make sense of a much more complex and bureaucratic form of democracy in which Parliamentary supremacy is only one important principle among many. The classic liberal view, although still regarded with respect and firmly established among the received ideas of British politics, is no longer particularly instructive as a guide to contemporary politics. It has been rendered rather obsolete by the enormously increased scope of modern

Figure 2.1 Classic view of the constitution

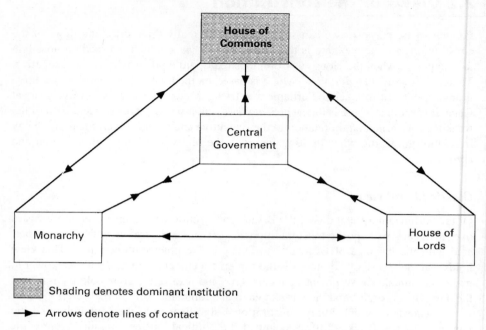

Shading denotes dominant institution

Arrows denote lines of contact

Government and by the power of political parties, pressure groups, the media and public opinion. This elitist Parliamentary model of the nineteenth century has had to give way to the claims of a more pluralist and populist kind of democracy at the end of the twentieth century.

Governmental view

Another well-known interpretation of the British constitution may be called the governmental view. This holds that the former power of the Monarch has been passed not to Parliament but to the Prime Minister and Cabinet, subject only to criticism in Parliament and periodic confirmation or rejection by the mass electorate at General Elections. It is a view usually associated with the writings of L.S. Amery and Herbert Morrison.[5] It maintains that the Government has a clear responsibility to govern and that the essential form of political accountability is the responsibility of the governing party to the electorate. Accordingly the role of the Opposition and all back-bench MPs is to act essentially as filters or megaphones between the Government of the day and the electorate. L.S. Amery was succinct when he wrote that 'the combination of responsible leadership by Government with responsible criticism in Parliament is the essence of our constitution'.[6]

Although this view, too, has to be qualified if we are to form an accurate impression of the way in which the British constitution really works, it has more validity than the classic liberal view, which is now characterised by sentimentality towards a vanished era of truly Parliamentary government. In the administrative and legislative spheres at any rate modern British Governments have had virtually unlimited power, provided they have had a reliable working majority in the House of Commons and as long as they have been careful to keep their Parliamentary supporters united behind them. Under the terms of the 1911 Parliament Act a Government can retain this power for a maximum term of five years before it is obliged to seek a fresh mandate from the electorate. In view of the notable imbalance of political resources between Government and Opposition, there is some truth in Lord Hailsham's allegation that the British political system is 'an elective dictatorship' tempered only by the minimal restraints of constitutional conventions and the governing party's normal desire to get re-elected.[7] The Governmental view is shown diagrammatically in Figure 2.2.

Figure 2.2 Governmental view of the constitution

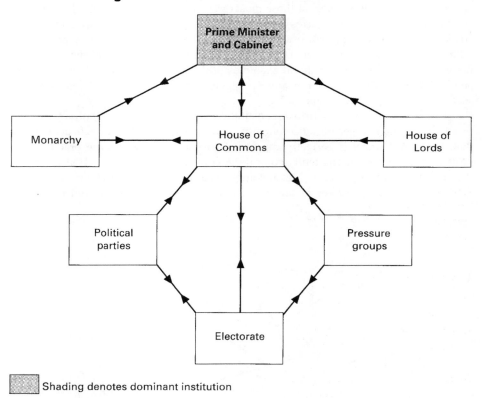

Shading denotes dominant institution

Arrows denote lines of contact

Empirical view

More accurate still in modern conditions is the empirical view of the constitution, which emphasises both the weakness of Parliament in relation to the Government of the day and the weakness of the Executive in relation to pressure groups, the media, public opinion and other actors on the national and international scene. It emphasises the way in which a deliberate extension of constitutional power can lead to a decline in effective power, no matter how great the Parliamentary majority or the political momentum of the party in office. This is essentially because, if a Government becomes over-extended in its ambitions or over-loaded in its commitments, it is likely to encounter so many real world obstacles and to create so many political enemies that it will be unable to achieve its objectives.

Indeed, a dispassionate reading of British constitutional history leads to the important conclusion that the most abiding political problem has been the gaining and retaining of public consent for the actions of any Government. Stage by stage from the thirteenth century to the present time, Governments in Britain, whether led by the Monarch or by a Prime Minister in Parliament, have had to cede and share power with the other great interests in the land – and nowadays increasingly with their partners in the European Union. Effective government has only been possible with the consent, or at least the tacit acquiescence, of those most directly affected by it or involved with it. Against this background it makes sense to regard successive British Governments as stable rather than strong, and to avoid confusing the concentration of responsibility with the concentration of power. Today public opinion, the influence of the media and the growth of European law are all examples of the powerful forces which condition and limit the exercise of power by any British Government. For a diagrammatic representation of this view see Figure 2.3.

Thus the contemporary British constitution is based on *two key paradoxes*. The first is the limited power of a theoretically supreme Parliament. This reflects the fact that, while Parliament is perfectly capable of passing any law, it is in practice able only to criticise and intermittently control the Government of the day. It also reflects the growing political power and legal competence of the European Union, which has tended to reduce the power of the national Governments within it and hence the

Figure 2.3 Empirical view of the constitution

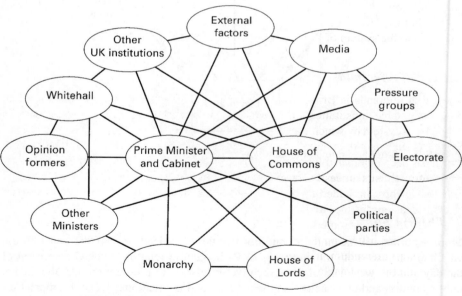

NB No dominant institution.
Everything influences and is influenced by everything else.

national Parliaments which claim to control them. The second is the limited power of the allegedly all-powerful Executive, which reflects the fact that, while a Government with a working majority in the House of Commons can invariably get its way in Whitehall and Westminster, little is achieved if its freedom of manoeuvre is unduly circumscribed by administrative constraints, media influence, interest group pressure or the impact of European law. This complicated network of informal checks and balances means that the evolving constitution continues to develop organically, but provides few constitutional safeguards against the arbitrary exercise of executive power.

Formal limitation of the power of any British Government is now more often sought and found in the rulings of the European Court of Justice or the European Court of Human Rights. On the other hand, informal constraints upon the power of all national Governments are to be observed most clearly these days in the capacity of the global financial markets to discipline any national authorities which lose credibility in the eyes of global investors, and in the enormous power of the global media corporations.

2.3 Pressures for change

Over the years constitutional changes have occurred piecemeal, even haphazardly, in response to the needs of public policy or the dictates of political necessity. No coherent pattern seems to have emerged and there has been no real attempt to co-ordinate the various initiatives which have been taken. Some have argued that there is an emerging constitutional crisis caused most notably by two factors: the challenge to British Parliamentary supremacy posed by the encroachment of European law, and the ever widening gap between the received ideas about Britain's 'unwritten constitution' and contemporary political realities. We shall look briefly at each of these matters in turn. However, before that we must consider the threat posed by the use of referenda to the system of Parliamentary government in Britain.

The use of referenda

The use of referenda in Britain in two celebrated cases in the 1970s produced some of the most notable constitutional developments of modern times.[8] 'Referendum' can be defined as a system by which a question is submitted to the direct vote of the whole electorate. As such, any referendum is still an unusual device in the British political system, which has been dominated for so long by the assumptions and practices of Parliamentary democracy. It sits uneasily with Britain's traditional constitutional arrangements, although it must be added that its apparently satisfactory use on a number of albeit limited occasions testifies to the robust flexibility of the British constitution.

In 1975 Britain's membership of the European Community (as the European Union was then called) on the terms 'renegotiated' by the Labour Government was put to a national referendum, mainly because the Labour Party was so deeply divided on the issue that it was unable to reach a collective decision which would bind the entire Cabinet, and because it was thought that this device would settle the issue once and for all for both main parties. Indeed, the Wilson Administration was so seriously split on the issue that it was necessary to suspend the normal convention of collective responsibility for the duration of the referendum campaign, so that Cabinet Ministers and others could argue freely against each other in public – something which had not happened since the open agreement to differ in the National Government (made up of both Labour and Conservatives) in 1931 on the issue of tariff reform.

In 1979 the legislation proposed by the Callaghan Government and passed by Parliament for the devolution of certain legislative powers to Scotland and Wales had to be put to separate referenda in each of those parts of the United Kingdom, because there seemed to be no other way of overcoming the persistent and effective Parliamentary opposition to the legislation from both sides of the House of Commons – but especially from the Government back-benches. As things turned out, the House of Commons passed an amendment to the legislation which insisted that, unless at least 40 per cent of those *entitled to vote* in each relevant part of the country supported the policy, the provisions of the legislation would not be put into effect. This proved to be a sufficient obstacle to the implementation of the legislation, since in neither Scotland nor Wales did as many as 40 per cent of those qualified to vote cast a 'Yes' vote.[9]

These two cases were seen by many people as valid precedents for the use of referenda on other issues, especially when the position taken by a majority in the House of Commons has been fiercely opposed by an irreconcilable minority in the governing party or has been apparently at odds with the view held by a majority of public opinion – in the latter case, for example, on the emotive issue of capital punishment. In this context there were strong calls for a national referendum on British adherence to the 1992 Maastricht Treaty from Margaret Thatcher and other members of a vociferous all-party campaign against Britain's participation in the latest stage in the process of ever deeper European integration. These calls were resisted by the Major Government which managed to win a crucial vote in the House of Commons on the matter. Nevertheless the issue has not gone away and it now seems certain that there will be a referendum on participation in a single European currency if the Government decided that Britain should join such an arrangement. Indeed, it would fit in with the general approach of the Labour Government which, in its first 13 months in office made use of referenda in Scotland and Wales (September 1997) and in greater London and Northern Ireland (May 1998).

The pressures for the use of referenda in these and other cases reflect a number of different factors. In part referenda are now seen as a way of enabling the governing party at any time to reconcile the irreconcilable on portentous issues, such as the nature and extent of Britain's relationship with the other member states of the European Union, where no satisfactory compromise formula seems to be available to the two sides of the argument within each of the main parties. In part the pressure for referenda reflects growing public impatience with the fastidious views of many MPs in all parties who refuse to toe a populist line on a number of emotive issues. In part it is testimony to the diminished status and authority of Parliament in the eyes of a much less deferential public and a largely hostile media. In relation to Britain's very tricky situation within the European Union (where the future project advocated by Britain's partners is unattractive to many in Britain, but the model preferred in Britain is not really on offer anywhere else in the European Union), the idea of holding further referenda has naturally appealed to the politicians in office at any time, whether Labour or Conservative, because such issues have threatened to divide and possibly destroy each main party when in office. The bleak fact is that Government and Parliament in Britain (and indeed in many other representative democracies) now lack the necessary authority to impose such decisions upon the people via the traditional Parliamentary procedures. In short, it crystallises the problem of democratic legitimacy in modern society.

The encroachment of European law

The challenge to British Parliamentary supremacy posed by the encroachment of European law is an issue with the most far-reaching constitutional implications. It has been highlighted by those in all parties who have opposed Britain's membership of the European Union (or at any rate Britain's deeper integration into the Union), just as it has tended to be played down by those who have favoured Britain's full participation at every stage of the European adventure. Now that Britain has been a member of the European Union for more than 25 years, virtually no one is seriously arguing the case for British withdrawal. Yet a number of politicians in all parties have been arguing for a redefinition of Britain's relations with her European Union partners along international rather than supranational lines.

On the assumption that Britain remains within the European Union, the likely result will be that the supremacy of Parliament at Westminster will become increasingly attenuated within the United Kingdom as the scope of European law is extended into more areas of British national life. More decisions of political importance will probably be taken at European level by the European institutions in which Britain will have no more than a minority stake, and more of the decisions in the Council of Ministers will probably be taken by qualified majority vote in view of the enormous difficulties of running a Union of fifteen or more member states on a basis of unanimity. The so-called 'democratic deficit', which recent European developments have revealed, is unlikely to be closed by Westminster and the other national Parliaments, but increasingly by the European Parliament with its growing powers of co-decision with the Council of Ministers. In an effort to staunch this integrationist tide some have advocated the doctrine of 'subsidiarity' which holds that no decisions should be taken at European level which could more appropriately be taken at national level or below. Yet by no means all Britain's European partners have seen things in this way or have been as determined to safeguard theoretical national sovereignty and actual national responsibility. Whatever the outcome of this titanic struggle between the supranationalists and the internationalists in the European Union, it is clear that it no longer makes sense to consider the British constitution in an exclusively national context.

Other pressures for change

The Conservative Government under Margaret Thatcher pushed through Parliament a wide range of legislation which, while not deliberately designed to bring about constitutional change, had some significant constitutional implications.[10] The 1979–83 Conservative Administration introduced legislation to restrict the already limited autonomy of local government. The 1983–87 Conservative Administration introduced further legislation to curb high spending local authorities and to abolish the Greater

London Council and the other Metropolitan County Councils. The 1987–90 Thatcher Administration introduced the highly controversial Community Charge (Poll Tax) into Scotland in 1989 and into England and Wales (but not Northern Ireland) in 1990, along with the Uniform Business Rate which replaced industrial and commercial rates.

Under John Major's leadership between 1990 and 1997 the sustained Conservative assault upon local government was diminished slightly, although tight financial control by central Government remained an important hallmark of Conservative policy. Between 1990 and 1992 the Community Charge was scrapped and the Council Tax introduced in its place with a greater emphasis upon property values (in 1991) rather than population as the basis for assessment. The issue of local government boundaries was addressed first by establishing the so-called Banham Commission to examine the issue in the various parts of the country and then by the creation of a number of all-purpose unitary authorities.

Whereas the Conservatives under John Major became more cautious in their attitude towards local government than they had been under Margaret Thatcher, they demonstrated their radical credentials more clearly in relation to extensive reform of the Civil Service. The result of this process (discussed more fully in Chapter 14) is that the Civil Service was reduced from over 700,000 in 1979 to under 500,000 by 1997 and that 132 Executive Agencies were established to deliver public goods and services more efficiently.[11]

From the late 1980s onwards an issue of more general constitutional importance was illuminated in a sharper light. This is the political problem posed by the ever widening gap between the received ideas about Britain's uncodified constitution and the contemporary political realities. One manifestation of this was the multi-party and non-party campaign under the banner of Charter 88 for comprehensive constitutional reform. This campaign was based on a 10-point programme which called, among other things, for a new Bill of Rights, an independent and reformed judiciary and proportional representation for elections to Parliament at Westminster.[12] Also important in this regard was the work of independent inquiry into constitutional reform carried out by the Constitution Unit over several years.[13]

Another manifestation of a more party political character was the extent of Scottish disgust with all things English and Conservative, which was evident from the dramatic SNP victory at the Glasgow Govan by-election in November 1988. In the eyes of many Scots this was a clear protest against both English Conservatism and the perceived ineffectiveness of the Scottish Labour Party at Westminster at the time. A good deal of renewed momentum was achieved by the SNP and from time to time it was seen as commanding strong support in opinion polls conducted north of the border.[14] These pressures gave a new sense of urgency to those who were campaigning for the establishment of a Scottish Parliament with its own law-making powers and certainly galvanised most of the other parties into supporting the so-called 'Claim of Right' for Scotland at the multi-party Constitutional Convention which was held in Edinburgh in March 1989. Indeed, the SNP has become the main challenger to the Labour Party in Scotland and it may prove difficult for Labour and its allies to resist the SNP pressure for Scottish independence.

Another constitutional issue which was brought to the fore during John Major's occupancy of 10 Downing Street was the constitutional future of Northern Ireland. The first break-through came in the form of the Downing Street Declaration of

15 December 1993, which was signed by John Major and Albert Reynolds on behalf of the British and Irish Governments. This led to exploratory peace talks both between London and Dublin and between each of the Governments and representatives of the Protestant/Unionist and Catholic/Nationalist communities in Northern Ireland. This 'peace process' bore fruit with the announcement of a complete ceasefire by the IRA in August 1994 and talks about talks at official level on the Northern Ireland issue. All these developments served to give the age-old Irish question renewed prominence in British politics and paved the way for the Good Friday Agreement in 1998 which offered real hope of a political solution to the intractable Irish problem.

Other developments also need to be taken into account, developments which have moved Britain's political culture away from informal understandings and precedents towards a more formal system of rules and regulations. These include the managerial revolution which has taken place in Whitehall as a direct result of the creation of 'Next Step' Executive Agencies (see Chapter 14); the declassification in 1992 of the Cabinet Office document 'Questions of Procedure for Ministers' (the rulebook for Ministers) and its subsequent emergence as a result of the Scott Inquiry into the arms to Iraq affair as an authoritative statement of Ministerial responsibility and account-ability to Parliament; and the tighter restrictions on the activity of MPs arising from the work of the Nolan Committee and the consequent appointment – from November 1995 – of a Parliamentary Commissioner for Standards. Some commentators have argued that these developments have created a framework for a written constitution and that, as a result, Britain can no longer accurately be described as having a completely uncodified constitution.[15]

These and other constitutional developments affecting Britain may have been mis-interpreted or even misrepresented in some cases. Yet they have encouraged some searching reconsideration of many basic constitutional assumptions in Britain, and strengthened the case of those arguing for specific and widespread constitutional reform. For example while the Liberal Democrats had always strongly argued for constitutional reform the Labour Party gradually took on board more and more of the reform agenda. Indeed the Labour Government elected in 1997 quickly set off on its objective of overhauling and modernising the British Constitution. Following referenda power was devolved to a Scottish Parliament, a Welsh Assembly and a London Mayor and Assembly; a new Northern Ireland Assembly and a Council of the Isles figured as part of the attempts to bring the Northern Ireland peace process to a successful conclusion. Proportional representation was introduced for the elections to the Scottish Parliament, the Welsh Assembly and the European Parliament, while a commission under Lord Jenkins gave advice on proportional representation for Westminster elections. The European Convention on Human Rights was incorporated into UK domestic law; freedom of information legislation was prepared; proposals for the modernisation of the procedures of the House of Commons were considered and reform of the House of Lords was brought forward. The Government signed the Council of Europe's 'Charter of Local Self-Government' designed to guarantee the freedom of local Councils from central Government interference and was apparently intent on moving power selectively from Whitehall to the regions of England – a policy which may lead to the creation of elected regional assemblies where there is local demand for it. These are changes which are moving the country towards a more federal – certainly a less overtly unitary – more written, codified constitution. Indeed, it is this perhaps, that will be – can be – seen as the basis of the 'Blair Revolution'; that the period of the late 1990s on into the twenty-first century will probably be seen as a period of significant institutional change in Britain, an incremental 'revolution' in the political values and methods of governing the country.

2.4 Conclusion

Some years ago Nevil Johnson argued that 'the gap between the theory and the reality of British political institutions and procedures has assumed serious dimensions' and 'the root of the political difficulty is to be found in a refusal to recognise that much of the traditional language of the British constitution ... has lost its vitality'.[16] This is a point of view which has become all the more persuasive as the British nation-state has been challenged by the European Union from above and by local loyalties, whether nationalist or regional, from below. In such dynamic conditions the preservation of traditional constitutional forms has become increasingly difficult, and consequently deliberate constitutional change has become increasingly necessary and has been pursued.

The clear conclusion is that constitutional change and reform is nearly always on the agenda of British politics. Sometimes it is there explicitly, because the politicians in office wish to change the constitutional arrangements. Sometimes it is there implicitly, because the policies of a radical Government have important constitutional implications. Sometimes it is forced onto the political agenda by nationalist movements within the United Kingdom or supranational developments within the European Union. In any event it is clear that change is constant, if not always predictable, in Britain's evolving constitution.

Suggested questions

1 What are the key features of the British constitution?
2 Which view of the British constitution accords best with contemporary political circumstances?
3 What difference is Britain's membership of the European Union likely to make to constitutional arrangements in Britain?

Notes

1. Although the European Convention on human rights was finally incorporated into domestic UK law in 1998 with the passage of the Human Rights Act, the British courts were not given the power to set aside primary legislation on the grounds of incompatibility with the Act, only the right to bring such incompatibility to the attention of Parliament. How this will work in practice, only practice will show.
2. William Blackstone, who was professor of Common Law at Oxford University, published his famous *Commentaries upon the Laws of England between 1765 and 1769*. In that work he presented a clear and systematic description of English law in the mid-eighteenth century. Walter Bagehot was equally famous in the nineteenth century for his great work, *The English Constitution*, which was published in 1867. This set out what he saw as the principles of British Parliamentary democracy at that time.
3. See W. Bagehot, *The English Constitution* (London: Fontana, 1978) and A.V. Dicey, *The Law of the Constitution* (London: Macmillan, 1959).

4. See R.H.S. Crossman's Introduction to W. Bagehot, *The English Constitution*, p. 35.
5. See L.S. Amery, *Thoughts on the Constitution* (Oxford: OUP, 1947), and H. Morrison, *Government and Parliament* (Oxford: OUP, 1959).
6. L.S. Amery, *Thoughts on the Constitution*, p. 32.
7. See Q. Hailsham, *The Dilemma of Democracy* (London: Collins, 1978) for an exposition of this argument.
8. For a fuller discussion of this subject see D.E. Butler and A. Ranney (eds), *Referendums: A Comparative Study of Practice and Theory* (Washington, DC: American Enterprise Institute, 1978), and V. Bogdanor, *The People and the Party System* (Cambridge: CUP, 1981), pp. 11–93.
9. In the event the vote in Scotland recorded 52 per cent of those who voted in favour and 48 per cent against, while the vote in Wales recorded a mere 20 per cent of those who voted in favour and 80 per cent against. This meant that in the Scottish case only 33 per cent of the qualified electorate voted 'Yes' and in the Welsh case only 12 per cent
10. For a fuller exposition of this argument see C. Graham and T. Prosser, *Waiving the Rules: the Constitution under Thatcherism* (Milton Keynes: Open University Press, 1988).
11. See Chapter 14 for further details.
12. Charter 88 was launched in London as a non-party political movement on 29 November 1988. It took the view that fundamental liberties were insufficiently protected by the British constitution, since liberty in Britain was based not so much on a set of rules as a state of mind. It therefore called for a codified constitution, electoral reform, a new Bill of Rights, reform of the House of Lords, reform of the judiciary, and more equitable power sharing between central and local government. The other seven points recommended in Charter 88 were: the subjection of executive and prerogative power to the rule of law; the introduction of freedom of information and more open government; the creation of a democratically elected, non-hereditary House of Lords; control of the Executive by a democratically renewed Parliament; legal remedies against the abuse of power by central or local government; a more equitable distribution of power between the various levels of Government; and a written and codified constitution anchored in the principle of universal citizenship.
13. The Constitution Unit was a research project set up in April 1995 to conduct an independent inquiry into the implementation of constitutional reform. It aimed to analyse proposals for constitutional reform, explore the connections between them and identify the practical steps involved in putting constitutional reforms in place. The unit was based at the Faculty of Laws, University College London, and was funded by a variety of charitable trusts and foundations.
14. For example, a System Three poll in March 1989 showed that 52 per cent of those questioned in Scotland supported the SNP policy of independence for Scotland within the European Union. In a Market Research Scotland poll published in *Scotland on Sunday* on 12 February 1995, 37 per cent favoured independence, 35 per cent favoured devolution, 19 per cent the unionist status quo and 9 per cent were undecided. More recently – 6 May 1998 – a Systems Three poll for the *Glasgow Herald* put support for the SNP, including its policy of independence, at 41 per cent; 5 per cent ahead of Labour on 36 per cent.
15. See P. Riddell, 'Cabinets, Codes and Counts', *The Times*, 13 May 1996.
16. N. Johnson, *In Search of the Constitution* (London: Methuen, 1980), p. 26.

Further reading

Alexander, R., *The Voice of the People. A Constitution for Tomorrow* (London: Weidenfeld & Nicolson, 1997).
Barnett, A., *This Time. Our Constitutional Revolution* (London: Vintage, 1997).
Benn, T., *Common Sense* (London: Hutchinson, 1993).

Bogdanor, V., *Power and the People. A Guide to Constitutional Reform* (London: Victor Gollancz, 1997).

Brazier, R., *Constitutional Reform* (Oxford: Clarendon Press, 1991).

Charter 88, Supplement to the Votes and Proceedings (London: House of Commons, 2 December 1988).

'Delivering Constitutional Reform' (London: The Constitution Unit, 1995).

Graham, C. and Prosser, T. (eds), *Waiving the Rules, the Constitution under Thatcherism* (Milton Keynes: Open University Press, 1988).

Hailsham, Q., *On the Constitution* (London: HarperCollins, 1992).

Hazell, R. (ed.), *Constitutional Futures. A History of the Next Ten Years* (London: The Constitution Unit, 1999).

Hennessy, P., *The Hidden Wiring: Unearthing the British Constitution* (London: Victor Gollancz, 1995).

Johnson, N., *In Search of the Constitution* (London: Methuen, 1980).

Norton, P., *The British Constitution in Flux* (Oxford: Martin Robertson, 1982).

Oliver, D., *Government in the United Kingdom* (Milton Keynes: Open University Press, 1991).

Ranney, A. (ed.), *The Referendum Device* (Washington, DC: American Enterprise Institute, 1981).

Wright, T., *Citizens and Subjects* (London: Routledge, 1994).

Website

The Constitution Unit   http://www.ucl.ac.uk/constitution-unit

3 The electoral system

The electoral system in Britain is the product of historical evolution and development. It began to be put on a democratic basis at the time of The Great Reform Act of 1832. This gave the right to vote to an additional half a million individuals who had not previously had it, taking the proportion of the enfranchised adult population to 5 per cent. Subsequent Acts carried forward the process of enfranchisement:

1867   *The Representation of the People Act* – which carried forward the principles of the 1832 legislation, increasing the electorate to number almost 2.5 million (13 per cent of the adult population).

1872   *The Ballot Act* – which introduced the principle of secret or confidential voting.

1883   *The Corrupt & Illegal Practices Act* – which made bribery and other corrupt practices at elections criminal offences.

1884   *The Representation of The People Act* – which extended the franchise to householders and tenements and to all those who occupied land or tenements with an annual value of not less than ten pounds. The main effect of this Act was to give the vote to working men in the counties, taking the total number of voters to 5 million, 25 per cent of the adult population.

1885   *The Redistribution of Seats Act* – which introduced the principle of equal electoral districts – equal in terms of numbers of voters – and to a great extent ensured single-member constituencies.

1918   *The Representation of the People Act* – which did away with virtually all restrictions on adult male suffrage and extended the vote to include 8.5 million women over the age of 30, creating an electorate of over 21 million people, or 75 per cent of the adult population.

1928   *The Representation of the People (Equal Franchise) Act* – which placed women on the same basis as their male counterparts, namely enfranchising virtually all those 21 years of age and over, leading to an electorate of 27 million potential voters, 99 per cent of the adult population.

1948   *The Representation of the People Act* – which further extended the principle of 'one person, one vote' by abolishing additional votes for university graduates and for those owning business premises and land in constituencies other than those in which they lived.

1969   *The Representation of the People Act* – which reduced the minimum age of voting from 21 to 18.

1985   *The Representation of the People Act* – which extended the right to vote to British citizens resident abroad for a period of up to five years from leaving the country.

1989   *The Representation of the People Act* – which extended the right to vote to British citizens living abroad to up to twenty years from leaving Britain, a potential electorate of over 1.5 million for the 1997 General Election, although by then only some 23,583 individuals had registered to vote.

The result of this is that there exists in Britain today a system of universal adult suffrage in which all British nationals – as well as citizens of the Irish Republic and of Commonwealth countries resident in the United Kingdom – aged 18 and over have the right to vote (including those British nationals living overseas and those temporarily on holiday abroad), with the exception of convicted felons, certified lunatics and peers of the realm. Although registration is compulsory voting is not (unlike, for example, in Australia, Belgium and Luxembourg).

Britain does not operate a system of fixed-term Parliaments with the dates of elections for the House of Commons known in advance – save for the fact that according to the Parliament Act of 1911, a Parliament cannot go on longer than five years (unless Parliament votes otherwise – as was the case in the two World Wars between 1914 and 1918 and between 1939 and 1945). Rather, the date for an election is set by the Prime Minister of the day. Traditionally, polling day is set on a Thursday. For example, the timing of the 1997 General Election was as follows:

March 17	Election date announced
March 21	Parliament prorogued (dismissed)
April 8	Parliament dissolved
April 11	Notice of the General Election published
April 14	Nominations for Parliamentary Candidates opened
April 16	Nominations for Parliamentary Candidates closed
May 1	Polling Day
May 7	Parliament re-assembled
May 14	Queen's Speech presented to the new Parliament

Traditionally, the four or five weeks of an election campaign are intensely busy for candidates, agents and voluntary helpers. Leaflets must be produced and delivered and envelopes addressed for leaflets being distributed by post. There are meetings to be organised, speeches to be written and made and press releases to be issued. Above all else there are people to meet; in short there is the task of going around the constituency seeking support from as many people as can be reached.

More recently, however, election campaigns have come to be dominated by the national, as opposed to the constituency-based, campaign. General elections have in many respects become contests between national parties, on national issues, fought out between national party leaders before the television cameras. See Figure 3.1 for an example of a day's campaigning schedule for the leaders of the three main parties in the 1997 General Election.

Figure 3.1 A day in the 1997 General Election campaign: the party leaders

John Major – Conservative

PROGRAMME FOR WEDNESDAY 30 APRIL 1997, LONDON AND EASTERN

MORNING

07.15	Briefing on the day's papers, No. 10 Downing Street.	**13.40**	Lunch in Langans restaurant with Duncan Revie, Tony Martin, Sepp Blatter, Keith Cooper, Director of Communications FIFA and Jeff Powell, *Daily Mail* Chief Sports Correspondent.
08.10	Briefing at No. 10.		
08.45	Depart No. 10 for Millbank.		
08.55	Arrive Millbank.		
09.05	Election Call (BBC programme).	**14.00**	Depart Wembley for Stevenage Town Centre to be met by Tim Wood, Candidate for Stevenage.
10.00	Depart Millbank for CCO (Conservative Central Office).		
10.05	Private meeting with Party Chairman	**14.45**	Arrive Town Square, Stevenage for walkabout. Possible Soapbox.
10.30	Briefing with top aides for Press Conference.	**15.15**	Depart Stevenage for Bedford.
11.00	Press Conference.	**16.00**	Arrive The Harpur Centre, Midland Road entrance to be met by: Cllr Robert Blackman, Candidate for Bedford; Mr John Hoskin, Manager of the Harpur Centre. Address gathering, walkabout. Walkabout in Harpur Centre to Harpur Square. No soapbox opportunity. Interview with regional media.
11.45	Interview with Channel 5.		

AFTERNOON

12.15	Depart CCO for Wembley		
12.45	Arrive Wembley Conference Centre		
13.20	Met by Duncan Revie. Photo opportunity with: Tony Martin, Chairman Soccerex; Sepp Blatter, General Secretary of FIFA; Rita Whelan, Show Director.	**16.30**	Depart Bedford for Huntingdon by car.
		18.30	Arrive The Old Bridge Hotel, Huntingdon.
13.30	Photo opportunity with FA dignitaries on the 2006 World Cup Bid Stand. Jack Charlton should be in attendance.	**19.00**	*Channel 4 News* with Jon Snow.
		19.30	Depart for Finings [their Huntingdon home] by car.

Tony Blair – Labour

PROGRAMME FOR WEDNESDAY 30 APRIL 1997

MORNING

06.30	TB depart home for LWT – (Driver).	**09.00**	TB/CB/Staff/Press/Richard Wilson depart Stansted for Prestwick.
06.50	Arrive London Television Studios underground.		
07.00	*GMTV* live with Eammon Holmes in studio.	**10.00**	TB/CB/Staff/Press arrive at Prestwick – direct transfer to helicopters.
07.08	Depart for MBT (Millbank Tower).		
07.15	Press Conference, MBT.	**10.30**	TB/CB arrive Crichton Hospital – met by George Robertson/Russell Brown PPC (Prospective Parliamentary Candidate) (2 snappers from local papers present to get shot of TB/CB meeting PPC).
07.50	TB/CB depart for Stansted in 30 seater bus – breakfast with Hugo Young/photographer. Interview for the *Guardian* en route.		

Figure 3.1 continued

11.00	TB/CB depart.		**14.50**	TB/CB escorted to main hall.

11.00 TB/CB depart.

11.05 TB/CB arrive Dock Park (crowds behind barriers).
TB/CB greets crowd behind tape. Press in pen opposite platform. (Pipe band playing) Estimated crowd 1000.

11.10 TB steps up onto platform. RW and CB to left of TB. GR, RB, C Browne, to right TB. Stewards release tape to allow crowd to come forward. TB Speech.

11.20 TB finishes speech. Leaves platform with party jazz band playing.

11.35 Arrive Rugby and showground – photo with 15 year old Ryan Cassidy for *Daily Record.*

11.40 TB/CB depart in helicopter for Teesside (approximately 50 minutes).

AFTERNOON

12.30 John Prescott and party will be waiting.

13.00 TB/CB/staff/John Williams & JP and staff board respective BBs [Battle Buses] for Stockton.
– *Mirror* interview with John Williams.

13.20 TB/CB/JP/ proceed on walkabout.

13.35 TB adresses crowd.

13.50 Board BBs and depart for Marton Manor School.

14.30 TB/CB arrive Marton Manor School, The derby, Marton, Middlesbrough – met by Andy Dunn, Head Teacher, (FULL PRESS OPPORTUNITY).

14.35 TB/CB escorted into school with reg & nat pool.
TB/CB escorted by Head Teacher only around two classes, 5–7 year olds in open plan classrooms.

14.50 TB/CB escorted to main hall. Children singing songs.
TB/CB sit down in empty seats in front row with parents.
(FULL PRESS OPPORTUNITY – behind tape on other side of hall.)

14.55 TB walks onto podium in centre of room and addresses audience – surrounded by children.

15.05 TB/CB depart.
Board BB and depart for Middlesbrough Police Station – MIKE OFF.

15.25 TB/CB and Helen arrive Middlesbrough Police HQ, Emily Road – met halfway down walk way by Chief Superintendent Maurice Jones, Det. Superintendent Ray Mallon & DI Russ Dalgliesh and lots of uniformed police.

15.30 TB/CB/Helen Mirren to briefing room where CID (Criminal Investigations Department) and DSU (Uniformed Support Unit) are putting in bids for manpower the following day.

15.40 TB/CB and HM escorted by Mallon into CID Room.
– Brief discussion about zero tolerance.

16.00 TB/CB transfer into Terry's Jag and depart for Myrobella – spot arranged.

16.30 TB/CB arrive Myrobella [Mr Blair's constituency home].

18.00 TB/CB arrive Labour Club.

18.20 TB speaks.
At end of speech TB/CB go out into main bar where there will be 2 pool crews – nat and reg.

18.45 CB/TB go back through function room to meet members.

19.00 TB/CB depart for home.

22.00 TB/CB to Labour club for drink.

KEY TB – Tony Blair, CB – Cherie Blair

OPERATIONAL NOTE – WEDNESDAY APRIL 30 1997

NEWS RELEASE NATIONAL MEDIA TEAM
HELICOPTER TOUR

MORNING

07.30	Pre-press Conference, Church House
08.00	Departs for Sutton, Gt Peter Street.
09.20	Press Conference.
10.00	Departs for Battersea Heliport.
10.30	Depart for Sutton (helicopter).
10.30	PA and journalists arrive Sutton.
10.50	Arrive Collingwood Recreation Gound, Sutton.
11.10	Depart for Portsmouth.
11.50	Arrive Portsmouth, South Sea Common, Serpentine Road, Portsmouth.

AFTERNOON

12.20	Depart for Eastleigh (helicopter).
12.30	Arrive Eastleigh, Flemming Park Sports Centre.
13.10	Depart for Christchurch (helicopter).
13.25	Arrive Twyneham School, Christchurch. Walkabout in Christchurch.
14.05	Paddy to return by car to helicopter.
14.10	Depart for Mid Dorset (by helicopter).
14.20	Arrive Mid Dorset, Ashdown School, Playing Field.
14.50	Depart for Exeter Airport.
15.25	Arrive Exeter Airport.
15.55	Depart Exeter Airport for Bideford.
16.20	Arrive Bideford, Victoria Park, Sports Ground, Bideford Town Centre.
16.30	Walkabout with Baroness Williams/Emma Nicholson.
17.05	Departs for Saltash (helicopter).
17.30	Arrive Saltash, School Playing Field, Saltash Community Centre, Meet the people.
17.55	Depart for Torquay, Torre Valley. South/North Playing Field, Torquay.
18.10	Arrive Torquay Rally. Rivera Centre, Forum Hall.
20.30	Depart Torquay.
23.30	Return to Vane Cottage [home].

Source: Parliamentary elections in Britain (London: Foreign and Commonwealth Office, 1998).

3.1 The system today

At the 1997 General Election, 3723 candidates stood for election to the House of Commons (824 more than in 1992), and 44,296,793 people were eligible to vote. The 659 constituencies varied considerably in population and geographical area, although the average electorate in each constituency was 67,218, ranging from 69,577 in England, through 66,122 in Northern Ireland and 55,563 in Scotland, to 55,338 in Wales. For example, the Western Isles with the smallest electorate (22,983) was one of the largest in geographical area (over 2000 square miles), whereas the Isle of Wight with the largest electorate (101,680) was geographically confined to quite a small area (147 square miles). The largest constituency was Ross, Skye and Inverness West covering some 3500 square miles (with an electorate of 55,639); one of the smallest was Kensington and Chelsea covering only 3.6 square miles (with an electorate of 67,786). In total, 537 of the constituencies fell within 10 per cent of the average, with 35 being 10–15 per cent over, 9 being 15–20 per cent over, and 3 being more than 20 per cent over the average. A further 45 were 10–15 per cent under the average, while 22 were 15–20 per cent under and 8 were more than 20 per cent under average.

These discrepancies derive mainly from the fact that the population has expanded in some parts of the country, for example, East Anglia and the South West of England – while it has contracted in other parts, such as the inner city areas of London, Birmingham and Liverpool. The Boundary Commissions, which are strictly independent bodies, attempt every 10 to 15 years to rectify the most glaring anomalies. Reports of the Commissions for England, Scotland and Wales were approved by Parliament in 1983; the report for Northern Ireland was approved in 1982. As a result of these, the number of Parliamentary constituencies was increased from 635 to 650 for the General Election of 1983. By 1992, following an interim review, an additional constituency had been added by dividing the Milton Keynes constituency into two. The most recent review was approved by Parliament in 1995, taking the number of Parliamentary constituencies from 651 to 659 for the 1997 General Election – these are shown on the map in Figure 4.1 (page 60).

Electoral mechanisms

Under the 'first-past-the-post' voting system currently used for Parliamentary elections in the United Kingdom, on election day voters go to the polls to cast their votes in secret by putting 'X' against one name on the ballot paper. Any other mark may produce a 'spoiled vote' which could be judged invalid at the end of the count. The marked ballot papers are folded and deposited by the voters in locked ballot boxes where they remain until the polling stations close at 10.00 p.m. (they open at 7.00 a.m.). The ballot boxes are then transported to a central point in the constituency (often a Town Hall) where the counting of the votes takes place under the supervision of the Acting Returning Officer (normally the Chief Executive of the local authority concerned). The results are declared at varying times depending on the nature and size of the constituency, usually not less than about three hours after the closing of the polls but sometimes not until the following day.

Since 1948 it has also been permissible to cast postal votes if the voters concerned apply to be put on their constituency postal registers at least two weeks before polling day. Those who qualify for postal votes include people prevented by the nature of their job from voting in person (for example, merchant seamen or long-distance lorry drivers), people who are too sick or handicapped to vote in person, and those who have moved out of the constituency but are still on the electoral register where they used to live, including those living overseas, provided they have not been away for more than twenty years. People away on holiday on polling day also qualify for postal votes or can get a friend or relative to cast a proxy vote for them, provided they complete in advance the necessary formalities specified in the applicable legislation. In the General Election of 1997 about 750,000 postal votes were cast, 2.4 per cent of the total vote. This was up from the 720,000 cast in 1992, but still down on the 793,000 cast in 1987. Traditionally postal voting has generally been reckoned to favour the Conservative Party because of its superior organisation; in 1992, however, the Labour Party was convinced that some of its gains were due to its more effective efforts to secure the postal vote[1], while in 1997 Labour was widely recognised to have made a particular effort to organise postal votes, especially in marginal constituencies.

Nonetheless, postal votes can only make a decisive difference to a result in very marginal constituencies, since in the vast majority of constituencies the number of postal votes ranges between only 500 and 1,500.[2]

In 1998 the Government established a working group to carry out a wide-ranging review of electoral arrangements with a view to recommending ways in which voting could be made easier and more attractive. Matters under consideration by the group included electronic or automated voting, universal postal votes, better access to polling stations, moving elections from the traditional Thursday to the weekend, setting up polling stations in supermarkets, the use of mobile polling stations and the feasibility of operating a 'rolling register' of electors. The current arrangements have evolved over many years during which time the nature of election campaigning has changed beyond all recognition. It seems likely – and, many have argued, desirable – that an independent Electoral Commission should be set up, independent of Government, to supervise electoral arrangements and related matters in the future.

Individuals who are British citizens, or citizens of another Commonwealth country or of the Irish Republic, may stand as candidates for election to the House of Commons, provided that they are not disqualified from so doing. Those *not* legally entitled to stand include:

1 undischarged bankrupts
2 individuals sentenced to more than one year's imprisonment (until pardon or completion of sentence)[3]
3 certified lunatics
4 members of the House of Lords
5 ordained clergy in the Church of England, the Church of Scotland, the Church of Ireland and the Roman Catholic Church
6 individuals holding offices stipulated in the House of Commons Disqualification Act 1975, including civil servants, certain local government officials, judges, members of the regular armed forces and members of the police service.

There is no age limit – either minimum or maximum – for candidates, although Members of Parliament cannot take their seat in the House of Commons until they are 21 years of age. Similarly, there is no residence requirement, either in the constituency concerned or indeed in the country.

In order to be able to stand, an individual must be both nominated and seconded and then supported by a further eight individuals whose names appear on the electoral register in the constituency concerned. In addition, candidates must deposit a sum of £500 with the Returning Officer, a sum which is refunded after the election if they obtain more than 5 per cent of the votes cast (1,599 candidates – 42.9 per cent of the total – 'lost their deposits' at the 1997 General Election). Since 1970 candidates have been allowed to put on the ballot papers not only their names (which appear in alphabetical order), but also a description of their party or political position in not more than six words–for example, 'Conservative', 'Labour Party candidate', 'Liberal Democrat'.

An example of a ballot paper is provided in Figure 3.2.

Each candidate is restricted by law to a maximum expenditure during the three to five weeks' campaign. For the General Election of 1997 this stood at £4,965 plus 5.6p for each name on the register of voters in a rural constituency, and £4,965 plus 4.2p for each name on the register of voters in an urban constituency.[4] This allowed a

Figure 3.2 Example of a ballot paper

	VOTE FOR ONE CANDIDATE ONLY	
1	**BURSTOW** (Paul Kenneth Burstow, of 114 Grove Road, Sutton, Surrey Liberal Democrat)	
2	**DUFFY** (James Duffy, of 6 Langley Avenue, Surbiton, Surrey, KT6 6QL Green Party)	
3	**HATCHARD** (Angela Rose Hatchard, of 5 May Tree Walk, Woodley Park, Lancashire, WN8 6UP Natural Law Party Candidate)	
4	**MAITLAND** (Olga Helen Maitland, of 21 Cloudesley Street, London, N1 0HX The Conservative Party Candidate)	
5	**MARTIN** (Geoffrey Clifford Martin, of 284 Gander Green Lane, Sutton, Surrey, SM3 9QF The Labour Party Candidate)	

From the 1992 General Election. Reproduced with the kind permission of the Returning Officer of the London Borough of Sutton.

maximum expenditure, on average, of £8,690 in a rural seat and £7,759 in an urban seat, although most candidates declare expenses of rather less than the legal maxima.[5] In addition candidates are entitled to post one communication relating to the election to each household in the constituency free of charge, providing it weighs no more than 57 grammes. The 'serious money' is spent by the political parties centrally on display posters and newspaper advertisements. This is shown in Figure 3.3.

Figure 3.3 Party election spending

1979
- LAB 4.5
- CON 6.5
- LD 0.6

1983
- LAB 4.3
- CON 7.1
- LD 3.6

1987
- LAB 7.4
- CON 14.1
- LD 2.8

1992
- LAB 12.2
- CON 12.7
- LD 2.1

1997
- LAB 26.0
- CON 28.0
- LD 3.0

Labour
Conservative
Liberal Democrat

All figures are £million and are at constant 1997 prices.

Source: Michael Pinto-Duschinksy, *Guardian*, 18 November 1997.

These are not enormous figures for a country with an electorate of more than 44 million.[6] The real explanation is that neither the parties nor the candidates have to spend large sums of money on buying TV time – indeed they are prohibited from doing so – unlike the position in the United States for example. Indeed, with figures such as these it appears that Parliamentary elections are fought on the cheap in Britain as compared with other countries.[7]

Each candidate has to have a designated agent who is legally responsible for seeing that all aspects of election law are observed and who, in an extreme case, could be sent to prison if found guilty of electoral malpractice by a court. The agent also serves in most cases as the local campaign manager for the candidate, although this is not part of an agent's legal duties. The bulk of the work in every election campaign is done by voluntary workers who are usually subscribing members of the party, but who may simply be sympathisers with the party cause or with the particular candidate.

First-past-the-post

The electoral system currently used for Parliamentary elections in the United Kingdom is commonly described as 'first-past-the-post'. This means that in each constituency the candidate with the largest number of votes wins the seat. Usually this has the effect of turning the largest single minority of votes cast in the nation into a clear majority of seats in the House of Commons for the largest single party. In this way the system has benefited the two leading parties and discriminated against the political fortunes of all other parties, unless their votes are geographically concentrated in a particular part of the country.

This pattern of discrimination has been discernible for years in the British electoral system. At the 15 General Elections since the Second World War no party has ever won even half the votes cast, and often far fewer.[8] Yet the winning party has seldom won fewer than half the seats in the House of Commons. Both the Conservative and Labour parties have benefited from this so-called 'multiplier effect' which can produce a sizeable majority of Parliamentary seats on the basis of a minority of the popular votes cast. For example, the Labour Party enjoyed a positive differential (that is, between the percentage of seats won and votes cast) of 14 per cent in 1945, 11 per cent in October 1974 and 20 per cent in 1997, while the Conservative Party enjoyed a positive differential of 8 per cent in 1959, 9 per cent in 1979, and 15 per cent in 1987. On the other hand, the Liberal Party has been the most notable victim of the system during the period since 1945. From 1945 to 1979, the Liberal share of the popular vote ranged from 2 per cent in 1951 to 19 per cent in February 1974. Yet the system prevented the Liberals from winning more than 2 per cent of the seats in the Commons even in their most successful attempt in February 1974. In the 1983 General Election, this multiplier effect worked even more dramatically against the interests of the Alliance of Liberals and Social Democrats which won 25 per cent of the votes cast but only 3 per cent of the seats in the House of Commons. In the 1987 General Election it was virtually the same story with the Alliance winning about 23 per cent of the votes cast, but still getting only 3 per cent of the seats in the House of Commons. In 1992 the Liberal Democrats secured 18 per cent of the vote but only 3 per cent of the representation in the House of Commons. In 1997 they received 16.8 per cent of the vote, securing them 6.9 per cent of the seats. Figure 3.4 demonstrates the multiplier effect at the 1997 General Election.

From this it can be seen that in 1997 it took 32,336 votes to elect a Labour MP, 58,199 votes to elect a Conservative MP and 113,975 votes to elect a Liberal Democrat MP. Plainly, the number of seats won is in no way proportional to the number of votes cast by the electorate. This was brought home particularly clearly in both 1951 and February 1974. In the General Election of 1951, the Labour Party obtained 231,067 more votes (0.8 per cent) than the Conservative Party, but the Conservatives won 26 more seats than Labour. Similarly – although the roles were reversed – in the General Election of February 1974, the Conservative Party secured 225,789 more votes (0.7 per cent) than Labour, but the Labour Party won four more seats than the Conservatives. These results occurred because the votes of one party – the Conservatives in 1951 and Labour in 1974 – happened to be more effectively concentrated in a number of marginal constituencies, thus giving the winning party an edge over the other main party in Parliament. Yet the system has never been arithmetically fair to all parties and it has always had a bias against second or third parties whose votes are not socially or regionally concentrated. Its political merits lie elsewhere, namely in the tendency for most General Elections to produce effective Parliamentary majorities for single-party Governments. This has enabled the electorate

Figure 3.4 Voting by party in 1997

Party	Number of votes	% of electorate	% of votes cast	% of seats won	Number of candidates	MPs elected
Labour	13,516,632	30.51	43.20	63.43	639	418
Conservative	9,602,857	21.68	30.70	25.04	648	165
Liberal Democrat	5,242,894	11.83	16.76	6.98	639	46
Scottish National Party	621,540	1.40	1.99	0.91	72	6
Plaid Cymru	161,030	0.36	0.51	0.61	40	4
Ulster Unionist	258,349	0.58	0.83	1.52	16	10
Democratic Unionist	107,348	0.24	0.34	0.30	9	2
UK Unionist	12,817	0.03	0.04	0.15	1	1
Social Democratic and Labour	190,814	0.43	0.61	0.46	18	3
Sinn Féin	126,921	0.29	0.41	0.30	17	2
Speaker	23,969	0.05	0.08	0.15	1	1
Independent	29,354	0.07	0.09	0.15	1	1
Referendum	811,827	1.83	2.60	–	547	–
UK Independence	106,028	0.24	0.34	–	194	–
Green	63,991	0.14	0.20	–	95	–
Alliance	62,972	0.14	0.20	–	17	–
Socialist Labour	52,110	0.12	0.17	–	64	–
Liberal	44,989	0.10	0.14	–	54	–
British National	35,833	0.08	0.11	–	57	–
Natural Law	30,281	0.07	0.10	–	196	–
Pro Life Alliance	18,545	0.04	0.06	–	53	–
Progressive Unionist	10,934	0.02	0.03	–	3	–
National Democrat	10,829	0.02	0.03	–	21	–
Scottish Socialist Alliance	9,740	0.02	0.03	–	16	–
National Front	2,716	0.01	0.01	–	6	–
Others	131,277	0.30	0.42	–	299	–
Total	31,286,597	70.6	100.0	100.0	3,723	659
Total electorate	44,297,793	100.0				

to hold the governing party to account for what happens, or fails to happen, during a particular Parliament.

Proportional representation

The characteristics of the British electoral system have led many people to argue strongly for the introduction of a system based on proportional representation.[9]

In December 1997 Tony Blair appointed a five-strong Independent Commission on the voting system with the remit to recommend an alternative to the existing system for Parliamentary elections to be put before the people in a referendum, opening up the possibility that a future General Election could be fought under the proportional system advocated by the Commission.[10] This needs to be seen not only in conjunction with the fact that in July 1997 the Government announced that a regional list system of proportional representation would be used for the 1999 elections to the European Parliament (as opposed to the traditional first-past-the-post system) but also with the fact that elements within the Scottish Parliament, the Welsh Assembly and the Greater London Assembly are to be elected using the party list system of proportional representation, while the Mayor of London is to be elected using the supplementary vote system (under which voters list their first and second choices, the latter coming into play to determine the outright winner if no candidate secures an overall majority amongst first choices). Indeed, there is no one type of proportional representation, rather a number of variants of the basic idea.

The 'purest' proposal is for proportional representation on the basis of a *Single Transferable Vote* in large multi-member constituencies. This would allow the electorate in each constituency to vote for individual candidates in order of preference. To secure election, a candidate would need to obtain a certain quota of votes (established by dividing the total number of valid votes cast by the number of representatives to be returned for the constituency plus one, and then adding one to this total). Thus in a five-member constituency in which 240,000 votes were cast, the number of votes required for the quota (and hence election) would be 40,001 or about 17 per cent of the votes cast:

$$\frac{240,000}{5+1} + 1 = 40,001$$

If five candidates obtain this number of first preference votes, this is the end of the process. If, however, fewer than five reach the quota, a process of transference, or redistribution, takes place. Firstly, the 'excess' votes of the candidates who have gained more votes than the quota are transferred on the basis of second preferences, with the amount by which the votes of such candidates exceed the quota determining the value of the second preference votes. Hence, if a candidate gains 1,500 first preference votes and the quota is 1000, a third of the votes has not been used. This candidate's second preference votes are therefore worth one-third of a vote each. As a result, if 600 second preference votes went to candidate 'X', candidate 'X' would be allocated an additional 200 votes to add to his or her total of first preference votes. After the second preference votes of those with more than the quota have been transferred, and if five candidates have not yet obtained the quota, then the candidate with the fewest first preference votes is eliminated and the votes transferred on the basis of second preferences. This process is then continued until enough candidates reach the quota and all seats are filled.

Under this system, every elected candidate could be said to have sufficient votes from the electorate (at least on the basis of second and subsequent preferences) and it would be possible for the voters to vote for individual candidates within the ideological range of any large party. For example, in a safe Conservative constituency the voters might choose two hard-line Conservatives, one moderate Conservative, one Liberal Democrat and one centre-Right Labour. In a safe Labour seat, they might equally choose one Left-winger and two mainstream supporters of the leader from Labour's ranks, one Liberal Democrat and one moderate Conservative.

This system of proportional representation was recommended by a Speaker's Conference in 1917. It was actually used in some of the multi-member University seats between 1918 and 1948; it was advocated by the Kilbrandon Commission in 1973 as part of the proposals for devolved Assemblies in Scotland and Wales; and it is currently used in Northern Ireland for elections to the Assembly, the European Parliament and for local government elections. It is also the system used for Parliamentary elections in the Republic of Ireland. It is estimated by many – certainly if current voting habits continued under a reformed system – that the likely outcome of a General Election fought on the basis of the Single Transferable Vote system would be Coalition Government – a Government made up of more than one political party, very probably including the Liberal Democrats.

Another variant of proportional representation which has been advocated is the *Additional Member System* (AMS). This system is used in the Federal Republic of Germany, where half of the Bundestag (Lower House) members are elected by plurality in single-member constituencies and the other half from party lists drawn up within each Land (state). The voters have two votes each: one for a constituency candidate and one for a regional party list. The former enables the voters to express their first preferences and, if it is in a good area for their party, to secure their first choice for Parliament by direct election. The latter enables the voters to express what amounts to a second preference, usually by voting for the party list of one of the smaller parties in an attempt to ensure that the major opponent of their first preference does not get elected. In other words, they cast their second vote for the party they dislike least in an attempt to exclude the party they dislike most. The system can often improve the Parliamentary prospects for the smaller parties (such as the Free Democrats or the Greens) which might not otherwise have enough concentrated voting strength to get any of their candidates elected on a basis of first-past-the-post. It is also qualified by the so-called 5 per cent threshold which prevents parties with less than 5 per cent of the popular vote or three outright victories on the basis of first-past-the-post from securing any representation at all in the Bundestag. This is the system that is to be used for elections to the Scottish Parliament, the Welsh Assembly and the Greater London Assembly.

Yet another variant is based upon the *Two-Ballot System* used in France. This uses single member constituencies, but requires a candidate to win over half the votes cast in order to be elected on the first ballot. Failure to do this triggers a second ballot in which the result is decided by simple plurality, that is to say first-past-the-post. To go forward to the second ballot (if there is no outright winner on the first ballot), candidates require at least 12.5 per cent of the votes cast in the first ballot. This eliminates a great number of candidates from smaller parties or political splinter groups and automatically clarifies the voters' choice at the second ballot. The great advantage of this system is that it ensures majority support at least for those elected on the first ballot. The most commonly recognised disadvantage is that it is capable of producing bipolarised distortions which make it possible for a candidate who came third on the first ballot to triumph on the second because some of the supporters of the candidates who came first or second may find the third placed candidate the least unacceptable of the candidates in the second round. In other words, at the first ballot the voters choose, whereas at the second they eliminate. This system certainly does not avoid the imbalance between votes obtained and seats won identified under the first-past-the-post system – a point underlined by the fact that in the 1981 elections to the French National Assembly, the Socialists secured 62 per cent of the seats on the basis of only 38 per cent of the votes cast.

A variation of this is the *Supplementary Vote System* (SV) under which voters mark their first and second choice candidates on the ballot paper. First preferences are counted and if one candidate gets 50 per cent of the vote or more, that person is elected. If no one gets 50 per cent of the vote, all of the candidates, except the two with the highest number of votes, are eliminated and second preferences on the ballot papers of those eliminated candidates are then allocated among the rest. Whoever has the most votes at the end of this process is declared the winner.

Two other systems should be noted. First, the *Alternative Vote System* (AV) – similar in some respects to the Supplementary Vote System – under which candidates contest single-member constituencies and voters mark the candidates in order of preference. If a candidate secures over half the votes cast, the candidate is elected; but if no candidate in a constituency does so, then the candidate with the fewest votes is eliminated and the votes redistributed according to the preferences indicated. This process continues until the support for a candidate passes the 50 per cent threshold. This system is currently in use for elections to the lower House in Australia.

Secondly, there is the *National Party List System*. Here the whole country could constitute a single constituency. Each party draws up a list of its candidates and the voters vote for the party they prefer. Once the votes have been counted, the parties are allocated seats in proportion to the number of votes they obtained. Hence, if a party gets 25 per cent of the vote, it gets 25 per cent of the seats, with individual candidates securing election according to their position on their party's list. This system is currently in use in Israel, Norway, Portugal and Turkey – in Israel it is used in its 'pure' form; the others use variants on the theme, for example by region and using thresholds. Some countries – for example Belgium, Denmark, Finland, the Netherlands, Spain and Sweden – use a variation of this system that enables voters to indicate a preference for candidates on the list. A variation of this system is the *Regional Party List System*, which is to be used in Britain for the elections to the European Parliament in 1999. (See Figure 3.5 for clarification of the regions.)

The Labour Party Manifesto for the 1997 election declared a commitment to a referendum on the voting system for the House of Commons, with an independent Commission on the voting system to be appointed to recommend a proportional alternative to the first-past-the-post system. A Commission was duly set up, under the Chairmanship of Lord Jenkins of Hillhead, in December 1997, and issued its report in October 1998. It recommended a two-vote mixed system – described as either limited AMS or AV top-up – with the majority of MPs (80–85 per cent) being elected on an individual constituency basis by the alternative vote system, with the remainder elected on a corrective top-up basis using open party lists in local areas. Nearly all the MPs in the minor parties favour a change, whereas this has been true of only some in the Labour Party and of very few in the Conservative Party. Whether or not we shall see the end of the first-past-the-post system for Parliamentary elections in the United Kingdom, only time will tell.

3.2 Criteria of assessment

In a celebrated text written more than 40 years ago W.J.M. Mackenzie suggested four criteria by which an electoral system could be assessed. These were the quality of those elected, the effectiveness of the legislature, the fairness of the electoral results, and the degree of public confidence inspired.[11] It may therefore be convenient to con-

Figure 3.5 The eleven Euro regions in the United Kingdom

number of MEPs

SCOTLAND
8

NORTH EAST
4

YORKSHIRE AND
THE HUMBER
7

NORTH WEST
10

EAST MIDLANDS
6

WEST MIDLANDS
8

EASTERN
8

WALES
5

LONDON
10

SOUTH WEST
7

SOUTH EAST
11

In 1998 the Government introduced a regional list system of proportional representation to select Britain's 84 Euro MPs at the elections to the European Parliament in June 1999. The country was divided into eleven large regions. Each region returns between four and 11 members.
The key difference is that the electorate votes for a party and not for an individual candidate. Each party puts forward a list of candidates for each region in its order of preference.
Seats allocated in proportion to each party's vote. Candidates higher up the lists therefore have a better chance of winning a seat. There was no change in Northern Ireland which has always been treated as a single region and where three MEPs elected under the single transferable vote system of proportional representation.

Source: The Times, 28 May 1998.

sider the British electoral system in the light of these four, admittedly rather ideal, criteria.

The quality of the MPs

Members of Parliament in Britain are not strictly representative of the general public in that they are usually better educated and financially better off than the electorate as a whole. Of course, these general observations should come as no real surprise since similar statements could be made about every national assembly throughout the world, including those in former Communist countries. Yet there remains a utopian bias in some quarters in favour of achieving a more 'representative' House of Commons – by which people usually mean one composed of those more like them!

Taking the House of Commons which was elected in May 1997, we find that 37 per cent of Conservative MPs and 45 per cent of Labour MPs came from what can be described as professional occupations, such as the law, education, medicine, accountancy and so on. In addition, 39 per cent of Conservative MPs and 9 per cent of Labour MPs had an occupational background in business. A further 23 per cent of Conservative MPs and 33 per cent of Labour MPs had their occupational background as political organisers, journalists and so on. Only 1 per cent (one) of Conservative MPs and 13 per cent (54) of Labour MPs could be categorised as manual workers. As far as the Liberal Democrat MPs were concerned, these categories accounted for 50 per cent, 24 per cent, 24 per cent and 2 per cent respectively.

Among Conservative MPs, 66 per cent had been educated at public school (with 13.7 per cent of those having been to Eton) and 81 per cent had experienced higher or further education, 51 per cent having been to either Oxford or Cambridge. Among Labour MPs only 16 per cent had received a public school education (and only 3 per cent of those had been to Eton), but 66 per cent had experienced higher or further education, although only 14 per cent had been to either Oxford or Cambridge. Among the Liberal Democrat MPs, 41 per cent had received a public school education (5 per cent at Eton), 70 per cent had received further or higher education, and 32 per cent had been to either Oxford or Cambridge.[12] Although the socio-economic differential has narrowed noticeably in recent years, it is nevertheless still apparent that Conservative MPs tend to come from more privileged backgrounds than their Labour and Liberal Democrat counterparts.

Certainly the House of Commons is far from being a microcosm of the population as a whole – a point which is most clearly evidenced by the fact that only 18.2 per cent of MPs elected in 1997 were women (although this was an increase on the 9.2 per cent figure in 1992), even though women comprised 52 per cent of the total electorate at the time; and by the fact that only 1.3 per cent were from ethnic minorities, even though ethnic minorities comprised 5.5 per cent of the population.

Of course, characteristics such as educational and occupational background are not necessarily signs of quality, and in any case the standard of MPs could always be higher. Yet quality is not really a function of the electoral system. It derives much more from the intermittent nature of Parliamentary work, the frustrations of life on the back benches, the unwillingness of many employers to encourage their employees to stand for Parliament, the increasing intrusion of the media into the private lives of public figures, and the low esteem in which politicians are held by the vast majority of the British people. All these factors may discourage many able people from standing for Parliament or even from entering active politics in the first place. Furthermore, in the front-bench-dominated political system that exists in Britain, no more than about 90 MPs are paid members of any Government and no more than about another 90 are involved in the tasks of front-bench Opposition. Thus the vast majority of MPs in the House of Commons at any time are obliged to busy themselves with other forms of political activity, such as liaising with outside interests or welfare work on behalf of their constituents. This may be appreciated by their contacts and expected by their constituents, but it does not necessarily attract the most talented people into Parliament.

Effectiveness of the legislature

There are many shortcomings in the British legislature, but they should not necessarily be attributed to the workings of the electoral system. One of the familiar charges levelled against the British system is that it makes it all too easy for one or other of the parties to win an overall majority in the Commons which can then be used to push through its partisan legislation, often against rather ineffective Parliamentary opposition and sometimes in defiance of the expressed wishes of the general public.

According to this argument, Parliament is actually too effective at churning out partisan, ill-considered legislation and too ineffective at controlling the actions of the Government of the day. If this is so, it is essentially because all MPs not in the Government have little involvement and no responsibility in the formative stages of policy and decision making. It is also because Government back-benchers are inhibited by party loyalty and political self-interest from pursuing continuous public criticism of their own Ministers. Parliamentary control is therefore left largely in the hands of the Opposition, which is usually unable to do more than kick up a fuss about controversial Government decisions or delay the contentious elements in the Government's legislative programme. The system is indeed one in which although the Opposition has its say, the Government gets its way, at any rate most of the time.

The British people expect their Members of Parliament to be doughty champions of their interests and unabashed spokesmen for their concerns. This is what they expect from an effective legislature. In practice, constituents are often disappointed to discover that the power of party loyalty usually overrides both more parochial and more altruistic considerations when it comes to votes in the House of Commons. The argument for this position is effectively that MPs on the Government side are elected principally to support Government policy as set out in the party Manifesto and other relevant documents and can only rarely go against that imperative without undermining what is described as 'the mandate theory' of Government (see pages 187–8) Thus, those opposed to or critical of the Government's programme may well win the argument, but usually lose the vote at the end of debates in Parliament.

Fairness of the results

It is here that we enter the area of greatest controversy about the British electoral system. While it enables the electorate to choose what is normally a single-party Government every four or five years at General Election time, it does not produce a House of Commons which is anything like an exact reflection of the votes cast for each party. Essentially, it is a system which enables the largest single minority of voters in the national electorate to bring about the return of single-party Government with an overall majority in the House of Commons. There is, in fact, a threshold of between 35 per cent and 40 per cent of the votes cast above which (especially in marginal seats with three or more candidates) a party has a good chance of capturing seats, but below which it is likely to fail to form the Government.

This situation arises because most General Elections in Britain tend to be contests between at least three parties in which the second and third ranking parties frequently split the losing vote between them, thus ensuring that neither has a real chance of defeating the leading party. Obviously there is always the possibility of tactical voting by the supporters of one or other of the losing parties, yet on the whole this has not made much difference to the results (except occasionally at by-elections), since none of the parties can be sure of delivering enough of its supporters to guarantee such an outcome. The same flaw affects the idea of an electoral pact between the various Opposition parties in which all but one of them would stand down in individual constituencies in favour of the party with the best chance of defeating the incumbent.

In the General Election of February 1974 the third party (the Liberals) received more than six million votes, a little more than half the votes received by either the Conservative or Labour parties, but won only fourteen seats in the House of Commons, less than one-twentieth of the seats secured by either of the two main parties. At the same time, and as previously pointed out, the party which won the election (Labour) did so with fewer popular votes than the party which came second in terms of Parliamentary seats (the Conservatives). In the 1983 General Election the discrepancy between votes and seats was even more striking: the Conservative Party secured 61 per cent of the seats on 42.4 per cent of the votes cast, the Labour Party got 32 per cent of the seats on 27.6 per cent of the votes cast, while the Alliance of Liberals and Social Democrats, although receiving 25.4 per cent of the popular vote – just 2.2 per cent less than Labour – won only 3.5 per cent of the seats, 28.5 per cent less than Labour. In the General Election of 1997, despite polling almost 5.2 million votes (39 per cent of the level of support obtained by the Labour Party), the Liberal Democrats still only obtained 46 seats in the House of Commons, 11 per cent of the Labour total of 418. In 1997 the Conservatives polled 30.7 per cent of the vote but received only 25.0 per cent of the seats; in Scotland they received 17.5 per cent of the vote and won not a single seat, whereas, in contrast, the Liberal Democrats received 13.0 per cent of the vote and won ten seats.

Of course, the results could be very different if the potential supporters of third parties, those who abstain from voting and those who are deterred from supporting their first preference for fear of casting wasted votes, were all to vote in accordance with their real political preferences. In that case, there would be a possibility of parties which previously came third coming first in many parts of the country. The most sensible conclusion is that in the scheme of things, fairness is not the prime consideration. The overriding purpose is to elect a Government with a sufficient Parliamentary majority to ensure its authority to govern throughout the period of a normal four or five year Parliament; in the first-past-the-post system this usually means single-party Government.

Public confidence inspired

It is difficult to produce reliable measures of public confidence in something as abstract as an electoral system. One way of assessing it is to note the degree of popular support for electoral reform as measured by opinion polls. This has consistently proved attractive to representative samples of the electorate as a whole.[13] Not that exact parallels can be drawn, but it is nonetheless interesting to point out that when consulted in a referendum in September 1992, the people of New Zealand voted overwhelmingly (84.5 per cent) to end their first-past-the-post electoral system, although it should also be noted that Kiwi public opinion – according to opinion polls – appears to have become more dubious with the benefit of experience.[14]

Another way of assessing public confidence in the electoral system is to log the performance of the two large parties at successive General Elections. In view of the fact that they have traditionally been associated in the public mind with adherence to the existing electoral system, a high level of support for both of them together could also be interpreted as support for the existing rules of the game. Doing this, we find that the proportion of the electorate voting for the Conservative and Labour Parties taken together fell consistently from 79 per cent in 1951 to 55 per cent in October 1974. It rose to 62 per cent in 1979, fell back to 51 per cent in 1983, rose again to 55 per cent in 1987, increased to 59 per cent in 1992, and fell back to 52 per cent in 1997. In the General Election of 1997, a sizeable proportion of the electorate (29.4 per cent) did not vote at all and the Labour Party won with the support of only 30.51 per cent of the total electorate.[15] In so far as any valid or lasting conclusion can be drawn from this evidence, it can hardly be that the British public has given a massive vote of confidence in the electoral system.

3.3 The debate

Firstly, supporters of the first-past-the-post system argue that the system works well, pointing out that it has led to stable Governments based on Parliamentary majorities of one party rather than Coalitions, which can be weak and ineffective. Single party Government is said to mean strong, accountable and responsive Government.

Critics of the present system counter this view in a variety of ways:

1. They argue that the system does not work well, pointing to the anomalies already referred to in this chapter as evidence of this.
2. They deny that stability is inherent in the system citing 1950–51, 1964–66, February and October 1974, and the periods 1976–79 and 1994–97 to back this up.
3. They point out that if by 'strong' Government is meant a Government that can force through unpopular legislation – such as the Poll Tax – then perhaps 'weak' Government, a Government that would have to listen to the views and opinions of others, would be no bad thing.
4. They assert that there is no justification for the view that proportional representation necessarily results in weak and unstable Government – citing the examples of Germany and Sweden to support the assertion.
5. They argue that the supporters of first-past-the-post are deluding themselves if they believe the system ensures decisive and strong action on the part of Government, and cite the weakness of John Major's Government at the time of the Parliamentary ratification of the Maastricht Treaty as evidence for their case.
6. They argue that the system encourages adversarial politics – citing the nationalisation, denationalisation, re-nationalisation and privatisation of the steel industry as one example of the damaging consequences of this approach to politics.
7. They point out that the first-past-the-post system is capable of creating Governments which behave like elective dictatorships, but which do so on a minority of the popular vote.

Secondly, supporters of the first-past-the-post system argue that electoral reform would lead to a Coalition Government and that this would place disproportionate power in the hands of the minor parties. It would be the minor parties which would dictate the outcome of elections, it would be the minor parties which would exert disproportionate influence on Government policy and it could be the minor parties which would determine the date and the occasion of the subsequent election. In short, the tail would be wagging the dog. To support this assertion they point to the role of the Free Democrats and the Green Party in Germany, parties which have often struggled to get even 10 per cent of the vote and yet one or other – traditionally the Free Democrats but more recently the Greens – have been an essential component of most postwar German Governments, and the New Zealand First Party in New Zealand following the 1996 election when, with only 13 per cent of the vote, the party leader, Winston Peters, was cast in the role of Kingmaker.

Those who argue for electoral reform respond by asking why this should be a problem if it ensures effective, successful Government – and cite the 'German Economic Miracle' as evidence of what can be achieved in such circumstances. Besides which, they go on to point out, 'deals' with minor parties are not unknown in the British political system, citing the Lib-Lab Pact of 1977–79 and the Conservative Government's dependence upon the Ulster Unionists at times during 1992–97. In their view, there is nothing inherently wrong in Coalition Governments, since the main political parties are Coalitions in themselves. In other words, the present system is based on intra-party coalitions, whereas a reformed system would depend on inter-party Coalitions

Thirdly, those who argue in favour of the current electoral system caution that any reform could lead to the rise of extremists – citing the rise of the Fascist Right in Germany (the DVU) and in France (The National Front) in the 1990s.[16]

Advocates of reform respond by observing that those who profess to be worried by the danger of Fascism and the extreme Right would do better to consider introducing formal checks and balances into Britain's constitutional arrangements – such as a written constitution and a new Bill of Rights. Without this there exists a system which allows, even facilitates, Government by a single party, with the support of about two-fifths of the popular vote, enjoying predominant power in Westminster. They go on to point out that an electoral system based on proportional representation would be an instrument which more accurately reflected the strength or weakness of the various political tendencies in society. It would follow, therefore, that if racist or extremist sentiment were present, it would be reflected through the electoral system.

Fourthly, supporters of the current electoral arrangements believe that reform would lead to weak Government.[17] To support this line they cite the examples of Italy and New Zealand: Italy where there were 55 Governments in the period 1945–1999 and where the politicians finally turned to the first-past-the-post system as a way out of the troubles associated with their previous proportional system; and New Zealand, which abandoned first-past-the-post in favour of a system modelled on that of Germany following a 54 per cent vote in favour of doing so in the referendum of 1993, but where by the end of 1997 most believed that the experiment had proved a spectacular failure and opinion polls showed that about 60 per cent of New Zealanders wanted the old system reinstated.[18]

Critics of the current British system would respond by observing that as far as Italy is concerned it has not adopted the first-past-the-post system entirely, but rather a mixed system in which 75 per cent of members of the Chamber of Deputies are elected by first-past-the-post and the remaining 25 per cent under a proportional system designed to ensure representation for those unlikely to win under pure first-past-the-post. They also point out that there were in fact more individuals in British Cabinets between 1944 and 1995 than in Italian Cabinets, thus casting doubt on the relative stability of the British system. With regard to the position in New Zealand, critics of the current British system point out that a change in the system used could, and probably would, result in a coalition government, with all that would entail – a fact that appears to have been ignored or misunderstood in New Zealand. Finally, they make the point that what happens in a particular society is usually more the product of that society than its electoral arrangements.

3.4 Conclusion

The British electoral system has come a long way since Queen Victoria confided to her diary that 'it seems to me a defect in our much famed constitution to have to part with an admirable Government ... merely on account of the number of votes'.[19] Nowadays, a General Election is usually seen as a public verdict on the record of the party in Government and the competing attractions of the various Opposition parties. Yet the mass electorate is politically sovereign only on condition that it exercises its sovereignty when invited to do so by the Prime Minister of the day and within the limits of political choice offered by the political parties at each General Election.

Modern British politics is essentially about the struggle for power between the political parties. Of course, there has always been some ideology in the political rhetoric and the party manifestos. Yet for most of those who reach the top of the political tree the ideological content has often been little more than a necessary part of the political ritual, the tribute which party leaders and others have had to pay to their more zealous followers and supporters, especially when in Opposition. Some would argue that this changed when Margaret Thatcher was Leader of the Conservative Party from 1975 to 1990. Yet the appeal of pragmatism usually trumps ideology if the latter is seen as a threat to a party's chances of gaining or retaining power, a fact that the case of Tony Blair and 'New' Labour would seem to highlight.

In short, the conduct of elections and the Parliamentary results which ensue are seldom more important than the actual behaviour of the parties either when elected into Government or when released for the self-indulgence of Opposition. While free elections on the basis of universal adult suffrage are an indispensable foundation for the electoral system, it is the quality of party politics between elections and the conduct of every Government in office which counts far more in British Parliamentary democracy.

Suggested questions

1   Describe the working of the British electoral system.
2   To what extent does the British electoral system satisfy the four criteria suggested by W.J.M. Mackenzie?
3   Analyse the arguments for and against a change to proportional representation in Britain.

Notes

1. See D. Butler and D. Kavanagh, *The British General Election of 1992* (London: Macmillan, 1992), pp. 243–44.
2. In the Cambridge constituency at the 1992 General Election the postal vote accounted for 10 per cent of the total vote (5,085 votes – an increase of 46 per cent over the 2,758 postal votes cast in 1987). It was a seat the Labour Party captured on a 6.4 per cent swing with a majority of only 580. At the 1997 General Election it is possible that the postal vote may have saved the Conservative incumbent in five constituencies, namely, Dorset South, Bedfordshire SW, Teignbridge, Lichfield and Hexham. See D. Butler and D. Kavanagh, *The British General Election of 1997* (London: Macmillan, 1997, p. 222).
3. This is stipulated in the Representation of the People Act, 1981, and was a direct result of the Bobby Sands case in Northern Ireland.
4. These figures are reviewed annually and increased if needs be in line with inflation. Under the Representation of the People Act, 1989, separate, higher, limits apply in the case of Parliamentary by-elections. In 1998 the basis was £19,863 plus 22.2p per elector in a rural constituency and 16.9p per elector in an urban constituency.
5. In 1997 the average expenditure of Conservative candidates was £5,600 (71 per cent), of Labour candidates £5,600 (71 per cent) and of Liberal Democrat candidates £3,200 (42 per cent). As far as victorious candidates were concerned the figures rose to 89 per cent, 77 per cent and 94 per cent respectively. See D. Butler and D. Kavanagh, *The British General Election of 1997*, p. 223.
6. The official expenses – the cost – of the 1997 General Election was about £52 million (quite apart from the annual cost of compiling the electoral register, which was £50 million in 1996–97), and are met by the Government out of the Consolidated Fund. This was a figure only slightly offset by the £799,500 received by the Treasury from lost deposits.
7. By way of international comparison it is interesting to note that in the United States it is estimated that the main parties spent $2.7 billion (£1.6 billion) on the 1996 presidential election campaign. Indeed, in the primary runoffs to secure the Democrat Party's California gubernotorial nomination in 1998 one of the candidates, Al Checchi, spent an estimated $50 million (£30 million), and another, Jane Harman, spent an estimated $25 million (£15 million), record spending, and neither secured the nomination, receiving only 13 per cent and 12 per cent of the vote respectively. (The individual who was nominated, Gray Davis, ran with the campaign slogan 'Experience that money can't buy'; spending an estimated $12 million (£7.2 million) he received 35 per cent of the vote.)
8. 1945, 1950, 1951, 1955, 1959, 1964, 1966, 1970, February 1974, October 1974, 1979, 1983, 1987,1992 and 1997.
9. See V. Bogdanor, *Power and the People* (London: Victor Gollancz), pp. 53–93 and V. Bogdanor, *What is Proportional Representation?* (Oxford: Robertson, 1984), for fuller discussion of proportional representation.
10. The members of the Commission were: Lord Jenkins of Hillhead (Chair), former Labour Cabinet Minister, co-founder of the SDP, and retired leader of the Liberal Democrat peers in the House of Lords; Lord Alexander of Weedon, Chairman of the Nat West Group and former Chairman of the Bar Council; Sir John Chilcot, Permanent Secretary at the Northern

Ireland Office 1990–97; Baroness Gould of Potternewton, Labour Party director of Organisation 1985–93 and a former member of the Plant Commission on Proportional Representation; David Lipsey, political editor of *The Economist*. The Commission's report was published in October 1998. See 'The Report of the Independent Commission on the Voting System', CM 4090-1 (London: Stationery Office, 1998).

11. See W.J.M. Mackenzie, *Free Elections* (London: Allen & Unwin, 1958), pp. 69–71.
12. See D. Butler and D. Kavanagh, *The British General Election of 1997*, pp. 186–209.
13. Polling for 'Make Votes Count' conducted in 1998 showed that 72 per cent would support elctoral reform. Even after hearing arguments for first-past-the-post, 57 per cent favoured reform. See Stephen Twigg, 'Votes for PR', *Guardian*, 20 June 1998.
14. See S. Collins, 'Vote for Change Overwhelming', *New Zealand Herald*, 21 September 1992.
15. The statistics on turnout at General Elections depend very much on the accuracy of the Electoral Register. On average, it has been little more than 90 per cent accurate and even less so in inner city areas where the population is very mobile. In addition, it has been claimed that there was an increase in the number of unregistered voters in the 1980s and 1990s as a direct result of individuals choosing not to register in an attempt to avoid paying the poll tax in the period 1988–92. In September 1994 a Labour Party report ('The Missing Millions: Disenfranchised Citizens') claimed that 20 per cent of people in their early 20s, nearly 25 per cent of black people and 38 per cent of those relying on a private landlord to fill in registration forms, did not appear on the electoral register. Despite campaigns like 'Rock the Vote' and 'Operation Black Vote' aimed to attract the missing young and ethnic minority voters, it is still estimated that some two million voters are not on the register. (See the Independent, 4 February 1998.)
16. See Rees-Mogg, W., 'The Primrose Path to PR', *The Times*, 26 March 1998.
17. See Mount, F., 'Say Hello to the Hell of PR Voting', *The Sunday Times*, 30 November 1997.
18. See Chapman, P., 'Voters get Cross with PR in New Zealand', *Electronic Telegraph*, No 930, 10 December 1997.
19. Quoted in E. Longford, *Victoria R.I.* (London: Weidenfeld & Nicolson, 1964), p. 518.

Further reading

Alderman G., *British Elections: Myth and Reality* (London: Batsford, 1978).
Blackburn, R., *The Electoral System in Britain* (London: Macmillan, 1995).
Bogdanor, V., *Power and the People* (London: Victor Gollancz, 1997).
Bogdanor, V.*, The People and the Party System* (London: CUP, 1981).
Bogdanor, V., *What is Proportional Representation?* (Oxford: Robertson, 1984).
Butler, D., *British General Elections Since 1945* (Oxford: Blackwell, 1989).
Butler, D. and Kavanagh, D., *The British General Election of 1992* (London: Macmillan, 1992).
Denver, D., *Elections and Voting Behaviour in Britain* (London: Phillip Allen, 1989).
Finer, S.E. (ed.), *Adversary Politics and Electoral Reform* (London: Anthony Wigram, 1975), *The Report of the Hansard Society Commission on Electoral Reform* (London: Hansard Society, 1976).
King, A. (ed.), *Britain at the Polls 1992* (London: Chatham House, 1993).
Lakeman, E., *Power to Elect: The Case for Proportional Representation* (London: Heinemann, 1982).
Norton, P., 'Does Britain Need Proportional Representation?', in Blackburn, R. (ed.), *Constitutional Studies* (London: Mansell, 1992).
Norton, P. and Gavin N.T. (eds), *Britain Votes 1997* (Oxford: University Press, 1997).
Plant, R. *The Plant Report on Electoral Reform* (The Labour Party/Guardian Newspaper, 1991).

Rawlings, H.F., *Law and the Electoral Process* (London: Sweet & Maxwell, 1988).
'The Report of the Independent Commission on the Voting System', CM 4090-1 (London: Stationery Office, 1998).

Website

BBC General Election 1997   http://www.bbc.co.uk/election97/

4 Voting behaviour

Voting behaviour in Britain since the Second World War (1939–45) has been characterised mainly by the tendency of the electorate at General Elections to divide between two main parties, namely the Conservative Party and the Labour Party. There have been occasions in recent history, however, when the formation of a three-party – or in Wales and especially in Scotland a four-party – system seemed to be imminent. For example, in the early 1970s there was a revival in the fortunes both of the Liberal Party and of the Nationalist parties, with the Liberal Party taking 19.3 per cent and 18.3 per cent of the national vote in the February and October 1974 General Elections respectively, with the Scottish Nationalists receiving 30.4 per cent of the vote in Scotland and Plaid Cymru 10.8 per cent of the vote in Wales in October 1974. Although the talk was of multi-party politics, by 1979 the fortunes of the minor parties had declined again.

Similarly, in the early 1980s, following the formation of the Alliance between the Liberals and the newly formed Social Democrats, it looked for a time as though the two-party mould of British politics would be broken. Yet in the event this was not to be the case. The Alliance split asunder in the wake of the 1987 General Election, when Dr David Owen and some Social Democrats refused to join the newly formed Liberal Democrats, and the leadership of the Labour Party appeared to rediscover the path of political moderation and common sense. In the 1997 General Election although the Liberal Democrats attracted 16.76 per cent of the popular vote nationally and 31.3 per cent in the South West of England (compared with 26.4 per cent for Labour), the Scottish Nationalists received 22.1 per cent of the Scottish vote (compared with 17.5 per cent for the Conservatives), and Plaid Cymru received 9.9 per cent of the Welsh vote, nonetheless, the traditional two-party model of voting behaviour seemed to have been reasserted, at any rate at General Elections on a nation-wide level – in contrast to local elections or Parliamentary by-elections when other parties have been more successful.

It is perhaps not altogether surprising that this should be so, since the dominance of two main parties (not always the same two parties) has clear antecedents in British political history and has been encouraged by the electoral system (see Chapter 3). In the late eighteenth and early nineteenth centuries there was a struggle for power between the Whigs and the Tories. In the late nineteenth and early twentieth centuries

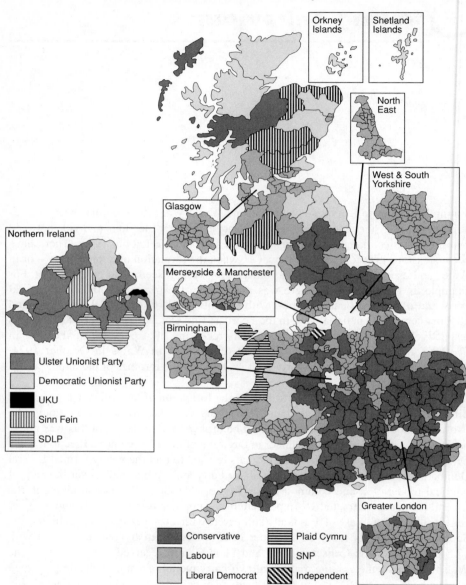

Figure 4.1 Political map of the United Kingdom
1997 General Election – constituency results

Orkney Islands

Shetland Islands

North East

West & South Yorkshire

Glasgow

Merseyside & Manchester

Birmingham

Northern Ireland

Ulster Unionist Party

Democratic Unionist Party

UKU

Sinn Fein

SDLP

Conservative

Labour

Liberal Democrat

Plaid Cymru

SNP

Independent

Greater London

there was a struggle between the Liberals and the Conservatives. During the first few decades of the twentieth century it was uncertain whether or not Labour would displace the Liberals as the main opponent of the Conservatives. However, since the end of the Second World War for many people the effective choice at all General Elections has been between the Conservative and Labour parties.

4.1 Groups in the electorate

It is possible to identify many different groups in the British electorate. The lines of political cleavage can be drawn in a number of different ways, according to various criteria. In this section we shall summarise the position according to the most widespread and familiar definitions.

Party loyalists

At General Elections since the Second World War the Conservative and Labour parties have been able to count on the loyal support of a significant number of core voters, individuals who have supported their party almost regardless of the issues or other factors. Estimates have put the number of core voters at between 6.5 million and 7.5 million for each main party. However, recent surveys have indicated that the proportion of the electorate strongly identifying with and consistently voting for one or other of the two main parties has declined. From the mid-1970s there has also been a significant number of voters who have consistently chosen to support first the Liberal Party and, more recently, the Liberal Democrats. Estimates have put this core Liberal vote at between 1 million and 1.5 million – a marked increase from the 1960s when it was between 0.5 and 0.75 million and indeed from the 1950s when it was as low as 0.25 million voters.

In Scotland and Wales there have been sections of the electorate which have voted consistently for the Nationalist parties, the Scottish National Party (SNP) and Plaid Cymru (PC). However, it is hard to ascertain how many of these voters can be considered 'core' supporters, since both the SNP and PC have always attracted substantial and varying protest votes and their electoral fortunes have fluctuated accordingly. At the 1997 General Election together they collected 782,570 votes, only 2.5 per cent of the total vote in the United Kingdom but 22.1 per cent in Scotland and 9.9 per cent in Wales.

The electorate in Northern Ireland (1,175,403 people in 1998) has traditionally been divided along religious lines, with a majority (50.6 per cent according to the most recent census) being Protestant and a minority (38.4 per cent) being Catholic – the remaining 11 per cent having no declared religious affiliation. Because of this, more than half have habitually voted for an assortment of Unionist/Protestant candidates (50.5 per cent in 1997), while the votes of most of the rest of the electorate have gone to the Nationalist/Republican/Catholic candidates, particularly the Social Democratic and Labour Party (SDLP) but also to Sinn Fein, the political wing of the IRA. In 1997 the SDLP received 24.1 per cent of the vote, while Sinn Fein received 16.1 per cent, Nationalist a total of 40.2 per cent. In addition there exists the non-sectarian Alliance Party which received 8.0 per cent of the popular vote in Northern Ireland in 1997.

In the elections to the Northern Ireland Assembly in 1998 the SDLP received 22.3 per cent of the vote and Sinn Féin received 17.6 per cent of the vote, a combined vote of 39.9 per cent. The Ulster Unionists obtained 21.3 per cent of the vote, with a total Unionist vote of 52.0 per cent.

Floaters and abstainers

The vital group of floating voters has varied in number and in composition at each General Election since the Second World War. This volatile section of the electorate, which by definition is never made up of exactly the same people from one General Election to the next, seems to have grown in size over the years. Over the period 1959–79 about half the electorate changed its voting behaviour at least once, if we include moves to and from abstention.[1] Over one-third of those who voted Labour in 1979 deserted the party in 1983, as did nearly one-quarter of those who voted Conservative, thus effectively determining the outcome of the 1983 election. At the 1987 General Election it was the Alliance of Liberals and Social Democrats which suffered most from the floating vote, losing nearly one-third of its 1983 vote to other parties or to non-voting. Each of the main parties also suffered from defectors, with the Conservatives losing 23 per cent of their 1983 vote to other parties and abstention and Labour losing 25 per cent in the same way. At the 1992 General Election, of those eligible to vote in both 1987 and 1992, 16 per cent moved from supporting one party to supporting another party and an additional 20 per cent moved to or from abstention. At the 1997 General Election it has been estimated that 23 per cent of those who had voted Conservative in 1992 voted for a different party, as did 7 per cent of the 1992 Labour vote and 31 per cent of the 1992 Liberal Democrat vote. Such floating voters therefore provide the key to electoral victory or defeat at every General Election.

In particular, the floating voters determine the electoral fortunes of the minor parties, since without the benefit of desertions from both main parties it would be difficult for them to collect many extra votes. Of course there is always the possibility that a third party can become one of the two leading parties in Parliament, provided it manages to break through a threshold of about 35 per cent of the votes cast, above which it is likely to win a substantial number of seats in the House of Commons but below which it is likely to languish in frustrating Parliamentary weakness. For example, the 16.76 per cent of the popular vote won by the Liberal Democrats in 1997 secured only 6.98 per cent of the seats in the House of Commons. (In 1983 the Alliance obtained 25.4 per cent of the vote but secured only 3.5 per cent of the seats.) Nonetheless, it is possible for a third party to make such a breakthrough. After all, it was in just such a manner that the Labour Party gradually displaced the Liberals during the first half of the twentieth century.

As for those who do not vote, for whatever reason, we discover that such people have accounted for between 16 per cent and 28.5 per cent of the total electorate at General Elections since the Second World War.[2] Since voting is voluntary in Britain, such non-voters can have a vital influence on the electoral outcome. For example, it has been estimated that differential non-voting had a vital influence on the results of the 1951, both the 1974 and the 1997 General Elections. It could have a similarly crucial influence on any future General Elections.

Social class as a basis for voting

Traditionally one of the most significant cleavages in the British electorate has been based on class factors of one kind or another. Indeed, in 1967 Peter Pulzer observed that 'class is the basis of British party politics; all else is embellishment and detail'.[3]

Yet the meaning of social class has changed and its correlation with voting behaviour has changed and diminished accordingly.

At General Elections since the Second World War the Conservative vote has usually consisted of perhaps two-thirds of the total middle-class vote and about one-third of the total working-class vote, according to the broadest definitions. The Labour vote has usually been made up of perhaps one-quarter of the total middle-class vote and more than one-half of the total working-class vote, according to the same broad definitions. The minor party votes in England have tended to be even less class-based (which has been part of their electoral problem), and in the other parts of the United Kingdom there has been no overwhelming class bias in the votes of the Nationalist parties.

There has always been a significant number of people whose voting behaviour could not easily be explained or predicted on traditional class lines. The most notable example has been that of the working-class Conservatives.[4] Typically, more than one-third of all Conservative votes at General Elections since the Second World War have come from working-class people. This means, for example, that at the 1983 General Election there must have been at least four million working-class people who voted Conservative, while at the 1987 General Election the party is estimated to have received as much as 37 per cent of the manual workers' vote – its best achievement among this group at any election since the Second World War. In the General Election of 1992 it is estimated that 46 per cent of the total Conservative vote came from within the working-class, 35 per cent of the working-class casting their votes for Conservative candidates. In view of the bottom-heavy shape of the social structure in Britain, it is evident that the Conservative Party could not be elected to office if it did not manage to attract a sufficient proportion of the working-class vote. Equally, it is clear that the Labour Party was badly damaged by the steady erosion of its working-class base in the 1980s.

In general, class-based voting of the traditional kind has weakened steadily in Britain over the years since the 1950s and 1960s, notably within the changing working class. In 1959 Labour's share of the vote of manual workers and their families was 40 per cent larger than its share of the vote of white-collar workers and their families. By 1983 the gap had narrowed to 19 per cent. The equivalent figure stood at 20 per cent in 1987 and 19 per cent in 1992. For a considerable period in the 1970s and 1980s the Labour Party lost working-class votes to the Conservatives. For example, at the 1983 General Election there was a swing from Labour to Conservative of 2 per cent among skilled manual workers and 4 per cent among semi-skilled and unskilled workers. At the 1987 General Election Labour concentrated on trying to recover the working-class support which it had lost in 1983, and to some extent it was successful in doing so. It increased its vote among the semi-skilled and unskilled manual workers and their families by 6 per cent, but it continued to lose the votes of skilled workers and their families, where the swing to the Conservatives was more than 2 per cent compared with 1983.[5] In 1992, however, there was a 3.5 per cent swing to Labour among skilled manual workers, which saw support for Labour move ahead of support for the Conservatives in this category; a trend which was underlined by the 1997 result which saw Labour 29 per cent ahead of the Conservatives within this category.

At the 1983 General Election it was the Alliance which was the main beneficiary of working-class desertions from Labour, since it gathered three times as many such votes as the Conservatives. Yet at the 1987 General Election Labour's fortunes varied as between the traditional and the new working class. It did well among the traditional unskilled manual working class at the expense of the Alliance, whereas among the new skilled working class both Labour and the Alliance lost votes to the Conservatives. While on average between 1945 and 1970 62 per cent of all manual workers had voted Labour, by 1983 Labour support from this quarter had fallen to 38 per cent. This represented nothing short of the transformation of working-class voting behaviour and was rightly described by Ivor Crewe as 'the most significant post-war change in the social basis of British politics'.[6]

The decline of traditional class-based voting in Britain could be attributed partly to the changing nature of the working class and partly to the desertion from Labour of the new skilled working class, especially those in this group who were owner-occupiers living in the south of England. A Gallup survey conducted at the time of the 1983 General Election showed that Labour trailed the Conservatives by 22 per cent among working-class owner-occupiers and by 16 per cent among working-class voters living in the south of England.[7] At the 1987 General Election Labour managed once again to achieve a strong position for itself among the traditional working class (especially those who were trade union members living in Scotland or the north of England), whereas among the new skilled working class it continued to lose support to the Conservatives. By 1992 Labour had recaptured lost ground, but still trailed behind the Conservatives among working-class owner-occupiers (39 per cent to 41 per cent) and among working-class voters in the south of England (38 per cent to 40 per cent).[8] The gradual shrinkage of its traditional support base and the obvious appeal of Thatcherite policies to these groups strengthened the hand of those arguing that Labour had to adapt – renew itself – to survive. In short, unless the party could move out from its traditional but shrunken social base it faced persistent defeat. It was from this analysis that 'New Labour' was born. The 1997 General Election showed that the Labour Party triumphed by maintaining its traditional support base but at the same time extending its appeal to the growing middle class in 'middle England'.

Gender and age differences in voting

Two further ways of categorising the electorate are by gender and age.[9] With regard to *gender differences in voting*, Labour have traditionally had a clear lead among male voters at General Elections since the Second World War, scoring a notable 19 per cent advantage over the Conservatives in 1945 and 1966. On the other hand, the Conservatives have traditionally had a clear lead among the female voters, scoring an almost as impressive 12 per cent and 13 per cent advantage over Labour in 1951 and 1955 respectively. At the 1979 General Election the Conservatives managed to maintain their strength among female voters with a 9 per cent lead over Labour, but since it was such a good result for the Conservatives, they also scored a 5 per cent lead over Labour among male voters. At the 1983 General Election this trend was reversed and, unusually, the Conservatives drew more of their support from men than from women. This was mainly because the Alliance made such inroads into the female vote, gaining 28 per cent of female support as compared with the 12 per cent achieved by the Liberals on their own in 1979. At the 1987 General Election all the parties drew their support about equally from men and women. In 1992, once again, more women voted

Conservative than did men, while more men voted Labour than did women. This modest gender gap closed in 1997 as more women than men moved to support New Labour, 10 per cent as against 7 per cent.

With regard to *age-related differences in voting behaviour*, Labour has traditionally done particularly well among voters under the age of 30, scoring a 28 per cent lead over the Conservatives in 1945, a 17 per cent lead in 1966 and a 16 per cent lead in October 1974. On the other hand, the Conservatives have traditionally done rather well among those in late middle age (50–64), scoring an 18 per cent lead over Labour in 1951, a 14 per cent lead in 1955 and a 13 per cent lead in 1959. The fortunes of the two main parties in the other age groups (30–49 and 65 plus) have been more evenly balanced. Whereas Labour did well among the 30–49 group in 1945 and 1966 with leads over the Conservatives of 16 per cent and 13 per cent respectively, the Conservatives did well among those over 65 in 1955, 1970 and February 1974 with leads over Labour of 9 per cent, 9 per cent and 14 per cent respectively. In 1979 Labour was able to retain a small lead of 1 per cent over the Conservatives among the 18–24 age group, notwithstanding the fact that it trailed the Conservatives by 7 per cent among voters of all ages and by 10 per cent among those aged 35 and over. At both General Elections in the 1980s Conservative voting support increased steadily with age, while Labour continued to do well among younger voters – for example, in 1987 Labour did best among voters in the 18–24 age group in which it secured the support of 40 per cent.[10] This general pattern was repeated in the 1992 General Election, although the Conservatives gained ground among the 18–29 age group (up 4 per cent over 1987), while Labour made additional headway particularly among those aged 30–44 (up 6 per cent over 1987) and those 65 and over (up 5 per cent over 1987), primarily at the expense of the Liberal Democrats. In 1997 there was a marked difference in the swing to Labour among different age groups, with those under 30 – already the most pro-Labour – swinging the most (+19 per cent), while Labour's share of the vote among those 65 and over actually fell (–2 per cent). It should also be noted that whereas half of Labour's voters were under 45, this was so of only a third of Conservative voters – reflecting perhaps the average age of Conservative Party members which had risen to 64.

Other sectional cleavages

There are, of course, other sectional cleavages in voting behaviour in Britain. In many ways these have become increasingly important over the years as the voters have become more volatile and instrumental in their voting behaviour.

First, there are the *geographical variations in voting behaviour*. Indeed, one of the most significant developments in recent British politics has been the emergence of a clear regional divide in voting. For example, at the 1979 General Election the Midlands and the South of England voted strongly for the Conservatives, especially in the new towns and the more prosperous working-class suburbs. On the other hand, South Wales, the North of England and much of Scotland remained largely loyal to the Labour Party.[11] At the 1983 General Election the Conservatives had a 38.6 per cent lead over Labour in the South East of England (excluding London), while Labour had a 5.6 per cent lead over the Conservatives in the North of England; indeed, the Conservatives led Labour in every region except the north of England and in Scotland

and Wales. Four years later in 1987 Labour made up some of its lost ground, coming out ahead of the Conservatives in the North West as well as in Yorkshire and Humberside and continuing to be ahead in the North, Scotland and Wales. The Alliance of Liberals and Social Democrats, although falling back slightly compared with 1983, continued to pose the main threat to the Conservatives in certain areas, out-polling the Labour Party in the South West (32.8 per cent as against 16.2 per cent), in the South East excluding London (26.9 per cent against Labour's 16.8 per cent) and in East Anglia (25.8 per cent against Labour's 21.7 per cent).

At the 1992 General Election the Labour Party increased its vote in every area of Great Britain except in Scotland, where its vote fell by 3.4 per cent. In each other area it rose by between 3.3 per cent (South West) and 7.4 per cent (East Midlands). Once again the party was ahead of the Conservatives in the North, the North West, Yorkshire and Humberside, Scotland and Wales. However, there was an increase in Conservative support in the North, Yorkshire and Humberside and in Scotland, with Scotland demonstrating a 2.5 per cent overall swing to the Conservatives. In all other areas there was a decline in the Conservative vote of between 0.2 per cent (North West) and 3.3 per cent (South West). Although the Labour vote in 1992 rose across the whole of the south and east of England, the party managed to win only an additional seven seats in these areas (excluding Greater London) and held only ten seats compared with 161 for the Conservatives. On the other hand, the Conservatives won no seats in the great northern cities of Liverpool, Manchester and Newcastle; only two in Edinburgh, none in Glasgow, and none in Cardiff. Although closing slightly, the North/South divide was again clearly apparent. The vote for the Liberal Democrats dropped in every region, from between 6.2 per cent (East Anglia) and 1.6 per cent (South West). If the South West and parts of the South East are excluded, their vote fell by between 6.2 per cent and 4.8 per cent.

Geographical variations in voting behaviour emerged as a significant factor in the Conservative defeat at the General Election of 1997. They can be seen clearly in Figure 4.2. The election left the Conservative Party for the first time ever without a single MP in Scotland and, for the first time since 1906, without a single MP in Wales. Although fielding candidates in nine of the constituencies in Northern Ireland, they also had no representation from there. Within England they secured no representation in some of the most populated areas – on Merseyside (16 constituencies), South Yorkshire (15 constituencies), West Yorkshire (23 constituencies) on Tyne and Wear (13 constituencies). Indeed, they won only two out of 28 seats in Greater Manchester, six out of 31 in the West Midlands and two out of 25 in Inner London. In short, in many respects, the Conservative Party had been reduced to an English rural rump, securing their lowest Parliamentary representation since 1906. The most significant regional factor which damaged the Conservatives was that the swing against them was greater in those areas where they had secured strong support in the Thatcher years, namely the South-East and the Midlands. Their regional support – excluding Northern

Figure 4.2 How Britain voted in 1997, region by region

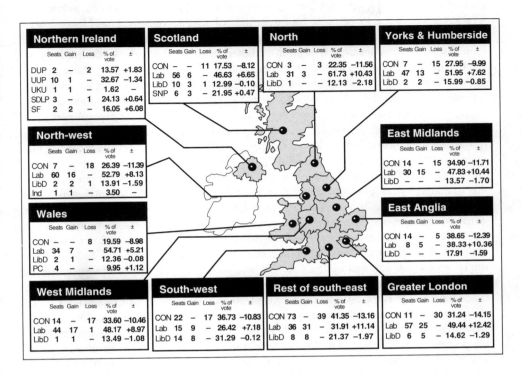

Northern Ireland

	Seats	Gain	Loss	% of vote	±
DUP	2	–	2	13.57	+1.83
UUP	10	1	–	32.67	–1.34
UKU	1	1	–	1.62	–
SDLP	3	–	1	24.13	+0.64
SF	2	2	–	16.05	+6.08

Scotland

	Seats	Gain	Loss	% of vote	±
CON	–	–	11	17.53	–8.12
Lab	56	6	–	46.63	+6.65
LibD	10	3	1	12.99	–0.10
SNP	6	3	–	21.95	+0.47

North

	Seats	Gain	Loss	% of vote	±
CON	3	–	3	22.35	–11.56
Lab	31	3	–	61.73	+10.43
LibD	1	–	–	12.13	–2.18

Yorks & Humberside

	Seats	Gain	Loss	% of vote	±
CON	7	–	15	27.95	–9.99
Lab	47	13	–	51.95	+7.62
LibD	2	2	–	15.99	–0.85

North-west

	Seats	Gain	Loss	% of vote	±
CON	7	–	18	26.39	–11.39
Lab	60	16	–	52.79	+8.13
LibD	2	2	1	13.91	–1.59
Ind	1	1	–	3.50	–

East Midlands

	Seats	Gain	Loss	% of vote	±
CON	14	–	15	34.90	–11.71
Lab	30	15	–	47.83	+10.44
LibD	–	–	–	13.57	–1.70

Wales

	Seats	Gain	Loss	% of vote	±
CON	–	–	8	19.59	–8.98
Lab	34	7	–	54.71	+5.21
LibD	2	1	–	12.36	–0.08
PC	4	–	–	9.95	+1.12

East Anglia

	Seats	Gain	Loss	% of vote	±
CON	14	–	5	38.65	–12.39
Lab	8	5	–	38.33	+10.36
LibD	–	–	–	17.91	–1.59

West Midlands

	Seats	Gain	Loss	% of vote	±
CON	14	–	17	33.60	–10.46
Lab	44	17	1	48.17	+8.97
LibD	1	1	–	13.49	–1.08

South-west

	Seats	Gain	Loss	% of vote	±
CON	22	–	17	36.73	–10.83
Lab	15	9	–	26.42	+7.18
LibD	14	8	–	31.29	–0.12

Rest of south-east

	Seats	Gain	Loss	% of vote	±
CON	73	–	39	41.35	–13.16
Lab	36	31	–	31.91	+11.14
LibD	8	8	–	21.37	–1.97

Greater London

	Seats	Gain	Loss	% of vote	±
CON	11	–	30	31.24	–14.15
Lab	57	25	–	49.44	+12.42
LibD	6	5	–	14.62	–1.29

Ireland – ranged from a high of 41.35 per cent in the South-East to a low of 17.53 per cent in Scotland. In contrast the regional support for the Labour Party ranged from a high of 61.73 per cent in the North to a low of 26.42 per cent in the South-West. For the Liberal Democrats these figures stood at 31.29 per cent (South-West) and 12.13 per cent (North).

Secondly, there are the *sociological differences in voting behaviour*, of which perhaps the most remarkable in recent years has been the cleavage between the traditional and the new working class. As a stereotype, the former group could be described as those who live in Scotland or the North of England, are Council tenants, trade union members and work in the public sector. Equally, the latter group could be described as those who live in the South and East of England, are owner-occupiers, non-trade-union members and work in the private sector, very often in a self-employed capacity.

At the 1983 General Election Labour led the Alliance by 23 per cent and the Conservatives by 21 per cent among voters who were Council tenants, while the Conservatives had a 19 per cent lead over the Alliance among working-class owner-occupiers and a 21 per cent lead over Labour in the same category. Among trade-unionist voters the Conservatives improved their position and came second to Labour with 31 per cent as compared with 39 per cent in that category. Yet the defection of trade-unionist voters was responsible for the biggest drop in any single category of the Labour vote (down by 14 per cent to 39 per cent), while the Alliance increased its support among trade-unionist voters by 12 per cent in line with its general performance in the electorate. Labour's strongest position was among those of the unemployed who decided to vote, with a 24 per cent lead over the Conservatives among the male unemployed and a 9 per cent lead among the female unemployed.

At the 1987 General Election Labour led the Conservatives by 34 per cent and the Alliance by 37 per cent among voters who were Council tenants, while the Conservatives had a 21 per cent lead over Labour and a 19 per cent lead over the Alliance among owner-occupiers in the working class. Among trade-unionist voters Labour improved its position compared with 1983 by establishing a 12 per cent lead over the Conservatives and a 16 per cent lead over the Alliance. Labour also improved its position among the unemployed, taking 56 per cent of the male unemployed vote and 54 per cent of the female unemployed vote, as against 21 and 23 per cent respectively for the Conservatives and 20 and 19 per cent for the Alliance. As far as socio-economic groups were concerned, as in 1983 the Conservatives attracted the votes of an absolute majority in both the AB-professional (57 per cent) and the C1-white collar (51 per cent) categories, and the largest following of any party amongst C2-skilled with 40 per cent as opposed to 36 per cent for Labour and 22 per cent for the Alliance. The Labour Party topped the poll among those classified as DE-skilled – attracting 48 per cent as opposed to 30 per cent for the Conservatives and 20 per cent for the Alliance. Although well behind the Conservatives, the Alliance out-polled the Labour Party in both the AB-professional and C1-white collar categories, securing 25 per cent support in both, in contrast to Labour's 14 per cent and 21 per cent respectively.

At the 1992 General Election the Conservative Party still led Labour among working-class home-owners, but only just (41 per cent to 39 per cent), with the Liberal Democrats way behind on 17 per cent, a drop of 10 per cent since 1983 and 6 per cent since 1987. Among owner-occupiers, Labour had also closed the gap, notwithstanding the fact that it was still substantial at 49 per cent for the Conservative and 30 per cent for Labour (a gap of 19 per cent), whereas the equivalent figures in 1983 had been 52 per cent and 19 per cent (a gap of 33 per cent). Labour's lead among working-class Council tenants was 36 per cent, with 58 per cent to the Conservatives' 22 per cent. Conservative support from trade unionists held steady, but a drop in support from this group for the Liberal Democrats – down to 19 per cent from 26 per cent in 1987 – ensured a rise in support for the Labour Party from 42 to 47 per cent. The Labour Party also secured an absolute majority of support among the unemployed, although there was a drop in the support for both Labour and the Liberal Democrats within this category and a rise in the support given to the Conservative Party.

As far as socio-economic classification was concerned, the 1992 result showed the Conservative Party still attracting majority support from among both the AB-professional and C1-white collar groups. Nonetheless, Labour was able to make inroads into both, increasing its support by 6 per cent and 4 per cent respectively. Among C2-skilled voters the Labour Party supplanted the Conservative Party as the recipient of the highest level of support from this group (41 per cent to 38 per cent), while it attracted the support of 50 per cent of those in the DE-skilled category. Support for the Liberal Democrats from both these final categories declined by 5 per cent as compared with 1987.

At the 1997 General Election Labour increased its share of the vote amongst each occupational category: 11 per cent among the semi-skilled and unskilled (DE), 13 per cent among skilled workers (C2), 22 per cent among white collar workers (C1), and 11 per cent among the professional and managerial category (AB). In contrast, the Conservative vote fell in each category: by 9 per cent, 13 per cent, 26 per cent and 14 per cent respectively. Consequently, those constituencies that had swung sharply towards the Conservative Party of Margaret Thatcher – those with a high concentration of clerical and skilled non-manual workers – shifted most strongly towards New Labour. Also of note in this respect is the fact that the swing to Labour among those with mortgages, namely 15 per cent, was higher than among either those who owned their homes outright (11 per cent) or those who were council tenants (10 per cent), possibly a consequence of the negative equity of the early 1990s and loss of faith in the economic competence of the Conservatives following 'Black Wednesday' (16 September 1992) and the forced withdrawal of the pound sterling from the Exchange Rate Mechanism of the European Monetary System.

In short, the British electorate no longer divides neatly into two traditional, class-based voting groups, essentially because British society is no longer like that. The voters have become less easy to categorise in sociological terms and less inclined to adhere to their traditional voting allegiances. In such circumstances predictions of voting behaviour along traditional lines on the basis of a simple split between middle class and working class are unlikely to be accurate in modern conditions. Greater account has now to be taken of the social mobility and the electoral volatility of modern British society.

A profile of the electorate between 1979 and 1997 is provided in Figure 4.3.

4.2 Main influences on voting

Traditionally it has been argued that there are three main influences on voting behaviour in Britain – political inheritance, self-interest, and the performance of the party in office.[12] Of course, there are other important influences on voting behaviour which cannot be ignored, such as policy and sentiment, image and technique and, as we have already observed, other social factors such as occupation, housing tenure, educational attainment, and neighbourhood or peer group pressures, also have an impact. We must therefore take account of a wide variety of influences if we are to form a complete picture.

Figure 4.3 Profile of the electorate 1979–1997

	Conservative					Labour					Liberal Democrat				
	1979	1983	1987	1992	1997	1979	1983	1987	1992	1997	1979	1983	1987	1992	1997
Total voters	45	44	43	43	31	38	28	32	35	44	14	26	23	18	17
Gender:															
Male	43	42	43	41	31	40	30	32	37	44	13	25	23	18	17
Female	47	46	43	44	32	35	26	32	34	44	15	27	23	18	17
Age group:															
First-time voters	N/A	N/A	N/A	35	19	N/A	N/A	N/A	40	57	N/A	N/A	N/A	21	18
18–24	42	42	37	35	27	41	33	39	38	49	12	23	22	19	16
25–34	43	40	39	40	28	38	29	33	37	49	15	29	26	18	16
35–54	46	44	45	43	30	35	27	29	34	45	16	27	24	19	19
55+	47	47	46	42	36	38	27	31	34	40	13	24	21	17	17
Occupational category:															
AB Professional/managerial	61	60	57	56	42	20	10	14	20	31	15	28	26	22	21
C1 Clerical/skilled non-manual (white collar)	52	51	51	52	26	29	20	21	25	47	16	27	26	19	19
C2 Skilled/manual	41	40	40	38	25	41	32	36	41	54	15	26	22	17	14
DE Semi-skilled/unskilled/pensioners etc.	34	33	30	30	21	49	41	48	50	61	13	24	20	15	13
Other categories:															
Home owners	53	52	50	49	35	29	19	23	30	41	14	28	25	19	17
Mortgage-payers	N/A	N/A	N/A	47	31	N/A	N/A	N/A	29	44	N/A	N/A	N/A	20	18
Council tenants	27	26	22	24	13	56	47	56	55	65	13	24	19	15	15
Trade Union members	33	31	30	30	18	51	39	42	47	57	13	29	26	19	20

Source: MORI

Political inheritance

The influence of political inheritance means the political attitudes and loyalties which voters derive from their parents and families. On the basis of surveys conducted in the 1960s Butler and Stokes were able to show a high correlation (typically over 75 per cent) between the voting behaviour of one generation and the next within family households.[13] This was not surprising at the time, in view of the well-established fact that the opinions of young people on most issues, whether political or not, tended to accord with those of their parents. Indeed there is still considerable inertia in the party political loyalties of many voters at General Elections, which in most cases reflects the voting habits derived from family inheritance and social surroundings. This can be seen most clearly in the few remaining tight-knit communities, such as the valleys in South Wales, where there is still effectively a one-party voting tradition (in this case for the Labour Party) in spite of the fact that modern social and geographical mobility has begun to erode it at the edges.

The key point at recent General Elections has been that it has not always been possible for either of the main parties to turn such traditional loyalties fully into a level of voting support commensurate with their party identifiers in opinion polls. For example, at the 1992 General Election 34 per cent of the electorate claimed to regard themselves as instinctively Labour supporters, and whereas 34.4 per cent of those who voted actually supported Labour candidates, this was the equivalent of only 26.7 per cent of the electorate.[14] Equally, evidence from the 1997 General Election shows that, despite securing 43.2 per cent of the vote, the Labour Party still appears to have a significant problem in mobilising some of its traditional support from within its heart-lands to come out and vote.[15] This is because the strength of voter commitment to either of the two main parties has become more attenuated over the years as a result of the long-run decline in party political allegiance and participation in Britain as in all other advanced societies. Indeed, this social development has tended to damage the electoral prospects of the Liberal Democrats most of all, since so much of their potential voting support as registered in opinion polls and at by-elections is significantly weaker and more transient than that given to either of the two main parties by their declared supporters.

Self-interest

The influence of self-interest derives very largely from the personal experience, favourable or unfavourable, consistent or contradictory, of millions of individual voters. For example, there is a fortunate minority of people in Britain who are born into well-off families, benefit from a good education, and manage to lead happy and successful lives. In the majority of cases such people have tended to vote Conservative. Equally, there is a large section of the public (typically several million) for whom life is a constant struggle against adverse material conditions. Their lives are characterised by financial insecurity, dependence on the state and its agencies, and impoverished expectations. In the majority of cases such people have tended to vote Labour, if they have decided to vote at all.

Certainly the majority of those in the AB-professional group and those cate-gorised as C1-white collar who traditionally voted Conservative are likely to have done so principally for reasons of self-interest, although they often describe their reasons for voting in terms of their conception of the national interest – 'what is good for me is good for Britain'. On this point, and as previously stated, the fact that Conservative support from within these two groups fell so sharply at the 1997 General Election can, at least in part, be accounted for by the loss of faith in the economic competence of the Conservatives following Black Wednesday in 1992.

Here it is worth noting that one of the objectives of New Labour was to appeal to these sections of the voting public. The modernisers in the party believed that unless the party moved to the new centre ground largely defined by Margaret Thatcher they would not – could not – win an election. 'Thatcher's people', the professionals and the new middle class – as well as aspirational members of the working class – would never be attracted to a party which appeared to be more interested in the poor and disadvantaged than those who wanted to 'get on'. It was for this reason that Tony Blair replaced the traditional values associated with 'old' Labour – those of redistribution and public ownership – with those of equal opportunity, enterprise and the market, albeit tempered with social justice and responsibility. The 1997 General Election result underlined the validity of this adventurous decision.

On the point of self-interest, it should also be noted that the Liberal Democrats now find their social base among the well-educated middle class – hence in making a Manifesto pledge in both 1992 and 1997 to earmark an increase of one penny in the pound on Income Tax to provide additional funding for education, they were playing to their natural supporters. This suggests that self-interest is not always a dominant influence on voting behaviour – people do not *necessarily* vote in accordance with their financial interests. Undoubtedly other factors, such as ideology and altruism, apathy and disillusion, play an important part as well.

Government performance

The performance of the party in office might seem to be an influence on voting behaviour too obvious to be worth stating, if it were not for the fact that it emphasises the importance of the growing tendency for many people to vote *instrumentally*. This is the technical term to describe what happens when millions of floating voters effectively strike a bargain with the politicians, whereby they reward the party in office with re-election or punish it with electoral defeat according to their assessment of its period in Government.[16]

This is certainly a view of voting behaviour which is widely held by practising politicians in Britain. It is also supported by the well-established axiom that parties in Government are more likely to *lose* an election than parties in Opposition are to *win* one. Hence, the Labour Government of James Callaghan 'lost' the 1979 General Election as a result of public hostility to the economic situation and the apparent power of the trade unions, culminating in the 'winter of discontent'. Equally, John Major 'lost' the 1997 General Election because the forced expulsion of sterling from the Exchange Rate Mechanism of the European Monetary System effectively destroyed notions of Conservative economic competence, because the Government was so openly divided on the issue of Europe, because of allegations of sleaze, and because after 18 years in office the Government appeared to be worn out; it was 'time for a change'. However, on neither occasion is it likely that there would then have been a change if there had not been an 'acceptable' alternative: the Conservative Party under Margaret Thatcher in 1979 and 'New Labour' under Tony Blair in 1997. The lack of an acceptable alternative was one of the reasons why it was possible for the Conservative Party to suffer a small but significant decline in its share of the votes cast between 1979 (44.9 per cent), 1983 (43.5 per cent), 1987 (42.3 per cent) and 1992 (41.9 per cent) and still win each election convincingly. In 1983 the Labour Party of Michael Foot was not seen as a viable alternative, and the Opposition was anyway fragmented between Labour and the Alliance of Liberals and Social Democrats. In 1987 the opposition was still fragmented and, besides which, the Labour Party was still seen as out of touch. In 1992, although Labour as a party was more acceptable, its leader, Neil Kinnock, was not seen by a sufficient number of voters as an acceptable alternative Prime Minister, while the issue that could have lost the election for the Conservatives, namely the Community Charge (Poll Tax), had been solved by a rapid change of policy following Margaret Thatcher's departure from 10 Downing Street.

Policy and sentiment

In recent years policy and sentiment have been increasingly important influences on voting behaviour in Britain. As the voters have become more volatile and instrumental in their attitudes, such factors have begun to weigh at least as heavily as traditional social allegiances.

Policy-based voting

Sarlvik and Crewe have shown that more than two-thirds of the votes for the three National parties at the 1979 General Election could have been predicated correctly on the basis of the view held by the voters on certain salient policy issues; and the correlation was over 90 per cent for Conservative and Labour voters.[17] They argued that this was a reflection of the fact that over the period 1964–79 there had been a dramatic decline in the level of popular support for three key Labour policies – further nationalisation, the reinforcement of trade-union power, and higher tax-financed spending on the Welfare State. These policies, which had commanded majority support in 1964 (at any rate among those voters who identified with the Labour Party), received less than 25 per cent support among Labour voters in 1979. Labour had therefore lost a great deal of its earlier policy-based appeal.

Yet nothing remains exactly the same in this area of analysis. After a period in the 1970s and 1980s when many of Labour's most salient policies were not popular with the electorate (for example, the commitment to higher direct taxation or support for unilateral nuclear disarmament), the party emerged from a period of comprehensive policy review with a range of more moderate and pragmatic – and as a result acceptable – policies. Neil Kinnock (1983–92), John Smith (1992–94) and Tony Blair (1994–) all deliberately sought to lead the Labour Party in a more modern and moderate direction. Tony Benn on behalf of the Left accused the leadership of 'diluting Socialism', declaring that 'the direction of the Labour Party now gives the impression of being superficial in analysis, weak in remedies, defensive in its posture and vague in its approach'.[18] The leadership hit back, with Neil Kinnock declaring that the party had to modernise, asserting that Labour politicians could not face the future with 'their heads in the clouds, ignoring the real world that people and parties and movements have to live in ... with their heads turned round, gazing longingly at the past, trying to call back yesterday'.[19]

This should remind us that all voters are less inclined than they used to be to vote in accordance with traditional class or family loyalties, and more inclined to vote in the light of which party most closely reflects their own interests and policy preferences. Indeed, evidence adduced by Sarlvik and Crewe suggested that voters' opinions on the policies and performances of each party are twice as likely to explain their voting behaviour as all their social and economic characteristics taken together.[20] A Gallup survey conducted for the BBC at the time of the 1983 General Election also showed that, when the voters preferred the policies of one Party but the leader of another, they decided in favour of the former by about four to one, a tendency which on that occasion worked principally to the advantage of the Conservatives.[21]

Yet in weighing the influence of policy on voting behaviour, it is important to distinguish between those policies which the voters, when questioned by opinion pollsters, may consider to be the best in the abstract or for the sake of the country, and those for which they actually vote in the privacy of the polling booth. At the 1987 General Election the Labour Party would have won if the voters had cast their votes in accordance with their altruistic policy preferences as expressed in answer to opinion polls at the time. The same thing was true at the 1992 General Election. For example, when Gallup asked the question 'Of all the urgent problems facing the country at the present time, when you decided which way to vote, which two issues did you personally consider most important?', 41 per cent of respondents mentioned health, 36 per cent mentioned unemployment, and 23 per cent mentioned education – all issues on which the Labour Party enjoyed a lead as the best party – yet the Conservatives still won the election quite comfortably.[22] Evidently, altruism does not necessarily translate into voting behaviour when the voters are choosing a Government at a General Election. The explanation for this has been provided by Ivor Crewe, who has pointed out that, when answering opinion pollsters, the voters respond altruistically and in the abstract, whereas when actually voting they tend to think much more instrumentally of their personal and family interests.[23]

Capricious sentiment

Hilde Himmelweit and others have shown that, 'although in practice both consistency (that is, party loyalty) and ideological thinking (that is, policy considerations) influence the decision to vote, each election is like a new shopping expedition in a situation where new as well as familiar goods are on offer'.[24] This means that evidence from recent General Elections can be interpreted and explained by using a consumer model of voting behaviour. Of course, a great deal depends on how the voters feel during the period just before and during an election campaign and on whether the public eventually decides to vote for positive or negative reasons or indeed to vote at all.

At the 1987 General Election, for example, the Conservative Party achieved a landslide majority in Parliament with almost the same share of the votes cast as in 1983. This was because the votes cast for the other National parties were fairly evenly divided between Labour and the Alliance, but even more because more than two-thirds of those who (according to opinion polls at the outset of the campaign) had seriously considered voting for the Alliance eventually did *not* do so on polling day, because they came to the conclusion that such action might give victory to whichever of the two main parties they disliked the most.

At the 1992 General Election a Mori survey found that 11 per cent of those who identified themselves as Liberal Democrat supporters a week before polling day switched to vote Conservative on polling day, as did 4 per cent of those who had identified themselves as Labour supporters. In addition 8 per cent of Labour supporters switched to the Liberal Democrats. The reasons for switching support were varied: 29 per cent said they did so because they liked the policies of the party to which they switched; 13 per cent said they did so because they disliked the policies of the other parties; 10 per cent said they did so because they liked the leader of the party to which they switched; and 56 per cent said they did so because they disliked the leaders of the other parties.[25] At the 1997 General Election when voters were asked which party they trusted most to take the right decision about the economy, Labour were placed ahead of the Conservatives by 44 per cent to 42 per cent; a stark contrast to the position in 1992 when the Conservatives had led Labour on the issue by 53 per cent to 33 per cent. Equally on the issue of income tax, traditionally one of the Conservative Party's strongest and which they had led Labour by 24 per cent in 1992 (55 per cent to 31 per cent), in 1997 Labour were ahead of the Conservatives – by 8 per cent – on this as well (44 per cent to 36 per cent).[26]

Image and technique

Party images and campaign techniques are some of the other significant influences on voting behaviour in this age of modern mass media. They have been identified by the political communications specialists of all the parties as crucial to electoral success in the modern age.

Party images

These are formed in the public mind by the party leaders themselves – for example, Lloyd George as the Welsh Wizard, Winston Churchill as the British Bulldog, Stanley Baldwin as the quintessential English country gentleman, Harold Macmillan as 'Super Mac', James Callaghan as 'jovial gentleman Jim', Margaret Thatcher as the 'Iron Lady'. More recently, we have seen the association of classlessness and geniality with John Major and vision and modernity with Tony Blair. Party images are also formed by the performance and behaviour of the parties whether in Government or Opposition. The party leaders and their media advisers work hard to preserve or improve their respective images. Indeed, the presentation of policy, if not policy itself, is usually influenced by professional assessments of the image it is likely to convey. Above all, the parties are careful to try to foster an image of unity in their own ranks and of disunity in the ranks of their opponents, since the appearance of disunity is invariably damaging to the electoral prospects of any party.

Party images are formed incrementally, even subliminally, over many years by what the parties do or fail to do when in Government and by the way they behave when in Opposition. For example, the Conservative Party undoubtedly benefited at both the 1983 and 1987 General Elections from Margaret Thatcher's acknowledged experience in high office and her resolute public image as someone who stuck to her guns when the going got tough – for instance, at the depth of the recession in the early 1980s, at the time of the Falklands crisis in 1982, and during the Westland affair in 1986. Equally, during the late 1970s and well into the 1980s the Labour Party suffered in the eyes of many people from a poor image which was the product of unconvincing leadership, party in-fighting and internecine ideological struggles. During the 1987 General Election the Labour Party strove very hard and quite effectively to present the party leader, Neil Kinnock, in a favourable and 'presidential' light, impressing many media professionals and party workers in the process; but even this was not enough to counter an adverse public image that had taken years to crystallise. Similarly, the Labour Party suffered in the 1992 General Election from Neil Kinnock's lack of credibility as an alternative Prime Minister and from John Smith's unwise decision as Shadow Chancellor to present an alternative tax-raising 'Budget' during the first week of the campaign.

In the 1997 General Election 69 per cent of voters believed that Labour was good for *all* classes, as opposed to 32 per cent who believed that this was true of the Conservatives. In contrast, whereas 68 per cent of voters believed that the Conservatives were good for only one class, only 31 per cent believed this of the Labour Party. Among Conservative defectors, 71 per cent said that the Conservative Party was good for only one class, whereas among those who moved to support the Labour Party 87 per cent believed that Labour was good for all classes. Clearly, the Conservative Party was associated in the eyes of many with only the rich, while New Labour had been able to break from its traditional association as the party of the trade unions, the working class, the inner city Council estates and the North; it constituted a sea-change in public perceptions. An aspect of this sea-change was seen in the images of the parties as being either united or divided, particularly if one bears in mind the traditional view which was of a united Conservative Party (loyalty was often said to have been the secret weapon of the Conservative Party) and a divided Labour Party. However, in 1997 only 16 per cent of voters believed that the Conservative Party was united – indeed, 93 per cent of Conservative defectors described the party as divided. Conversely, 66 per cent of voters described Labour as united, a figure which rose to 83 per cent among New Labour converts.[27]

Campaign techniques

These can also have an important influence on voting behaviour, especially since many of the floating voters do not make up their minds until the final stages of the campaign. The parties therefore make every effort during the campaign to get as much good media coverage as possible and to present both their leaders and their policies in the most favourable light. Yet, in spite of these often expensive efforts, the actual conduct of the campaign seldom makes a decisive difference to the electoral outcome. For example, although it was widely agreed that the Labour leadership fought a brilliant media campaign in 1987, it seems clear that this had little or no effect on the battle with the Conservatives for first place, but a considerable effect on the battle with the Alliance for second place. On the other hand, in the 1992

General Election campaign the Conservatives had some success with their vivid posters (put up on 4500 sites) and newspaper advertising drawing attention to what they described as 'Labour's Double Whammy' – namely, higher taxes and higher prices – and asserting that the average voter would pay over £1000 a year more in tax under a Labour Government. Indeed, Labour campaign strategists in 1997 were determined to learn the lessons of the 1992 campaign and not to make the same mistakes again, namely failing to counter the accusations over tax and being unprepared for the late swing away from the party. Hence Labour pledged not to raise marginal rates of Income Tax in the life-time of the following Parliament and to accept Conservative public spending limits for two years, all in a convincing effort to 'square' the national press.

The 1997 Labour campaign also demonstrated the increasing importance of technology in targeting voters and in being able to respond rapidly to the arguments of the other parties, of having a clear and straightforward message and the importance of discipline and being able to stay 'on message'.

In the case of the minor parties, which in normal times do not get much media attention, effective campaign techniques can be more significant in drawing helpful attention both to their leaders and to their policies – as was shown by the positive impact of the Liberal Leader, Jeremy Thorpe, in the February 1974 General Election and by Paddy Ashdown for the Liberal Democrats in 1997.

The candidates

In normal circumstances party has a much greater pull than does the personality of individual candidates, party image nationally has a greater impact on the result in an individual constituency than the local activity of any candidate, and national issues tend to take precedence over local ones. Consequently, conventional wisdom has held to the view that individual candidates are unlikely to count for more than possibly 500–1000 votes. This may not seem very much, but it could have a decisive impact on a result in a marginal constituency. However, the significance of candidates can have a greater impact on the result than the conventional wisdom allows. This is particularly so in by-elections, as was apparent for example in the Winchester by-election in November 1997. Here the sitting Conservative MP, Gerry Malone, had been defeated in the General Election by the Liberal Democrat, Mark Oaten, by a margin of two votes and had consequently challenged the result in the courts on the grounds of ballot-paper irregularities, the courts ruling that the contest should be re-run. Although there were a variety of factors involved, the contest was nevertheless fought to a very considerable extent on the alleged unpopularity of Gerry Malone, with the result that the Liberal Democrat held the seat – on a near 20 per cent swing from the Conservatives – with a majority of 21,556. Other examples would include the cases of Wallace Lawler at Birmingham Ladywood (1969), Cyril Smith at Rochdale (1972), Dick Taverne at Lincoln (1973) and Peter Tatchell at Bermondsey (1983). Circumstances can arise which result in individual candidates having a significant impact at the time of a General Election also, a factor that was underlined by the contest between Martin Bell and Neil Hamilton at Tatton in 1997.

Other influences on voting

In one of the most authoritative studies of voting behaviour in Britain, Heath, Jowell and Curtice demonstrated the advantages of drawing multi-dimensional maps of the electorate.[28] Using this technique, it is possible to take full account of all the various cleavages in the electorate and go beyond the familiar criteria of social class and electoral geography. A modern list of the other variables should include the influence of neighbourhood, occupation, housing tenure, share ownership, educational attainment, gender, and racial identity. On this last point, for example, it appears from survey data that at the 1992 General Election 79 per cent of ethnic minority voters voted Labour, 10 per cent voted Conservative and 9 per cent voted Liberal Democrat. In 1996/97 survey data showed that 70 per cent of Asian and 86 per cent of black voters intended to vote Labour as opposed to 25 per cent and 8 per cent respectively intending to vote Conservative.[29] Although better-off ethnic minority voters are relatively less likely to vote Conservative than their white counterparts (29 per cent against 43 per cent in 1992), the end of Labour hegemony among ethnic minority voters has been predicted.[30] Indeed, the Commission for Racial Equality calculated that as many as 40 Parliamentary constituencies would not be retained by the Labour Party if Asian, Afro-Caribbean and other ethnic minority voters divided their loyalties in the same proportions as white voters.[31]

In short, there is a wide variety of influences on voting behaviour in Britain. The traditional influences – that is, political inheritance, self-interest, and the performance of the party in office – are still of fundamental importance. Yet the more ephemeral influences (for instance, policy and sentiment, image and technique) have made themselves increasingly felt in recent years and have assumed a growing importance as the voters have shown more volatility in their voting behaviour and as General Election campaigns have become more presidential both in style and in content. The use of such modern techniques emphasises the manipulative aspects of modern party politics and reminds us of the influence of the mass media. Yet in spite of such new developments, it is clear that British electoral politics have not been completely Americanised, not least because of the tight legal limits on the amount which each Parliamentary candidate may spend on election expenses during the rather brief General Election campaigns in Britain, and the fact that it is impossible for the parties under British electoral law to purchase broadcasting time on the electronic media.

4.3 Conventional wisdom

Undoubtedly, what the 1997 General Election did was to show that a number of tenets of conventional wisdom about electoral and party politics in Britain were no longer true.

First, it was apparent that a belief in the inevitability of the electoral cycle – whereby a Government suffers 'mid-term' unpopularity only to recover as a General Election approaches – was misplaced.

Second, it was apparent that the perception of the Conservative Party as the most formidable machine for fighting elections in Europe was similarly misplaced as they were outclassed throughout by both the Labour Party and the Liberal Democrats.

Third, the image of the Labour Party as a party weighed down by ideological and historical baggage and of the Conservative Party as unhindered by any such disadvantage, was turned on its head. 'New' Labour appeared to be just that, while the Conservative Party gave every impression of being 'a rabble without a cause', an ideological entity without an ideology, unsure of its post-Thatcherite purpose. As one commentator observed at the time, 'Tony Blair was as liberated from his party's past as John Major was hemmed in by his.'[32]

Fourth, the image of the Labour Party as the party of splits, divisions and internecine disputes and of the Conservative Party as the party whose secret weapon was loyalty was similarly turned upside-down. As had been observed by Martin Kettle of the *Guardian*:

> For most of post-war British history, it has been the Conservative and not Labour who have been the disciplined party. Loyalty and conformism came as naturally to most mid-20th century Tories as argument and independence did to Labour supporters of the same era ... Today it is Labour which behaves more like a Californian cult, its members ready to do, say and even to wear whatever the all-knowing leader Tony Blair demands, whereas the Conservatives long ago abandoned much of the old deference that once held their party together.[33]

Fifth, the idea that 'it's the economy, stupid', namely that incumbent Governments win or lose dependent on the strength of the economy at the time of the General Election, was shown to be inaccurate as the undoubted strength of the economy during the period 1993–97 was undermined by the voters' memory of 'Black Wednesday' in 1992 which had cast serious doubt on any claims to competence in office which the Conservatives might otherwise have enjoyed.

Putting these various factors together, one can conclude that it was John Major's misfortune to be the leader of a deeply divided party with no real sense of direction, seemingly bereft of new ideas and tarnished by sleaze and public boredom. Conversely, it was Tony Blair's good fortune to be the leader of a party chastened by long years in Opposition and at last hungry for power, disciplined in its behaviour, efficient in its operations, focused in its goal, furnished with new ideas and a sense of direction, and to find himself in that position at the very time large numbers of voters were looking for an acceptable alternative to the discredited Tories.

4.4 Continuing uncertainties

There are some continuing uncertainties which are likely to have a significant influence on the outcome of future General Elections in Britain:

- Will the voters be more or less concerned with issues of policy?
- Will a substantial part of the middle class continue to vote Labour or Liberal Democrat?
- Will the Conservative vote continue to decline among the new working class?
- Will men and women come to have less differentiated political leanings?
- Will ethnic minority voters continue to divide their loyalties differently from their white counterparts?

- Will the electorate become more or less volatile in its voting behaviour?
- Will the Liberal Democrats and the Nationalists continue to attract sizeable levels of support, or will they suffer significant defections?
- Will voting turn-out at General Elections grow or decline?
- To what extent will there be signs of political alienation?
- What effects will flow from change in the electoral system?

However tentatively, it is worth exploring some of these important questions.

Instrumental or expressive voting

There was a time in the late 1950s and early 1960s when some observers proclaimed the end of ideology in Britain and other advanced Western countries.[34] More recently, however, ideology and policy considerations have become once again a significant influence on voting behaviour. This is consistent with the evidence for so-called *instrumental voting*, whereby voters assess the policies, attitudes and images of the various parties and then cast their votes in the light of their own interests.

From the late 1970s and throughout the 1980s it seems that the positions taken by the different parties on the main issues of policy had a significant effect on voting behaviour at General Elections. This was brought about partly by the continuing fragmentation of the traditional working class, which created a rootless, upwardly mobile group whose voting behaviour was particularly susceptible to instrumental appeals from the politicians to their particular interests. It was also a reflection of the increasing sophistication of all those voters who regarded their decisions at General Elections as really another form of consumer choice. For such people, as long as there appeared to be an attractive political product on offer, a significant number of them measured its claims against not only their own policy preferences but also their assessment of their own interests. In such a political beauty contest between the parties, the voters' perceptions of political issues and of their own interests in relation to party policies have a significant effect on election results.

On the other hand, there is considerable evidence in support of the so-called *expressive interpretation of voting* – that is to say, the tendency of many in the electorate to vote in accordance with the norms and values of the principal social group to which they belong. According to this theory of voting behaviour, many of the preferences which are expressed in opinion polls by reference to voter predilections for particular party policies are actually little more than rationalisations of more basic interests, or a cover for a dominant social identification. In other words, if voting behaviour is determined principally by social identity, then one need only look at the changing class proportions within society to be able to forecast likely outcomes.

Labour and the growing middle class

It is worth noting that, over the last decade and more, even when the Labour Party has fared badly at General Elections, its middle-class voting support has held up rather well. There is no complete explanation for this, although it may partly be explained by Labour's strong support among white-collar workers in the public sector – for example, teachers and health service workers. Indeed it is something that has been strengthened as Labour has managed to broaden its appeal to encompass more issues of concern to the growing middle-class electorate, such as law and order, the quality of public services, protection of the environment, and greater economic opportunities for women. The 1997 General Election provided real evidence of Labour's success in reassuring the growing middle class.

Of course, another explanation for this phenomenon is simply that, as the electorate as a whole becomes more middle class, so Labour voters are likely to become more middle class as they move up the economic and social ladder. Even though their improved material circumstances and middle-class life-style might be thought to be more consistent with voting Conservative, such voters remain loyal to their social origins and principles and so vote New Labour.

Conservatives and the fragmented working class

It is striking that, in spite of presiding over the two worst economic recessions since the Second World War, namely in 1980–82 and 1990–92, the Conservative Party was still able to retain the support of a significant number of working-class voters. In the 1980s this support was critically dependent on the party's ability to maintain a reputation for competence in office, something which was severely dented during the early and mid-1990s and which was a factor in the desertion from the party of large numbers of such voters in the 1997 General Election. Such support also depended on the image of the party in the eyes of the so-called authoritarian working class – that is, those working-class voters who are attracted by whichever party takes the toughest line on issues, such as law and order, immigration, trade-union reform and defence. The headway made by Tony Blair and New Labour on these very issues showed that the Conservative party could not afford to take such support for granted.

In 1979 the Conservatives benefited from widespread revulsion at the trade union excesses during the so called 'Winter of Discontent'. In 1983 they benefited from the patriotic appeal of victory in the Falklands and from a divided Opposition. In 1987 they benefited from a rising tide of prosperity and a divided Opposition. In 1992 they benefited from a new leader, the absence of the Poll Tax, an electorate still reluctant to trust the Labour party, and once again a divided Opposition. They lost in 1997 because their image of integrity in office had been tarnished by sleaze, because their reputation for economic competence had been smashed by the fiasco of Black Wednesday, and because New Labour was able to portray itself rather more convincingly as the party for those with ambition and drive. In order to have a good chance of winning in the future, the Conservatives will need to regain a good part of the working-class vote which they won in 1979, 1983, 1987 and 1992 but which deserted them in 1997.

Gender differences in voting

Gender differences in voting, whereby women were more likely than men to vote for the Conservative Party, have been a feature of electoral behaviour since both men and women were given the vote in Britain. Indeed, Winston Churchill is said to have remarked that had he known how many women were going to vote Conservative, he would have been more inclined to give them the vote at an earlier stage. The Conservative advantage among female voters reached its peak in the 1950s, fluctuated in the 1960s and 1970s and had disappeared altogether by 1987 when they received the support of 43 per cent of the votes from both women and men. There was nonetheless a comparative advantage as women were still then more likely to vote Conservative than Labour (32 per cent) or Liberal Democrat (23 per cent). The gender gap was apparent again in 1992 when 44 per cent of women as opposed to 41 per cent of men voted Conservative. However, a significant development at this time was that although older women – especially pensioners – preferred the Conservative party, younger women actually sided with Labour; indeed, among younger voters generally more women than men voted Labour.

During the 1997 General Election the Labour party sought to make a concerted effort to attract the votes of women, not only by fielding more female candidates than ever before (159, 24.8 per cent) and fielding many of them in targeted winnable seats, but also paying particular attention to differences in women's and men's media preferences and coming forward with a set of policy proposals specifically designed to appeal to women. It was an approach which reaped rich rewards as 44 per cent of women voted Labour compared with 32 per cent who voted Conservative.

Quite what factors will come to the fore to influence gender preferences at future General Elections is difficult to predict. It does appear, however, that the Conservative party no longer enjoys an automatic, natural advantage among women voters; indeed, if any party does, it is the New Labour party of Tony Blair.

Electoral volatility

At the 1997 General Election there was further evidence of electoral volatility to add to the body of evidence provided by analysis of elections since the mid-1970s. For example, it has been estimated that during the campaign as many as 7.1 million voters changed their minds. Figure 4.4 shows electoral volatility between the 1992 and 1997 General Elections.[35]

Similarly, it has been estimated that 25 per cent of the electorate decided how they would cast their vote in the final week of the campaign – indeed, 11 per cent did so on polling day itself. Of those who ended up voting Liberal Democrat, only 34 per cent had made up their minds to do so before the campaign got underway, against 58 per cent of Conservatives and 65 per cent of Labour voters. By the middle of the campaign the Liberal Democrats had persuaded another 25 per cent of their eventual voters to back them, but as many as 41 per cent of Liberal Democrat voters made up their minds to support the party only in the last week of the campaign; indeed, 16 per cent decided to do so only in the last 24 hours. The volatility of the electorate during the 1997 General Election campaign is shown in Figure 4.5.

In future, the impact of electoral volatility will depend on the net effect of a number of different factors. It is likely that increased volatility will be encouraged by the relative weakening of traditional associations between class and party, the growing tendency for voters to cast their votes instrumentally, the advent of capricious 'consumer' voting, and the unsettling influence of the media on the opinion polls and voting behaviour. On the other hand, volatility could decrease if there were to be a general recognition of the futility of casting votes for smaller parties or a sustained secular trend towards a sea-change in voting behaviour of the kind which can occur in Britain every twenty years or so. Only time will tell.

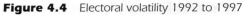
Figure 4.4 Electoral volatility 1992 to 1997

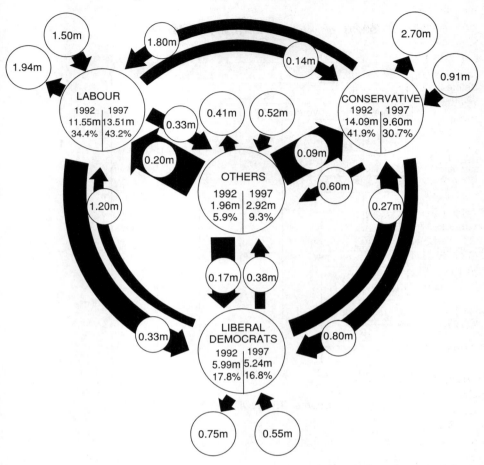

Note:
Width of arrows represents number of voters

Net voter movement:	Labour	Conservative	Liberal Democrat	Other
Added (first time voters/ previous abstensions)	1.50	0.91	0.55	0.52
Subtracted (died/abstained)	1.94	2.70	0.75	0.41
Switched to	3.20	0.50	1.30	1.31
Switched from	0.80	3.20	1.85	0.46
Net balance (+/–)	+1.96	–4.49	–0.75	+0.96

Source: BBC/NOP poll, May 1997; May 1997 Election Results Analysis, Peter Kellner, *Observer*, 18 May 1997.

Figure 4.5 Electoral volatility in 1997

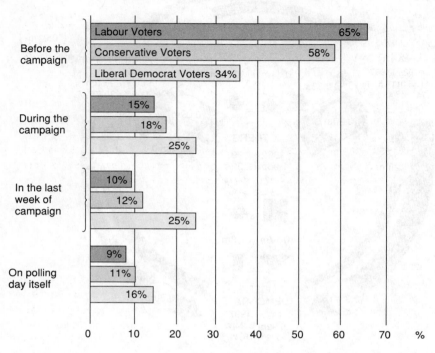

The decision
Q *When did you decide which party to vote for?*

Source: BBC/NOP poll, May 1997

Participation or alienation

If political participation is measured simply in terms of the turn-out at General Elections since the Second World War, we can see that it has fluctuated between a high point of 84 per cent in 1950 and a low point of 70.6 per cent in 1997, with an average of 76.2 per cent over the entire period. In 1970 and 1983 for seasonal reasons (both elections were held in June, when many people were on holiday) and in October 1974 for reasons directly connected with public alienation from the political process (two General Elections in one year), the number of those not voting rivalled or exceeded the number of those who voted for the party which came second. Given that the two-party struggle has been a dominant characteristic of the British political system since the war, these facts could be interpreted as signs of real alienation from the political process.

It is also reasonable to argue that such signs of disenchantment with the two large parties are not necessarily signs of dissatisfaction with the electoral system or alienation from the entire political process. Indeed, it is worth remembering that many individual party candidates regularly get more than 50 per cent of the votes cast in their own constituencies. Yet there can be no escape from the fact that the struggle for power between the two leading parties has been the dominant characteristic of the British political system since the Second World War, so perhaps the conclusion is justified.

There are ebbs and flows in the tide of support for the two main parties. In 1951 they secured between them 96.8 per cent of the popular vote. This declined gradually to 87.5 per cent in 1964, rose to 89.8 per cent in 1966 and stood at 89.4 per cent in 1970. It fell sharply to 74.9 per cent in February 1974 and 75.0 per cent in October 1974. It rose again in 1979 to 80.9 per cent, but fell again in 1983 to 70.0 per cent. It increased to 73.1 per cent in 1987 and to 76.3 per cent in 1992 but fell back to 73.9 per cent in 1997. It remains to be seen whether the 'traditional' duopoly will reassert itself at the expense of the smaller parties or whether the position can be reversed by the minor parties. On this point it should perhaps be noted that in 1997 the combined Conservative and Labour share of the vote was still lower than at any General Election between 1929 and February 1974. Thus any conclusion that the 1997 Election heralded a return to two-party politics is probably premature.

4.5 Conclusion

In conclusion, it can be said that the main influences on voting behaviour in Britain are political inheritance, self-interest, and the performance of the party in office. Nevertheless these are often subjective influences which can depend on the conclusions which individual voters draw from their own experience and observation of the political scene. From a more objective point of view, it seems clear that social class, economic occupation, housing tenure, educational attainment and geographical location are among the most important influences on the way people cast their votes at General Elections. Furthermore, the voters do not cast their votes in a vacuum. They go to the polls (or decide not to bother) after weeks and months of verbal bombardment by the politicians and the media as well as assiduous attention from the opinion pollsters. All these various forces help to form the views of the voters, whose voting behaviour has become more volatile and even capricious in consequence.

There is still some validity in the view of Jean Blondel, who wrote years ago that, 'the simple division between working and middle class ... contributes to the clearest cleavage in British political attitudes and voting behaviour'.[36] Yet such a statement no longer tells us all we need to know about voting behaviour in contemporary Britain. This is because the traditional working class has become significantly smaller while the middle class has grown, in each case as a function of changing patterns of employment. Whatever happens in the minds of the voters, it is well to remember that there are few, if any, certainties in voting behaviour in Britain.

Suggested questions

1   What are the main divisions in the British electorate?
2   Which are the most significant influences on voting behaviour in Britain?
3   Is social class still a decisive factor in determining the outcome of elections in Britain?

Notes

1. B. Sarlvik and I. Crewe, *Decade of Dealignment* (London: CUP, 1983), p. 66.
2. Since about 6 per cent of the names on the Electoral Register are redundant (i.e. dead, double-counted, emigrated, etc.), the true level of non-voting is somewhat lower than the usual figures suggest.
3. P. Pulzer, *Political Representation and Elections in Britain* (London: Macmillan, 1967), p. 98.
4. For a fuller discussion of this subject see R.T. McKenzie and A. Silver, *Angels in Marble* (London: Heinemann, 1968), and J.H. Goldthorpe, *Social Mobility and Class Structure in Modern Britain* (Oxford: Clarendon Press, 1980).
5. See I. Crewe, 'A New Class of Politics', *Guardian*, 15 June 1987.
6. *Guardian*, 13 June 1983.
7. *Ibid.*
8. See Mori poll, *The Sunday Times*, 12 April 1992 and Gallup Post Election Survey 10–11 April 1992.
9. The evidence on differences in voting behaviour by gender and age has been written up in successive Nuffield Election Studies since 1950. The figures given here are derived from those studies.
10. See the Gallup Survey commissioned by the BBC and published in the *Guardian*, 15 June 1987.
11. For detailed breakdown of regional variations in voting behaviour see successive Times Guides to the House of Commons which are published after each General Election.
12. See, for example, A.H. Birch, *The British System of Government*, 8th edn (London: Allen & Unwin, 1990), pp. 78–82.
13. See D.E. Butler and D. Stokes, *Political Change in Britain*, 2nd edn (London: Macmillan, 1974, pp. 48–66).
14. See A. Heath, R. Jowell, J. Curtice with B. Taylor, *Labour's Last Chance? The 1992 Election and Beyond* (Aldershot: Dartmouth, 1994).
15. See J. Curtice and M. Steed, The Results Analysed, pp. 299–300 in D. Butler and D. Kavanagh (eds), *The British General Election of 1997*, (London: Macmillan, 1997).
16. See A. Heath et al., *How Britain Votes* (Oxford: Pergamon Press, 1985).
17. See B. Sarlvik and I. Crewe, *Decade of Dealignment*, pp. 247–344.
18. Tony Benn, *Guardian*, 11 April 1988.
19. Neil Kinnock, *The Sunday Times*, 12 June 1988.
20. See B. Sarlvik and I. Crewe, *Decade of Dealignment*, p. 113.
21. *Guardian*, 14 June 1983.
22. See D. Kavanagh, 'Spirals of Silence', *Guardian*, 21 April 1992.
23. *Guardian*, 16 June 1987.
24. H.T. Himmelweit et al., *How Voters Decide* (London: Academic Press, 1981), p. 14.
25. See R. Worcester, 'Don't Blame the Opinion Pollsters', *The Times*, 13 April 1992.
26. See P. Kellner, Why the Tories were Trounced, pp. 108–122, in P. Norris and N.T. Gavin, *Britain Votes 1997* (Oxford: Oxford University Press, 1997).
27. *Ibid.*
28. See A. Heath et al., *How Britain Votes*, pp. 170–175.
29. See S. Saggar, 'Racial Politics' pp. 185–199, in P. Norris and N.T. Gavin, *Op Cit.*
30. Patrick Edwards, Director, Greater London Action for Racial Equality. Cited in *Guardian*, 6 August 1994.
31. See 'Connections', Commission for Racial Equality, August 1994.
32. D. Macintyre, *Independent*, 4 April 1997.
33. M. Kettle, 'Exit the Looney Left, Enter the Rabid Right', *Guardian*, 1 April 1997.

34. See, for example, D. Bell, *The End of Ideology*, revised edition (London: Collier)
35. As is the case with any such exercise, a margin for error must be accounted for. Others, drawing on the same hard data may produce slightly different estimates. Nonetheless, it is impossible to produce figures vastly different from those using the information available.
36. J. Blondel, *Voters, Parties and Leaders* (Harmondsworth: Penguin, 1974), p. 86.

Further reading

Butler, D.E. and Jowett, P., *party Strategies in Britain: A Study of the 1984 European Elections* (London: Macmillan, 1985).

Butler, D.E. and Kavanagh, D., *The British General Election of 1992* (London: Macmillan, 1992).

Crewe, I., Gosschalk, B. and Bartle, J. (eds), *Political Communications* (London: Frank Cass, 1998).

Franklin, M., *The Decline of Class Voting in Britain* (London: University Press, 1985).

Goldthorpe, J.H., *Social Mobility and Class Structure in Modern Britain* (Oxford: Clarendon Press, 1980).

Heath, A. et al., *Understanding Political Change: the British Voter 1964–1987* (Oxford: Pergamon Press, 1991).

Heath, A. et al., *How Britain Votes* (Oxford: Pergamon Press, 1985).

Himmelweit. H.T. et al., *How Voters Decide* (London: Academic Press, 1981).

King, A. (ed.), *New Labour Triumphs: Britain at the Polls* (Chatham, NJ, USA: Chatham House, 1998).

McCormack, U., *Playing at Politics; First Time Voting in the 1997 UK General Election* (Politeia, 1998).

Miller. W.L. et al., *How Voters Change* (Oxford: Clarendon Press, 1990).

Norris, P. and Gavin, N.T. (eds), *Britain Votes 1997* (Oxford: University Press, 1997).

Robertson. D., *Class and the British Electorate* (Oxford: Martin Robertson, 1983).

Rose. E. and McAlister, I., *Voters Begin to Choose* (London: Sage, 1986).

Sarlvik. B. and Crewe, I., *Decade of Dealignment* (London: University Press, 1983).

Scarborough, E., *Political Ideology and Voting* (Oxford: Clarendon Press, 1984).

PART 2

Sources of Power, Pressure and Opinion

5 The political parties

In Britain there is a system of party government – government by and through political parties. Parties are at the very centre of the system: national, organised, disciplined political parties. The rise of parties changed the nature of elections, altered the relationship between Members of Parliament and their constituents, determined the position of Prime Minister and Cabinet and transformed the House of Commons. As a result political parties have had a dominant influence upon the whole nature of the British political system.

5.1 Origins and historical development

Although groups identified as either Whigs or Tories could be found in Parliament as early as the seventeenth century, parties in the modern sense only appeared in the nineteenth century as a direct consequence of Parliamentary reform. Due to successive extensions of the franchise (see Chapter 3), factions or groups within the House of Commons were increasingly obliged to organise outside Parliament in an attempt to secure the necessary voter support at elections.

The 1832 Reform Act led to the creation of a number of 'societies' whose function it was to arrange for the registration of voters sympathetic to their cause. The Tories established a central organisation to co-ordinate their efforts in this regard in 1832, and were followed two years later by the Whigs. However, it was the consequences of the 1867 Representation of the People Act which triggered the creation of parties in their modern form. The 1867 Act created a larger electorate, too large to deal with effectively in the traditional ways of personal influence, bribery, intimidation, and so on. Consequently, national party organisations were created through which widespread electoral support could be mobilised – seeking to secure the election of 'our' party and the defeat of 'their' party, with politics becoming a matter of 'us' against 'them'. Thus the National Union of Conservative Associations was established in 1867 and the National Liberal Federation ten years later. The age of nationally organised and relatively disciplined political parties had arrived in Britain.

Against this background it is easy to see that British politics is party politics which takes place in what is, fundamentally, a two-party system. In this chapter, therefore, we shall focus principally on the Labour and Conservative parties, as they have been the two most significant political forces in Britain, at any rate since the Second World War. Beyond them we shall look at the smaller parties, whether those with an aspiration throughout Britain – such as the Liberal Democrats – or those with a more geographically limited vocation, such as the nationalist parties in Scotland and Wales. We shall also consider briefly the parties in Northern Ireland and the fringe parties in the rest of the United Kingdom – the Greens, the British National Party and so on.

At the outset it is worth trying to offer a common definition which can be applied to every political party to a greater or lesser extent. In the eighteenth century Edmund Burke defined a political party as 'a body of men united for promoting by their joint endeavours the national interest upon some particular principle in which they are all agreed'.[1] Today, however, there are difficulties with such a definition, not least because it places such an emphasis on agreements freely entered into between relatively independent individuals – an emphasis which no longer reflects the realities of modern British politics. Political parties in Britain, as elsewhere in the democratic world, are nowadays more like organised coalitions, each containing a wide spectrum of ideology, principle, opinion and belief. As a result, a rather better definition of a political party in modern conditions might be: 'an organised and relatively disciplined group of people who freely combine to advance a set of political attitudes or beliefs with a view to translating them via success at elections into administrative decisions or legislative actions'. In other words, all parties try to influence and a few aspire to win the democratic power of Government.

In 1998 the *Registration of Political Parties Act* came into force, establishing a register of political parties, made necessary by the adoption of party list systems for elections to the European Parliament, the Scottish Parliament and the Welsh Assembly, and with the objective of protecting parties from spoiler candidates who use deliberately confusing descriptions on the ballot paper. Although voluntary in nature, the incentive to register is, first, to protect its name – a candidate requires a registered party's permission to use its name or any form of words which might lead voters to associate a candidate with any particular registered party – and, secondly, as a registered party be eligible to make party political broadcasts.

5.2 Ideological principles

Since the Second World War it has been the Labour and Conservative Parties which have dominated the British political scene. They have brought to British politics two distinct ideological traditions within which their respective political principles have been advanced in the light of circumstances prevailing at the time.

The Labour Party

From the outset, and certainly ever since the party constitution was adopted in 1918, the Labour tradition was based on a commitment to the ideology of Socialism. Yet from the beginning the importance of ideology was balanced to some extent by the more pragmatic outlook of the Fabians and Christian Socialists. It was also tempered by trade-union scepticism towards some Socialist principles. Nevertheless, as Samuel Beer observed, 'if the implication of sudden and violent change is extracted … it is correct to say that the meaning of Socialism to the Labour Party was a commitment to ultimate social revolution'.[2] To the Labour Party this always meant more than a commitment to the public ownership of the means of production, distribution and exchange, as laid down originally in Clause IV of the party constitution. It also meant a commitment to a form of moral collectivism which drew on the reserves of fellowship and fraternity traditionally associated with the trade union movement.

The Socialist tradition continued in the modern Labour Party. For example, the October 1974 Labour Manifesto contained a clear commitment to 'an irreversible shift in the balance of wealth and power' in favour of working people. The fact that the Labour Party, when in office, has not always acted in a particularly Socialist way has merely engendered disillusion and recrimination among its more zealous members. It was for this reason that the Party swung markedly to the Left following defeat at the 1979 General Election. Many activists in the constituency Labour parties gave strong support to the campaign of Tony Benn and others on the left of the Party in favour of constitutional changes within the Labour movement designed to make Labour MPs more accountable to the ideological elements in the constituency parties and to diminish the more cautious influence of the Parliamentary leadership on Labour policy. As a result the Left was able to secure radical alterations to the Party constitution in 1981, alterations which provided for the mandatory reselection of sitting MPs and election of the Leader and Deputy Leader of the party by an electoral college made up of the trade unions (40 per cent), the Parliamentary Labour Party (PLP) (30 per cent) and the constituency parties (30 per cent). During this period the position of the Left within the party was strengthened by the election of Michael Foot as Leader and by the decision of a number of Labour MPs to join the newly formed Social Democratic Party. Labour's Manifesto for the 1983 General Election was the most Left-wing in its history and as such was described at the time by one critic in the party – Gerald Kaufman – as 'the longest suicide note in history'.

Within days of the election defeat in 1983 Michael Foot resigned the leadership of the party and after four months of campaigning Neil Kinnock, another leading Left-winger but politically more realistic and about 30 years younger, was elected to succeed him. He accepted the proposition that the party's chances of returning to power would be determined largely by its ability to formulate credible and coherent policies that were neither a source of intra-party strife nor repugnant to the electorate at large. To this end the decision was taken to concentrate less on policy and more on campaigning, the leadership being determined to rebuild the party with a more modern image and more moderate policies. It was for this reason that Labour policy commitments to withdraw Britain from the European Community, to re-nationalise privatised industries, and to repeal aspects of Conservative industrial relations legislation were abandoned or toned down, although the commitment to nuclear disarmament remained for a while longer.

Following yet another electoral defeat for the party at the 1987 General Election, Neil Kinnock and his fellow 'modernisers' realised that in order to have a chance of defeating the Conservatives in future, it was necessary further to modernise both the party's internal structures and its policies. In attempting to achieve these objectives, they followed three courses of action.

First, they introduced a wider franchise for the selection and reselection of party candidates in order to stop small groups of hardline activists dominating the process and to make constituency parties more representative of ordinary Labour supporters and the party more attractive to the voters. Secondly, they restructured the National Executive Committee (NEC) to give the Shadow Cabinet and the PLP more power and the NEC and the Party Conference less power for similar reasons. *Thirdly*, they initiated a wide ranging policy review designed to produce a set of modern policies for the 1990s which would improve Labour's chances of returning to office.

The Policy Review was overwhelmingly endorsed at the 1989 Labour Conference. Having dropped the Socialist policies which were perceived as having made Labour unelectable, Neil Kinnock felt able to declare that the party was 'fit for Government'. Undoubtedly the party was more united than it had been for many years and it had become a more formidable contender for power than it had been for a considerable time. Although the Policy Review did not offer a completely new definition of Labour's ideological principles for the 1990s, it did convey to the British electorate the symbolically important fact that the party had modernised its stance and abandoned old-fashioned Socialism.

Following yet another defeat for the Labour Party at the 1992 General Election, Neil Kinnock resigned as Leader and John Smith was elected in his place. The new Leader, who was also a 'moderniser', immediately decided to build on the reforms of his predecessor by pledging to abolish trade-union block votes within the Labour movement and to introduce the principle of 'one member one vote' into the party's own decision making. After a fierce and often passionate debate at the 1993 Labour Conference, delegates voted in favour of One Member One Vote (OMOV) for the selection of Parliamentary candidates, reform of the system for electing the Leader and Deputy Leader, and the abolition of the union block vote in Party Conference decisions. In short, although the party remained the political voice of the trade unions, the relationship between the two was put upon a modern and politically acceptable basis of individual membership and voluntary participation.

Thus by the time of John Smith's untimely death in May 1994 and the election of Tony Blair as his successor in July 1994, the Labour Party had moved a very long way from the old-fashioned Socialism for which it had stood – at least rhetorically – in the 1970s and early 1980s. Indeed, Tony Blair appeared so moderate and pragmatic on some issues – such as education and law and order – that it seemed possible sometimes that Labour might position itself to the right of the Conservatives on particular issues where majority public opinion held such a position. However, Tony Blair was careful to say that Labour's redefinition of its policy had not altered its traditional commitment to social justice. Rather it had balanced that commitment with honest recognition of the new economic and political realities both in Britain and world-wide. Labour rhetoric came to include frequent references to '*partnership*' between the public and private sectors of the economy, '*fairness*' in taxation and social security arrangements, and '*democracy*' in relation to health and education and the oversight of extra-governmental organisations.

In the late 1990s it could be said that the party favours:

- the use of the tax and social security systems for some redistribution of income and wealth from the better off to the poor;
- higher public spending on the National Health Service, pensions, education, and social security but targeted for the most effective purposes;
- more purposeful intervention in industrial and regional policy by a strengthened Department of Trade and Industry;
- the introduction of a minimum wage and of positive workers' rights;
- nursery places to be provided for all four-year olds and class sizes to be cut to 30 or fewer for all pupils of 5, 6 and 7 years of age;
- reduced waiting lists at NHS hospitals;
- the establishment of elected assemblies in Scotland and Wales;
- the reform of the House of Lords and procedural changes in the House of Commons;
- closer co-operation with Britain's partners in the European Union including UK participation in the Social Chapter;
- willingness to retain Britain's nuclear deterrent until such time as it might be abandoned in the context of multilateral nuclear disarmament.

Following a long series of electoral defeats, Labour made a significant shift towards a more moderate and pragmatic policy stance. Since 1983 three successive Labour Leaders have sought to maximise the party's chances of returning to power and clearly believed that this could not be achieved on the basis of old-style Socialism. The party's willingness to accept many of the economic and social changes made by the Conservatives during the 1980s is somewhat reminiscent of Conservative willingness in the late 1940s to accept many of the changes made by the postwar Labour Government. In each case the principal Opposition Party recognised that there had been a sea change in the conventional wisdom and assumptions of British politics which it had to accept if it were to persuade the voters of its suitability for Office.

The Labour Party's shift towards pragmatism and moderation was particularly noticeable on some sensitive and important issues, such as trade union reform and wider home ownership; but it became increasingly evident right across the board. For example, mainstream Labour attitudes on public ownership, taxation and consumer rights became more cautious and less doctrinaire than previously, and Tony Blair and John Prescott (his Deputy) were even able to persuade the party to accept a new, more modern definition of Clause IV of the 1918 party constitution, namely one which declared that the party sought to create a community in which power, wealth and opportunity are in the hands of the many not the few, and where rights enjoyed reflect the duties owed. In short, Neil Kinnock, John Smith and Tony Blair all seemed determined to let no ideological shibboleths stand in the way of the return to power of a modern and voter-friendly Labour Party on a modern and pragmatic platform. Indeed throughout the run-up to the 1997 General Election Tony Blair's efforts to make the Labour Party electable continued apace. It was for this reason that he matched the Conservatives with a pledge to hold a referendum on British participation in the European single currency, and why Gordon Brown announced that there would be no increase in the rates of Income Tax for five years under a Labour Government. Indeed, bearing in mind the effectiveness of the Conservatives' attempts to portray the Labour Party as a 'tax and spend' party in the 1992 election, they went even further by announcing that they would abide by the Conservative Government's spending plans for the first two years of a Labour Government.

In short, the Labour Party – the party for so long committed to the public owner-ship of the means of production, distribution and exchange – transformed its image, structure and policy in order to re-position itself on the new centre ground of British politics largely defined by Margaret Thatcher. This has been supported by a series of organisational changes which have given greater authority to the leader and by a mastery of the techniques of modern media-focused campaigning.

The Conservative Party

The Conservative tradition stresses the importance of strong Government, in the sense that Conservatives believe that a Government should act with determination and self-confidence based on the democratic legitimacy which it derives from its Parliamentary majority in the House of Commons. Conservatives have traditionally been suspicious of political ideology of an imperative or all embracing kind, although during Margaret Thatcher's period as Leader (1975–90) many observers doubted the validity of such a proposition. In the opinion of Samuel Beer, the ideas of independent authority for the Executive, class rule by those deemed best equipped to govern, pragmatic decisions of a non-ideological character and strong determined Government were all discernible in Conservative political thought for a long time.[3]

Occasionally in the course of its long history the Conservative Party has been swept along on the wave of some particular ideology, but such periods have not usually lasted or brought enduring political success. Joseph Chamberlain, a refugee from the Liberal Party, did not get very far with his campaign for tariff reform during the early years of the twentieth century. Edward Heath felt obliged to reverse the radical free market policies on which he and his colleagues had entered office in 1970. Yet, even though a conscious political ideology does not seem to belong in the Conservative tradition, the party appeared much more ideological in the 1980s – certainly in its free-market rhetoric and occasionally in its actions. This reflected the influence of what was then called the New Right on Conservative thinking. Pressure groups outside Parliament, such as the Institute of Economic Affairs and the Adam Smith Institute, and factions within Parliament, such as the self-styled No Turning Back Group of radical Conservative back-benchers, combined to push the party's policy and decision-making in a markedly more right-wing direction and to give extra political impetus to the Thatcherite revolution.

In present circumstances the Conservative Party is reviewing nearly all its poli-cies, but the following broad strands seem likely to endure:

- the maintenance of sound money (sometimes called 'monetarism');
- the control of public expenditure;
- the reduction of tax rates on income, when it is prudent to do so;
- the pursuit of a range of 'supply side' reforms designed to maintain Britain's com-petitiveness in the global economy;

- greater freedom of choice for consumers, parents, and patients;
- a more selective approach towards social security and unemployment benefit;
- a tough approach towards law and order;
- strict controls on immigration;
- the maintenance of the nation's defences against terrorism and external military threats;
- a cautious, even nationalistic, attitude towards British membership of the European Union.

The party has also traditionally made a point, even a fetish, of trying to preserve party unity (or at least the appearance of unity), since it is well aware of the political disadvantages of obvious disunity. Indeed, loyalty to the leader and the consequent image of unity was at one time said to be the Party's 'secret weapon'. Nevertheless, this did not prevent the conduct of a bitter (though often coded) argument between the Thatcherites and the non-Thatcherites about the pace and scale of supply side reform (such as privatisation), nor did it prevent frequent outbreaks of internecine strife within the party about the nature and extent of Britain's commitment to the future development of the European Union – particularly with regard to a single European currency – during the 1990s. The former argument was largely resolved in favour of the Thatcherites, since most of the prominent 'Wets' were sacked or had retired from the Cabinet by the end of the 1980s and the rest of the party came to recognise the force of three successive General Election victories under the leadership of Margaret Thatcher. With regard to the latter argument, it was one of the factors that led to the removal of Margaret Thatcher as party leader and Prime Minister in 1990, and proved to be the most disruptive issue for the party during the leadership of John Major (1990–97).

For much of his time John Major sought to hold back the mounting pressure within the party in favour of ruling out altogether British membership of a single European currency – committing the party to hold a referendum on the issue was part of this policy – and by the time of the 1997 General Election the party was sounding its most sceptical line to date not simply on the issue of economic and monetary union but on European matters generally. To his pro-European critics in the party John Major was seen as the Canute of his day; to his anti-European critics in the party he was simply seen as lacking the Eurosceptic credentials of his predecessor. In attempting to hold both wings of the party together John Major pleased neither. In opposition following the 1997 General Election and under a new leader, William Hague, it was still apparent that the fault lines in the party on the issue of Europe had not gone away, although the new leader's clearer line that UK entry into EMU should not be contemplated for ten years was more in tune with majority opinion within the much reduced Parliamentary party as well as within the wider party, a fact highlighted by the result of the internal party ballot on the issue in 1998 which strongly endorsed his position.

During Margaret Thatcher's period as leader of the party (1975–90), the emphasis in Conservative rhetoric was put on the paramount importance of individual attitudes and behaviour in response to material incentives and legislative penalties. Leading party spokesmen were at pains to emphasise the comparatively limited role of the state and other public agencies, but equally to stress that the law should be clearly defined and strongly enforced in those areas in which state power could legitimately be exercised. There were also sustained attempts to reward individual success and to penalise failure, whether in education, work or life in general. Above all, the Conservatives sought to persuade people not to look to the Government for salvation, but to take responsibility for themselves and their families.

With the election of John Major a more emollient style of leadership and a less exclusive approach to politics was apparent. Nonetheless, there was considerable continuity of policy, especially in respect of the party's commitments to sound money, reducing the size of the public sector and concentrating social security on those who needed it most. Under John Major the Conservatives presented a less ideological and more pragmatic profile. The slogans and ideas most closely associated with John Major's period as Prime Minister included:

- his declared wish to create 'a nation at ease with itself';
- the concept of 'the Citizens Charter' designed to make the providers of public services more responsive to the needs and expectations of citizens as customers and consumers;
- the aspiration that Britain should be 'at the heart of Europe' (but without any commitment to further integration);
- a rather counterproductive call to get 'back to basics' in such areas as education and law and order.

John Major's critics in the media and in his own party accused him of having insufficient political conviction and failing to demonstrate real leadership qualities. In these respects unfavourable contrasts were drawn with his predecessor, notwithstanding the fact that he was chosen to succeed Margaret Thatcher in 1990 very largely because he was different in style and character.

The 1997 General Election result left the Conservative Party devastated and despairing and, with John Major stepping down as leader, plunged it into its fourth leadership election in less than eight years. It was not only the loss of office – difficult enough in itself after 18 years – nor the scale of the defeat – described as 'the most catastrophic electoral showing for 165 years[4] – but the specifics of the defeat: the fact that seven Cabinet Ministers lost their seats, including the Foreign Secretary, Malcolm Rifkind, and Defence Secretary, Michael Portillo, both of whom would have been leadership contenders had they held their seats; as well as results which saw Sir Marcus Fox, Chairman of the 1922 Committee, lose his seat on a 13.79 per cent swing, Norman Lamont, the former Chancellor, lose his seat on a 15.75 per cent swing and the failure to hold on to Margaret Thatcher's old Finchley seat. As one senior Conservative put it, 'it was a disaster of biblical proportions'.[5]

The new leader, William Hague, declared that he and party members knew why the Conservatives had lost the election: 'People thought that we had lost touch with those we always claimed to represent. Our Parliamentary party came to be seen as divided, arrogant, selfish and conceited. Our party as a whole was regarded as out of touch and irrelevant.',[6] and pledged himself to 'transform the world's oldest and most successful political party into a modern fighting force equipped for the battles of the 21st century.'[7]

The Liberal Democrats

The Liberal Democrats were formally launched on 3 March 1988, under the slogan 'The New Choice – The Best Future', born out of the decision by the old Liberal Party and the Social Democratic Party (SDP) to merge their two separate parties – previously co-operating as *the Alliance* – into a single entity. Under their leader, Paddy Ashdown, the party sought to establish a distinctive political profile. In doing so, it identified four pillars of policy:

- investing in the future by allocating more public funds to education, health and the nation's technological base;
- modernising and defending democracy by developing a new concept of citizenship;
- developing a more ambitious environmental policy;
- laying great stress on Britain's international vocation and responsibilities.

Within its new concept of citizenship, the party was strongly committed to:

- the achievement of a fairer voting system;
- devolution of power to Assemblies in Scotland, Wales and the regions of England;
- greater power for individuals through the introduction of employee councils at their place of work;
- the introduction of legislation guaranteeing freedom of information;
- a new Bill of Rights.

Above all, they advocated a less divisive and more decentralised approach to solving the continuing problems of British politics within the context of the European Union, to which they showed more commitment than either of the two main parties.

Having abandoned not only their original strategy of replacing Labour as the Centre-Left alternative to the Conservative Party, but also their subsequent stance of equal distance between the two main parties, the Liberal Democrats entered the 1997 General Election in the hope that it would produce a Parliament in which no single party had a majority but where they would be left holding the balance. Although they saw their share of the national vote go down slightly on their 1992 showing, the focused nature of their campaign strategy – targeting some 50 constituencies – enabled them to increase their Parliamentary representation from 20 to 46 MPs, giving them their best result in seventy years. Nonetheless, with an overall Labour majority of 178 they were further from holding the balance of fewer than before. Paddy Ashdown, the Party Leader at the time, pledged to make the party the most constructive voice within the opposition. In this they were determined to confront Labour Ministers on issues such as education and health – on which during the election campaign the Liberal Democrats had promised higher public spending financed by tax increases – and to do so also on constitutional matters on which they believed that they had made the running over many years.

However, with New Labour having moved onto much of the ground previously occupied by the Liberal Democrats and recognising the fact that by the time of the next election much of what the party has fought for over the years could actually be achieved – electoral reform, devolution, a Bill of Rights, freedom of information, higher spending on education and health, greater participation in Europe – the party is aware that it faces a struggle to remain distinctive, with its own identity. It is for this

Figure 5.1   Party policies at the 1997 General Election

Constitution

CONSERVATIVE Evolutionary, rather than revolutionary, change. Plan to give Parliament more time to consider legislation by extending Queen's Speech programme to cover firm programme for year ahead, and provisional programme for the year after.

LABOUR Referendums offered on Scottish, Welsh and London devolution, and Proportional Representation for general elections. Abolition of hereditary peers' rights in Lords. Reform of party funding. Freedom of Information Act. More freedom for councils. Human rights guarantee.

LIB DEM Smaller, stronger Commons. Ten-year plan for elected Lords. Proportional Representation. Four-year Parliaments. Party-funding cleansed. Bill of Rights. Freedom of Information. Scottish and Welsh home rule. Stronger local government; London authority. Ulster power-sharing executive.

Defence

CONSERVATIVE Encouragement of further development of cadet forces. No need for defence spending review. Will resist attempts to bring Western European Union under control of EU.

LABOUR Retention of Trident, though nuclear weapons to be included in multilateral negotiations 'when satisfied with verified progress towards our goal of global elimination'. Strategic defence, security, and spending review promised.

LIB DEM Retain Trident, with restricted warhead capacity, until international multilateral nuclear disarmament can be achieved. Retain defence capability at current level. Strengthen UN peacekeeping. Control of arms sales, and ban landmines.

Education

CONSERVATIVE School performance targets, with action taken to bring under-performers up to mark. Inspection of local education authorities, with remedial action when required. More delegation to schools; more specialist schools and a grammar school, if wanted, in every major town. Nursery vouchers, education or training credits to be introduced.

LABOUR Nursery places to be provided for all four-year-olds. Class sizes to be cut to 30 or fewer for all pupils of 5, 6, and 7, financed by phase-out of assisted places scheme. Ministers to close and restart failing schools. Open University-style University of Industry.

LIB DEM Nursery education for children of 3 and 4 whose parents want it, as first call on £2bn annual spending programme. Five-year pledge: to limit class sizes to 30 for all children 5–11; and spend £500m on school repair backlog. Double year-one spend on school books and equipment.

Europe

CONSERVATIVE Positive vision of partnership of nation states; no further extension of qualified majority voting, or erosion of veto. Strong defence of frontier controls. Demand exemption from Working Time Directive. Will not join fudged Euro currency. Membership only by referendum approval.

LABOUR Rapid completion of single market, high priority enlargement, urgent reform of CAP, greater democracy in EU bodies, retain national veto over key national interest issues, and signing of Social Chapter. Triple lock on single currency membership: Cabinet, Parliament and referendum.

LIB DEM Referendum for substantial change in relationship. PR for 1999 European parliamentary elections. Enlargement, with more majority voting; keeping veto for constitution, budget, pay and social security. Aim to join single currency, but in line with convergence criteria and only with referendum majority.

Health

CONSERVATIVE Annual increases in real resources for NHS. Hospital league tables to inform patient and GP choice. Practice-based cottage hospitals. Nurse prescribing to be extended. No long-stay mental hospital to be closed without adequate community care alternative. Private Finance Initiative to 'unleash' modernisation funds.

LABOUR First £100m saved on ending internal market bureaucracy to take 100,000 off waiting lists. No-wait cancer surgery. Annual real terms increase in NHS spending. Action on mixed-sex wards. Ban on tobacco advertising. Independent food standards agency. New Minister for Public Health.

LIB DEM Free eye and dental checks and freeze on prescription charges. Three-year target of six-month limit on hospital waiting lists. Invest £200m annually to recruit more frontline staff. End two-tier NHS and local pay bargaining. Six-month freeze on finance-driven closures.

Crime

CONSERVATIVE Mandatory prison sentences for persistent burglars and drug-dealers; automatic life terms for anyone convicted of second serious sexual or violent crime. Extra 10,000 public place CCTV cameras by 1999. Voluntary ID cards. Speedy court sanctions for young offenders, including electronic curfews and Parental Control Orders.

LABOUR Halving of time to get persistent young offenders from arrest to sentence. Parental responsibility orders, to make parents face up to child's misbehaviour, community safety orders for bad neighbours, and child protection orders for youngsters left out too late at night. Free vote on total handgun ban.

LIB DEM Extra 3,000 police officers on beat within a year. Encourage community sentences as alternative to prison, using prison where essential for public protection or effective punishment. Councils to get crime prevention powers. Royal Commission on drugs. Witness and victim support schemes to be developed.

Economy

CONSERVATIVE Tight control on public spending with five-year goal of reducing government expenditure below 40 per cent of national income. Maintaining inflation target of 2.5 per cent or less. Aim to virtually eliminate public borrowing by 2000. Maintain lowest European tax burden.

LABOUR Inflation target 2.5 per cent or less. Greater independence for Bank of England. Public debt at 'stable and prudent level', borrowing only to invest, 'over economic cycle'. Review of Whitehall assets. Maintenance of current, two-year spending plans. High and stable employment.

LIB DEM Bank of England independence; accountable to Parliament for keeping inflation low. Lower inflation and stable exchange rate best served by single currency membership. Public borrowing should not exceed investment 'over economic cycle'. Public-private investment partnerships. Savings encouragement. Investment and economic stability.

Environment

CONSERVATIVE 'Tough but affordable' targets to improve air quality. Sustained improvements in water quality, at affordable pace. Encouragement of low-pollution vehicles. Continuing exploration of polluter pays principle. Product labelling to show environmental impact of how goods made.

LABOUR All departments to promote environmental policies, with parliamentary audit. Integrated transport policy. Review of vehicle excise duty to promote low-emission vehicles. Tough regulation of water industry. Tax penalties for pollution. Moratorium favoured on 'large-scale sales' of Forestry Commission land.

LIB DEM Cut car tax to £10 for cars up to 1600cc, while gradually increasing fuel duty 4p per litre. Urban road pricing to finance public transport. Carbon tax to finance VAT and employers' NICs cut. Countryside Management Contracts to help farmers to protect vital habitats.

Housing

CONSERVATIVE Aim to raise £25bn over decade for rundown housing estates where tenants agree switch to private sector landlords. Rough Sleeper Initiative to be extended from London to other big cities. Aim for at least 60 per cent of all new homes to be built on derelict urban sites.

LABOUR Phased release of council house sale receipts to be re-invested in housing. Action on gazumping. Tenant agreement to be sought for private finance improvement of public housing. Commonhold ownership of blocks of flats, and easier purchase of freehold by leaseholders. New council duty to protect homeless.

LIB DEM Phased release of council house sales receipts for housebuilding. Mortgage Benefit to replace MIRAS for first-time buyers; eventual merger of Mortgage and Housing Benefit 'focused on those most in need'. Help for homeless, streetsleepers, and action on empty homes. Strengthen tenants' right to repair.

Jobs

CONSERVATIVE Exemption from European Working Time Directive to be demanded. Project Work, 'workfare' programme to be extended, if economically viable, to cover longterm unemployed nationwide. Developing scheme to use private and voluntary sectors to get people off welfare and into work.

LABOUR Windfall tax to finance welfare-to-work scheme for 250,000 under-25s, unemployed for more than six months. Six-month tax rebate for employers taking on long-term unemployed. Special Employment Zones to co-ordinate benefits, training and jobhunting. Special help for lone parents.

LIB DEM Help for long-term unemployed with self-financing Benefit Transfer Programme, turning benefits

for one-year jobless into employers' incentive to recruit and train. Citizen's Service scheme to give youngsters up to two years', environmental, conservation, crime prevention, social services, housing renovation, and armed services work.

Pensions

CONSERVATIVE All youngsters entering work to get personal pension fund, with rebate on National Insurance Contributions. More flexibility for personal pension holders to continue investing even if subsequently join company schemes. Easier set-up for small employer personal pension plans.

LABOUR Basic state pension to be increased 'at least in line with prices'. Private, state-approved second pension scheme proposed, offering high value-for-money standards. Action to stop pension mis-selling. Help mooted for million pensioners not claiming Income Support entitlement.

LIB DEM Guaranteed minimum standard of living in retirement. Additional top-up pension for those with incomes below Income Support. Phase-out of expensive contributory system. Flexible decade of retirement from 60. Expansion of personal and occupational pension schemes, replacing SERPS.

Privatisation

CONSERVATIVE London Underground and Parcelforce. Preserve national identity, universal service and distinctive characteristics of Post office Royal Mail while considering options – including 'different forms of privatisation' – for providing private capital and management.

LABOUR 'We will ensure that self-financing commercial organisations within the public sector – the Post Office is a prime example – are given greater commercial freedom to make the most of new opportunities.' Privatisation not mentioned.

LIB DEM London Underground to be retained. Existing utility regulators combined in Office of Utility Regulation, ensuring excess profits used to cut prices and improve services.

Tax

CONSERVATIVE Around 2m one-taxpayer couples to get extra £17.50 from transfer of married partner's unused tax allowance to working spouse, where partner looking after dependants. Five-year Parliament, 'aim' to reduce basic rate income tax to 20p. Cuts in burden of capital gains tax and inheritance tax 'as prudent'.

LABOUR Five-year pledge of no increase in income tax rates. Long-term

objective of 10p starting rate income tax. VAT on domestic fuel and power reduced to 5 per cent. No extension of VAT to food, children's clothes, books, newspapers or public transport fares. Windfall tax on privatised utilities.

LIB DEM Penny on basic rate income tax – 24p – to raise £2bn a year for education. Higher rate of 50p for taxable income over £100,000. That finances raising of tax threshold by £200, taking 470,000 out of tax. Fivepence on packet of cigarettes to pay for health package.

Transport

CONSERVATIVE Complete 'successful transfer' of British Rail, followed by plans to privatise London Underground, with recycling of proceeds to modernise network within five years, and regulation of fares to ensure no rise above inflation for four years. Road-building programme to be sustained.

LABOUR More effective regulation of privatised railways, with new rail authority back-up. Unpersuaded on case of 44-tonne lorries. Strategic review of roads programme. New public-private partnership for London Underground, with no sell-off. Proper, local regulation of bus services.

LIB DEM Treble rail freight and double passengers by 2010, withholding subsidies from Railtrack if targets not met, with possible renationalisation of controlling interest in Railtrack in event of 'persistent failure'. Urban road-pricing to help pay for 'clean and rapid' public transport. Public-private partnership investment.

Unions

CONSERVATIVE Public protection from 'abuse' of union power by removal of legal immunity from court action for strikes which have 'disproportionate or excessive effect', allowing public and employers to seek injunctions to stop such strikes. Strike ballots to be repeated at regular intervals.

LABOUR Union legislation of 1980s to stay on ballots, picketing and industrial action, but where majority of 'relevant workforce' vote for representation, union should be recognised. 'Full consultation on the most effective means of implementing this proposal.' Minimum wage to cut taxpayer subsidy to low-pay employers.

LIB DEM New rights to consultation and participation in decisions. Promotion of profit-sharing and employee share-ownership. Extension of EU Social Chapter benefits to all employees, 'while resisting the adoption of new rules that unnecessarily harm job opportunities.'

Source: Independent 'Guide to the Election', April 1997

THE POLITICAL PARTIES 115

reason that the party has embarked on efforts to construct a new distinctive agenda. Early in 1998 eight Commissions were set up to review policy, namely on the economy, social security, home affairs, foreign affairs, health, education, the environment and the constitution. It appears that there are three themes running through these reviews, first the concept of a 'contract' between the tax-payer and the Government which will empower the individual; the need to change the relationship between national and local government, and thirdly, the need for further protection of civil liberties in modern society.

In January 1999 Paddy Ashdown announced that he would step down as Liberal Democrat leader in June 1999. The choice of leader is likely to determine the future direction of the party and its prospects for success.

The Nationalist parties

Formed in 1928 (but under its current name from 1934) the *Scottish National Party* (SNP) has been motivated principally by the quest for Scottish independence and has therefore been able to encompass a broad ideological spectrum of opinion on nearly all other issues. During the 1980s and 1990s most of the party was able to unite on the basis of opposition to English, Conservative rule from London, hostility to the position of the Labour Party as the leading party in Scotland, and the aspiration for an independent Scotland within the European Union.

Plaid Cymru, the Welsh Nationalist Party, was founded in 1925 and has an ideology which is based on its determination to preserve the Welsh language and culture as the foundation of a distinctive Welsh identity within the United Kingdom. The party has both a radical and a moderate wing, with the former being in favour of certain forms of direct action in protest against the English dominance of Wales (for instance on the issues of Welsh water for English cities or English second homes in Wales) and the latter seeming more content to use the traditional channels of Parliamentary influence and the opportunities provided by devolution to advance the Welsh nationalist cause.

Northern Ireland parties

In Northern Ireland the majority Protestant community is represented at Westminster by various factions of the Unionist cause – the *Ulster Unionist Party* (UUP), the *Democratic Unionist Party* (DUP), and the *UK Unionists*. All of them stand, to a greater or lesser extent, for continued Protestant supremacy and the maintenance of Northern Ireland as an integral part of the United Kingdom. The minority Catholic community is represented mainly by the *Social Democratic and Labour Party* (SDLP), which has campaigned to improve the economic and social conditions of its supporters and which favours closer links between Northern Ireland and the Irish Republic as a step towards eventual Irish unity by consent. A smaller part of the Catholic community gives its support to the much more radical *Sinn Féin*, the political wing of the Irish Republican movement in the north, which campaigns openly for the withdrawal of British troops from Northern Ireland and the subsequent establishment of a united Ireland – a policy which from the late 1960s through into the 1990s they sought to achieve by all means at their disposal, including the use of force. In addition to the Protestant/Unionist and Catholic/Nationalist parties there is the non-sectarian *Alliance Party of Northern Ireland*. Launched in 1970, it has not been successful in Westminster elections and attracted only 8.0 per cent of the Northern Ireland vote in 1997.

Many of the Unionists came to adopt an increasingly 'garrison' mentality, not least because they came to feel that the constitutional position of Northern Ireland had been placed in jeopardy, firstly by the 1985 Anglo-Irish Agreement between the British Government and the Government of the Irish Republic, secondly by the Downing Street Declaration signed by the British Prime Minister and the Irish Taoiseach on 15 December 1993, and thirdly by the whole 'peace process', culminating in the Belfast Agreement, the agreement reached at the multi-party talks in April 1998 and ratified by referendum in May 1998.

The Fringe Parties

There are many fringe parties in British politics – indeed, a total of 1,678 candidates (a record number) stood under a minor party or independent label in the General Election of 1997. Some of the smallest, particularly those from the extremes of both Right and Left, wax and wane with bewildering frequency. On the extreme Right, the *British National Party* (BNP), the *National Democrats* and the *National Front* are based on a white racialist ideology which is heavily tinged with xenophobia and impatience with the democratic methods of Parliamentary politics. On the extreme Left, the *Communist Party of Great Britain* – formed in 1920 – was one of the most unreconstructed and Stalinist parties in the whole of Western Europe, since it strongly opposed any firm Western response to the Soviet military threat and any liberalising tendencies in the Soviet Union or Eastern Europe. However, in 1991, seeking to shed its Stalinist image and to be seen as 'an open democratic party of the new, pluralistic and radical Left', the party re-named itself the Democratic Left. Also on the extreme Left are the *Socialist Labour Party* under its leader Arthur Scargill, President of the National Union of Miners, which was formed in 1996 as a socialist alternative to New Labour and which fielded 64 candidates; and both the *Socialist Party of Great Britain* and the *Workers' Revolutionary Party*, which were distinguishable from the old Communist Party mainly by their attachment to the idea of workers' control in industry and commerce and by their more favourable attitude towards reform in what was once the Soviet Union.

In a different category altogether there is the *Green Party*, which stands for an ecological approach to all political issues. Formed as the People's Party in 1973, it became the Ecology Party in 1975 and changed to its current name in 1985. It reached considerable prominence in the late 1980s, riding the wave of a buoyant popular environmentalism which swept across Europe at the time. Indeed, in the 1989 elections to the European Parliament it secured 14.5 per cent of the votes cast (20 per cent in the south-east of England), coming second in six seats out of 78 in Britain and third in 61. However, because of internal disputes and structural weaknesses, the re-emergence of the Liberal Democrats, the effects of the recession and the fact that the other parties sought to display their own 'green' credentials; the party proved unable to build on this performance, and in the 1992 General Election its average share of the vote in the 253 seats which it contested was only 1.3 per cent. In 1997, fielding only

95 candidates and advocating policies to withdraw from the European Union, scrap nuclear weapons and take the railways back into public ownership, it secured 0.2 per cent of the vote, an average of 673 votes per candidate.

In the 1997 General Election the largest number of fringe party candidates – 547 (32.6 per cent) – were those from the *Referendum Party*, the Eurosceptic party formed, funded – to the tune of some £20 million – and led by Sir James Goldsmith. The policy was to secure a referendum with the questions 'Do you want the UK to be a part of a federal Europe? Or do you want the UK to return to an association of sovereign nations that are part of a common trading market?' The party polled 811,827 votes, 2.6 per cent of the total on an average vote of 3.1 per cent, saving 42 deposits – with its highest votes being 9.2 per cent in Harwich and 8.0 per cent in Folkestone & Hythe. The party was seen to be a spoiling factor by some of the defeated Conservatives, because in 24 of the constituencies in which the Conservative Party was defeated – 19 to Labour and 5 to the Liberal Democrats – the vote for the Referendum Party was greater than the size of the Conservatives' 1992 majority. Nonetheless, it is difficult to confirm such an assertion, not least because, according to the exit polls, less than half of the votes for the party came from those who had previously voted Conservative.

Perhaps the most remarkable individual result of the 1997 General Election was that in the Tatton constituency where a majority of 22,365 for the sitting Conservative member and former Corporate Affairs Minister, Neil Hamilton, was turned into a majority of 11,077 for the Independent 'anti-sleaze' candidate Martin Bell, the former BBC correspondent, who became the first independent to be elected to the House of Commons since 1950.

The 1997 General Election also saw 196 candidates stand under the label of the *Natural Law Party*, a group whose campaign was designed to promote 'vedic science' espoused by Maharishi Mahesh Yogi as the solution to the world's problems, but which on average obtained only 0.7 per cent of the votes cast, 0.1 per cent of the total. Also on the fringe can be found a selection of 'loonies' – the *Official Monster Raving Loony Party*, the *Fancy Dress Party*, the *Miss Money Penny's Glamorous One Party*, and others – all individuals who have sought to get involved simply for the fun of it and who have undoubtedly added a touch of colour to British elections.

Aside from the *Referendum Party*, the most successful of the other fringe parties in the General Election of 1997 was the Liberal Party, a group of dissident Liberals who had refused to go along with the 1988 merger with the SDP. They fielded 54 candidates and secured an average of 1.8 per cent of the votes cast in those constituencies, saving two deposits with 9.6 per cent and 6.6 per cent of the vote respectively.

Apart from Martin Bell winning in Tatton – and of course Betty Boothroyd being re-elected as The Speaker in West Bromwich West – three fringe party candidates secured more than 10 per cent of the vote: R. Silvester (Labour Change) and S. Edwards (National Democrat) both in West Bromwich West, securing 23.3 per cent and 11.4 per cent respectively, and Tommy Sheridan (Scottish Socialist Alliance) the anti-Poll Tax campaigner who again contested Glasgow Pollock – on this occasion not from prison – and who obtained 11.1 per cent of the vote.

5.3 Political functions

The political parties in Britain perform a range of political functions. Essentially these can be reduced to one primary function and a number of subsidiary functions, all of which contribute to the working of the British political system.

Primary function

The primary function of the main political parties in Britain, as Robert McKenzie made clear, is to sustain competing teams of potential leaders in the House of Commons in order that the electorate as a whole may choose between them at periodic General Elections.[8] Indeed, any attempt by the parties to play a more prominent role in their own right would cut across the chain of responsibility from Cabinet to Parliament to electorate which is fundamental to the British system of Parliamentary democracy. In the British political system constitutional power resides essentially with the Prime Minister and Cabinet, supported by a working majority in the House of Commons. In these circumstances the supreme function of the parties is bound to be the gaining and retaining of public consent for the exercise of such power. Any other conception of their paramount task would be inaccurate and improper, according to the conventional wisdom.

Subsidiary functions

All the parties perform similar subsidiary functions which vary in importance depending on the particular circumstances of the time. First, they encourage public interest and participation in the process of politics. In other words, they provide permanent structures within which individuals and groups can act if they wish to play a part in politics at the local, national or European levels.

Secondly, the parties reflect, moderate and direct into constitutional channels the views and interests of a wide range of sectional groups. Of course, pressure groups have a powerful independent existence in their own right within the political system. Yet the existence of the parties enables and encourages all sectional groups to act in a constitutional manner and leads them to pay more attention to Parliament than might otherwise be the case.

Thirdly, they provide legitimate frameworks for the ventilation, discussion and criticism of political issues. This function has been more prominent in the Labour and Liberal Democrat parties than in the Conservative Party, because the former believe in the virtues of considerable grass roots influence on the process of policy making, whereas the latter has traditionally allowed only a very limited role for its activists in this sphere. However, in the 1980s this contrast became somewhat less marked, since Conservative activists felt encouraged by Margaret Thatcher and her like-minded Parliamentary colleagues to make more forcefully known their support for radical policies, especially when such developments appeared to be blocked or delayed by some of the more traditional figures in the Parliamentary party. Consequently, Margaret Thatcher's successors, John Major and William Hague have had to take account of the party rank and file to a greater extent than any of their predecessors, a fact emphasised at the 1993 Conference when John Major felt obliged to reduce the pressure on his position as Leader with a direct appeal to the basic instincts of traditional Conservative supporters by calling for a return to core Conservative values, in 1997 when William Hague sought the endorsement of the party in its first ever ballot on the leadership, and in 1998 when William Hague sought to stamp his authority on the party on the issue of the Single European Currency through a ballot of party members. On the other hand, although the annual Conference is theoretically the supreme policy-making body within the Labour movement, its 'decisions' can be heavily influenced and even manipulated by the Leader, the NEC and the Parliamentary Party, and the power of Conference has been reduced still further by Tony Blair's latest round of party reforms.

Lastly, and by no means least important, the political parties exist to build up membership, raise money, select candidates and organise political campaigns at local, national and European levels. The key to all of this activity is money and consequently all of the political parties put considerable effort into fundraising. Traditionally the Labour Party has been heavily reliant on the financial support of affiliated trade unions, support which provided 80 per cent of the party's income in the 1960s. More recently as a direct result of a conscious effort to move away from a position of financial dependence on the unions, this has declined to between 60 and 50 per cent in the early-to-mid 1990s and to 30 per cent by 1998. In addition to money from the unions, 40 per cent of its income comes from small donations, mainly from party members, 20 per cent from large donors and 10 per cent from other activities such as the sale of policy papers and so on.

In the Conservative Party a great part of the income has traditionally been provided by industry and commerce, a source which accounted for 60 per cent of its income in the 1970s. In the late 1990s, however, with corporate donations being described as in 'terminal decline'[9] this figure had declined to about 20 per cent. Aside from this, income is derived from donations from members and supporters, from the fundraising efforts of the voluntary workers in the Constituency Associations and from miscellaneous party activities.

The Liberal Democrats seek to raise money both locally and nationally in broadly similar ways, except for the fact that they do not receive official trade union support and their support from business has always been limited.

In modern political conditions all parties find it increasingly difficult to keep going financially at a time when the costs of political activity are rising and the membership of political parties has dwindled in a disturbing way. For example, the Conservative Party claimed a membership of 2.8 million in 1953, a figure which had declined to just under 1.5 million in 1979 and just under 400,000 by September 1997, and it was believed by many that the real figure was in fact substantially lower than this.[10] Similarly, although the Labour Party claimed over one million members in 1953, this had declined to something under 300,000 towards the end of 1994. It subsequently rose to 405,238 in early 1998, although it fell back to 385,000 by mid-1998. The Liberal Democrats claimed a membership of 100,000 in 1998. As far as the costs of political activity are concerned – as outlined in Chapter 3 – the 1997 General Election campaign cost the parties centrally some £57 million, 52 per cent more than in 1992.

Figure 5.2 shows annual party income and expenditure for the three main parties in 1997.

Figure 5.2 Party consolidated income and expenditure accounts for the year ended 31 December 1997

	Labour	Conservative	Liberal Democrat
Income (£m)			
Subscriptions	1.9	–	1.3
Constituency quota	–	1.1	–
Application fees	6.4	–	–
Donations	14.5	38.2	2.5
Other	1.3	3.2	–
Total	24.1	42.5	3.8
Expenditure (£m)			
Premises	1.4	0.9	0.3
Staff	9.0	7.1	0.8
Publications	1.3	1.1	0.1
Research	0.3	1.0	0.1
Other	4.6	–	–
Total	16.6	10.1	1.2
Campaigns			
• newspaper advertising	0.8	3.2	–
• outdoor advertising	4.8	11.1	0.1
• other advertising	0.1	0.1	–
• publications	1.0	1.0	0.2
• direct mail	0.7	2.2	0.2
• telemarketing	0.2	–	0.3
• party political broadcasts/videos	0.5	0.5	0.2
• other	6.8	10.2	1.3
Total campaign spending	14.9	28.3	2.3
Total	31.5	38.4	3.5

Note:
Expenditure figures for the Conservative Party are for 1996–97.
Source: *The Funding of Political Parties in the United Kingdom*, Fifth Report on the Committee on Standards in Public Life, Cm 4057–1 pp. 30–44 (The Stationery Office).

Since the publication of the Houghton Report in 1976, there has been the additional possibility for the Opposition parties to receive financial support from public funds in proportion to the votes which they secured at the previous General Election.[11] In the year following the 1997 General Election the Conservative Party received £1.6 million of public money to support their opposition work in Parliament and the Liberal Democrats received £400,000.

Throughout the 1990s there was mounting disquiet on the whole matter of party funding following a series of allegations and revelations concerning donations made to the Conservative Party, not least substantial donations from foreign sources, some of which could only be described as 'dubious' (such as the £440,000 given by Asil Nadir, the Cypriot businessman who fled the United Kingdom following the collapse of his Poly Peck empire and allegations of fraud; the £250,000 given by Mohamed Al-Fayed, the owner of Harrods, who later went on to release details of the cash-for-questions scandal; and the £1 million given by Ma Ching-Kwan the Hong Kong publishing tycoon whose father was a suspected drugs trafficker and a fugitive). The disquiet continued following the 1997 election when it became public knowledge that a gift of £1 million to the Labour Party had been made by the head of Formula 1 motor racing, Bernie Ecclestone, with resulting allegations that the money had influenced the Labour Government's decision to seek an exemption for Formula 1 from a European tobacco advertising ban, an action that had been contrary to their previously stated policy on the matter. In March 1998 the Committee on Standards in Public Life, under the chairmanship of Lord Neill, launched an inquiry into the whole question of party funding. Questions considered included a ban on foreign donations and the identification of those who donate more than £5000 in any one year (both changes already implemented by William Hague in the Conservative Party), a limitation on the amount of money a party can spend during an election campaign (with suggested limits ranging between £2 million and £15 million), the provision of free access to advertising space and hoardings, and direct state funding for the parties.

5.4 National organisation

In matters of national party organisation there has traditionally been a notable contrast between the Conservative Party, which was created from the centre and the top down, and the Labour Party which was created from the grass roots up. The Conservative organisation was originally intended to act as the handmaid of the Parliamentary Party, whereas the Labour organisation was conceived as the servant of the National Executive Committee and ultimately the annual Party Conference. Such contrasting origins and traditions have left their mark on the way in which each of the main parties is organised today. Having said this, however, it should be pointed out that Neil Kinnock, who led the Labour Party between 1983 and 1992, made significant organisational changes in the Labour Party which brought it more under the sway of the Parliamentary leadership, changes which both his successors, John Smith and Tony Blair, have been able to take further. Similarly, on becoming leader of the Conservative Party in 1997, William Hague set off on a course of radical structural reform of a party organisation essentially unchanged since its inception in 1867.

The Labour Party

A diagram of the Labour Party organisation is provided in Figure 5.3.

For much of its history the Labour Party organisation was under the control of the General Secretary, who was the senior paid official responsible to the National Executive Committee, which was accountable in its turn to the annual Party Conference. In view of the dual hierarchy in the party, the Leader of the Party and

Figure 5.3 Labour Party organisation

senior Parliamentary colleagues could be at odds over matters of policy and procedure with prominent members of the National Executive Committee, who were often backbench MPs of a more radical disposition elected to the NEC by the constituency Labour Parties, as was the case during the Labour Governments in the 1970s.

However, under Neil Kinnock's leadership (1983–92) and thereafter under the leadership of both John Smith (1992–94) and Tony Blair (1994–), serious efforts were made by the Parliamentary leadership to regain effective control of the NEC and the party organisation which served it. This has meant not only much greater emphasis on attractive presentation of united Labour policy, but also much greater influence from the centre than was formerly the case in the Labour movement. It was for this reason that in 1990 a new policy-making process was established consisting of a Joint Policy Committee – including the Leader, the Shadow Cabinet (the Cabinet when in Government) and the NEC – and a National Policy Forum. It was an attempt to ensure that policies which came before Conference had emerged from an inclusive process, consultation and deliberation; in short, an attempt to find a balance between the aspirations of the party activists and the realities of Government. One aspect of this new approach saw the party's draft manifesto, *New Labour New Life for Britain* subjected in 1996 to a full ballot of individual members. This attracted a 95 per cent 'yes' vote (218,023 votes) on a 61 per cent turnout. The declared intention for the future is to create structures and provide mechanisms through which everyone in the party will have the opportunity to participate in the policy-making process.

The staff at Labour Party headquarters, including the Research Department, are responsible to the General Secretary and perform a range of support functions. The Party Chairman, who normally holds office for one year only, is usually the member of the NEC with the longest continuous membership of that body and with responsibility to the party as a whole rather than to the Leader of the Party.

The Labour Party Conference has traditionally been a powerful gathering. Its claim to a real political role was based on the fact that it is constitutionally and formally the policy-making body of the party, while the party in Parliament is theoretically little more than the Parliamentary arm of the entire Labour movement.[12] The Conference is presided over by the Chairman of the Party, who is assisted by a Conference Arrangements Committee composed of representatives of all the main sections of the Labour movement. In the past the Conference was dominated by the block votes of the trade unions. For example, the Transport and General Workers Union had a block vote of about 1.2 million and the Amalgamated Engineering Union had one of about 840,000 votes. By comparison, neither the smaller trade unions nor the constituency parties had much voting power at Conference, although they could make their influence felt with extra militancy. The Conference was composed of mandated delegations which were expected to vote in accordance with the decisions previously taken by the organisations which they represented. However, in 1993 the union block vote was abolished with union delegates thenceforth being free to vote independently and with the proportion of union votes falling to 50 per cent of the total. Labour Members of Parliament can attend Conference, but unless they are members of the NEC, they do not usually play a prominent part in the proceedings.

The NEC has traditionally been a powerful body which has claimed to act in the name of the entire Labour movement between annual Conferences. It includes representatives of the affiliated trade unions, the constituency parties, the Women's Section, the Youth Movement, other affiliated Socialist societies, together with automatic representation for the Leader, the Deputy Leader, the General Secretary and the Party Treasurer. It acts in the name of the Conference and carries on the business of the party from one year to the next. It has also had a constitutional claim to a major role in party policy-making and to participation with the Cabinet or Shadow Cabinet in the preparation of the Party Manifesto – both somewhat diluted following the creation of the Joint Policy Committee and the National Policy Forum and the use of membership plebiscites. In the past there has been the possibility of tension between it and the leadership of the Parliamentary Party. In recent years, however, and particularly under the leadership and reforms of Tony Blair, such tensions have not come to the forefront.

In the House of Commons the Parliamentary Labour Party is led by the Leader. When the party is in Opposition, the leader chairs the Parliamentary Committee (Shadow Cabinet) which is the executive committee of the party in Parliament in those circumstances. Constitutionally the position is slightly different when the party in is Government as the leader is Prime Minister and his most senior colleagues are members of the Shadow Cabinet. Since 1970 the weekly meetings of the entire PLP have been chaired by an elected Chairman who is usually a senior back-bencher. Back-benchers involve themselves with various subject groups, depending on their particular policy or constituency interests. In both cases, however, they have relatively little formative influence over the process of policy making.[13]

In Opposition, the members of the PLP vote every year for those of their colleagues who aspire to places in the Shadow Cabinet. The top 15 are elected and the Leader is then free to distribute the portfolios between them. The junior Shadow spokesmen are appointed by the Leader according to the usual criteria of political clout, personal merit and regional or ideological balance. In Government, the Party Leader is, of course, Prime Minister and therefore free to allocate the real Ministerial responsibilities as appropriate, subject to the usual political considerations of ideological and regional balance within the party. However, in particular response to pressure in the early 1980s – when Tony Benn and others on the Hard Left of the party urged that members of a Labour Cabinet should be elected by the PLP rather than appointed by the Prime Minister of the day – provision is now made for all the elected members of the Shadow Cabinet to become members of the Cabinet automatically when the party moves into Government, although not necessarily in the Ministerial posts which they had been shadowing.

From 1922 to 1980 the Leader of the Party was elected exclusively by the PLP. However, after the 1979 General Election, the Hard Left of the party was successful in its long-running campaign to take this power out of the exclusive hands of Labour MPs. Following an agreement at Bishops Stortford in 1981, this power was entrusted to an electoral college in which the three main sections of the Labour movement were represented. Following changes in 1993 the college votes are divided into thirds with individual party members accounting for one-third, Labour MPs and MEPs accounting for one-third, and trade union members (plus the members of other affiliated organisations) all voting individually accounting for the remaining one-third. Candidates for the leadership must be MPs and their nominations must be supported by at least one-eighth of the PLP.

The Conservative Party

Following the 1997 General Election defeat, the election of William Hague as Leader and subsequent organisational reforms designed to renew the party, the three separate and distinct pillars of the old party – the Parliamentary Party, the voluntary party and the professional party (Central Office) – were drawn together in a single structure. Consequently, today the Conservative Party is managed by a single governing body – the Board – under a single constitution (watched over by a Constitutional College) with a national membership and provision for direct membership involvement and participation. Indeed, the reforms themselves were put to a postal ballot of all members in 1998, receiving approval by 110,165 votes to 4425; a margin of 96.1 per cent to 3.9 per cent. See Figure 5.4 for a diagram of Conservative Party organisation.

The idea behind the creation of the Board was that of unity; to create for the first time a single, unified Party. It is for this reason that the Board is the supreme decision-making body in all matters relating to Party organisation and management. It comprises the Chairman of the Party – who chairs its meetings – a Deputy Chairman, the Treasurer, the Leader of the Party in the House of Lords and a senior member of the professional staff – all of whom are appointed by the Party Leader – as well as the Chairman of the 1922 Committee, the President and Chairman of the National Convention, three members elected from the National Convention, an elected representative of the Party in Scotland, the Welsh Co-ordinating Chairman and the Chairman of the Association of Conservative Councillors. An additional member can be appointed by the Party Leader, subject to the endorsement of the Board, and one by the Board subject to the approval of the Party Leader.

Another guiding principle of the Hague reforms was that of decentralisation. Consequently, Constituency Associations remain an important focus and the role of Constituency Chairman has been enhanced. Above the constituency is the area level with Area Councils and Area Executives, the principal link between the Board and Constituency Associations. However, there is also a Regional level providing for co-ordination of activity and policy formulation. Important in all of this has been the establishment of the National Conservative Convention to provide a focus for the views of party members and to act as a link between the leadership and the membership. The annual Party Conference continues to be the main party gathering of the year.

Another important principle said to underpin the Hague reforms was that of democracy; in short, giving power to the membership of the party. Consequently, the membership has already been asked to endorse William Hague as leader, vote on the principles of Party reform and vote on policy concerning the Single European Currency. In addition they have been given greater involvement in the selection of candidates and the vote in future leadership elections. A part of this approach has also been to provide for greater involvement by the membership in the development of policy. As a result the Conservative Policy Forum (CPF) has been established to provide for the involvement of party members – via Regional Policy congresses and regular surveys – in discussing and formulating policy proposals. The CPF itself has been given considerable input into the annual Party Conference agenda.

Figure 5.4 Conservative Party organisation

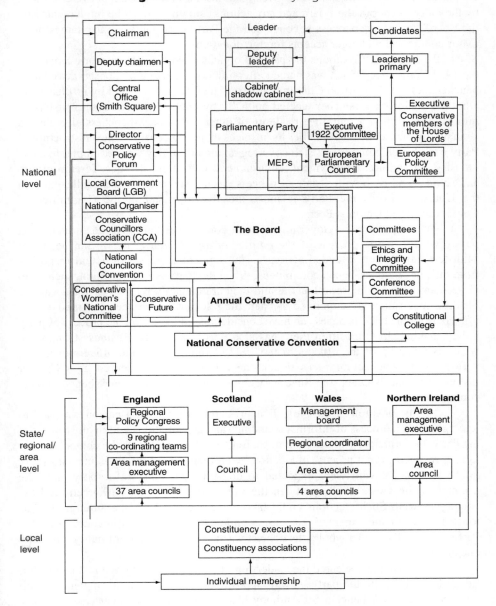

Also important in the Hague reforms were the principles of integrity and openness. The party knew that it had been damaged by the accusations of sleaze in the run-up to and during the 1997 General Election. Consequently, an Ethics and Integrity

Committee has been established to investigate instances of misconduct referred to it by the Party Leader or the Board and any action it stipulates must be implemented by the Board. As far as openness is concerned the Party now publishes the names of its major donors and no longer accepts foreign donations.

In the House of Commons the party is organised within a framework capped by the 1922 Committee, which was named after a famous meeting of Conservative back-benchers held at the Carlton Club in that year. The Committee is led by its chairman, who is a senior back-bencher elected annually by back-bench colleagues. It has an influential Executive Committee made up of other senior back-benchers also elected annually by their colleagues. Under its auspices there is a considerable substructure of Party back-bench committees each covering an area of policy – for example, finance, industry, agriculture, employment, environment, education, defence, foreign affairs and so on – and each with a slate of officers elected annually by their colleagues. In the House of Lords the Party is more loosely organised in the Committee of Conservative and Unionist Peers.

When the party is in Government, such committees can have an influence on policy via the subtle process of *the politics of anticipated reaction*, that is, when Ministers adjust their intended actions in the light of expected or actual responses from the relevant back-bench committees. When the Party is in Opposition, such com-mittees are probably more influential and they are certainly busier, since the various Shadow spokesmen are appointed to chair the relevant committees and their fellow officers from the back-benches can have considerable influence on the process of party policy making. In Opposition there has also been a so-called Business Committee which is made up of the officers of the 1922 Committee and the officers of all the various back-bench committees under one rubric. This has served as a broader institutional link between the Shadow Cabinet and the various back-bench subject committees.

As for the position of the Party Leader, before 1965 such a person was said to 'emerge' from a process of informal soundings and consultations within all sections of the Party, but principally in the Commons. Between 1965 and 1998 the choice of Party Leader resulted from a process of election by all members of the Parliamentary Party in the Commons, who were expected to consult each other informally and take account of the views of the party in the Lords, the European Parliament and the country as well. Such elections could take place every year in the autumn. Yet, as long as the Leader maintained the confidence of senior colleagues and the Parliamentary Party as a whole, the contest was merely an annual formality with only one nomination.

Margaret Thatcher secured the leadership in 1975 by challenging the then Leader, Edward Heath, while the party was in Opposition. She remained unchallenged until 1989 when the back-bencher Sir Anthony Meyer challenged her unsuccessfully. The following year, 1990, Michael Heseltine challenged her and, although obtaining only 152 votes to her 204 on the first ballot, secured enough support under the rules to ensure a second ballot, thus undermining her position to such an extent that she with-drew from the contest. On the second ballot – which allowed new candidates to enter the contest – John Major came top of the poll with 185 votes and secured the leader-ship because the other candidates did not press their rights to initiate a third ballot, even though he had not achieved a large enough margin of victory to rule it out. Following considerable media speculation that John Major was to be challenged for the leadership of the party in 1992, 1993 and 1994, and as a direct result of mounting speculation in 1995, John Major himself resigned as Party Leader in June 1995, challenging critics to 'put up or shut up'. This brought forth a challenge from John Redwood, but John Major secured re-election on the first ballot.

Following the election of William Hague as Party Leader in 1997, both the rules for initiating and the mechanism for conducting a leadership election were changed. First, the Party Leader can only be removed following a vote of no-confidence by a majority of Conservative MPs. Secondly, the Party Leader is to be elected by the entire party membership on the basis of one-member-one-vote following a primary election among Conservative MPs to select a short-list of candidates to place before the entire party membership.

Main party contrasts

The traditional organisation of each of the main parties reflected the contrast between the traditionally hierarchic principles of the Conservative Party and the traditionally democratic aspirations of the Labour Party. In the former case, this meant that party decisions were normally taken expeditiously and implemented without undue debate or difficulty. In the latter case, it meant that the origins of party decisions were often blurred and the implementation occasionally challenged by some of those involved. In short, the Conservative Party tended to be more amenable to firm leadership from the top, whereas the Labour Party often seemed temperamentally and organisationally averse to it. Nonetheless it has been observed that in the post-Thatcher Conservative Party and the Blair-led Labour Party these traditional views are no longer accurate; indeed, some might say that the defining characteristics of the two parties have been reversed.

The problem for Labour was that it had been difficult adequately to control a party which served a movement which had aspired to be both ideological and democratic, although the ideology of democratic Socialism held that there was no conflict between these two characteristics. The problems of the Conservatives have been more subtle, but just as real on occasions. In spite of their autocratic style and tradition, the management of the party has been by no means trouble-free. For example, exposure to a hostile Party Conference can be an unpleasant and tricky ordeal for even the most senior and experienced politicians, especially when the representatives have bayed for blood on the more atavistic issues, such as decolonisation in the 1950s, Rhodesia in the 1960s, law and order in the 1980s, and Europe in the 1990s.

In the Labour Party power has traditionally been diffuse, certainly from the adoption of the party constitution in 1918, since it was shared between the PLP on the one hand and the affiliated trade unions and constituency parties on the other. This uneasy alliance has been balanced sometimes in favour of the extra-Parliamentary elements and sometimes in favour of the PLP. In the 1970s and early 1980s great efforts were made by the constituency parties to seize a larger share of power, heavily encouraged by Tony Benn who sought to make them his own power-base within the Labour movement, and to strengthen the NEC against the PLP. Power has tended to reside with the

Parliamentary leadership more when the party has been in Government and less when it has been in Opposition. A great deal has depended on the inclinations and ambitions of the leading figures in the movement at different times. Yet, as we have seen in the cases of Neil Kinnock and Tony Blair, if a Labour Leader is determined to assert authority, this can certainly be done.

In the Conservative Party effective power has traditionally been wielded mainly by the Leader, and to a lesser extent by the other senior Parliamentary figures, in Government or Opposition. The senior figures in the hierarchy of the National Union were soothed with knighthoods rather than seriously consulted on matters of policy and on the whole the voluntary side of the party knew its place in the scheme of things. Yet even a powerful Conservative Leader could not afford to ignore party opinion, since the activists could put pressure on back-benchers who then felt obliged to lobby Ministers when in Government or Shadow spokesmen when in Opposition. It has also been noticeable over the years that Conservative Leaders seem to have been more vulnerable than their Labour counterparts to political 'assassination' when they fail to win General Elections or are directly involved in other events politically calamitous for their party. Quite how this balance will play itself out in the party of William Hague – in the era of 'unity, decentralisation, democracy, involvement, integrity and openness' – only the passage of time will show.

The Liberal Democrats

The organisation of the Liberal Democrats is federal in nature, in that there are autonomous parties in England, Scotland and Wales, each with its own national offices, staff and conferences. The party in England is further sub-divided into 12 regional parties. The Federal Conference, which meets twice a year, is composed of representatives from the constituencies, the Parliamentary Party, associated organisations – such as those representing youth – and the officers of the national organisation. The party's Federal Executive, the Federal Policy Committee and the Federal Conference Committee all report to it. See Figure 5.5 for a diagram of Liberal Democrat Party organisation.

Responsibility for developing and presenting party policy, including the preparation of the General Election Manifesto, is placed on the Federal Policy Committee. This is composed of the Party Leader, the Party President, five representatives of the party in both Houses of Parliament, three representatives from local authority Councillors, two representatives each from the Scottish and Welsh parties, and thirteen members elected by the Federal Conference. Responsibility for directing, co-ordinating and implementing the work of the Federal Party falls to the Federal Executive, a body formed on a similar basis to the Federal Policy Committee. Its tasks include setting up a Finance and Administration Committee to manage the finances and direct the administration of the Federal Party, including its headquarters at 4 Cowley Street, London SW1, and the appointment of a General Secretary. Party headquarters is divided into seven Departments – membership and direct mail, finance, campaigns and elections, policy, Conference, party newspaper, and the General Secretary's Department.

Elections for the position of Leader of the Party are held every two years, unless postponed by a vote of two-thirds of the Federal Executive. Apart from this, an elec-

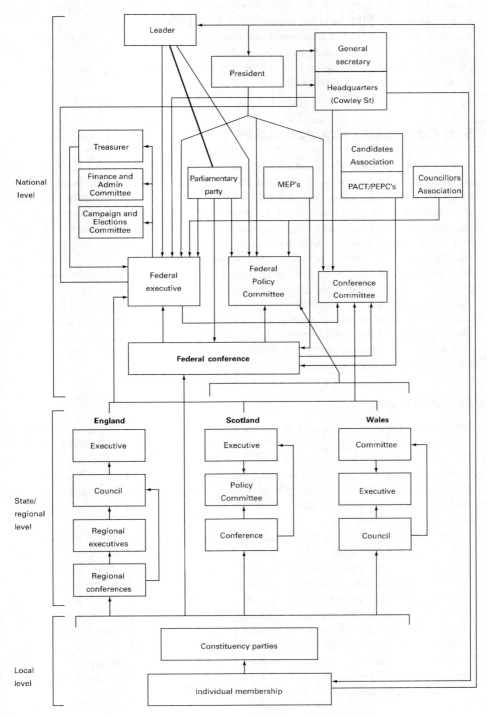

Figure 5.5 Liberal Democrat Party organisation

tion can be held either at the Leader's own request or following the loss of the Leader's Parliamentary seat, or a vote of no confidence in the Leader by a majority of Liberal Democrat MPs, or at the request of 75 local parties. Candidates for the leadership have to be an MP, to be proposed and seconded by MPs and to be supported by at least 200 party members in at least 20 local parties or associated organisations. The election of the Leader is carried out on the basis of one member one vote via a postal ballot of the entire party membership.

5.5 Constituency activities

It is when we consider the constituency activities of the parties that we notice more similarities than contrasts, in spite of the wide variety of people who are involved. For example, both of the main parties and the Liberal Democrats have sought to ensure and maintain political activity in all the constituencies, except in Northern Ireland.[14] Nevertheless, all three parties have tended to focus their resources and concentrate their efforts rather more directly than this blanket approach might suggest. In particular, the Liberal Democrats have concentrated their efforts and resources in relatively few constituencies where they already have local support and where their electoral prospects appear to be quite good – an approach which reaped rich rewards in the 1997 General Election. Constituency organisations vary in size from a mere handful of members in areas where parties are weak to as many as several thousand in the strongest areas of the large parties.[15] In all cases they exist to serve the campaigning and fundraising purposes of the parties and to enable them to contest local, Parliamentary and European elections.

Financial support

Unlike local party organisations in the United States, constituency parties in Britain try to remain solvent and operational throughout the time between General Elections. They are assisted in doing this by the need to contest local and European elections at regular intervals and occasionally Parliamentary by-elections as well. Yet they rely for their continued existence on individual and corporate subscriptions and donations made possible by the voluntary efforts and fund-raising activities of the party workers.

In the *Labour Party*, although trade union sponsorship of MPs was discontinued in 1995 some constituency organisations – about 100 in 1997 – receive financial support from local trade union branches through what are known as 'Constituency Plan Agreements'. The bulk of the money is raised from membership subscriptions, donations and various forms of fundraising activity. In the *Conservative Party*, a considerable portion of the income at constituency level comes from local business and commercial interests, although the bulk of the money is raised from individual subscriptions and voluntary fund-raising activities of all kinds. The *Liberal Democrats* have sought to maintain similar activities at constituency level in order to perform similar political functions, but they often have had to struggle to maintain viable levels of income and support.

Local membership

Political parties can grow and prosper only if their grassroots are vigorous and healthy. Traditionally active Local Associations were the necessary foundations on which a national party existed and flourished, with a party seeking to have one in each Parliamentary constituency. Today, although still important, their importance has been reduced due to the fact that the parties all operate national centralised membership schemes.

The active members of the various constituency parties come from many different walks of life. In all parties they tend to hold political views which are more zealous and uncompromising than those of the electorate in general. Indeed, if this were not the case, it is unlikely that many of them would be sufficiently motivated to join in the first place or to remain as paid-up members of their political party.

It is difficult to generalise about the membership of constituency parties, since a wide variety of people become involved in politics at the local level at one time or another. With regard to Conservative Party membership, the 'typical' Conservative member is retired, middle class, Protestant and white, with 49 per cent being female and 51 per cent being male. The average age of members had been found to be 62, while 43 per cent are aged 66 or over. Only 5 per cent of its membership is below the age of 35 and only 1 per cent is aged 25 or less. Indeed, failure to appeal to a younger generation is a serious problem for today's leadership. It is a failure underlined by the fact that there are currently fewer than 3000 Young Conservatives compared with 160,000 in 1949. Although membership numbers have declined generally, this had fallen at a greater comparative rate over the same period of time, namely by 98.1 per cent as compared with 85.7 per cent.

Two-thirds of Conservatives see themselves as belonging to a particular class, with 75 per cent of these describing themselves as middle class. In total 8 per cent fall into the category of traditional working-class manual workers. Only 29 per cent of members are still in work, the remainder being classified as retired. Of those in work more than half are part of the salariat, with teachers forming the largest single group, then financial service workers, and with marketing and public relations executives as well as central and local government administrative workers forming sizeable groups. Typists, clerks and so on – what can be termed routine white collar workers – account for 18 per cent of the membership and proprietors of small businesses a further 13 per cent. In all, 70 per cent of members own stocks and shares. Aside from this, the available material shows that 99 per cent of the membership is white and 1 per cent Asian. Over 75 per cent are Protestant, with 10 per cent being Catholic. Only 12 per cent have a university degree and 31 per cent have no educational qualifications at all. Surveys of Conservative members show that 40 per cent are not active members and that, amongst the 60 per cent who are active, 20 per cent are 'very active' and 80 per cent are 'active to some degree'.[16]

With regard to membership of the Labour Party, recent research has sought to make a distinction between 'old Labour' – those who joined the party before 1994 – and 'new Labour' – those who joined the party after 1994. From the data provided we can see that new Labour members are younger, although they still rank overall as middle-aged. Amongst new Labour 25 per cent are aged 35 or below, compared with 12 per cent for old Labour; the average age of new Labour members is 48 compared to

54 amongst old Labour. As far as gender is concerned, 63 per cent of new Labour members are male and 37 per cent are female, compared with 60 per cent and 40 per cent respectively amongst old Labour members. The party – old and new – tends to be middle class with 60 per cent of new Labour members and 67 per cent of old Labour members coming from among the white-collar professional salariat, with a high proportion of individuals working in the public sector among both new and old members. Only 2 per cent of both new and old Labour members are classified as small business-people. A total of 38 per cent of old Labour members belong to a trade union, compared with only 29 per cent of new Labour members. As far as education is concerned, 30 per cent of new Labour and 37 per cent of old Labour are graduates. New Labour members are more strongly in favour of the free market than old Labour (32 per cent as opposed to 23 per cent), are more inclined to believe in the incentive effects of low rates of income tax (30 per cent as opposed to 21 per cent), are more inclined to be 'tough' on law and order issues (between 58 and 61 per cent compared with figures between 46 and 51 per cent) and are rather more sanguine on the matter of private education (only 21 per cent definitely wanting to abolish it compared with 31 per cent of old Labour members) In short, new Labour members are more conservative than old Labour members. They are also less likely to be active within the party – 43 per cent less active than old Labour members – and less partisan – with only 38 per cent of new Labour members as opposed to 58 per cent of old Labour members describing themselves as 'very strong' Labour and with 9 per cent as opposed to 4 per cent describing themselves as 'not very strong' Labour.[17]

Detailed information on the membership of the Liberal Democrat Party is not so readily available. What is known, however, is that the male/female ratio amongst the membership is 51:49 and that 2 per cent of the membership is under 25 years of age, 15 per cent are aged 25–40, 33 per cent are aged 41–55, 31 per cent are aged 56–70 and 19 per cent are over the age of 70. It can also be said that members tend to be drawn from a wider cross-section of the population and include many people who are not so closely identified with obvious class interests as well as some who have not previously been active in party politics at all. By defining 'activists' as those who hold office within the party, or who are elected as local authority Councillors, some 10 per cent of the party's membership is active. However, such a narrow definition clearly very seriously underestimates those who have some level of activity in the party. Survey evidence has shown that over 70 per cent of members define themselves as being active in some way.

In the final analysis however, no generalisations about party membership are really satisfactory, not least of all because the figures for membership are very fluid. For example, in 1997 some 55,438 members of the Labour Party, 13.6 per cent of the total, failed to renew their membership, although this was a figure more than compensated for by new members joining. All that can be said with any certainty is that the trends over the years have been characterised by a steady erosion of active support for each of the two main parties and by significantly changing social composition in each case. As far as membership is concerned, the numbers who join have fallen sharply from the high point of the 1950s (see p. 106). It is also noticeable that over the period since the early 1970s the Conservative Party has become less dominated at constituency level by traditional middle-class people, while the Labour Party in the constituencies has become less the party of the working class and the trade unions than it was before. Such social changes at constituency level have had an important effect on the character of each of the parties in Parliament. The Conservative Party has moved noticeably 'down market' in its composition and attitudes, while the Labour Party has become less closely associated with the interests and outlook of the traditional working class, extending its appeal to the growing middle class.

Political power

In so far as members of constituency parties exercise effective political power, they do so mainly through their right to select and, occasionally, deselect Parliamentary (and local government) candidates. In view of the fact that roughly two-thirds of all the seats in the Commons have been considered 'safe' for one or other of the two main parties, the power to select and deselect the candidate has often amounted to the ability to determine the choice of the MP in many parts of the country. For example, prior to the 1997 General Election the Bolton North East Labour Party deselected David Young, while, in the Conservative Party, three sitting MPs were deselected, namely: David Ashby in Leicestershire North West, Sir Nicholas Scott in Kensington and Chelsea, and Sir George Gardiner in Reigate. The power to select and deselect has been the real foundation of political power at constituency level and it has had to be taken very seriously by MPs and candidates alike. In addition party members are involved in choosing the Party Leader. Labour members have a share in the electoral college which chooses the Party Leader, while in the Liberal Democrats and now in the Conservative Party the leader is essentially elected on the basis of one member one vote. In all the political parties it is now accepted that ordinary party members should have some real influence on the process of policy making.

In the *Conservative Party* the key constituency bodies are the Executive Councils of perhaps 30 to 80 members, composed partly of Association Officers, but mostly of representatives of the various wards or branches in the constituency. In the Labour Party the key constituency bodies are the General Management Committees, which are composed in the same sort of way, but which are often somewhat smaller.

Candidate selection

In each of the main parties the candidates for Parliament chosen by the 'selectorates' have tended to be rather different both from the groups which select them and from the electorate as a whole. There has been a tendency over the years for social convergence between the Parliamentary candidates of the two main parties. This has often meant the selection of middle-aged, middle-class white men with families in preference to women, blue-collar workers or people from the ethnic minorities.

However, in recent times it has become increasingly necessary to qualify this overall description. In the *Conservative Party* there is nowadays a wider variety of candidates for Parliament. Although the privileged origins of some Conservative aspirants remain very noticeable, there has also been a growing number of self-made men and a few women who have managed to fight their way into Parliament. In the *Labour Party* the changes have been even more dramatic in recent years. Nowadays many more Labour candidates have been selected from the ranks of the 'talking classes' in white-collar and public-sector occupations to the exclusion of many of the more traditional types from the old-fashioned working class. In the late 1970s and early 1980s this coincided with a marked shift towards more radical attitudes in constituency Labour parties which put a greater emphasis on the selection of candidates who were eager (or at least prepared) to carry out the wishes of the party activists. Indeed, a preference for radical minority activists (whether feminists, blacks or gays) became increasingly evident in the London Labour Party and in some other areas where such people got themselves entrenched in local parties. However, from the middle 1980s the Labour leadership began to take a greater interest in candidate selection, especially at by-elections which attracted more than the usual amount of national media attention, and in the run-up to the 1997 General Election, at the behest of Walworth Road, a growing number of Labour constituency parties practised something akin to positive discrimination in favour of women candidates. At the time of the 1997 General Election 24.8 per cent of all Labour candidates were women.

The position has been rather different as far as the *Liberal Democrats* are concerned. Traditionally the Liberal Party attracted men and women of broadly liberal outlook who wished to see the liberal point of view translated into public policy. However, it did not lay great insistence on strict adherence to party orthodoxy. This approach has continued in the Liberal Democrats, although it has been tempered by a degree of hard-nosed political realism and a willingness to follow the line laid down by the leadership, both of which characteristics were brought to the party from the former SDP.

While the nature and strength of a candidate's commitment to party ideology seems to have become more important in determining an individual's progress in all parties, it is no longer usually the case that the wealth or family connections of an aspiring candidate have much bearing on the chances of success at constituency level (although it must be said that there have been a few husband-and-wife or other family combinations in the House of Commons). Since the late 1940s all parties have set low limits on the personal donations which candidates or MPs may make to their constituency parties, so it is no longer possible to purchase a nomination, as it used to be, at any rate in the Conservative Party before the Second World War. Yet some candidates still have a better chance of success than others, especially at by-elections, when the parties wish to take no unnecessary chances, and in the competition for the safest seats.

In the *Labour Party* candidates seeking selection have to be nominated by at least one branch of the constituency party. At the national level there is a list of approved Parliamentary candidates which is kept at party headquarters in London following endorsement of the names by the NEC. Nonetheless some candidates who emerge as 'local favourites' of their constituency parties do not appear on the national list, but nevertheless are usually endorsed by the NEC if they are selected. In exceptional cases the modern Labour Party has actually limited the range of local choice or even imposed a candidate on the local party in order to avoid the selection of a candidate believed to be detrimental to the party's chances at a by-election.[18] Between 1993 and 1996 (when an Industrial Tribunal ruled the process to be illegal) positive discrimination in favour of women was exercised in candidate selection, a move designed to ensure that more women would be elected to Parliament.

In the *Conservative Party* there is also a list of approved Parliamentary candidates which is kept centrally at party headquarters in London. In order to get on this list aspirants have to go through a complicated process of written submissions and personal interviews, as well as a subsequent assessment process. In some cases these stages can prove more difficult than the later appearance before Constituency Selection Committees. Traditionally each Constituency Association has had the unfettered right to select anyone it liked, even if the person concerned was not on the centrally approved list of Parliamentary candidates at the time, or indeed was deemed unacceptable to the national Party leadership. This fact came sharply into the spotlight at the time of the 1997 General Election when the Beckenham Association reselected Piers Merchant – despite allegations in the press that he had had an affair with a 17 year old night-club hostess – and the Tatton Association reselected Neil Hamilton – despite his being at the centre of the 'cash-for-questions' row – notwithstanding the fact that the national Party made it known to the local Associations concerned that they would prefer these two candidates *not* to be reselected, because of the adverse national impact such selections would have. Consequently, some of the Hague reforms – such as the creation of the Ethics and Integrity Committee with power to suspend and even expel miscreants – have been intended to strengthen the hand of the centre in this respect.

In the *Liberal Democrats* responsibility for the shortlisting of candidates rests with the executive committee of the local party or a shortlisting sub-committee appointed by it. All candidates must be on the party's list of approved candidates, a process which involves a series of oral and written interviews, tests and submissions. Unless a sitting MP or previous candidate is reselected, the process involves drawing up a shortlist incorporating a specified number of candidates which, subject to there being a sufficient number of applicants, must include at least one member of each sex. Each member of the party in the constituency has a vote in the process and the choice of candidate is determined by proportional representation.

5.6 Conclusion

Political parties are central to the British political system. Indeed, there exists in Britain a system of government by and through political parties. Having said this, however, there are a number of factors present which have already caused difficulties for the political parties and which could in the future undermine their position of dominance. The factors include:

- declining membership of political parties;
- declining popular attachment to political parties;
- the myriad of other opportunities for activity and public participation in which increasingly, non-political interests dominate;
- the growing detachment of pressure groups from their previously close association with the political parties;

- the increasing de-alignment of newspapers with a particular political party;
- the growing importance of the media as channels for all political messages.

A further challenge to political parties is posed by the increasing use of referenda within the political process. A final point to note would be the fact that political parties themselves are today far less self-contained and self-reliant than ever before, a consequence of the use of think-tanks for the development of policies and the full panoply of the communications and public relations industries – pollsters, media advisers, so-called 'spin doctors' and so on – for campaigning and contesting elections.

Nonetheless, in Britain it is political parties which compete for power and the maintenance of party discipline is a very important factor in determining a party's chances at General Elections. Quite simply, a party divided against itself cannot win; a party divided will always be defeated – as Labour found to its cost in the 1980s and the Conservatives learned in 1997.

In Government, the tasks of the victorious party are three-fold:

- to ensure that the policies on which it was elected are translated into administrative decisions or legislation as appropriate;
- to ensure that the Government's measures are supported and carried whenever there are key votes in Parliament;
- to propound and defend the merits of Government policy both through the media and in direct contacts with members of the public.

In Opposition, the task of the defeated parties is simpler in that, apart from licking their wounds and sorting out their internal difficulties, their main duties are to criticise and oppose the Government of the day, and to elaborate alternative policies and political stances which can be put before the electorate in the run-up to the following General Election. In this context it is important to note that the second largest party in the House of Commons becomes the *official Opposition* and thus shares with the Governing party the responsibilities of conducting Parliamentary proceedings in an effective and business-like manner, which normally allows the Government of the day to get its way in the end while allowing the Opposition full opportunities to play its constitutional roles of criticism, scrutiny and occasionally delay.

While the two main parties differ quite considerably in their history, ideology and constituency membership, they are more similar in many other respects than some accounts have suggested. When in Opposition, each Party has tended to use distinctive political language and to develop a distinctive political style in order to differentiate itself from the party in Government and often from its own record or behaviour in previous times. When in Government, each party has traditionally behaved in a broadly responsible and moderate way and each has pursued policies which belonged within the framework of the postwar consensus.

From the early 1970s a number of significant developments in each of the main parties led them both to depart quite markedly from their previous adherence to the postwar consensus. The Labour Party began to change significantly when in Opposition from 1970 to 1974, as Tony Benn and others on the Left of the Party began to denigrate the 1964–70 Labour Government for its failure to be sufficiently

Socialist. The Conservative Party began to change when in Opposition from 1974 to 1979 as Sir Keith (later Lord) Joseph and Margaret Thatcher (later Baroness Thatcher) began to redefine the purposes and priorities of Conservatism in contradistinction to the policies pursued during the second half of the 1970–74 Conservative Government. As a consequence of these movements of opinion, the ideological gap between the two parties became wider during most of the 1970s and 1980s.

The position began to change yet again in the late 1980s. One result of winning three General Elections in a row was to make the Conservative Party increasingly radical and self-confident in its Thatcherite beliefs. On the other hand, another consequence of this chain of Conservative victories was to force the Labour Party under successive Leaders to reconsider and revise many of its previously Socialist policies in a determined and conscious attempt to make its appeal more credible to the mass electorate. The situation changed once again with the downfall of Margaret Thatcher in November 1990 and the election of John Major to the leadership of the Conservative Party in her place. One consequence of the change was to make the Conservative Party itself, as well as the public at large, much less clear about what it stood for or where it was going. Whereas there was a body of doctrine which could be described as 'Thatcherism', and although some of this undoubtedly outlasted Margaret Thatcher's period as Leader – indeed, in many respects politicians in all of the mainstream parties had come to accept the essential tenets of the Thatcherite agenda to the extent that a new Thatcherite consensus had emerged – pundits and practitioners alike searched in vain for a coherent set of political principles and beliefs which could legitimately be described as 'Majorism'. When set alongside the fact that the process of revisionism within the Labour Party started by Neil Kinnock and continued under John Smith was carried forward by Tony Blair, some observers began to doubt whether there was much that was authentically either Left or Right of centre on offer to the public from either of the two main parties at the General Election of 1997. Indeed, Labour's victory in that election was, in a bizarre, even perverse, way evidence of the success of Conservatives under Margaret Thatcher in the 1980s. In no small measure her assault on the postwar consensus and her three electoral victories in a row laid the basis for a new bi-partisan consensus and made her the midwife to New Labour.

As for the future, much will depend on exactly how firmly embedded in the national consciousness this new post-Thatcherite consensus really is. Much will depend on the extent to which Tony Blair is able to deliver the promises of New Labour. Similarly, much will depend on whether William Hague can improve the electoral fortunes of his party from the shattering defeat of 1997. The extent to which the successor to Paddy Ashdown as Leader of the Liberal Democrats is able to make an impact will also be a factor. Much will also depend on events and influences outside the control of politicians, such as the workings of global markets and the practices of global media. Indeed, a durable or definitive conclusion is not possible, since in party politics, as in life, it is the journey and not the arrival which matters.

Suggested questions

1 What are the principal functions of political parties in the British political system?
2 'British politics is party politics.' What factors lie behind such a view?
3 Where does real power lie in the Conservative and Labour parties?

Notes

1. E. Burke, 'Thoughts on the Cause of the Present Discontents' (1770), Works vol. I, see G.H. Sabine, *A History of Political Theory*, 3rd edn (London: Harrap, 1968), p. 611.
2. S. Beer, *Modern British Politics*, p. 135.
3. S. Beer, *Modern British Politics* (London: Faber, 1969), p. 247.
4. *The Times*, 3 May 1997.
5. Jackson Carlaw, vice chairman, Scottish Conservative Party, *Guardian*, 3 May 1997.
6. William Hague, Address to Conservative Party Conference, 7 October 1997, *The Times*, 8 October 1997.
7. William Hague, Address to Conservative Party Conference, 10 October 1997, *The Times*, 11 October 1997.
8. See R.T. McKenzie, *British Political Parties*, 2nd edn (London: Heinemann, 1963), p. 645.
9. Evidence from Lord Parkinson, Conservative Party Chairman, to the Neill inquiry into political funding, 22 April 1998, *Independent*, 23 April 1998.
10. In the ballot of Conservative members to endorse William Hague as leader and to solicit support for his reform proposals, although a total of 399,203 ballot papers were distributed only 179,013 were returned.
11. See the 'Report of the Committee on Financial Aid to Political Parties', Cmnd 6601 (London: HMSO, 1976).
12. For further discussion of this subject see L. Minkin, *The Labour Party Conference* (Manchester University Press, 1980).
13. This is because in the Labour Party the NEC shares the policy-making role with the Parliamentary leadership.
14. From the late 1980s there was pressure from grass-roots Conservatives in Northern Ireland to recreate Conservative Associations in the Province which could again be affiliated to the National Union. This idea was approved in principle at the 1989 Conservative Party Conference. As a result Conservative Party candidates contested eleven of the seventeen Parliamentary constituencies in Northern Ireland at the 1992 General Election (securing 5.7 per cent of the votes cast) and nine of the eighteen at the 1997 General Election (receiving 1.5 per cent of the votes cast).
15. In 1998 the top Labour constituency was Ealing Southall with 3980 members, the top Conservative constituency was Kensington & Chelsea with 2629 members (although Beaconsfield was said to have 'close to 3000, members), and the top Liberal Democrat constituency was North Devon with 823 members.
16. See Seyd, P., Whiteley, P. and Parry, J., *Labour and Conservative Party Membership: Social Characteristics, Political Attitudes and Activities* (Aldershot: Dartmouth, 1996).
17. *Ibid.*
18. One of the best examples was when Robert Kilroy-Silk resigned as Member of Parliament for Knowsley North in 1986, having made allegations about Militant infiltration into his constituency party. He was succeeded by George Howarth who was imposed on the local party by the national hierarchy of the party at Walworth Road in London.

Further reading

Blake, R., *The Conservative Party from Peel to Major* (London: Heinemann, 1997).
Cook, C., *A Short History of the Liberal Party 1900–1997* (London: Macmillan, 1998).
Davies, A.J., *To Build a New Jerusalem* (London: Michael Joseph, 1992).
Driver, S., *New Labour: Politics after Thatcherism* (London: Pluto, 1998).
Ewing, K., *The Funding of Political Parties in Britain* (Cambridge: University Press, 1987).

'The funding of political parties in the United Kingdom', fifth report of the Committee on Standards in Public Life CM 4057-1 (London: Stationery Office, 1998).

Gamble, A., *The Free Economy and the Strong State* (London: Macmillan Education, 1988).

Ingle, S. *The British Party System*, 2nd edn (Oxford: Basil Blackwell, 1990).

Mandelson, P. and Liddle, R., *The Blair Revolution* (London: Faber & Faber, 1996).

Norton, P. (ed.), *The Conservative Party* (London: Prentice Hall / Harvester Wheatsheaf, 1996).

Pelling, H., *A Short History of the Labour Party*, 10th edn (London: Macmillan, 1993).

Pinto-Duschinsly, M., *British Political Finance* (Washington DC: American Enterprose Institute, 1982).

Riddell, P., *The Thatcher Era and Its Legacy* (Oxford: Basil Blackwell, 1991).

Seldon, A. (ed.), *UK Political Parties since 1945* (Hemel Hempstead: Philip Allan, 1990).

Seldon, A. and Ball, S. (ed.), *Conservative Century: The Conservative Party Since 1900* (London: University Press, 1994).

Seyd, P., Whiteley, P. and Parry, J., *Labour and Conservative Party Membership: Social Characteristics, Political Attitudes and Activities* (Aldershot: Dartmouth, 1996).

Seyd, P., Whiteley, P. and Richardson, J.J., *True Blues: The Politics of Conservative Party Membership* (Oxford: Clarendon Press, 1994).

Shaw, E., *The Labour Party Since 1945* (Oxford: Basin Blackwell, 1996).

Shaw, E., *The Labour Party Since 1979: Crisis and Transformation* (London: Routledge, 1994).

Stevenson, J., *Third Party Politics Since 1945: Liberals, Alliance and Liberal Democrats* (Oxford: Basil Blackwell, 1993).

Wright, T. and Carter, M., *The People's Party* (London: Thames and Hudson, 1997).

Young, H., *One of Us*, revised edition (London: Pan Books, 1990).

Websites

Conservative Party   http://www.conservative-party.org.uk/

Labour Party   http://www.labour.org.uk/

Liberal Democrats   http://www.libdems.org.uk/

Plaid Cymru   http://www.plaid-cymru.wales.com/

Scottish National Party   http://www.snp.org.uk/

Sinn Féin   http://www.irlnet.com/sinnfein/index.html

Social Democratic & Labour Party   http://www.sdlp.ie/sdlp/

Ulster Democratic Unionist Party   http://www.dup.org/

Ulster Unionists Party   http://www.uup.org/

6 Pressure groups

In the British context pressure groups have been defined variously as:

- 'organised groups possessing both formal structure and real common interests in so far as they influence the decisions of public bodies' (W.J.M. Mackenzie);[1]
- 'any organised group which attempts to influence Government' (Moodie and Studdert-Kennedy);[2]
- 'organisations ... trying to influence the policy of public bodies in their own chosen direction, though never themselves prepared to undertake the direct Government of the country' (Samuel Finer);[3]
- 'an association of individuals joined together by a common interest, belief, activity or purpose that seeks to achieve its objectives, further its interests and enhance its status in relation to other groups, by gaining the approval and co-operation of authority in the form of favourable policies, legislation and conditions' (Peter Shipley).[4]

Thus a pressure group is any group in society which, through political action, seeks to achieve changes which it regards as desirable or to prevent changes which it regards as undesirable.

The expression 'pressure groups' is a comprehensive term which subsumes both sectional interest groups and more widely based attitudinal cause groups. The former are usually well-established groups advocating or defending a vested interest. The latter can be ephemeral organisations which may decline or disappear when their goals have been achieved, although in modern times they have played an increasingly influential and continuous role in the political process. However, the term presupposes that all pressure groups are *promotional* in the sense that they seek to promote their various objectives in the most effective possible ways. It also implies that they are *irresponsible* in the strict sense that they are not democratically accountable to the general public. It is the political parties which have to accept that form of responsibility and which are vulnerable to the verdict of the electorate at every General Election, and at other elections to a lesser extent as well.

In attempting to achieve their objectives, pressure groups seek access, either directly or indirectly, to the political and governmental systems in order to influence the whole policy-making process. In essence this means seeking to influence the formation, process and administration of policy by means of contacts with Ministers, civil servants, MPs, peers, devolved Parliaments and Assemblies, local authorities, political parties, other groups, the media, the general public and, increasingly, with individuals, institutions and other groups elsewhere in the European Union.

Pressure groups reach into every area of political, economic and social life. Their activity, indeed their active co-operation, is often an essential prerequisite for the smooth working of national Government. According to *group theory*, individual representation is not realistic in modern society, but collective representation can be for people as home owners, car drivers, employers, consumers, teachers, doctors and so on. Consequently, the state does respond to pressure groups through which the interests and opinions of different people can be both expressed and given direction. The 'father' of group theory was Arthur F. Bentley, who wrote in 1908 that it was only through the analysis of group activities that one could achieve a true knowledge of government.[5] For Bentley politics was about groups and their effects on each other and on Government – 'the tool of the strongest groups'. His argument, however, took insufficient account of the impact of political parties and of elections on policy making, since pressure groups have to function within a framework which is shaped and influenced by both.

Nonetheless, pressure groups are still an important and influential part of the British political system. Traditionally, the British have been an organised people and, in many respects, the nation's history can be seen to have been one of competing sectional interests – competition, for example, between craft and merchant guilds, professional groupings, landowners, factory owners, railway developers and trade unions – all continuously striving to influence, or even dominate, the course of national politics. Equally, British history has seen the continuous pursuit of ideals and causes, as witness, for example, the cause group campaigns to abolish slavery, end child labour, extend the franchise, or improve prison conditions.

6.1 Classification of groups

When looking at pressure groups, it is necessary to make a preliminary distinction between *Interest Groups* (sometimes known as sectional groups) and *Attitude Groups* (sometimes known as cause groups). The former are often defensive in their functions and closely involved with the institutions of central Government. The latter often begin as institutional outsiders, but some of them have attained a degree of prominence which virtually requires their views to be taken into account. In practice, of course, there is considerable overlap between the two types of group and some find a place in both categories.

Interest groups

Interest groups are all those whose basis of association is a common interest, usually economic or vocational. Put simply, they exist to promote the interests of their members. The best example of an interest group would be a trade union, an employers' association or a professional association. As far as trade unions are concerned, there are a large number of these bodies in Britain, such as:

- UNISON (an amalgamation of NALGO, NUPE and COHSE, all public service unions) – membership 1,300,451.
- the TGWU (Transport and General Workers Union) – membership 881,357.
- the AEEU (Amalgamated Engineering & Electrical Union) – membership 720,296.
- the MSF (Manufacturing Science & Finance Union) – membership 429,602.
- the TUC (Trades Union Congress), the trade association for 73 independent trade unions, essentially a union of trade unions – with a combined membership in 1998 of 6.6 million.[6]

With regard to employers' associations, there is the CBI (Confederation of British Industry), which exists primarily to ensure that Governments understand the intentions, needs and problems of British business. With a membership of more than 250,000 firms, employers' associations and trade associations covering 50 per cent of both the UK's workforce and output, it is the leading 'voice' of business in Britain. Modern rivals for the CBI include the Chambers of Commerce and the Institute of Directors, and there are many more trade associations which speak for different sectors of British industry and commerce. Mention should also be made of the NFU (National Farmers' Union) which has a membership of 68,817 throughout England and Wales, 75 per cent of the total number of farmers. With regard to professional associations, prominent examples would include the Royal College of Nursing which represents nurses, the Law Society for solicitors and the Bar Council for barristers, to name but a few. A vast array of other groups would also be classified as 'interest groups', such as the Society of Authors, the Royal British Legion, the Association of Licensed Taxi Drivers, the Scottish Whisky Association and the AA (Automobile Association).

Attitude groups

Attitude groups are those which seek to achieve objectives based on shared attitudes or beliefs, rather than common material interests. The activities of such groups are directed towards the advancement of particular causes. For example, there are the groups dedicated to:

- the cause of environmental protection, such as:
  - Friends of the Earth – 200,000 members
  - Greenpeace – 200,000 members
  - The National Trust – 2.5 million members
  - The Council for the Protection of Rural England – 46,000 members
- to prison reform, such as The Howard League for Penal Reform – 3000 members and supporters
- electoral reform, such as The Reform Society – 2000 members
- nuclear disarmament, such as The Campaign for Nuclear Disarmament, CND – 35,000 members.

Many attitude groups seek to do battle on behalf of those who find it difficult or impossible to fight for themselves. Examples would include:

- animal welfare groups, such as:
  - Royal Society for the Prevention of Cruelty to Animals, the RSPCA – 81,000 members
  - The League Against Cruel Sports – 35,000 members and supporters
- child welfare groups, such as The Child Poverty Action Group – 5000 members.[7]

There are also a wide range of attitude groups which campaign for moral causes, such as those arguing for or against legal abortion, those arguing for or against smoking, and those which have been involved for or against legal Sunday trading. The examples given are no more than the tip of a very large iceberg. Indeed, no one really knows how many pressure groups there are, although one reputable source lists some 6800 national and voluntary organisations in Britain.[8] Not all of these would necessarily fall within everyone's definition of a pressure group, but the figure gives some idea of the scale of what is involved, not least because it does not include local organisations.

Mention should also be made of 'NIMBY' – Not In My Back Yard – groups. These are groups which oppose particular technology and other developments – such as new power stations, motorways or rail links – because of the perceived adverse effects on their own quality of life at local level, and yet support (or at least take routine advantage of) such developments when sited elsewhere.

From this it is apparent that pressure groups differ widely. They can be international, national or local, large or small, permanent or temporary, proactive or reactive, rich or poor, powerful or weak, successful or unsuccessful, or any possible combination of these.

6.2 Main functions

In the contemporary British context pressure groups have a number of main functions.

They act as intermediaries between the Government and the public. This is a role which has become more important as the scope and complexity of politics have increased and as it has become more difficult for the political parties on their own to perform all the representative functions. This means that they act as spokesmen and negotiators on behalf of clearly defined sectional interests – for example, the National Farmers' Union on behalf of farmers, or the British Medical Association on behalf of doctors. It also means that they help all Governments to develop and implement their policies by entering into detailed consultations on proposals for administrative action or legislation and subsequently by delivering a measure of public consent to the output of the policy and decision making process. For example, Shelter has had considerable influence on housing legislation over the years, the Child Poverty Action Group has consistently pressed for improvements to help the poor and especially families with children, and the Magistrates' Association is regularly consulted about the development of the criminal law by the Home Office and the Lord Chancellor's Department.

They act as opponents and critics of Government, especially when the interests of those whom they claim to represent are threatened by Government policy. For example, the British Medical Association was in the forefront of the campaign to resist the Conservative Government's reforms of the National Health Service in the late 1980s and early 1990s, while the Bar Council and the Law Society lobbied heavily against some of the Major Government's proposals for reform of the legal profession. Some people might argue that, in behaving like this, they are duplicating or even usurping the rightful role of the political parties. Yet that would really be an outdated point of view in a modern, pluralist democracy. As Robert McKenzie pointed out long ago, 'the voters undertake to do far more than select their elected representatives; they also insist on their right to advise, cajole and warn them regarding the policies which they should adopt and they do this for the most part through the pressure group system'.[9]

They have acted as extensions or agents of Government. This is a role which has grown in importance whenever the tendency towards corporatism has grown in British society.[10] For example, the British Medical Association had a number of expert and advisory functions under the auspices of the 1946 National Health Service Act. The National Farmers' Union had a number of analogous functions under the auspices of the 1947 and 1957 Agriculture Acts. The Law Society is responsible for administering the system of state-financed legal aid. Perhaps the most familiar example of corporatism, especially under Labour Governments during the 1960s and 1970s, has been the prominent role played by the TUC and the CBI both as economic interest groups and as virtually obligatory partners with Government in nearly all matters to do with the management of the economy and often much else as well. Examples would include the special employment and training measures which were administered by the Manpower Services Commission set up in 1973, or the regulations made by the Health and Safety Executive under the auspices of the 1974 Health and Safety at Work Act. In addition, there are occasions when the Government makes grants to a pressure group so that it can provide a particular service. For example, Relate, the national marriage guidance organisation, has been the recipient of grants for the advice centres it runs, while Government Departments make grants to a number of pressure groups for research relating to public policy.

They have acted occasionally as substitutes for or outright opponents of Government itself. This is a very rare occurrence in British politics and it is not a role which even the most powerful groups are keen to play, since it can so easily engender a serious and lasting public backlash. If it happens, it is usually the result of either a breakdown of Government authority in certain areas of policy or the deliberate implementation of some form of syndicalism.[11] To some extent the former conditions applied in certain circumstances during the serious trade union disruption of essential public services which took place during the 'winter of discontent' in 1979. The latter conditions applied on a local scale during the time of the Meriden Co-operative in the late 1970s, when the workers themselves took over and ran their own motor cycle factory for a while until market forces and Japanese competition got the better of them.

They act as publicists and purveyors of information in order to promote a particular point of view or defend a particular standpoint. For example, during the 1980s the Campaign for Nuclear Disarmament was very active in its efforts to secure favourable media coverage and publicity for its cause of unilateral nuclear disarmament in Britain as an example to the rest of the world. It sought to do this by organising public meetings, mass demonstrations and other carefully planned media events, as well as by producing a wide range of campaign material and propaganda. Equally, some environmental groups, such as Friends of the Earth or Greenpeace, have used similar techniques in their successful campaigns for environmental improvement, for example the use of returnable bottles, the preservation of rare animal species or the abandonment of the fast-breeder reactor programme in Britain. The Child Poverty Action Group is an unabashed user of publicity as a battering ram for change. As one of its early directors made clear, 'our main aim is to shift Government, not to chat with civil servants – coverage in the media is our strategy'.[12] Equally, from its formation in 1966 the housing group Shelter showed itself to be a most effective publicist of the dreadful housing conditions in which many millions lived and the need for substantial improvement. More recently animal welfare groups such as Compassion in World farming, have used publicity to considerable advantage in their campaign against the live animal export trade.

In nearly all cases the most familiar and successful techniques involve staging media events to attract publicity and then further steps to capitalise on the public attention thus gained by advancing persuasive arguments in suitable supporting material. The publicity techniques may involve an unlikely combination of endorsement by show-business personalities and follow-up with detailed and well-researched arguments. Sometimes those concerned even go so far as to undertake difficult or dangerous stunts in order to capture media attention; for example, the Greenpeace campaigns to save whales and seals by sailing small boats into the hunting areas in order to disrupt the activities to which they objected and their occupation of the Brent Spar oil-storage installation in 1995 as part of a campaign to prevent it being dumped in the Atlantic. The media coverage achieved for campaigns of this kind is not an end in itself, but rather a means of getting such issues onto the political agenda and of putting pressure on politicians and others to take appropriate action. Some other cause groups are essentially defensive. These have included the Wing Airport Resistance Association which helped to prevent the siting of a third London airport at Cublington in Buckinghamshire, and the M23 Action Group which helped to persuade the Government to drop its plans to extend a motorway through residential Wallington in South London.

Pressure groups offer an alternative career path into public life for those who may not be completely enamoured with conventional party politics. Examples of individuals who attained national prominence through such pressure group activity include Jonathon Porritt through Friends of the Earth; Des Wilson through Shelter and later the Campaign for Lead-Free Air; Frank Field through the Child Poverty Action Group; Joan Ruddock through CND; and Mary Whitehouse through the National Listeners and Viewers Association.

6.3 Channels of influence

There are many channels of influence open to pressure groups through which they can try to achieve their objectives. These channels relate very closely to the various institutional structures through which decisions are taken and to the nature of the British political system itself. As a result, groups in Britain attempt to exert influence through five basic channels, namely:

- directly on public opinion;
- indirectly via the choice of candidates for public office;

- shamelessly via financial contributions to party funds;
- predictably via pressure during the legislative process;
- continuously via expert and technical representations to civil servants in Whitehall.

Pressure groups attempt to influence public opinion through all the media of mass communication – notably press, television, and radio – and use all the techniques of the public relations industry. The purpose of such pressure is either to persuade the public to act directly – for example, the RSPCA's campaign to persuade shoppers not to buy products from companies that did not meet the animal protection group's criteria for 'cruelty-free' animal testing – or to mobilise them politically and so achieve a group's objectives via effective influence on Whitehall and Westminster. Obtaining favourable publicity and mobilising public sympathy may not in itself be enough to ensure a permanent solution to the problem identified. For example, in the late 1960s the National Campaign for the Homeless (Shelter) produced publicity of considerable emotional power which aroused widespread public concern for the homeless, but action by Government to eradicate the problems identified did not follow. Research in the early 1990s showed that Britain still had one of the highest rates of homelessness in the European Union.

Groups can seek to exert influence on the selection of candidates for public office. The most obvious example in this respect is provided by 'constituency plan agreements' between trade unions and certain constituency Labour parties, whereby some trade union financial support goes towards constituency activities in return for which a trade union secures representation on the general management committee of the Constituency Labour Party. This was the system devised to replace direct trade union sponsorship of Labour MPs, a practice which was discontinued in 1995. Some other groups encourage their members, if already involved in a political party, to participate in candidate selection in an attempt to ensure that candidates well disposed to their objectives are selected. Examples of this practice can be found in the groups on either side of the argument over blood sports and country pursuits. The effect, however, is usually only marginal, since it is such an indirect and uncertain method. It should also be pointed out that some groups can, and increasingly do, put forward their own candidates at elections. The most obvious case in point would be that of the billionaire financier Sir James Goldsmith's Referendum Party at the 1997 General Election. Although the party put up 547 candidates, the fact was that it was a single-issue party whose goal was to bring about a referendum on the issue of Europe, not to govern the country. Another example from 1997 would be the Pro-Life Alliance which sought the repeal of the Abortion Act and the Human Fertilisation and Embryology Act and which fielded 53 candidates in the General Election of that year.

Groups still make financial contributions to political parties in the hope that their money will buy political influence. An example of this type of activity would be the large sum of money – estimated at more than £20 million – spent by Sir James Goldsmith on the Referendum Party at the 1997 General Election. Nonetheless, the most familiar example is provided by the open and well-established financial support by many trade unions to the Labour Party. Yet in the 1980s and 1990s greater media and public attention was paid to the more opaque financial support from certain companies, entrepreneurs and commercial interests to the Conservative Party. These donations constitute a sizeable part of the party's national income – estimates vary, but suggest a figure of at least 50 per cent. The interesting question here is whether and, if so, to what extent such financial support really succeeded in buying effective influence. In trying to reach a sensible conclusion on this, it is worth noting, for example, that when in 1991 British Airways, a long-term contributor to Conservative Party funds, announced that it would no longer do so because of the Government's alleged failure to defend the BA interest in the negotiations on international air routes and access to Heathrow, Ministers paid no obvious heed to such shameless pressure from Lord King, the Chairman of the company. This issue came into focus early on in the life of the Labour Government of Tony Blair when it was revealed that the head of Formula 1 motor racing, Bernie Ecclestone, had donated £1 million to the Labour Party amidst allegations that the money had influenced the Government's decision to seek an exemption for Formula 1 from a European tobacco advertising ban. The allegations were strenuously denied but the money was returned and Tony Blair appeared on television to apologise for the way the matter had been handled. (Bernie Ecclestone later revealed that he made the contribution because he was impressed with Tony Blair's leadership of the Labour Party, not least by his decision to retain a top rate of personal income tax at 40 per cent, and he wanted to reinforce Tony Blair's independence in a party still substantially dependent on finance from trade unions.[13])

Pressure groups seek to exert influence during the passage of legislation through the House of Commons and the House of Lords. They attempt to influence MPs and Peers in a variety of ways. They may, for example, deluge Members of either House with letters from the public urging their point of view or arrange for a mass lobby of Parliament which entails large numbers of people seeking to present their views directly to MPs and Peers at Westminster. They can prepare detailed briefs for Parliamentary debates, a tactic used to great effect, for example, by the Haemophilia Society in 1987 when it persuaded a large number of MPs to press the Government to provide special financial help to the 1200 haemophiliacs who had become HIV positive – and hence vulnerable to AIDS – as a result of receiving contaminated blood and plasma in the course of NHS treatment. Many groups maintain close personal contacts with individual MPs and Peers, either directly or through the growing band of professional lobbyists. This practice can both advance the interests of the groups concerned and provide useful information and advice for Members of both Houses of Parliament, especially those in Opposition, who do not normally have the benefit of Civil Service advice.[14]

Groups seek continuously to make expert and technical representations to the civil servants in Whitehall. These civil servants are there to provide policy and administrative advice to Governments of all political complexions. As the tasks of modern Government have become more technical and complex, the necessity for close liaison between the Whitehall bureaucratic machine and a myriad of pressure groups has increased. The resulting relationship is a two-way affair: pressure groups seek information on decisions which may affect their areas of interest and try to ensure advantageous decisions, while civil servants on behalf of their political masters seek data and expert advice as well as the cooperation of groups in the implementation of policy.

All these different channels of influence for pressure groups are not, of course, mutually exclusive. Very often a group will be engaged, for example, in discussions with a Government Department about a particular legislative proposal while at the same time trying to influence MPs and Peers by mounting a publicity campaign.

However, this account does demonstrate, albeit in a rather schematic form, the range of opportunities which pressure groups seek to exploit in the British political system.

6.4 Organisation and power

Pressure groups in Britain are organised in almost as many ways as there are different groups. The pattern of organisation which evolves and the degree of power which can be exerted depend on a number of different factors. It is therefore worth considering the various aspects in turn.

Nature and scope of membership

When the interests of the membership are material and immediate, a group will usually reflect them and concentrate most of its resources on defending them by whatever means are available. For example, for many years until the coal dispute of 1984–85, the National Union of Mineworkers (NUM) proved its ability to exploit both the strength of its organisation and the concentration of its interest as a way of gaining substantial material rewards for its members. The result was that the miners managed to stay consistently at or near the top of the industrial earnings league and all Governments treated them with wary respect. On the other hand, when the interests of the membership are diffuse and varied, it is usually more difficult for a group to exert direct and immediate influence on behalf of its members. For example, the Consumers' Association, which has about 800,000 subscribing members, has been more successful in raising the profile of consumer interests and consumer rights in general than in defending the position of individual consumers. Nevertheless, the high quality and well publicised research done by organisations of this kind can have a considerable impact on firms and on Government.

The power of a group depends to a considerable extent on both the coverage and the cohesion of its membership. If a group has a clear identity and purpose and if it manages to attract into its membership a high proportion of those eligible to join, it can be said to have a good coverage and is likely to be effective in defence of its members' interests. This has been borne out by the British Medical Association (BMA) which over the years has had over 80 per cent of all practising doctors in membership and which showed its political muscle during the late 1980s and early 1990s at the time of considerable public debate about the then Government's reforms of the National Health Service (NHS). On the other hand, if a group seeks to represent a wide range of interests, it is likely to have little natural cohesion and to be rather ineffective in defence of its members' interests. For example, neither the TUC, which seeks to represent 73 affiliated trade unions and 6.6 million individual trade unionists, nor the CBI, which seeks to do the same for more than 250,000 subscribing companies and employers' and trade associations, has been really effective on behalf of its members, since the need to be inclusive has weakened the cohesion and hence the effectiveness of each organisation. The TUC has had the added problem that the membership of trade unions declined by 45 per cent – more than 5.5 million members – between 1979 and 1998, while the CBI has had the obvious difficulty of trying to represent employers both large and small in both the private and public sectors. For these reasons, among others, neither organisation has been particularly powerful or effective in recent times.

Loyalty of the rank and file

The degree of loyalty shown by the rank and file towards their leaders and spokesmen is another aspect of the relative power or weakness of any group. Certainly such loyalty cannot be taken for granted in an age of greatly diminished deference. However, in most circumstances, the leaders of a pressure group have more scope for initiative if they are in the job for life and not subject to periodic recall or re-election, an advantage long enjoyed by several prominent trade union leaders. It is also the case that the leadership enjoys more latitude if the material interests of the rank and file are not directly threatened by any policy initiatives. For example, Clive Jenkins' advocacy of an embargo on the sale of equipment to South Africa under apartheid was tolerated and even supported as long as the members of his trade union (then called the Association of Technical and Managerial Staff) had no material interest that could be threatened by such a stance.

On the other hand, when the activities of pressure group leaders seem likely to prejudice the interests of the ordinary members, the rank and file are quite likely to reject the lead which is given. For example, Clive Jenkins was allowed to indulge in left-wing posturing on virtually any policy issue except the idea of nationalising the banks and insurance companies, since that would have posed a direct threat to the jobs of many of his union's members. Equally, Arthur Scargill, as President of the NUM, was opposed by a majority of his own members when he was precipitate in seeking their endorsement for a political campaign of industrial action against the 1979–83 Conservative Government and succeeded only in splitting his union in 1984–85 when he persuaded his Executive to launch an all-out strike against threatened pit closures without first securing the support of his members in a union ballot. In 1979 the NUM, with a membership of 372,122, was widely regarded as providing the 'shock troops' of the Labour movement. However, by 1998 it could claim only 5001 members, a fall of 98.7 per cent. The UDM (Union of Democratic Mineworkers) had a membership of 3000. Although much of this decline has been due to broader factors, such as the general state of the economy and the specific competitiveness of the British coal industry,[15] it is undoubtedly the case that the trade-union leadership – both in style and content – has also been a contributory factor, and this serves as a pointer to how *not* to lead a pressure group.

Political leverage

The power of pressure groups also depends on the degree of political leverage which they can exert. If a group is in a position to exert significant leverage, it can be truly formidable. Such leverage can take the form of an ability to deny to the rest of society the provision of goods or services which the community cannot easily do without and which others are not able to supply. For example, power station workers or air traffic controllers can be in such a position, as can computer operators in the Civil Service or safety workers in the water industry. Currency speculators and company treasurers can also wield comparable financial power in the money markets which amounts to a form of highly effective political leverage. In 1989 the brewing industry showed its ability to sway the then Conservative Government, partly through its ability to exploit a clever and hard-hitting advertising campaign, partly through an adroit use of political contacts, and partly because many Conservative back-benchers realised the significant part which it played in providing financial support for the party.[16]

This kind of leverage on its own may not be sufficient for the attainment of a pressure group's objectives without the support of other attributes of group power, such as Civil Service contacts, the ability to use the media effectively and financial or political clout. Yet it can achieve a great deal in a complex, modern society in which such groups can sometimes be in a position to hold the rest of the community to ransom. Only very rarely does it consist in the ability to create completely new balances of power in society which allow one particular group or interest to coerce the rest. On such occasions the Government of the day may have to use the full powers of the modern state – for instance, a massive police presence or even military units – in order to counter one brand of ruthlessness with another. No system of democratic Government can afford to tolerate, still less allow itself to be defeated by, groups using the sort of leverage through violence or coercion which has become all too familiar in parts of the world today.

Certainly some groups have used campaigns of civil disobedience as a way to try and achieve their aims. The Suffragettes were an early example. More recently there has been:

- the wide-scale campaign for the non-payment of the Poll Tax;
- some virulent activity engaged in by the campaign against the Child Support Agency;
- the port demonstrations co-ordinated by CIWF (Compassion in World Farming) against the live animal export trade in 1994–95;
- the action taken by Welsh farmers against McDonalds over their purchases of British Beef in 1998;
- the activity of DAN (Disabled People's Direct Action Network) which has fought hard in recent years to change the face of disability activism – such as lying on the pavement outside Downing Street in pools of blood-red paint.

Other groups have become involved – some intentionally, others unintentionally – in direct action which has involved violence. Examples of this are:

- the picket-line violence at Grunwick in 1977, at Warrington in 1983, at Wapping in 1987, and during the miners' strike in 1984–85;
- the inner city riots of the early 1980s, the Poll Tax riot in Trafalgar Square in 1990, and the riot against the Criminal Justice and Public Order Bill in 1994;
- the actions of the Animal Liberation Front involving arson attacks in the early 1990s;
- some of the excesses witnessed at the direct action campaigns against the Newbury bypass, the Exeter-Honiton A30 extension scheme, the Twyford Down cutting and the Manchester Airport extension in the mid-to-late 1990s.

It is perhaps worth noting that in most cases the use of civil disobedience is effective in advancing the interests of the groups concerned, whereas degeneration into violence is invariably counterproductive.

Civil Service contacts

The strength and frequency of contacts with the Civil Service is another aspect of the power and influence of groups. As J.J. Richardson and A.G. Jordan have pointed out, 'it is the relationships involved in committees, the policy community of Departments and groups, the practices of co-option and the consensual state which account better for policy outcomes than examinations of party stances, Manifestos or Parliamentary influence'.[17] On the whole, established groups prefer to have a continuous, quiet influence on the process of Government rather than an intermittent and noisy impact based on the use of media publicity and the staging of public demonstrations. Widely publicised campaigns are something of a last resort for groups, which normally succeed in keeping in close touch with the Civil Service and the rest of the policy-making community. They use their reliable and frequent contacts with Whitehall and the expertise of their own professional staff to influence Ministerial decisions and the detailed content of legislation. In such cases resorting to widely publicised campaigns is almost an admission of failure.

A number of groups secure official representation on advisory committees established within the orbits of Whitehall Departments and in this way are able to support and monitor the detailed aspects of policy implementation. This gives them extra status and recognition in Whitehall, rights of access to Ministers when the need arises, and opportunities for consultation and influence not available to others outside the charmed circle of customary consultative arrangements in central Government. For example, the National Farmers' Union (NFU) was deeply involved in the development and application of British agricultural policy from the 1947 Agriculture Act to Britain's entry into the European Community in 1973. Since then it has had to concentrate more on trying to influence the development of the Common Agricultural Policy, principally in representations to the European Commission and European Parliament through the European farmers' organisation, COPA. Equally, in the 1960s and 1970s, the CBI and the TUC both managed to establish the convention that they should be widely and frequently consulted by central Government on all matters of direct interest and concern to them. However, between 1979 and 1997 neither body was made so welcome by successive Conservative Governments, which had come to power determined to reduce their status and influence over policy and which did so.

Obviously the nature and extent of such consultation has varied from time to time and from Government to Government, depending on the priorities and objectives of the Ministers concerned. Following the establishment of the National Economic Development Council ('Neddy' in popular parlance) in 1962, it was generally accepted practice that what were called 'the two sides of industry' should be consulted by Government on a frequent and extensive basis. Many of these consultations were formalised within the Neddy framework and took place within a large number of so-called sector working parties. Other contacts took place directly between Whitehall officials and representatives of trade unions and trade associations. Such habitual consultation, which was for many years an important element of the policy and decision-making process, was downgraded by the Conservatives from 1979. For example, in 1987 it was announced that 'Neddy' would meet only four times instead of ten times a year as previously; and in December 1992 'Neddy' was abolished altogether.

However, there have been examples of very close and continuous consultation between privileged interest groups and Government Departments even under Conservative Administrations in the 1980s and 1990s whose Ministerial rhetoric often inveighed against such corporatist contacts. The classic case has probably been the relationship between the Road Transport Federation, the principal lobby group for the road freight interest, and the Department of Transport which, until a shift of policy in 1994, had consistently pushed ahead with the road building programme seemingly in defiance of the Treasury, the competing railway lobby and the general environmental interest. Another example would be the Prison Reform Trust, which has established a niche role despite having neither a large membership nor significant financial resources; the Home Office always consults the Trust when considering policy on prisons.

Publicity value

The publicity value of the causes espoused by different groups is another factor which influences the success or failure of such organisations. For example, the favourable publicity secured by Age Concern in its campaign in the 1970s to get a better financial deal for pensioners was clearly beneficial to that particular cause, although the political priorities of the 1974–79 Labour Government had a lot to do with the outcome as well. Equally, the publicity traditionally secured by the Child Poverty Action Group for poor families with children or by Shelter for the homeless was beneficial to those particular sections of society, at any rate as long as Ministers were either sympathetic to their arguments or embarrassed into action. An example of this last point occurred in 1977 when the then Labour Government was preparing to go back on its previous commitment to introduce a Child Benefit scheme. The Child Poverty Action Group leaked Cabinet minutes to this effect and the resulting protests forced the Government to back-track and introduce the scheme after all. In the early 1980s the Campaign for Lead-Free Air (CLEAR) was able to make considerable headway towards achieving its goal as a result of the publicity arising first from the leaking of a letter from the Government's Chief Medical Officer to the effect that lead in petrol was permanently reducing the IQ of many children, and then from the report of the Royal Commission on Environmental Pollution which confirmed the dangers to children and called for the banning of lead in petrol. In 1998 the Countryside Alliance – not least via a march through London which drew an estimated 250,000 people – raised the profile of a whole range of rural concerns, placing the countryside firmly on the political agenda.

On the other hand, the publicity secured by the Campaign for Nuclear Disarmament in the late 1950s and early 1960s had little effect on public policy at the time, other than to harden the resolve of the then Conservative Government to oppose such a policy. In general, the publicity gained by a group for its cause depends on the spirit of the times as much as its technical skill in using the media to its own advantage. Thus the public demonstrations and other media events organised by CND and other 'peace groups' in the early 1980s seem to have had more effect on public opinion than the Aldermaston marches of the 1950s, although while Margaret Thatcher was Prime Minister they made relatively little headway in influencing the Conservative Government in Britain. Besides which, much of their thunder was stolen by the dramatic disarmament initiatives of President Reagan of the United States and President Gorbachev of the former Soviet Union.

Financial power

The mere possession of wealth and financial power cannot buy success in pressure group politics, although it obviously helps to pay the bills and to finance the necessary publicity. An examination of the available evidence suggests that not even the most lavishly funded campaigns achieve their objectives simply because they can out-spend their opponents – as the billionaire Sir James Goldsmith found in 1997 when he spent £20 million and failed in his efforts to secure a referendum on Britain's future in the European Union. This may reflect the way in which the British party system shields politicians from the full force of group pressures or it may be a tribute to the probity and impartiality of the British Civil Service. Whatever the reasons, it is difficult to point to any occasions when money on its own has bought success for a pressure group.

For example, there is no conclusive evidence that the expensive 'Mr Cube' campaign of Tate & Lyle and other sugar producers against the proposed nationalisation of the sugar refining industry in the late 1940s had a decisive influence on the subsequent decision of the Labour Government not to proceed with such a policy after the 1950 General Election. Indeed the much stronger explanation is that the collapse of Labour's Parliamentary majority, from 146 to 5, made it seem politically imprudent for the Government to proceed further with this particular case of nationalisation. Similarly, there is no conclusive evidence that the fact that the 'Keep Britain In' campaign outspent the 'National Referendum Campaign' (those campaigning for British withdrawal) by ten-to-one (£1,481,583 to £133,630) had a decisive effect on the way in which the British people voted in the 1975 Referendum on Britain's membership of the European Community. Rather, it appears to have been the coalition of political authority represented by the leading personalities of the pro-European campaign which had the most positive impact on the result, since their public reputations then compared very favourably with those of the leading personalities on the anti-European side of the argument.[18]

During the long period of Conservative rule from 1979 until 1997, critics of the Government argued that its health policy was undermined by the financial and political power of the tobacco industry which successfully resisted pressures for a complete ban on all tobacco advertising. Similarly, they argued that its macro-economic policy was distorted by the excessive influence of the property and construction sector which became the most overheated part of the economy in the late 1980s. The former example may provide a valid case study of the financial power of a sectional interest group and its ability to influence Government policy. The latter example is better defined as a case study of how this particular sector of industry and the Ministers who championed it overplayed their hand to the eventual detriment not only of those directly concerned but also the British economy as a whole when the recession hit in the early 1990s.

Voting power

As for the power of groups to deliver votes at elections, twentieth-century British history has shown that the pull of party consistently triumphs over the pull of groups.

Ever since the emergence of recognisably modern political parties during the last quarter of the nineteenth century, the nature of the British first-past-the-post electoral system and the influence of strong party discipline has left all groups with a poor chance of striking effective political bargains with individual Members of Parliament or Parliamentary candidates. Yet this is not to say that certain influential groups cannot exercise considerable influence on the parties, especially when the latter are in Opposition and unshielded by Civil Service advice.

Unlike the situation in the United States, individual politicians in Britain do not have to construct precarious platforms of electoral support by seeking to appeal directly to powerful interest or cause groups in their constituencies. If their party has been in office, they tend to concentrate on presenting the record of their party in the most favourable light. If their party has been in Opposition, they tend to demonstrate how bad things have been under the stewardship of their opponents and how they could do much better if given the chance. Yet this is not to say that it is ever sensible or prudent for politicians to ignore the pressure of groups which are active or influential in their own constituencies.

Of course, there remains the special case of trade union influence on the Labour Party.[19] This stems from the fact that the creation of the Labour Party at the end of the nineteenth century was largely the work of the trade unions and ever since then trade union influence within the wider movement was often significant and occasionally decisive. However, in the 1990s the links between the Labour Party and the trade unions became the focus of considerable debate, and there was even some talk of a 'friendly divorce'. Nonetheless, the connection is one of the defining links in British politics, and although it has changed and may change further, it is doubtful that it will be ended. Yet no matter how close and crucial the relationship between the Labour Party and the trade unions has been in the past, it would be unwise to generalise from it when assessing the role of other pressure groups in the British political system.

6.5 Involvement in politics

Since the British political system is pluralist, liberal, and democratic, it affords many opportunities for the involvement of pressure groups in the policy and decision-making process.[20] Indeed, it is impossible fully to describe political activity in Whitehall and Westminster without giving an account of the part played by pressure groups. They have become seemingly inevitable participants in the process of official consultation and as such they contribute to the maintenance of public consent for the acts of Government. Their involvement in the policy and decision-making process is shown diagrammatically in Figure 6.1.

Policy germination

At the initial stage of policy germination the main role of pressure groups is to identify problems and to get issues onto the political agenda. This is something which they can do rather well and which they are sometimes even encouraged to do by Ministers.

Figure 6.1 Pressure group involvement in politics

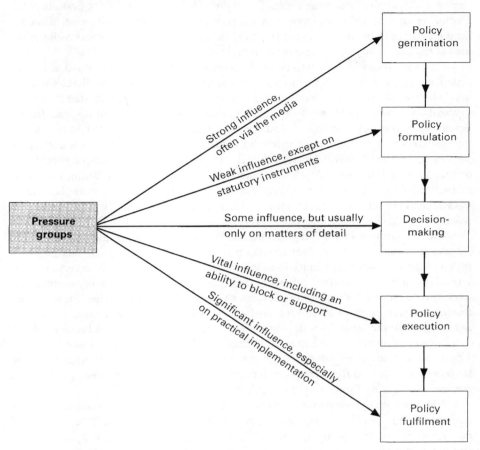

This is because the latter often prefer to appear to be responding to external pressures rather than taking unprompted initiatives. For example, the National Society for Clean Air (previously the Smoke Abatement Society) was to a considerable extent instrumental in getting the problems of air pollution onto the political agenda in the 1950s. It then conducted a sustained campaign of publicity and persuasion which helped to bring about the passage of the Clean Air Act in 1956. Equally, the Institute of Economic Affairs can claim much of the credit for getting the policy of privatisation onto the political agenda in the 1980s, since it had been campaigning for this for years beforehand especially in influential Conservative circles.

In playing their part at this early stage of the policy and decision-making process, pressure groups depend very heavily on their ability to excite the interest of the media. Without such media assistance many of the campaigns would never get off the ground at all. For example, the creation of the Department of the Environment in 1970 was to a considerable extent a political response to the pressure exerted over many years by the Conservation Society and other environmental groups who had wanted their concerns more clearly represented in Whitehall. It was also a response to the growing public interest in environmental matters which later found international expression at the 1972 Stockholm Conference. Equally, in the 1980s and early 1990s, Friends of the Earth, Greenpeace and other environmental pressure groups had a significant influence on the pace and direction of various 'green' initiatives, not only at national level but also at the European and wider international levels as well.

Pressure groups also need to persuade powerful politicians of the good sense and timeliness of their cause. For example, the Road Haulage Association (RHA) worked very closely with leading figures in the Conservative Party when the latter were in Opposition between 1945 and 1951 and was able to persuade them of the case for the denationalisation of its industry. The result of this pressure was seen in the partial denationalisation of the industry by the Conservative Government soon after its victory at the 1951 General Election. Equally the proponents of employee share ownership, such as Job Ownership Ltd, worked hard and continuously during the 1980s and early 1990s to persuade the Conservative Government to giver further legislative backing and tax relief to a cause which chimed in well with Conservative thinking on worker participation and wider share ownership.

The introduction in 1997 of a Pre-Budget Report setting out areas for consultation – coming out in November, four months prior to the March Budget – has provided groups with a greater opportunity to influence the Government's income and expenditure plans than ever before. Previously, with the Budget in November, submissions tended to be made after the August/September holidays, by which stage it was usually too late to have much of an impact. In 1998 the Chancellor, Gordon Brown, spelled out in advance the areas in which he sought input – such as tax and benefit reform, measures to promote investment and the closing of tax loopholes – and received some 1,500 submissions from interested groups, including the TUC, CBI, AA, RAC, the Brewers and Licensed Retailers Association, the Royal Society for Protection of Birds and the Engineering Employers' Federation.

When pressure groups wish to get issues onto the political agenda, the most effective approach is usually to persuade officials in the relevant Whitehall Department of the importance of their particular problem or interest and then to follow up with expert and detailed advice on how it might be tackled in ways which would be congruent with the principles of the Government of the day. A notably successful practitioner of this technique was the National Farmers' Union (NFU) which over the years from the 1947 Agriculture Act until British entry into the European Community in 1973 enjoyed an exclusive and almost symbiotic relationship with the Ministry of Agriculture. This relationship influenced the outcome of every annual farm price review and was also credited with having given rise to the 1957 Agriculture Act, which gave the NFU an even more entrenched consultative role.

The other principal way of achieving such an objective is for a group to get on a common wavelength with leading figures in the governing party and then provide them with new ideas which can be presented as a logical development of their existing policies. Once again a good example of the effectiveness of this technique is provided by the way in which so called political 'think-tanks', like the Institute of Economic Affairs and the Centre for Policy Studies, managed to play the role of intellectual pathfinders for the free market policies of the Conservatives in the 1980s, or Demos and the Institute for Public Policy Research which have been influential upon the development of New Labour's so-called 'third way' policies in the late 1990s.

Policy formulation

Pressure groups can also have influence, but not such an important role, at the stage of policy formulation. When a political party is in Opposition, policy formulation is mainly the work of its leading personalities, who are assisted by officials from the party organisation. When a party is in Government, it is mainly the work of civil servants in the Departments concerned. Yet in each case those who formulate policy may well consult pressure groups, provided the latter can be trusted to preserve the necessary confidentiality and are able to supply useful expert advice or information.

The role of groups can be especially significant when policy needs to be formulated as new legislation. For example, the Town and Country Planning Association has made frequent representations over the years and some of its ideas have been incorporated in planning legislation; the Society of Conservative Lawyers had some real influence on the policy formulated by the Conservative Party in Opposition during the late 1970s and this made a significant contribution to the subsequent British Nationality Act of 1981; the Constitution Unit – a research project set up in 1995 to conduct an independent inquiry into the implementation of constitutional reform – had a very real impact on the way in which the constitutional reform agenda of the Labour Government which came into office in 1997 was implemented. There is therefore a role for pressure groups to play at the stage of policy formulation, although it is not usually as prominent as at other stages of the process.

Decision making

In a strict sense pressure groups have no direct involvement at the decision-making stage of the political process, since this is essentially a matter for elected politicians. Yet even such an apparently clear-cut statement does not fully reflect the various ways in which political decisions are actually taken in modern Britain. For example, many Ministerial decisions are really taken by civil servants acting in the name of Ministers, notably in the detailed and complex area of delegated legislation. Groups with the necessary expertise and access to officials can play an influential part in this aspect of decision making. Examples could be found in the close and frequent contacts between the Law Society and the Lord Chancellor's Department, the Local Authority Associations and the Department of the Environment (now the Department of the Environment, Transport and the Regions), or the British Medical Association and the Department of Health. However, it is necessary to note that the influence of all these groups declined under the Conservative Government of Margaret Thatcher (1979–90), not least because Ministers were engaged in measures of radical reform affecting each of these vested interests.

Since the introduction of new legislation also involves important decision making of a kind, pressure groups can play an influential part at this stage of the political process as well. For example, the 1982 Criminal Justice Act was influenced, at least in important matters of detail, by the persistent representations made during the committee stage of the legislative process by groups such as the Magistrates' Association and the National Association for the Care and Resettlement of Offenders (NACRO). Equally, the Committee of Vice-Chancellors and Principals (CVCP) waged an effective and successful campaign in 1993–94 to persuade Ministers at the Department for

Education to modify their legislative proposals for the reform of student unions by accepting the political goal (however reluctantly), but then offering a more sensible way of implementing the policy in practice. Similarly, the Finance Bills which pass through the House of Commons every year and which contain legislative changes of considerable importance can be influenced in matters of detail by pressure groups with interests to defend or causes to advance. For example, the Institute of Chartered Accountants and other professional bodies were instrumental in persuading Treasury Ministers to drop a clause from the 1994 Finance Bill concerning Inland Revenue rights of access to confidential papers in the possession of accountants and other financial advisers, pending further detailed consultations with the interested bodies designed to refine and improve the measure. In these various ways groups can be involved to some extent at the decision-making stage.

Policy execution

The real test of effective power for all modern Governments is how well they manage to execute their policies. Ministerial decisions or Acts of Parliament are not worth very much if they cannot be implemented in practice, either because of administrative impracticality or because the people who have to execute them decide to withdraw their co-operation.

Formidable delaying power is available to civil servants. If senior civil servants wish to delay the decisions of Ministers, there are many ways in which they can do so. The most gentle technique is simply to go slowly in the administrative implementation of what has already been decided. Another is to support further consultations on the detailed implementation of policy with the groups directly affected. Yet another is to put up their own Minister to argue with Ministerial colleagues that the time is not ripe for a decision in the first place. Most drastic of all is the tactic of deliberate non-cooperation, which was used in many parts of the Civil Service during the long dispute over pay and conditions in 1981. This did temporary damage to the efficiency of Government and led, for example, to long delays in the collection of some public revenues and the payment of some social security benefits.

The role of groups can also be vital, since their active co-operation or passive acquiescence is often a condition of the satisfactory execution of policy. For example, in the early 1990s the National Union of Teachers (NUT), the National Association of Schoolmasters/Union of Women Teachers (NAS/UWT) and the Association of Teachers and Lecturers refused to co-operate with the Conservative Government's plans for national curriculum assessment, boycotting the tests involved. It was a course of action that forced the Government to make significant concessions. Similarly, the BMA initially advised its members not to co-operate with the Health Authorities and others in implementing the Conservative Government's plans for the reform of the National Health Service in the late 1980s. In all such cases acquiescence in Government policy by the relevant practitioners or workers is an important condition of successful policy execution. Such examples emphasise the key point that one of the main tasks of Ministers is to assess the limits of what is 'politically possible' in a given situation at a given time. In making such assessments, it is clear that the co-operation of the relevant civil servants and interest groups is a distinct advantage and their non-cooperation a serious liability in the execution of policy.

Policy fulfilment

A similar point can be made about the final stage of policy fulfilment. Few policies can be brought to fruition without the active co-operation or at least the passive acquiescence of the groups most directly affected. Ministers and civil servants commit serious mistakes if they are ever tempted to equate the political process solely with what happens in Whitehall and Westminster. In modern political conditions there are also many external factors which can influence the success or failure of a given policy. For example, the world-wide commodity price explosion of 1972–73 damaged the counter-inflation policies of the 1970–74 Conservative Government, while the limitations imposed on national sovereignty by the 1986 Single European Act restricted the Major Administration's room for manoeuvre in negotiating with its European partners in the run-up to the 1992 Treaty of Maastricht. Similarly, in September 1992 the Conservative Government proved unable to sustain its monetary policy in the face of a tidal wave of sterling being sold on the foreign exchanges, and was forced to suspend British membership of the Exchange Rate Mechanism of the European Monetary System by the power of market forces. Such examples inevitably extend the scope of the present discussion beyond the sphere of national politics. Yet it is undeniable that, in what is an increasingly interdependent world, political issues have to be considered in a much wider context if we are to take full account of all the limitations on the alleged autonomy of national Governments.

Politicians in office may imagine that they have become the undisputed masters of the political scene. Yet they always do well to remember that in modern political conditions they need the co-operation of interest groups and the support of other external influences if they are to have a reasonable chance of fulfilling their policies.

6.6 Conclusion

The effectiveness of a pressure group does not depend simply on its size, its privileged contacts or its financial resources. It depends, rather, on a wide variety of internal and external factors. Internal factors include size, unity of purpose, leadership quality, organisational competence and financial backing. External factors include the nature of the political environment, the strength of other competing groups and the attitudes of the media and the general public. Politicians take all such factors into account when deciding on the weight and significance to accord to the representation of particular groups.

In Britain support for pressure groups, particularly attitude groups, has burgeoned in the past 40 years, not least because of increasingly widespread disillusion among the public at large with the established political parties. As active participation in party politics has continued its long-term decline, this has been matched by an equally impressive growth in pressure group participation. For example, Friends of the Earth increased its membership from 1,000 in 1971 to stand at 200,000 in 1998, while the membership of the National Trust is now larger at 2.5 million than any other voluntary organisation in the country and more than six times larger than either the Labour or the Conservative parties. In these circumstances there are reasons for regarding the activities of pressure groups as broadly beneficial to the British political system and other reasons for regarding them as rather harmful.

On the positive side, there are at least four points which can be made:

1. they can provide the Government of the day with expert information and advice which would not necessarily be available from other sources;
2. they can provide frameworks for public participation in the political process between General Elections by all who are unwilling or unable to channel their energies through one or other of the political parties;
3. they help to define and focus public attention on issues which may not be ripe for decision but which need nevertheless to be placed on the political agenda;
4. they can provide a form of institutional ratification and public consent for the actions of Government which can assist Ministers in the difficult tasks of policy execution and fulfilment.

On the negative side, there are at least four reasons for regarding pressure groups with suspicion if not distaste:

1. they tend to give too much weight in the political process to the importance of the concurrent majority – that is, the various sectional groups in Britain's pluralist society – to the detriment of the Parliamentary majority – that is, the part of the electorate which voted for the winning party in the House of Commons at the preceding General Election;
2. they can become accomplices in a system of government which is based on exclusive, metropolitan circles of policy and decision making and which may act to the detriment of everyone else;
3. they have reinforced the tendencies towards corporatism in British society and during the 1970s in particular this worked to the detriment of Parliament and the traditions of British Parliamentary democracy;
4. as Douglas Hurd (Lord Hurd of Westwell) put it in 1986, when reflecting on his experience as Home Secretary, 'the weight of these groups, almost all of them pursuing a legitimate cause, has very substantially increased in recent years and adds greatly not just to the volume of work but also to the difficulty of achieving decisions in the general interest'.[21]

Pressure groups have undoubtedly injected considerable vitality into contemporary British politics, providing their members with real access to and influence on the political system, and the general public with information, advice and ideas which would probably not be forthcoming from modern political parties. Without the activities of pressure groups (aided and abetted by the media), the political process would be heavily stacked in favour of the Government of the day and this would not be good for the health of British democracy.

In conclusion, it is necessary to assess the role of pressure groups in parallel with an assessment of the political parties. Both categories of institution play vital roles of mediation and representation which contribute to the working of the British political system. Whereas pressure groups are not democratically accountable in the way that political parties have to be, they do share common aspirations to reflect and defend the views and interests of their members. In this way they bring a measure of public consent to the working of the political process and help to endow it with a measure of legitimacy which otherwise it might not have. On the other hand, they have been seen by Ministers as 'serpents' which can prevent political decisions being taken in the general interest. Either way, they are among the most significant sources of power, pressure and opinion in the British political system.

Suggested questions

1   What are the main functions of pressure groups in British politics?
2   Which factors make some pressure groups more powerful than others?
3   At what stages in the political process do pressure groups exert their most effective influence?

Notes

1. Quoted in R. Rose (ed.), *Studies in British Politics*, 3rd edn (London: Macmillan, 1976), p. 343.
2. G.C. Moodie and G. Studdert-Kennedy, *Opinions, Publics and Pressure Groups* (London: Allen & Unwin, 1970), p. 60.
3. S.E. Finer, *Anonymous Empire*, revised edition (London: Pall Mall, 1966), p. 3.
4. P. Shipley (ed.), *Directory of Pressure Groups and Representative Associations* (London: Wilton House, 1976), p. 3.
5. A.F. Bentley, *The Process of Government* (Cambridge, Mass.: Harvard University Press, 1908).
6. Membership figures are those provided by the Trades Union Congress in July 1998.
7. Membership figures are those of June 1998, except those for the League Against Cruel Sports where 1996 figures apply because of refusal to state the more recent number.
8. G.P. Henderson and S.P.A. Henderson (eds), *Directory of British Associations and Associations in Ireland*, 14th edn (London: CBD Research, 1998).
9. Quoted in R. Kimber and J.J. Richardson (eds), *Pressure Groups in Britain* (London: Dent, 1974), p. 280.
10. *Corporatism* is a term which has often been used pejoratively by those who believe that democratic representation should be territorially based on constituencies rather than functionally based on the various sectional interests in society. For our purposes here it is taken to mean the tendency in modern British politics for Government to deal directly with the 'social partners' (that is employers and trade unions) to the detriment perhaps of the elected Members of Parliament. See R.K. Middlemass, *Politics in Industrial Society* (London: Deutsch, 1979), for a fuller discussion of this subject.
11. *Syndicalism* is a term which was used originally to describe the movement among industrial workers at he end of the nineteenth century (especially in France) of which the primary aim was the transfer of the means of production, distribution and exchange from capitalist owners to groups of workers at factory level. On the British experience of syndicalism see B. Holton, *British Syndicalism, 1900–14* (London: Pluto Press, 1976).
12. Quoted in 'A Nation of Groupies', *The Economist*, 13 August 1994.
13. See 'Ecclestone: I gave Blair £1M to keep taxes down', *Guardian*, 13 May 1998.
14. See M. Rush (ed.), *Parliament and Pressure Politics* (London: OUP, 1990).
15. It is interesting to note that there were over one million miners working in more than 1000 mines in the late 1940s, each producing an average of one ton of coal per person shift. By 1998 there were 18,000 miners in only 22 mines, but each was producing an average of nearly 20 tons of coal per person shift.
16. See J. Warner, 'The clout of the beerage', *Independent*, 18 July 1989.

17. J.J. Richardson and A.G. Jordan, *Governing Under Pressure* (Oxford: Martin Robertson, 1979), p. 74.
18. See D. Butler and U. Kitzinger, *The 1975 Referendum* (London: Macmillan, 1976), p. 285.
19. See H. Pelling, *A History of British Trade Unionism* (London: Macmillan, 1963), and H. Pelling, *A Short History of the Labour Party* (London: Macmillan, 1965), for a fuller account of this relationship.
20. See Chapter 19 for a fuller description of the policy and decision-making process in Britain.
21. Lecture to the Royal Institute of Public Administration, 19 September 1986.

Further reading

Baggott, R., *Pressure Groups Today* (Manchester: University Press, 1995).
Brennan, T., *Pressure Groups and the Political System* (London: Longman, 1985).
Byrne, P., *The Campaign for Nuclear Disarmament* (London: Croom Helm, 1988).
Crouch C. and Dore, R. (eds), *Corporatism and Accountability: Organised interests in British Public Life* (Oxford: Clarendon Press, 1990).
Grant, W., *Business and Politics in Politics in Britain*, 2nd edn (London: Macmillan, 1993).
Jordan, A.G. and Richardson, J.J., *Government and Pressure Groups in Britain* (London: OUP, 1987).
Lowe, O. and Goyder, J., *Environmental Groups in Politics* (London: Allen & Unwin, 1983).
Marsh, D., *The New Politics of British Trade Unionism: Union Power and the Thatcher Legacy* (London: Macmillan, 1992).
Mazey, S., and Richardson, J.J. (eds), *Lobbying in the European Community* (London: OUP, 1993).
Middlemass, K., *Power, Competition and the State*, vol. 3: *The End of the Post-War Era* (London: Macmillan, 1991).
Miller, C., *Lobbying Government* (Oxford: Basil Blackwell, 1987).
Smith, M., *Pressure Power and Policy* (Hemel Hempstead: Harvester Wheatsheaf, 1993).
Rush, M. (ed.), *Parliament and Pressure Politics* (London: OUP, 1990).
Whiteley, P. and Winyard, S., *Pressure for the Poor: The Poverty Lobby and Policy Making* (London: Methuen, 1987).
Wilson, D., *Pressure, the A to Z of Campaigning in Britain* (London: Heinemann, 1984).

Websites

Amnesty International   http://www.amnesty.org
Charter 88   http://www.charter88.org.uk
Confederation of British Industry   http://www.cbi.org.uk/
Electoral Reform Society   http://www.gn.apc.org/ers/
European Movement   http://www.euromove.org.uk
European Policy Forum   http://www.epflpd.org.
Friends of the Earth   http://www.foe.co.uk/
Greenpeace   http://www.greenpeace.org/uk/
Trades Union Congress   http://www.tuc.org.uk/

⑦ The media

In considering the media in Britain, we are concerned with more than neutral channels of communication. We are examining some of the most influential participants in the political system, even though they have no formally recognised place in British constitutional arrangements. For better or worse we live in a mass media age which is characterised by the widespread use (and abuse) of the various channels of communication for a broad range of political and other purposes. Politicians need the media more than ever and seek every opportunity to get their messages across to the public. Equally, those who own or work for the media are not too shy to exert a real influence on the political process in Britain and all other countries.

7.1 The current situation

The current situation in all parts of the media is particularly dynamic and consequently in a state of flux. The following paragraphs can therefore offer only a snapshot taken at a particular time and the information provided should be seen in that light. In the press, some publications come and go, some change hands, and nearly all have to adapt or modify their appeal in response to technological change or market pressures. The trend towards multi-media companies under multi-national ownership has been growing fast with the result that it is almost a misnomer to refer any longer to 'the British media'. In the electronic media, national boundaries and jurisdictions mean even less and the emergence of huge multi-national media corporations with global reach, such as News Corporation (including News International), Worldcom, Bertelsmann, The BBC or CNN, means that people in Britain and elsewhere are increasingly living in what Marshall McLuhan described many years ago as 'a global village' of instantaneous mass-media communications. The effects of these developments on politics and culture in Britain, as in other countries, have yet to be fully understood.

The press

The current situation in the British press is that there are five daily national broadsheet newspapers, five of the tabloid variety, four Sunday national broadsheet newspapers, and five of the tabloid variety. There is only one significant evening newspaper in London, the *Evening Standard*, but there are a number of successful daily newspapers in other parts of the country – for example, the *Western Morning News*, the *Yorkshire Post*, the *Manchester Evening News* and the *Glasgow Herald*. There are a number of weekly newspapers which give prominence to political issues – for example, *The Economist*, the *Spectator* or the *New Statesman*. There are also a number of more academic periodicals which specialise in political issues, such as *Political Quarterly*, *Parliamentary Affairs*, *Government and Opposition* and *Public Administration*. Mention should also be made of the Communist daily newspaper, the *Morning Star*, the satirical and anti-Establishment periodicals, such as *Private Eye*, and the publications of the political fringe, such as *Militant* and *Socialist Worker* on the far Left or *Spearhead* on the far Right. There is, therefore, a wide variety of political points of view expressed in the British press, although it is worth noting that some of the most widely read publications are not really political at all – for example, *Radio Times*, *Woman's Own* or *Hello!*

Until the 1980s one common denominator for nearly all the British press was the difficulty of making a profit. This was due to old-fashioned management practices and chaotic labour relations, and it brought in its wake increasing concentration of ownership as titles were forced to amalgamate or close. When the national newspapers were based in Fleet Street, virtually every attempt by management to introduce new technology was fiercely and effectively resisted by the powerful print unions. It was only after a new breed of tougher newspaper owners had founded or bought some of the titles, such as Eddy Shah with *Today* and Rupert Murdoch with the *Sun*, that things began to change in a radical way. A number of bitter industrial disputes were fought between the traditional print unions and the new owners when the latter set out to break the trade union stranglehold by moving their production facilities to new lower cost locations in the East End of London, and by introducing the latest technology which enabled journalists to write and produce their own copy with only a minimum requirement for traditional printers' skills. These bitter struggles exemplified both the ingrained resistance to change which had characterised the industry in the past and the inevitability of such change once a determined employer, such as Rupert Murdoch, decided to break ranks with the more traditional newspaper proprietors and to bust the previous, mutually destructive arrangements between employers and trade unions in the industry.

Since that time there has been a new climate of fierce commercial competition in the British newspaper market which has enabled those proprietors with the deepest purse, such as Rupert Murdoch from Australia or Conrad Black from Canada, to put enormous competitive pressure not only on each other but also on their weaker competitors. The rival newspaper and media empires have engaged in fierce price wars designed to secure the largest possible share of what has become a highly competitive market and eventually to eliminate at least the weakest competitors in the various sectors of the market. Against this background it is not surprising to find that only eight multi-national companies, dominated in a number of cases by very wealthy individuals or families, own all the mass circulation newspapers in Britain, and that one person – Rupert Murdoch – controls a huge multi-media empire world-wide and owns more than 35 per cent of the British national press. A table of the various national newspapers with their circulation figures and political leanings is set out in Figure 7.1.

Figure 7.1 Main national newspapers in Britain

Title	Foundation date	Ownership Group	Chairman	Political leaning	Average daily circulation (Jan–June 1998)	Market share (%)
Broadsheet Dailies:						
The Times	1788	News Corporation Ltd (Rupert Murdoch)		Right wing Euro-Sceptic	769,742	5.97
Guardian	1821	Guardian Media Group plc (Bob Gavron)		New Labour	400,005	3.10
Daily Telegraph	1855	Hollinger Inc. (Conrad Black)		Conservative	1,066,675	8.28
Financial Times	1888	Pearson plc (Lord Blakenham)		Business European	361,779	2.81
Independent	1986	Independent Newspaper Group (Tony O'Reilly)		Centre Left	224,559	1.74
Tabloid Dailies:						
Daily Mail	1896	Daily Mail & General Trust plc (Lord Rothermere)		Thatcherite Conservative	2,312,168	17.95
Express	1900	United News & Media plc (Lord Hollick)		Thatcherite Conservative	1,133,356	8.80
Mirror	1903	Mirror Group plc (Victor Blanc)		Labour	2,340,080	18.16
Sun	1969	News Corporation Ltd (Rupert Murdoch)		Chauvinist Populist	3,701,446	28.73
Daily Star	1978	United News & Media plc (Lord Hollick)		Thatcherite Conservative	574,086	4.46
Broadsheet Sundays:						
Observer	1791	Guardian Media Group plc (Bob Gavron)		Centre Left	403,300	2.85
Sunday Times	1822	News Corporation Ltd (Rupert Murdoch)		Radical Conservative Republican	1,320,265	9.33
Sunday Telegraph	1961	Hollinger Inc. (Conrad Black)		Conservative Euro-Sceptic	833,878	5.90
Independent on Sunday	1990	Independent Newspaper Group (Tony O'Reilly)		Centre Left	255,664	1.81
Tabloid Sundays:						
News of the World	1843	News Corporation plc (Rupert Murdoch)		Chauvinist Populist	4,165,320	29.45
People	1881	Mirror Group plc (Victor Blanc)		Labour	1,716,906	12.14
Express on Sunday	1918	United News & Media plc (Lord Hollick)		Thatcherite Conservative	1,033,241	7.30
Sunday Mirror	1963	Mirror Group plc (Victor Blanc)		Labour	1,970,869	13.93
Mail on Sunday	1982	Daily Mail & General Trust plc (Lord Rothermere)		Thatcherite Conservative	2,192,294	15.50

Source of circulation figures: Newspaper Publishers Association

The electronic media

In television the situation at the time of writing is that five terrestrial channels provide a national service covering the entire country. There are the two BBC channels with BBC1 being a channel of broad appeal, broadcasting over 1,000 hours of features, documentaries and current affairs programmes, along with nearly 1,000 hours of drama and entertainment, more than 650 hours of sport and almost 400 hours of children's programmes; while BBC2 is a channel of innovation and flexibility catering for special audience interests. There are three commercial channels with ITV (Channel 3) providing a diverse programme service designed to appeal to a wide range of viewers' tastes and interests, about one-third of whose output is made up of informative programmes – news, documentaries, current affairs – with the remainder consisting of drama, entertainment, sport and children's programmes; Channel 4 offering innovation and original programmes with a distinctive character designed to appeal to a wide range of minority audiences; and Channel 5, which provides an output of light entertainment, films and soaps.[1]

The BBC makes and broadcasts most of its own material from a vertically integrated broadcasting organisation employing thousands of journalists, technicians and programme makers. It is financed from the proceeds of an annual licence fee (costing £101.00 for colour and £33.50 for black and white in 1999–2000), which is levied by law on all who own a television set. In contrast, commercial television is financed by the proceeds of advertising carried during and between its programmes. Its output is produced by 15 regional programme companies, each with an exclusive franchise for part of the country for an agreed contractual period (usually ten years). The BBC is run by a Director-General and management team, who are in their turn answerable to the Chairman and Board of BBC Governors chosen on rotation by the Government of the day, but representing a wide range of backgrounds, opinion and experience. On the other hand, the commercial television companies are answerable to the Independent Television Commission (ITC) which is there to play much the same buffer role as the BBC Board of Governors in relation to any political pressures from the Government of the day. On the BBC, news is gathered by its own correspondents and broadcast by its own producers and technicians; whereas on commercial television the news is gathered by Independent Television News (ITN), a separate non-profit making organisation established for the purpose and jointly owned by the programme companies. See Figure 7.2 for a simplified chronology.

Satellite television has been one of the growth areas of the media in Britain and around the world over the past few years. At the time of writing there are over 30 satellite channels available in Britain to over five million people who currently pay subscriptions for them. These include the Sky channels partly owned by Rupert Murdoch; various film, sport and special interest channels; and CNN, the world-wide news channel owned by Ted Turner in the United States. There has also been a rapid growth of cable television in Britain in the 1990s with an increasing number of people – currently 2.75 million – choosing to pay for connection to cable networks, partly because these seem to offer more local services than broadcasting, but mainly because modern cable technology can offer a range of facilities for private households, including telephony, interactive shopping, banking and distance learning.

Digital television, a new way of broadcasting television signals with no picture interference and far superior sound quality to the traditional analogue system became a

Figure 7.2 The electronic media in Britain: a simplified chronology

1904	*Wireless Telegraphy Act* required that all wireless transmitters and receivers be licensed by the Post Office
1922	*British Broadcasting Company* established a cartel of radio manufacturers and licensed to broadcast with revenue derived from licence fees payable by wireless users to the Post Office
1923	*Sykes Committee* established by the Post Office to consider the collection and distribution of licence fees and royalties, and all other aspects of broadcasting
1925	*Crawford Committee* established to suggest guidelines for the future of broadcasting
1927	*British Broadcasting Corporation* established with John Reith as its first director-general
1938	*Resignation of John Reith* as director-general
1946	*Labour White Paper* on broadcasting policy favoured 'some element of competition' in the expanding field of television
1954	*Television Act* provided for the establishment of Independent Television, a new commercial TV channel financed from the proceeds of TV advertising, and the Independent Television Authority, a new regulatory body to oversee commercial TV in Britain
1955	*Start of Commercial Television* broadcasting and of Independent Television News
1962	*Pilkington Committee Report* on the future of broadcasting in Britain
1963	*Television Act* on broadcasting standards and practice
1964	*BBC 2* launched as a new television channel
1967	*Introduction of colour television* on BBC 2 and the re-naming of BBC Light Programme, Third Programme and Home Service as Radios 2, 3 and 4
1969	*Colour television* introduced on BBC 1 and ITV
1972	*Independent Local Radio* launched and Independent Television Authority re-named the Independent Broadcasting Authority
1977	*Annan Committee Report* on the future of broadcasting
1981	*Broadcasting Complaints Commission* brought into operation
1982	*Channel 4*, the second commercial TV channel in the UK, began broadcasting
1984	*Sky Channel*, the first TV channel in the UK, began broadcasting
1985	*Cable Authority* began granting franchises and regulating the new cable services in the UK
1986	*Peacock Report* published on the financing of the BBC
1988	*Broadcasting Standards Council* brought into operation and the House of Commons agreed to the televising of its proceedings on an experimental basis
1989	*Televising of the House of Commons* made permanent
1990	*Broadcasting Act* created the Independent Television Commission to replace the Independent Broadcasting Authority and the Cable Authority, and to license and regulate all commercial television services
1991	*Radio Authority* established to license, regulate and oversee the expansion of commercial radio and to introduce three new national radio channels
1991	*European Broadcasting Directive* came into force in the UK, together with the Council of Europe Convention of Trans-frontier Television
1992	*Department of National Heritage* created to take over ministerial responsibility for broadcasting policy from the Home Office
1995	*Conservative proposals on Media Ownership* and longer-term regulatory issues
1995	*The Learning Zone* – a night-time education and training service – was launched by BBC 2
1996	*New BBC Royal Charter* came into effect, enabling the service to continue as Britain's main public service broadcaster until 2006
1996	*Broadcasting Act* set up a flexible regulatory framework for the introduction of digital terrestrial broadcasting – at least 18 national digital television channels and 12 digital radio services – and paved the way for more broadly based competitive media groups
1997	(March) *Channel 5*, the third commercial TV channel in the UK, began broadcasting
1997	(April) *The Broadcasting Standards Commission* (BSC) was established
1997	(June/July) *Licences* to operate commercial digital television multiplexes were awarded by the ITC
1997	(July) The Department of National Heritage became the *Department for Culture, Media and Sport* (DCMS)

Figure 7.2 continued

reality in the late 1990s. Both the BBC and ITV will be adjusting to broadcast digitally, while Sky Digital, offering 140 channels by satellite, began broadcasting from 1 October 1998, and OnDigital, jointly owned by the two largest ITV companies (Carlton Communications and Granada) and offering 30 channels through existing aerials, began broadcasting from 15 November 1998. Cable companies such as Cable & Wireless, Telewest and NTL prepared for digital services to come on line during 1999.

In short, digital television introduces a huge range of channels to the public and, beginning in 1999, 'interactivity', meaning that televisions will be used as two-way channels of communication, including television shopping, banking, e-mail, and – in some cases – access to a television version of the World Wide Web.

On radio the BBC has five national channels – Radio 1 to 5 – which each cater for a different segment of the wide range of public interests and tastes. Radio 1 provides mostly popular music and is aimed very much at a younger audience. Radio 2 provides middle-of-the-road music programmes and light entertainment of one kind or another. Radio 3 caters for minority interests of a more high-brow and cultured variety, as well as providing such traditional services as commentaries on Test Match cricket. Radio 4 provides most of the solid news, information and analysis of arts and current affairs, as well as some high-quality drama and popular entertainment. Radio 5 provides 24-hour sports and news coverage. The BBC World Service broadcasts to more than 150 countries in 46 languages around the world and sets a standard of radio reporting and analysis which is widely admired.

There are three independent national radio services: Classic *FM* broadcasting classical music, news and information; Virgin *1215* broadcasting broad-based pop and rock music; and Talk Radio *UK* which is a speech-based service. Local radio services are provided in Britain from 43 BBC local radio stations, and from some 200 or so commercial local radio stations which are financed, like commercial television, from the proceeds of advertising carried on air during and between the programmes. Local radio of both kinds broadcasts a great deal of popular music and other mass appeal programmes designed to ensure an adequately large audience. Yet it also concentrates to a considerable extent on covering local and community issues and for these purposes puts considerable emphasis on public phone-in programmes and other forms of local audience participation. Many would argue that this has been a healthy development which has boosted a sense of community and democracy in parts of the country where previously it was rather lacking.

7.2 The problems of the press

The problems of the press are both internal and external. For the purposes of this chapter, however, we shall be concerned mainly with the ways in which the activity of the press and some of its methods of work cause disquiet, even hostility, among politicians and public alike. Most people in Britain are content that there is a free press;

but, if there is a common thread of public criticism, it is invariably that the press is too 'free', namely that it may have become too powerful and too invasive of people's privacy. This was an argument that came very much to the fore in the aftermath of the death of Diana, Princess of Wales. On the other hand, editors and journalists are often more concerned to defend the rights and independence of the 'Fourth Estate' against what they are sometimes inclined to see as tyrannical Ministers and draconian laws. In this age-old struggle between politicians and the press, there has often been a good deal of hypocrisy and double standards on both sides. This has made it hard to get at the truth at times. Nevertheless the following section attempts to cover the salient issues and perennial problems.

Influence and bias

All the national newspapers have political reporters and commentators who usually take distinctive lines on the political issues of the day. In the popular or tabloid newspapers, however, the main purposes are to entertain the readers and maintain or boost the circulation, so that advertisers do not take their custom elsewhere and profits can be increased. The result of these commercial imperatives is that the coverage of political issues is usually not very extensive and certainly not very subtle. Instead the emphasis is put on presenting news and opinion in stark and eye-catching ways with the use of dramatic photographs, screaming headlines and vivid language.[2]

As a general rule, the influence of the tabloid press seems to vary inversely with the knowledge or interest of its readers. For example, the *Mirror*, which has consistently supported the Labour Party at General Elections since the war, seems to have a significant influence upon the voting behaviour of its readers by persuading many of them, if wavering, to remain loyal to their traditional Labour allegiance. Equally, when the *Sun* (which had previously – from 1979 – supported the Conservative Party) gave strong and unequivocal support to Tony Blair at the 1997 General Election. This appears to have influenced the voting behaviour of many of its readers at that election, although there were other factors which probably had a greater influence on the extent to which both skilled and unskilled workers and their families switched to Labour in that watershed election. Thus it may be that the relatively frivolous nature of such 'newspapers' in normal times and the relative ignorance or lack of interest in politics among their readers actually increase the political influence which they can have if their editors decide to pull out all the stops in favour of a particular political party at election time. Indeed, following the *Sun*'s call to its readers to support John Major rather than Neil Kinnock in 1992 and the ensuing Conservative victory, the newspaper proclaimed 'It's the Sun wot won it'. However, few readers of the tabloid press seem to pay much attention to the political line taken by the newspaper that they habitually read and the political influence of such organs seems to have been exaggerated by journalists and politicians alike. The academic research shows that newspapers have no measurable effect on the way their readers vote.[3] The readers are demonstrably more interested in the sport, scandal and soft pornography which dominate so many pages. The editors clearly know what sells such newspapers and invariably allocate their column inches accordingly.

The quality national newspapers devote much more space to political reporting and comment, and certainly they all aspire to influence the political process in their chosen directions. Their influence is usually of a subtle and indirect kind in that they seek to persuade the politicians themselves, civil servants involved in the policy process and the wide variety of other interest groups and opinion formers who are involved directly or indirectly in British politics. Thus well known commentators, such as Andrew Marr in the *Observer*, Peter Riddell in the *Times* and Hugo Young in the *Guardian*, can have real influence from time to time on the evolving political debate. Similarly, leading articles, political features and even letters to the editor in such newspapers are taken seriously and often carry weight in Whitehall and Westminster. Such columns are rather like a house notice board for the political class and they have some disproportionate impact in view of the elitist and metropolitan character of so much political opinion formation in Britain.

Many on the Left of British politics have argued that there is a persistent bias in the national press in favour of the Conservatives and against the views and interests of the Labour Party. It certainly used to be true that the *Mirror* was the only national daily newspaper which consistently supported the Labour Party as a matter of editorial policy. Apart from its sister paper, the *Sunday Mirror*, all the other national newspapers could be divided essentially between those which were still broadly in favour of policies derived from the postwar consensus (for example, the *Guardian* and the *Observer*) and those which were invariably pro-Conservative (for example, the *Express* and the *Sunday Telegraph*). However, this traditional pattern was undermined and consequently altered by two factors: firstly, the financial shock and political set-back of 'Black Wednesday' on 16 September 1992 when Britain was forced out of the European Exchange Rate Mechanism by enormous turbulence in the global currency markets; and, secondly, the Blairite transformation of the Labour Party. The first seriously damaged the political credibility of the Conservative Government, the second made a Labour alternative acceptable. Indeed, throughout the 1992–97 period it was the Conservative Party, and especially its leader John Major, who were the target for considerable press criticism and abuse.

Privacy and public interest

One of the strongest political and public concerns about the press is the way in which it is seen to invade people's privacy and make some lives miserable as a result of various forms of media intrusion – whether telephone tapping, bugging with directional microphones, photography with telephoto lenses, or intimidatory 'door-stepping' of people in the news. Although the concern is often voiced by and on behalf of politicians, it is a problem which can afflict many other people as well, including members of the Royal Family, television personalities, sports stars and a whole range of show business people (most of whom would not make such a lucrative living if they were not so frequently in the public eye). It can also afflict regular members of the general public from time to time – the so-called 'innocent by-standers of life' – if and when they are involved in some particularly newsworthy event, such as the death of a child, a 'lucky' win on the National Lottery, the loss of a loved one in a terrorist outrage, or some other personal tragedy. In nearly every such case self-righteous editors and investigating journalists seek to justify their actions by claiming that 'the public has a right to know' and that their journalism is 'in the public interest'. Sometimes this may, indeed, be true; but more often the real (unadmitted) explanation is that sensational journalism boosts the circulation of the newspapers which get scoops and hence increases both the advertising revenue and the profits of the media corporations which stand to benefit.

There is no denying the fact that significant numbers of the public are 'interested' in such squalid journalism, since the circulation figures of the newspapers concerned invariably increase dramatically when they serialise a colourful political memoir, such as Alan Clark's *Diaries*, or publish the transcript of sensational revelations about the Royal Family, such as the so-called Camillagate Tapes, which purported to record in lurid and highly compromising detail some private telephone conversations between the Prince of Wales and his friend Mrs Camilla Parker Bowles. Nor is there much doubt that many prominent figures in public life benefit – at any rate financially – when they sell their stories to the press, as less prominent people also do when they succumb to the lure of so-called cheque-book journalism.

It is more questionable, however, whether what interests the newspaper-buying public is always 'in the public interest', since such vivid and sensational journalism manifestly damaged the reputation of the Royal Family in the 1990s and did not exactly assist John Major to govern the country with confidence at a time when an unusually large number of his political colleagues were exposed by the media in compromising circumstances. Indeed on this last point the attack on the *Guardian* in April 1995 by the then Chief Secretary to the Treasury, Jonathan Aitken – in which he spoke about 'the cancer of bent and twisted journalism' and 'the fight against falsehood and those who peddle it' – was seen by some as an attempt by the Government at the time to halt the debilitating attacks on Ministers over allegations of 'sleaze' which had led to 17 resignations during the first four and a half years of John Major's premiership.[4] Those who hold a brief for the Fourth Estate will invariably say, when challenged, that members of the Government and all in public life deserve all they get when their indiscretions or wrong doings are exposed. Yet there was not always such open warfare between journalists and those in public life, as can be seen from the much more discreet way in which journalists and editors declined to report or publish all that they knew to be true of Edward VIII, Harold Macmillan, or President Kennedy. The inescapable conclusion is that the press, like the public, has become much less deferential to politicians and others in public life; and that the competitive pressures upon all editors to 'publish and be damned' are now compelling in a world of intense media competition in which any newspaper which acts 'responsibly' by withholding a sensational story will almost certainly lose ground commercially to one of its rivals which is not so fastidious.

In the contemporary British context, the question has arisen, therefore, as to what – if anything – can or should be done about these problems. In April 1989 the Conservative Government charged the Calcutt Committee with the difficult task of examining the issues and making recommendations on 'what measures (whether legislative or otherwise) – were needed to give further protection to individual privacy from the activities of the press and improve recourse against the press for the individual citizen, taking account of existing remedies including the law on defamation and breach of confidence'.[5] In an attempt to pre-empt Calcutt the newspaper editors agreed a Code of Practice and appointed in-house ombudsmen to consider readers' complaints. In fact Sir David Calcutt's Committee decided to give the press 'one last chance' at self-regulation and, as part of this, urged that a new 'authoritative, independent and impartial' body – a Press Complaints Commission – be established to oversee this self-regulation, warning that if it did not perform adequately it should be replaced by a statutory tribunal with statutory powers and implementing a statutory code of practice.[6]

The Press Complaints Commission (PCC) came into being in January 1991 and soon claimed that it was proving itself to be effective.[7] However, the following year brought forth a succession of sensational press stories on the private lives of a number of national political figures – not least stories which had been obtained via the use of bugging devices and other questionable methods – as well as a considerable focus of attention on members of the Royal family and particularly the status of the marriage of the Prince and Princess of Wales, which reached a crescendo with the serialisation in the press of Andrew Morton's book *Diana: Her True Story*. Notwithstanding the fact that the Chairman of the PCC described the press coverage involved as 'an odious exhibition of journalists dabbling their fingers in the stuff of other people's souls',[8] the resulting lack of action – restraint by the press – made the PCC look at best ineffectual and at worst ridiculous.

The Minister responsible for the media at the time, David Mellor, described the newspapers as 'drinking in the last chance saloon' and in July 1992 commissioned Sir David Calcutt to conduct another inquiry specifically into press self-regulation. Not long after, David Mellor was obliged to resign as a result of extensive press publicity of the circumstances surrounding an extra-marital affair. Sir David produced his second report in 1993 in which he called for a compulsory system of press controls operated by an official Press Tribunal.[9] The Government – after a considerable lapse of time and following press hostility to the report's recommendations – rejected the proposals for regulation, confirming instead the principle of self-regulation;[10] in short, the last chance saloon was given a substantial extension to its drinking hours.

Events took another turn following the death of Diana, Princess of Wales, at the end of August 1997. This was due in part to the perceived implication that elements within the press had been involved in some of the circumstances leading up to the tragedy. Lord Wakeham, who had taken over as Chairman of the PCC in 1995, initiated a review of the rules covering the use of 'intrusive' paparazzi photographs, but this was hardly sufficient and the climate was changing. The Foreign Secretary observed that 'we will have to reflect' on whether the love and affection with which the British people regarded the Princess 'was truly reflected in the behaviour of the British press towards her',[11] and the Prime Minister declared that 'the newspaper industry should be looking at lessons that should be learnt'.[12] Certainly, few who heard the words of the Princess's brother, Earl Spencer, at her funeral service in Westminster Abbey when he spoke of 'the treatment that she had received at the hands of the newspapers' and of Diana as 'the most hunted person of the modern age'[13] – could have failed to appreciate the impact of what he said, although it may still have been shrugged off by those against whom his words were directed.

Towards the end of September 1997 Lord Wakeham put forward a number of proposed amendments to the press Code of Practice to protect privacy. These included proposals to ban the publication of pictures obtained illegally or through persistent pursuit or stalking; to tackle the problem of 'deeply intimidating' media scrums; to extend the protection of children; to give a wider definition of what constitutes 'private property'; and to define private life in terms of people's health, home life, family relationships and personal correspondence into which the press should not intrude without an excuse of overriding public interest. These proposals were accepted by the industry's Code Committee in December, and came into effect in January 1998. The Code is reproduced as Figure 7.3.

Figure 7.3 Press Code of Practice

All members of the press have a duty to maintain the highest professional and ethical standards. This code sets the benchmarks for those standards. It both protects the rights of the individual and upholds the public's right to know. The code is the cornerstone of the system of self-regulation to which the industry has made a bindinf commitment. Editors and publishers must ensure that the code is observed rigorously not only by their staff but also by anyone who contributes to their publications.

It is essential to the workings of an agreed code that it be honoured not only to the letter but in the full spirit. The code should not be interpreted so narrowly as to compromise its commitment to respect the rights of the individual, nor so broadly that it prevents publication in the public interests.

It is the responsibility of editors to co-operate with the PCC as swiftly as possible in the resolution of complaints. Any publication which is criticised by the PCC under one of the following clauses must print the adjudication which follows in full and with due prominence.

1. Accuracy

(i) Newspapers and periodicals must take care not to publish inaccurate, misleading or distorted material, including pictures.

(ii) Whenever it is recognised that a significant inaccuracy, misleading statement or distorted report has been published, it must be corrected prominently and with due prominence.

(iii) An apology must be published whenever appropriate.

(iv) Newspapers whilst free to be partisan must distinguish clearly between comment, conjecture and fact.

(v) A newspaper or periodical must report fairly and accurately the outcome of an action for defamation to which it has been a party.

2. Opportunity to reply

A fair opportunity to reply to inaccuracies must be given to individuals and organisations ehen reasonable called for.

*3. Privacy

(i) Everyone is entitled to respect for his or her private and family life, home, health and correspondence. A publication will be expected to justify intrusions into any individual's private life without consent.

(ii) The use of long-lens photography to take pictures of people in private places without their consent is unacceptable.

Note: Private places are public or private property where there is a reasonable expectation of privacy.

*4. Harassment

(i) Journalists and photographers must neither obtain nor seek to obtain information or pictures through intimidation, harassment or persistent pursuit.

(ii) They must not photograph individuals in private places (as defined in clause 3 note) without their consent; must not persist in telephoning, questioning, pursuing or photographing individuals after having been asked to desist; must not remain on their property after having been asked to leave and must not follow them.

(iii) Editors must ensure that those working for them comply with these requirements and must not publish material from other sources which does not meet these requirements.

5. Intrusion into grief or shock

In cases involving grief or shock, enquiries must be carried out and approaches made with sympathy and discretion. Publication must be handled sensitively, but this should not be interpreted as restricting the right to report judicial proceedings.

*6. Children

(i) Young people should be free to complete their time at school without unnecessary intrusion.

(ii) Journalists must not interview or photograph children under the age of 16 on subjects involving the welfare of the child or of any other child, in the absence of or without the consent pf a parent or other adult who is responsible for the children.

(ii) Pupils must not be approached or photographed while at school without the permission of the school authorities.

(iv) There must be no payment to minors for material involving the welfare of children nor payment to parents or guardians for material about their children or wards unless it is demonstrably in the child's interest.

(v) Where material about the private life of a child is published, there must be justification for publication other than the fame, notoricty or position of his or her parents or guardian.

7. Children in sex cases

1. The press must not, even where the law does not prohibit it, identify children under 16 who are involved in cases concerning sexual offences, whether as victims or as witnesses.

2. In any press report of a case involving a sexual offence against child:

(i) The child must not be identified.

(ii) The adult may be identified.

(iii) The word "incest" must not be used where a child victim might be identified.

(iv) Care must be taken that nothing in the report implies the relationship between the accused and the child.

*8. Listening devices

Journalists must not obtain or publish material obtained by clandestine listening devices or by intercepting private telephone conversations.

*9. Hospitals

(i) Journalists or photographers making enquiries at hospitals or similiar institutions must identify themselves to a responsible executive and obtain permission before entering non-public areas.

(ii) The restrictions on intruding into privacy are particularly relevant to enquiries about individuals in hospitals or similar institutions.

*10. Innocent relatives and friends

The press must avoid identifying relatives or friends of persons convicted or accused of crime without their consent.

*11. Misrepresentation

(i) Journalists must not generally obtain or seek to obtain information or pictures through misrepresentation or subterfuge.

(ii) Documents or photographs should be removed only with the consent of the owner.

(iii) Subterfuge can be justified only in the public interests and only when material cannot be obtained by any other means.

12. Victims of sexual assault

The press must not identify victims of sexual assault or publish material likely to contribute to such identification unless there is adequate justification and, by law, they are free to do so.

13. Discrimination

(i) The press must avoid prejudicial or pejorative reference to a person's race, colour, religion, sex or sexual orientation or to any physical or mental illness or disability.

(ii) It must avoid publishing details of a person's race, colour, religion, sexual orientation, physical or mental illness or disability unless are directly relevant to the story.

*14. Financial journalism

(i) Even where the law does not prohibit it, journalists must not use for their own profit financial information they receive in advance of its general publication, nor should they pass such information to others.

(ii) They must not write about shares or securities in whose performance they know that they or their close families have a significant financial interests, without disclosing the interest to the editor or financial editor.

(iii) They must not buy or sell, either directly or through nominees or agents, shares or securities about which they have written recently or about which they intend to write in the near future.

15. Confidential sources

Journalists have a moral obligation to protect confidential sources.

*16. Payment for articles

(i) Payment or offers of payment for stories or information must not be made directly or through agents to witnesses or potential witnesses in current criminal proceedings except where the material concerned ought to be published in the public interest and there is an overriding need to make or promise to make a payment for this to be done. Journalists must take every possible step to ensure that no financial dealings have influence on the evidence that those witnesses may give. (An editor authorising such a payment must be prepared to demonstrate that there is a legitimate public interest at stake involving matters that the public has a right to know. The payment or, where accepted, the offer of payment to any witness who is actually cited to give evidence must be disclosed to the prosecution and the defence and the witness should be advised of this.)

(ii) Payment or offers of payment for stories, pictures or informationmust not be made directly or through agents to convicted or confessed criminals or to their associates – who may include family, friends and colleagues – except where the material concerned ought to be published in the public interest and payment is necessary for this to be done.

*The public interest

There may be exceptions to clauses marked * where they can be demonstrated to be in the public interest.

1. The public interest includes:

(i) Detecting or exposing crime or a serious misdemeanour.

(ii) Protecting public health and safety.

(iii) Preventing the public from being misled by some statement or action of an individual or organisation.

2. In any case where the public interest is invoked, the PCC will require a full explanation by the editor demonstrating how the public interest was served.

3. In cases involving children, editors must demonstrate an exceptional public interest to override the normally paramount interests of the child.

Source: The Press Complaints Commission

Nonetheless, notwithstanding the fact that the press had sought, in some respects at least, to clean up its act in the immediate aftermath of the death of Diana, Princess of Wales, few observers believed they had witnessed a permanent change of character. Indeed, it was not long before the press could be seen to have returned to its bad old ways.

Although the Labour Government said that it had no plans to legislate on privacy, it did bring forward legislation to incorporate the European Convention on Human Rights into domestic law; and Article 8 of the Convention confers the right to respect for private and family life, home and correspondence. The Human Rights Act 1998, which brought this change into effect, seems still to leave unresolved a number of key questions: (1) can there be an effective right to privacy; (2) if so, who can claim such a right and to what extent; and (3) how can suitable redress be provided for those who believe that their privacy has been intolerably invaded?

Certainly everyone should be able to expect a high degree of privacy about those aspects of their lives in which public disclosure could be severely prejudicial to their interests – for example, sensitive information about their medical condition or their tax position. This means that doctors or tax inspectors are usually under a rigorous duty of confidentiality to patients and tax-payers respectively. However, those who *choose* to enter public life or who accept a position of public responsibility cannot reasonably expect so much privacy, at any rate in connection with their public duties. Furthermore, public figures who sound off on issues of personal morality or integrity – as certain politicians have chosen to do in the past – should not be surprised if this tempts the media to explore their lives for sensational double standards between their public pronouncements and their private practices.

The challenge in this area is to draw a convincing and generally acceptable line between those in public life and everyone else, and then perhaps a further line for those in public life between the 'public' and 'private' aspects of their lives. In practice, the latter distinction has proved almost impossible to sustain, because any journalist exploring a good story will tend to argue that a revelation drawn from the private life of someone normally in the public eye *necessarily* has a bearing upon either that person's fitness to hold public office or the public's ability to put its trust in the person concerned. In such testing circumstances those actively engaged in public life and, regrettably, often their families too are regarded by the media as fair game whenever any newsworthy information is uncovered about them. It is therefore difficult to see how there could be an enforceable statutory right to privacy covering all aspects of people's lives and certainly not for those who have chosen to be in public life.

In seeking appropriate means of redress for those whose privacy has been intolerably invaded, a distinction should be drawn between the existing *voluntary* restraints upon the press symbolised by the self-regulation of the Press Complaints Commission and any more exacting forms of press regulation which may be imposed by Parliament in future. At the time of writing, the consensus of political opinion in all parties appears to be a sense of caution towards any compulsory system of press controls. Consequently, it seems unlikely that the Government will introduce new legislation specifically and significantly to curtail press freedom, which is what any new law to protect privacy would inevitably entail. Furthermore, the few leading figures in the Fourth Estate who have expressed some sneaking sympathy with the view that excesses by parts of the media have made statutory regulation more likely, have also made the point that it would be easier to countenance new statutory controls if there were already in the background a codified constitution containing fundamental safeguards for freedom of expression (such as the First Amendment to the American constitution) and legislation guaranteeing freedom of information, which is now promised by the Labour Government.

Secrecy and censorship

Another important characteristic of the British press is that it has been more inhibited than in most other Western countries by the traditional secrecy of British Government and the restrictive attitudes in Whitehall towards the unauthorised disclosure of official information. Such secretive habits were established years ago and have persisted at least since the 1911 Official Secrets Act which in Section 2 was meant to deter public servants (including Ministers) from communicating and journalists or others from receiving any official information whose disclosure had not been authorised, that is to say deliberately released by Ministers or by senior civil servants acting on their behalf. There has been, of course, a certain Alice in Wonderland quality about this aspect of the law which for years allowed Ministers to authorise their own indiscretions (if it suited their political purposes), but which equally allowed the system to come down like a ton of bricks on any unfortunate participant in the Whitehall or Westminster game caught disseminating or receiving information that Ministers wished to be kept secret. Over the years the effect of this legislation was to discredit the whole idea of official secrecy in Britain without removing the need for occasional, often farcical prosecutions. This bred an understandably cynical response among all journalists and even some public servants.

Thus there was a widespread welcome when the then Conservative Government introduced a new Official Secrets Bill in November 1988.[14] This was designed to remove the 'catch-all' provisions in Section 2 of the 1911 Act and replace them with provisions which restrict the application of the criminal law to specific categories of official information – such as defence, security and intelligence, international relations, law and order, and the interception of communications (phone tapping or letter opening). However, it has since become perfectly obvious that the effect of the new law upon the press and the rest of the media is actually more restrictive, although less capricious, than the discredited law which it replaced. It is therefore hard to argue that much, if anything, has been gained for the cause of journalistic freedom.

The same cautious and restrictive attitudes which have inhibited freedom of the press, are evident in the so-called 'D Notice' system which is designed to prevent publication in the press or broadcasting in the electronic media of sensitive defence information by the simple expedient of issuing a private written warning from an official committee consisting of officials and journalists together. While these obscure arrangements have certainly been successful over the years in achieving a degree of self-censorship among those journalists who cover defence and security issues, the opaque nature of the restrictive arrangements and the unpredictability of intervention by the D Notice Committee have bred further cynicism among those most directly affected.

Similarly restrictive attitudes are reflected in the libel and copyright laws in Britain, which have also had the effect of inhibiting aggressive and fearless reporting, especially when the subject under journalistic investigation is an individual or a company which has the wealth and self-confidence to use the law to the full. These laws confer extensive powers of prior restraint and hence effective censorship upon those who wish to prevent publication or broadcasting of anything which their lawyers advise may be libellous or defamatory, by the simple expedient of obtaining a High Court injunction to stop it. They also permit wealthy or determined individuals to go to Court to obtain 'justice' in libel cases and, if successful in their suits, to secure from juries orders for damages which have been known to reach half a million pounds or more.[15] While there is an obvious need for people to be able to protect themselves from libel or defamation in the media, or even intolerable invasion of privacy as discussed above, it is generally unsatisfactory that only the rich, the powerful and the well-connected seem able to avail themselves of the protection of the law in this way, while the rest of the population is neither adequately protected from journalistic excesses nor sufficiently compensated by journalistic vigilance for the public good.

Freedom of information

Concerted attempts have been made over the years to deal with the problems of secrecy and censorship which affect the British press and other media by introducing proposals designed to promote freedom of information and by pursuing a vigorous pressure group campaign towards this end. In 1978 a report by 'Justice', the British Section of the International Commission of Jurists, recommended a Code of Practice on the disclosure of official information for all Government Departments and other public bodies to be supervised by the Parliamentary Commissioner for Administration (the Ombudsman).[16] At about the same time a Liberal MP, Clement Freud, introduced a Private Member's Bill designed to legislate for freedom of information along the lines of detailed proposals made a year or so earlier by the Outer Circle Policy Unit.[17] Since that time other back-benchers in all parties have tried to introduce legislation along similar lines and in limited areas (for example, environmental information) they have been successful. Yet no all-encompassing Freedom of Information Bill has reached the statute book in Britain, although the Labour Government announced that a draft Freedom of Information Bill would be given pre-legislative scrutiny during the 1998–99 session, with a view to legislating during the 1999–2000 Session.

Those who have favoured reforming the law have wanted to do so in such a way that a public right of access to official information would be enshrined in statute law and the onus put on public authorities to satisfy the Courts of any justification for non-disclosure. This principle is the reverse of that contained in existing legislation, which holds that all classified information should remain restricted unless its release has been specifically authorised either by a Minister or by a Court. The reformers have also wanted to give British citizens the right to see their personal files and to establish a reliable register of all official files, except those which involve the security of the state. They have favoured the establishment of some form of appeals procedure against refusal to supply official information and the introduction of a judicial remedy for aggrieved citizens in cases of proven non-compliance with the law. Only certain categories of information – including some defence and security material, information involving commercial confidentiality, and information which must be safeguarded for reasons of privacy – would be exempt from the provisions of such legislation.

Apart from the traditional unwillingness of most Ministers and civil servants to respond positively to such proposals, the main argument used against them was the alleged extra cost to public funds needed to apply such legislation. It was also pointed out that in those countries where such legislation has been implemented – for example, Sweden and the United States – the actual experience has been that pressure groups and commercial interests have made much greater use of it than individual citizens. At bottom, the idea has provoked the fundamental antipathy of Ministers, civil servants and most other public officials in Britain towards the disclosure of any official information other than that which is unavoidably forced upon them (for example, in public inquiries), or whose release is believed by Ministers to be advantageous to the Government's cause.

Nonetheless, the Labour Government which was swept into power in 1997 was pledged to introduce Freedom of Information legislation, and in December 1997 published a White Paper – entitled 'Your Right to Know' – on the subject. The Minister responsible stated that the statutory right of access offered by the proposals would 'transform the culture of Government and make it more open and accountable'.[18] Maurice Frankel, Director of the Campaign for Freedom of Information, observed that 'the White Paper goes further than we had thought any British Government would be willing to go'.[19] In short, the Government proposed to give the public a statutory right of access to official records and information, not only from Government departments and local authorities, organisations such as the National Health Service and bodies like the Atomic Energy Authority, but also from privatised utilities. There were to be certain bodies excluded, such as the Intelligence Services, and a number of areas protected, such as national security, personal privacy and commercial confidentiality. In addition, it was proposed that an Information Commissioner be appointed to adjudicate and enforce rights of access and that a new criminal offence be introduced for wilful or reckless destruction, alteration or withholding of records from the Commissioner.

The extent to which the proposals outlined in the White Paper will be enacted into the law of the land only time will tell. Suffice it to say that the longer the delay, the greater the likelihood that the proposals will be watered down. It is, however, expected that draft proposals will be outlined during the 1998–99 Session and that legislation will be introduced during the 1999–2000 Session, with the resulting measures coming into effect in 2000/1.

The role of the Lobby

A paradoxical aspect of the position of the press in Britain is that, whereas there is so much emphasis on secrecy and censorship in the formal and legal arrangements, in practice a great deal of information is made available to the press and electronic media on what are called 'Lobby terms'.[20] This practice involves supplying accredited Lobby journalists (that is, those entitled to frequent the Members' Lobby and other restricted parts of the Palace of Westminster) with privileged and unattributable information and comment on the strict understanding that there is no disclosure of sources or direct attribution of comments. The practice has spread beyond the precincts of the Palace of Westminster to every part of Whitehall, so that every Department (and especially

10 Downing Street) has contacts with certain journalists who are the privileged recipients of official information and guidance which is regularly given to them. Indeed, most Ministers and even some officials see it as an important part of their jobs to keep at least a few journalists well informed of what is happening or about to happen in their areas of responsibility. Equally, the journalists concerned find it convenient to take advantage of this form of news management by Government and by Parliament, since it ensures a steady flow of news, gossip and opinion.

This Lobby system has advantages for both the providers and the recipients of such privileged information. For Ministers and officials it can be an effective way of defusing potentially difficult issues through judicious and timely leaks, so that when the information is formally released, much of its adverse publicity impact has been removed. A good example of this technique would be the early leaking of rising unemployment figures or an early indication of bad trade figures, so that the markets do not respond adversely when the figures are formally released. The system is also used to fly kites for new policy initiatives in order to get some idea of how they might be received by the media and the public. Occasionally it is used to pursue in the media policy arguments or personality conflicts which are taking place behind closed doors in Whitehall or Westminster. For example, the Press Office at 10 Downing Street was known to guide journalists towards taking an unfavourable view of Ministers who had incurred Margaret Thatcher's personal displeasure and senior Ministers or their political aides are widely believed to brief the media against each other in Tony Blair's Labour Government.[21]

It is a moot point whether the use of Lobby techniques and indeed the entire Lobby system are really desirable. Some national newspapers have challenged it. For example, the *Independent* and the *Guardian* boycotted the unattributable briefings at 10 Downing Street for a period in the late 1980s and early 1990s, but still kept their Lobby correspondents and made use of information gathered on 'Lobby terms'. Yet the vast majority of political journalists have been prepared to play the game, since it can help them to get a good story and occasionally to increase the circulation of their newspapers. The attractions for politicians are more obvious unless and until the shroud of anonymity is lifted to the embarrassment of those who have been too indiscreet in the past.

7.3 The problems of the electronic media

The problems of the electronic media are both technological and ideological. They are technological in the sense that there are a number of developments in train which, even if Government and Parliament were to take no action, would significantly affect the media environment now and in the future. For example, the technologies of television and telecommunications are fast converging, so that by one means or another the limitations traditionally imposed by broadcasting spectrum scarcity are likely to be overcome or by-passed. This means that a wider range of programmes and services will be made available locally, nationally and internationally; and these services are likely to have improved sound and visual quality. It also means that the range of programme content could be widened as the technology of encryption enables direct payment by subscription to register customer choice in a cost-effective way.

Perhaps most significant of all, with the spread of cable, satellite and digital television and the growth of global media companies, national media frontiers are becoming porous and may even disappear with uncertain consequences for public taste, national culture and regulatory arrangements. Eloquent concern has already been expressed in many quarters about the need to safeguard quality, to prevent excessive concentration of ownership and to work out new regulatory arrangements, increasingly at international level, to match the global reach of the new technologies and the global structure of the largest media companies. So far at least, the global media companies seem to be winning.

The problems are ideological in the sense that the previous Conservative Government in Britain seemed convinced that 'the growth of [media] choice means that a rigid regulatory structure neither can nor should be perpetuated'.[22] As far as the Labour Government which came into office in 1997 was concerned, it became apparent that it shared its predecessor's approach in this regard. This almost *laissez-faire* attitude is in stark contrast to that of the French or Chinese Governments which have been taking both administrative and legislative action to safeguard their respective national cultures against what they see as undesirable external influences upon their societies projected by the global (usually Anglo-Saxon) media. In most cases the approach of recent British Governments has been one consistent with an overall policy of de-regulation, although it has equally asserted that 'rules will still be needed to safeguard programme standards on such matters as good taste and decency, and to ensure that the unique power of the broadcast media is not abused'.[23] Both the quotations just given are drawn from a single paragraph in the 1988 Broadcasting White Paper and reveal the tensions, not to say contradictions, which have existed – indeed, still exist – in Government policy between the urge to liberalise and the attempt to regulate, however difficult the latter may prove to be in such a rapidly changing, market-led and technologically driven sector.

Much of the policy set out in 1988 has been overtaken by events, notably by the fact that terrestrial broadcasting is being challenged and in some cases overtaken by new satellite, cable and digital technologies. The last Government appeared to believe that the circle could be squared by having both less regulation and better regulation – the latter being defined as 'lighter, more flexible, more efficiently administered' regulation. It remains to be seen whether this synthesis of opposites will be effective in practice. Much will depend on how well the Department for Culture, Media and Sport (the Department with the regulatory responsibilities for the media in Britain) manages to resist the pressures from elsewhere in Whitehall (notably the Treasury and the Department of Trade and Industry) for a market-driven response to developments in the media. Still more will depend on actual technological developments in the global marketplace which are likely to render ineffective, even obsolete, any national regulations or conscious efforts by Governments to steer media outcomes.

The power of television

The power of television has affected many aspects of British life and in the political sphere notably the style and nature of political debate. As Anthony Smith has observed, television has become a well from which society draws many of its common allusions (illusions?) and an important source of social reference points.[24] This means that, in considering the power of television, we need to look not so much at its impact on voting behaviour (which until recent times appears to have been minimal) as its capacity to influence the way in which the political debate is conducted both between elections and during election campaigns.

In essence, political issues are often treated as if they were simply another form of public entertainment and politics as a rather esoteric spectator sport. This has encouraged the tendency for politicians to perform before the people rather than reason with them. The respectable argument for this practice is that it serves to grab and hold the attention of what might otherwise be an uninterested and cynical viewing public. Yet while it may produce a greater public awareness of some political issues, it does not necessarily raise the level of public understanding and may even produce a bias against it.[25]

In so far as television has had a discernible effect on political allegiance in Britain, it seems to have been one of reinforcement rather than conversion, although the early studies on this subject seemed also to suggest that the direct effects on voting behaviour were rather slight either way. For example, Trenaman and McQuail in their pioneering study of the 1959 General Election (the first televised campaign in Britain) showed that the main effect of television was simply to increase the store of information and opinion available to the electorate.[26] In a follow-up study of the 1964 General Election, Blumler and McQuail showed that the only other discernible effect was to boost slightly the popularity of the Liberal Party by giving it an abnormal degree of media exposure.[27] In 1981 television coverage of the newly formed Social Democratic Party seemed to have a similar, but temporary effect which assisted it in early by-elections. However, with the notable increase in voter volatility since the mid-1970s, it seems plausible that the impact of television on elections has become greater than it was when the conventional wisdom on this matter was established.

Nowadays saturation coverage characterises the portrayal of General Election campaigns on television and it seems that the British public may have had enough of it. For example, during the 1987 campaign Gallup polls discovered that 69 per cent of its samples expected there to be too much political coverage on television (getting in the way of or displacing their favourite regular programmes), while another opinion poll discovered that 27 per cent thought there should be no election coverage at all![28] Certainly the widely held opinion among the psephological experts was that Labour had 'won' the media battle against the Conservatives hands down, but this did not seem to make any difference to the level of support for Labour which was the same on polling day as it had been at the beginning of the campaign. After the 1992 General Election the standard view of the experts was that while television coverage may have shaped the rhythm and pattern of the campaign, it had much less influence on the final outcome; except that in as much as the campaign had a presidential quality, the Conservatives clearly 'won' with John Major much more credible in the role of Prime Minister than Neil Kinnock could ever be.[29] Similarly, during the 1997 General Election campaign, although television coverage was more voluminous, substantial and detailed than ever before, this is not to say that it was at all decisive. Indeed, television's most important contribution to the election arguably lay rather more in its day-to-day coverage during the months and years leading up to the campaign proper – coverage of 'Black Wednesday', Europe and the divisions in the Conservative Party, the issue of sleaze, and the transformation of the Labour Party under Tony Blair into

'New Labour', events which all became firmly embedded in the consciousness of the voting public. In fact it has been suggested that the news coverage during the campaign itself was more negative than in previous campaigns and that, consequently, many voters may have been turned off by it.[30]

One of the most significant effects of television on British politics has been manifest in the style and methods of political argument and election campaigning. Since the 1964 General Election campaign, the parties have held daily press conferences each morning during the formal campaign period. This development, amplified by the nightly news bulletins on BBC and ITN, has had the effect of focusing public attention on the party leaders and a few of their most senior colleagues. The emphasis on a presidential style of campaigning has been increased by the presence of a veritable media circus with the party leaders as they go on tour around the country. All of this has diminished the role and importance of most Parliamentary candidates, except in very marginal seats or in rather special circumstances – such as in Tatton in 1997 – or at highly publicised by-elections. It has also diminished still further the value of public meetings as a form of political campaigning, although again there are partial exceptions to this rule in some rural constituencies with small cohesive communities and at significant by-elections.

Equally significant in its effect on British politics has been the tendency for television to personalise, trivialise and sensationalise nearly every political issue. It does this almost unconsciously in that programme producers will tend to prefer staging interviews with the party leaders rather than with other lesser political figures. Indeed, the producers cannot really be more high-minded or restrained than this, since they are in competition with the tabloid press and other parts of the media which are inclined to be sensational in their treatment of all issues. Banner headlines which scream messages such as 'Major on the ropes' or 'Blair miles ahead', set a vivid standard with which television feels obliged to compete. Furthermore, it is thought appropriate to translate the antagonistic conventions of the House of Commons into the television and radio studios, and leading television interviewers, such as Jeremy Paxman or John Humphrys, regard their clashes with the Party Leaders as a central part of the political ritual in modern politics.

Influence, bias and agenda setting

Just as some on the Left of British politics have been concerned about anti-Labour bias in the national press, so others in all parties have maintained that television is far from being a neutral medium of mass communication. According to this argument, the political effect of television is no longer simply to reinforce existing values and preferences in society, but actually *to set the agenda* of political discussion. Public faith in the impartiality of television news is said to be misplaced on the grounds that true objectivity can never be achieved by those who produce and edit the programmes. The Glasgow Media Group, in particular, has argued that the news is not really 'the news', but an arbitrary selection and presentation of certain information and opinion according to the undeclared criteria and preferences of those who produce and present the programmes.[31] It is interesting that these Left-wing academics are not alone in their suspicion of television decision-makers, but are joined in such feelings by a whole swathe of Right-wing political opinion which is equally convinced that the programme-makers in general and the BBC in particular are out to do them down by innuendo and any other methods which come to hand.

If there really is such a media conspiracy against the politicians, it is worth noting that the sense of paranoia is experienced by Left and Right alike. The counter-argument, which has been put by Martin Harrison and Alastair Hetherington, is essentially that political bias on television is in the eye of the viewer, just as on radio it is in the ear of the listener.[32] Such sceptics have pointed out that everything really depends on the broadcast material selected for analysis and that in the case of the Glasgow Media Group the academics concerned were essentially displaying their own prejudices. Equally, there are many on the Conservative side of the argument who believe that they had cause to complain about the iconoclastic and even subversive nature of some television programmes. For example, the BBC *Panorama* programme 'Real Lives', which was screened in 1986, purported to equate the life and motivation of an acknowledged IRA terrorist with that of an Ulster loyalist, thus leaving the viewers with the clear impression that the one was morally indistinguishable from the other. Similarly, the *This Week* programme 'Death on the Rock' analysed the way in which three suspected IRA terrorists were killed on a street in Gibraltar in broad daylight by members of the Special Air Service (SAS) and conducted its analysis in such a provocative and controversial way that there was a considerable political row followed by a highly controversial coroner's inquest.

During the period 1992–97 Conservative politicians certainly felt persecuted by the media and convinced that the real agenda of some newspaper editors and programme makers was to topple John Major, if not to bring about the defeat of the Conservatives at the ensuing General Election. In most cases leading media people reply to such political charges by arguing either that they are simply holding up a mirror to some politically uncomfortable reality or merely pursuing their vocation as investigative journalists or both. In the final analysis most political reporting and editorialising is a matter of taste and judgement rather than right or wrong – unless, of course, there is a well-founded suspicion that the law may have been broken. In most cases discipline is imposed by the professionalism of the media people themselves and only in the last resort by the Courts. An example of this 'last resort' occurred in March 1995 when the BBC was forced to abandon plans to screen in Scotland – three days before Local Elections – a *Panorama* interview with John Major after this was challenged in the Courts by both the Labour and Liberal Democrat parties and a judge ruled that the programme breached the strict impartiality rules governing the BBC.

The power of radio

Radio is also a powerful medium which has its effect on both politics and society in Britain. The programmes broadcast by the BBC on its five national channels serve to entertain, inform and educate the public. Taken together they seek to offer a balanced media output, but one which has moved some distance from the original Reithian objectives for the BBC which were to keep a broadly *equal* balance between entertainment, information and education.

The expansion of local radio since the late 1960s has also left its mark upon the development of British popular culture and indeed on British society as a whole. The BBC now has a total of 43 local radio stations including 38 serving England and the

Channel Islands, and 'national' stations covering Scotland, Wales and Northern Ireland, including Welsh and Gaelic language stations. However, the BBC's efforts in local radio are now dwarfed by the 200 or so commercial radio stations which cover virtually every locality in the United Kingdom.

This explosion of local radio in all parts of the country has given a real boost to local consciousness and some of the more colourful local personalities (political and otherwise) have thrived in the new atmosphere which has been created. Apart from heavy doses of popular music and other forms of popular entertainment, the stations tend to broadcast a large number of chat shows, quiz games and phone-in programmes which provide opportunities for members of the public to air their views and prejudices, while politicians and other public figures have extra opportunities to demonstrate their activity and concern. Thus local radio has undoubtedly contributed to the vitality of British life and often it provides the most vivid forum for local political debate. Yet the real reason for the expansion has been the opportunity for commercial profit.

In the future, radio in Britain will have further opportunities for development and expansion. The commercial sector will benefit from the lighter regulatory regime of the Radio Authority, while the BBC will continue to be responsible for public service broadcasting. There will be less spectrum scarcity and more wave-lengths available for new services, including community and special interest radio stations. All of this means that there will be more opportunities for media entrepreneurs to make money out of commercial radio, more competition for the BBC which may feel obliged to dilute its commitment to the public service ethos in order to retain a significant share of a much larger total radio audience, and new opportunities for pressure and cause groups to peddle their ideas (as happens now in the United States with the so-called media evangelists) in a more pluralist and less regulated media environment. Many of these developments may affect the nature of British politics; all of them will affect the quality of life in Britain.

The impact of new technologies

It is already clear that new technologies have had and will continue to have a very significant impact upon the development of the media in Britain. The availability of more radio frequencies, as well as the growth of satellite, cable and digital transmission of television, will make many more services technically possible whether for a local, national or supranational audience. The main constraint on the pace and scale of these developments is likely to be the ability to make them commercially viable within a reasonable period rather than any serious doubts about their technical feasibility or their political acceptability.

If everything goes well and the new technologies are developed along the benign lines foreseen by their most enthusiastic proponents, we could see the development of a society which was described by a former Minister for Information Technology as 'better informed ... more relaxed, less formal, more mobile, less enamoured with structure, more skilled, less ridden with class and social differences, and full of scope for more individuality'.[33] Yet if things go differently and the new technologies are developed overwhelmingly for short-term commercial gain and subsequently perhaps for manipulative purposes either by powerful media corporations or by public authorities at a national or supranational level, then individual freedom could be eroded, social variety could be stifled and totalitarian tendencies could spread.

The traditional distinction between television and telecommunications is becoming increasingly blurred and may even be eliminated altogether by technological developments. This has meant that there is a larger range of home-based educational opportunities available than ever before, new opportunities for teleworking and buying and selling directly from home, and a variety of new consumer services such as electronic mail, Internet and telebanking on offer. The progressive introduction of pay-as-you-view television programmes[34] will increasingly limit universal public access to programmes which hitherto have been virtually free goods provided to every household with a television set, assuming only the payment of a very cost-effective licence fee. Members of the public are likely to resent having to pay explicitly for mass audience programmes which previously they were able to enjoy 'free' at the time of screening (for example, great sporting events[35]) and even those with minority interests and enthusiasms (for example, opera, ballet or vintage cars) may prefer going to real events or perhaps buying or renting videotapes of the same rather than paying quite substantial subscriptions in order to be able to watch encrypted, live programmes.

It is too soon to tell what will be the full consequences of these new media technologies upon British society and British politics. Taking a favourable view, it is possible to foresee a future in which a more open and competitive media market can be achieved which will give both viewers and listeners greater choice and greater influence without detriment to the range or quality of the services provided. Taking an unfavourable view, these developments could lead to a waste of scarce resources, the erosion of social diversity and significant damage to the popular culture.

The decision to encourage the development of cable technology in Britain can now be seen to have been of considerable significance.[36] Initially the market for cable services and systems did not expand as rapidly as the then Conservative Government had expected. This led the Labour Party to commit itself to the promotion of cable technology on a much more ambitious scale so as to achieve a national fibre-optic communications network (an 'information super highway').[37] As the British economy recovered from the long recession of the early 1990s, the commercial prospects for cable services improved dramatically. With more and more households willing to pay for cable television and related services, the result was that many (including foreign owned) companies entered the market.

The growth of Direct Broadcasting by Satellite (DBS) has also been impressive after a shaky start during the early years of commercial operation in Britain. In recognition of the high initial development costs of satellite technology, the 1984 Cable and Broadcasting Act provided for the companies concerned a 15-year contract period rather than the 8-year franchises awarded to the cable companies. This apart, the general approach of Government has been that the market should determine how far and how fast satellite television develops in Britain. Considerable investment has already been made in this technology in Britain and elsewhere in Europe, which underlines the point that the regulatory arrangements – like the technology – are likely to be further developed on an international or even supranational level.

At present the Independent Television Commission (ITC) is responsible for licensing and regulating commercial television services – including cable and satellite services – operating in or from Britain. Regulation is exercised by various codes, namely on programme content, advertising, sponsorship and on technical standards. Under the European Community Broadcasting Directive (1997) and the Council of Europe Convention on Transfrontier Television, both of which Britain has implemented, participating countries are obliged to allow the retransmission of programmes originating from other participating countries and must ensure that their own programmes abide by certain minimum standards as far as both advertising and sponsorship are concerned as well as content with regard to taste and decency – especially as far as sex and violence are concerned. Within Britain the Broadcasting Standards Commission (BSC), established in 1997, has its own code on the portrayal of violence and sexual conduct and on standards of fairness, taste and decency. They monitor and report on what the broadcasters are doing in these regards and issue guidance which is usually followed.

It is clear that the extensive commercial development of modern technology has had and will continue to have far-reaching implications for traditional ideas of national sovereignty and cultural identity. The British people have already begun to experience the invasive consequences of 'junk' or 'tabloid' television often – and sometimes unfairly – associated with programmes made in or inspired by the United States. Such problems could be even more serious for other Governments, especially in fragile or rootless societies. In the global media village more and more programmes are likely to be standardised and monoglot, purveying mid-Atlantic mediocrity designed to appeal to the lowest common denominator. The possible implications for the quality of life in Britain and other countries are potentially very disturbing.

7.4 The media and politics

There is no doubt that the media have come to play an increasingly important part in the British political system over the last 40 years or so. The journalists, editors, presenters and producers no longer carry conviction if they claim that all they are doing is to reflect what is happening in British politics and society. Indeed, the more thoughtful members of the media professions readily acknowledge their ability to influence the agenda of politics and recognise the tensions which media priorities can create between them and the politicians.

There are really five main points which need to be made about the role of the media in modern British politics. *First*, it is argued by politicians and others in the public eye that the media, and especially television, give a distorted impression of politics and the political world, since bad news is nearly always given precedence over good news, disunity over unity, gossip and speculation over solid reporting and analysis. These media tendencies are usually more noticeable in the tabloid press and television, but even the so-called quality media are not above a little distortion or oversimplification when it suits them. The usual explanation is that the imperatives of the market and the need to compete for fickle public attention require the media to behave in this way. Whether sincerely given or not, it seems that these explanations will become even more valid as the liberalisation of the media market proceeds still further.

As we noted earlier in this chapter, such media distortions can take the form of perceived bias in the reporting of the activities and policies of the political parties.

More often, however, the distortion is of a different kind, namely the tendency to per-sonalise and sensationalise complicated political issues for the sake of gaining and retaining the attentions of the public. This was evident, for example, in the tendency of the media to portray the Thatcher Government in presidential terms and to overem-phasise the gladiatorial nature of the conflict between the two main parties. It was also evident in the sustained campaign in many parts of the media between 1992 and 1997 to denigrate John Major and to try to force him out of office by presenting his prag-matic approach to politics as the absence of leadership. Of course, the media profes-sionals will reply that this sort of presentation merely reflects political realities, equates with the importance attached to leadership by members of each main party, and was borne out by the views of the public as expressed in the 1997 General Election. While there is some force in all these pleas in mitigation, it remains an observable fact that a great deal of the media coverage of British politics has oscillated between occasional sycophancy and frequent character assassination, with the empha-sis increasingly on the latter.

Secondly, it is argued by political scientists and others that the media have an unrivalled capacity to set the agenda of politics – often in co-operation, it must be said, with energetic campaigning groups. In one sense this is a more weighty point than the first, since it emphasises what can be one of the most constructive roles played by the media in the British political system. The positive result of this can be that public attention is drawn to new or difficult issues which might not otherwise receive the attention which they deserve from the political parties or established sec-tional interests. Two examples of issues which have been dramatised by the media in this way are the environmental issues of 'green' politics and the wide range of issues which go under the heading of consumer politics. Clearly, if the Fourth Estate is doing its proper job in areas of this kind, it is likely to warn the public of impending prob-lems and probe beneath the surface of events in attempts to reveal what is really happening.

Probably the main reason why some people are made uneasy by this aspect of the media is that they may hold the rather old-fashioned view that political parties should be the sole – or at least the principal – organisations with the right to initiate new policies. In reality there is bound to be considerable interplay between the politicians and the media in the process of political agenda-setting, as we shall see in more detail in Chapter 19. This is not because politicians are bereft of new ideas, but rather because (for those in opposition or on the back-benches) the process of Government policy making is typically opaque and exclusive.

Thirdly, whenever the party in power at Westminster has a comfortable majority in the House of Commons, those in the media can be tempted to take the view that they have a duty to provide effective opposition – certainly effective scrutiny, espe-cially if the politicians on the Opposition benches appear temporarily unwilling or unable to do so. Such a view was widely held in media circles during most of the 1980s when the Conservatives had large majorities in the House of Commons and the Labour Party seemed preoccupied with trying to sort out its own problems. In such circumstances there was a real temptation for those in the media to try to fill the gap left by an ineffective and demoralised Opposition. Certainly this was how the situation was seen at the time by many Conservative politicians. A similar situation arose following the 1997 General Election, except that on this occasion it was the Labour Party which had a large majority in the House of Commons and the Conservatives who were ineffective and demoralised in Opposition. After an initial 'honeymoon' period elements within the media certainly appeared to believe that it was their duty to provide if not effective Opposition then certainly effective questioning and scrutiny.

Of course, all Governments, when they become deeply unpopular, are tempted to conclude that the media are to blame for their difficulties. This was very evident during the time of the second Wilson Administration (1966–70), especially following the mortal blow to Labour's prestige inflicted by the 1967 devaluation of Sterling – the second time such a thing had happened to a Labour Government since the Second World War. Such attitudes of persecution and paranoia were equally evident during John Major's period at 10 Downing Street, especially following 'Black Wednesday' on 16 September 1992 when Sterling was forced out of the European Exchange Rate Mechanism and subsequently devalued by 15 per cent. On the other hand, leading figures in the media have had cause from time to time to resent Government attempts at political spin and message-projection – attempts in short to manage the news or manipulate the media for party political purposes. While there can be no final or definitive assessment of this controversy, most neutral observers would probably agree that it is not healthy for a Parliamentary democracy if the media became effectively the real Opposition to the Government of the day.

Fourthly, it is argued by some of a traditional disposition that the media in Britain and other modern societies can have a deleterious effect upon the quality of life by producing various forms of cultural pollution. This fear is felt particularly in relation to the possible effects of weakening the regulatory framework within which the media operate and it is reinforced by the evidence of lower cultural standards associated with the tabloid press and equivalent television.

It was clear from the 1988 Broadcasting White Paper and subsequent statements made by Ministers that the Home Office (at the time the responsible Department) fought a strong rearguard action against the liberalising instincts of 10 Downing Street and the Department of Trade and Industry. Yet the outcome, so far as commercial television was concerned, was clearly favourable to the free play of market forces. As the *Financial Times* observed in a critical editorial not long afterwards, 'British broadcasting faces a future in which bottom line considerations will increasingly dictate the contents of programmes'.[38] Set against this, Channel 4 was shielded to some extent from the full force of commercial competition, and the traditional financial framework of the BBC (based on the annual licence fee) was subsequently safeguarded until at least 2002.[39]

Notwithstanding these few reassurances for the traditionalists, there remains a real fear in some quarters that the quality of British broadcasting may deteriorate during the transition from the former paternalistic duopoly of the BBC and ITV to a much more open free market constrained by only the lightest regulation. Even the Peacock Committee, whose work provided much of the stimulus for the 1988 White Paper, had emphasised the importance of achieving an appropriate balance between taxation, advertising revenue and viewer subscriptions when constructing a sound financial base for British broadcasting in the future. Yet in spite of this advice, Conservative Ministers at the time approved a future for British broadcasting which has in many respects put the new media entrepreneurs very much in the driving seat. Worries are therefore likely to remain that the few remaining islands of real broadcasting quality – such as Radio 3, BBC2 and Channel 4 – may not survive very long in a sea of mass media mediocrity.

Fifthly, strong concern has been expressed in many quarters that heavy concentrations of media ownership could develop unless effective rules are laid down and enforced to prevent such outcomes. In 1989 the then Home Secretary, Douglas Hurd, made it clear to the House of Commons that 'we should regard it as quite unacceptable if British broadcasting were allowed to be dominated by a handful of tycoons or international conglomerates'.[40] The Government therefore promised effective rules to safeguard diversity of ownership and editorial stance, and Ministers made it clear that excessive cross-media holdings would be prevented. Specifically, it was laid down in subordinate legislation that no single media group would be allowed to own two large television or radio franchises and that no British national newspaper group would be allowed to have more than a 20 per cent stake in any satellite company, terrestrial television or radio franchise.[41]

However, a Government review of ownership regulation in 1995 concluded that the rules needed to be relaxed, both within and across different media sectors, and that this would reflect both the needs and the aspirations of the industry allowing British media companies to grow and compete more effectively in the international market and to do so against the background of accelerating technological change. As a result the Broadcasting Act of 1996 scrapped restrictions that limited independent television companies to owning two ITV licenses, replacing it instead by a limit of up to 15 per cent of the total audience, and permitted newspaper groups to control ITV companies for the first time, subject to a 'public interest' criteria.

However, few knowledgeable observers have been convinced that it will be easy to ensure high quality and diversity of ownership once the free play of market forces takes full effect. Apart from other considerations, it is difficult to argue that regulations should be strictly imposed at a national level in Britain when many of the new technologies can only effectively be regulated at a Continental or even a global level. In many ways the idea of national media could become as obsolete as the idea of national Capitalism, and if so we shall all have to adjust our traditional assumptions.

In short, in considering the evolving relationship between the media and politics, a great deal depends on the mixture of interest, temperament and ideology which prevails at any time. In the 1980s and 1990s Conservative Ministers argued that by giving more power of choice to readers, listeners and viewers, it is possible to engender greater diversity and commercial opportunity without sacrificing quality. Their critics and others of a sceptical disposition have maintained that there is a real danger of the dynamics of fierce commercial competition reducing real consumer choice and diminishing quality. Only time will tell which side of the argument is proved right. It could be that in Britain and other countries we are witnessing an explosion of consumer choice and commercial opportunity, but it could equally be that the Philistines are at the gates.

7.5 Conclusion

We have seen in this chapter how the power of the media in Britain is in one sense greater, but in another sense not so great as it was in previous times – for example, during the heyday of the press barons, Rothermere, Northcliffe and Beaverbrook, in the early part of this century. Today television in particular has a strong influence on the context and style of British politics, especially during election campaigns. On the other hand, the media do not entirely determine public opinion and they cannot really topple Governments as, it might be argued, they were able to do on certain occasions in the mid-nineteenth century.

Certainly television has an unsettling and pervasive influence on the British political system. For most politicians it has acted like a lamp to moths with the result that they have often seemed fatally attracted to its light. In many ways radio and television studios have replaced the Chamber of the House of Commons as the principal battle-ground of British politics. This would not matter very much if it were not for the fact that in the minds of the general public television in particular has gained an aura of impartiality and authority not enjoyed to anything like the same extent by the other forms of media. Thus the power, and the responsibility, of television with its ability to influence the political agenda is now an important factor in any modern democracy.

On the positive side of the argument, it is worth underlining the fact that television has provided greatly increased scope for communication between opinion formers and decision makers on the one hand and the general public on the other. This is definitely a plus factor in a less deferential and more participatory democracy. Yet even this advantage of the modern media may prove a disappointment if the rapid exploitation of the new commercial opportunities creates more scope for media mediocrity. The existing tendencies towards bias, triviality and sensationalism seem unlikely to disappear, since they are not even generally acknowledged by most of those who work in the media. In these circumstances the onus of proof is on the leading lights of the media to demonstrate that these concerns can be allayed and that the new technologies and commercial opportunities can be developed in ways which will enhance the quality of life and the vitality of British democracy.

With these general considerations in mind, it is possible to summarise the overall contribution of the media to the British political system as (1) the encouragement of a greater awareness of political issues among the general public, and (2) the influencing of the political agenda through media choices of the issues and personalities to be dramatised. The latter is especially significant in the context of pressure group politics where so many different and competing interests vie for the attention of politicians and public alike. It also reminds us that political priorities are often influenced not so much by the intrinsic importance of particular issues as by the nature and extent of the coverage given to them by the media.

Of course, the influence of the media extends well beyond the sphere of party politics, since it has a demonstrable effect on the values, assumptions, attitudes and behaviour of millions of individual people. For example, the media have contributed to the mindless materialism of modern society by reinforcing the widely held assumptions that individual status and social progress should be measured principally in terms of the income people receive and the money they spend. They have also influenced public attitudes towards Government and other public agencies by raising expectations that problems exposed or discussed in the media will therefore be swiftly addressed and solved. More positively, the media have raised the level of public awareness and prompted urgent official responses to many of the problems and injustices of the modern world – for example, famine, environmental degradation or assaults on human rights in many parts of the world. They can therefore be a force for good as well as harm.

In short, while the media have undoubtedly made it more difficult for Governments to govern by highlighting the flaws and shortcomings in public policy and the politicians responsible for it, and by encouraging a level of public expectations which no Governments have been able to satisfy; they have also communicated a great deal of useful information and opinion to the general public, and probably raised the levels of public consciousness in certain areas in ways which have been beneficial for democracy. In forming conclusions on their role in Britain or any other comparable country, it is as well to remember that in a free society the media are always more likely to be critics than buttresses of those in power, and it is right that this should be so in a pluralist, liberal democracy.

Suggested questions

1 Describe the changing structure and ethos of the media in Britain.
2 How influential is the British press?
3 In what ways do radio and television influence the practices of British politics?

Notes

1. Figures published in the national press for the week ending 17 May 1998, for example, showed that the most popular programmes on BBC 1 and ITV were the soap operas *East-Enders* and *Coronation Street* with 14.42 million and 16.65 million viewers respectively. On BBC 2 and Channel 4 there was a wider range of programmes with ratings at lower but nonetheless impressive levels of between 3 million and 6 million viewers – for example, *Have I Got News for You* (5.93 million) *Top Gear* (4.14 million) and *The Antiques Show* (4.31 million) on BBC 2 and *Tourist Trap* (4.4 million) and *Countdown* (3.07 million) on Channel 4. The most widely watched programme on Channel 5 was *Buster*, attracting 1.79 million viewers.

2. Among the most famous headlines of recent years have been those which appeared in the *Sun*, such as 'Gotcha' at the time of the sinking of the Argentinian cruiser Belgrano during the 1982 Falklands conflict, and 'Up yours Delors' at the time of maximum conflict between Jacques Delors, President of the European Commission, and the British Conservative Government.

3. See J. Curtice, 'Is the *Sun* shining on Tony Blair? The Electoral Influence of Newspapers in Britain since 1992', *Harvard International Journal of Press and Politics* (Boston, Mass.: Harvard University Press, 1997).

4. The fact that the libel action that he subsequently brought against the *Guardian* and *World in Action* collapsed in June 1997, exposing him as corrupt, and his later – 1999 – plea of

guilt to perjury tended to detract from the argument. Nonetheless, it was and is an argument many would adhere to.

5. Quoted in the *Report of the Calcutt Committee on Privacy and Related Matters* (London: HMSO, 1990).
6. David Calcutt *Report of the Committee on Privacy and Related Matters* (London: HMSO, 1990).
7. See: 'Press Complaints Commission', Report Number 1, January–June 1991 and Report Number 2, July–September 1991.
8. Lord McGregor, Press Complaints Commission statement, *The Times,* 9 June 1992.
9. David Calcutt *Review of Press Self-Regulations* (London: HMSO, 1993).
10. *Privacy and Media Intrusion: The Government's Response* (London: HMSO, 1995).
11. Robin Cook, 1 September 1997; *Independent,* 2 September 1997.
12. Tony Blair, speaking on BBC Television's *Breakfast with Frost,* 7 September 1997.
13. Earl Spencer, Funeral Address, 6 September 1997; *Sunday Times,* 7 September 1997.
14. This later became part of the law of the land as the 1989 Official Secrets Act.
15. For example, in July 1987 Jeffrey Archer (as Lord Archer then was) was awarded £500,000 in damages against the *Star* which had libelled him with allegations about an assignation with a prostitute, and in December 1988 Elton John secured £1 million from the *Sun* in an out-of-Court settlement for an alleged libel.
16. *Freedom of Information* (London: Justice, 1978).
17. *An Official Information Act* (London: Outer Circle Policy Unit, 1977).
18. David Clark, House of Commons, 11 December 1997; *Independent,* 12 December 1997.
19. Maurice Frankel, *Independent,* 12 December 1997.
20. For a fuller discussion of the Lobby system see J. Margach, *The Anatomy of Power* (London: Star, 1981), pp. 125–55.
21. The most obvious example of this was the rivalry – dating back to the 1994 Labour leadership contest – between the Blairites who supported Tony Blair and the Brownites who supported Gordon Brown. Often played out through unauthorised press briefings, it came to a head in late December 1998 with the events surrounding the resignation of Peter Mandelson as Secretary of State for Trade and Industry and resulted in the resignation of Charlie Whelan as Gordon Brown's press secretary early in January 1999.
22. See 'Broadcasting in the Nineties – Competition, Choice and Quality', Cmnd 517, November 1988, para. 2.5.
23. *Ibid.*
24. A. Smith, *The Politics of Information* (London: Macmillan, 1978), p. 5.
25. This point was well made some five years ago by John Birt and Peter Jay writing in *The Times* (28 February, 30 September and 1 October 1975).
26. See J. Trenaman and D. McQuail, *Television and the Political Image* (London: Methuen, 1961).
27. See J.G. Blumler and D. McQuail, *Television in Politics* (London: Faber, 1968).
28. See M. Harrison on broadcasting in D.E. Butler and D. Kavanagh, *The British General Election of 1987* (London: Macmillan, 1988), p. 139.
29. See D.E. Butler and D. Kavanagh, *The British General Election of 1992* (London: Macmillan, 1992), p. 253.
30. See H.A. Semetko, M. Scammell and P. Goddard, *Television,* in P. Norris and M.T. Gavin (eds), *Britain Votes 1997* (Oxford University Press, 1997), pp. 101–7 and M. Harrison on *Politics on the Air* in D.E. Butler and D. Kavanagh *The British General Election of 1997* (London: Macmillan, 1997), pp 133–55.
31. See Glasgow Media Group, *Bad News* (London: Routledge & Kegan Paul, 1981), pp. 12–13.

32. See M. Harrison, 'TV News, Whose Bias?' (Hermitage, Berkshire: Policy Journals, 1985), and A. Hetherington, *News, Newspapers and Television* (London: Macmillan, 1985).
33. Kenneth Baker, 'Towards an Information Economy'; speech to the British Association for the Advancement of Science, 7 September 1982.
34. The first example of this in Britain occurred in March 1996 when Sky asked its subscribers to pay an extra £9.95 to watch Frank Bruno defend his world heavyweight boxing title against Mike Tyson.
35. Indeed, it was as a result of strong public and Parliamentary concern that the Broadcasting Act 1996 prohibited subscription channels from gaining exclusive access to a number of 'listed' sporting events, namely, the FA Cup Final, the Scottish FA Cup Final (in Scotland only), the World Cup Finals, the Derby, the Grand National, the Wimbledon tennis finals weekend, England's home cricket test matches and the Olympic Games. In June 1998 following the recommendations of the Gordon Committee set up to look at the future of listed events, Chris Smith, the Culture, Media and Sport Secretary, announced the creation of an A-List of events – events which had to be made available to terrestrial broadcasters – and a B-List of events – events which could be available for satellite broadcast, provided highlights were made available soon after the event to terrestrial broadcasters. The A-list of events included the Olympic Games, World Cup football, European Football Championships (finals, semi-finals and home nation matches), FA Cup Final, Scottish Cup Final (in Scotland), the Grand National, the Derby, Wimbledon tennis finals, the Rugby World Cup Final and the Rugby League Challenge Cup Final. The B-list of events included England's domestic cricket Test matches and World Cup final, semi-finals and home nation matches, non-finals play at Wimbledon, Five Nations rugby matches involving the home countries and all other matches in the Rugby World Cup tournament, World Athletics Championships, the Commonwealth Games, the Open Golf Championship and the Ryder Cup.
36. See 'The Development of Cable Services and Systems'; Cmnd 8866 (London: HMSO, 1983).
37. The Labour Party – prior to the 1997 General Election – reached an agreement with British Telecom and the cable companies to connect up schools, libraries, colleges and hospitals to the information superhighway, and for them to do so free of charge.
38. *Financial Times*, 14 June 1989.
39. See 'The Future of the BBC'; Cmnd 2621 (London: HMSO, 1994), para. 5.10.
40. *Hansard*, 8 February 1989, col. 1011.
41. In spite of these Government decisions, Ministers in the Thatcher Administration seemed prepared to allow News International to be an exception to the general rule, since the company was permitted to establish Sky Television while retaining its ownership of 37 per cent of the national press in Britain.

Further reading

Crewe, I., Gosschalk, B. and Bartle, J. (eds), *Political Communications* (London: Frank Cass, 1998).

Curran, J. and Seaton, J., *Power without Responsibility*, 3rd edn (London: Routledge, 1991).

Dyer, C., 'Analysis: Privacy' in The *Guardian*, 19 December 1997.

Hargreaves, I., *Sharper Vision* (London: Demos, 1994).

Harris, R., *Good and Faithful Servant* (London: Faber, 1990).

Hetherington A., *News, Newspapers and Television* (London: Macmillan, 1985).

Ingham B., *Kill the Messenger* (London: Fontana, 1991).

Margach, J., *The Anatomy of Power* (London: Star, 1981).

Marr, A., *Ruling Britannia* (London: Michael Joseph, 1995).

Negrine, R., *Politics and the Mass Media in Britain*, 2nd edn (London: Routledge, 1995).

Sampson, A., *The Essential Anatomy of Britain* (London: Hodder & Stoughton, 1992).

Seaton, J. and Pimlott, B., *The Media in British Politics* (Aldershot: Gower, 1987).

Seymour-Ure, C., *The British Press and Broadcasting since 1945* (Oxford: Blackwell, 1991).

Tunstall, J., *Newspaper Power: The New National Press in Britain* (Oxford: Clarendon Press, 1996).

Watts, D., *Political Communication Today* (Manchester: University Press, 1997)

8 Public opinion

The term 'public opinion' has no generally accepted fixed and definite meaning. Certainly the diversity that exists reflects the different views taken at different times by different people, depending upon the society in which they lived and the political outlook which they had. Whereas Jeremy Bentham (1748–1832) defined it as 'a system of law emanating from the body of the people',[1] Robert Peel (1788–1850) defined it as 'that great compound of folly, weakness, prejudice, wrong feeling, right feeling, obstinacy and newspaper paragraphs'.[2] Dean Inge (1860–1954) saw it as 'a vulgar, impertinent, anonymous tyrant',[3] while Oscar Wilde (1854–1900) described it as 'an attempt to organise the ignorance of the community and to elevate it to the dignity of physical force'.[4]

Nicolas Sebastien Chamfort (1741–1794) asked simply 'How many fools does it take to make a public?'[5] and William Hazlitt (1778–1830) observed that 'there is not a more mean, stupid, dastardly, pitiless, selfish, spiteful, envious, ungrateful animal than the public'.[6] A.V. Dicey (1835–1922) declared public opinion to be 'a mere abstraction', and 'not a power which has any independent existence', defining it simply as 'a general term for the beliefs held by a number of human beings',[7] and more particularly as 'the wishes and ideas as to legislation held by the majority of those citizens who have … taken an effective part in public life'.[8] V.O. Key (1908–1963) was perhaps more cynical when he defined it as 'those opinions of private persons which Governments find it prudent to heed'.[9]

In Britain in the nineteenth century public opinion was usually considered to be synonymous with the views of the relatively small number of people who were enfranchised and so able to have effective political influence, at least at election time. Nowadays it is generally accepted that public opinion includes the views and prejudices of all adults, no matter how shallow or fitful or indeed non-existent their involvement in politics.

Broadly speaking, public opinion can be described as what people think ought to be done – or ought not to be done – on a particular issue at a particular time. On those matters which impinge on the concerns, interests or emotions of the public it is likely that enough individuals will react in the same way for their collective private opinions to constitute a manifestation of public opinion. As a result, public opinion can be seen as being the views expressed by an aggregation of individuals. It is a point of view – an opinion – held in common by a number of people – the public – on issues of social, economic or political significance. Thus, for the purposes of this chapter, public opinion is defined as *the sum of opinions held on social, economic and political issues by the entire population*. Having said this, however, there are of course many different components of public opinion which vary from issue to issue and from time to time. As Richard Rose put it, 'there is not a single public with which the Government seeks to communicate; there is a variety of publics distinguishable by their degrees of organisation, their policy preferences and their knowledge or interest in political issues'.[10] The composition of public opinion is therefore more akin to a mosaic than to a well-defined or predictable diagram. It is nevertheless possible to show the flow of public opinion in diagrammatic form, and this is done in Figure 8.1.

Figure 8.1   The flow of public opinion

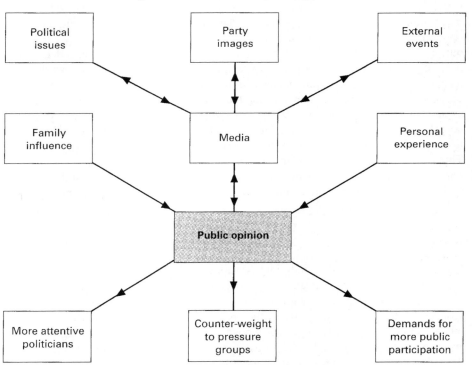

8.1 The formation of opinion

Inheritance and experience

Expert studies have shown that public opinion is formed from a myriad of private opinions, whether personal or group opinions. Such private opinions are often formed quite early in life, usually when people first become aware of political issues. They tend to be derived principally from family influence and personal experience, with the pressures from school, work, friends and neighbours all playing a part.

In the 1960s Butler and Stokes wrote an important book in which they demonstrated the strength of *family influence* as a factor in voting behaviour.[11] Although the growth of electoral volatility from the 1970s indicated that its significance had declined, young people today still derive many of their attitudes and opinions from their parents, and family influence remains one of the more constant factors in the development of every young generation. Of course, there have always been young people who reject the attitudes and opinions of their parents, either as part of a transient adolescent rebellion or as a function of economic and social mobility. Yet on the whole family influence still plays a major part in the formation of opinion.

As for the influence of *personal experience*, it is obvious that this has a significant impact on the formation of individual opinions. Few people form their opinions on political issues on a basis of detached or altruistic ratiocination, since this is a luxury which is usually available only to those whose material circumstances and educational background allow them to adopt such a Platonic stance. For most people individual opinions are formed in the light of the fortune or misfortune which they experience during the course of their lives, whether at home, at work or at leisure. Indeed, it has been argued that it is the formative experience of young adults which has the most lasting influence on their opinions later in life. This is known as 'the cohort theory' of opinion formation and it certainly seemed to fit those who came of age in 1945 as well as those who did so in the late 1950s. Some would argue that the theory is still valid, notably in the tendency during the late 1980s and early 1990s for those in their twenties and thirties to reject old-style Socialism and accept many of the tenets of Thatcherite Conservatism. A cautious conclusion must be that formative experience remains important as an influence upon the formation of opinion, but that the pace and scale of economic and social change in the modern world has generated much greater volatility than in the past.

Issues and images

Opinions are also formed by individual responses to political issues and party images. Traditionally the psephological evidence seemed to suggest that people tend to reconcile their political opinions with their party allegiances, rather than the other way around. In the 1950s and 1960s neither policy nor ideology seemed to mean very much to the average British citizen whose political opinions and voting behaviour appeared to be largely unaffected by such considerations. Yet evidence drawn from the 1970s and 1980s suggests that *political issues* do have an impact on the formation of public opinion and hence on voting behaviour. For example, Ivor Crewe concluded that 'it was issues, not organisation or personalities, that won the [1979] election for the Conservatives'.[12] Indeed even those who voted Labour on that occasion often preferred Conservative policies, although evidently not enough to persuade them to align their votes with their policy preferences. For much of the 1980s the nature and extent of trade union power was one of the major issues in the political debate and on the whole its salience worked in favour of the Conservatives who were seen to adopt a consistently tougher stance in relation to the trade unions. The same might be said of the issue of nuclear weapons on which the Labour leadership had, perhaps reluctantly, to concede points to the Conservative position.

Yet, in considering the influence of political issues upon opinion, we need to distinguish between the bread-and-butter issues of daily life (such as inflation, jobs, health, education and pensions) upon which most people have strongly held views which influence their voting behaviour, and the more esoteric issues of policy (for example, the control of money supply or theories of nuclear deterrence) upon which some people hold opinions, but which tend not to interest the vast majority. In considering the influence of issues in the latter category, it is as well not to exaggerate the authenticity or originality of the views held by the general public.

Among the more ephemeral considerations which influence the formation of public opinion, *the images* of the parties and especially of their leaders constitute another important factor in modern political conditions. For example, for decades the Conservative Party managed to preserve an image of competence in Government which led many people to support it even when it might not have appeared particularly warm or sympathetic to most of the general public. Several of its leaders – such as Winston Churchill, Harold Macmillan and Margaret Thatcher – were respected and even occasionally revered for their achievements in office, although they did not necessarily engender feelings of warmth or affection in the hearts and minds of many people. In the mid and late 1980s, the party's reputation for competence in Government was tarnished by the 1986 Westland Affair, the unwelcome surge in inflation and interest rates, and by the introduction of the Poll Tax. Similarly, under the much criticised leadership of John Major, the party's reputation for competence suffered further damage, particularly during the passage of the legislation to align UK law with the 1992 Maastricht Treaty and, more especially, when Britain was forced to leave the European Exchange Rate Mechanism of the European Monetary System in September 1992.

On the other hand, the Labour Party has traditionally had an image of understanding and concern for ordinary people which has helped it to retain the voting loyalties of a large part of the electorate. This achievement was partly a reflection of the positive personal image of several of its leaders – such as Clement Attlee, Hugh Gaitskell, and Harold Wilson – but mainly a tribute to the image of the Party as the Parliamentary vanguard of the entire Labour movement at a time when the latter had authenticity, fraternity and solidarity. From the middle 1970s, however, Labour had more trouble with its image, particularly during the brief period of Michael Foot's leadership in the early 1980s, and it required all the media and presentational skills of Labour image-makers to attempt to recreate and present a positive, modern image for the party. They did so with considerable success, to the extent that by the middle 1990s, under the leadership of Tony Blair, the party appeared new and responsible and in 1997 swept back into office on a tide of popular approval.

Notwithstanding the wonders that the image-makers and spin doctors can perform, it should be borne in mind that it is the performance and credibility of the Government of the day – any Government – which is likely to be decisive in the battle for the hearts and minds of the British people and which mainly determines the outcome of General Elections. In Britain, as in other countries, Governments tend to lose elections rather than Opposition parties to win them.

The power of the media

As we saw in Chapter 7, perhaps the most influential factor in the formation of public opinion in Britain today is the power of the media to reflect, explain or distort the most important political issues and personalities at any time. For example, during the 1980s and into the 1990s most of the tabloid press conducted a ruthless and single-minded campaign to portray the Labour Party as completely beholden to the trade unions and the trade unions as stereotypically mindless and militant. Such a campaign would not have been remotely credible to the general public if certain trade union leaders – for example, Arthur Scargill of the National Union of Mineworkers (NUM) – had not played into the hands of the newspaper proprietors by behaving in a manner which might have been calculated to lend credence to their caricatures. Yet undeniably the public's image of the so-called 'loony Left', whether identified with some of the trade unions or some of the Town Halls up and down the country, was heavily influenced, even determined, by the columns and pictures in the *Sun*, the *News of the World*, the *Mail on Sunday*, the *Express* and other such newspapers. Conversely these same newspapers and others like them consistently indulged in sycophancy towards Margaret Thatcher in a crude and sustained attempt, one must suppose, to keep the Conservatives in office. By contrast, following the 1992 General Election most of these same newspapers turned viciously against John Major, criticising him mercilessly for what they alleged were his failures of leadership. Following the Conservatives' loss of the 1997 General Election, a number of observers and commentators were quick to attribute the outcome at least in part to this improbable switch by the so-called 'Tory press' into the camp of Tony Blair and 'New Labour'.

As for radio and television, the part which these broadcast media play in the formation of public opinion is generally agreed to be more insidious, even manipulative. It consists essentially of helping to set the political agenda by influencing the relative salience of different political issues as they waft in and out of the public's consciousness. It is not so much that influential programmes, like *Today*, *Panorama* or *News at Ten*, consciously set out to tell the general public what to think about a given politician or political issue; but rather that they set the framework of values, assumptions and information within which the public has to try to make up its own mind. In a world in which real public interest in politics is desultory and attention spans are alarmingly short, this form of media influence is obviously both ephemeral and unpredictable. Indeed it may well be that the influence of the media is greater via mass entertainment programmes, such as *EastEnders*, *Casualty, Brookside, Coronation Street* or *The Archers*, than it is via the more serious programmes which are specifically designed to inform and educate the public. In any event we cannot review the various factors which influence the formation of public opinion in Britain today without laying great stress on the role of the mass media.

8.2 The sources of opinion

Public opinion is an amorphous and infinitely malleable concept. Like information on the electronic superhighway, it will pass on by without being picked up unless the proper receiving apparatus is available, switched on and tuned in. The opinions of the public are communicated to politicians in a variety of ways, although it is perhaps more accurate to say that politicians perceive public opinion from a number of different sources. Eleven can be identified: General Elections, by-elections, European and local elections, referenda, opinion polls, focus groups, surveys and enquiries, direct contact with the public, organised groups, political parties, and the media, and it is important to look at each of these in turn.

General Elections

Political leaders are continually conscious of the fact that their performance is constantly subjected to evaluation by the public. They are also acutely aware that the decision about whether or not they hold office ultimately depends on the judgement of the public as expressed at a General Election. The significance of this was witnessed in the political demise of Margaret Thatcher and the rise of John Major, when a party in Government deposed one leader and chose another in order that it should remain – or at least have a better chance of remaining – the party of Government. Just as Harold Macmillan replaced Anthony Eden in 1957 when the party believed that it was staring defeat in the face, so too John Major replaced Margaret Thatcher in 1990.[13] For politicians, nothing concentrates the mind more than the prospect of defeat at the next General Election.

Also important in this context is the theory of the 'mandate'. The idea here is that at the time of a General Election each political party publishes its programme – its Manifesto – outlining in general terms what it proposes to do and what policies it will pursue, if it were to form the Government. The assumption is that the voters will read the various Manifestos and will make up their minds on how to cast their votes accordingly, based on their assessment of and support for the policies outlined. This process is then presumed to grant to the newly elected Government the seal of public approval to implement the policies concerned – the public gives a mandate to the Government to act as it said it would do.

In the past there have been instances of General Elections being called specially so that the Government of the day might obtain an electoral mandate on a particular issue. For example, in the two elections of 1910 the Liberal Government under H.H. Asquith sought the backing of the electorate for its 1909 budget and plans to limit the powers of the House of Lords.[14] Similarly, in 1923 Stanley Baldwin sought to appeal to the people quite specifically for a mandate on the introduction of tariff protection.[15] In October 1931 the National Government, which had come into being in August, went to the country seeking what was described at the time as 'a doctor's mandate', in order to deal with the economic crisis from a position of strength, namely with the support of the public behind it.[16] More recently, in February 1974, Edward Heath, in the midst of an industrial confrontation with the NUM, dissolved Parliament more than one year before he needed to in order to secure a new mandate to strengthen the Government's hand in dealing with the industrial conflict and the wider consequences of the 1973–74 world oil crisis.[17]

A problem arises with regard to the concept of the mandate, however, if it is taken to its logical conclusion, namely that a Government can only introduce measures that have previously been placed before the electorate. It is for this reason that Governments have tended to show a rather more wide-ranging understanding of what is entailed, namely that the role of the electorate is to choose the Government not the Government's policies. Hence a Government obtains a general mandate to govern for a maximum period of time (limited to five years by the 1911 Parliament Act) and is less committed to specific policies. As a consequence the doctrine of the mandate cannot be applied too literally or without qualification to allow for changing economic and political circumstances.

In addition it is anyway necessary to question the very basis of the theory, for although the parties lay their policy proposals before the electorate, the extent to which the public studies them, let alone understands them, is doubtful. Besides which, voters are not able to pick and choose, save between parties: Manifestos are set menus; the public cannot choose to eat à la carte.

Finally, there is the matter of the ability of the electoral system itself to reflect accurately the wishes of the voters. For example, in the 1951 General Election more people voted Labour than voted Conservative, yet the result produced a Conservative Government. Similarly, in the General Election of February 1974, more people voted Conservative than voted Labour, but the result brought the Labour Party to power. More particularly, no Government since 1935 has secured a majority of the *popular* vote and yet, with only one exception (February 1974), every Government has been backed by a majority in the House of Commons. These matters have been dealt with fully in Chapter 3, so it is not necessary to repeat the arguments here, except to say that, for a variety of reasons, British elections may not produce results which reflect the wishes of the public – indeed the reverse is possible.

By-elections

If in the period between General Elections a Member of Parliament dies or resigns, a new election – known as a by-election – is held in order to fill the resulting vacancy. By-elections have become ways in which the popularity, or otherwise, of the Government of the day is put to the test, they are invariably fought on national issues and their results are often interpreted as reflecting public opinion as a whole. This is so even though most individual constituencies are far from perfect samples of the country at large, the number of people casting a vote is likely to be no more than 45,000–55,000, there may be particular factors involved with regard to one or other of the candidates, and there may be issues specific to the area concerned which affect the way people vote.

Whether or not by-elections are an accurate reflection of public opinion, politicians certainly take them seriously. For example, in October 1933 a by-election occurred in East Fulham. It was a seat that had been held by the Conservatives in 1931 with a majority of 14,521; it was captured by the Labour candidate on a disarmament platform with a majority of 4840, a massive switch of votes in just two years. The Prime Minister, Stanley Baldwin, took the result as evidence of a pacifist wave sweeping the country and it subsequently influenced his whole approach to the issue of rearmament.[18] Similarly, the Orpington by-election in March 1962 – which saw a Conservative majority over Labour of 14,760 turned into a Liberal majority of 7855 – provided a shock to the then Prime Minister, Harold Macmillan. When on 12 July 1962 the Conservatives were beaten into third place at a subsequent by-election in North-East Leicester, Harold Macmillan responded by carrying through a very extensive cabinet reshuffle – the so-called 'night of the long knives' in which he dismissed a third of his cabinet.[19] On the other hand, there is the case of the Hull North by-election which took place early in 1966. This produced an increased majority for the Labour Party and was undoubtedly an important factor in persuading the Prime Minister, Harold Wilson, to call a General Election – the result of which was the return of the Government with a considerably enhanced majority.

Two more examples are interesting. At the Beaconsfield by-election in May 1982, which took place following a series of sensational by-election victories for the Liberals and Social Democrats, the Conservatives held the seat with ease thanks largely to the patriotic surge of support for the governing party associated with its decision at that time to send a British Task Force to the Falkland Islands following the Argentinian invasion in April 1982.[20] Then there was the Ribble Valley by-election in March 1991, when a Conservative majority of 19,528 was turned into a Liberal Democrat majority of 4,601, although the seat had been the Conservative Party's tenth safest. Described at the time by the victorious candidate as 'the poll-tax by-election', it was seen by many as a referendum on the issue. This strengthened the hand of those within the Government who were seeking an alternative to the Poll Tax, enabling them finally to grasp one of the nettles that had so damaged Margaret Thatcher. As a result, the Cabinet agreed the following month to replace the Poll Tax with a new Council Tax, which turned out to be a more acceptable alternative.[21]

European and local elections

Just as the results of by-elections are seen as snap-shots of public opinion, so too are the results of European and local elections, which often tend to be fought on national issues with the popularity of the national Government of the day being judged in the process. For example, the campaign for the local elections of May 1990 was widely portrayed as being a referendum on the performance of the Conservative Government in general and Margaret Thatcher in particular. In the event, the results were cleverly presented by Kenneth Baker, then Conservative Party Chairman, as nothing like as bad as expected in view of the fact that the party's overall losses were actually less than predicted and the Conservatives had managed to retain control of two of their 'flagship Councils', Wandsworth and Westminster. In this case the Conservative Party may have lost the electoral battle, but it won the propaganda war and the immediate effect was to reduce the pressure on Margaret Thatcher's leadership, at least for a time.

Similarly, the elections to the European Parliament in June 1994 came after a series of electoral setbacks for the Conservative Party – the loss of the Newbury and Christchurch by-elections to the Liberal Democrats in May and July 1993, and widespread losses to the Liberal Democrats in the May 1993 and May 1994 local elections – all of which put considerable pressure on the leadership of the Prime Minister, John Major. The expectation in some quarters was of electoral annihilation for the Conservatives and widespread gains by the Liberal Democrats. As things turned out, however, the results were not as bad as originally feared, not least because the Liberal Democrats did not make widespread gains. The immediate conclusion of many Conservative MPs was that they could breathe more easily and, as a result, back-bench pressure on John Major was temporarily reduced.

Referenda

Britain has only had one *national* referendum since the Second World War. It was held in June 1975 on the issue of whether or not the country should remain in the European Economic Community, and produced, on a turnout of 65 per cent, a majority of almost two to one in favour of Britain's continued membership of the EEC.[22] There have, however, been seven *regional* referenda – two in Northern Ireland (1973 and 1998), two each in Scotland and Wales (1979 and 1997) and one in London (1998).

The 1973 Northern Ireland referendum was on the question: 'Do you want Northern Ireland to remain part of the United Kingdom?' Over 600,000 people voted, with about 58 per cent of the whole electorate casting its votes in the affirmative.[23] In 1998 the referendum was on the agreement reached at the multi-party talks and saw 951,845 individuals, 80.98 per cent of the electorate, cast their votes, 71.12 per cent in support of the agreement, and 28.88 per cent against.[24]

The referenda in Scotland and Wales in 1979 were on whether or not to establish Assemblies with devolved powers in both Scotland and Wales. In Wales only 12 per cent of the electorate voted in favour, compared with 47 per cent who voted against. In Scotland 33 per cent of the electorate voted in favour and 31 per cent against. However, because the legislation had stipulated that at least 40 per cent of the electorate in each case would have to give its approval for the legislation to be implemented, the policy of devolution was not put into effect.[25]

The second Scottish referendum took place on 11 September 1997, with a turnout of 60.16 per cent. Of those voting, 74.29 per cent voted for a Scottish Parliament (as opposed to 25.71 per cent voting against), and 63.48 per cent of those voting voted for the Parliament to be given tax-varying powers (as opposed to 36.52 per cent against). The second Welsh referendum was held on 18 September 1997 on the issue of whether there should be a Welsh Assembly. With a turnout of 51.3 per cent, 50.3 per cent voted in support of the creation of an Assembly and 49.7 per cent against. It was a clear, indeed some would say emphatic, result in Scotland, but the closest of results in Wales. Nonetheless, both voted in favour of the proposals on offer, and so the Government moved ahead with the necessary legislation to create both a Scottish Parliament and a Welsh Assembly, with a view to both coming into being in 2000.

On 7 May 1998 the people of London were asked 'Are you in favour of the Government's proposals for a Greater London Authority made up of an elected Mayor and a separately elected Assembly?' On a turnout of 34.13 per cent, 72 per cent voted in the affirmative and 28 per cent in the negative. Amongst those who voted it was an overwhelming victory for the 'yes' campaign. The Government moved to introduce the necessary legislation with a view to the GLA taking over in 2000.[26]

The reasons for holding the first of these referenda owed little or nothing to the idea that the people ought to be consulted because of the importance of the issues involved. Rather they were the result in 1975 of deep and irreconcilable divisions within the governing party and in 1979 of the Parliamentary circumstances in which a minority Labour Government was seeking to legislate on an issue which divided its own back-bench supporters. Similarly, the Northern Ireland referendum of 1973 can only be understood in the light of the troubled circumstances prevalent in the Province at the time. However, it was a rather different matter with regard to the various referenda of 1997 and 1998. These were held in Scotland, Wales and London specifically with a view, firstly, to confirming popular demand and, secondly, to strengthening the legitimacy of the proposals concerned and speeding their passage through Parliament. With regard to the Northern Ireland referendum, this was deemed necessary so as to show that the future of the Province was being determined by the consent of the people.

Perhaps here it should be noted that the Labour Government which came into office in 1997 is also committed to holding two national referenda, one on the electoral system used for elections to the House of Commons and one on Britain joining the single European currency.

While on the subject of referenda, it is also necessary to point out that just as elections are seen by some as distorting rather than reflecting public opinion, so the same point can be made about referenda, not least because of the difficulty of putting complex issues before the public for a simple 'Yes' or 'No' answer. There is also the traditional view that the use of referenda is contrary to the theory of British Parliamentary democracy. This is a matter to which we shall return later in the chapter.

Finally within this section it is necessary to include a brief account of a number of initiatives during the 1980s which extended the principle of consultation through the use of local votes in a number of areas. For example, the Housing Act 1988 provided for Council tenants to 'choose' a landlord by allowing them to vote to transfer to a Housing Association, Trust or private landlord. Similarly, the Education Act 1988 provided for schools to 'opt out' of Local Authority control via an affirmative vote amongst parents. Finally, the Conservative Government under the leadership of Margaret Thatcher introduced a whole series of legislative measures of trade union reform, among which the Trade Union Act 1984 stipulated that trade unions should hold secret ballots before taking industrial action.

Public opinion polls

Essentially, public opinion polls are a means by which an attempt is made to measure the attitudes, behaviour, beliefs, intentions and opinions of the public. Political opinion polls are primarily concerned with voting intentions and opinions relating to current issues and personalities. Their purpose is to enable conclusions to be drawn about the opinions and intentions of the public as a whole by analysing and presenting data drawn from small, though representative, samples. As a result they have emerged as a means by which the incoherent opinions of the public are formulated and then communicated to those active in the political process.

Opinion polls have undoubtedly contributed to Government action, or inaction, in some cases. For example, they were a significant factor in the debate concerning abortion law reform in the mid-1960s. A series of opinion polls was commissioned by the Abortion Law Reform Association and the findings were used to demonstrate to the Government and to Parliament that public opinion was on the side of reform. Similarly, it is apparent that Government activity in important areas of policy has been influenced by opinion polls. For example, opinion poll findings which demonstrated the great unpopularity of the Poll Tax were influential in persuading the Conservative Government under Margaret Thatcher to modify the impact of the tax in ways designed to reduce its adverse impact.[27]

Overall it can be said that although politicians pay close attention to opinion polls, the action which they take is not necessarily based on them. The clearest case in which public opinion as revealed by opinion polls has been conspicuously and continuously ignored is on the issue of capital punishment. To begin with, in 1965 the death penalty was abolished provisionally for a five-year period by a free vote in the House of Commons – a decision taken in the face of considerable public opposition evidenced by overwhelming opinion poll majorities of 80 per cent or more in favour of its retention.[28] Despite the fact that every poll taken since that time has also revealed a large majority of the population in favour of restoring the death penalty, Parliament has repeatedly and clearly voted against such a step. A different example can be drawn from the sphere of European policy. Parliament voted against the holding of a referendum on the ratification of the Maastricht Treaty despite public opinion poll evidence that a large majority of the public were in favour of such a step.[29] More recently it was asserted that the Labour Government ignored public opinion – as portrayed in the public opinion polls – when it refused to find Parliamentary time during 1997–98 for a Private Member's Bill to ban fox-hunting.[30]

Focus groups/people's panels

During their years in Opposition (1979–97) the Labour Party began to use focus groups – groups drawn from individual members of the public – to test reaction to existing and suggested policy. These market research-led techniques were seen by many as important components not only in the modernisation of the Labour Party but in the party's subsequent return to power. In office the Government sought to carry the idea forward, setting up a 5000 strong 'people's panel': A representative sample of the population was drawn up to ensure that individual groupings – such as ethnic minorities, different age groups, disabled people and so on – were included, with a view to testing public attitudes to the Government, what it does and the services it offers. This testing is done in a number of ways:

- via general surveys conducted over the telephone;
- through the use of small focus groups of about ten individuals;
- by using larger 'citizens' juries', where those selected spend several days answering detailed questions.

The criticism of this approach arises from the belief that it bypasses open, public consultation in favour of a closed process dominated by market research analysts, pollsters and spin doctors and that it is the job, indeed duty, of politicians to give a lead and not simply to follow; the view that politicians ought to do more than simply seek to be popular.

Surveys and enquiries

At the turn of the century a number of social enquiries into living conditions which involved extensive house-to-house surveys – such as Charles Booth's *Life and Labour of the People of London* (1897) and Seebohm Rowntree's *Poverty: A Study of Town Life* – had a significant impact on the climate of political opinion at the time and provided much factual support for the drive towards social reform and public welfare.

More recently, Lord Scarman's *Report into the Brixton Disorders of 10–12 April 1981* owed a lot to the oral evidence provided by more than fifty witnesses, including police officers, journalists, members of the emergency services and residents of the area who had witnessed the course of events, as well as written evidence from 284 organisations and individuals and some 450 letters from members of the public.[31] Described by the *Daily Mirror* as 'one of the great social documents of our time', it influenced the subsequent political debate on the inner cities, the police and the ethnic minorities. The same could be said of the Report of the Archbishop of Canterbury's Commission on Urban Priority Areas (*Faith in the City*, 1985), which drew extensively on evidence taken by the Commission all over the country.[32]

As the range of Government activity has become greater and the role of Government correspondingly larger, so the requirement for information has grown, both to estimate social needs and to monitor the effects of Government action. Fundamental to this process is the Census carried out every ten years, the most recent in 1991. In addition, the Office for National Statistics carries out surveys and research on a regular and continuing basis which provides essential factual information for policy makers in Government. The Family Expenditure Survey and the International Passenger Survey are both examples of this work. Individual Government Departments are also involved in gathering data. For example, the Department of Transport's Cross Channel Passenger and Freight Traffic Report of 1996 was an extensive and detailed analysis of people who cross the English Channel.[33] We should also mention in this context the public opinion research done for large-scale planning inquiries, such as those which examined proposals for a Third London Airport, the Sizewell B nuclear power station, and the Channel Tunnel Rail Link. All of these investigations were intended to contribute to the quality of policymaking. In addition it is not uncommon for the views of the public to be sought as part of a process of general consultation during the policy making process. For example, in 1997 the Government sought to test public opinion on the matter of women serving as front line troops in the army, while in 1998 the Human Genetics Advisory Commission (HGAC) and the Human Fertilisation and Embryology Authority (HFEA) published a document – also on the World Wide Web – which asked a series of questions on the matter of therapeutic cloning and invited responses from the public on this morally difficult issue.[34]

Direct contacts between MPs and the public

There are a variety of opportunities available to Members of Parliament directly to ascertain the views of the public. First, there are the letters which MPs receive both from their constituents and more widely from the general public. A typical MP now receives more than 150 letters a week, receiving in one day the amount of correspondence which would have been received in one week in the 1960s. Sir Robert Rhodes James, MP for Cambridge between 1976 and 1992, calculated that he received and replied to 249,000 letters from his constituents, an average of 300 letters a week, and that answering them sometimes took three hours a day.[35]

Secondly, Members of Parliament are lobbied with increasing frequency by sometimes very large delegations which turn up at the Palace of Westminster demanding to see their MP (or indeed any MP) and put their case. Thirdly, nearly all MPs now hold what are described as 'surgeries' or 'advice bureaux' in their constituencies either once a week or twice a month. These provide yet another source of information on public feelings, although because of their self-selecting characteristics, such aggrieved constituents may not be representative of the broader swathe of public opinion.

Organised groups

Pressure groups have been covered in Chapter 6, so it is sufficient here simply to point out that individuals can join with others of a like mind in an attempt to get a particular opinion or set of opinions across to politicians of all parties and to the Government of the day and by so doing seek to secure political action consistent with those opinions. Having said this, it is interesting to record a cautionary note struck by Jack Straw when Home Secretary in 1998, when he warned that 'elected politicians should be ever wary of the dangers of becoming the agents of sectional interests and of ignoring the concerns of those who elect them. One need only look at how unsuccessful the Labour Party was throughout the 1980s to see that.'[36]

Political parties

Political parties were covered in Chapter 5, so we need merely point out here that individuals can join the political party whose broad ideological approach most closely matches their own and then work within its structures in an attempt to influence party policy and perhaps public policy as well.

The media

Although the subject of the media has been covered in Chapter 7, it is nonetheless necessary briefly to mention two matters in this chapter. First, there is the issue of the extent to which the media truly reflects public opinion. Certainly members of the public have access to the media via, for example, the letters pages of newspapers and magazines, radio phone-in programmes and public participation programmes on television. Yet all of this is only a tiny proportion of total media output and may not reflect much more than the views of those who push themselves forward.

Secondly, there is the issue of the extent to which the media are simply acting as neutral channels of communication between the Government and the governed, or rather are seeking to lead, form, mould and even distort public opinion. On this last point, it is argued by some that the only reality is that created by the media, since it is the media which assess what the people think and want and then relay the results to others. However, others (especially those actively engaged in politics) contend that reality is often very different from what the media choose to convey at any time and that all politicians have to deal with the problems caused by media distortions and consequently public misconceptions. The simple conclusion must be that both sides of this argument have valid points and that wisdom consists in eschewing dogmatic or permanent conclusions.

8.3 The effects of opinion

More deferential politicians

Public opinion in Britain has a variety of political effects. It is arguable that one effect has been to make most politicians more deferential to the wishes of the electorate. While this tendency may seem to have reached its zenith in the time of Harold Wilson, who as Leader of the Labour Party (1963–76) paid assiduous attention to opinion polls and other psephological data (such as by-election and local election results), it has remained significant at all times in postwar politics, especially when General Elections are imminent. Certainly it has been true in the negative sense that leading politicians both in and out of office usually take considerable care not to put forward policies or take positions which seem destined to encounter powerful opposition from public opinion. Even the redoubtable Margaret Thatcher, who more than any other leader sought to do what she believed to be right regardless of the political consequences, adjusted Conservative policy on some occasions in order to take account of the public responses which might have been expected if she and her Ministerial colleagues had pressed ahead with certain radical policies in an unaltered form.[37]

It has of course been true in the positive sense as well. For example, when in 1993 the then Conservative Chancellor Norman Lamont announced the introduction in two stages of VAT on domestic fuel – 8 per cent from 1994 and 17.5 per cent from 1995 – the size of the public lobby against the move took the Government by surprise and eventually forced it to retract, so that only the first stage of the tax was ever imposed. Similarly, it was the public response to the Dunblane shooting in 1995 that led the Government of the day to introduce tough gun-control legislation and the Labour Opposition of the time to pledge to introduce a complete ban on all handguns in general civilian use; a pledge they later fulfilled when in Government.

This draws our attention to the elusive and controversial concept of *political impossibility* which has played such an important part in so many political calculations by leading politicians over the years. In essence it can be defined as the influence on political decision-makers of anticipated public reaction. Some have argued that this is a harmful influence on politics, since it can prevent the adoption of radical policies which may be justified as an appropriate response to many of Britain's deep-seated national problems. Others have argued that it is a beneficial influence, since it can be seen as a contribution to British national cohesion, especially during difficult periods of disappointment and relative decline when a less sensitive political approach could prove very damaging. The argument is really between those who regard the conservatism of British public opinion as something of a saving grace, since it constitutes a significant obstacle to the ambitions of the zealots in each main party; and those who see it as a tragedy, since it has often constituted a virtually insuperable barrier to radical action. If the overriding priority is to guard against radical change, then the former view ought to be commended; if it is to make radical change, then the latter view ought to prevail. In any event the outcome is likely to depend on the personal temperament of the leading politicians who have to carry the responsibility of Government.

Under Margaret Thatcher's leadership in the 1980s the Conservative Government tended to press for what it believed to be right almost regardless of the immediate political consequences. Under John Major's leadership in the 1990s the approach was much less ideological and more pragmatic in a way strangely reminiscent of Harold Wilson's period as Prime Minister. John Major's supporters justified his pragmatism on two principal grounds. First, he was elected leader of his party in 1990 precisely because he was not Margaret Thatcher, and secondly, he had to give his highest priority to holding his party together – something which was made that much more difficult after the 1992 General Election when the Conservative majority in the Commons was reduced to a small fraction of the majority that Margaret Thatcher had enjoyed.

Both in Opposition and in Government Tony Blair has been highly sensitive to polling information and he has sought to be in tune with the instincts of the general public. Indeed he observed that: 'Supposing you are running Marks & Spencer or Sainsbury or whatever it is, you will be continually trying to work out whether your consumers are satisfied with the product that they are getting. I don't think there is anything wrong with Government trying to do that in the same way.'[38]

A counterweight to pressure groups

Another important effect of public opinion has been the way in which it has provided a useful counterweight to the influence of pressure groups in the British political system. As we noted in Chapter 6, there have been times when it has become very difficult for any Government to resist the claims of certain powerful interest groups, such as the National Union of Mineworkers in the 1970s or the British Medical Association in the late 1980s, without appealing over the heads of the group concerned to the general public. This is essentially what Edward Heath sought to do when he called a General Election in February 1974 on the issue of 'who governs?' It is also what the 1979–83 Conservative Government sought to do when it introduced legislation to provide for secret ballots in trade unions affairs. In each case the intention of Ministers was to appeal over the heads of obstructive interest groups to the wider public in an effort to fulfil their political purposes. Of course, the success of this tactic depends on the power of the opposing interest group and the degree of public sympathy or support which it can generate for its cause. For example, the NUT's campaign against the Conservative Government's attempts to introduce national curriculum assessment in the early 1990s depended on the credibility of its propaganda, the willingness of its members to remain solidly behind the union line and the sympathy of parents.

Whenever politicians of the Right or Left invoke the views of the wider public in support of their cause, it is usually a sign that they have been obstructed or opposed by a small but powerful group which seeks to set its sectional interest above that of the general community. This has been as true when Labour Ministers in the 1970s complained about the pernicious influence of the City of London as when Conservative Ministers in the 1980s criticised the abuse of trade union power. In each case they sought to defend the principle that general public opinion has more inherent legitimacy than any sectional group. On the whole it is hard to oppose this principle, since general public opinion has a sounder and more altruistic record than sectional groups on most political issues. Yet every political system also needs safeguards against the tyranny of the majority (or even of a minority of the electorate exploiting a Parliamentary majority), since in most societies there have been times when majority opinion has been unfair or unenlightened and temporarily defeated minorities have needed protection against it. Thus a balance has to be struck which allows fair opportunities for both majority and minority opinion, while retaining a democratic presumption in favour of the former.

The influence of opinion polls

Yet another effect of public opinion has been to give political opinion polls an influence out of all proportion to their true value. Such polls have become the most systematic expression of public opinion between General Elections. When sensibly interpreted, they can provide a useful navigational aid for politicians, whether in Government or Opposition. The systematic analysis of opinion poll data has enabled the parties to identify key target groups of voters – for instance, the wives of blue collar workers in the case of the Conservative Party, or the public sector salariat in the case of the Labour Party – and then to concentrate and organise their efforts with particular target groups in mind. Opinion polls also guide the Prime Minister of the day in making the decision about when to call a General Election and they can affect the morale of party activists if the findings are either very good or very bad for a particular party or its leader.[39] While opinion polls are not normally used to determine policy or decision making, it is understandable that they should influence both the development and the presentation of policy. On the other hand, there is a widely held view among practising politicians that both local and European elections (but not usually Parliamentary by-elections) are a better guide to the public mood, if not necessarily an infallible indicator of voting behaviour at a future General Election.

Special considerations apply to the role of opinion polls during election campaigns. Some experts have argued that the polls produce a bandwagon effect which assists the party that seems to be on a winning streak. Others have argued for the backlash effect which leads doubting voters to rally to the party that appears to be the underdog. One thing seems certain, however, and that is that opinion polls can have a much more powerful effect on the actual result at by-elections than at General Elections, since on such occasions they signal to the local electorate which is the best vehicle for effective tactical voting and, as a result, political protest. This was certainly evident during the Bermondsey by-election in 1983, the Greenwich by-election in 1987 and the Glasgow Govan by-election in 1988.[40]

The use of referenda

Still another effect of public opinion is visible in the way in which the growing self-confidence and declining deference of the general public has led to periodic demands for national referenda. These demands have arisen on a variety of political issues, notably those which demonstrate that Parliamentary opinion is out of tune with public opinion, for example on the emotive issue of capital punishment. Of course, national referenda have certainly not been a defining characteristic of the constitutional arrangements in Britain and most MPs in all parties have been determined to see that this remains the position. Yet there is always a temptation for political demagogues or other publicity seekers to break ranks with their colleagues in Parliament by calling for national referenda on certain issues when they believe that the results of a plebiscite would be in their favour, as Margaret Thatcher and others did by campaigning for a referendum on British ratification of the 1992 Maastricht Treaty.

The important and much publicised referenda on Britain's membership of the European Community in 1975, on devolution to Scotland and Wales in 1979 and 1997 and on a Mayor and Assembly for London in 1998 are still generally considered to have been exceptions which prove the rule. The publicly stated reason for holding referenda in these special cases was that they were conducted on constitutional issues of great importance in which the very future of Parliament itself was involved. However, this would not explain why there was no such referendum on the issue of the ratification of the Maastricht Treaty, an issue which undoubtedly presaged major constitutional change. Rather, the actual reasons for holding referenda in 1975 and 1979 owed more to the intra-party political and Parliamentary circumstances of the times; those of 1997 and 1998 owed more to the principle of consent, but nonetheless grew out of the experiences of these earlier examples. Despite the fact that the Labour Government which came into office in 1997 promised referenda on the electoral system and on joining the single European currency, the holding of referenda are clearly exceptions to the general rule that Britain is a Parliamentary rather than a plebiscitary democracy. On the other hand, it is possible that, as such precedents have been set, it may prove increasingly difficult for Members of Parliament to resist future demands for referenda on a wide range of political issues, especially when a majority in the House of Commons is seen to be out of tune with the overwhelming opinion of the general public, when public feelings are running high, or when powerful cause groups succeed in persuading the public.[41]

The impact of direct action

Finally, we should not neglect the impact of direct action as a powerful form of non-verbal and non-literate political communication. We should note the fact that at various stages in British history public protest, whether spontaneous or induced, has played an important, sometimes decisive, part in the expression of public opinion. We need only instance:

- Wat Tyler and the Peasants' Revolt in 1381;
- the Peterloo Massacre in 1819;
- the Chartist Movement in the 1840s;
- the Suffragette demonstrations in the early 1900s;
- the Invergordon 'mutiny' in 1931;
- the Jarrow and other unemployment marches in the 1930s.

More recent examples of the power of direct action would include:

- the inner city riots in the summer of 1981;
- the miners' dispute of 1984–85;
- the Greenham Common demonstration against American cruise missiles in the mid-1980s;

- the campaign of civil disobedience against the Poll Tax in the late 1980s;
- the demonstrations against the actions of the Child Support Agency in 1993–94;
- the activity of animal welfare protesters against the live animal export trade in 1994–95;
- the actions of anti-road building protestors in 1996–97.

Nowadays lawful public demonstrations are usually organised for publicity purposes by minorities who feel strongly about an issue, but who also feel excluded from the regular channels of influence and representation in society. The fact that some people have recourse to such methods may cast doubt upon the validity of their arguments, but more often it reflects their assessment of the chances of attaining their objectives by more orthodox institutional means, such as Parliamentary pressure or official contacts in Whitehall. For example, those who believed in the merits of unilateral nuclear disarmament chose to squat outside the Greenham Common air base or to march in large processions through London, since they did not believe that the more conventional means of putting their case would have had any impact on the decision makers. Similarly the Muslim demonstrations in London, Bradford and other cities against Salman Rushdie and his 'blasphemous' novel *The Satanic Verses* illustrated the anger and frustration of the minority Muslim community at the apparent inability of Parliament to respond to their deeply felt concern. Public demonstrations of this kind have always been a recognised way of seeking publicity for a grievance or support for a cause, and most are conducted in a peaceful and law-abiding manner. Yet they do not always succeed in influencing political decisions in their chosen direction, since the impact on the general public is often adverse and occasionally counterproductive.

8.4 Public opinion in context

The question has often been asked about the circumstances in which politicians should follow, lead, educate, cajole or simply ignore public opinion. The issue is certainly not new. Edmund Burke writing to his constituents in 1774 stated what is the classic case for representatives arriving at their own judgement, completely independent of what their constituents' views might be. His view was that: 'Your representative owes to you not his industry only, but his judgement; and he betrays, instead of serving you, if he sacrifices it to your opinion.'[42] It is this approach, this reasoning, which has been cited by MPs over the years when refusing to bow to the demands of public opinion for the restoration of capital punishment, for example. The traditional position in Britain is simply stated – namely that the public is expected at a General Election to choose the party which it wishes to see in Government until the next General Election, not to assume responsibility for any part of the Governmental process once in operation. As one quality newspaper explained, 'it is the job of Members of Parliament to understand and decide on issues after open debate and with due regard for the opinions of the voters'.[43]

The alternative view is one derived from the philosophy of Jean-Jacques Rousseau who declared that: 'the deputies of the people are not and cannot be their representatives, they can only be their commissioners, and as such they are not qualified to conclude anything definitely. No act of theirs can be a law, unless it has been ratified by the people in person; and without their ratification nothing is a law.'[44] This view (often described as 'direct democracy') has never gained much support in Britain, not least because it clearly conflicts with the concept of Parliamentary supremacy. Yet it seems likely to gain ground in the future given that the British people are becoming less deferential to leaders and already appear less prepared to give the benefit of the doubt to Members of Parliament at Westminster.

Traditional discussion of the part that public opinion ought to play in the formation of public policy tends to assume that members of the public have valid opinions to communicate. Such an assumption, however, is not necessarily borne out by experience. It should also be recognised that the relationship between public opinion and decision making is two-way with the flow of influence rarely, if ever, running smoothly from the former to the latter. Indeed, no simple causal relationship is apparent. Public opinion never moves in a single direction without setting up contradictory and countervailing forces. Nor does it exist in a vacuum. Rather it is an integral and inseparable part of any political system, even when suppressed by an authoritarian regime.

It follows that any correspondence between public opinion and political action tends not to be exact or immediate. Public opinion – in the sense of a viewpoint widely held – is only likely to have an effect, whether positive or negative, if channelled or exploited by politicians, pressure groups or the media. It is more often a factor of constraint, setting limits to what is acceptable in a pluralist society rather than providing new opportunities for action by decision makers or opinion formers. Indeed, all Governments have to make calculations when deciding on their courses of action (or inaction), as to whether or not the public will wear it. In this sense the art of governing in a Parliamentary democracy is the ability to calculate when too many people will say 'no', but before they have an opportunity to do so.

Consensus and controversy

There has been both consensus and controversy in British politics since the Second World War. Generally, Governments have relied to a very great extent on at least the tacit acquiescence, if not the positive consent, of the various groups and interests with which they have to deal; and on the whole they have preferred discussion, compromise and agreement to the imposition of policy on unwilling institutions, groups or interests.

The 1945–51 Labour Government under Clement Attlee established the postwar consensus under which Britain was governed for more than a quarter of a century thereafter. There were six main elements in this consensus:

1. a mixed economy with extensive state intervention, including a large industrial public sector;
2. a commitment to maintain full employment;
3. an extensive welfare state – with provisions 'from the cradle to the grave';
4. progressive taxation with high marginal rates in order to pay for public expenditure;

5. acceptance of the trade unions as legitimate economic and social partners in the process of Government;
6. a belief that Government should pay at least lip service to a fairer and more equal society.

In short, there was a belief in activist Government; a belief that it was the function of Government to find solutions to problems, whenever and wherever they arose.

Although this consensus was either modified or extended by successive Governments of both parties, there was no substantial or sustained challenge to it until the mid-1970s.[45] In these circumstances the political argument was largely confined to disputes about the best way to manage the mixed economy and to distribute the fruits of economic growth. Admittedly, there were some deep divisions of opinion about some issues, notably in the sphere of foreign policy. For example, the Suez expedition in 1956, the process of decolonisation in the late 1950s and early 1960s, and Britain's relationship with the European Community all caused serious dissension between and within the main Parties. Yet such arguments took place against a background of basic agreement on many other issues of fundamental importance.

This particular view of the world was challenged during the latter part of the 1960s and finally defeated in the mid-1970s. There were a number of powerful reasons for this:

1. Inflation began to soar in the mid-1970s as a consequence of the quadrupling of the price of oil in the world energy crisis of that time.
2. As the recession went deeper, the economy began to contract and the public finances plunged into debt.
3. In the new climate of monetarism imposed by the IMF in 1976, Keynesian remedies came to seem as part of the problem rather than the solution.
4. First the Labour Government and then the Conservative Government after 1979 were faced with the problems of managing, or even lowering, public expectations in the light of the new realities.

In such circumstances it was not surprising that the postwar consensus came to an end. The Labour Party moved to the Left and the Conservative Party to the Right, thus producing a degree of political polarisation in the early 1980s which had not been seen in Britain since the 1930s. Margaret Thatcher and her political supporters in the Conservative Party, matched by the so-called 'hard Left' in the Labour Party, were the outward and visible manifestations of this period of political polarisation.

From 1979 to 1990 the three successive Thatcher Administrations effectively demolished much of the postwar economic, social and political order. As Norman Tebbit, one of Margaret Thatcher's political allies, explained at the time: 'our task is to establish the new political consensus within which our opponents, too, must work'.[46] The commitment to full employment was abandoned, the battle against inflation was given priority, the role and responsibilities of the State were deliberately reduced, and the power of the trade unions was curbed. In the process public attitudes and perceptions were changed, leading to a greater sense of economic realism, more respect for market forces and greater acceptance that people should not look to Government for solutions to every problem. By the end of the 1980s the result was the establishment of a new 'common ground', one with which the Government's opponents were obliged to come to terms. Among the political casualties were the old Labour Party, which lost a considerable part of its support to the newly formed 'Alliance' of Liberals and Social Democrats, and the so-called 'Wets' within the Conservative Party who had sought, but failed, to uphold the principles of the postwar consensus.

On becoming Leader of the Labour Party in 1994 Tony Blair was convinced that it was necessary, indeed crucial, to the future success of his party to change the perceptions of the electorate as to where the Labour Party stood on the main issues. This involved adopting centre-Right positions on key issues, such as taxation and public spending, the role of markets, the powers of trade unions, privatisation and law and order. In short it involved the acceptance of at least some of the tenets of the Thatcherite legacy. The resulting policy revolution within the Labour Party was implemented with considerable skill and efficiency and reaped the rewards of a resounding victory at the General Election of 1997.

However, nothing ever stands still in British politics, so we should not be surprised to notice that the new middle ground seems to be occupied by all three main parties which acknowledge the new, post-Thatcherite consensus. The guiding principles seem to include a readiness to accept most of the implications of living in a market economy, off-set in Labour's case by an urge to intervene (at any rate at the European level) and to redistribute income and wealth via a 'fairer' tax and social security system; in the Conservative case by a wish to regulate the liberalised economy no more than strictly necessary and to concentrate social provision principally upon those who really need it; and in the Liberal Democrat case by the concept of empowering the individual through the creation of a contractual relationship between tax payer and Government, by seeking to change the relationship between Whitehall and Town Hall; and by focusing particularly on civil liberties.

Informed opinion and mass opinion

Differences between the Left and the Right are not the only significant cleavages in British public opinion. There is also the important gulf which exists between informed opinion and mass opinion.

Informed opinion may be defined as opinion held by the minority of people who are 'in the know' about political issues and whose views are usually, but not always, the result of a recognisably rational process of thought. Typically it is the opinion of politicians at Westminster, civil servants in Whitehall, political journalists, pressure group spokesmen and those prominent in some other walks of life, such as public corporations, local Government, medicine, education, the law, the church and the City. In view of the metropolitan character of British political opinion, it often derives disproportionately from interacting London elites, although it can also be influenced by ephemeral intellectual trends which often originate in the universities and in so-called 'think tanks', such as the Institute for Economic Affairs, the Institute for Public Policy Research, Demos, and the Social Market Foundation. It is therefore essentially the opinion of the current Establishment and its licensed critics.[47]

Mass opinion, on the other hand, is often little more than ignorant sentiment, although it is usually based on significant attitudes, beliefs and ideas which are rooted in popular experience. This means that it has often to be conjured up before it can be said to exist. As V.O. Key observed, 'public opinion does not emerge like a cyclone and push obstacles before it; rather it develops under leadership'.[48] The extent of public ignorance about the basic facts of politics obviously contributes to this situation and has been a matter of record for some time. For example, in 1964 almost a quarter of a representative sample did not know that the coal industry had been nationalised for nearly 20 years. In 1971 another opinion poll showed that only 13 per cent of those questioned could name the six member states of the European Community at a time when the British Government was engaged in widely publicised negotiations for British entry. In 1978 only 46 per cent of those questioned in a national poll could give the name of their MP and a poll in 1979 showed that 77 per cent of those questioned did not know what was meant by the acronym NATO – 30 years after the foundation of the North Atlantic Treaty Organisation.

The high level of public ignorance of the facts of politics has persisted ever since. For example, in June 1986 when presented in a MORI Poll with photographs of all the leading Conservative politicians, a representative sample of the public were 100 per cent correct only in their recognition of Margaret Thatcher, 66 per cent correct with Norman (later Lord) Tebbit, and 51 per cent correct with Sir Keith (later Lord) Joseph. Yet in all other cases less than half of the public correctly identified such senior figures as the Foreign Secretary, the Chancellor of the Exchequer, and the Home Secretary. Recognition of politicians was no better at local level, since a Gallup Poll in April 1988 showed that 44 per cent of a representative sample could give neither the name nor the party affiliation of their local Councillor.

As for the major issues of policy, a Gallup Poll in June 1988 showed that only 29 per cent of a representative sample knew what was meant by the much publicised date of '1992', while 15 per cent associated it incorrectly with the Poll Tax and 42 per cent confessed to having no idea at all. In an NOP survey in 1995 almost a third of under 35s questioned put their apathy about politics down to 'not knowing enough about it'. Also in 1995 the MORI 'state of the nation' poll for the Joseph Rowntree Reform Trust revealed that 53 per cent of women and 35 per cent of men were prepared to admit that they 'know nothing or had never heard' of proportional representation; that 54 per cent of women and 34 per cent of men were equally ignorant of the European Union; and that 43 per cent of women and 29 per cent of men knew absolutely nothing about the House of Lords. In 1998 in a survey of young people aged 16–24 commissioned by the British Youth Council, 10 per cent of respondents were unable to name the Prime Minister, 60 per cent were unable to name the Leader of the Conservative Party, 85 per cent were unable to name the Home Secretary and 97 per cent were unable to name the Health Secretary.

Bearing in mind all the political communication which takes place, it is perhaps a little difficult to understand why such a degree of public ignorance and apathy has persisted. The explanation could be that those politicians and others who have something to say are not saying it with sufficient clarity or repetition. It could be that the channels of communication in the mass media are defective for this purpose. It could even be that the public is perfectly able to hear, but not really prepared to listen because of a widespread mood of cynicism and even alienation from the whole process of party politics. Simple observation would suggest that politicians and other opinion formers try hard to impart a great deal of fact and opinion to the general public, perhaps even too much for easy assimilation. It would also suggest that the media, and especially television, are more pervasive and influential than ever before.

Yet it is equally clear that these factors do not necessarily produce a well-informed or enlightened public.

It is possible to identify several plausible reasons for this unsatisfactory state of affairs. It may be because the conduct of political argument on aggressive party lines is not the best way of explaining to the public many of the complicated issues raised in contemporary politics. It may also be because the imperatives of modern journalism and the fierce commercial competition in the media have discouraged editors and producers from giving sufficient coverage or adequate explanation of many difficult political issues. After all, the popular national newspapers are more noted for their coverage of sport, scandal and sex than for intelligent or subtle discussion of important political issues. Equally, the radio and television programme makers are more concerned to compete for a mass audience and to win the battle of the ratings than to provide much serious coverage of political news and views. As for the attitudes of the general public, anecdotal evidence suggests that most British people are largely uninterested in party politics, are suspicious of the apparent untrustworthiness of politicians, and feel cynical, even perhaps alienated, from the whole process whenever they do pay attention. If these understandable public reactions to the volume of information made available and the intractability of most of the problems are taken into account, it would seem to be more a case of a public which is not very keen to listen than of politicians and other opinion formers who are not trying to communicate.

In short, mass opinion on most political issues consists of a large component of ignorance, a considerable lack of interest, a high degree of cynicism, a certain amount of prejudice, an assortment of received ideas, a smattering of popular mythology, a dose of wishful thinking, and considerable rationalisation of personal experience. If this appears to be something of a caricature, then it must be said that there is not much evidence from opinion polls or other systematic sources to disprove it. It seems to be the political reality in Britain, and it will probably continue to be the case until such time as a more positive and less cynical political culture develops.

8.5 Conclusion

Governments are undoubtedly influenced by public opinion. However, the extent to which they choose to pay attention to public opinion depends on how important a part they consider public opinion plays in the resolution of a particular issue.

The extent to which a Government follows public opinion will depend on how it interprets the views of informed opinion. The opinions expressed from these quarters certainly carry considerably more weight than mass opinion. Besides which, it must always be remembered that public opinion is only one of the pressures and constraints operating on Government in the highly complex world of policy and decision making. It is the task of the Government of the day to determine the relative importance of each factor. It is likely, for example, that the constraints imposed by the markets or by the international environment will have considerable influence on national decisions in the modern world. Nonetheless, it is evident that all those involved in political decision making have to take full account of public opinion. Where they differ is over their definitions of public opinion, how it should be measured and assessed and the significance to be attached to what they find out. The fact that in many cases Governments have felt obliged to make decisions which are consistent with perceived public opinion at the time, is an indication of the importance of public opinion in the British political system. The conclusion must be that public opinion in Britain influences, but is not necessarily a determinant of, what happens in British politics. The degree of its importance depends mainly upon three factors: its *intensity*, its *durability* and its *specificity*. The more intense, durable, and specifically focused it is, the greater the degree of influence it is likely to have.

Whatever shape it takes or force it demonstrates, public opinion in Britain can be regarded as a source of political legitimacy, a counterweight to the influence of pressure groups, a form of political intelligence and occasionally even a 'Court of Appeal' in matters of strong public concern or great importance. Yet its true value is limited by the fact that, in complex issues of national policy, it is usually not based on sufficient knowledge or experience and is often more of an echo than an inspiration for the positions taken by leading politicians and other opinion formers. It is undoubtedly a dynamic factor in the working of the British political system, since it involves a constant and continuous process of two-way communication between the politicians and the people.

Political leadership will always have a major part to play in the formation of public opinion. Yet, if such leadership is to be really effective, it will have to make itself felt beyond the limited confines of Whitehall and Westminster. Metropolitan elites will need to leave the corridors of power and make more frequent contact with the general public in all parts of the country. In any event all opinion-formers will need to have a clearer idea of what they want to say and how best to say it. The key people in the media will need to offer more political news and views and to present such material in balanced and responsible ways. Schools and other institutions of learning will need to put more emphasis on political literacy in all its forms. Yet, even assuming a reasonable degree of success with all these endeavours, the politicians will still have to keep their fingers crossed and hope that the British people really want to play an active part in the nation's pluralist political process.

Suggested questions

1 How is public opinion formed and influenced in Britain?
2 What are the ways in which public opinion is brought to the attention of politicians in Britain?
3 What are the effects of public opinion on British Government and politics?

Notes

1. B. Parekh (ed.), *Bentham's Political Thought* (London: Croom Helm, 1973), p. 212
2. Quoted in A.H. Birch, *Representative and Responsible Government* (London: Allen & Unwin, 1964), p. 172.
3. Cited in A. Andrews, *Quotations for Speakers and Writers* (London: Newnes Books, 1969), p. 376.
4. *Ibid.*
5. *Ibid.*
6. *Ibid.*

7. See A.V. Dicey, *Introduction to the Study of the Law of the Constitution*, 10th edn (London: Macmillan, 1967), pp. 59, 60, 71–85.
8. See A.V. Dicey, *Law and Opinion in England in The Nineteenth Century* (London: Macmillan, 1905), p. 10.
9. V.O. Key, *Public Opinion and American Democracy* (New York: Knopf, 1961), p. 14.
10. R. Rose (ed.), *Studies in British Politics*, 3rd edn (London: Macmillan, 1976), p. 254.
11. See D.E. Butler and D. Stokes, *Political Change in Britain*, 2nd edn (London: Macmillan, 1974), pp. 19–151.
12. In H.R. Penniman (ed.), *Britain at the Polls, 1979* (Washington, DC: American Enterprise Institute, 1981), p. 282.
13. See N.D.J. Baldwin, *The Conservative Party: An Instinct to Survive* (Barnstaple: Philip Charles Media, 1990).
14. See R. Jenkins, *Mr Balfour's Poodle* (London: Heinemann, 1954).
15. See K. Middlemass and J. Barnes, *Baldwin: A Biography* (London: Weidenfeld & Nicolson, 1969).
16. *Ibid.*
17. See J. Campbell, *Edward Heath: A Biography* (London: Capes, 1993).
18. See I. Bulmer-Thomas, *The Growth of the British Party System* (Vol. II) (London: John Baker, 1965), pp. 103–4.
19. See A.H. Home, *Macmillan* (Vol. II) (London: Macmillan, 1984), pp. 331–51.
20. See J. Bruce-Gardyne, *Mrs Thatcher's First Administration* (London: Macmillan, 1984), pp. 113–14.
21. See C. Cook and J. Ramsden, *By-elections in British Politics* (London: University College Press, 1997), p. 261.
22. See D. Butler and U. Kitzinger, *The 1975 Referendum* (London: Macmillan, 1976).
23. See W. Whitelaw, *The Whitelaw Memories* (London: Aurum Press, 1989), pp. 108–9.
24. See N.D.J Baldwin, *British Government and Politics, The Modern Studies Association Yearbook, 1998/98* (Scotland: MSA, 1998).
25. See V. Bogdanor, *The People and the Party System* (London: Cambridge University Press, 1981).
26. See N.D.J. Baldwin, *op cit.*
27. See M. Thatcher, *The Downing Street Years* (London: HarperCollins, 1993), pp. 642–67.
28. See F. Teer and J.D. Spence, *Political Opinion Polls* (London: Hutchinson, 1973), p. 138.
29. For example, a MORI poll of June 1993 showed 73 per cent of respondents in favour of a referendum as opposed to 18 per cent against and 9 per cent 'don't knows'.
30. See F. Abrams, 'Public Opinion on Fox-Hunting Being Ignored', *Independent*, 4 April 1998.
31. *The Scarman Report* (London: HMSO, 1981).
32. *Faith in the City: A Call for Action by Church and State* (London: Church House, 1985).
33. *Cross-Channel Passenger and Freight Traffic Report* (London: HMSO, 1992).
34. See N. Hawkes, 'Advisers Seek Public's View on Cloning Human Tissue', *The Times*, 30 January 1998.
35. R. Rhodes-Jones, 'Politics in the Postbag', *The Times*, 22 October 1992.
36. J. Straw, writing in *The Times*, 8 April 1998.
37. For example, Mrs Thatcher and her ministerial colleagues deliberately postponed an all-out confrontation with Arthur Scargill and the National Union of Mineworkers until 1984, when all the relevant preparations for a long industrial dispute had been made by the Government and the electricity utilities.
38. Tony Blair, *The Jimmy Young Programme*, BBC Radio 2, 29 July 1997.
39. It was the fact that the Conservatives trailed a long way behind Labour in the opinion polls during the final 16 months of Mrs Thatcher's leadership which, more than anything else,

was responsible for the Cabinet-led back-bench revolt which brought about her downfall in November 1990.

40. See P. Norris, *The Volatile Electorate: British By-elections since 1900* (London: Oxford University Press, 1990).
41. For a fuller discussion, see D.E. Butler and A. Ranney (eds), *Referendums: A Comparative Study of Practice and Theory* (Washington, DC: American Enterprise Institute, 2978).
42. F.O. Goman, *Edmund Burke: His Political Philosophy* (London: Allen & Unwin, 1973), pp. 55–6.
43. The *Independent*, 17 June 1992.
44. J.J. Rousseau, *The Social Contract* (New York: Harper, 1949), p. 85.
45. See D. Kavanagh and P. Morris, *Consensus politics from Attlee to Thatcher* (Oxford: Basil Blackwell, 1989).
46. Norman Tebbit, *The Times*, 7 October 1987.
47. See A. Sampson, *The Changing Anatomy of Britain* (London: Hodder & Stoughton, 1982) and *The Essential Anatomy of Britain* (London: Hodder & Stoughton, 1992), for a vivid description of the Establishment in Britain.
48. V.O. Key, *Public Opinion and American Democracy*, p. 285.

Further reading

Broughton, D., *Public Opinion Polling and Politics in Britain* (London: Prentice Hall/Harvester Wheatsheaf, 1995).
Clemens, J., *Polls, Politics and Populism* (London: Gower, 1983).
Cook, C. and Ramsden, J. (eds), *By-Elections in British Politics* (London: University College Press, 1997).
Johnson, N., *In Search of the Constitution* (London: Methuen, 1980).
Jowell, R. et al., *British Social Attitudes* (London: Gower, 1990).
Ranney, A. (ed.), *The Referendum Device* (Washington, DC: American Enterprise Institute, 1981).
Teer, F. and Spence, J.D., *Political Opinion Polls* (London: Hutchinson, 1973).
Worcester, R.M. and Harrop, M. (ed.), *Political Communications* (London: Allen & Unwin, 1982).
Wybrow, R.J., *Britain Speaks Out, 1937–87* (London: Macmillan, 1989).

PART 3

Parliament

Parliament

9 The Monarchy

There was a time not many years ago – certainly the late 1970s (1977 was Queen Elizabeth II's Silver Jubilee) and the early 1980s (1981 saw the wedding of Prince Charles to Lady Diana Spencer) – when the institution of Monarchy was sure of itself, widely admired and overwhelmingly popular; in short, it stood at the apex of British society. The fact that the Monarch was a constituent part of the British system of government tended to be glossed over, even ignored altogether. Indeed, part of the success of constitutional monarchy in Britain is that it ceased – in one sense at least – to be politically important, the system became one in which 'the Queen reigned but did not rule'. It cannot be glossed over, let alone ignored, today. The difficulties arising from problems in the personal lives of members of the Royal Family – highlighted by the breakdown in the marriage of the Prince and Princess of Wales – came to a head in the 1990s reaching a crescendo in the immediate aftermath of the tragic death of Diana, Princess of Wales, in 1997. Consequently, the institution of Monarchy and the role of the Royal Family in Britain today has come to be at the very centre of public debate.

It is important to place the Monarchy in its contemporary context, and it is the object of this chapter to do this. Before doing so, however, some knowledge of the past is necessary, because in order to be able to understand and appreciate the position of the Monarchy within today's constitutional framework, some knowledge of its history and consequent development is essential. In Britain continuity and change have gone hand-in-hand. Continuity has been the dominant feature of British constitutional development, yet this has not meant the absence of change as age-old institutions have evolved and adapted to fulfil purposes often very different from those for which they were originally created. As a result there is often a striking contrast between the theory and practice of the British Constitution. Nowhere is this more true than in the case of the Monarchy.

In formal terms the Monarchy is one of the institutions of Parliament. With a Queen on the throne every Government is 'Her Majesty's Government', the Opposition is 'Her Majesty's Loyal Opposition' and the Monarch still has an important, if largely formal, part to play in Britain's constitutional arrangements. It is the Queen who opens each new session of Parliament, who reads 'the Queen's Speech' from the throne on such occasions, and who gives her Royal Assent to Bills, without which they could not become Acts of Parliament and hence the law of the land.

9.1 Origins and historical development

In Saxon times kings were guided by the 'Witan' or 'Witenagemot', an assembly of the most important men – lay and ecclesiastical – in the kingdom. The membership was not static and consisted of those individuals whom the King chose to summon to the three or four meetings held annually. As Ronald Butt put it, 'his natural advisers were the elders; the men of strength, standing, influence, experience and knowledge'.[1] Those present included the chief officers of the Royal Household and others who held high state office, the 'Earldormen' who represented central Government in the shires, Bishops and other senior churchmen, and the principal men who held land directly from the King. The functions of the Witan were ill-defined, but included 'discovering and declaring' the law, in other words being a consultative and law-consenting assembly. In addition, the Witan sat as the King's Supreme Court of Justice. Its actual power was inversely proportional to that of the King at any given time. Together the King and the Witan were the highest authority in the nation.

A new stage in the development of the nation's political institutions was ushered in when Duke William of Normandy defeated Harold, the Saxon claimant to the throne, at the battle of Hastings in 1066. William the Conqueror (as he came to be known) launched a series of campaigns which, in the fullness of time, left him in undisputed control of the country. It was William's claim that he had succeeded to the throne through inheritance. As a result he laid claim to an element of continuity and sought to maintain many of the laws of his Saxon predecessors. At the same time, however, he brought with him from Normandy a new approach to government, namely the feudal system, whereby the greater part of the country was governed by tenants-in-chief, or barons, who held their land directly from the King on condition that they defended the conquered territory for the King. By the time of the Domesday survey of 1085–86, only about eight per cent of the land remained in English hands; indeed, of the tenants-in-chief only two appear to have been English.

The Norman barons assembled in the Court of their sovereign to regulate the affairs of their tenancies, settle disputes between each other and organise the military subjection of the conquered lands. The tenants-in-chief thus assembled – both lay and ecclesiastical – became known as the *Magnum Concilium* or Great Council. This gathering assisted the King in determining state policy, supervised the work of public administration, acted as the highest Court of Justice, and made or modified the laws of the land. It met only three or four times a year, and then only for a matter of days at a time. For this reason there grew up the *Curia Regis* or 'Court of the King' – an inner circle of the Great Council – whose function it was to assist the sovereign on a day-to-day basis during the long periods when the Great Council was not assembled.

This system of government worked well for a while, but towards the end of the twelfth century tensions between the King and his 'great men' began to increase. Matters were brought to a head by the abuse of autocratic power by King John. Consequently the barons seized an opportunity in 1215, when the King's position was weakened by war and misrule, to force him to sign a *Magna Carta* or Great Charter, setting out some clear principles and safeguards against further abuse of power by the Monarch. The intention of the barons was not to create a new system of government, but rather to ensure better government under the existing system. The agreement foreshadowed three of the main principles upon which the development of Parliament was later to be based, namely that:

1. the King himself was subject to the law;
2. the King could only make law and levy taxation with the consent of the governed;
3. the King's subjects did not owe the King absolute or unconditional obedience.[2]

In short, it asserted the limited nature of kingship – the principle of conditional or 'constitutional' Monarchy which was to be the mainspring of Parliamentary action against the Crown in the seventeenth century.

Within three months of the King's seal being affixed to Magna Carta, however, the concordat which it was supposed to symbolise broke down. John died in October 1216 to be succeeded by Henry III, then a boy of nine. Henry occupied the throne for the next 56 years during which time politics were dominated by the struggle between the Crown and the barons. The relationship between the King and the barons deteriorated eventually to the point of armed conflict in which the barons under Simon de Montfort were victorious. In 1265 de Montfort convened a Parliament (literally a 'talking gathering') which was attended not only by the barons, clergy and knights of the shires, but also by two burgesses from each of the Boroughs known to be supportive of the baronial cause. This occasion has since been widely recognised as the real beginning of Parliament at Westminster, and it is the recognition of this date which allows the British Parliament to claim that it is one of the oldest Parliaments in the world.

During the decades and centuries which followed, the holding of 'Parliaments' containing representatives of the counties and towns became the accepted custom and practice and 'Parliament' itself became a feature of the governmental system. At no time was Parliament definitively established, it merely evolved as a consultative forum for the King and the politically important sections of his realm. By about 1485 – the beginning of the Tudor period – it may be said that the institutional foundations of Britain's constitutional Monarchy had been laid. See Figure 9.1 for a chronological table of Monarchs.

The Tudor Monarchs found that there was political advantage for them in having their national policies – such as Henry VIII's break with the Catholic Church or Elizabeth I's determination to oppose the Spanish kings – supported and endorsed by the people's representatives in Acts of Parliament. For this reason no Tudor Monarch sought to dispense with Parliament and each member of the dynasty in turn put its support to good use. However, sessions of Parliament were infrequent and brief. Even during the 45-year reign of Elizabeth I, when Parliament counted for more than had previously been the case, the two Houses (Lords and Commons) were in session on average for little more than three weeks a year. During this period, the House of Lords became predominantly a secular body, while the House of Commons was increased in size by more than a third to about 300 members. By the end of the sixteenth century Parliament had become second only to the Monarch as a power in the land.

Constitutional tensions came to the fore under the Stuarts, especially James I and Charles I, who laid claim to the 'divine right of kings' and sought to reduce or deny the privileges acquired by Parliament under the Tudors. The mounting disagreements between Crown and Parliament eventually led to the Civil War (1642–49), the triumph of the Parliamentary forces, the execution of Charles I and the abolition of the Monarchy itself. For the next few years the country was ruled by Oliver Cromwell in what was called a Protectorate. It was not until after Cromwell's death in 1658 that the

Figure 9.1   British Monarchs since the Norman conquest

The Normans		The Stuarts	
William I (the Conqueror)	1066–1087	James I	1603–1625
William II	1087–1100	Charles I	1625–1649
Henry I	1100–1135	*The Interregnum*	
Stephen	1135–1154	Oliver Cromwell	1649–1658
Henry II	1154–1189	Richard Cromwell	1658–1660
Richard I (the Lionheart)	1189–1199	Charles II	1660–1685
John	1199–1216	James II	1685–1688
		William III & Mary II	1689–1702
The Plantagenets		Anne	1702–1714
Henry III	1216–1272		
Edward I	1272–1307	**The Hanoverians**	
Edward II	1307–1327	George I	1714–1727
Edward III	1327–1377	George II	1727–1760
Richard II	1377–1399	George III	1760–1820
		(Regency 1811–20)	
Lancaster		George IV	1820–1830
Henry IV	1399–1413	William IV	1830–1837
Henry V	1413–1422		
Henry VI	1422–1461	**Saxe-Coburg and Gotha /**	
		1917: Windsor	
York		Victoria	1837–1901
Edward IV	1461–1483	Edward VII	1901–1910
Edward V	1483	George V	1910–1936
Richard III	1483–1485	Edward VIII	1936
		George VI	1936–1952
The Tudors		Elizabeth II	1952–
Henry VII	1485–1509		
Henry VIII	1509–1547		
Edward VI	1547–1553		
Mary I	1553–1558		
Elizabeth I	1558–1603		

Monarchy was restored, Charles II assuming the throne for the Stuarts in 1660. However, the relationship between the Monarch and Parliament was not a great deal better than before the Civil War and matters worsened under James II as he sought to reassert the divine right of kings. The eventual result was that Parliament and people combined against the King who fled the country in 1688 and was replaced by William of Orange (from Holland) and his English wife Mary – daughter of Charles I – in 1689. This peaceful transfer of constitutional power from one Monarch to another – but actually from the Monarchy to Parliament – has been described by Whig historians as 'the Glorious Revolution'. The new constitutional settlement was given statutory recognition in the 1689 Bill of Rights. The 'pretended power' of the Crown to suspend or dispense laws, or to govern without the consent of Parliament was declared illegal, as was the levying of taxation by Royal prerogative without the authority of Parliament. The 1689 Bill of Rights and the 1701 Act of Settlement confirmed the victory of Parliament in the struggle against the Crown. Constitutional Monarchy was developed in place of the unfettered rights of Kings and Queens, and Parliamentary supremacy in the government of the country was well and truly established.

From the beginning of the Hanoverian dynasty in 1714, the role of the Monarch was reduced still further. George I (1714–1727) was a German, speaking no English and knowing nothing of English ideas and ways. George II (1727–1760), although more interested in his adopted land, lacked the ability to make himself felt in government affairs. In these circumstances the powers which their predecessors had so jealously sought to preserve fell into disuse or into the hands of the English aristocracy who effectively ran the country throughout the eighteenth century. George III (1760–1820), perhaps more English than Hanoverian, tried to recapture the Royal position that had been lost. His influence on Government and politics was far greater than that of his two predecessors to the extent that in 1780 the House of Commons felt driven to declare that the 'influence of the Crown has increased, is increasing, and ought to be diminished'.[3]

After the resignation of Lord North as Prime Minister in 1782, the tide turned back in favour of Parliament, and during the last decades of his reign, the King was discredited by madness. By then a satisfactory way of running the Government without the active participation of the Monarch had been developed. This fact, soon to be buttressed by successive extensions of the franchise in the nineteenth century, meant that no Monarch could turn back the clock. Admittedly, Queen Victoria (1837–1901) occasionally sought to play a partisan political role, but her attempts were increasingly marginalised by a long chain of Prime Ministers who countered her ambitions by variously ignoring, opposing or flattering her. The result is that since Victorian times no British Monarch has been seriously tempted to step outside the bounds of constitutional Monarchy.

9.2 Powers and functions

The Monarchy has long been regarded as one of the 'dignified' rather than 'efficient' parts of the constitution, to use Walter Bagehot's nineteenth-century terminology. As a result the powers which the Monarchy possesses today are more theoretical than real. They are based upon convention and residual Royal prerogatives, namely the residue of discretionary or arbitrary authority legally left in the hands of the Monarch. This means that they can only be used within the confines of well-established custom and practice. If such conventions were ever broken by the Monarch, it would discredit and possibly do fatal damage to the institution of the Monarchy itself. If the Monarch were to exercise constitutional power without reference to acknowledged advisers – including notably the Prime Minister of the day – it could provoke a constitutional crisis.

Today the powers and functions of the Monarchy essentially fall under two broad headings which can be termed the *political* and the *symbolic*. The constraints placed upon independent action by the Monarch in the political sphere have traditionally bolstered the strength of the Monarchy in the symbolic sphere. We shall now address the *political sphere* and deal with each power or function under that heading.

The choice of Prime Minister

Whereas George III chose and dismissed Prime Ministers almost at will, the last Monarch to choose a Prime Minister without advice was Queen Victoria in 1894, and today Elizabeth II is 'free' to choose as Prime Minister only the elected leader of the party which commands majority support in the House of Commons. It would only be in the exceptional circumstances of a so-called 'hung Parliament' – that is, one in which no single party has an overall majority in the Commons – that the Monarch could be faced with alternatives, either calling upon the leader of the largest single party to form a minority Government or possibly looking for a senior political figure with a better chance of forming a Government which could command the support of a majority in the Commons.

During the first 20 years after the war, however, the position was more shaded, at any rate in relation to the choice of Conservative Prime Ministers. In January 1957, when Anthony Eden became too ill to continue as Prime Minister after the debacle of the Suez expedition, the Queen took advice from Sir Winston Churchill and the Marquess of Salisbury before inviting Harold Macmillan to form a new Government. In October 1963, when Harold Macmillan became seriously ill and a successor had to be found for the position of Prime Minister, the Queen again took advice – this time from Harold Macmillan himself in hospital – before inviting Lord Home to form a new Government. In both cases a new leader of the Conservative Party was said to have 'emerged' from the process of informal soundings which characterised the decision making of the party in those days. On the last occasion, the behaviour of the so-called 'magic circle' was strongly criticised by Iain Macleod and Enoch Powell, who subsequently both refused to serve in the Administration of Sir Alec Douglas-Home (the style to which Lord Home reverted after renouncing his peerage in order to sit in the Commons as Prime Minister).

Since 1965 in the case of the Conservative Party and 1922 in the case of the Labour Party, there have been systematic arrangements to ensure that a new leader is rapidly elected to succeed one who retires or dies. The result is that the role of the Queen is now confined to choosing as Prime Minister whoever has already been elected as leader of the governing party – hence John Major became Prime Minister in 1990 with his election as leader of the Conservative Party following Margaret Thatcher's decision to stand down. Of course, when there is a clear change of Government following a decisive result in a General Election, the Queen sends for the leader of the victorious party and invites that individual to form a new Government – hence Tony Blair was sent for in May 1997.

There has always been the possibility of a more significant role for the Monarch at a time of national crisis or when a General Election has produced a 'hung Parliament'. An example of the first eventuality occurred in 1931 when George V was instrumental in encouraging the formation of the National Government under Ramsay MacDonald in order to get through the Commons the deflationary economic measures which had not been acceptable to a significant part of the Parliamentary Labour Party when it had been in power on its own.[4] Another example occurred in 1940, when George VI had some influence on the choice of Winston Churchill to succeed Neville Chamberlain as Prime Minister after the latter had been discredited by the significant number of abstentions within the Conservative Parliamentary Party at the end of a crucial debate of confidence on the conduct of the war.[5]

An example of the second eventuality occurred in February 1974 when it seemed possible for a while that the Queen could have been drawn into party political controversy by Edward Heath's attempt to retain power for the Conservatives by offering a pact (and seats in his Cabinet) to the Liberals after his party had been defeated at the General Election. As things turned out, it proved impossible for the then Liberal leader, Jeremy Thorpe, to persuade his party to do such a deal with the Conservatives. Thus a few days later Harold Wilson was duly invited by the Queen to form a minority Labour Government.[6]

Certainly the scenario of a hung Parliament – the prospects of which could increase if a proportional voting system were to be adopted for Westminster elections – is one which could give rise to the Monarch being involved in some very awkward decisions which could have very far-reaching political consequences. In such a situation the Monarch would be expected to send initially for the leader of the largest single party in the Commons who would then have to see whether a minority Government could be formed or whether some sort of understanding with one or more of the other parties was possible. Either course would be quite plausible and it would only be in the unlikely event of complete Parliamentary deadlock that the Monarch might be advised to send for another party leader or political figure to form a viable Government – rather than agree to a dissolution very soon after the previous General Election. Whatever happened, the Monarch might be obliged to play a significant, even decisive, role in the process of Government formation. This is not something which either a Monarch or a Monarch's advisers would relish, since it might well cast doubt on the traditional impartiality of the Monarchy in party political matters. Nonetheless, the possibility remains that the Monarch might have to exercise the discretion which constitutionally rests in the Monarch's hands if there seemed to be no alternative.

Dissolution of Parliament

It is now a well-established convention that the Monarch can only dissolve Parliament at the request of the Prime Minister in office within the five-year maximum life span of a Parliament. It is necessary to go back to the reign of Queen Anne to find the last example of a Monarch exercising this Royal prerogative in an independent way. Even in 1913, when it was argued by some that George V might have been within his constitutional rights to have dissolved Parliament in order to give the electorate a chance to pronounce upon the Liberal Government's Bill for Irish Home Rule, A.V. Dicey, the eminent constitutional expert, was not prepared to recommend such a step to the King for fear that it would compromise the neutral constitutional position of the Monarchy.

Since that time various views have been advanced about the power of dissolution. One view, which was advocated by some after the very close General Election result in 1950, holds that if the Prime Minister in office is not prepared to recommend a dissolution in circumstances where it might be considered in the national interest to have one, then the Monarch is entitled to seek other leading figures in the Commons who might be prepared to recommend such a course. In the event such a view did not prevail in 1950 and it has not prevailed ever since. The Monarch is therefore bound by the established view and obliged to accept only the advice of the Prime Minister in office.

There may be a valid distinction, however, between the Monarch's constitutional right *to refuse* a dissolution on the grounds that it would lead to a premature and unnecessary General Election and the now unsustainable claim by any Monarch *to impose* a dissolution against the wishes of the Prime Minister in office. As far as the right to refuse a dissolution is concerned, no such request has been refused since the middle of the nineteenth century, although dissolutions have been refused more recently by Governors-General acting on behalf of the Monarch in Commonwealth countries. As for the right to impose a dissolution upon the Government of the day – in essence the dismissal of the Government – no British Government has been dismissed by the Monarch since George III dismissed the Fox–North Coalition (under the titular leadership of the Duke of Portland) in 1783.

There is another way in which the Monarch could become involved in controversy surrounding a dissolution. This would be if the Monarch suggested a dissolution – and hence a General Election – before agreeing to a request from the Government to exercise the Royal prerogative. This was the position in 1910 under both Edward VII and George V with regard to Herbert Asquith's request to create enough new Liberal peers to ensure the passage of the Parliament Bill in the House of Lords. On that occasion, successive Monarchs made it clear that they would not feel justified in creating new peers until the electorate had a chance to express its views on the issue in a General Election.[7] In practice, of course, the exercise of any such form of Royal initiative today would run the serious risk of totally discrediting the whole idea of constitutional Monarchy in Britain. It would involve the Monarchy in apparently taking sides in the political battle and that would destroy one of its vital assets, namely political impartiality.

Notwithstanding the conventional wisdom on this matter, there are some conceivable circumstances in which a Monarch might be justified in exercising the Royal prerogative of dissolution in defiance of the wishes of the Prime Minister in office. For example, if it became clear in the course of a 'hung Parliament' that a minority Government had outlived its usefulness and was simply standing in the way of a timely General Election which might produce a clearer Parliamentary result, those who advise the Palace on constitutional issues might be prepared to emphasise the arguments for such a dissolution. Such a course of action might also have to be considered if the Government broke the most basic of electoral rules, namely the five-year maximum life-span of a Parliament, without the necessary all-party support for doing so, as existed, for example, during both World Wars.[8]

Another possibility is that an unpopular Prime Minister might carry out a threat to call a General Election in mid-Parliament rather than agree under pressure from senior Cabinet colleagues either to change policy or even to resign as Prime Minister. In such circumstances established political conventions would support the position of the Prime Minister, even if there appeared to be sufficient support in the governing party for a change of policy or a new Prime Minister or both. Whatever might be the private views of the Monarch and the Monarch's advisers, it seems clear that they would be obliged to grant the wish of the Prime Minister in office, however unpopular that might be with most of the governing party. It would therefore be for the governing party to sort out its own problems of policy and personality rather than for the Monarch to intervene in the dispute. It must be stressed, however, that these are all hypothetical circumstances which would be most unlikely to arise in modern political conditions.

If the Monarch did proceed along these lines, it is likely that no more than a pyrrhic victory would be won, since such steps would almost certainly lead to a 'Monarch versus the people' clash at the ensuing General Election. This would probably be won by the aggrieved party and might put in jeopardy the very continuation of

Britain's constitutional Monarchy. Indeed, the exercise of Royal prerogative by the Governor-General in Australia in 1975 – when Sir John Kerr dismissed Gough Whitlam's Labour Government – was undoubtedly an important factor behind the rise of Republican sentiment in that country. The practical conclusion is that the Monarch in Britain today has no sensible alternative to accepting the advice of the Prime Minister in office, whatever might appear to be the arguments for doing otherwise. Nonetheless, a former Cabinet Secretary has argued that the right to refuse a request for a dissolution still exists: 'It seems to me that it's not just theoretically correct, but common sense that the Sovereign should have the right to withhold consent to a request for a dissolution, if only as a check upon the irresponsible exercise of the Prime Minister's right to request one, however improbable such a contingency might be.'[9]

Assent to legislation

Royal assent to legislation is another aspect of the Monarch's prerogative which has become purely formal over the years. In the seventeenth century Charles II managed to postpone or quash Bills of which he disapproved by the simple expedient of mislaying them. Queen Anne was the last British Monarch to veto legislation outright when in 1707 she withheld assent from the Scottish Militia Bill. George III certainly encouraged the House of Lords to reject the India Bill in 1783, while George IV managed to delay legislation on Catholic emancipation by letting it be known that he was not happy with the idea. Queen Victoria was the last Monarch seriously to consider withholding assent, although there is some evidence that in 1913 George V toyed with the idea of refusing assent to the Government of Ireland Bill which was then being put through Parliament under the Parliament Act of 1911.

During Elizabeth II's Silver Jubilee speech to Parliament on 4 May 1977 – at a time when the question of legislating for devolution to Scotland and Wales was very firmly on the political agenda – the Queen declared: 'I cannot forget that I was crowned Queen of the United Kingdom of Great Britain and Northern Ireland. Perhaps this Jubilee is a time to remind ourselves of the benefits which union has conferred, at home and in our international dealings, on the inhabitants of all parts of this United Kingdom.'[10] Some took these words to be a warning shot fired across the bow of those politicians who sought in any way to weaken the unity of the Kingdom, concluding that the Queen was in fact pointing to a possible future use of the Royal veto, one used to uphold her coronation oath. Nevertheless, no such veto was used and the legislation involved received Royal Assent in 1978.[11]

The granting of Royal Assent has become a mere formality. Any attempt to make it otherwise would prompt a constitutional crisis and, consequently, all involved would go to great lengths to avoid any such eventuality. In short, it is today a well established convention that the Monarch accepts and acts upon the advice of Ministers.

Creation of peers

The Monarch has the power to create new peers and in certain cases it is believed that the Palace still has some influence over the final selection from the various names proposed. Certainly there was a time when the use of this particular Royal prerogative was formidable indeed. For example, in 1711–12 Queen Anne, on the advice of her Ministers, created twelve new peers precisely to ensure ratification by the House of Lords of the Treaty of Utrecht. In 1831 even William IV's threat (at the instigation of his Whig Prime Minister, Lord Grey) to create new peers helped to ensure the passage of the first Reform Bill against fierce Tory opposition. In 1911 the willingness of George V to create as many as 400 new Liberal peers (discreetly made known by the Prime Minister, Herbert Asquith) caused the hereditary majority of Conservatives in the upper House to give way to the Liberal majority in the House of Commons over what was to become the 1911 Parliament Act.[12]

Whereas in the past Monarchs took a keen interest in such matters – Queen Victoria, for example, refused to sanction the creation of individual peers on a number of occasions during her reign – in contemporary circumstances the creation of new peers by the Monarch has become little more than a constitutional formality. Appointments to the peerage are normally made twice a year when the names of the newly created peers appear in the Honours Lists. The appointments are made on the basis of advice given and co-ordinated by the Prime Minister in office, although anyone can make suggestions which are then discreetly sifted and assessed by a small unit of civil servants attached to 10 Downing Street before the Prime Minister of the day makes the formal recommendations.

Since 1964, life peerages have been the usual order of the day, mainly because successive Prime Ministers since that time have not felt generally inclined to recommend the creation of any more hereditary peerages. Yet this is no more than a convention of fairly recent times and as such it has been capable of modification. For example, immediately after the 1983 General Election William Whitelaw and George Thomas were made hereditary peers on the recommendation of Margaret Thatcher. The former was in recognition of William Whitelaw's long and distinguished service to the Conservative Party and the nation, culminating in his period as Deputy Leader of the party from 1975 to 1983 and to enable him to take over as Leader of the Lords. The latter was in recognition of George Thomas's distinguished period as Speaker of the House of Commons from 1975 to 1983. In each case the Queen complied with the Prime Minister's wishes, as is now customary in such matters, although the element of controversy in restoring the principle of hereditary peerages was reduced by the fact that William Whitelaw had no male heir, only daughters who were not eligible to inherit the title, and George Thomas was a bachelor. More recent departures from the modern norm in favour of life peerages were the granting of an hereditary Earldom to Harold Macmillan – who had male heirs – in 1984, and to Prince Andrew on the eve of his wedding to Sarah Ferguson in 1986.

Some argue, however, that difficulties could arise for the Monarch if a future Government were committed to the abolition of the House of Lords and hence the creation of a unicameral Parliament. This would probably entail the creation of a very large number of new peers whose sole task on taking their seats in the House of Lords would be to vote for a House of Commons Bill designed to bring about their abolition.[13] In such circumstances much would depend on whether the Monarch considered that the Government had a clear mandate for such a far-reaching constitutional change. If so, the Monarch and the Monarch's advisers would probably conclude that there was no alternative but to go along with the idea. Yet it is not absolutely certain that the Monarch would acquiesce in this procedure, since the Monarch might be convinced that the demise of the House of Lords foreshadowed the demise of the Monarchy itself. What is clear is that any attempt by the Monarch to block such a measure would probably have fatal consequences for the future of the Monarchy itself.

Granting of honours

The Monarch is also formally involved in the granting of honours, both civilian and military, to those whom it is customary for the nation to recognise and reward in this way. As with the creation of peerages, this usually happens twice a year when the Honours Lists are published. However, there can be special investitures to recognise special events: for example, the honours awarded to those whose acts of conspicuous gallantry had been recognised during the 1982 Falklands campaign and the 1990–91 Gulf War. In nearly all cases the system is a popular and effective way of recording public recognition for those who have made notable contributions to the well-being of British society and who have shone in various walks of life. It also adds lustre to the institution of Monarchy and provides regular opportunities for rewarding service to the community in ways which do not involve bribery or corruption.[14]

Nearly all such honours are awarded by the Monarch on the formal recommendation of the Prime Minister who, in turn, is advised by a small Civil Service unit attached to 10 Downing Street. Once again this unit sifts and assesses a wide range of recommendations made by MPs and others. Even so, a few honours have remained in the personal gift of the Monarch – for example, the Order of the Garter, the Order of the Thistle, the Order of Merit, and the Royal Victorian Order. Usually these awards have no political significance, but are simply a way of signifying the Monarch's personal recognition of an outstanding person, such as Mother Theresa, the Catholic nun who worked for the hungry and the destitute in Calcutta until her death in 1997 and who was awarded the Order of Merit by the Queen on her visit to India in 1983, or Nelson Mandela, President of South Africa, who was awarded the Order of Merit by the Queen during her state visit to that country in 1995. Very occasionally such awards do have political significance, albeit marginally, as was the case in 1990 when the Queen awarded Margaret Thatcher the Order of Merit following her resignation as Prime Minister, and Denis Thatcher an hereditary Baronetcy in recognition of his role in support of his wife; or in 1998 when the Queen invested Emperor Akihito of Japan with the Order of the Garter during a state visit to Britain, despite the hostility from former prisoners of war of the Japanese who have been seeking a full apology and financial compensation.

Public appointments

The Monarch plays a formal role in a vast range of public appointments, since all important posts in the Civil Service, the police, the judiciary, the BBC and the Church of England are filled in the name of the Monarch, not to mention, of course, the Ministerial appointments in every Government. Once again such appointments are usually made on the basis of advice given or co-ordinated by the Prime Minister, often with the help of the small Civil Service unit attached to 10 Downing Street which processes the recommendations from all quarters. Senior appointments in the Diplomatic Service are made on the advice of the Foreign Secretary, in the Armed

Services on the advice of the Defence Secretary, in the police on the advice of the Home Secretary, and in the judiciary on the advice of the Lord Chancellor. However, many other senior Ministers effectively have considerable power of public patronage which they exercise in the name of the Monarch and every Prime Minister takes a close personal interest in all the main appointments.

In these circumstances it is not surprising perhaps that some concern has been expressed from time to time about the nature and scope of such political patronage, which is Royal in name but Ministerial in fact.[15] Concern arises over the apparent lack of public scrutiny or subsequent democratic accountability of such public appointments, not to mention the implications for public expenditure in the wide range of public bodies to which such people are appointed. The problem is compounded in the eyes of many observers when such public appointments appear to be made – to a considerable extent at least – on party political criteria. Yet this kind of political patronage has not led the critics to attack the Monarchy, since it is well understood that the Monarch is merely acting as a dignified rubber stamp for appointments which are not really within her control.

Mercy and pardon

The prerogatives of mercy and pardon are still vested in the Monarch, who is entitled to exercise them on the advice of the Home Secretary of the day. Yet since the House of Commons voted in 1965 to abolish the death penalty on a provisional basis, and since that decision has subsequently been confirmed in successive free votes over the years, it now seems that this particular aspect of the Royal prerogative has fallen into disuse. Pardons are granted only after conviction and sentence in rare cases when there is some special reason why a sentence should not be carried out or a conviction should be quashed – for example, a discovery that the evidence on which a conviction was based is actually false. Thus the exercise of this aspect of the Royal prerogative has been both formal and rare.

Other formal functions

In Britain the Government of the day enjoys not merely powers derived from Parliament but also those that it exercises in the name of the Crown, namely what are known as the powers of the Royal prerogative. This enables a Government to act in a variety of ways without requiring the prior and formal approval from Parliament. In such cases the Monarch is acting as a splendid and dignified veil for decisions which are actually taken by Ministers in the Government of the day.

In the conduct of foreign policy *the Royal prerogative to conclude treaties* enables Ministers to reach legally binding agreements with other Governments or international organisations without having to secure the *prior* approval of Parliament. For example, the 1972 Treaty of Accession which took Britain into the European Community was signed by Edward Heath as Prime Minister in Brussels without the Government having had to secure the prior approval of Parliament at Westminster. The same procedure applied to the 1986 Single European Act and the 1992 Treaty of Maastricht, both of which involved initiatives taken by Ministers in the name of the Crown which had the effect of committing the United Kingdom to certain highly controversial courses of action *before* Parliament had an opportunity to give a formal opinion. Unlike the position in the United States, where treaties negotiated by the Administration have to secure the 'advice and consent' of the Senate *before* they can become American law, or the position in the European Union where the European Parliament has to give its formal opinion *before* the Council of Ministers and the Commission can conclude a new European treaty in the name of the European Union, the position in Britain is that only if treaties have legislative consequences in the United Kingdom does the Government have to involve Parliament. Even then, this need only be done *after* a treaty has been signed by a Minister on behalf of the Crown. Indeed, one can go further: during the passage of the legislation implementing the 1992 Treaty of Maastricht one Minister appeared to suggest that it would be quite possible to ratify the Treaty by means of the Royal prerogative, irrespective of the decision of Parliament.

A *declaration of war* is made officially in the name of the Monarch, although in the nuclear age such formalities would be of little real interest if time were very short. In the event of a war which directly affected Britain, it would be for the Prime Minister and a few senior colleagues and military advisers to take all the key decisions. Such decisions would merely be made known to and later ratified by the Monarch as and when appropriate. In the case of the 1982 Falklands conflict, Britain did not declare war on Argentina, since there were compelling technical and legal reasons for not doing so in the light of British diplomatic efforts at the United Nations and elsewhere. Although the Queen was not therefore required to sign a declaration of war, she was kept informed by the Prime Minister at every stage of the conflict.

Colonial constitutions are promulgated or changed in the name of the Monarch. For example, the constitution of Zimbabwe, which British Ministers under Lord Carrington had negotiated with the representatives of all the parties at Lancaster House in 1979–80, was eventually promulgated in the name of the Queen and later given statutory authority in the Zimbabwe Independence Act of 1980.

The creation of public corporations is also done in the name of the Monarch through the granting of Royal Charters to the bodies concerned. For example, the BBC became a public corporation by Royal Charter in 1926. The various 'new towns', such as Milton Keynes, which were built over the years since the Second World War, were established in a similar way.

Governments can also *create, abolish or merge Departments* by Royal prerogative – as in 1974 when a new Energy Department was set up, or in 1992 when the Energy Department was merged with Trade (and later Industry), or when the Department for National Heritage was created in 1992 (later to be called the Department for Culture, Media and Sport).

The significant growth of so-called QUANGOs (Quasi-Autonomous Non-Governmental Organisations)[16] under recent Governments has been another aspect of central Government activity facilitated by the use of the Royal prerogative. This may have simplified the procedures of public appointments by Ministers, but it assisted the 'unelected state' to grow without undue hindrance from Parliament or other elected bodies and, consequently, has been the subject of some criticism.[17] Indeed, the use of the powers of the Royal prerogative can be extremely controversial as Margaret Thatcher and her Government found when they used it to remove the right of trade union membership from employees at GCHQ, the Government's Communications

Headquarters at Cheltenham, in 1984. This right was restored by the Labour Government which was returned to power in 1997, again through exercising the powers of the Royal prerogative. Alleged misuse of the Royal prerogative was also one of the questions raised during the Scott Inquiry into the Conservative Government's handling of the 'Arms to Iraq' affair over the period 1984–90.[18]

Unpublicised functions

Within the political sphere the Monarch also performs some unpublicised functions, the most notable of which are the regular and confidential conversations with the Prime Minister of the day. On such occasions the Monarch enjoys what Walter Bagehot once described as 'the right to be consulted, the right to encourage and the right to warn'.[19] In modern circumstances these rights are exercised during private meetings every week at Buckingham Palace (when the Monarch is in residence) and once a year for a week-end in the late summer when the Monarch is resident at Balmoral in Scotland.

Queen Elizabeth II's experience of the affairs of state is unrivalled in modern times, since in more than 45 years on the throne she has been served by ten different Prime Ministers and 17 different Governments. She came to the throne in 1952 when Winston Churchill was Prime Minister, President Truman occupied the White House and Stalin still ruled in the Kremlin. She has the undisputed right to see all state papers and in consequence she is almost certainly better informed about key political developments than virtually anyone else in Britain. Her private advice to all Prime Ministers must be invaluable in view of the length and variety of her experience of matters of state. Indeed one former Prime Minister apparently accepted the analogy of paying a weekly visit to a psychiatrist and admitted that he could say things to the Queen that he could not say even to his closest political colleagues.[20] The functions of the Monarchy are summarised in Figure 9.2.

Figure 9.2 Functions of the Monarchy

Political functions	Symbolic functions
Royal Assent to Bills	State Opening of Parliament
Dissolution of Parliament	Head of the Commonwealth
Choice of Prime Minister	State visits abroad
Creation of peers	Entertaining foreign heads of state in UK
Granting of Honours	Patronage of good causes
Public appointments	Visits to all parts of UK
	Military ceremonial
	Religious ceremonial
Formal functions	**Unpublicised functions**
Conclusion of treaties	Personal contacts with the Prime Minister
Declaration of war	Confidential advice to the Government
Introduction or amendment of colonial constitutions	
Establishment of public corporations	**Quasi-judicial functions**
Creation/abolition of Government Departments	Prerogative of mercy
	Prerogative of pardon

Symbolic functions

The Monarch and other members of the Royal Family play an important symbolic role in many different ways. For example, Queen Elizabeth II and Prince Philip have made frequent State visits to countries in all parts of the world. Queen Elizabeth II has also played an important role at successive Commonwealth Conferences and in entertaining foreign Heads of State or Government when they visit Britain. In all such activities the Monarch and other members of the Royal Family are serving the national interest, as defined by the Government of the day. As far as the Monarch's travels are concerned, Royal trips abroad are judged to be good for British foreign policy and for the promotion of British trade. Furthermore, the making or withholding of a Royal visit can be used by the British Government as a way of indicating approval or disapproval of political regimes in other countries. For example, in 1995 the Queen paid official visits to President Yeltsin in Russia and President Mandela in South Africa, while in 1998 there were visits to Brunei, Malaysia, France and Belgium.

In relation to the Commonwealth, Queen Elizabeth II plays a particularly significant role as titular head of that free association of nations and she is known to attach particular personal importance to it. This has involved her and other members of the Royal Family in travelling tens of thousands of miles to different parts of the world to see and be seen by many thousands of people in the 53 member states of the Commonwealth (54 including Britain, in sixteen of which the Queen is Head of State). It has also led her to attach considerable personal importance to her annual Christmas broadcasts to the people of Britain and the Commonwealth.

Within Britain the Monarch and other members of the Royal Family are involved by custom and tradition, and often at the instigation of the Government of the day, in the promotion of good causes and in various forms of public ceremonial designed to raise the morale or reinforce the unity of the British people. For example, the Queen usually leads the nation in paying respect to the dead of two World Wars, and other conflicts in which the British armed services have been involved, at the Cenotaph in Whitehall on Remembrance Sunday every year. The Queen and other members of the Royal Family also pay conspicuous visits to all parts of the United Kingdom, including notably those where the people have suffered from natural disaster (as when hundreds of school children were killed by a coal-tip landslide at Aberfan in 1966) or been involved in serious social unrest (as in the inner city areas of London, Bristol and Liverpool after the 1981 riots).

Members of the Royal Family also make an important contribution to the work and activities of a large number of charities. Indeed, in 1997 25 per cent (667) of all engagements carried out by members of the Royal Family within the United Kingdom were carried out on behalf of charities. In these and many other ways the Monarchy makes a valuable contribution to the underlying cohesion and morale of the people in the United Kingdom. See Figure 9.3 for a summary of the Royal Family's working year.

9.3 Financing the Monarchy

Although any well-researched attempt at a comprehensive cost–benefit analysis of the British Monarchy would almost certainly show that it generates a financial profit for

Figure 9.3 The Royal Family's working year

	Official visits, opening ceremonies and other engagements	Receptions, lunches, dinners and banquets	Other engagements, including investitures, meetings attended and audiences given	Total number of engagements in the United Kingdom	Engagements while abroad on official tours	Total
Queen Elizabeth II	133	73	234	440	55	495
Duke of Edinburgh	165	148	50	363	174	537
Queen Mother	29	15	11	55	0	55
Prince of Wales	215	91	67	373	161	534
Duke of York	96	42	12	150	173	323
Prince Edward	36	34	7	77	112	189
The Princess Royal	301	103	62	466	213	679
Princess Margaret	–	–	–	32	–	32
Duke of Gloucester	115	36	34	185	86	271
Duchess of Gloucester	74	29	14	117	62	179
Duke of Kent	154	41	24	219	32	251
Duchess of Kent	–	–	–	5	–	5
Princess Alexandra	78	25	17	120	35	155
Total	1396	637	532	2602	1103	3705

Source: *The Times*, 2 January 1999.

the nation, for many years the annual publication of the Civil List (the grants from tax-payers for the upkeep of the Royal Family) tended to provoke considerable media and public interest – and in many cases criticism – not least because of the Queen's great private wealth and tax-free status at the time. In 1990, in an attempt to defuse these issues an agreement was reached between the Queen and the Government setting an annual sum of £7.9 million on the Civil List to be averaged over the period 1991–2000 for the support of the Queen, with further annual allowances totalling £1.88 million net to be paid to the Duke of Edinburgh, the Duke of York, the Queen Mother, Princess Margaret, the Princess Royal and other active members of the Royal Family. The income of the Prince of Wales and his two sons, Prince William and Prince Harry, is derived from the rental income and other revenues of the Duchy of Cornwall and so he was not part of this settlement.[21] In addition, the costs of maintaining the Royal residences (except for Balmoral and Sandringham), the Royal Flight and the Royal Yacht *Britannia* were to continue to be met from public funds.

Unfortunately for the Monarchy, the fate of the Royal Family seemed to go from bad to worse in the early 1990s. One result of this was that in November 1992 it was announced – on the initiative of the Queen herself – that the Monarch would start paying Income Tax on her private fortune and that she would finance the Civil List payments made to members of her family other than herself, her husband and her mother.[22] This unexpected announcement seemed to meet much of the public criticism head on, as did the announcement in June 1994 – again on the Queen's personal initiative – that the Royal Yacht *Britannia* would be decommissioned in 1997 and the Royal Family would in future pay for their private use of the Queen's Flight. In short, the methods of financing the British Monarchy have changed very significantly in the 1990s as the Royal Family and the whole institution of Monarchy have come under much more widespread media exposure and public criticism. See Figure 9.4 for a summary statement of the financing of the Monarchy.

Figure 9.4   Financing the Monarchy[A]

Item	1990 Settlement*	1998
Civil List[B] (palace staff etc.[C])	£7,900,000	£7,900,000
Queen Elizabeth, The Queen Mother[D]	£643,000	£643,000
Prince Philip, Duke of Edinburgh[D]	£359,000	£359,000
Other members of the Royal Family[D]	£879,000	–
Other Royal expenditure[E]	£3,850,000	£3,400,000
Spent by Whitehall Departments:[F/G]		
Palace maintenance (D of E/DETR)	£25,650,000	£19,600,000
Royal yacht (MoD)	£9,272,000	Decommissioned in 1997
Queen's flight (MoD)[F]	£6,745,000	⎫
Royal train (D of T/DETR)[F]	£2,276,000	⎬ £17,300,000
Civil air fares (MoD)[F]	£825,000	⎭
Publicity (COI)[G]	£376,000	£471,000
Overseas visits (FCO)	£33,807	⎫
Honours administration (Treasury)	£190,000	⎬ £469,764
Equerries (MoD)	£192,000	⎪
Yeomen of the Guard (D of E/DETR)	£48,000	⎭
Security	Classified	Classified
TOTAL	£59,238,807	£50,142,764

Notes:
*See Report of the Royal Trustees, 15 October 1990 (London: HMSO, 1990).
A   These costs should be set against the annual revenue of the Crown Estates (£55 million in 1989–90; some £113.2 million in 1997–98) surrendered to the Exchequer – 'for the benefit of the taxpayer' – by each Sovereign at the beginning of each reign since 1760.
B   The figure of £7.9 million is an annual estimate over the period 1991–2000, and is arrived at by adopting the sum of £5.9 million from 1990, allowing for capital expenditure on information technology, and increasing the total by 7.5 per cent a year for inflation. The figure for each year is then adjusted downwards by a percentage factor each year to reflect efficiency savings.
C   Staff costs represent approximately 70 per cent of this total.
D   Calculated on the same principle as B, above.
E   Those expenditures incurred by the Queen as a consequence of her position as sovereign which are not met by the Civil List.
F   Buckingham Palace took direct control of the Royal travel budget in 1997.
G   Buckingham Palace took direct control of the communications budget in 1998.
Note: The Queen's personal expenditure as a private individual is met from her own resources and, consequently, does not form a part of these figures. (See Note 21 at end of this chapter).

As far as scrutiny of the costs of Monarchy are concerned, in 1998 the Queen agreed to allow Parliament's financial watchdog, the National Audit Office, direct access to the finances of the Royal palaces, the Queen's Flight and the Royal Train and authorised the publication of the accounts for the Royal travel allowance, both marked improvements in the transparency and openness of spending of taxpayers' money in support of the Royal Family.

9.4 The Monarchy, the media and the public

Traditionally, the Monarchy has been one of the most revered of Britain's national institutions. An opinion poll in 1969 demonstrated considerable public support for the Monarchy in that only 13 per cent thought it should be ended, 30 per cent thought it should continue as it was, and 50 per cent thought it should continue but change with the times (7 per cent had no opinion).[23] A similar opinion poll in 1980 showed that the appeal of the Monarchy was derived to a significant extent from the fact that it was usually projected to the people as the 'Royal Family', which 80 per cent of those questioned thought to be 'a marvellous example to everyone of good family life'.[24] The same poll also showed that 90 per cent preferred the idea of Monarchy to a Republic of the French or American type. This was a point emphasised by another poll in 1984 in which 77 per cent of the respondents considered that Britain would be worse off and only 5 per cent thought that Britain would be better off as a Republic.[25]

From the mid-1980s however, both the respect for and the popularity of the Monarchy plummeted, with polls showing that those who considered that Britain would be better off without the Monarchy had increased to 13 per cent in 1987, 20 per cent in 1992 and 27 per cent in 1995.[26] By 1996 for the first time the balance of public opinion was that Britain would *not* have a Monarchy in 50 years' time, with a poll showing that only 33 per cent believed that the Monarchy had a long-term future, while 43 per cent believed that it did not.[27]

The institution and its leading personalities became subjected to an unprecedented degree of media scrutiny, disclosure and criticism. In March 1992 it was confirmed that the Duke and Duchess of York were to separate. Equally, there was increasing concern about the marriage of the Prince and Princess of Wales. Media speculation and public prurience reached fever pitch with the publication of a book by Andrew Morton entitled *Diana: Her True Story*, in which it was claimed that the Princess of Wales was 'trapped in a loveless marriage' and was so unhappy that she had attempted to commit suicide on six occasions. In November 1992, during a Royal visit to South Korea, the awful relationship between the Prince and Princess of Wales became painfully apparent to TV audiences, thus increasing speculation about separation and even divorce for the Royal couple.

Throughout this time some Members of Parliament were agitating for a reduction in the financial privileges enjoyed by the Monarchy. Such agitation reached a peak after a fire destroyed part of Windsor Castle on 20 November 1992 and the Government announced that it would cover all the costs involved in repairs and restoration. On 24 November 1992, in a speech at the Guildhall, the Queen spoke of how the year of her fortieth anniversary on the throne had deteriorated from a celebration to what she termed an *'annus horribilis'* (awful year). She admitted that the Monarchy and other institutions were not above reproach, but suggested that less savage and more constructive criticism would be appreciated. The year ended with the *Sun* newspaper's premature publication of the Queen's Christmas broadcast, and 1993 began with the Monarch successfully suing the paper for breach of copyright – an action which was settled out of court in the Queen's favour.

From the mid-1980s, therefore, the gap between myth and reality in public perceptions of the Monarchy widened and people were clearly made aware of the fact that the

Royal Family consisted of frail human beings rather than impeccable public symbols. As a result, the moral authority of the Monarchy sharply declined. However, as British society became less deferential, it became harder, even impossible, to maintain the magic and the mystery surrounding the British Monarchy. As Jack Straw wrote in 1993: 'it is increasingly clear that the current Royal system, with its large number of participants and its emphasis on show business, has little serious future [...] there is little mystery about a soap opera'.[28] Paddy Ashdown, then Leader of the Liberal Democrats, called for much of the pomp and circumstance surrounding the Monarchy to be stripped away, while Dr John Habgood, then Archbishop of York, raised doubts about the Monarch's continuing role as 'Defender of the Faith' and Head of the Church of England.[29] Some opinion formers, such as Ludovic Kennedy, even argued that the Monarchy had had its day and the time had come for a Republic.[30] In 1996 the *Independent on Sunday*, in a banner edition declared simply that it was 'Time for a Republic'.[31]

Monarchy and the death of Diana

The news of the death of Diana, Princess of Wales, in a car crash in a Paris underpass at the end of August 1997 stunned Britain as no event had done since the assassination of President Kennedy in 1963. Although she held no official position – following the divorce she was no longer a member of the Royal Family – in life and even more so in death she acquired the same iconic significance as Kennedy. After a brief shining moment the candle had burned out, but the legend of 'the people's Princess' never would. The event was a tragedy that touched the hearts of many millions of people, and the Prime Minister spoke of 'a nation in shock'.

To begin with there was a growing sense of anger at the apparent manner of her death – killed in a high-speed chase escaping from a group of paparrazzi photographers. It appeared that she died as she had lived, hounded by and in the full glare of the media. Public anger was initially directed towards the press, but as officials debated the complexities of protocol for the funeral and the Royal Family – on holiday in Balmoral – sought to deal with the tragedy with traditional stoicism and dignity; the focus of public criticism, even anger, shifted to the Royal Family itself and their failure to make any public expression of grief over the death. Diana had always put emotional needs before duty; for others in the Royal Family it had always been the other way round, in public if not in private. In the face of massive displays of very public outpourings of grief throughout the country, one commentator wrote simply that 'the Windsors still don't understand us' and noted that: 'Having lost its most popular member, the Firm has made the kamikaze decision to distance itself still further.'[32] A leading editorial declared, 'If only the Royals dared weep with the people'[33] and it was said that a period of profound reflection in and about the future of the House of Windsor was necessary.[34]

Grudgingly and gradually – that was certainly the perception of many – the Monarchy began to compromise in the face of public pressure as first it was announced that the funeral route would be lengthened from that which had originally been stated, then more and more books of condolence were put out for the public to sign, and then it became apparent that both protocol and tradition were in many respects at least to be set aside for the funeral itself. But protocol dictated that the Royal Standard flew at the top of the mast at Balmoral while no flag at all flew over

Buckingham Palace, and this became the focus for a 'People v. the Palace' campaign in the press. The headline of the *Daily Mail* said simply, 'Let the flag fly at half mast',[35] the *Express* demanded, 'Show us you care',[36] the *Sun* asked 'Where is our Queen? Where is our flag?',[37] the *Mirror* urged, 'Speak to us Ma'am',[38] while an editorial in *The Times* noted, 'Queen and Country: a bond that weakens behind the closed doors of Balmoral'.[39] On the day before the funeral the Queen broadcast live to the nation. Then came the events of the funeral itself, the Royal Family standing in the street and bowing their heads as the cortege drove past, the Union flag flying at half-mast over Buckingham Palace, Elton John singing in Westminster Abbey, Earl Spencer's address and the applause for its hard-hitting message.

At the end of it all the Prime Minister, Tony Blair, observed that: 'As a result of what happened, we have changed.'[40] Indeed for many British people Britain felt like a subtly different country as the events unfolded and the reaction to them – and the reaction to the reactions – altered perceptions and understandings. The people in a strange bout of collective emotion rather than by any conscious plan seemed to know what they wanted; conversely, it was the oldest national institution of all, the Monarchy, that gave every impression of being unsure of itself. Consequently the events surrounding 'the people's funeral' for 'the people's Princess' – the tens of thousands who lined up to sign the books of condolences, the arrays of bouquets of flowers, the Queen's broadcast, the flag finally flown at half-mast over Buckingham Palace, the more than a million who thronged into London, the many millions who watched the funeral on television, the song sung by Elton John, the clapping following Earl Spencer's funeral address, the people lining the route from London to Althorp House and throwing yet more flowers onto the cortege – were all signs of a very British revolution, where nothing had changed yet nothing would be the same again.[41]

During her broadcast following the death of Diana, the Queen noted that 'there are lessons to be drawn from [Diana's] life and from the extraordinary and moving reaction to her death.'[42] Indeed, the death brought pressure on the Royal Family to reinvent itself, to adapt or die. But this in fact had always been the watchword of the British Monarchy: it continued to exist in Britain because of its very ability to adapt, to move with the times, to adjust to the demands of the media and the people. Indeed, the events following Diana's death should be seen not as the beginning of the end for the Monarchy, but simply as one more recent stage in its evolutionary development. As one observer noted, 'What happened in the end was a triumph for Royalty, not the disaster many diagnosed at first; proof of Royalist ardour, not the beginning of the end of the magic;'[43] a viewpoint that was later supported by the opinion polls.[44]

Letting daylight in on magic: the dangers of de-mystification

It is apparent from developments over recent years that public attitudes towards the Royal Family as public figures and the British Monarchy as an institution have become much less positive, certainly ever since the media began to give saturation publicity to the events leading up to and surrounding the breakdown of the marriages of the Prince and Princess of Wales and of the Duke and Duchess of York. These developments, along with apparently lurid revelations about the personal lives of some of those involved, severely tarnished the 'ideal family' image which advisers at Buckingham Palace had earlier sought to present. The result was a combination of prurience and ridicule which led some observers to speculate that Monarchy itself had had its day.

Obviously it has been enormously difficult, particularly for the younger generation within the Royal Family, to live anything resembling a 'normal' life when they have had to do so in the glare of such unremitting and intrusive media publicity. However, in an age when the traditional 'nuclear family' has become a minority model rather than the social norm and when as many as one in two new marriages are destined to end in divorce, it may be that a more tolerant and indifferent public is simply amused and titillated by what has befallen certain members of the Royal Family. Furthermore, it should be noted that it has been possible for some members of the Royal Family to overcome their personal problems and go on to restore their reputation in the eyes of the public through assiduous good work and public service, as Princess Anne, the Princess Royal, has shown so emphatically.

When in 1969 Queen Elizabeth II first decided to accept the advice that she should allow the television cameras in to show not only her public face but also her more private and family activities, a fateful decision was made from which it has been difficult to retreat, even though at times she must have been sorely tempted to do so. To begin with, all went well in that the Silver Jubilee celebrations in 1977 and the Royal Wedding in 1981 of Prince Charles and Lady Diana Spencer demonstrated a flair for publicity and spectacular ceremonial which worked positively for the Monarchy and indeed the whole Royal Family. Such glittering pageantry, as well as the more homely Christmas broadcasts by the Queen to the nation and the Commonwealth, did much to tighten the bonds of sentiment and loyalty between the Royal Family and the wider public. Yet, as we can now see with the advantage of hindsight, there was always a risk in this strategy, namely, that the greater sense of familiarity which the Queen and their extended family engendered by allowing the mass media to pry and eavesdrop on their lives would breed, if not contempt, then a larger degree of public cynicism and hence a loss of public respect not only for members of the Royal Family but also the institution of Monarchy. Distance and mystique were previously important – some would say vital – elements in the public appeal of the Monarchy. As Walter Bagehot observed, 'Above all things our Royalty is to be reverenced, and if you begin to poke about it you cannot reverence it ... we must not let daylight in on magic'.[45] Now that the media have to a large extent demystified the public image of the Monarchy – now that daylight has been let in on the magic – it will be much more difficult to restore a sense of public deference and to reinforce the sense of public respect which is still felt for the Queen herself.

Nevertheless the scenes associated with Diana's death and funeral derived from her affiliation with Royalty – she had been wife to the future King, she was mother to a future King, she had been (and to many people at the time of her death she still was) a Royal Princess. By the end of 1997 the proportion of those who believed that Britain would be better of without the Monarchy had fallen to 15 per cent, those expressing approval of Prince Charles had risen to 61 per cent (from 46 per cent in August 1997)[46] and during 1998 there were already signs of 'William-mania', public fascination with all things to do with Prince William.

It should always be remembered that on many occasions before in its long history the Monarchy has engendered great controversy and experienced extensive public criticism, and yet has managed to survive such crises. For example, the Prince Regent and William IV were deeply unpopular and heavily ridiculed in the early nineteenth century; Edward VII, as Prince of Wales, was the butt of many jokes and much public ribaldry; and Edward VIII effectively split public opinion down the middle during the Abdication Crisis in 1936 when he chose marriage to an American divorcee, Wallis Simpson, in preference to the throne. It may well be, therefore, that the Monarchy will survive its present troubles as well and that in some years' time all the controversies of the 1980s and 1990s will be largely forgotten. After all, the present Queen is not only one of the most respected Monarchs in the world, but also likely to remain on the throne as long or longer than her illustrious predecessor Queen Victoria. This very longevity and continuity in the person of the Queen herself is likely to stand the institution of Monarchy in good stead and may be enough in itself to counter and eventually defeat the waves of strident media criticism and malicious innuendo against the most vulnerable or foolish members of the Royal Family. Time alone will tell.

9.5 Conclusion

The Monarchy still holds the supreme position at the apex of British society, yet it does so at the expense of its previous claims (before 1837) to wield real political power. Today it serves as a powerful symbol of continuity and community which is particularly valuable to the nation in difficult or troubled times – as long as it judges the public mood correctly.

The Monarchy also provides an excellent example of the many paradoxes which abound in the British political system. It is an inherently conservative institution which can facilitate change. Whatever else may be altered, the Monarchy still appeals to most people as an unchanging icon, a reassuring symbol. Such seemingly permanent and unchanging institutions can make it easier for people to accept even radical change in other areas of their lives. The Monarchy therefore plays an important part in preserving the cohesion of British society and it contributes significantly to the sense of underlying national unity which helps to hold the British people together. Its reputation in the eyes of a significant number of British people was damaged during the 1980s and 1990s by revelations about the private lives of some members of the Royal Family and by its actions in the immediate aftermath of the death of Diana, Princess of Wales. Consequently it will not be easy or perhaps even possible to restore the Monarchy to the position it once held in the hearts and minds of the British people. Nonetheless, it is deeply rooted in the British psyche and cannot be ignored.

Suggested questions

1 What are the functions of the British Monarchy?
2 Does the Monarch have any real power in Britain today?
3 'The Queen reigns but does not rule.' What does this mean?

Notes

1. R. Butt, *A History of Parliament: the Middle Ages* (London: Constable, 1989), p. 2.
2. *Ibid.*, p. 60
3. The Dunning Motion – a resolution by John Dunning in April 1780 and approved by 233 votes to 190. See: J. Brooke, *King George III* (London: Constable, 1992), pp. 201–18.
4. See F. Hardie, *The Political Influence of the British Monarchy 1868–1952* (London: Batsford, 1970), pp. 150–3, and W.I. Jennings, *Cabinet Government* (London: Cambridge University Press, 1951), pp. 40–2.

5. See S. Bradford, *George VI* (London: Weidenfield & Nicolson, 1989), pp. 310–12.
6. See J. Campbell, *Heath* (London: Nonathan Cape, 1993), pp. 616–18
7. See. F. Hardie, *The Political Influence of the British Monarchy 1868–1952*), p. 67.
8. The Parliaments elected in 1910 and in 1935 were each extended by all-party agreement, in the former case until 1918 and in the latter case until the 1945 election which took place soon after the agreed ending of the 1940 Coalition Government.
9. Lord Armstrong of Ilminster. Cited in P. Hennessy and S. Coates, 'The back of the Envelope: Hung Parliaments the Queen and the Constitution', Strathclyde Analysis Papers, No. 5, 1991, p. 10.
10. Elizabeth II's Silver Jubilee address to Parliament, 4 May 1977. See B. Pimlott, *The Queen* (London: HarperCollins, 1996) pp. 446–7.
11. Because the Welsh voted against what was on offer and because in Scotland the 40 per cent threshold was not met (see p. 186) neither the Welsh Act (1978) nor the Scotland Act (1978) were put into effect; indeed, both were subsequently repealed.

    While considering the issue of Royal Assent it is interesting to note a recent Belgian experience: In April 1990 both Houses of Parliament approved the legalisation of abortion during the first 12 weeks of pregnancy. King Baudouin, a devout Catholic, refused for reasons of conscience to sign such a law but, in order to avoid the constitutional crisis that would have resulted from such an action, abdicated (4 April). This enabled the Government to declare (under Article 79 of the constitution) that the King was temporarily incapable of ruling and, consequently, promulgated the new law during the King's 'absence' from the throne. The following day (5 April) King Baudouin (under Article 82 of the constitution) reassumed the mantle of Monarch following a request for him to do so from a special joint session of Parliament. In short, a solution to the problem was found in a novel, though effective, way.
12. Some historians have argued that in 1831 the threat of the mob and in 1911 the threat of rebellion in Ireland also played a part in persuading the Conservative peers to give way to the Government of the day in the Commons.
13. This was the proposal advocated in the late 1970s by the Labour politician Tony Benn – he suggested the creation of 1000 Labour peers.
14. Although there have been occasions in the past when the honours system was abused for political purposes – for example, by Lloyd George as Prime Minister when Maundy Gregory was active on his behalf in offering peerages in return for financial support.
15. Among those who have expressed concern about this are Tony Benn in *Arguments for Democracy* (London: Jonathan Cape, 1981), and P. Holland and M. Fallon in *Public Bodies and Ministerial Patronage* (London: CPC, 1978).
16. See Chapter 15 for a full discussion of Quangos.
17. See F.F. Ridley and D. Wilson (eds) *The QUANGO Debate* (Oxford: University Press, 1995) pp. 128–144, 145–162 and 163–181.
18. See A. Tomkins, *The Constitution after Scott: Government Unwrapped* (Oxford: University Press, 1998).
19. W. Bagehot, *The English Constitution* (London: Fontana/Collins, 1963) p. 111.
20. A point made by Dr David Butler in correspondence with one of the authors.
21. Total Duchy of Cornwall Estate income – from land and property in 22 counties – for the 1997–98 financial year amounted to £14,101,000 including some £11,246,000 from lettings of agricultural, commercial and residential properties and £2,074,000 from investments on the Stock Exchange and interest on cash holdings. Operating costs over the same period stood at £7,096,000, leaving a surplus of £7,005,000. As a Crown body the Duchy is tax-exempt, but the Prince of Wales voluntarily pays income tax – currently at 40 per cent – on his income from it, tax being calculated after deducting official expenditure, the biggest element of which is his staff of about 70 at St James's Palace and Highgrove House. Source: *The Times*, 24 June 1998.

22. In 1998 *The Sunday Times* calculated the Queen's private fortune to be some £250 million, comprised of an investment portfolio of £70 million, property of £100 million and jewellery, art and racing interests worth £80 million. See 'Rich List 1998', *The Sunday Times*, 19 April 1998, p. 20.
23. *The Sunday Times*, 23 March 1969.
24. *Now*, 8 February 1980 (a weekly news magazine which later ceased publication).
25. *The Times*, 22 April 1984.
26. ICM Polls, *Guardian*, 9 January 1995.
27. MORI/*Independent on Sunday*, 18 February 1996.
28. *Guardian*, 19 January 1993.
29. *Guardian*, 25 January 1993.
30. See 'Who should be President of Britain?', *The Times*, 18 January 1992.
31. *Independent on Sunday*, 18 February 1996.
32. Suzanne Moore, *Independent*, 3 September 1997.
33. *Independent*, 3 September 1997.
34. Editorial, *Independent*, 2 September 1997.
35. *Daily Mail*, 4 September 1997.
36. *Express*, 4 September 1997.
37. *Sun*, 4 September 1997.
38. *Mirror*, 4 September 1997.
39. *The Times*, 4 September 1997.
40. Tony Blair, *Breakfast with Frost*, BBC1 TV, 7 September 1997.
41. See Elaine Showalter, 'Storming the Wintry Palace', *Guardian*, 6 September 1997; editorial, *Sunday Times*, 7 September 1997 and Steve Crawshaw, 'People Power Never Before Seen in Quiet Cosy Britain', *Independent*, 6 September 1997.
42. Broadcast, BBC1 TV, 5 September 1997.
43. Hugo Young, 'The Saving of the Monarchy', *Guardian*, 8 September 1997.
44. See MORI poll, *The Times*, 24 December 1997.
45. Walter Bagehot, *Op. Cit.*, p.120.
46. MORI poll 12–15 December 1997, *The Times*, 24 December 1997.

Further reading

Bagehot, W., *The English Constitution* (London: Fontana/Collins, 1963).
Barnett, A., *Power and the Throne: The Monarchy Debate* (London: Vintage, 1994).
Bradford, S., *Elizabeth* (London: BCA, 1996).
Bogdanor, V., *The Monarchy and the Constitution* (London: OUP, 1995).
Borthwick, R., *Long to Reign Over Us? The Future of the Monarchy* (London: John Stuart Mill Institute, 1994).
Borthwick, R., *The Monarchy* (Barnstaple: Philip Charles Media, 1990).
Dimbleby, J., *The Prince of Wales* (London: Little Brown, 1994).
Flamin, R., *Sovereign* (London: Bantam, 1991).
Hall, P., *Royal Fortune: Tax, Money and the Monarchy* (London: Bloomsbury, 1992).
Hardie, F., *The Political Influence of the British Monarchy 1868–1952* (London: Batsford, 1970).
Holden, A., *The Tarnished Crown* (London: Bantam, 1993).
Keay, D., *Elizabeth II: Portrait of a Monarch* (London: Ebony Press, 1992).
Pimlott, B., *The Queen* (London: HarperCollins, 1996).
Ziegler, P., *Crown and People* (London: Collins, 1978).

Website

The Queen   http://www.royal.gov.uk/

10 The House of Lords

As we saw in Chapter 9, an important – possibly the most important – feature of the British constitution is its capacity gradually to adapt to changing circumstances. In this respect the House of Lords is a microcosm of the British constitution, since throughout its long history it has been able to do just this. In contrast to other Second Chambers elsewhere in the world which have been specifically created with powers and composition clearly defined in basic constitutional documents, the House of Lords is the product of history. It was not created by Founding Fathers or under a Basic Law; it has simply developed and changed organically in the soil of British history. This is not to say that its evolution has been linear or continuous; on the contrary, it has been haphazard, spasmodic and uncertain. Yet it has survived for a very long time and its evolutionary adaptability will probably enable it to survive a good while longer.

10.1 Origins and historical development

As the product of evolution rather than deliberate creation, it is not possible to say exactly when the House of Lords originated, for Parliament as a whole had no single genesis. Rather it came into being gradually 'from the medieval Court and Council where Plantagenet kings consulted the great men of the realm to secure support and offer their people justice'.[1] Nonetheless, as we saw in the previous chapter, it is possible to find the deepest roots of the British Parliament in the consultative customs of the Saxon kings who took periodic advice and support from the 'Witan'.

From the late thirteenth century onward there was a gradual and halting alignment of the membership of Parliament into two principal groups: the House of Lords and the House of Commons – the former composed of men who attended in response to individual summons from the Monarch, and the latter of people elected in the Counties and Boroughs who attended in a representative capacity. By 1485 – at the outset of the Tudor period – the institutional foundations of Parliament had been laid. As we also noted in the previous chapter, the power of Parliament (especially the Commons) made steady progress throughout the Tudor period, to such an extent that the historic clash in the seventeenth century with the pretensions of the Stuart Monarchy became inevitable. In consequence the nation experienced a Civil War (1642–49), the execution of the King (1649), an interregnum under Oliver Cromwell (1649–58), the restoration of Charles II as King (1660), and the so-called 'Glorious Revolution' (1688–89) before a new constitutional order was firmly established.

As the principle of representative and responsible government developed in the eighteenth century, the power of control over the Executive fell increasingly to the House of Commons rather than the House of Lords. It was to the Commons, not the Lords, that individual Ministers and the Government collectively came to be held responsible. However, the Lords did not meekly accept the constitutional superiority of the Commons, and the leading territorial magnates in the upper House managed to retain effective control over the lower House by controlling the processes of election to many seats in the Commons, especially the so-called pocket or rotten boroughs. The personification of this manipulative power in the second half of the eighteenth century was the Duke of Newcastle who, in co-operation with his noble friends and relatives, managed to control as many as 80 to 100 seats in the House of Commons – enough 'placemen' to ensure that he and his faction either formed or dominated many Administrations.

The Reform Act of 1832, which enlarged the electorate from about three to five per cent of the adult population and which abolished many of the rotten boroughs, deprived the House of Lords of much of the political power which it had enjoyed in the eighteenth century. The Tory peers had strongly opposed it, but in the end were forced to concede to a combination of Liberal reformers in both Houses (led by Earl Grey) and popular pressure from what was called 'the mob' – that is, angry public demonstrations in favour of reform. The Monarch, William IV, also played a significant part on the side of reform by indicating his willingness to create a large number of new peers who, if necessary, could have swamped the die-hard opposition in the Lords. In the event, this threat, along with the other pressures mentioned, was sufficient to get the legislation passed.

The expansion of the suffrage and the development of more modern electoral arrangements between 1832 and 1867 gave the House of Commons a growing claim to genuinely representative credentials. At the same time, the power of the landed interest was in decline in the wake of the growth of the industrial towns and, after the repeal of the Corn Laws in 1845, the enormous impact of free trade on the economy and society. These and other factors brought about a gradual shift of political power away from the House of Lords to the House of Commons – for example, the proportion of peers in the Cabinet declined from about three-quarters to about a third of the total. During these years the House of Lords was able to head off challenges to its legal powers and to the hereditary basis of its membership as long as the peers were content to play second fiddle to the Commons. Indeed, in many ways the leading figures in the Lords were careful not to alienate or challenge their counterparts in the Commons for fear of provoking further instalments of constitutional reform which would have weakened their institutional position still more. As Walter Bagehot explained the position of the Lords in 1867: 'the House has ceased to be one of the latent directors, and has become one of the temporary rejecters and palpable alterers' (of legislation passed by the Commons).[2] He went on to describe the House of Lords as a Chamber with powers of delay and revision, but little else and concluded that: 'its danger is not in assassination, but atrophy; not abolition but decline'.[3]

It was not long, however, before the validity of Bagehot's observations was challenged, since during the last decades of the nineteenth century and the first decade of the twentieth century there was recurrent conflict between the Tory and Unionist majority in the Lords and the Liberal majority in the House of Commons. This finally came to a head in the constitutional crisis of 1909–11. In 1893 the Conservative and Unionist majority in the Lords had heavily defeated William Gladstone's Liberal attempt at Irish Home Rule. In 1906 the Liberal Education Bill had been very drastically amended by the Lords, and consequently abandoned by the Commons. The Lords had rejected the Land Valuation Bill in 1907 and again in 1908, the Licensing Bill in 1908, and finally (and fatefully) the Liberal Finance Bill of 1909. The quarrel between the two legislative Chambers – a quarrel, in Winston Churchill's words 'often threatened, often averted, long debated, long delayed, always inevitable' – had come to a head at last.[4]

The House of Commons immediately voted to declare the House of Lords' action unconstitutional and a breach of privilege. Parliament was then dissolved. In the ensuing General Election the Liberals were returned to power, although with a much reduced majority. However, when the Parliament Bill to curb the power of the Lords was introduced into the Commons in April 1910, the Liberals were able to count on Labour and Irish Nationalist support. The first consequence of the new Parliamentary arithmetic was that the 1910 Liberal Budget was passed by the Commons and then accepted by the Lords without a vote. However, owing to the death of King Edward VII on 6 May 1910, the Parliament Bill itself was not proceeded with. Following the failure of attempts to negotiate an agreed settlement at a constitutional Conference, the Liberal Government decided that a second General Election should be held in 1910 before it could legitimately proceed with the Bill. The Prime Minister (Herbert Asquith) also obtained a promise from the new King, George V, that should the Liberals win the election he would agree to create enough new Liberal peers to overcome the die-hard Conservative opposition to the Bill in the Lords. The new House of Commons (elected in November 1910) was almost identical in composition with the old, so the Liberals remained in office, reintroduced the Parliament Bill and promptly secured a Parliamentary majority for it in the Commons. This time the Lords gave it a Second Reading, but watered it down in Committee. On its return to the Commons, the lower House refused to accept most of the amendments proposed by the Lords and promptly returned it to the peers. On 10 August 1911, after considerable behind the scenes activity and argument within the Conservative and Unionist peers, the majority in the upper House were reluctantly prepared to accept the Bill as it then stood as the lesser of two evils. Consequently, the Lords voted not to insist on their amendments by 131 votes to 114, with some 300 Conservatives abstaining.[5]

The *1911 Parliament Act* removed the Lords' power to reject Money Bills, while their powers to veto ordinary Public Bills were replaced with a power of delay for a maximum of two years. This meant that if a Bill were approved by the Commons in three successive Sessions, it automatically became law at the end of that time whether or not their Lordships were content. Together with the reduction in the maximum permitted span of a Parliament from seven to five years, this meant that any Bill passed by the Commons in the first two sessions of a five-year Parliament would inevitably become the law of the land if insisted on by a majority in the Commons. Although the Bill curbed the powers of the Lords, the composition of the upper House was not addressed, any more than the whole issue of the appropriate functions for a curtailed second Chamber.

In 1917 a constitutional Conference of 32 distinguished individuals under the chairmanship of Viscount Bryce was set up with the object of finding solutions to the problems of reforming both the powers and the composition of the House of Lords. In its report the following year it proposed that a reformed upper House should have three-quarters of its members indirectly elected by MPs on a regional basis, while the remaining quarter should be chosen by a joint committee of both Houses. As far as powers were concerned, it proposed that legislation which was the subject of dispute between the two Houses should be submitted to a 'free conference', consisting of a small number of Members from each House who should be given very great power in determining whether or not the legislation should pass and in what form. There was, however, a substantial dissenting minority within the Bryce Commission and this disagreement was sufficient to prevent the Government of the day from acting on its majority recommendations. Even though many other proposals were made between the wars for reforming the House of Lords and the Labour Party Conference became committed to the abolition of the second Chamber, the constitutional position remained unchanged until after the Second World War.

In 1945 the victorious Labour Government did not put forward any proposals for reform or abolition of the House of Lords, since it had many other more pressing legislative priorities – such as the creation of the National Health Service, various nationalisation Bills, and the legislation to bring about independence for India. Furthermore, the Conservative peers under the leadership of Lord Salisbury adopted a deliberate convention of self-restraint under which they did not oppose at Second Reading any legislative measures emanating from the 1945 Labour Manifesto, although they were prepared to press amendments to Labour Bills in the name of 'improving' the legislation. By 1947, however, the mood of the Conservative majority in the upper House had changed and it became clear that, at any rate in relation to the proposed nationalisation of the iron and steel industries, the Conservative peers were prepared to use their inbuilt majority against such legislation. Faced with this threat from their Conservative opponents in the Lords, Labour Ministers secured approval in the Commons for a further Parliament Bill designed to reduce the delaying power of the upper House to one year. In spite of efforts to find a compromise between the respective majorities in the two Houses, agreement proved impossible. The Government went ahead without all-party agreement, using provisions of the 1911 Parliament Act to ensure the passage of what was to become the *1949 Parliament Act*. This effectively reduced the period of delay to less than thirteen months, cut from three to two the number of Sessions in which a disputed Bill had to be passed by the Commons, and from three to two years the period of maximum delay following Second Reading in the Commons. Once again, however, the Act did nothing to change the composition or the functions of the second Chamber. When the Labour Party lost office and the Conservative Party returned to power in 1951, the whole issue of comprehensive reform fell out of the reckoning.

A number of minor reforms did, however, take place during the late 1950s and early 1960s. In 1957 daily allowances were introduced for travel to and from and attendance at the House of Lords. In 1958 the *Life Peerages Act* made possible the creation of Life Peers (that is, peerages which cannot be inherited), including peerages for women in their own right. In 1963 the *Peerage Act* enabled female hereditary peers to sit and allowed hereditary peers to renounce their titles – while in no way impinging on the rights of their heirs and successors – in order to make themselves eligible for membership of the House of Commons.[6] In the wake of these minor changes, the right of hereditary peers to sit in the House of Lords remained, as did the rights of the House as a whole to reject subordinate legislation, Private Bills and Bills to confirm provisional Orders. In addition, the minimal delaying power which the upper House still possessed not only gave the Peers the ability to dislocate considerably the Government's legislative programme, but also, in the final year of a Parliament, to defeat a Government Bill in its entirety.

The 1964 General Election saw the return of a Labour Government, which in the 1966 General Election managed to increase its majority in the Commons to nearly 100. One result of this was the subsequent introduction of the ill-fated *Parliament (No. 2) Bill* in 1968, which involved both a reduction in the total number of peers and an attack on the hereditary principle. The Bill secured a comfortable majority on Second Reading in the House of Commons. However, when it went into Committee on the floor of the House (as is conventional with constitutional measures), it was effectively defeated by a sustained and devastating filibuster by back-benchers on both sides of the Commons led by Enoch Powell and Michael Foot. Such traditionalists in the Commons opposed further reform of the House of Lords mainly on the grounds that a reformed second Chamber was likely to be a strengthened second Chamber, whereas they were determined to preserve the primacy of the House of Commons. In the face of this time-consuming and highly effective opposition, the Wilson Government abandoned the Bill, leaving the upper House still unreformed in both composition and functions.[7]

10.2 Composition

In 1998 the membership of the House of Lords was still divided between ecclesiastical and lay members, formally described as 'Lords Spiritual' and 'Lords Temporal'. The *Lords Spiritual* are the senior clergy of the Church of England, namely the Archbishops of Canterbury and York, the Bishops of London, Durham and Winchester, and the 21 most senior among the other diocesan Bishops. They cease to be Members of the House when they retire as Bishops and so are the only Members who are not Members until they die. They sit on the Bishops' bench and do not take a party whip. The *Lords Temporal* are the peers of England, Scotland, Great Britain and the United Kingdom. All peers of this type who are aged 21 or over, not bankrupt, of British Commonwealth or Irish nationality, and have not been convicted of treason (until pardon or completion of sentence) are entitled to take their seats in the House of Lords. The various categories of the peerage are shown in Figure 10.1.

Hereditary peers

In 1998 the vast majority of Members of the House of Lords were hereditary peers, namely those whose title was held by virtue of inheritance. Most hereditary peerages

Figure 10.1 Composition of the House of Lords: 19 November 1998

Peerage category	No.	%
Hereditary peers (male)	733	56.62
Hereditary peers (female)	16	1.23
Created hereditary peers (all male)	9	0.69
Life peers (male)	387	29.84
Life peers (female)	87	6.71
Law Lords (all male)	39	3.01
Bishops (all male)	26	2.00
Total	1297	100.00
of whom:		
Lords without writs of summons	68	5.24
Peers on leave of absence	63	4.86

pass through the male line, although certain peerages can pass through the female line in default of a male heir, while special provision has occasionally been made for a title to pass to a female – for example that of Earl Mountbatten of Burma in 1979. Only since the passage of the 1963 Peerage Act have female holders of hereditary peerages been able to sit in the House of Lords.

The peerage is an ancient order – for example the Baronies of de Ros and Mowbray date back to 1264 and 1283 respectively, the Earldom of Shrewsbury to 1442 and the Dukedom of Norfolk to 1483, each of which still has a title holder today. However, very few peerages which are still extant date back that far in British history and most of them have been created since the beginning of the nineteenth century; indeed, many such peerages were created during the early years of the twentieth century. Very few hereditary peerages have been created since 1964, because successive Prime Ministers since that time have believed (in line with public opinion) that such creations were 'a thing of the past'. Labour Prime Ministers have been ideologically opposed to the expansion of the hereditary peerage, while most Conservative Prime Ministers have not wanted to appear provocative on the issue. Yet there have been a few notable departures from this custom and practice. For example, in June 1983 William Whitelaw (Deputy Leader of the Conservative Party 1975–83) and George Thomas (Labour Speaker of the House of Commons 1975–83) were created hereditary peers on the recommendation of Margaret Thatcher, and in February 1984 Harold Macmillan finally accepted the hereditary Earldom of Stockton which he had previously declined on ceasing to be Prime Minister in October 1963.

It should not be assumed that all hereditary peers are mere 'backwoodsmen', since some of them have played a distinguished part in British Government. For example, Lord Home was Foreign Secretary in Administrations led by Harold Macmillan and Edward Heath; Lord Shackleton was a senior member of Harold Wilson's Administration (1964–70); and Lord Carrington was Defence Secretary in Edward Heath's Administration (1970–74) and Foreign Secretary under Margaret Thatcher (1979–82). The hereditary peerage has also produced some able and enthusiastic younger peers who have been useful and effective Ministers in successive Governments.

Life Peers

Life Peers are those whose title is limited to the lifetime of the title-holder. They fall into two categories: those created under the 1876 *Appellate Jurisdiction Act* and those created under the *1958 Life Peerages Act*. The former Act provided for a limited number of Lords of Appeal in Ordinary (Law Lords) who are appointed to hear and determine judicial appeals. The general category of Law Lords also includes those other peers who have held or are currently holding high judicial office in a superior Court – for example, present and former Lords Chancellor.

The 1958 Life Peerages Act enabled distinguished men and women from many walks of life to have peerages conferred on them in recognition of their political or public services to the nation. Such Life Peers may be former civil servants or diplomats; distinguished soldiers, sailors or airmen who rose to the highest military ranks; successful industrialists or prominent trade union leaders; distinguished scientists or other academics; renowned actors or other leading figures from the world of the arts and the media. In 1998 there were 103 women peers, an increase compared with earlier times, but still rather a small number and only 7.94 per cent of the total membership.

By far the largest single category of life peers is composed of politicians who have previously sat in the House of Commons or been active in local government. In the former case, they tend to have been either retired Ministers or previously eminent back-benchers whom the Prime Minister of the day and the other party leaders wish to reward with a seat in the Lords and whose political skills can be kept in play in the upper House. In the latter case, they tend to have been distinguished figures from the world of elected local government whose experience in that sphere is seen as an attribute for membership of the Lords. In both cases we can agree with Ian (now Lord) Gilmour who observed that: 'the House of Lords does something to reduce the hazards of a political career and embalms without burying a number of useful politicians'.[8]

Political affiliations

In 1998 the Conservative and Unionist peers were by far the largest grouping in the House of Lords, accounting for 36.78 per cent of the total eligible membership. The Conservative ranks in the upper House were disproportionately made up of hereditary peers (62.68 per cent) while the much smaller Labour contingent was mainly composed of life peers (89.77 per cent). The ranks of Liberal Democrat peers have tended to be drawn in approximately equal parts from hereditary and life peers. There was also an increasingly significant and influential group of non-party and cross-bench peers, who represented not only the interests of the law and the church, but also independent-minded laymen.[9] See Figure 10.2 for information on political affiliations in the House of Lords.

Any analysis of political affiliations in the House of Lords has to take account of a number of variables, such as the subject under discussion, the persuasive power of

Figure 10.2 Political affiliation in the House of Lords: 19 November 1998

Party/group	No.	Total %
Conservative	477	36.78
Labour	176	13.57
Liberal Democrat	69	5.32
Cross-bench	277	21.36
Non-party	71	5.47
No declared political affiliation	227	17.50
Total	1297	100.0

certain individuals, the day of the week and even the hour of the day. When these factors are taken into account, it becomes apparent that the *complete* Conservative control of the upper House, which was evident in the early and middle part of the century, has since disappeared. Gone are the days when a Conservative Government need have no fear of defeat in the Lords. Indeed, in the years between 1979 and 1997 the Lords were a frequent embarrassment, irritant and even obstruction to successive Conservative Administrations. Thus, although in the past there was an in-built Conservative majority in the Lords, by the late 1990s there was at best only a *potential* Conservative majority in the upper House. Certainly it was still easier for the Conservatives to win divisions than it was for Labour, but such outcomes were no longer inevitable. In short, one of the little-known secrets of the contemporary House of Lords was that *no single party could rely unreservedly on its support.*

Whatever the party political implications of recent developments in the House of Lords, it is as well to note that political divisions on party lines in the upper House are not usually as sharp or bitter as they can be in the Commons. This is apparent in the often relaxed and courteous style of debate in the Lords. Furthermore, most of the speech-making and legislative work is done by perhaps 150 to 200 particularly active peers, although a larger number usually take part in divisions. There have been occasions over the last five decades when the membership sought to amend or delay Labour Government legislation of which it disapproved and a surprising number of occasions on which similar treatment was meted out to Conservative legislation. Yet, as we shall see later in this chapter, the Conservative peers were usually rather careful not to use even the limited constitutional power which has been left to the Lords in ways which would have provoked a Labour Government or seriously embarrassed a Conservative Government. This is essentially because the House as a whole had an instinct for self-preservation and peers of all affiliations recognised that incautious action on their part could lead to significant constitutional conflict with the Commons and even perhaps the eventual abolition of the second Chamber.

10.3 Powers and functions

The classic statement of the powers and functions of the second Chamber in the British political system was made in the Bryce Commission Report of 1918.[10] The present activities of the House of Lords can be considered in the light of the four powers and functions identified in that report. These were:

1. *The power of legislative delay* – the ability to delay for about one year the passage of a Bill approved by the Commons.
2. *The power of legislative scrutiny and revision* – the ability to amend and improve a Bill inadequately drafted or considered by the Commons.
3. *The power of well-informed discussion and deliberation* – the ability to debate the issues of the day in a better-informed and less partisan way than is often the case in the Commons.
4. *The power to initiate non-controversial legislation*, thus relieving the Commons of at least some of the legislative burden at the beginning of every session of Parliament.

To this list suggested by the Bryce Commission in 1918 we should add:

5. *The judicial powers and functions of their Lordships*, exercised by the so-called Law Lords sitting in either one or two Appellate Committees.
6. *The scrutiny powers and functions*, exercised by special committees of peers established for the careful consideration of Private Bills, delegated legislation flowing from Whitehall Departments, and draft European Legislation flowing from European institutions in Brussels.

Legislative delay

In theory, the power of legislative delay is used by the Lords when they refuse to approve legislation already passed by the Commons. The 1911 Parliament Act laid the foundation for this by enabling the Lords to delay legislation (with the exception of Money Bills) for up to two years. Subsequently the 1949 Parliament Act reduced the delaying period to one year. In practice, since 1911 this power has been used only sparingly, because the latent Conservative majority in the upper House has been well aware of the danger that excessive use of this power could hasten the day when a Labour Government might decide to reform radically or even to abolish the Lords altogether. The only Bills which passed into law under the terms of the 1911 Parliament Act were the *1914 Welsh Church Act*, the *1914 Government of Ireland Act*, and the *1949 Parliament Act*.

Until the *1991 War Crimes Act*, no Bills passed into law under the terms of the 1949 Parliament Act. However, the House of Lords did seek to use its constitutional delaying power on two occasions in the mid–1970s when the then Labour Government pressed ahead with highly contentious legislation (namely the *1975 Trade Union and Labour Relations Bill* and the *1976 Aircraft and Shipbuilding Industries Bill*) at a time when it had little or no overall majority in the Commons. In both these cases, the Labour Government called the peers' bluff by reintroducing the legislation a second time under the terms of the Parliament Acts. This proved sufficient to persuade their Lordships to back down and each of these Bills duly became law at the second time of asking. A similar situation arose in 1998 when the Labour Government sought to introduce a closed-list system for elections to the European Parliament (the *European Elections Bill*), and the peers persistently voted against such a change, ensuring that the legislation fell at the end of the Session. The Government reintroduced the Bill in the 1998–99 Session under the terms of the Parliament Acts, and the peers backed down. The moral of the tale is that the majority in the Commons can always get its way in the end if it really wants to do so, although Conservative Governments in particular have felt obliged to take account of opposition to their legislation in the Lords and to respect the limited delaying power still available to the upper House.

Legislative scrutiny and revision

The power of legislative scrutiny and revision exercised by the House of Lords has often been regarded as its most important function, especially when dealing with particularly complex or controversial Government Bills. This is mainly because MPs very often make inefficient use of the Parliamentary time available in Standing Committees when they are supposed to scrutinise and debate Bills clause by clause and line by line. The result is that there is often a need for additional legislative revision. This falls on the House of Lords, where many of the necessary amendments and new clauses are introduced by Ministers when the Government has had second thoughts about aspects of its own legislation.

Sometimes this is in response to suggestions made in the House of Commons or to sustained pressure from interest groups which have lobbied for or against aspects of the legislation. Sometimes it is simply a matter of doing in the Lords what should have been done in the Commons, if there had been enough Parliamentary time to do so and if all parties when in Opposition did not spend so much of the time in committee simply filibustering on the early clauses of Government Bills. Although the close scrutiny of Bills involves a great deal of often painstakingly dull work, it is clear that the House of Lords performs an essential and invaluable Parliamentary function in this respect. In doing so, it does invaluable work which would otherwise have to be done by the House of Commons or which would simply be left undone to the detriment of the quality of legislation. It also helps to see that the Courts do not have to spend too much of their time subsequently clarifying the original intentions of Parliament via the medium of case law.

It is argued by some that when acting as a revising chamber, the House of Lords has sometimes been involved in wrecking Government legislation from the lower House of which a majority of their Lordships may strongly disapprove. In 1969, for example, the Conservative peers insisted on amendments to the *House of Commons (Redistribution of Seats) No. 2 Bill*, the purpose of which legislation was to free the Labour Home Secretary, James Callaghan, from the legal obligation to lay before Parliament the reports of the independent Parliamentary Boundary Commissions. The amendments had the desired effect for the Conservatives in that the Labour Government backed down and the danger of 'gerrymandering' of constituency boundaries by Labour was averted.

Deliberative function

The deliberative function of well-informed debate on the great issues of the day is another worthwhile aspect of the activities of the House of Lords. This is because the level of knowledge and the standard of argument in the upper House is often very high and because the issues are usually approached in a serious and relatively dispassionate way. Indeed, the Lords can often find time to debate important and topical issues which might not get an airing in the more partisan and busy conditions of the Commons. In such debates the Lords can also draw on the great knowledge and experience which is available in their ranks, especially among the life peers who include Fellows of the Royal Society, leading industrialists and others of great intellectual and professional distinction. This is therefore one of the ways in which their Lordships can have considerable influence in Whitehall and Westminster and on the climate of informed opinion in the country as well.

Initiation of non-controversial legislation

The initiation in the Lords of Bills dealing with subjects of a comparatively non-controversial character (and in this respect it means controversial on politically partisan lines) is a particularly appropriate procedure when dealing with Government legislation which is both complex and technical, such as Bills on data protection, energy conservation and patent law for example. The reason for introducing such legislation in the upper House is that such Bills, having been fully discussed and put into a well considered shape prior to submission to the House of Commons, may have an easier passage through the House of Commons than would otherwise be the case. The view often held is that because the work on such legislation is dull and not advantageous politically, members of the House of Lords are better suited to carry out the work than are members of the House of Commons. It is also pointed out that when such Bills are examined first by the Lords, this saves the House of Commons a considerable amount of legislative time.

Judicial powers and functions

Theoretically, there is no distinction between the House of Lords in its judicial role as the final Court of Appeal in Britain and in its other activities. In practice, the judicial proceedings are quite separate from all other proceedings as only the Law Lords participate in hearing appeals, legal sittings are separate from the sittings of the whole House, and the Law Lords may sit in their judicial capacity even after the House has been prorogued or dissolved.

Judgments on appeal to the Law Lords are delivered by members of the Appellate Committee meeting in the Chamber of the Lords, but since 1963 these have taken the form of a written opinion from each individual judge. Usually appeals are heard by a committee of five Law Lords and decisions are reached by a majority. The judgments have great authority and have influenced the development of English law over centuries. For a long time the Law Lords regarded themselves as bound by legal precedents established in their earlier decisions, but since 1966 they have been prepared occasionally to modify that doctrine by departing from their previous decisions when it has appeared right to do so. (See Chapter 17 for more on this subject.)

Scrutiny powers and functions

The House of Lords is actually quite effective at scrutinising the activities of the Executive in Britain. There are several ways in which their Lordships do this beyond their normal participation in debates and in the legislative process. For example, peers may ask up to four Questions for oral answer each day that the House is sitting, each of which can lead to Supplementary Questions. Unstarred Questions, Private Notice Questions and Questions for written answer are also available. In addition, the most important statements of Government policy made in the House of Commons are usually made simultaneously in the House of Lords and on such occasions peers have the opportunity to probe or criticise Ministerial decisions. In recent years, the House of Lords has also made very good use of its Select Committees which, in some cases, have built up unrivalled reputations for their expert knowledge and the quality of their reports. Examples in recent years would include Science and Technology (1979–) including its sub-committees (which in 1998 investigated both the Management of Nuclear Waste and the Medical and Recreational use of Cannabis), Unemployment (1979–82), Overseas Trade (1984–85), Murder and Life Imprisonment (1988–89), Relations between Central and Local Government (1995–96) and the Public Service (1996–98). In all these ways members of the House of Lords scrutinise the activities of the Executive, sometimes more effectively than their counterparts in the House of Commons.

There are three other forms of scrutiny exercised by the House of Lords most of which are highly technical, but nevertheless rather important in the overall process of Parliamentary control. These are the careful scrutiny of Private Bills, of delegated legislation (Statutory Instruments) flowing from Whitehall Departments under previous primary legislation and of draft European legislation flowing from the European institutions.

Private Bills (which are Bills to alter the law relating to a particular locality or to confer rights or relieve liabilities from a particular person or category of persons) may be assigned to a committee of five peers for detailed consideration once the legislation has been through the earlier stages of public notification and Second Reading. Such committees have some of the attributes of quasi-judicial proceedings in that the promoters and opponents of Private Bills are usually represented by legal counsel and may call evidence in support of their arguments. Once this committee stage is successfully concluded, the Bill is reported to the House where its subsequent stages are similar to those of a Public Bill.

In the case of *Delegated Legislation (Statutory Instruments)*, the original Act may confine to the House of Commons the responsibility for scrutiny, as is the case with all fiscal measures. However, in most other instances the Lords have the same scrutiny powers as the Commons. These powers are usually exercised by the Delegated Powers and Deregulation Committee and by the Joint Committee on Statutory Instruments (consisting of seven peers and seven MPs). The former has the duty to report whether the provisions of any measure inappropriately delegate legislative power, while the latter has the duty to consider whether or not the attention of both Houses should be drawn to a particular Statutory Instrument on any of a number of different grounds. These include, for example, whether it would impose a charge on public funds, whether it would be retrospective in its effects, whether its publication has been unjustifiably delayed, or whether there are doubts about it being *ultra vires* – that is, outside the acknowledged legal competence of the Minister and Department concerned. In short, the Joint Committee may report on a Statutory Instrument on any one of such technical grounds, as long as it does not seek to address the merits or demerits of the policy.

In spite (or perhaps because) of the fact that there is a large and growing number of Statutory Instruments issued by central Government, very few are referred by the Joint Committee for further debate in this way. However, those which are subject to the negative procedure and those subject to the positive procedure which have been reported on unfavourably by the Joint Committee, can be prayed against', which means made the subject of a critical motion put down by peers or MPs for debate on the floor of either House. The main effect of these procedures, in which peers play a full part, is to keep Whitehall officials up to the mark by discouraging them from drafting sloppy or unjust secondary legislation.

As for Parliamentary scrutiny of *European legislation* (that is, Directives issued by the European institutions), Committees of each of the two Houses of the Westminster Parliament have been in existence since 1974 with scrutiny powers and functions similar to those of the Joint Committee just described which deals with national Statutory Instruments. In fact, the House of Lords Select Committee on the European Communities (as it is known) more than matches the House of Commons Select Committee on European Legislation, and is considered by many knowledgeable observers to be unrivalled in its expertise and depth of scrutiny of European legislation. The Lords Committee has a membership of 18, but is able to co-opt others on to its sub-committees (there were 49 co-opted members in 1998) of which there are six, namely:

- *Economic and Financial Affairs, Trade and External Relations* (Sub-committee A);
- *Energy, Industry and Transport* (Sub-committee B);
- *Environment, Public Health and Consumer Protection* (Sub-committee C);
- *Agriculture, Fisheries and Food* (Sub-committee D);
- *Law and Institutions* (Sub-committee E);
- *Social Affairs, Education and Home Affairs* (Sub-committee F).

Both the Lords' and Commons' committees are continuously involved in the scrutiny of draft European legislation, and both may report to their respective Houses with recommendations that particular legislative proposals should be debated in plenary session. Thus the House of Lords plays a leading role in this increasingly important area of Parliamentary activity.

Overall assessment

In many ways, in spite of its anachronistic image, the House of Lords is still in a position to act as an important constitutional check and as a safeguard of judicial independence in Britain. This significant role for the Second Chamber derives at least partly from the fact that the consent of the Lords is required before the lower House can extend the life of an elected Parliament beyond five years (as happened in both World Wars); and the fact that High Court judges can only be dismissed on an address to the Monarch from *both* Houses of Parliament, thus giving the Lords an effective veto against any serious attempt at political interference with the independence of the judiciary.

However, the position of the House of Lords in Britain's constitutional arrangements does not depend only, or even mainly, on these two aspects of its powers and functions. It derives at least as much from the weight of British history and the fact that custom and practice in Britain have ensured a bi-cameral legislature capped by a constitutional Monarchy. The three elements of this institutional structure need to be considered as a whole. Yet within this framework, the House of Lords is now the weaker partner vis-à-vis the House of Commons and, as Janet Morgan warned their Lordships some years ago: 'it is only by monitoring their own behaviour and remaining sensitive to their image in the world outside [Westminster] that they can avoid infringing a web of sanctions explicitly formulated or implicitly understood'.[11]

10.4 The work and impact of the Lords

As far as the work of the House of Lords is concerned, the first thing to be aware of is the fact that a substantial proportion of the membership chooses either not to attend or to attend only occasionally. For example, during the 1997–98 Session 20.75 per cent of their Lordships did not attend at all, while a further 3.25 per cent attended only a single sitting. In all 58.34 per cent of those who did attend did so on fewer than a third of the 228 possible sitting days. It is apparent, therefore, that there is a marked difference between the total potential participation and the actual participation.

Nevertheless, the introduction of life peers gradually caused the style and working methods of the House to alter. This reflects the fact that a large proportion of the Life Peers are former MPs, former leading lights in local government or people with other kinds of party political experience. More and more of the peers drawn from these categories have tended to approach their role as members of the House of Lords with a degree of political professionalism not shared by all their hereditary counterparts. Indeed, in most cases they are now appointed to the upper House on the recommendation of the respective party leaders in the Commons to be what are openly called 'working peers' – to differentiate them from others who are appointed more in recognition of their previous distinguished contributions to British national life in spheres which are not necessarily related to party politics. In this respect, the character of the House of Lords has gradually changed and its membership and behaviour have moved closer to the character of the House of Commons – with the obvious differences that none of their Lordships is currently elected to the second Chamber and in the Lords there are a significant number of independents (the cross-benchers). The changing nature and scope of work in the House of Lords is shown in Figures 10.3 and 10.4.

It is clear from these tables that the number of peers attending sittings has greatly increased and that their Lordships are spending more time in Parliament and are involved in more Parliamentary business than before. Whereas peers could at one time count on working only Tuesday to Thursday with each working day often confined to the hours between 4.00 p.m. and 7.00 p.m.; currently the House sits more often, the working week has expanded, and the sittings go on much longer to accommodate the greater volume of legislation and other Parliamentary business. Logically, therefore,

Figure 10.3 Sessional statistics, 1950–1951 to 1997–1998

Statistical item	1950/51	1960/61	1970/71	1980/81	1990/91	1997/98
Average daily attendance	86	142	265	296	324	417
Number of sitting days	100	125	153	143	137	228
Number of sitting hours	294.45	599.00	966.53	919.53	885.52	1604.21
Average length of sitting	2.57	4.47	6.18	6.25	6.28	7.02
Sittings after 10 p.m.	1	5	38	53	42	102
Monday sittings	0	21	22	28	29	49
Friday sittings	–	–	–	11	9	14

Note:
The 1970/71 and 1997/98 Sessions were longer than usual because they began after 1 June and 1 May elections respectively.

Figure 10.4 The work of the House of Lords, 1950–1951 to 1997–1998

Type of Work	1950/51	1960/61	1970/71	1980/81	1990/91	1997/98
Starred questions (a)	119	290	511	537	531	832
Questions for written answer	38	73	283	857	1304	5729
Unstarred questions	12	12	39	31	42	129
Motions leading to debate	(b)	(b)	46	47	71	96
Public Bills Introduced:						
Government Bills (c)	6	7	11	12	10	15
Private Members Bills	2	2	14	23	8	22

	1951/52	1962/63	1970/71	1980/81	1990/91	1997/98
Amendments made:						
Government Bills (Commons)	30	456	558	418	544	2097
Private Members Bills (Commons)	27	29	15	49	24	9
Government Bills (Lords)	75	283	207	940	1012	1741
Private Members Bills (Lords)	0	8	75	53	5	149
Totals	132	776	855	1460	1595	3996

(a) In 1954 the limit was put up to three per day on any Sitting Day; previously it had been three only on Tuesdays and Wednesdays. In 1959 the limit was raised to four per day on any Sitting Day.
(b) Figures not available.
(c) Excluding consolidation bills.

the procedures of the House of Lords have gradually been changed to meet the new requirements. Their Lordships have seemed keen to do this and, since the House is a self-regulating institution with relatively few Standing Orders, it has been able to respond more flexibly to changing needs and requirements.

Throughout the 1980s, when a determined and sometimes highly ideological Conservative Government had a commanding position in the House of Commons, the House of Lords often asserted its constitutional independence. During that time the peers sought to provide some of the effective scrutiny and opposition which they felt that the House of Commons was unable to provide. For example, in March 1980 the Education (No. 2) Bill, which was later to become the 1981 Education Act, ran into trouble with their Lordships on a clause which sought to allow Local Education Authorities to impose transport charges for children in rural areas. The proposal offended both rural and religious interests in the Upper House and in any case had been strongly attacked in the Commons when 13 Conservative MPs had voted against it and 16 more had abstained. The campaign was led in the Lords by the Duke of Norfolk, supported by two former Conservative Secretaries of State for Education, and in the end the Government was heavily defeated by 216 votes to 112 with no fewer than 38 Conservative peers voting against the Government. The sheer scale of the defeat and the prospect of having to face further back-bench dissent in the Commons and a second defeat in the Lords encouraged Ministers to climb down. No further attempt was made to resurrect the clause and the Treasury was obliged to forgo an estimated public expenditure saving of up to £30 million. In all, 50 defeats, ten of them significant, were inflicted on the Conservative Government by the Lords in the 1979–83 Parliament. Most were on specific points of particular concern to their Lordships – for example, the treatment of pensioners and the disabled, rural issues, respect for existing minority rights, and matters of constitutional etiquette.

During *the 1983–87 Parliament* further Government defeats in the Lords ensued – a total of 62. Perhaps the most significant was when the Government's plan to cancel the May 1985 elections to the Greater London Council and six other Metropolitan County Councils was defeated by 191 votes to 143 on a Labour amendment which came before the House in its deliberations on the 1984 Local Government (Interim Provisions) Bill. The Government then offered a compromise in the light of the defeat which allowed the existing Councils to continue for an extra year, but which still cancelled the election due in 1985. Such an example clearly indicated that the Lords have been both willing and able to administer salutary and timely rebuffs to Conservative and Labour Governments alike.

During *the 1987–92 Parliament* the Lords inflicted 72 defeats on the Government with an additional 62 defeats during *the 1992–97 Parliament*. For example, in April 1991 during consideration of the Criminal Justice Bill the peers defeated the Government by passing an amendment to do away with the mandatory life sentence for murder, an amendment which the Government later overturned in the Commons. In 1993, during passage of The Railways Bill, the peers voted to give British Rail an equal chance to bid for rail franchises alongside the private sector, twice defeating the Government on the issue and thus ensuring that the Government later came forward with a compromise solution. In 1994 the Police and Magistrates' Courts Bill and the Criminal Justice and Public Order Bill both suffered defeats or forced concessions at the hands of their Lordships – for example, on the proposed power for the Home Secretary to appoint Police Authority chairmen; to end local government majorities on Police Authorities; to introduce a new offence of male rape; to challenge in the Courts the film censor's criteria on video violence, and to allow judges to draw the attention of juries to a defendant's exercise of the traditional right to silence when charged with a criminal offence.

During the first Session of the *Parliament elected in 1997* the Lords inflicted defeats on the Government on the Referendum (Scotland and Wales) Bill over both the date for the referendums and the exact wording of the taxation part of the Scottish question, on the Education (Schools) Bill over the details of the scrapping of the Assisted Places Scheme, on aspects of the Firearms (Amendment) Bill for example over exemptions for the disabled, and on the Greater London Authority (Referendum) Bill on the timing of the referendum. In addition there were defeats on the Human

Rights Bill exempting churches, religious charities and church schools from the legislation and the Competition Bill – the peers voting by 121 votes to 93 (in a division which saw 23 Labour peers vote against their own Government) to outlaw predatory pricing in the newspaper industry, and also to protect community pharmacists from being undercut by supermarkets selling cheap drugs. There were also defeats to the Teaching and Higher Education Bill on the abolition of state maintenance grants for students (143 votes to 102), on tuition fees at Scottish Universities – the peers pressing the issue and defeating the Government on three separate occasions (by 134 votes to 89, 212 votes to 89 and 319 votes to 108), and on the powers of the General Teaching Council, (137 votes to 112). In addition, there was a defeat on the Crime and Disorder Bill when the peers voted by 290 votes to 122 to remove an amendment added to the Bill by a large majority in the House of Commons, namely one which reduced the legal age of consent for homosexuals from 18 to 16. The Government – convinced that they would be unable to alter the view of the peers and that, if they were to try, they risked losing the whole Bill – did not try to reinstate the amendment, an action that ensured that the remainder of the legislation reached the statute book on time. They did however pledge to introduce legislation to reduce the legal age of consent for homosexuals from 18 to 16 in the following Session. Most significantly of all, the peers voted on five separate occasions against the closed-list system for elections to the European Parliament, as laid down in the European Elections Bill, a course of action which ensured that the Bill was – for that Session at least – lost. (Under threat of the procedures laid down in the Parliament Act the peers backed down, the legislation becoming law in the 1998–99 Session.)

In all these cases their Lordships demonstrated considerable self-confidence in playing one of their legitimate roles as a constitutional critic and check on the power of the Government of the day. Yet it must equally be pointed out that Governments have usually been able to overcome such objections in the Upper House by using Parliamentary power in the lower House when they have really needed to do so.

10.5 Proposals for change

There is a lively and continuing debate about the future of the House of Lords which has taken place within and between all parties. Proposals for change have tended to fall into one or more of four broad categories:

1. Abolish the House of Lords altogether, creating a unicameral Parliamentary system, as was the case for a few years following the execution of Charles I in 1649.
2. Abolish the House of Lords, but create in its place a wholly new body with different composition, powers and functions.
3. Change the composition of the House of Lords, but keep its powers and functions as they are.
4. Reform both the composition and the powers and functions of the House of Lords.

Set against all these various forms of possible change, of course, is the conservative view (with a small 'c') that the House of Lords should be left as it is now ('if it ain't broke, don't fix it'). The Labour Party has wavered over the years between a wish to reform it, a wish to replace it, and a wish to abolish it altogether. Those Conservatives (with a capital 'C') who are interested in this matter have tended to press for reform of the upper House in order to strengthen and entrench its position in relation to the Commons. The Liberal Democrats have tended to see reform of the House of Lords as part of a new constitutional settlement in a much wider context.

Labour proposals

The Labour Party has traditionally been less interested in reform than in abolition of the House of Lords. As long ago as 1907 Labour members of the House of Commons moved a resolution declaring that 'the upper House, being an irresponsible part of the Legislature and of necessity representative only of interest opposed to the general well-being, is a hindrance to national progress, and ought to be abolished'. In 1918 the party went on record as being opposed not only to the continuance of the House of Lords as at the time constituted, but to the existence of any second Chamber however consti-tuted, taking the line of the oft-quoted Abbé Siéyès – who drafted Constitutions for revolutionary France – namely that 'if a second Chamber dissents from the first, it is mischievous; if it agrees with it, it is superfluous'. Indeed, in 1934 the Party Conference pledged itself to the total abolition of the House of Lords.

Notwithstanding these facts, no Labour *Government* has ever come forward with proposals to abolish the Lords. The first and second Labour Administrations – 1924 and 1929–31, both under Ramsey MacDonald – were minority Governments and could do little, least of all embark on major constitutional reform. The Attlee Government of 1945–51 introduced and passed into law the Parliament Act of 1949 which reduced the period of time the House of Lords could delay legislation from, essentially, two years to one year – the Act itself having to be implemented under the terms of the Parliament Act of 1911 – but sought to do nothing else on the matter. Although the Wilson Government of 1964–70 did instigate a serious attempt at reform of both the composition and the powers of the Lords – firm proposals being brought forward by way of the Parliament (No. 2) Bill during the 1968–69 Session – the pro-posals received a critical, even hostile, reception in the House of Commons and the legislation was ultimately dropped.

During the period of the Wilson and Callaghan Governments in the 1970s – 1974–76 and 1976–79 respectively – and as a direct result of the difficulty the Government had in the House of Lords with a number of key items of its legislative programme – many in the Labour Party came to the conclusion that it was time to abolish the House of Lords. In the words of Eric Heffer speaking in 1976: 'It is an out-dated, superannuated body, and we should get rid of it at the earliest possible opportu-nity,'[12] This was the conclusion reached by the party as a whole the following year when the Annual Conference voted by 6,248,000 votes to 91,000 for a motion declar-ing that 'This Conference believes that the House of Lords is a negation of democracy and calls on the Government, the Parliamentary Party and the National Executive Committee to take every possible step open to them to secure the total reform of Parliament into an efficient single-chamber legislating body without delay.'[13]

No action was taken to achieve such an objective, superficially because of lack of legislative time owing to the devolution legislation of the period, but more particularly because the then Prime Minister, James Callaghan, was opposed to such a course. Indeed, during proceedings to draw up the Party's 1979 election Manifesto, he twice threatened to resign if the Manifesto proposed the abolition of the House of Lords. Consequently, it promised not outright abolition, only the abolition of its power of delay.

By the time of the 1983 General Election, however, under the leadership of Michael Foot – one of those who had been most opposed to the reform attempt of the late 1960s because he saw it as strengthening the position of the House of Lords – the Party committed itself in its Manifesto to 'abolish the undemocratic House of Lords as quickly as possible'.

Although the 1987 election Manifesto – under Neil Kinnock's leadership – did not mention the House of Lords, by 1992 the Party was advocating the replacement of the House of Lords with a new elected second chamber with power to delay – for the lifetime of a Parliament – legislation that threatened to reduce individual or constitutional rights.

On becoming Labour Leader following the untimely death of his predecessor John Smith in 1994, Tony Blair indicated a degree of caution towards the idea of wholesale Lords reform. However, on 7 February 1996, delivering the John Smith Memorial Lecture, Tony Blair pledged that a Labour Government would act to end the system under which individuals wielded power simply by right of birth: 'Are we going to continue alone of all the democracies to have laws passed by an upper chamber, a majority of whose members are there by birth not merit, perhaps because 300 years ago their ancestor was the mistress of a Monarch?' As one leading newspaper explained, it was an approach which placed hereditary peers 'on notice to quit'.[14] He advocated a two-stage approach to reform. In the first stage, the right of hereditary peers (some 750 individuals in all) to sit and vote in the upper House would be removed, turning the House of Lords into a body of 'the distinguished and meritorious'. In the second stage, an elected element would be introduced into the membership, though keeping some peers chosen because of their expertise and others because of their non-party status (namely some cross-bench element). To many people the impression given was that whereas the first stage was a priority for an incoming Labour Government, this would not be the case for the second stage of reform.

In outlining his thinking behind this policy, Tony Blair observed that while there were over 300 official Conservative hereditary peers, there were only 12 Labour and 24 Liberal Democrat hereditary peers. He went on to note that there were several hundred other hereditary peers who rarely attended, but if they did, 'we can be sure very few would side with Labour or the Liberal Democrats'. The situation, he declared, was, 'plainly and incontrovertibly politically biased', and he concluded by saying that 'there are no conceivable grounds for maintaining this system'. Nevertheless, he went on to state that a Labour Government would be prepared to allow some of the hereditary peers who made a regular contribution in the House of Lords to become life peers. He also made it clear that the Law Lords would remain as members of a reformed upper House.

Early in 1999 the Government published a White Paper 'Modernising Parliament: Reforming the House of Lords' outlining its step-by-step approach to reform.[15] Step one was the removal of the right of hereditary peers to sit and vote in the House of Lords with legislation to achieve this being introduced during the 1998–99 Session. As far as step two was concerned – a transitional House – the Government declared itself 'minded to accept' the proposal that a small number of hereditary peers be allowed to sit temporarily as members. It also pledged that no one party would be in a position to dominate the transitional House and that steps would be taken to reduce the unfettered power of the Prime Minister to nominate those to be appointed to life peerages, pledging to establish an independent Appointment Commission to recommend non-political appointments. Step three was the creation of a Royal Commission – under the chairmanship of Lord Wakeham – to examine a range of possible alternatives for longer-term reform covering role and functions as well as composition.[16] The White Paper set out four main options for future composition for the Royal Commission to consider, namely, a nominated chamber, a directly elected chamber, an indirectly elected chamber and a mixed chamber, and charged it to consider reform in the context of the planned devolved Parliament for Scotland and Assembly for Wales and the Northern Ireland Assembly, the incorporation of the European Convention on Human Rights into United Kingdom law, and what were described as 'developing relations' with the European Union. Step four would see the Royal Commission's recommendations being considered by a Joint Committee of both Houses of Parliament to examine in more detail the Parliamentary aspects of any proposed reform. Step five would be legislation to implement the resulting proposals designed to 'renew the House of Lords as a modern, fit and effective second chamber of Parliament for the 21st century'.

Within the Labour Party there are those who favour outright abolition and a single chamber Parliament. They see Tony Blair's proposals as, at the very least, an irrelevance; one MP declared that the policy was nothing short of a sellout. The critics are also concerned that the proposals, certainly for a transitional House, will simply create another giant Quango. Some question the staged approach and doubt whether much, if any, thought has been given to when and how an elected element could be introduced. Others fear that any moves in the direction of an elected second chamber will pose a threat to the position of the House of Commons.

It may well be that a Blair Government will find, as others have found before, that the road to Lords reform, although paved with good intentions, offers no easy solutions. Although the idea of a staged approach to reform, with the first stage being achieved by a simple, single-clause Bill to remove the hereditary right to attend, may be attractive in its apparent simplicity, there will be those who will seek to make it anything but simple when the legislation is debated in both Houses, and not all of the critics will be from outside Labour's ranks.

Conservative proposals

Traditionally there have been elements within the Conservative Party which have been quite interested in reforming the House of Lords, since they have seen such ideas as a way of putting the upper House on a more secure constitutional basis. Winston Churchill and L.S. Amery were among those who flirted in the 1920s with the idea of turning the Lords into a more functional body capable of directly representing both sides of industry as well as the hereditary peerage.[17] In the late 1940s and early 1950s the Marquess of Salisbury, as Conservative Leader in the Lords, concentrated on encouraging his noble colleagues to exercise political self-restraint, especially when they faced the radical postwar Labour Government. For example, agreement was reached not long after the 1945 General Election that the upper House, with its overwhelming Conservative majority, would not divide on the Second Reading of any Government Bill which had been foreshadowed in the 1945 Labour Party Manifesto.

In 1977 Lord Carrington, then Conservative Leader in the Lords, proposed the creation of a reformed second Chamber whose members would have been elected by proportional representation from large regional constituencies. His argument was that such a Chamber would reflect public opinion rather differently from the Commons, since the type of constituencies, the method of election and the timing of the elections would all have been different from those of the lower House. His main objective was to produce a reformed second Chamber with sufficient democratic legitimacy to survive and prosper as a constitutional check or counterweight to the House of Commons. In 1978 a Conservative committee chaired by Lord Home produced another set of reform proposals which recommended that the membership of the Lords should be reduced to about 400, of which one-third would have been nominated by the political parties and two-thirds elected on a basis of proportional representation from about 250 large territorial constituencies.[18] However, neither of these proposals – or anything resembling them – was brought forward during the long period of Conservative rule between 1979 and 1997. This was mainly because successive Conservative Governments did not give a high priority to Lords reform and because the vast majority of the Conservative Party in the Commons was opposed to the introduction of proportional representation.

In Opposition following the 1997 General Election and with Lords reform very firmly on the agenda of the new Labour Government, some Conservatives again turned their attention to reform proposals, with elements on both the Right and the Left demanding a clear policy in favour of a fully or partly elected second chamber. For example, Andrew Tyrie of the Conservative Policy Forum argued for a mainly elected upper House with the same powers of scrutiny and revision as the House of Lords,[19] while Nick Kent of the Tory Reform Group advocated a 350-strong second chamber made up of about 160 members elected regionally for nine-year terms, about 90 appointed life peers, bishops and other religious leaders, Law Lords and representatives from British territories overseas.[20] In July 1998 William Hague announced the establishment of a Constitutional Commission on the House of Lords under the chairmanship of the former Lord Chancellor, Lord Mackay of Clashfern, to consider all options for reform.[21]

Liberal Democrat proposals

Liberal Democrats have sought to place the 'modernisation' of what they describe as 'Britain's antiquated and ineffective constitution' at the head of their policy priorities. They have therefore advocated reform of the House of Lords as part of a new constitutional settlement incorporating a codified constitution, an entrenched Bill of Rights, home rule for Scotland and Wales, regional Assemblies throughout England, and proportional representation for all elections. As far as the second Chamber is concerned, they advocate transforming the House of Lords into a directly elected Senate with the task of representing the various nations and regions of the UK. Members of such an upper House would be elected by Single Transferable Vote for fixed terms of six years, with one-third retiring every two years. They would be empowered to delay legislation, with the exception of Money Bills, for up to two years and would have a power of veto over proposed constitutional changes emanating from the lower House.[22]

10.6 Conclusion

A study of the House of Lords in recent years provides clear evidence that it is not in danger of atrophy or decline; indeed, quite the reverse. The House of Lords has demonstrated a remarkable ability to evolve and adapt to changing circumstances. This stems very largely from its extraordinary character, a character derived from the fact that it has never been the brainchild of constitutional draftsmen, but has been shaped by a small number of Parliamentary Statutes and influenced by tradition, custom and practice dating back at least to medieval times.

The House of Lords, as it exists today, is thus the product of a long evolutionary process. It may appear to be an illogical institution in that it is hard to believe that anyone would set out to establish a second Chamber quite like it. Yet its unusual character can be regarded as a strength in that it encompasses a delicately balanced combination of real effectiveness and curtailed powers which makes a significant contribution to the work of Parliament and the British political system. If it did not exist, it would almost certainly need to be replaced with a new Parliamentary institution of comparable purpose and utility.

Suggested questions

1   Analyse the composition of the House of Lords in Britain today.
2   What are the functions of the House of Lords and how well is it able to perform them?
3   What are the implications of reforming or abolishing the House of Lords?

Notes

1. R. Butt, *A History of Parliament in the Middle Ages* (London: Constable, 1989), p. 1.
2. W. Bagehot, *The English Constitution* (Glasgow: Fontana/Collins, 1963), p. 128.
3. *Ibid.*, p. 149
4. Quoted in R. Rhodes James (ed.), *Churchill Speaks* (Leicester: Windword, 1981), p. 178.
5. See R. Jenkins, *Mr Balfour's Poodle* (London: Collins, 1954).
6. The 1963 Peerage Act was the direct result of the efforts of Tony Benn, who had inherited the title of Viscount Stansgate, to get the law changed so that he and other hereditary peers could disclaim their titles and consequently no longer be disqualified from standing for election or re-election to the House of Commons. In 1998 ten individuals had disclaimed their titles – although two of these sat in the Lords as life peers.
7. For a full account see J. Morgan, *The House of Lords and the Labour Government 1964–70* (Oxford: Clarendon Press, 1975).
8. I. Gilmour, *The Body Politic* (London: Hutchinson, 1969), p. 302.
9. The term 'cross-bencher' is used to describe those peers who are not formally aligned with any political party, but who belong to an unofficial group which meets each week, with a convenor in the chair to discuss forthcoming business. These members receive written notice of future business, the difference between this and a party whip being that it is issued without the additional matters on divisions and so on which are included in a party whip.
10. See 'Report on the Reform of the Second Chamber', Cmnd 9038 (London: HMSO, 1918).

11. J.P. Morgan, *The House of Lords and the Labour Government, 1964–70* (Oxford: Clarendon Press, 1975), p. 8.
12. E. Heffer, 919 *H.C. Debs.*, c.1906–1907, (22 November 1976).
13. Report of the 76th Annual Conference of the Labour Party, pp. 270–5; p. 270.
14. See *The Times*, 8 February 1996.
15. White Paper, *Modernising Parliament: Reforming the House of Lords*, CM 4183 (London: Stationery Office, 1999).
16. Aside from its Chairman, the former Conservative Minister Lord Wakeham, the membership of the Royal Commission comprised: Ann Beynon, National Manager of BT Wales; Lord Butler of Brockwell, the former Cabinet Secretary; Baroness Dean, the former Trade Union leader; the Right Reverend Richard Harris, Bishop of Oxford; Lord Hurd, the former Conservative Northern Ireland, Home and Foreign Secretary; Gerald Kaufman, the senior Labour MP; Anthony King, Professor of Government at Essex University; Bill Morris, General Secretary of the Transport and General Workers Union; Kenneth Munro, Chairman of the Centre for Scottish Public Policy and a former European Commission representative in Scotland; Dawn Oliver, Professor of Constitutional Law at University College London; and Sir Michael Wheeler-Booth, former Clerk of the Parliaments.
17. See L.P. Carpenter, 'Corporations in Britain, 1930–45' in the *Journal of Contemporary History,* 11 (1976), pp. 9–14; and references to 'Industry and the State' published in 1927 by Harold Macmillan and others.
18. See *The House of Lords: Report of the Conservative Review Committee*, Chairman: The Lord Home of the Hirsal, March 1978.
19. A. Tyrie, *Reforming the Lords: A Conservative Approach* (London: Conservative Policy Forum, 1998).
20. N. Kent, *Enhancing our Democracy: Reforming the House of Lords* (London: Tory Reform Group, 1998).
21. *The Times*, 14 July 1998.
22. See 'Here We Stand: Proposals for Modernising Britain's Democracy', Liberal Democrat Federal White Paper, No. 6, September 1993.

Further reading

Bagehot, W., *The English Constitution* (London: Fontana, 1978).
Baldwin N.D.J., *The House of Lords* (Barnstaple: Philip Charles Media, 1990).
Bromhead, P.A., *The House of Lords and Contemporary Politics* (London: Routledge & Kegan Paul, 1958).
Constitution Unit, *Reform of the House of Lords* (London: The Constitution Unit, 1996).
Dickson, B. and Carmichael, P. (eds), *The House of Lords: Its Parliamentary and Judicial Roles* (Oxford: Hart Publishing, 1999).
Griffith, J.A.G., Ryle, M. and Wheeler-Booth, M.A.J., *Parliament: Functions, Practice and Procedures* (London: Sweet & Maxwell, 1989).
Initial report of *The Constitutional Commission to Consider Options for a New Second Chamber* (Chair: Lord Mackay of Clashfean), (London: Constitutional Commission, September 1998).
Limon, D. and McKay, W.R., (eds) *Erskine May's Treatise on the Law, Privileges, Proceedings and Usage of Parliament* (22nd ed), (London: Butterworths, 1997).
Morgan, J.P., *The House of Lords and the Labour Government, 1964–70* (Oxford: Clarendon Press, 1975).
Norton, P. (ed.), *Parliament in the 1980s* (Oxford: Basil Blackwell, 1985).
Shell, D., *The House of Lords* (2nd ed) (Oxford: Philip Allan, 1992).
Shell, D. and Beamish, D. (eds), *The House of Lords at Work* (Oxford: Clarendon Press, 1993).

Smith, E.A., *The House of Lords in British Politics & Society 1815–1911* (London: Longman, 1992).

Wells, J., *The House of Lords* (London: Hodder & Stoughton, 1997).

White Paper, 'Modernising Parliament: Reforming the House of Lords', CM 4183 (London: Stationery Office, 1999).

Website

Parliament   http://www.parliament.uk

11 The House of Commons

Unlike the Monarchy or the House of Lords, the House of Commons still has real power in the British political system, at any rate on those occasions when it is willing and able to use it. Yet the nature of its power is different from what it was in the nineteenth century when most of the traditional notions about the House of Commons were established. The modern House of Commons is neither the Government of the country nor even the principal place where official decisions or legislative proposals are conceived. It is essentially the sounding board for popular representation and redress, one of the stages on which the party battle is fought, the principal forum within which legislation and other decisions of Government are scrutinised, and the framework for Parliamentary control of the Executive – one of the tasks which it shares with the House of Lords.

The essential purposes of the House of Commons have not changed significantly since the last quarter of the nineteenth century. W.I. Jennings described them as being 'to question and debate the policy of the Government and in doing so to bring home ... the unpopularity (or popularity) of a particular line of policy'.[1] L.S. Amery described them as being 'to secure full discussion and ventilation of all matters ... as the condition of giving its assent to Bills ... or its support to Ministers'.[2] Such descriptions are still broadly valid today.

11.1 Composition

At the General Election of 1997 a total of 418 Labour Members of Parliament (MPs) were elected, along with 165 Conservatives, 46 Liberal Democrats, 6 Scottish Nationalists, 4 Welsh Nationalists (Plaid Cymru), 10 Ulster Unionists, 2 Democratic Unionists, 1 UK Unionist, 3 Social Democratic & Labour, 2 Sinn Féin, 1 Independent and the Speaker, giving a House of Commons composed of 659 members elected on a uniform national franchise from single member constituencies with an average of 67,218 electors. The Speaker and three Deputy Speakers are all elected MPs. The current Speaker, Betty Boothroyd, prior to being elected Speaker by MPs was a Labour MP. The Speaker and the Deputy Speakers – one Labour MP and two

Conservative MPs – take no partisan part in the proceedings (unless a vote is tied, in which case they are expected to vote for the *status quo*), since they are responsible in the chair for seeing that the rules of order are maintained. Thus, at the 1997 election the Labour Government secured an overall Parliamentary majority of 179. Early in 1999, following the defection to their ranks of a Conservative MP, Peter Temple-Morris, and the expulsion from the party of one of their own MPs, Tommy Graham, this remained at 179.

MPs as representatives

Members of Parliament can be seen as more or less representative in two quite different senses. *First*, we can consider the educational and occupational backgrounds of individual MPs. This reveals that all sorts and conditions of men and a small, but growing, number of women can be found in the House of Commons. We can illustrate the point by using figures derived from the 1997 General Election results. These show that 37 per cent of Conservative, 45 per cent of Labour and 50 per cent of Liberal Democrat MPs came from professional occupations, while only 1 per cent of Conservative, 2 per cent of Liberal Democrat and 13 per cent of Labour MPs came from traditional working-class occupations. In addition, 39 per cent of Conservative, 24 per cent of Liberal Democrat and 9 per cent of Labour MPs came from a business background. These figures demonstrate the growing *embourgeoisement* of the political class which is turning the House of Commons steadily into a meritocracy. This process has been further stimulated by the fact that 81 per cent of Conservative, 70 per cent of Liberal Democrat and 66 per cent of Labour MPs had experienced further or higher education – one of the most significant predictors of upward social and occupational mobility. Of the Conservative MPs, 50.9 per cent had been to university at Oxford or Cambridge, as had 32.6 per cent of Liberal Democrat MPs, whereas the comparable figure for Labour MPs was only 14.6 per cent. Equally, there was a significant divergence in the proportions of those who had been to public schools (private education) with 66 per cent of Conservative MPs, 41 per cent of Liberal Democrat MPs, but only 16 per cent of Labour MPs having done so.

Thus British MPs as a whole are still something of an elite in educational and occupational terms, although notably less so than they were some years ago. Of course, much depends on whether one refers to the individuals concerned or to their family backgrounds. If the latter criterion is adopted, the social and class differences between the parties remain greater – a fact which is best explained in this context by the rapid upward social mobility experienced by many people in Britain in recent years. In general, however, it is evident that as the middle class as a whole has become larger, so, predictably, its contingent of MPs has become larger as a direct reflection of changes in society as a whole. Equally, the influence of the prestigious public schools and the universities of Oxford and Cambridge has continued to decline – even in the Conservative Party – with the result that there is growing educational and social convergence between the Parliamentary representatives of the three main parties. This has greatly diminished the presence of MPs from each end of the conventional social spectrum.

Secondly, we can consider the extent to which the composition of the House of Commons reflects the composition of the electorate as a whole and especially those sections of the population which traditionally have been under-represented in nearly all the leading British institutions.[3] The most obvious example of a disproportion between representation at Westminster and in the population as a whole is that of *women*, who account for 52 per cent of the electorate but only 18.2 per cent (120) of all MPs. In the past this has been largely due to the prejudices of Conservative women on constituency selection committees who have seemed opposed to choosing those of their own sex as candidates for winnable seats, and the male chauvinism of many traditional Labour activists when choosing candidates for winnable Labour seats. However, in recent years things have begun to change in this respect – at any rate in the Labour and Liberal Democrat parties where there is now a degree of positive discrimination in favour of women candidates. Such developments have been less noticeable in the Conservative Party where the proportion of women MPs is now significantly smaller than in the Labour Party – 7.8 per cent as opposed to 24.1 per cent – in spite of the experience and example of Margaret Thatcher.

Another marked disparity (as we have already noted in Chapter 3) is that those who vote for the Liberal Democrats are penalised by the 'unfair' working of the British electoral system which discriminates against all third parties unless their votes are geographically concentrated (and sometimes even then). Consequently at the 1997 General Election the Liberal Democrats got 16.76 per cent of the votes cast across the nation, but only 6.98 per cent of the seats in the House of Commons. Moreover, some other groups in the electorate are under-represented in the House of Commons – for example, those under 30 years or over 80 years of age. The 1997 election saw the return of one MP over the age of 80 – Sir Edward Heath – and ten under the age of 30. In fact the Labour and Conservative Parliamentary parties have a broadly similar age profile, with approximately 75 per cent of their MPs being in their forties and fifties in 1997. The Liberal Democrats had the youngest age profile with 37 per cent of their MPs being in their thirties. On the other hand, there are groups which seem to be over-represented in the House of Commons; notably lawyers, consultants, and company directors in the Conservative Party; and lecturers, journalists and public sector white-collar workers in the Labour Party. Nevertheless many MPs develop a wide range of interests (both paid and unpaid) during their time in the House and this can turn them into quite prominent 'virtual representatives' of various categories and interests in the electorate.[4]

Front-benchers

In 1998 paid office-holders in the Government (those who are entitled to sit on the Government front bench) accounted for about 90 of the 418 Labour MPs. This figure included 14 Government Whips who facilitate the business in the Commons, but who do not speak in debates or share in the running of Government Departments in the way that other Ministers do. The so-called payroll vote (that is, those who are expected to support the Government on all occasions) is now supplemented by about 46 Parliamentary Private Secretaries (PPSs) who sit on the second bench just behind their Ministers and who are expected to be completely loyal to the Government in the same way as the Ministers whom they serve. At the heart of the Government front bench is the Cabinet which (in June 1998) had 22 members, of whom 20 sat in the Commons, since only the Lord Chancellor and the Leader of the Lords sat in the upper House.[5]

On the Opposition side, the Conservative front bench is made up of the Shadow Cabinet and other more junior spokesmen who support their more senior colleagues. The Conservative Shadow Cabinet consists of 20 senior members of the Parliamentary Party, all appointed by the Leader of the Party. Beneath the Shadow Cabinet there are about 20 to 25 junior spokesmen who are appointed by the Leader usually after consultation with senior colleagues to share the front bench duties of shadowing the various Ministers. In addition, there are about 10 Opposition Whips led by the Opposition Chief Whip who, together with the Leader of the Opposition and the Opposition Pairing Whip, are the only members of the Opposition to receive additional salaries from public funds in recognition of their additional Parliamentary responsibilities.

Back-benchers

The 460 or so MPs who have no direct involvement in Government or in the tasks of front-bench Opposition make up the generality of back-benchers. Some are senior, have been in the House a long time, may well have been Ministers at an earlier stage in their careers, and wield a good deal of influence within their parties. A few carry considerable weight in the House as a whole and still attract a larger than normal audience of their colleagues when they speak in debate. However, by far the greater number of back-benchers are relatively junior and have been in the House for only a short period.[6] They try to make their way in politics as well as they can. This means that they are likely to spend a great deal of their time trying to attract the attention and approval of their party Whips by playing an active and helpful part both in proceedings in the Chamber and in Committee 'upstairs'.

The principal duty of back-benchers when their party is in Government is to support it with their votes in the division lobbies and, to a lesser extent, with their voices during Parliamentary proceedings. When their party is in Opposition, their principal task is to harry the Government on every suitable occasion both in the Chamber and in Committee 'upstairs'. Some back-benchers may choose a more notorious and difficult path by becoming rebels within their own party, as the so-called Euro-sceptics did within the Conservative Party in the 1990s. Others come to be seen by the party hierarchy (and are often dismissed) simply as mavericks or eccentrics. Such deviant behaviour is not normally recommended for those who are ambitious for Ministerial office, but there are some formidable exceptions who usually get taken into Government before long in order to turn them into team players rather than the rebels which they are in danger of becoming.

The life of a back-bencher in the modern House of Common is usually more fun in Opposition than in Government. This is because, in the former case, there are more opportunities to play a prominent part in the party battle (since by definition there are always fewer MPs on the Opposition benches than on the Government side) and to make a favourable impression on the party leadership. It is also because nothing which is said or done by Opposition back-benchers matters very much and such politicians can therefore enjoy (at least at Westminster, if not in their constituencies where their role is different) the luxury of considerable irresponsibility. When their party is in Government, back-benchers have to tread the much more difficult, narrow path between sycophancy and rebellion. In such conditions they can be forgiven for thinking that all their Whips really want is their presence in the division lobbies at the appointed times to support the Government.

Certainly back-benchers in both main parties have cause to complain about the privileges granted to Privy Councillors (that is, very senior back-benchers nearly all of whom have held Ministerial office at an earlier stage in their careers) and to the spokesmen of minor parties, since both categories are almost certain to be called to speak in debates at favourable times and to catch the Speaker's eye if they wish to intervene at Question Time or following Ministerial Statements. This is mainly a reflection of the seniority principle which influences the pecking order at Westminster and indeed in virtually every other Parliament around the world. It is also a reflection of the well established Westminster convention that the Speaker should try to ensure a hearing for minority points of view and indeed for dissidents within the main parties as well. For example, the so-called Maastricht rebels were able to speak frequently and sometimes at length during the course of the legislation to implement Britain's adherence to the Maastricht Treaty in the early 1990s, and back-benchers who intend to abstain or vote against their party (especially if it is in Government) will normally be given a chance to explain their reasons during the course of the relevant debate.

Pay and conditions of work

All MPs receive a Parliamentary salary from public funds (£43,860 in 1997–98; £47,008 from 1 September 1999) which is linked to a percentage of the pay awarded to civil servants in Grades 5 to 7, together with a Parliamentary allowance for office costs of up to £47,568 (in 1997–98). They are also entitled to free, first class travel within the United Kingdom as long as they are on Parliamentary or constituency business, and to one free trip a year to the institutions of the European Union or the national Parliament of any EU state. At Westminster they do not have to pay for telephone calls within the United Kingdom and have the benefit of free, first-class post for written communication with their constituents and others (for example, public bodies) in connection with their constituency duties. For those with motor cars there are generous mileage allowances for travel to and from (and within) their constituencies. Inner London MPs qualify for a London allowance (£1406 in 1997–98), while all other MPs are entitled to claim a so-called Additional Costs Allowance (up to a maximum of £12,717 in 1997–98) which is supposed to take account of the extra costs of having to have two homes as a function of Parliamentary life.

Ministers, who have the same constituency duties as their back-bench colleagues (excluding peers), receive various levels of salary from public funds according to their positions in the Government, together with their Parliamentary salaries. In 1999–2000 Ministerial salaries ranged from £160,011 for the Lord Chancellor (the senior legal officer in the land who is more highly paid than the Prime Minister) to £25,319 for a junior Minister.[7]

Compared with their counterparts in comparable democracies, British Ministers and Members of Parliament do not enjoy very lavish salaries. However, their overall package of pay and allowances is probably as good as the average in many other countries. Ever since MPs began to award themselves significant pay and allowances in 1964, the issue has been controversial and ostensibly unpopular with the media and the general public. In spite of the automatic link between the pay of MPs and a percentage of Civil Service pay at a determined level and in spite of the work of the Top Salaries Review Board which makes recommendations on Ministerial pay, it seems that there is never a right moment for Members of Parliament, Ministers (and indeed peers who can claim daily allowances for their attendance at the House of Lords) to increase their remuneration even if only in line with the cost of living. The situation was exacerbated in the middle 1990s by a succession of sensational revelations in the media of MPs allegedly being prepared to take money from outside interests in return for asking Parliamentary Questions, and this opened up a much wider debate about the propriety or otherwise of MPs having paid outside interests in addition to their public duties. All outside interests (both paid and unpaid) are supposed to be declared in the Register of Members' Interests which is kept up to date by a senior Parliamentary clerk and to begin with the principle of full, voluntary disclosure was thought to be sufficient. However, public interest in these matters became much more acute in the middle 1990s, following a succession of sensational revelations previously referred to, and this led to the establishment of a Committee on Standards in Public Life (the Nolan Committee) in 1994. The following year the House of Commons agreed that MPs could *not* be advocates for causes in the House if such causes provided them with any personal financial benefit. They also agreed, following recommendations of the Nolan Committee, to establish a Parliamentary Commissioner for Standards, an individual who can advise MPs on standards of conduct and who is responsible for conducting investigations into alleged breaches of the rules. The Commissioner (Sir Gordon Downey, more recently Ms Elizabeth Filkin) reports to the House of Commons Select Committee on Standards and Privileges.

Apart from the Speaker and the three Deputies, the only MPs not in the Government who have additional salaries paid from public funds are the Leader of the Opposition (£55,000 in 1997–98), the Opposition Chief Whip (£31,125 in 1997–98) and the Opposition Pairing Whip (£20,029 in 1997–98). Once again their total remuneration is increased in each case by their Parliamentary salary to which they are entitled in respect of their duties as constituency MPs. In addition, there is financial assistance from public funds to Opposition parties to assist them to carry out their Parliamentary activities.[8] These financial arrangements symbolise the longstanding commitment in Britain to the idea of constitutional Opposition and give financial expression to the traditional term 'Her Majesty's Loyal Opposition'. Indeed, Britain was the first Parliamentary democracy to make such financial arrangements for leading members of the Opposition in recognition of their constitutional duty to oppose the Government of the day.

The conditions of work for MPs have improved dramatically over the last thirty years, although some of the arrangements reflect the lingering amateurism which still characterises some of the more traditional habits and assumptions at Westminster. For example, when the Chamber of the House of Commons was rebuilt after the Second World War, it was decided to leave the size and shape as it had been before the German attack which had destroyed it, namely rows of opposed benches and a total seating capacity of no more than two-thirds of those entitled to take a seat. This was consciously done to reflect both the combative nature of British Parliamentary politics and the conversational, occasionally intimate, atmosphere of many debates and other proceedings.

Although some nearby buildings at 1 Parliament Street and 7 Millbank were refurbished for MPs and their personal staff in the late 1980s and early 1990s and although a completely new Parliamentary office building is due to be completed by 2000, there is nonetheless a shortage of suitably equipped office premises for individual MPs at Westminster and a number of them still have to make do with a desk, telephone and filing cabinet in rooms shared with their colleagues. The traditional approach to these matters has reflected a certain caution on the part of successive generations of MPs at the prospect of having to defend the spending of large amounts of taxpayers' money on facilities for themselves, and this has been reinforced by the reluctance of every British Government to encourage MPs not in the Administration to become professional, full-time politicians capable of monitoring the Executive on anything like equal terms.

Furthermore, most MPs now have such a burden of constituency work and committee work at Westminster that they spend relatively little time in the Chamber, except when present for Questions to Ministers or particular debates in which they hope to take part. Of course, this trend has been somewhat modified by the televising of the Commons, which has lured many more MPs into the Chamber, at any rate during prime time (that is, when the media are paying attention) since they hope to be seen in glorious political action by their constituents and the general public. Nevertheless it remains broadly true that until quite recently MPs have had to perform an increasingly varied and time-consuming range of political tasks in physical conditions which were largely unchanged since the mid-nineteenth century when the present Palace of Westminster was built.

11.2 The power of the Commons

The tasks of the House of Commons are diffuse, variable and rather difficult to define in a permanent and authoritative way. They are not set out in any single document or defined in any Court ruling. In cases of dispute the most reliable guide is *Erskine May*, the reference book which covers the whole of Parliamentary procedure in the lower House according to the precedents established over centuries by successive Speakers and codified by successive Clerks of the Commons.[9]

Theory and practice

In theory, the House of Commons has very great power in the British constitution. This could be said to include the power to make and unmake Governments, to topple Prime Ministers, to safeguard the liberties of British subjects, to bring to light and remedy injustices, and even to legislate itself out of existence or the country into a dictatorship.

In practice, the power of the Commons is usually subsumed in the power of the Government of the day, which governs through Parliament as long as it retains the voting support of an overall majority in the House of Commons. It is usually misleading to refer to the powers of the Commons in any way which implies that such powers can be divorced from those of modern single-party Government which has been the norm in recent times. In normal Parliamentary conditions, when one of the main parties on its own has an overall majority in the Commons, the power of the House as a representative institution seeking to monitor and control the Government of the day is wielded principally by the Opposition parties in their constant efforts to draw attention to the shortcomings of Government policy and to criticise, delay and occasionally obstruct the progress of Government legislation. There is, however, an important, if delicate role for Government back-benchers as representatives of those in the electorate who voted for the party in office and as critics of Government policy when they believe it is reneging on party commitments or falling short of public expectations.

Only on rare occasions this century has the power of the House of Commons really made itself felt. One of the most famous examples was in May 1940, when the poor result of a vital confidence debate on the conduct of the war (when the Chamberlain Government won the vote with a reduced majority, but entirely lost the argument and the mood of the House) led Neville Chamberlain to resign as Prime Minister and so make way for Winston Churchill to succeed him as the country's wartime leader. Another memorable example was in March 1979 when, at the end of a confidence debate following the so-called 'Winter of Discontent', all the Opposition parties united to defeat what was by then a minority Labour Government and so precipitated the May 1979 General Election which brought the Conservatives under Margaret Thatcher to power.

A more recent example of Parliamentary power was the ability of the small band of Euro-sceptics on the Conservative back-benches to threaten and almost to defeat the Government legislation to give legal effect to the Treaty of Maastricht in Britain. In this case a disparate group of between ten and twenty back-benchers, often in tactical alliance with the Labour Opposition, were able to alarm and annoy Ministers for months on end while the Bill concerned was slowly grinding its way through the legislative process. The practical effect of this sustained Parliamentary campaign – which had some powerful support in parts of the media and in many Conservative-held constituencies – was to debilitate and discredit John Major's Administration and, in so doing, to sow the seeds of its subsequent loss of authority in the country at large and its eventual loss of office in 1997. On the whole, however, all such examples of raw Parliamentary power have been rare in modern times, since on most occasions Governments have been able to count on the voting support and loyalty of their own back-benchers in order to ensure their survival in office at least until the subsequent General Election.

The power of influence

In most normal circumstances the House of Commons has to rely on the power of influence – that is, influence on Ministers in the Government, influence on the policies of the Government, and influence on the media and public opinion. Effective influence in the Commons is frequently exercised in a discreet manner *before* the event, whether in party committees, formal delegations or informal conversations. On the other hand, the exercise of overt Parliamentary power (as in the examples already given earlier in this chapter) is usually confined to the comparatively rare occasions when the authority of a Minister or sometimes of the Government as a whole is in jeopardy or may even have broken down. For example, when it became clear at the beginning of April 1982 that Ministers in the Foreign Office and the Ministry of Defence had lost the confidence of the bulk of the Conservative Parliamentary Party following the

Argentinean invasion of the Falkland Islands, Lord Carrington and most of his Ministerial team at the Foreign Office resigned and John Nott at the Ministry of Defence offered his resignation, but had it refused at the time by Margaret Thatcher because the nation was by then effectively at war with Argentina. In crude and capricious Parliamentary conditions this was a vivid example of the power of the Commons or, more precisely, the power of Government back-benchers when they are no longer prepared to support Ministers because of grievous failures of policy – perceived or actual.

Another example is provided by the case of Nicholas Ridley, Secretary of State for the Environment from 1986 to 1989, who became increasingly accident prone and unpopular with the electorate because of his obvious disdain for the usual shibboleths of 'green' politics. His incorrigible attitudes made life very difficult for Conservative back-benchers who conveyed their anxiety to the Conservative Whips with increasing frequency and intensity. The result was that by 1989 Margaret Thatcher was left with no alternative but to move him from the Department of the Environment in her Cabinet reshuffle of July that year, even though he remained one of her personal favourites. More recent examples of Ministerial vulnerability to Parliamentary displeasure – notably from the Government back-benches – are provided by the cases of Norman Lamont and Harriet Harman. The former, when Chancellor, came to seem increasingly inept and accident prone, especially during the long economic recession of the early 1990s. Conservative MPs were bombarded with demands from their constituents and from the wolf-like media for a human (political) sacrifice. The situation became even more embarrassing following Black Wednesday on 16th September 1992 when Britain was effectively ejected by the financial markets from the European Exchange Rate Mechanism to which the Government's entire anti-inflation policy had been anchored – at least rhetorically. Although Norman Lamont clung onto office as Chancellor of the Exchequer for a few more months, his case became hopeless and his eventual fate was sealed. Accordingly, John Major unceremoniously sacked him in May 1993. The latter, when Secretary of State for Social Security in the Labour Government which came into office in 1997, never recovered her authority after a major political row over cuts in lone parent benefit and the perceived threat of widespread withdrawal of some disability benefits and, as a result, was dismissed by Tony Blair in his first reshuffle in July 1998. Both cases exemplify the political truth that when a Minister becomes a significant liability or embarrassment to the party in office and especially to Government back-benchers, sooner or later the unfortunate individual will be obliged to resign or will get the sack.

Over the long period since the Second World War such examples of raw Parliamentary power have been relatively rare, although more recently in the febrile atmosphere of mass media politics the vulnerability of errant or fallible Ministers appears to have increased. Certainly such things seem to happen faster and with greater sensationalism these days than was the case even twenty years ago and in this respect, as in many others, the nature of British politics has changed significantly over the years. Nowadays Parliamentary reputations are built up and then demolished, sometimes with alarming rapidity. The more that certain Ministers are thrown into the limelight, the more rapidly they seem to become vulnerable to destruction at the hands of the media and their own back-bench 'colleagues'. This was clearly highlighted by the examples of Ron Davies, who resigned as Welsh Secretary in October 1998 following a 'moment of madness' on Clapham Common; of Peter Mandelson, who resigned as Secretary of State for Trade and Industry in December 1998 following publication of details concerning a home loan he had obtained from Geoffrey Robinson; and of Geoffrey Robinson, who resigned as Paymaster General in December 1998 when the Mandelson home loan raised one too many questions about his business dealings. In all such cases the most decisive criteria for Ministerial survival are the degree of political embarrassment caused to the rest of the Government, the extent to which Government back-benchers are prepared to weather it, and whether the Prime Minister eventually wishes to sacrifice or stand by the Minister in question. In each and every case the chain of events and the eventual outcome is subtly different, although it may not seem that way to the victims of such political 'assassination'.

The background reality which lies behind all this is that at nearly every General Election since the Second World War the electorate has voted and the electoral system has worked in such a way as to ensure that one of the main parties has had an overall majority in the Commons large enough to withstand most back-bench rebellions and the political erosion which takes place due to death and retirement during the normal span of a Parliament. In such circumstances the power of the Commons has not normally been manifested in successful attempts to censure Ministers, still less to defeat Governments. Instead it has been exercised through constant back-bench influence on Ministers and the constant interplay between Governments striving to get their policy approved and their legislation onto the Statute book and Oppositions striving to criticise their actions and delay or frustrate their progress.

Parliamentary culture

The House of Commons has sometimes been described as 'the best club in London', although doubtless there would be many members of other clubs, such as Whites or the Garrick, to challenge this claim. However, it does say something about the Parliamentary culture in Britain. It is an atmosphere in which the cut and thrust of the party battle is balanced by a political camaraderie which often makes it easier to form friendships across the floor of the House than with other members on the same side. It is an institution which relies on the assumption that all its members are 'honourable' (although this may have become harder to sustain in the context of Parliamentary 'sleaze' in the middle 1990s) and all are equal in terms of democratic legitimacy.

Yet in an institution in which there are supposed to be no second-class members, it is remarkable how some are more equal than others, and how front-benchers and Privy Councillors seem to get all the best parts. The main explanation, of course, is that traditional Parliamentary procedure, much of which dates from the 1880s, assumes that debate and discussion will be conducted largely by the political giants of the day and that the rest will be content with minor roles as spear-carriers or cheer leaders. This established tendency is reinforced by the simple fact that the Chamber itself is rather small (deliberately so) and that no more than about two-thirds of those entitled can possibly find a seat on the green benches when the House is full – for example, on Budget Day or on Wednesday during Prime Minister's Question Time. In short, there are only limited opportunities for MPs to shine during prime Parliamentary time at Westminster and most of these are taken by senior Ministers and their 'shadows' on the Opposition front bench.

Another interesting aspect of Parliamentary culture in the House of Commons is the extent to which the institutionalised, almost ritual, party conflict is organised by the party whips working through what are known as 'the usual channels'. This phrase is a euphemism for the sometimes heated and vigorous discussions which take place behind the scenes and off the record between the two front benches. Without the benefit of such discussions, which can include the Prime Minister and the Leader of the Opposition on occasions, the whole place would probably grind to a halt.[10] As it is, the essential deal between the two sides is based on two key assumptions: (1) that the Government must 'get its business' (that is, get its legislation passed more or less intact); and (2) that the Opposition must have full opportunities to oppose and, within limits, to decide what is newsworthy and urgent or what is uncontentious and acceptable and hence suitable for full cooperation between the parties. In support of this generally pragmatic approach to the conduct of Parliamentary business is the basic British idea that it is the duty of Her Majesty's Loyal Opposition to oppose the Government of the day, coupled with the understanding that there are few problems which cannot be solved in Parliament by the so-called 'business managers' on each side acting in tacit co-operation.

Indeed, the co-operative principle is reflected in the attitude and behaviour of individual MPs who strive very hard as soon as they get to Westminster to secure 'a pair' – that is, a Member on the other side of the House who will agree on specific occasions (normally two-line whips) to stay away from the division lobbies when the votes are called, so that the overall result of the vote is not affected. Such 'pairing' is an invaluable practice for those with long Parliamentary careers and can serve to mitigate what would otherwise be the tedium and exhaustion of staying up half the night to vote on matters about which most Members may know little and care even less. However, such personal arrangements (which have to be registered with the Whips on each side) are only allowed to operate on the less contentious items of Parliamentary business which usually attract no more than a two-line whip – signifying that in the eyes of the parties the issue is not at the heart of the party political battle. See Figure 11.1 for typical 'whips' giving guidance to Labour and Conservative MPs.

A final aspect of Parliamentary culture which is worth mentioning is the fondness of MPs in all parties, but especially on the Conservative side, for dining clubs and informal political gatherings of all kinds. It is sometimes said that the morning and afternoon hours at Westminster resemble those of a coffee shop or works canteen, while the evening hours are often whiled away in the Smoking Room (where fewer people now actually smoke), on the Terrace overlooking the Thames in summer, or around various dining tables among self-consciously exclusive groups of like-minded MPs. In the Labour Party the various groups usually like to meet and talk in the Tea Room – a canteen and sitting area confined to MPs and officers of the House. In the Conservative Party they prefer the Members' Dining Room or private rooms on the Terrace level or even their London homes. The common denominator on all these occasions is the self-indulgent exchange of political gossip and ideas, something which is the very stuff of politics in all Parliamentary assemblies around the world.

The views of these internal party groups, as and when they are clarified, are propounded and taken forward by the MPs concerned who usually lose little time in passing on the essence of their discussions to their party whips and sometimes, in suitably veiled form, to lobby journalists. It is in these ways that much political opinion at Westminster is moulded and developed. If a full account is to be given of life in the

Figure 11.1 Typical party 'whips'

(a) Labour

PARLIAMENTARY LABOUR PARTY

MONDAY, 8TH JUNE 1998

The House will meet at 2.30 p.m.

1. Social Security and Ministers for Women Questions.

Tabling for Defence, President of the Council and House of Commons Commission.

2. TEACHING AND HIGHER EDUCATION BILL [LORDS]:
(Stephen Byers and Kim Howells).

PROGRESS ON REMAINING STAGES.

YOUR ATTENDANCE FOR A RUNNING WHIP FROM 3.30 PM AND UNTIL THE BUSINESS IS CONCLUDED IS ESSENTIAL.

PROVISION WILL BE MADE FOR THE TEN O'CLOCK RULE TO BE SUSPENDED.

TUESDAY, 9TH JUNE

The House will meet at 2.30 p.m.

1. Environment and the Regions and Transport Questions.

Tabling for Scotland and Lord Chancellor's Department.

2. Ten Minute Rule Bill:

Youth Parliament - Andrew Rowe.

3. TEACHING AND HIGHER EDUCATION BILL [LORDS]:
(Rt. Hon. David Blunkett and team).

CONCLUSION OF REMAINING STAGES (FOR THREE HOURS).

4. EUROPEAN COMMUNITIES (AMENDMENT) BILL:
(Doug Henderson).

CONSIDERATION OF SUPPLEMENTAL ALLOCATION OF TIME MOTION.

5. EUROPEAN COMMUNITIES (AMENDMENT) BILL:
(Doug Henderson).

CONSIDERATION OF A LORDS AMENDMENT .

YOUR ATTENDANCE FOR A RUNNING WHIP FROM 3.30 PM AND UNTIL THE BUSINESS IS CONCLUDED IS ESSENTIAL.

PROVISION WILL BE MADE FOR THE TEN O'CLOCK RULE TO BE SUSPENDED.

Continues overleaf.

WEDNESDAY, 10TH JUNE   The House will meet at 9.30 a.m.

Private Members Business

1. 9.35 - 11.00   Jim Fitzpatrick   Leasehold reform.

    11.00 - 12.30   Peter Brand   Preventative health care and home
                                              insulation.

2. Chancellor of the Duchy of Lancaster and Prime   Tabling for Wales and Prime Ministe
    Minister's Questions.

3. Ten Minute Rule Bill: Restoration of Damage to Sites of Spe
                                               Scientific Interest - Candy Atherton.

4. NORTHERN IRELAND (SENTENCES) BILL: SECOND READING.
    (Rt. Hon. Mo Mowlam and Adam Ingram).

    YOUR ATTENDANCE AT 9.00PM FOR 10.00PM IS ESSENTIAL.

THURSDAY, 11TH JUNE   The House will meet at 2.30 p.m.

1. Education and Employment Questions.   Tabling for Treasury.

2. Debate on the PROSPECTS FOR THE CARDIFF EUROPEAN COUNCIL on a Motion for the
    Adjournment of the House.
    (Rt. Hon. Robin Cook and Doug Henderson).

    YOUR ATTENDANCE IS REQUESTED.

FRIDAY, 12TH JUNE

The House will not be sitting.

                                                NICK BROWN

Source: The Labour Party

(b) Conservative

The House will meet:

MONDAY, 8th June at 2.30 p.m. for Social Security Questions.
Tabling for Defence, President of the Council and House of Commons
Commission Questions.

Teaching and Higher Education Bill (Lords): Progress on remaining
stages.

Important divisions will take place, and your attendance at 5.30 p.m.

and until the business is concluded is essential.

TUESDAY, 9th June at 2.30 p.m. for Environment and the Regions and
Transport Questions.
Tabling for Scottish and Lord Chancellor's Department Questions.

10 Minute Rule Bill: Youth Parliament. (Mr Andrew Rowe).

For three hours,
Teaching and Higher Education Bill (Lords): Conclusion of remaining
stages.

Thereafter,
Consideration of Supplemental Allocation of Time Motion relating to the
European Communities (Amendment) Bill.

European Communities (Amendment) Bill: Consideration of a Lords
Amendment.

Important divisions will take place, and your attendance at 3.30 p.m.

and until the business is concluded is essential.

Note: A Motion to suspend the Ten O'Clock
Rule may be moved at 10.00 p.m.

PLEASE TURN OVER

WEDNESDAY, 10th June at 9.30 a.m.

PRIVATE MEMBERS' DEBATES

9.35-11.00am	Jim Fitzpatrick	Leasehold Reform.
11.00-12.30pm	Dr Peter Brand	Preventative health care and home insulation.
12.30-1.00pm	Mr Ian Pearson	Planning guidance on the use of sports grounds.
1.00-1.30pm	Mr Richard Spring	The provision of magistrates' courts in Suffolk.
1.30-2.00pm	Mrs Claire Curtis-Thomas	Mr Ray Herring and the Merseyside Police.

At 2.30 p.m. PROMPT
Chancellor of the Duchy of Lancaster's Questions and Prime Minister's
Questions.
Tabling for Welsh Questions and Prime Minister's Questions.

10 Minute Rule Bill: Restoration of Damage to Sites of Special
                     Scientific Interest.   (Ms Candy Atherton)

Northern Ireland (Sentences) Bill: 2nd Reading and Money Resolution.

Your attendance is requested.

Source: The Conservative Party

House of Commons, attention should be paid to these political groupings within at least the two main parties. In the Labour Party – when in Opposition – the Tribune Group and the Campaign Group each organise their own slates of candidates for the annual elections to the Shadow Cabinet. In the Conservative Party, the 92 Group, the Reform Group, the Macleod Group, One Nation, The Progress Trust and the No Turning Back Group have been among the much more numerous informal groupings which compete for influence over party policy and appointments.

11.3 Main functions

In 1867 Walter Bagehot suggested that the House of Commons needed to perform the following functions if it was to do its duty: 'elect a Ministry, legislate, teach the nation, express the nation's will and bring matters to the nation's attention'.[11] If we were to translate his words into modern terms, we would say that the House of Commons has to provide most of the Ministers in any Government, to scrutinise and pass legislation, to give a lead to public opinion on the great issues of the day, and to seek redress for the grievances and concerns of the general public. There are, of course, other vital functions performed by the modern House of Commons, notably Parliamentary control of the Executive and party political conflict on the Parliamentary stage. Yet the essential functions of the House have not changed very much since the time when Walter Bagehot made his authoritative observation. The functions of the Commons are summarised in Figure 11.2.

Representation and redress

The oldest function of Members of Parliament is to represent the interests of their constituents and to seek redress for their grievances by the Government of the day.

Figure 11.2 Functions of the House of Commons

Representation and redress	**The party battle**
On behalf of constituents	In the chamber
On behalf of interest	In Committees
On behalf of causes	In the media
The legislative process	**Parliamentary control**
First reading	Debates in the chamber
Second reading	Oral and written questions
Committee stage	Select Committee work
Report stage	Representations to ministers
Third reading	Representations to agencies

This function, which has been performed ever since the establishment of Parliament in the thirteenth century, is still a vital task for MPs in modern conditions. There are a number of different ways in which it is carried out. These range from having a quiet word with a Minister in the division lobby to signing an Early Day Motion with other MPs in order to signal the breadth and depth of support for a particular cause or concern.

They include such techniques as:

- writing a letter to a Minister enclosing documentary evidence of a constituent's complaint;
- leading a delegation to lobby a Minister in Whitehall;
- putting down a Parliamentary Question for written answer in order to get a Ministerial response on the record in *Hansard*;
- putting down a Question for oral answer in order to be able to make a point in a supplementary question on the record in the Chamber;
- applying to the Speaker for an Adjournment Debate at the end of the day's Parliamentary proceedings or an Emergency Debate immediately after Oral Questions and any Ministerial Statements.

As must be evident from this brief description, there are many channels of representation available to MPs when performing this aspect of their duties. It is normal for them to begin with one of the lower key methods and to resort to the more dramatic ones only if the former do not have the desired effect. This wide range of possible techniques for publicising the concerns or grievances of their constituents gives back-bench MPs a real degree of influence in their representations to Ministers and civil servants.

If MPs did not speak up and intervene on behalf of their constituents when the latter feel frustrated by the bureaucracy of central Government or other public agencies, many people might conclude that Parliamentary democracy was a bit of a sham and withdraw their support for it. Even as things stand, the general public has a pretty cynical attitude towards the role and utility of MPs and it is not usually until people experience a positive response from their MP that they are prepared to reconsider their habitually low opinion of the political process. On the other hand, when a conscientious MP is able to provide effective help for a constituent, it can make the beneficiary of such political action more likely to appreciate the value of having an MP in the first place. To the extent that MPs exert themselves in this way – and nearly all of them do

– it provides at least one recognisable justification for the British Parliamentary system.

The party battle

Another function of Members of Parliament is to act as combatants for their party when it is in Government and critics or opponents of the Government when their party is in Opposition. The party battle, which was particularly polarised in the 1970s and 1980s, has been deplored in many quarters, especially by the minor parties whose interests are not very well catered for in the procedural arrangements at Westminster. However, there are some points to be made in its favour. It encourages the voters to take an interest in national politics between General Elections, to consider at least two sides to every political argument and to pay some attention to topical policy issues. Without the drama of the party battle at Westminster and, of course, in the columns and studios of the media, the political process would lose much of its vitality and the influence of the bureaucracy would increase. While there are those who would welcome such an alternative way of conducting British political life, even they would have to concede that it would probably produce a less accountable and less democratic form of government.

Although in Britain many people pay little or no attention to the processes of politics, there would probably be even less public interest and even more public apathy without the stimulus and often annoyance of the party battle. Evidence over a long period suggests that the degree of success or failure of the Opposition parties in criticising the Government of the day and putting forward their own proposals does have a cumulative effect on public opinion and subsequently on the voting behaviour of at least the more attentive voters. Opposition parties very often fail to get all the publicity which they would like (especially for their own policy proposals), but they are often successful in sowing the seeds of doubt and resentment about the performance of the party in office in the minds of the voters. In this way, more than any other, there tends to be a negative bias in the British party battle which breeds zero sum attitudes in the minds of many voters. Yet it is hard to see how things could be otherwise as long as Britain retains its present 'winner takes all' electoral system.

The legislative process

Another well-recognised, but not always well-understood, function of Members of Parliament is the scrutiny and passage of legislation. It is the function most often mentioned by members of the public when asked to describe the activities of Parliament. Over the years it has absorbed an increasing proportion of Parliamentary time as the scope and complexity of legislation have increased and as the public – notably pressure groups – have made greater demands on Governments of all political persuasions.

The legislative process in the Commons begins with First Reading. This is the name of the formal stage at which printed copies of a Bill are made available in the Vote Office for all MPs and others who are interested to read and consider it. After an appropriate interval, this is followed by Second Reading (usually about two weeks later) when a wide ranging debate takes place for about six hours during which the broad purposes of a Bill are discussed and at the end of which a vote is usually taken which shows whether or not the House approves of a Bill in principle. This is the stage of the debate when the senior Minister in charge of a Bill sets out the broad arguments for it, the chief Opposition spokesman sets out the broad arguments against it (unless a Bill is wholly uncontentious, in which case detailed criticism and constructive suggestions are more likely to be offered), interested back-benchers on both sides of the House make national or constituency points, and junior Ministers and Opposition spokesmen wind up the debate during the final hour by answering (or sometimes ignoring) the various points made by others during the course of the debate. At the end of such debates on all Government Bills the votes are whipped, which means that MPs are expected to support the position of their own party, unless they have overwhelming reasons for doing otherwise – for example, conscientious objections to a Bill or overriding constituency reasons for opposing it.

Assuming that a Bill is approved by the House at Second Reading, it is then referred to a committee, usually a Standing Committee 'upstairs' where it is debated in detail and at length by a committee of between sixteen and fifty MPs chosen to reflect the party balance in the House as a whole.[12] This means that a typical Standing Committee may be made up of two or more Ministers in charge of the Bill, a Government Whip and perhaps a dozen or more back-benchers on the Government side, ranged against a variety of Opposition MPs who will invariably include two or more Opposition spokesmen and an Opposition Whip as well as a number of interested Opposition back-benchers who between them usually share the burdens of scrutinising and opposing the Bill.

The task of a Standing Committee is to debate and scrutinise a Bill clause by clause and line by line. This usually involves the members of the Opposition side putting down a considerable number of critical or even wrecking amendments, some merely probing but some seeking to alter fundamentally or even destroy the effect of a Bill. The Ministers in charge of a Bill have to answer each separate debate and, if necessary, to persuade their own back-benchers to vote against any amendments unacceptable to the Government if the Opposition is not prepared to withdraw them at the end of each debate. Once all the debates on amendments and on each clause 'stand part' have been concluded, new clauses can be proposed and debated, provided they fall within the scope of the long title of a Bill.

In the case of unusually complex and controversial Bills, the later stages in committee often have to be timetabled as long as the Government can persuade the House as a whole to vote for a so-called 'guillotine' motion at the end of a three-hour debate in the Chamber, thus ensuring that the proceedings are timetabled for the remainder of the committee stage. This procedural device is supposed to ensure that all parts of a Bill are discussed, however briefly, and that the passage of a Bill through committee is not unreasonably delayed by Opposition filibustering. Yet even with the benefit of this timetabling procedure, some Bills may involve a committee stage of a hundred hours or more and large parts of some Bills may still not be adequately discussed in important respects.

After an appropriate interval (usually several weeks to give time to officials and legislative draftsmen to take account of amendments put forward in committee), the Bill is then returned to the floor of the House for the final Commons stages of Report and Third Reading. These are usually taken on the same day and may last for six hours or more – in other words, at least one full day's debate in the Chamber. The Report stage is the time when the House as a whole (especially those who did not serve on the Standing Committee) have a chance to speak and vote on any new amendments or new clauses which have been accepted by the Speaker for debate on the floor of the House. It is out of order for opponents of a Bill to go over ground already traversed during earlier stages of the legislative process. Third Reading, which follows immediately, is usually no more than a fairly brief debate on the general merits or demerits of a Bill as it then stands, and provides what is usually a final opportunity for the House as a whole to record its views. The debate is concluded by yet another vote on the main principles of the Bill in which MPs tend once again to vote on party lines.

By this stage of the legislative process the House of Commons has usually concluded its scrutiny of a Bill, unless subsequently the House of Lords insists on making some substantial amendments which Ministers decide to resist. If this happens the Commons have later to give further consideration to the Bill as amended by their Lordships. If all the Lords amendments are acceptable to the Commons (which really means to the Government of the day), the lower House simply sends a message to the Upper House signifying its agreement. If, however, some of the Lords' amendments are not acceptable to the governing party in the Commons, the lower House sends a message containing its reasons for disagreement and possibly some counter amendments of its own. It is then for the Lords to decide whether to persist with their opposition to the Commons or to give way gracefully in the light of the fact that under the constitutional provisions of the 1911 and 1949 Parliament Acts, the House of Commons can ultimately get its way. On nearly all occasions since 1949 – indeed, ultimately, on all but one occasion – their Lordships have considered discretion to be the better part of valour and accordingly have given way to the will of the majority in the Commons (see Chapter 10, p. 239).

Since nearly all Lords amendments are inspired by the need for technical or drafting improvements in Government Bills (nearly all of which are made at the instigation of Ministers in the light of criticisms voiced during earlier stages of the legislative process), such amendments usually cause no difficulties in the lower House. They merely underline the usefulness of having a bi-cameral legislature. Once a Bill is out of the Lords, it is virtually complete and awaits only the formality of Royal Assent by the Queen. The whole process from First Reading to Royal Assent normally takes between six months and one year. However, it can be speeded up dramatically in cases of emergency legislation – for example, Bills to deal with terrorism or civil disorder which (with the benefit of agreement between the parties) can be put through all stages of the legislative process in 24 hours if necessary.

Parliamentary scrutiny and control

Yet another vital function of Members of Parliament is to scrutinise and seek to control the activities of the Executive. This is probably the most necessary, but also the most difficult function to be performed by the House in modern conditions, essentially because there is no formal separation of powers in Britain between the Executive and the Legislature as there is in so many other comparable countries. This means that in Britain the Government of the day – provided it has a secure overall majority in the House of Commons – is more often able to dominate Parliament rather than the other way around.

Traditionally, it was assumed that Ministers' responsibility to answer the questions and debating points of Members of Parliament constituted adequate and respectable Parliamentary control of the Executive. Yet with the remorseless extension of the perceived responsibilities of Government over the last 60 years, it has become painfully clear that this traditional and complacent assumption does not meet public expectations and needs to be reinforced if central Government and its Agencies are to be properly scrutinised, let alone controlled by the elected representatives of the people. The fundamental problem here is that with typical British ambiguity there is a clash between two different versions of democratic legitimacy – that of the party elected into office at the previous General Election to govern the country for a period of years according to the principles and policies which it put before the electorate, and that of the House of Commons as a whole as the overall, democratic manifestation of the will of the people at a particular time.

In modern times Parliamentarians (that is, members of both Houses) have sought to square this circle by making increasingly full and effective use of Select Committees. In the House of Commons these are committees reflecting broadly the political balance in the House at any time which are charged by the House as a whole with scrutinising and controlling the activities of the Executive in given policy areas. Originally, in the nineteenth century, they were set up by the House *ad hoc* to look closely into particular issues of public concern – for example, Britain's military shortcomings in the Crimean War. They can also be traced back to the attitudes of William Gladstone and other Parliamentarians in the 1850s who, in their determination to guarantee the probity and efficiency of public expenditure, established the Public Accounts Committee as a permanent Committee of the House of Commons designed to enable the House as a whole to be satisfied that public money was being correctly and properly spent.

From these nineteenth-century beginnings through to modern times, the fortunes of Select Committees have waxed and waned. They have tended to be more powerful when the Government of the day has had only a very small majority in the Commons or no majority at all (as in the late 1970s), but considerably less powerful when the Government of the day has had a commanding majority which it could use, if necessary, to steamroller any flickering challenge from largely impotent Select Committees. Indeed, for many years there has been a whole school of thought – represented by people such as Tony Benn and the late Enoch Powell, for example – that holds that the correct way to scrutinise and control the Executive is on the floor of the House and that Select Committees are little more than a self-important and time-consuming distraction from what should be the cockpit of Parliamentary control in the Chamber.

Against this background it was fortuitous and somewhat surprising that the incoming Conservative Government in 1979 decided to propose a comprehensive reform of the Select Committee structure which was willingly accepted by most Government back-benchers and certainly by the Opposition parties.[13] Following this fundamental reform, there is now one of these all-party and largely non-partisan committees for each area of central Government activity, as well as a number of non-Departmental committees which have deeper roots in Parliamentary soil as has already been explained. These Select Committees, each of which is usually composed of between eleven and seventeen MPs broadly reflecting the party political balance in the House as a whole, meet regularly (perhaps two days a week when the House is sitting and on other occasions as well) to oversee and investigate their particular area of Government activity. In the course of their investigations, which can include foreign travel, they can call for persons and papers, and their findings are normally written up in substantial reports drafted by their clerks and expert advisers and usually redrafted and amended by members of the committee. Once published in the form of reports to the House as a whole, such documents are intended to inform both Parliamentary and public debate. Occasionally, they can have real influence on the course of Government policy.[14]

In normal circumstances Select Committees have no legislative role, so they are not really analogous to the Congressional Committees in the United States. However, on a few occasions they have been used as Parliamentary mechanisms for the exploration of policy options at a pre-legislative stage.[15] Whatever their shortcomings and inhibitions, they do represent a systematic attempt to improve Parliamentary scrutiny and control of the Executive and its Agencies in Britain, which has come to seem all the more necessary as it has been increasingly recognised that the traditional forms of Ministerial accountability to the House as a whole do not guarantee the achievement of this important Parliamentary objective.

In recent years the influence (if not the power) of Select Committees has increased in that their public hearings are quite often televised and hence attract a degree of extra media and public interest. This makes them more formidable interlocutors for Ministers and senior civil servants and a more central part of the whole Parliamentary publicity machine. The Chairmen of such committees can become (or may already be) influential and newsworthy MPs who are often called to speak early in debates on the floor of the House and can be much in demand for media interviews. Yet it would be a mistake to believe that this extra visibility for Select Committees has altered to any real extent the fundamental imbalance of power in the House of Commons between a self-confident Government with a secure Parliamentary majority and the rest of the House, no matter how effective the Opposition may be or how keen certain MPs may have become to use Select Committees and other Parliamentary procedures more effectively to hold Ministers and the Executive to account.

The experience of the Westland Crisis in 1986 and other clashes between Members of Parliament and the Executive before and since underlines the fact that Parliamentary control of the Executive in Britain is not, and may never be, as effective as its proponents or some members of the general public would like.[16] In the final analysis, Select Committees, and indeed Parliament as a whole, are likely to remain relatively weak when faced with a strong and determined Government which is confident of its ability to use its voting support on the floor of the House to overcome any challenge. The only circumstances in which this situation might be changed would be if a Government were committed to, or had imposed on it by dint of its minority status in the Commons, a new constitutional settlement including extensive Parliamentary reform, a new Bill of Rights, an independent Supreme Court, legislation to guarantee freedom of information, and the introduction of proportional representation for elections to Westminster. In the past such comprehensive reforms have seemed most unlikely. However, at least some such reforms are being implemented by the Labour Government which came into office in 1997 as part of its self-conscious programme of 'modernisation'.

As Professor Bernard Crick wrote about thirty years ago, we should not read too much into the idea of Parliamentary control in Britain because it means 'influence not direct power, advice not command, criticism not obstruction, scrutiny not initiative, and publicity not secrecy'.[17] Yet even these attenuated forms of Parliamentary control should not be underestimated in a political system which has never been characterised by clear-cut and unambiguous power relationships. Furthermore, a degree of Parliamentary control to match that exercised by Congress in the United States would only be possible in Britain if it were decided to move to an explicit separation of powers set out in a newly codified constitution and guaranteed by an independent Supreme Court. Such revolutionary change is unlikely to be brought about in a political system in which it is the Government of the day and the official Opposition front bench (the putative alternative Government) which effectively control the nature and scope of Parliamentary power. The irony is that it is in the name of 'Parliamentary supremacy' that Governments still dominate the political sphere in Britain, although this observation has increasingly to be qualified in the light of constitutional developments in the European Union which are affecting the political system in Britain.

11.4 The progress of reform

The progress of Parliamentary reform has been limited by the fact that the power of Parliament in Britain has usually been a euphemism for the power of Government ruling through Parliament. It has also been limited by the inherent tension between the interests of the Executive and those of the Legislature which is supposed to control it – in other words, between actual and potential Ministers on the one hand and all back-benchers on the other. In most normal circumstances, when the governing party has an overall majority in the House of Commons, any reform (that is, strengthening) of the power of the Commons is likely to mean a relative weakening of the power of Government. The only developments which are really likely to alter this state of affairs would be the introduction of electoral reform, together with a number of institutional and constitutional reforms. Since those who believe that they benefit from the present arrangements (the two front benches and a few self-styled 'great Parliamentarians') have been sceptical of the advantages of making such radical changes, it is easy to see why the cause of Parliamentary reform has only made modest headway over the years.

Although the progress of Parliamentary reform has been slow and the reforms made have been rather marginal, experience in the late 1990s has shown that it is possible to achieve reform. The new, generally warmer disposition towards the cause of Parliamentary reform has stemmed largely from the changing composition and outlook of all parties, but especially among Labour and Liberal Democrat MPs who, at least in their more 'modern' elements, have become increasingly impatient with those of their colleagues who cling to the traditional ways of doing things at Westminster. Reformist pressures have come strongly from the growing contingent of women MPs who have generally been very critical of the unsocial hours and archaic procedures of Parliament which militate against anything like a normal family life. Reform has also been spurred by the gathering institutional and legislative implications of Britain's membership of the European Union, notably the need for national Parliaments to equip themselves better to deal in a timely fashion with the spate of European legislative proposals emanating from the European institutions and with those European competences which may be 'repatriated' to the member states under the doctrine of subsidiarity.[18]

In February 1992 the so-called Jopling Report of an all-party Committee chaired by a former Conservative Chief Whip recommended a number of far-reaching procedural reforms, including the time-tabling of all Government Bills and a variety of other proposals designed to enable the House to rise no later than 10.30 p.m., while allowing for the standard half hour for adjournment debates.[19] On this occasion the response from the Conservative side, both front-bench and back-bench, was generally favourable, while the die-hard tendency on the then Opposition side seemed to be overcome by the party leadership. The result, after some prevarication and delay, was that the House eventually debated and approved a package of procedural reforms in the spirit of the Jopling Report on 19 December 1994.[20]

The key points in the Reforms were:

1. the curtailing of debate on the Ways and Means Resolutions of Money Bills to a maximum of 45 minutes;
2. reference of most Statutory Instruments and European legislative proposals to a Standing Committee on Statutory Instruments with any debates on the floor of the House normally being limited to ninety minutes;
3. the House would no longer sit on eight Fridays during the annual session, which MPs could then be sure of reserving for their constituency commitments;
4. the House would meet in plenary session every Wednesday between 10.00 a.m. and 2.30 p.m. to debate matters on an adjournment motion (in other words, unwhipped business);
5. the subjects for debate on Wednesdays would be chosen by ballot and the rest of the time on Wednesdays would be concerned with Questions to Ministers and other normal Parliamentary business in the Chamber.

The spirit and purpose of this package of Parliamentary reform was to reduce somewhat the time-consuming demands of debates and votes in the Chamber, to provide more clear time for MPs to be in their constituencies during Parliamentary sessions, and to limit proceedings late in the evening so that all MPs could normally leave Westminster after voting at 10.00 p.m. – if not earlier when the business of the House permits. Belatedly, therefore, it was an attempt to modernise and humanise some of the House's antiquated procedures and to limit its secular tendency to sit for longer hours to less and less good effect.

Following the General Election of 1997, a new Select Committee on Modernising the House of Commons was established under the chairmanship of the then Leader of the House, Ann Taylor, with a remit to improve the quality of legislation by:

• allowing more effective consultation and scrutiny;
• reviewing the structure of the Parliamentary year;
• overhauling the process for scrutinising European Law;
• strengthening the ability of MPs to call Ministers to account.

The first report of the Committee recommended a more open and formal approach to timetabling; increased consultation on draft Bills and more pre-legislative scrutiny, including by Select Committees; more effective use of Standing Committees; and the carry-over of Bills from one Parliamentary session to another.[21] Cumulatively these proposals are – potentially at least – very far-reaching; it is up to the Government, the Whips and of course to Members of Parliament themselves to see that they have positive effects in practice.

The other area of procedural reform in which the House of Commons has made significant strides in recent years has been in the sphere of financial procedure. As long ago as 1980 the so-called Armstrong Report produced by a Committee chaired by a former Cabinet Secretary recommended that the Commons consider both sides of the public accounts together and that such a unified Budget should be heralded a few months before by a 'green Budget' setting out the Chancellor's provisional ideas for revenue raising and public expenditure in the following year.[22] The essential ideas behind this proposal were that a unified Budget would be a more coherent way of presenting the public accounts than the traditional practice of dealing with revenue and expenditure in different Whitehall cycles, and that opportunities should be created for Parliament and other interested bodies to influence the fiscal policy of any Government at an earlier and more formative stage of policy making.

Subsequently, the first Thatcher Administration (1979–83) went some way towards accepting these ideas by increasing the range and quality of financial information made available to the House of Commons in the annual economic forecasts published by the Treasury. This reformed procedure was brought into effect for the first time in 1982 and subsequent Autumn Statements published by the Treasury became enlarged and more informative documents as a result. However, it was not until the first Major Administration (1990–92) that the Government accepted the idea of having a unified annual Budget, although it rejected the idea that this great Parliamentary occasion should be preceded a few months before by a provisional 'green Budget'. The result was that in 1993 there were two Budgets in the year (one on the old basis in the spring and one on the new basis in the autumn) and from 1994 a unified Budget was presented by the Chancellor in November soon after the opening of each annual session of Parliament.

Needless to say, not everyone at Westminster was content with the new arrangements. MPs in all parties called for an extra debate on the economy each July to replace the debate on the Autumn Statement which used to take place in November or December, and for the annual Finance Bill to be split into two parts – a relatively brief 'political' Bill containing the really controversial measures and a much longer and more technical Taxes Management Bill designed to keep the Inland Revenue administration cost-effective and up to date. The Major Government accepted the former suggestion, but rejected the latter on the grounds that it was based on an artificial and untenable distinction in tax law.

Under New Labour, the Chancellor, Gordon Brown, has persisted with unified annual budgets; but he has moved the budget date back to the spring and introduced the practice of making 'green' budget proposals for prior consultation several months before. It remains to be seen if these new arrangements will prove durable and successful.

The impact of radio and television

Since November 1989 the proceedings in the Chamber of the House of Commons and sometimes 'upstairs' in Select Committees have been broadcast on radio and television. The idea had been under discussion in Britain at least since the 1960s and had been promoted by both media and academic interests with growing support from MPs in all parties. For a long time there was nothing more adventurous than a limited experiment which began in the late 1970s with live radio transmission of a few particularly newsworthy exchanges or debates in the Commons. This tended to concentrate on Prime Minister's Questions and a few significant debates or Parliamentary occasions of particular media interest, such as the Chancellor's annual Budget Statement, the May 1978 debate on nuclear fuel reprocessing, the April 1982 debate on the outbreak of conflict over the Falkland Islands, and the January 1986 debate on the Westland crisis.

The present position on radio is that producers use edited extracts from the tape recordings of proceedings in the Chamber and in committee 'upstairs' as the raw material for programmes which are usually broadcast after the event, such as the BBC programmes *Today in Parliament* or *The Week in Westminister*. On television it has been possible since November 1989 for the general public both in Britain and abroad (courtesy of the C Span channel on satellite television) to watch coverage of proceedings both in the Chamber and 'upstairs' in committee. Although originally accepted only as an experiment, the House voted on a free vote in July 1990 to make the arrangements permanent and it now seems inconceivable that the television cameras will ever be withdrawn.

No one can be absolutely sure what will be the long-term effects of allowing television cameras into the House of Commons and it is probably still too soon to suggest a definitive conclusion. On the one hand, the proponents of televising the Commons have argued that it brings the proceedings closer to the public – indeed, right into the sitting-rooms of people in Britain and abroad – and thus can enhance public understanding and support for the working of British Parliamentary democracy. They have also argued that, if the House had continued to resist the televising of its proceedings, it would have condemned itself to increasing quaintness and irrelevance in the eyes of people everywhere who have become used to being able to watch all the leading political figures perform in front of the cameras.

The opponents of televising the Commons, on the other hand, have argued that it can have the effect of trivialising and sensationalising the proceedings, partly because the media are always more interested in the trivial and the sensational than the dull but worthy aspects of what happens and partly because many MPs are not able to resist the temptation of playing to the gallery of perhaps millions of viewers on big occasions. The opponents have also argued that, notwithstanding the special arrangements which were made to limit what may be shown by the cameras (for example, no reaction shots of anyone unless an MP is specifically referred to by the MP who has the floor at the time), eventually the imperatives of 'good television' (from the producer's point of view) are likely to predominate over a more restrained approach to portraying Parliamentary practice. They have had to admit, however, that many of their worst fears have not actually been borne out in practice and that both Parliament and people have emerged relatively unscathed from the experience so far. Indeed, it could be said that life at Westminster continues very much as before.

11.5 Conclusion

The House of Commons has a range of powers and functions which can be formidable or merely nominal, depending on the Parliamentary arithmetic at any time and the mood or inclinations of the 659 MPs. In what might be described as normal circumstances, when the governing party has an effective overall majority, the Government of the day is able to get its way on the things which really matter, provided only that it retains the confidence and voting support of its back-benchers. In the rarer circumstances when the result of a General Election has produced a very small majority for the governing party or even a so-called 'hung Parliament' (in which the Government has no overall majority), there can be a serious risk of defeat at the hands of combined Opposition parties. Indeed, even when a Government has a modest, but sufficient overall majority, it can still encounter great danger in Parliament if a significant and cohesive group of its own back-benchers are in revolt on a political issue where they have a good slice of public opinion on their side – as John Major and his Ministerial colleagues discovered in the early 1990s when the 'Euro-sceptics' on the Conservative back-benches harried and nearly brought down the Government during the passage of the legislation designed to bring British law into line with the 1992 Maastricht Treaty.

There are many paradoxical aspects of the House of Commons which ought to discourage sweeping generalisations. All that can really be said is that the House carries out its various tasks with varying degrees of efficiency and success. It is reasonably effective as a forum for popular representation and redress. It is best known as a dramatic stage for party political conflict, especially now that it is broadcast to a potentially large audience by radio and television. It is quite good at the detailed scrutiny of legislation (although it still does not make the most efficient use of this time), but almost incapable of modifying legislation against the wishes of the Government of the day unless a large enough group of party rebels are prepared to stick to their guns to the point of defying the party Whips. It is gradually becoming more effective as a mechanism for the scrutiny and control of the Executive, although in this respect it cannot emulate the power and independence of the American Congress as long as there is no formal separation of powers in Britain.

In short, while the House of Commons is theoretically supreme in the British political system, in practice it is usually controlled by the Government of the day in tacit collusion with the official Opposition. In other words, the power of all MPs – and especially the preponderance of back-benchers – is severely limited by the rules and conventions of Britain's 'front-bench constitution'. This position is unlikely to change significantly unless and until there is agreement to far-reaching reforms of Britain's electoral and constitutional arrangements. Such changes are unlikely to be made unless a new Parliamentary consensus emerges to support them, even though the present Government may come to believe that it has a mandate for such radical action.

However, the scope for delay and obstruction remains very great, especially since there are probably enough entrenched traditionalists in all parties to thwart the most ambitious plans of the Parliamentary and constitutional reformers. In these circumstances it is unwise to make dogmatic statements about the House of Commons, not least because the mood and priorities of every Parliament can change and in politics no one can really foretell the future.

Suggested questions

1   To what extent do Members of Parliament reflect the views and interests of their constituents?
2   How well does the House of Commons perform its main functions?
3   What changes need to be made to improve Parliamentary control of the Executive?

Notes

1. W.I. Jennings, *Parliament*, 2nd edn (Cambridge: CUP, 1969), pp. 7–8.
2. L.S. Amery, *Thoughts on the Constitution* (Cambridge: CUP, 1947), p. 12.
3. Ethnic minorities have been significantly under-represented in all parties in Parliament. Recently, however, the Labour Party particularly has made some successful efforts to recruit more MPs from Asian and Afro-Caribbean backgrounds, a record nine being elected in 1997 including, for example, Keith Vaz from Leicester and Diane Abbott from Hackney. In fact, in 1997 a record 44 candidates from within the ethnic minorities were picked by the three main political parties, up from 24 in 1992, 14 fielded by Labour, 11 for the Conservatives and 19 by the Liberal Democrats.
4. 'Virtual representation' was best defined a long time ago by Edmund Burke in 1797 when he wrote in a letter to Sir Herbert Langrishe that it was 'representation in which there is a communion of interests and a sympathy in feelings and desires between those who act in the name of any description of people (that is, MPs) and the people in whose name they act (that is, particular sections or interests in the community), though the trustees (the MPs) are not chosen by them (but by the voters)'. Today 'virtual representation' raises topical and controversial issues about the outside interests of MPs.
5. When the Labour Party is in Opposition and, consequently, forms a Shadow Cabinet, 15 members of it are elected each year by their colleagues in the Parliamentary Party. In addition, five others sit *ex officio*, namely, the Leader, the Deputy Leader, the Chief Whip, the Chairman of the Parliamentary Party and the Leader of the Opposition in the Lords (who is formally co-opted by the Party Leader).
6. The new intake of MPs at the 1997 General Election – some 260 individuals – was a postwar record, comprising 39.4 per cent of the House of Commons. These new members accounted or 44 per cent of the Parliamentary Labour Party, 25 per cent of the Conservative ranks, and 63 per cent of the Liberal Democrat membership. In no Parliament since 1945 had there been such a wholescale renewal of parliamentary personnel.
7. In 1997–98 the Prime Minister, Tony Blair, declined the full salary to which he was entitled, namely £100,000, drawing instead a salary of £58,557. Similarly, Cabinet Ministers decided to accept salaries of £43,991 (Commons) and £58,876 (Lords) rather than the full entitlement.
8. This annual financial assistance stood at £3254 for every seat won at the 1997 General Election, plus £7.04 for every 200 votes. This formula ensured that during 1997–98 the Conservative Party received £874,930 and the Liberal Democrats received £334, 233. There is also some limited financial assistance provided to the main Opposition parties in the

House of Lords – the Conservative Party receiving £102,600 and the Liberal Democrats receiving £30,780 in 1997–98.

9. The latest (22nd) edition of *Erskine May* was published in 1997 and was edited by Sir Donald Limon, then Clerk of the House of Commons, and W.R. McKay, then Clerk Assistant, later Clerk of the House of Commons. It is particularly useful as a work of reference on current procedure and practice in the Commons.

10. Indeed, following the Conservative Government's decision to guillotine the Statutory Sick Pay Bill in December 1993, the then Leader of the Opposition, John Smith, withdrew all official pairing for divisions in the House and became un-cooperative in dealings through 'the usual channels'. This gesture of Opposition displeasure with the Government lasted only until the following spring, but it did serve as a reminder of the extent to which the House of Commons can only operate satisfactorily by consent and tacit co-operation between the two front benches.

11. W. Bagehot, *The English Constitution* (London: Fontana, 1978), p. 170.

12. Constitutional measures – such as the Maastricht Bill or the legislation to set up a Scottish Parliament and a Welsh Assembly – have to be taken in a committee of the whole House in the chamber.

13. Since 1979 there has been the following Select Committees: Agriculture; Defence; Education; Employment (Education and Employment were later merged, but with separate Education and Employment Sub-Committees being set up); Energy (now absorbed by Trade and Industry); Environment (later merged with Transport); Foreign Affairs; Health and Social Security (since split into two committees); Home Affairs; Scottish Affairs; Trade and Industry; Transport (merged with Environment in 1997 to form the Environment, Transport and Regional Affairs Select Committee – but with separate Sub-Committees for both the Environment and Transport); Treasury and Civil Service (later split between Treasury and Public Administration); and Welsh Affairs. Following the 1992 General Election additional Select Committees were established to cover National Heritage (re-named Culture, Media and Sport in 1997); and Science and Technology. In 1994 Northern Ireland was added to the list of Select Committees as part of the price exacted by the Ulster Unionists for their support of the Conservative Government at that time. In 1997 new Committees on International Development, Modernisation of the House of Commons and on sustainable development – known as the Environmental Audit Committee – were added.

    The non-departmental Select Committees, which in many cases have been long established, are: Parliamentary Commissioner for Administration; Public Accounts; Statutory Instruments; European Legislation; Consolidation Bills; Procedure; Standards and Privileges; and Broadcasting of the House. The arrangements for all Select Committees are co-ordinated by a liaison committee composed of the chairman of all the various committees. There are also some 'domestic' committees dealing with the internal arrangements of the House of Commons, such as Information; Accommodation; Administration; and Catering.

14. For example, the Foreign Affairs Select Committee published a very influential report on the misuse of ODA support for the Pergau Dam project in July 1994, the Social Security Select Committee had a good deal of influence on the reform of the Child Support Agency in 1993–94, and the Treasury and Civil Service Select Committees helped to shape the new Code for the Civil Service in November 1994–January 1996.

15. Examples of this sort of work are now rather dated, but in the 1970s Select Committees were occasionally used to investigate ideas for further fiscal legislation – for instance, Coroporation Tax in 1970–71, Tax Credit in 1972–73 and Wealth Tax in 1974–75.

16. The different, but overlapping aspects of the Westland crisis were examined by no fewer than three Select Committees – Defence; Trade and Industry; and Treasury and Civil

Service. See especially the Defence Select Committee Report entitled 'Westland plc, the Government's Decision Making', HC 519 (1985–86), for further details.

17. B. Crick, *The Reform of Parliament,* rev. edn (London: Weidenfeld & Nicolson, 1968), p. 80.
18. See Chapter 18, for further discussion of the doctrine of 'subsidarity'.
19. See 'Select Committee Report on the Sittings of the House (1991–92)', HC 20, (London: HMSO, 1992).
20. See *Hansard* 13 July 1992, Cols 833–907.
21. See 'First Report from the Select Committee on Modernising the House of Commons (1997–98)', HC 190, 29 July 1997 (London: HMSO, 1997).
22. See W. Armstrong et al., *Budgetary Reform in the United Kingdom* (Oxford: OUP, 1980) for a fuller exposition of these ideas.

Further reading

Biffen, J., *Inside the House of Commons* (London: Grafton Books, 1989).

Cowley, P. (ed.), *Conscience and Parliament* (London: Frank Cass, 1998).

Drewry, G. (ed.), *The New Select Committees*, rev. edn (Oxford: OUP, 1989).

Garrett, J., *Westminster: Does Parliament work?* (London: Gollancz, 1992).

Griffith, J.A.G. and Ryle, M., *Parliament, Functions, Practice and Procedures* (London: Sweet & Maxwell, 1989).

Heatherington, A. et al., *Cameras in the Commons* (London: Hansard Society, 1990).

Limon, D. and McKay, W.R. (eds), (22nd edn), '*Erskine May's Treaties on the Law, Privileges, Proceedings, and Usage of Parliament*' (London: Butterworth, 1997).

Norton, P., *Does Parliament Matter?* (London: Harvester Wheatsheaf, 1993).

Norton, P., *The Commons in Perspective* (Oxford: Martin Robertson, 1981).

Radice, L., *Member of Parliament* (London: Macmillan, 1987).

Riddell, P., *Parliament Under Pressure* (London: Victor Gollancz, 1998).

Ryle, M. and Richards, P.G. (eds), *The Commons under Scrutiny* (London: Routledge & Kegan Paul, 1988).

Silk, P. and Walters, R. (4th edn) *How Parliament Works* (London: Longman, 1998).

Walker, R. and Criddle, B., *Almanack of British Politics,* 5th edn (London: Routledge, 1996).

Walkland, S.A. (ed.), *The House of Commons in the Twentieth Century* (Oxford: Clarendon Press, 1979).

Website

Parliament   http://www.parliament.uk

PART 4

Central Government

12 Prime Minister and Cabinet

12.1 Historical development

The use of the term *Prime Minister* was no more than a tenuous convention from the time of Robert Walpole (1721–42) to the time when Lord North insisted that his Administration resign *en bloc* in 1782 when he lost favour with King George III. In fact, it is worth noting that the term 'Prime Minister' when used to describe both Harley and Godolphin during the reign of Queen Anne (1702–14) was actually used as a term of abuse; an insult to signify that the politician concerned was seen as being in the pocket of the Monarch and as little more than the Monarch's messenger. Indeed, on a number of occasions during the eighteenth century, the most powerful politician of the time, Lord Chatham, was actually the leading Secretary of State in various Administrations headed by others, such as Lord Pelham or Lord Newcastle. Until the beginning of William Pitt's Administration in 1784, all Prime Ministers were chosen because of their good relationships with the Monarch and they survived in office because of their ability to manage the House of Commons.

The term *Cabinet* is older in origin and was first used during the reign of Charles II. At that time the King used to summon a few favoured members of his Privy Council for consultations in his private apartments and such courtiers became known as members of his 'Cabinet' after the French word for 'private quarters'. For a time they were also known as the 'Cabal', which was an acronym for the names of those involved – Clifford, Arlington, Buckingham, Ashley and Lauderdale.

The office of Prime Minister and the institution of the Cabinet evolved together throughout the nineteenth century. Until the 1832 Reform Act the Prime Minister and Cabinet were answerable to the Monarch almost as much as they were to Parliament. The extension of the franchise in 1832 meant that the Prime Minister and Cabinet became more answerable to and dependent upon shifting majorities in the House of Commons. Further changes occurred after the 1867 Reform Act as the growing power of nationally organised political parties began to limit the independence of individual MPs. One of the consequences was to accord increased political stature to the main party leaders, such as William Gladstone and Benjamin Disraeli, who alternated as Prime Minister for nearly twenty years. In 1878 the title of 'Prime Minister' was officially recorded in a public document for the first time when Benjamin Disraeli signed the Treaty of Berlin on behalf of the British Government. Another equally important development during this period was the growth of the power of the Cabinet in relation to the House of Commons. Thus by the time of Lord Salisbury's second Administration (1886–92) Britain had moved essentially from Parliamentary government of the classic type to Cabinet government of the modern type – that is, government *through* Parliament rather than government *by* Parliament.

Statutory recognition of the office of Prime Minister was not formally complete until 1937 when the Ministers of the Crown Act provided the Prime Minister of the day with a salary and a pension from public funds. Yet to this day the powers and responsibilities of the Prime Minister have not been defined in statute. Like the institution of the Cabinet, the office of Prime Minister provides a classic example of the importance of conventions in British constitutional arrangements. Figure 12.1 lists all British Prime Ministers since Sir Robert Walpole.

In theory, the Cabinet now constitutes the supreme decision-making body in the British political system. Yet in practice, as we shall see, the Prime Minister can be more than first among equals in any modern British Government. In political terms the most effective sanctions against Cabinet decisions of which people may disapprove are a decisive back-bench revolt in the governing party or the verdict of the electorate at the subsequent General Election. The Prime Minister and the Cabinet are also influenced in an imprecise but real way by the shifting views and feelings of their back-bench supporters in the House of Commons; the need to take account of the Opposition's demands which can affect the progress of Government legislative business in Parliament; their relations with party activists, pressure groups and the media; and their assessment of public opinion on any given issue at any given time. All these factors can qualify and refine the power and authority of the Prime Minister and Cabinet in modern conditions.

12.2 The Cabinet and its support

The Cabinet in modern Britain has been composed of between nineteen and twenty-four senior Ministers (including the Prime Minister) who meet every Thursday morning (but not usually throughout August) around the large coffin-shaped table in the Cabinet room at 10 Downing Street. It subsumes a large network of committees, both Ministerial and official, and it depends for its efficient operation upon the work of the Cabinet Secretary and 56 other civil servants in the Cabinet Office.[1] The latter is the administrative nerve-centre of central Government and responsible for recording all Cabinet and Cabinet committee decisions, and then communicating them to those who need to know in the various Departments in Whitehall. The Cabinet Secretariat also has an important role in progress chasing, scheduling meetings, setting agendas, checking that papers are circulated in good time and cover the subject properly (for example, financial and European aspects), and briefing the chairmen of the committees concerned.

Certain very senior Ministers have a place in every Cabinet – for example, the Chancellor of the Exchequer, the Home Secretary and the Foreign Secretary. Some other Ministers have a place by dint of the area of the country which their Department represents – for example, the Secretaries of State for Wales, Scotland, and Northern Ireland. Occasionally some important Ministers, such as the Secretary of State for Transport, have been included in the Cabinet at one time and excluded from it at

Figure 12.1 *Prime Ministers since Robert Walpole*

Sir Robert Walpole (Whig)	1721–42	Edward Stanley, 14th Earl of	
Spencer Compton, Earl of		Derby (Con)	1858–59
Wilmington (Whig)	1742–43	Henry Temple, 3rd Viscount	
Henry Pelham (Whig)	1743–54	Palmerston (Lib)	1859–65
Thomas Pelham-Holles, Duke of		Earl Russell (Lib)	1865–66
Newcastle (Whig)	1754–56	Edward Stanley, 14th Earl of	
William Cavendish, 4th Duke of		Derby (Con)	1866–68
Devonshire (Whig)	1756–57	Benjamin Disraeli (Con)	1868
Thomas Pelham-Holles, Duke of		William Ewart Gladstone	
Newcastle (Whig)	1757–62	(Lib)	1868–74
John Stuart, 3rd Earl of Bute (Tory)	1762–63	Benjamin Disraeli, Earl of	
George Grenville (Whig)	1763–65	Beaconsfield (Con)	1874–80
Charles Wentworth, 2nd Marquis		William Ewart Gladstone	
of Rockingham (Whig)	1765–66	(Lib)	1880–85
William Pitt, Earl of		Robert Gascoyne-Cecil, 3rd	
Chatham (Whig)	1766–68	Marquis of Salisbury (Con)	1885
Augustus Fitzroy, 3rd Duke of		William Ewart Gladstone	
Grafton (Whig)	1768–70	(Lib)	1886
Frederick, Lord North (Tory)	1770–82	Robert Gascoyne-Cecil,	
Charles Wentworth, 2nd Marquis of		3rd Marquis of Salisbury (Con)	1886–92
Rockingham (Whig)	1782	William Ewart Gladstone (Lib)	1892–94
William Fitzmaurice, 2nd Earl of		Archibald Primrose, 5th Earl of	
Shelburne (Whig)	1782–83	Rosebery (Lib)	1894–95
William Cavendish-Bentinck, 3rd Duke		Robert Gascoyne-Cecil, 3rd	
of Portland (Coalition)	1783	Marquis of Salisbury (Con)	1895–1902
William Pitt, the younger (Tory)	1783–1801	Arthur James Balfour (Con)	1902–05
Henry Addington (Tory)	1801–04	Sir Henry Campbell-Bannerman	
William Pitt, the younger (Tory)	1804–06	(Lib)	1905–08
William Wyndham,		Herbert Henry Asquith (Lib)	1908–16
Lord Grenville (Whig)	1806–07	David Lloyd George	
William Cavendish-Bentinck,		(Coalition)	1916–22
3rd Duke of Portland	1807–09	Andrew Bonar Law (Con)	1922–23
Spencer Perceval (Tory)	1809–12	Stanley Baldwin (Con)	1923–24
Robert Jenkinson, 2nd Earl of		Ramsay MacDonald (Lab)	1924
Liverpool (Tory)	1812–27	Stanley Baldwin (Con)	1924–29
George Canning (Tory)	1827	Ramsay MacDonald (Lab)	1929–31
Frederick Robinson,		Ramsay MacDonald	
Viscount Goderich (Tory)	1827–28	(National)	1931–35
Arthur Wellesley, Duke of		Stanley Baldwin (National)	1935–37
Wellington (Tory)	1828–30	Neville Chamberlain	
Charles, 2nd Earl Grey (Whig)	1830–34	(National)	1937–40
William Lamb, 2nd Viscount		Winston Churchill	
Melbourne (Whig)	1834	(Coalition)	1940–45
Sir Robert Peel, 2nd		Clement Attlee (Lab)	1945–51
Baronet (Tory)	1834–35	Sir Winston Churchill (Con)	1951–55
William Lamb, 2nd Viscount		Sir Anthony Eden (Con)	1955–57
Melbourne (Whig)	1835–41	Harold Macmillan (Con)	1957–63
Sir Robert Peel, 2nd Baronet (Tory)	1841–46	Sir Alec Douglas-Home (Con)	1963–64
Lord John Russell (Whig)	1846–52	Harold Wilson (Lab)	1964–70
Edward Stanley, 14th Earl of		Edward Heath (Con)	1970–74
Derby (Con)	1852	Harold Wilson (Lab)	1974–76
George Gordon, 4th Earl of		James Callaghan (Lab)	1976–79
Aberdeen (Coalition)	1852–55	Margaret Thatcher (Con)	1979–90
Henry Temple, 3rd Viscount		John Major (Con)	1990–97
Palmerston (Lib)	1855–58	Tony Blair (Lab)	1997–

another, depending on the competing claims of other Departments and the personal preferences of the Prime Minister of the day. In a few rare cases a senior Minister may belong to the Cabinet, but draw no public salary for it. This may be because the Prime Minister of the day has decided to breach the upper limit on the permitted number of such positions (currently 23), but more usually it reflects the convention that party political appointments to the Cabinet (such as the Chairman of the governing party) should be paid from party rather than public funds. Although the Government Chief Whip is not usually a formal member of the Cabinet – an exception was Ann Taylor under Tony Blair – the occupant invariably attends all Cabinet meetings – as indeed does the Prime Minister's Parliamentary Private Secretary (the channel of communication with Government back-benchers) and under Tony Blair the Prime Minister's Press Secretary as well.

The Cabinet meets formally once a week about eleven months a year (usually not in August) and for up to ninety minutes at a time, although extra meetings are arranged as and when the need arises. Owing to the size of the Cabinet, there is no question of all its members taking a full part in all the items under discussion. In what might be described as normal circumstances, some members of the Cabinet remain silent because their Department is not involved in the issue under discussion and some may be unavoidably absent on the day in question (which is quite often the case with the Foreign Secretary). In such circumstances the Minister concerned may submit views in writing to the Prime Minister, so that these can be taken into account in any discussion. It is just as well that the Cabinet proceeds in this way, since if every Cabinet Minister spoke on every item of Cabinet business, the agenda would never be covered in the time available. At the invitation of the Prime Minister other non-Cabinet Ministers (for example, the Law Officers) may attend and speak at Cabinet meetings when their views are needed.

Cabinet Committees are an essential and integral part of Cabinet government. They are usually composed of the relevant Ministers according to the subject under discussion and chaired by the Prime Minister or another senior Cabinet Minister, such as the Lord Chancellor, the Deputy Prime Minister or the Chancellor of the Exchequer. They are normally empowered to take decisions on behalf of the entire Cabinet. Only in cases of serious disagreement are matters referred back to the full Cabinet for final resolution. Few substantial issues are considered by full Cabinet which have not already been dealt with in some way in bilateral meetings between the Prime Minister and the relevant Departmental Minister or by the relevant Cabinet committee. Thus one of the main purposes of such meetings is to reach decisions which can then be put to full Cabinet simply for formal ratification. When Cabinet committees cannot reach agreement or when the issues under discussion are too important to be settled at a smaller meeting, the whole Cabinet has to argue things out in order to reach conclusions which then bind the entire Government.

Cabinet committees can conveniently be divided between *Standing Committees* – such as the Economic Committee, the Home and Social Affairs Committee, the Overseas and Defence Committee and the Legislation Committee – and the *Ad Hoc Committees,* which are usually classified under 'Miscellaneous' or 'General' headings and which remain in being only as long as is necessary to resolve a particular issue. Many of the Standing Committees and the sub-committees spawned by them are chaired by the Prime Minister, although interestingly Tony Blair is content to let the Chancellor chair the Economic Committee. Decisions reached in such committees do not necessarily require subsequent ratification by the Cabinet as a whole, but are usually reported to the full Cabinet.

Miscellaneous or General Committees are normally chaired by either the Prime Minister or another senior Cabinet Minister and they meet for as many discussions as necessary in order to resolve the matters at issue. For example, in the 1980s such committees dealt with the Royal Navy's replacement of the Polaris weapons system with Trident, the abolition of the Greater London Council and the other Metropolitan Councils, the imposition of public spending cuts, the de-indexing from average earnings of social security benefits, the annual rate support settlement for local authorities, and the reform of the National Health Service. In the 1990s such committees dealt with the treatment of refugees arriving in Britain from the former Yugoslavia and the replacement of the Poll Tax with the Council Tax. Under New Labour such committees have considered issues relating to biotechnology and genetic modification and have sought to drive action to prevent damage from the failure of electronic systems related to the year 2000 date change. It is normal for the decisions of such committees to require subsequent approval by the full Cabinet or at least one of its Standing Committees. Yet in all cases the key to the successful working of such committees is that they are empowered to take decisions on behalf of the whole Cabinet and in most cases they do so without any political or constitutional difficulty.

Senior civil servants and the military Chiefs of Staff are not formally members of the Cabinet or its committees, at any rate in peace-time. Yet the Chief of the Defence Staff regularly attends the main Overseas and Defence Policy Committee of the Cabinet, although not formally a member of it. In the broader framework of Cabinet government, junior Ministers play a frequent and useful part in Cabinet committees where they can relieve senior Ministers of many of the burdens of collective decision making. Indeed, junior Ministers are the workhorses of the Cabinet committee system and they can make or mar their reputations when performing this aspect of their Ministerial duties. For an illustration of the range and scope of the Cabinet committee system see Figure 12.2.

Support in Whitehall

Meetings of the Cabinet and its committees would not proceed as smoothly as they usually do if it were not for the fact that the Ministerial meetings are prepared and supported by official meetings of senior civil servants from the various Departments concerned. It is this parallel structure of official committees which keeps Government business moving along and makes it possible for the Cabinet and its committees to dispatch a great deal of Government business in a rather expeditious way. Cabinet Office officials usually chair these official committees which are intended to maximise the areas of potential inter-Departmental agreement and to define, if not minimise, the areas of potential disagreement. Since each Department tends to respect the interests and responsibilities of every other Department and since there is an established pecking order in Whitehall with 10 Downing Street and the Treasury at the top and the smaller or newer Departments at the bottom (for example, the Welsh Office or the Department for Culture, Media and Sport); the outcome of inter-Departmental discussions at official level often reflects the balance of bureaucratic power in Whitehall. This may facilitate the collective decision-making process, but it can also make for minimalist, inter-Departmental compromises which may lower the quality or reduce

Figure 12.2 Ministerial Committees of the Cabinet

Ministerial Committee on Defence and Overseas Policy (DOP)
Terms of reference
To keep under review the Government's defence and overseas policy

Ministerial Committee on Constitutional Reform Policy (CRP)
Terms of reference
To consider strategic issues relating to the Government's constitutional reform policies

Ministerial Sub-Committee on House of Lords Reform (CRP(HL))
Terms of reference
To consider policy and other issues arising from the Government's plans for reform of the House of Lords and to make recommendations to the Ministerial Committee on Constitutional Reform Policy

Ministerial Committee on the Intelligence Services (CSI)
Terms of reference
To keep under review policy on the security and intelligence services

Ministerial Committee on Northern Ireland (IN)
Terms of reference
To oversee the Government's policy on Northern Ireland issues and relations with the Republic of Ireland on these matters

Ministrial Committee on Home and Social Affairs (HS)
Terms of reference
To consider issues of home and social policy

Ministerial Committee on the Environment (ENV)
Terms of reference
To consider environmental policy issues

Ministerial Committee on Local Government (GL)
Terms of reference
To consider issues affecting local government, including the annual allocation of resources

Ministerial Committee on Economic Affairs (EA)
Terms of reference
To consider issues relating to the Government's economic policies

Ministerial Committee on Energy Policy (EA(N))
Terms of reference
To consider the principles and objectives which should underlie the United Kingdom's energy strategy; and make recommendations for an energy strategy to the Ministerial Committee on Economic Affairs

Ministerial Committee on Public Expenditure (PX)
Terms of reference
To review public expenditure allocations and make recommendations to the Cabinet

Ministerial Committee on The Queen's Speeches and Future Legislation (QFL)
Terms of reference
To prepare and submit to the Cabinet drafts of the Queen's speeches to Parliament and proposals for the Government's legislative programme

Ministerial Committee on Devolution to Scotland and Wales and the English Regions (DSWR)
Terms of reference
To consider policy and other issues arising from the Government's policies for devolution to Scotland and Wales and the regions of England and to promote and oversee progress of the relevant legislation through Parliament and its subsequent implementation to the Ministerial

Ministerial Committee on Legislation (LEG)

Terms of reference

To examine all draft Bills; to consider the Parliamentary handling of Government Bills, EU documents and Private Members' business, and such other related matters as may be necessary; and to keep under review the Government's policy in relation to issues of Parliamentary procedures

Ministerial Sub-Committee on European Issues ((E)DOP)

Terms of reference

To consider questions relating to the UK's membership of the EU and to report as necessary to the Ministerial Committee on Defence and Overseas Policy (DOP)

Ministerial Sub-Committee on London (GL(L))

Terms of reference

To co-ordinate the Government's policies on London, and report as necessary to the Ministerial Committee on Local Government (GL) and the Ministerial Committee on Devolution to Scotland, Wales and the English Regions (DSWR)

Ministerial Sub-Committee on Welfare to Work (EA(WW))

Terms of reference

To develop policies to get people from welfare to work and to report as necessary to the Ministerial Committee on Economic Affairs (EA)

Ministerial Sub-Committee on Incorporation of the European Convention of Human Rights (CRP(EC))

Terms of reference

To consider policy and other issues arising from the Government's decision to legislate for the incorporation of ECHR in UK law and to promote and oversee progress of the relevant legislation through Parliament and its subsequent implementation, reporting as necessary

Committee on Constitutional Reform Policy

Ministerial Sub-Committee on Freedom of Information (CRP(FOI))

Terms of reference

To consider policy and other issues arising from the Government's decision to legislate on freedom of information; to promote and oversee progress of the relevant legislation through Parliament and its subsequent implementation; and to report as necessary to the Ministerial Committee on Constitutional Reform Policy

Ministerial Sub-Committee on Drug Misuse (HS(D))

Terms of reference

To co-ordinate the Government's national and international policies for tackling drugs misuse, and report as necessary to the Ministerial Committee on Home and Social Affairs (HS)

Ministerial Sub-Committee on Health Strategy (HS(H))

Terms of reference

To oversee the development, implementation and monitoring of the Government's health strategy; to co-ordinate the Government's policies on UK-wide issues affecting health; and to report as necessary to the Ministerial Committee on Home and Social Affairs (HS)

Ministerial Sub-Committee on Women's Issues (HS(W))

Terms of reference

To review and develop the Government's policy and strategy on issues of special concern to women; to oversee their implementation; and to report as necessary to the Ministerial Committee on Home and Social Affairs (HS)

Ministerial Group on Food Safety (MISC1)
Terms of reference
To co-ordinate Departmental consideration of issues arising from the establishment of a Food Standards Agency and other aspects of food safety, and to make recommendations to the Ministerial Committee on Home and Social Affairs

Ministerial Group on Youth Justice (MISC2)
Terms of reference
To oversee the Government's programme for reform of youth justice, including the preparation of proposals for agreement by the Ministerial Committee on Home and Social Affairs

Ministerial Group on Utility Regulation (MISC3)
Terms of reference
To oversee an inter-Departmental review of regulation of the utility industries, to consider issues arising from the review and to report to the Ministerial Committee on Economic Affairs (EA)

Ministerial Group on the Millennium Date Change (MISC4)
Terms of reference
To drive action across the public and the private sectors to ensure that the national infrastructure is not damaged by the failure of electronic systems related to the year 2000 date change

Joint Consultative Committee with the Liberal Democrat Party (JCC)
Terms of reference
To consider policy issues of joint interest to the Government and the Liberal Democrat Party

Source: Adapted from *Vacher's Parliamentary Companion*

the effectiveness of the decisions actually taken. In other words, a significant political price can be paid for the collegiate conventions of Whitehall government.

The outcome of Cabinet discussions and of inter-Departmental discussions at official level is also affected by the relative standing and authority of the various Ministers whose Departments are involved in a political issue at a given time. Thus if the Chancellor of the Exchequer and the Chief Secretary have won battles with their Cabinet colleagues over the control of public spending, the Treasury is likely to be even more formidable than usual in its dealings with other Departments. Equally, if Foreign Office Ministers have been proved wrong, or even had to resign, over sensitive issues – for example, the Argentinian invasion of the Falkland Islands in April 1982 – then that Department will find its authority and standing in Whitehall at least temporarily diminished. About the only sure rule in British central Government is that it is usually wise to enlist the support of 10 Downing Street in any important inter-Departmental battle.

In the process of central Government the Cabinet Office has a vital role to play in ensuring fast and efficient communication of inter-Departmental decisions to all who need to know of them throughout Whitehall. This central secretariat, which consists mainly of Civil Service high-flyers seconded from other Departments, communicates Government decisions in the form of extracts from Cabinet or Cabinet committee minutes to those parts of the central Government machine which have to act on them. This means that in the first instance such decisions are communicated to the Private Offices of the Ministers involved in the implementation of the policy and then further relayed from there within the respective Departments. Such minutes are drawn up by officials of the Cabinet Office under the overall supervision and direction of the Cabinet Secretary. It is open to the Prime Minister, or indeed any other Cabinet Minister, to see the minutes in draft, to point out errors and then ask for suitable amendments. Yet if this is to be done, it has to be done quickly. Consequently, requests are not frequently made and even less frequently granted. In short, Cabinet Office officials keep a tight and effective grip on this aspect of Cabinet government.

Following the 1997 Election victory the Prime Minister, Tony Blair, appointed Peter Mandelson – a key architect of the 'New Labour' project and MP for Hartlepool – as Minister without Portfolio based in the Cabinet Office, with the task of developing and co-ordinating policy across Government Departments and with responsibility for policy presentation. It was a clear attempt to ensure that the perceived failings of previous Governments – namely the lack of central direction and frequency of the arguments between various Departments of State – would not be features of the Blair Government.[2] In July 1998 Tony Blair, in his first reshuffle, appointed Jack Cunningham as Minister for the Cabinet Office with a seat in the Cabinet – with the task of strengthening Government policy making – particularly in this respect co-ordinating closer workings between the Cabinet Office Secretariat, the No. 10 Policy Unit and the Treasury on long-term policy – preventing bottlenecks arising in the process of policy co-ordination and removing unnecessary diversions from a focused pursuit of the Government's objectives. It was also announced that a powerful new Performance and Innovation Unit was to be established in the Cabinet Office with a right to range across Whitehall Departmental boundaries, propose new policies, improve the delivery of existing objectives, and secure increased co-ordination and improved practical delivery of policy and services which involve more than one governmental organisation.

10 Downing Street

In addition to the formal structure of Cabinet government just described, successive Prime Ministers since Lloyd George (1916–22) have taken steps to have other sources of advice and support available to them at 10 Downing Street, and today there is a network which includes the Private Office, the Press Office, the Appointments Office, the Parliamentary Private Secretaries, the Political Office and the Policy Unit.

The *Private Office* is traditionally headed by a Principal Private Secretary, with additional private secretaries for Parliamentary affairs, home affairs, economic affairs and two for foreign affairs. The individuals concerned are Civil Service high-fliers whose task is to handle, sift and determine the relative importance of all official papers destined for the Prime Minister. Under Tony Blair the Office is headed by his Chief of Staff, Jonathan Powell.

The *Press Office* – headed by a Press Secretary (traditionally a civil servant) – organises the Prime Minister's dealings with the media and has became an increasingly important aspect of activity since its first appearance on the scene in 1931. Some noted examples include Joe Haines (a former journalist) for Harold Wilson (1969–70 and 1974–76), Bernard Ingham (a former journalist) for Margaret Thatcher (1979–90) and Alistair Campbell (a former journalist) for Tony Blair (1997–).[3]

The *Appointments Office* – headed by a senior civil servant and staffed by civil servants – deals with the various appointments which fall within the remit of the Prime Minister, but which are in essence non-political, such as appointments within the Church of England for example. The total staff costs for Number 10 were £3.4 million in 1996–97 and £4.1 million in 1997–98. Estimated costs for 1998–99 were £4.9 million.

The task of the Prime Ministers' *Parliamentary Private Secretaries (PPS)* is to keep the Prime Minister in touch with backbench opinion in the House of Commons. Ian Gow was particularly effective in this role for Margaret Thatcher during the period 1979–83. John Major as Prime Minister also appointed a PPS from the House of Lords. In 1997 Tony Blair appointed two PPSs, Bruce Grocott and Anne Coffey.

As far as the *Political Office* is concerned, it is responsible for dealings between the Prime Minister and the party organisation and for events and activity of a party political nature. Consequently, it is paid for out of party rather than public funds.

Over the years Prime Ministers have often relied on a particular individual or key individuals. For example Lloyd George had the services of a so-called 'Kitchen Cabinet' of advisers and cronies during the First World War and immediately after. During the Second World War Winston Churchill had the help of Lord Cherwell (known as 'the Prof'); after the war Clement Attlee had assistance from Francis Williams (a political journalist); Harold Macmillan derived support and comfort from John Wyndham (an aristocratic personal friend); Harold Wilson during his four terms as Prime Minister (1964–66, 1966–70, February to October 1974 and 1974–76) had personal support from Marcia Williams (his Political Secretary); Margaret Thatcher had Charles Powell as well as several personal advisers including Sir Anthony Parsons (a retired diplomat) and Sir Alan Walters (an academic economist); while Tony Blair has relied on Jonathan Powell (his Chief of Staff), Peter Mandelson (as Minister without Portfolio) and Anji Hunter from his Political Office (responsible for presentation and planning).

Since 1974 there has also been a *Policy Unit* in 10 Downing Street consisting normally of fewer than a dozen advisers brought in to serve the Prime Minister of the day and to assist with political tasks. The personnel of this Unit have varied from Government to Government, depending on the outlook and preferences of the Prime Minister of the day. For example, Harold Wilson and James Callaghan depended quite heavily on Dr Bernard Donoghue, an academic from the London School of Economics; Margaret Thatcher had advice and support from Sir John Hoskyns, a businessman, Ferdinand Mount, a journalist, John Redwood, a banker and later a politician, and Brian Griffiths, an academic and lay preacher; John Major depended on the advice and support of Sarah Hogg, a journalist, and Norman Blackwell, a management consultant; Tony Blair has relied on Geoff Mulgan, formerly Director of DEMOS, Roger Liddle, formerly of the SDP, and David Miliband, formally of the Institute for Public Policy Research. Whether such advisers are installed in the Policy Unit or work more informally for the Prime Minister of the day in a 'kitchen cabinet', their contributions to the policy-making process can be very significant. They often act as speech-writers and help the Prime Minister of the day to develop a distinctive personal agenda, and they can act as political trouble-shooters, when necessary, between conflicting interests in the Government. The Prime Minister's support structure is outlined in detail in Figure 12.3.

12.3 Prime Ministerial power

The Prime Minister of the day could be described as the most powerful person in Britain. Certainly the reality of Prime Ministerial power has been recognised for some

Figure 12.3 The Prime Minister's Support Structure (1998)

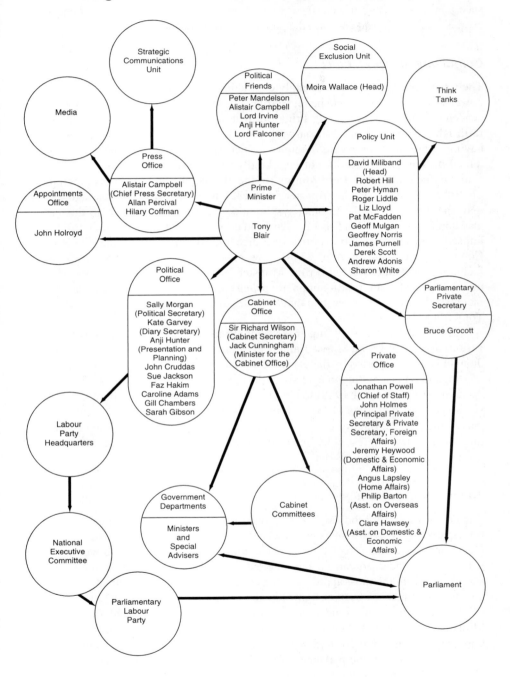

time by practising politicians and academic observers alike. Yet the nature and extent of such power is a matter of controversy and there are some significant constraints on its exercise, no matter who occupies the premises at 10 Downing Street.

Conflicting interpretations

There have been at least two strongly conflicting interpretations of Prime Ministerial power in Britain. On the one hand, Harold Wilson concluded that 'the predominantly academic verdict of overriding Prime Ministerial power is wrong'.[4] In making this forthright comment, Lord Wilson was probably reflecting on his own experience of having to preside over several Labour Cabinets which contained powerful and determined personalities who did not take kindly to excessive Prime Ministerial leadership. On the other hand, Lord Morley (in the nineteenth century) in his biography of Sir Robert Walpole (Prime Minister from 1721 to 1742) wrote as long ago as 1889 that 'the flexibility of the Cabinet system allows the Prime Minister [in this case he was thinking rather of his Liberal friend and colleague William Gladstone] to take on himself a power not inferior to that of a dictator, provided always that the House of Commons will stand by him'.[5] This view has had its strong adherents ever since, including Sir Anthony Eden (Prime Minister 1955–57) – who wrote in his Memoirs that 'a Prime Minister is still nominally *primus inter pares* [first among equals], but in fact his authority is stronger than that'[6] – Margaret Thatcher (1979–90) and seemingly Tony Blair (1997–).

The best way of assessing these conflicting interpretations is to examine the various aspects of Prime Ministerial power in order to see which of the two schools of thought is best supported by the evidence of history. Yet even at this early stage in our investigation it is tempting to agree with the common sense view expressed by Herbert Asquith (Prime Minister 1908–16) in his Memoirs which he wrote more than seventy years ago that 'the office of Prime Minister is what its holder chooses and is able to make of it'.[7] In the light of the long history of the office, it is difficult to dissent from this concise view expressed by one of its most distinguished occupants. The scope of Prime Ministerial powers is outlined in Figure 12.4.

The power of patronage

The Prime Minister of the day has the power of political patronage. This is manifested principally in the power of appointment to and dismissal from Ministerial posts in Government. Having accepted the Royal commission to form a new Government, the party leader concerned can fill the hundred or so Ministerial posts in the Commons and the Lords in the most appropriate ways. Yet for reasons of practical politics there are always a number of senior figures in any party who virtually select themselves for Ministerial office and some others whom it would be imprudent for any Prime Minister to exclude. Other considerations which come into play in the course of Government formation are regional balance, ideological balance and simply age, as well as political debt and personal loyalty. Thus, although Prime Ministers have done almost as they liked when making Ministerial appointments, their freedom of manoeuvre has always been limited in practice by common prudence and sensible calculation of their own strength or weakness at any time.

Figure 12.4 Prime Ministerial powers

Patronage
- Appoints Government Ministers
- Dismisses Government Ministers
- Appoints senior civil servants
- Dispenses a large number of honours
- Appoints to a large number of paid public posts

Within Parliament
- Party leader
- Appoints Government Ministers
- Dismisses Government Ministers
- Can dissolve Parliament

Within party
- Party leader
- Power of patronage
- Can determine the date of the General Election

Within Government
- Head of Government – sets agenda and priorities
- Appoints and dismisses Government Ministers
- Determines membership of Cabinet committees
- Determines membership of mini-Cabinets/ inner-Cabinets
- Draws up the Cabinet agenda
- Summons Cabinet meetings
- Chairs Cabinet discussions
- Summarises Cabinet 'conclusions'
- Sends 'minutes' (directives) to Ministers

On the national and international stage
- Natural focus of publicity
- Nation's chief representative in international relations
- Controls use of nation's nuclear weapons

Equally, the Prime Minister can ask for the resignation of any member of the Government at any time on the grounds that the Minister concerned is not up to the job or is too old to continue or the office is needed for someone else. Although the most usual motives for Prime Ministerial dismissal of a senior Minister are to improve the general effectiveness and political balance of the Cabinet, there have been occasions when the Prime Minister of the day has deliberately sought to create a more politically congenial array of senior Ministers. For example, in September 1981 Margaret Thatcher sacked three Cabinet Ministers (Lord Soames, Sir Ian Gilmour, and Mark Carlisle) at least two of whom she found ideologically uncongenial, and appointed three new ones (Nigel Lawson, Norman Tebbit, and Lady Young) at least two of whom were very close to her own brand of Conservatism. John Major, by contrast, was more loath to use his power of dismissal and tended to do so only when the passage of events forced it on him. For example, when he sacked Norman Lamont as Chancellor of the Exchequer in May 1993, it was a belated attempt to placate public hostility to the pain caused by the economic recession of the early 1990s, and his extensive reshuffle of July 1995 was a clear attempt to put a new face on the Government following his own re-election as Leader of the Conservative Party in the same month.

The Prime Minister of the day also has a wider and more general power of political patronage which stems from the right to advise the Monarch on public appointments made in the name of the Crown. This means that a large number of important and influential positions in the higher ranks of the British Establishment and nowadays at the top of the large and growing number of Quangos (Quasi-autonomous non-governmental organisations) – are effectively in the gift of the Prime Minister of the day and senior Ministerial colleagues when they fall due for appointment or replacement. For example, the Permanent Secretaries of Whitehall Departments, Bishops in the Church of England (albeit on the advice of the Ecclesiastical Appointments Committee), the Governor of the Bank of England, the chairmen of public bodies such as the BBC or the ITC, and key appointments to a host of other public bodies all depend to a considerable extent on finding favour with the Prime Minister of the day, although other senior Ministers obviously have a good deal of influence in their own Departmental spheres. In view of the influential nature of many of these positions these appointments can have great significance. Thus Prime Ministerial patronage, whether exercised positively in favour of some or negatively to blackball others, is a formidable and growing aspect of Prime Ministerial power in Britain.

Power within Government

It probably does not need saying that the Prime Minister of the day normally has considerable power within the Government. Indeed, many would argue that a strong Prime Minister has the ability to dominate the Government by personally setting its strategic agenda and political priorities. This is done in a number of different ways, all of which are facets of Prime Ministerial power. It is achieved through:

- the Prime Minister's control of the Cabinet agenda;
- the right to establish Cabinet committees and to pick their membership;
- the right to chair the most important committees and discussions;
- the right to summarise the conclusions of Cabinet meetings;
- the right to have the best available advice from the Civil Service and outside;
- the ability to take an overall and non-Departmental view of political issues;
- the power of Ministerial appointment and dismissal;
- the pre-eminent position in the eyes of the media and the public;
- the leadership of the governing party in the House of Commons.

During the 1980s when Margaret Thatcher was at 10 Downing Street, the power of the Prime Minister within the Government increased very largely at the expense of the Cabinet as a whole. This happened for a number of reasons. It was partly an obvious consequence of Margaret Thatcher having led her party to three consecutive General Election victories. More insidiously, however, it was a consequence of her ability gradually to transform the membership of the Cabinet over a period of years from one which she largely inherited from Edward Heath to one which she could call her own, because all but one of its members (Sir Geoffrey Howe, as Lord Howe of Aberavon was then) owed their positions in Cabinet directly to her. It was also a consequence of her marked preference for bilateral meetings with key Ministers as an effective and disciplined way of resolving policy problems rather than having recourse to the more traditional but less controllable methods of Cabinet committees or full Cabinet meetings. No one should really have been surprised by these developments, since Margaret Thatcher gave due warning of her intentions and her preferred method of working in Government when she told Kenneth Harris in a famous newspaper interview given before the Conservatives came to power in 1979 that 'it [her Administration] must be a conviction Government – as Prime Minister I could not waste time having any internal arguments'.[8]

During John Major's period at 10 Downing Street (1990–97), the power of the Prime Minister within the Government was not so obvious – indeed, he sometimes seemed to be almost a prisoner of some of his senior colleagues or of rebel backbenchers in his own party. This should not have come as a surprise either, partly because from the beginning of his time as Prime Minister he set out to be more colle-giate in his approach to leadership than his combative predecessor, but mainly because during his time as Party Leader and Prime Minister the Parliamentary arithmetic was much less comfortable for the Conservatives than at any time when Margaret Thatcher was Prime Minister. These plain facts did not, however, prevent the media and some of his Parliamentary colleagues from contrasting him unfavourably and unfairly with his predecessor and almost certainly contributed to his remarkably low rating in the public opinion polls and the subsequent heavy defeat of 1997.

Under Tony Blair we have again seen a 'presidential' approach to the premier-ship; indeed, perhaps more than ever before. Although Margaret Thatcher was 'presi-dential' in her personal style and personal approach, Tony Blair from the outset sought to be 'presidential' not merely in style and approach but also institutionally. The appointment in 1998 of Jack Cunningham as Minister for the Cabinet Office charged with the task of ensuring that the Prime Minister's (not the Government's) objectives were delivered was an important sign of this.

Nonetheless, the extent and nature of Prime Ministerial power within Government can change frequently and sometimes almost without warning – as was the case with John Major's loss of authority following 'Black Wednesday' on 16 September 1992. Such power has been a matter of continuing controversy under all Prime Ministers. In the space of even a few months – let alone a few years – the perception of a given Prime Minister can change dramatically, as even the careers of Winston Churchill, Harold Macmillan and Margaret Thatcher showed so clearly.

Furthermore, the available evidence is often relayed by observers or participants in the process of British politics who are strongly committed for or against a particular Prime Minister (or indeed by former Prime Ministers themselves), while most academic accounts are largely speculative in view of the unreliable quality of their sources. The honest investigator is left with not much more than a series of impressions of one Prime Minister as compared with another or of the same Prime Minister at different phases of electoral and political fortune. The dilemma is that those who might be reliable and fairly objective witnesses of the drama do not normally gain real first-hand access to the political theatre, whereas those who were privileged to be on stage at the relevant time have not usually been the most reliable witnesses – especially when writing their memoirs some time afterwards. Since no final or definitive conclusions can therefore be drawn, it would be wise to rest on the observation that Prime Ministerial power in Government has varied greatly from one Administration to another and indeed from one time to another during a particular Prime Minister's tenure of the office.

Power in Parliament

Most Prime Ministers have usually had formidable power and authority in Parliament. This is partly because the power of appointment to and dismissal from posts in the Government can do so much to determine the political fortunes of MPs in the governing party, and partly a reflection of their leading role in the gladiatorial battles between the parties both in the House and in the media. Clearly the extent and nature of such power has varied from time to time, depending on the personal fortunes of each Prime Minister and the political standing of the governing party at any time. Much also depends on the extent to which the Prime Minister can rely on the loyalty and support of Parliamentary colleagues, the efficiency and subtlety of the Government Whips, and the personal standing of the Prime Minister in the eyes of the media and the general public.

On the whole, Conservative Prime Ministers seem to have been more powerful in relation to their Parliamentary followers than Labour Prime Ministers in relation to theirs, although there have been exceptions to the rule from time to time. The general position reflects the contrasting origins, organisation and instincts of each main party. Whereas the Conservative Party has been *traditionally* both hierarchical and deferential towards its leader, the Labour Party has tended to be more democratic in its aspirations and egalitarian in its attitude towards the leader. In most cases this has made it easier for Conservative Prime Ministers to preserve their Parliamentary authority than for Labour Prime Ministers to preserve theirs, although the contrast should not be exaggerated. Not only is it true that there have been relatively strong and decisive Labour Prime Ministers – for example, Clement Attlee from 1945 to 1950, Harold Wilson from 1964 to 1967 and Tony Blair since coming to power in 1997 – it is also true that there have been relatively weak and indecisive Conservative Prime Ministers – for example, Sir Anthony Eden from 1955 to 1957, Sir Alec Douglas-Home from 1963 to 1964 and John Major from September 1992 to 1997. We should also bear in mind that all political relationships in Britain have become much less deferential over the years and that the media have become more powerfully destructive, so it is not surprising that the authority of all modern Prime Ministers is probably not as secure as their illustrious, but less widely criticised predecessors.

In general, all peace-time Prime Ministers in Britain during the twentieth century have been able to exercise predominant power in Parliament as long as they have retained high standing in the eyes of the media and the public, and have been able to count on the loyal support of the vast majority of their own back-benchers.[9] In many ways the exceptions have been more interesting than the rule. For example, there were several times after the devaluation of the pound in 1967 when Harold Wilson had to head off the threat of serious revolts against his damaged political authority – which came from those of his Cabinet colleagues who were particularly close to the trade unions (such as James Callaghan) and from those who more or less openly resented his leadership or coveted his job (such as Roy Jenkins). Equally, there were times during John Major's tenure at 10 Downing Street when he was openly defied by some of his Cabinet colleagues (notably Michael Portillo, Peter Lilley and John Redwood) and by troublesome back-benchers on issues such as the preservation of the UK against threats alleged to emanate from Britain's deeper involvement in European integration and from the so-called 'peace process' in Northern Ireland. Indeed, the sniping at John Major became so damaging in 1994 and 1995 that he felt obliged to resign the leadership of the Conservative Party in June 1995 in order to challenge his adversaries in the party 'to put up or shut up'. In the event his gamble paid off and he was re-elected Leader of his party by a convincing margin against his sole challenger, John Redwood. This did not, however, silence his critics on the back-benches for long, and the image created by their constant criticism was undoubtedly a factor in the Conservative defeat of 1997.

Party political power

It must also be obvious that the Prime Minister of the day can have great power over the fortunes and destiny of the governing party. In the Conservative Party, this stems from the degree of deference traditionally accorded to the party leader, especially when that person is also Prime Minister – although this is undoubtedly less nowadays than in the past. In the Labour Party, the party political dominance of the leader has not usually been so clear-cut – although it is undoubtedly greater in the 1990s than ever before – since within the Labour movement even Prime Ministerial power has had to be shared with the rest of the Parliamentary Party, the affiliated trade unions and the constituency parties, all of whom have acknowledged roles even under the newly reformed Labour party constitution. Furthermore, Labour Prime Ministers have quite often had problems with the National Executive Committee of the party, since nearly all the members of this committee have their own independent power bases within the Labour movement. Whereas the authority of any Conservative Prime Minister is usually recognised, if sometimes resented, within the party, the paramount position of Labour Prime Ministers has not always been recognised and, indeed, has often been challenged by party colleagues both in private and in public. Nevertheless, we should not over-simplify this distinction between the two main parties, since John Major found it difficult to lead his Party whereas Tony Blair has appeared to dominate his.

In terms of the party political context, the power of any British Prime Minister is probably at its greatest (and certainly most lonely) in the exclusive right of the occupant of the office to recommend to the Monarch the time of dissolution within the five-year maximum span of a Parliament. The exercise of this aspect of Prime Ministerial power can have lasting effects for good or ill on the political fortunes of the party and the destiny of the country. It is a formidable power, as Margaret Thatcher demonstrated in 1983 and 1987, when on each occasion she called an election a year before she had to, which contributed to the continuation in office of the Government which she led. Nevertheless it is a power with a double edge, as can be illustrated by a few historical examples.

In 1951 Clement Attlee decided to call a General Election, even though the Labour Government which he led had an overall majority of five in the Commons and more than three years of its full Parliamentary term still to run.[10] The result of the election was a narrow victory for the Conservatives and the beginning of thirteen years of Conservative rule. In February 1974 Edward Heath decided to appeal to the country by holding a General Election on the issue of 'who governs?' He was persuaded to do this by Conservative Central Office even though the Government which he led had a comfortable majority in the Commons and nearly 18 months of its Parliamentary term still to run. The result was a narrow victory for the Labour Party (largely on the issues of industrial peace and the rising cost of living) and the beginning of more than five years of Labour rule. His unwise and premature decision also had lethal consequences for his own position in the party and within little more than one year he had lost the leadership.

On the other hand, James Callaghan appeared to err in the other direction when he decided *not* to call a General Election in October 1978 against the advice and instincts of nearly all his senior colleagues and contrary to the confident expectations of many of his most powerful trade union allies. The main political consequence was that the Labour Party missed what was probably its best opportunity to win another term of office at a time when there was relative industrial peace and some evidence of economic recovery. When the postponed General Election did eventually take place in May 1979, it was against a background of the so-called 'Winter of Discontent' with the trade unions and the Parliamentary defeat of the Labour Government in the Commons on a vote of confidence in March 1979. The result of these events was the election of a Conservative Government under Margaret Thatcher and the beginning of eighteen years in opposition for Labour. In all these cases it can be argued that this particular aspect of Prime Ministerial power had very significant political consequences.

Power on the national and international stage

In contemporary political conditions Prime Ministers in Britain – as in other democracies – have considerable power and prestige on the national and international stage, even allowing for demystified public attitudes and widespread public cynicism. Of course, the symbols and trappings of Prime Ministerial power should not be confused with the substance. Yet they are significant nevertheless as part of the aura of power which tends to surround all heads of Government in the modern media age. Certainly this particular aspect of power can be strongly reinforced by the excessive attention which the media sometimes devote to nearly every aspect of a Prime Minister's life. It is also dramatised by the need for the Prime Minister of the day to attend frequent summit meetings with counterparts in other countries, all of which serve to elevate the leading figures to a political level well above other Ministers.

On the other hand, we have seen in the cases of Harold Wilson after the 1967 devaluation of the pound and John Major after the 1992 departure of Britain from the European Exchange Rate Mechanism, the media (and hence public opinion) have a marked tendency to turn swiftly against such leaders whom they may have admired only a little while before. As far as the media are concerned, this may happen because they believe they have genuine cause to reassess the competence or integrity of the Prime Minister in question, or, more cynically, it may be because it suits their commercial purposes (that is, boosting circulations or editorial egos in apparently equal parts) to build up even the most senior politicians only to have the pleasure of knocking them down some time later. Either way, these characteristics underline the strong trend towards presidentialism in Britain and many other Parliamentary democracies – something which has become more visible than ever in the political presentation and public perception of Tony Blair as a truly 'presidential' Prime Minister.

Needless to say, these aspects of Prime Ministerial power are enhanced every time there is a real international crisis or a requirement for particularly swift or decisive national leadership. This is especially true in time of war, but it is also true in relation to matters of national security in time of peace. For example, it is normally the Prime Minister of the day who has to act decisively in the event of a spy scandal or a major industrial crisis which threatens essential services. Equally in foreign affairs, it is for the Prime Minister to give a clear lead when British national interests are threatened – as Sir Anthony Eden did at the time of the Suez crisis in 1956 or Margaret Thatcher did at the time of the conflict over the Falkland Islands in 1982 or Tony Blair has done in relation to threats from the dictators in Serbia and Iraq. Similar requirements for Prime Ministerial leadership have applied to the so-called 'peace process' in Northern Ireland as we have seen since the Downing Street Declaration in December 1993. They would also apply in the now unlikely event of Britain being involved in a possible nuclear confrontation or having to respond to the threat of nuclear blackmail from a maverick dictator or terrorist group.

12.4 Cabinet Government

It is difficult to consider the idea of Cabinet Government in Britain in a way which separates it from the role of the Prime Minister. Yet there are some important points about the ideas of Cabinet government and collective responsibility which serve to illustrate some of the limitations on the exercise of Prime Ministerial power. Many years ago Walter Bagehot focused attention on the Cabinet describing it as 'a hyphen which joins, a buckle which fastens the legislative part of the state to the executive part of the state. In its origin it belongs to the one, in its functions it belongs to the other'.[11] In the 1960s John Mackintosh provided a useful framework of analysis when he argued that the main tasks of the British Cabinet were 'to take or review the major decisions (of central Government), to consider (though not necessarily at the formative stage) any proposals which might affect the future of the Government, and to ensure that no Departmental interests are overlooked thus giving the work of Government a measure of unity (and coherence)'.[12] It may, therefore, be helpful if we consider each of these aspects in turn.

Important decision making

In theory, the Cabinet is the most important decision-making body in British central Government. It is supposed to play this vital role because there is no other institution so well placed or qualified to meet the need for decisive arbitration at the apex of central Government. After all there is formally no chief executive in British central Government and all executive power is vested by statute in the various Secretaries of State and other Ministerial heads of the Whitehall Departments. Thus whatever the impact of real Prime Ministerial power, the Cabinet is supposed to be the most important decision-making body and to give institutional expression to the principle of collective responsibility.

On the other hand, some have argued that in modern times it has invariably been the Prime Minister of the day who has taken all the really important political decisions, albeit usually after appropriate discussion with senior Ministerial colleagues. There is historical evidence to support this view in the 1947 decision to develop a British nuclear weapons capability, the 1956 decision to invade the Suez Canal Zone, the 1982 decision to send a Task Force to recapture the Falkland Islands, and the 1993 Downing Street Declaration on the future of Northern Ireland. The argument is also borne out when speed of response is an essential factor in Government decision making, as was the case, for example, with the decision in September 1992 to leave the European Exchange Rate Mechanism. Yet all these essentially Prime Ministerial decisions had to be cleared with a few very senior Ministers and advisers and were subsequently endorsed by the whole Cabinet.

There are several reasons why the Prime Minister of the day usually comes out on top in the decision-making process of British central Government. The main reason is that in every modern Cabinet the Prime Minister has usually been more than first among equals. This is partly for the reasons already given in the earlier section on Prime Ministerial power, but also because the Civil Service is accustomed to dealing with Ministers in an hierarchical way. Indeed, it is usually convenient to have a Prime

Minister who is regarded as being head and shoulders above the rest of the Cabinet, since this provides opportunities for competing Ministers to outflank or trump the efforts of their colleagues by securing the support of 10 Downing Street at a decisive stage in any important inter-Departmental argument.

Nearly every Cabinet in modern times has divided quite conveniently into two layers: a 'first eleven' of very senior Ministers who carry real weight and authority in the Government and a 'second eleven' who, although in charge of Departments and holding Cabinet rank, count for less in any Government. At one time in the early 1950s Winston Churchill sought to formalise this division by nominating a few 'Overlords' from among his most senior Cabinet colleagues to supervise and co-ordinate the work of clusters of other Cabinet Ministers. The experiment did not really work and was soon abandoned because of Ministerial resentment and jealousy. In the late 1960s Harold Wilson also experimented with the idea of creating an 'inner Cabinet' composed of fewer than half a dozen of Labour's real political heavyweights at that time. Once again the idea did not really work in practice for similar reasons and was soon abandoned. More recently, Michael Heseltine's appointment as 'First Secretary of State' and Deputy Prime Minister in John Major's July 1995 reshuffle provided another example of a move in this direction, as did Tony Blair's appointment of John Prescott as Deputy Prime Minister and Secretary of State for the Environment, Transport and the Regions in 1997 with a wide remit across the Government.

In every Cabinet it is the Prime Minister who usually holds most of the high cards in dealings with Cabinet colleagues. The Prime Minister can determine the member-ship of Cabinet committees – at any rate at the margin – by including additional members who can be relied on for their support, although the bulk of the membership of such committees is really determined by the nature and scope of the issues under discussion. The Prime Minister can exploit the use of bilateral meetings with individ-ual Ministers in order to divide and rule any collective opposition within the Cabinet to preferred policies. Indeed, as long as a political axis is preserved between the Prime Minister and the Chancellor of the Exchequer, there are few, if any, occasions on which the two of them are likely to be defeated by the rest of the Cabinet.

All of these realities are underpinned by the doctrine of *collective responsibility*. This means that the invidious choice facing any member of the Cabinet (or indeed any other Minister or PPS) who is really unhappy about an aspect of Government policy is either to threaten resignation, with the high risk that such a threat might be called, or to keep quiet and so risk losing political credibility if it is widely known in Westminster and Whitehall that the Minister concerned is at odds with Government policy. Clearly this can never be an attractive choice, yet on most occasions in modern times Ministers faced with this dilemma have chosen the latter course and remained within the Government. All of which really underlines that it is not sensible for even a very powerful Cabinet Minister to threaten resignation unless the Minister concerned is fully prepared to carry out the threat, especially since all the actors in the drama of modern British politics are aware that few resignations, even from the Cabinet, have enhanced the prospects of the individual taking such a momentous step. In most cases in modern times it has proved to be a ticket to political obscurity.

To find examples of senior Cabinet Ministers who chose to resign on significant issues of policy, in the *Conservative Party*, it is necessary to go back to Anthony Eden who resigned in opposition to the policy of appeasement in 1938, or Peter Thorneycroft who resigned because of his inability to carry the Prime Minister and other Cabinet colleagues with him on his policy of public expenditure cuts in 1958. Yet notwithstanding this, Ministers in successive Conservative Governments during the period 1979–97 were notably accident-prone and media calls for resignation were frequent.

The resignation of Lord Carrington and Ministerial colleagues at the Foreign Office in April 1982 was relatively unusual in that it was a direct and immediate atonement for the policy failure of their Department to foresee or prevent the Argentinean invasion of the Falkland Islands, even though it was widely agreed that the Ministry of Defence was equally culpable. The dramatic resignation of Michael Heseltine in January 1986 was also partly on policy grounds when he concluded that he was losing his argument in favour of a European future for Westland Helicopters, but it was mainly an act of exasperation at the way in which Margaret Thatcher had conducted Cabinet government over many years. The resignations of Nigel Lawson in 1989 and Norman Lamont in 1993 exemplify somewhat different phenomena. Nigel Lawson had become increasingly exasperated during his later years as Chancellor with the baleful influence of Sir Alan Walters over Margaret Thatcher, but – more importantly – he and his powerful neighbour in Downing Street had eventually drifted apart on one of the key issues of economic policy, namely the weight to be given to stability of the exchange rate in the conduct of monetary policy. Norman Lamont who had offered to resign on the ignominious 'Black Wednesday' in September 1992, became understandably resentful about having to take subsequent sole blame for the unpopular effects of Britain's membership of the European Exchange Rate Mechanism – a policy which he claimed he had not really believed in even when he was having staunchly to defend it.[13] Most dramatic – and consequential – of all recent examples was the resignation of Sir Geoffrey Howe as Leader of the House and 'Deputy Prime Minister' in November 1990, an act which gave him the opportunity to make an uncharacteristically electrifying personal statement to the House of Commons indicting Margaret Thatcher and her whole approach to political leadership especially on European policy, and thus precipitating her downfall.

These various examples of Conservative Cabinet resignations, demonstrate two different general phenomena. The cases of Lord Carrington and Norman Lamont were in their different ways clear examples of the need for ritual sacrifice to atone for policy failures by the Government as a whole. The cases of Michael Heseltine, Nigel Lawson and Geoffrey Howe, however, were in their different ways all expressions of exasperation at having to deal with Margaret Thatcher as she became increasingly obdurate and unreasonable on matters of policy. Thus issues of policy and personality were inextricably connected, as is so often the case in politics.

In the *Labour Party*, it is customary to refer to the cases of Aneurin Bevan, Harold Wilson, and John Freeman in 1951 who resigned against the Treasury's insistence on introducing charges for false teeth and spectacles within the National Health Service, and George Brown in 1968 who resigned in a fit of pique against Harold Wilson's continued prevarications on European policy. In both these celebrated cases clashes of personality and the influence of personal ambitions were bound up with differences of fundamental importance. It was no coincidence that Aneurin Bevan and Hugh Gaitskell (the Labour Chancellor in 1951) were obvious rivals for the succession to Clement Attlee, and that George Brown had been defeated by Harold Wilson in the 1963 Labour leadership contest following Hugh Gaitskell's untimely death.

As interesting and revealing, however, were the counter-examples of Michael Foot and Tony Benn, two of the leading Left-wingers in the 1974–79 Labour Governments of Harold Wilson and James Callaghan, neither of whom resigned from the Cabinet at any stage – even when faced with the appalling need (from a Socialist point of view) to make deep and immediate cuts in public expenditure at the behest of the International Monetary Fund in the autumn of 1976.[14] These cases demonstrate not only the addiction to high office of even previously rebellious individuals, but also the cunning and good sense of successive Labour Prime Ministers in keeping some of their most potent, potential adversaries inside rather than outside the tent, in the words of the traditional Arab proverb.

Given all the effective constraints and inhibitions of collective responsibility, there has been a tendency in all British Governments for disaffected or unhappy members of the Cabinet to convey their disapproval of certain aspects of Government policy either via private and unattributable conversations with Lobby journalists (see Chapter 7, pp. 161–162) or in carefully coded public speeches designed to be just within the bounds of collective responsibility, while marking out important differences designed to distance them from the prevailing Government orthodoxy. The use of such techniques can be regarded as a tribute to the durability and elasticity of collective responsibility in British central Government, but it can also end in tears.

The latitude provided by these techniques was used with impunity by Tony Benn during the period in the 1970s when he was the self-styled Socialist *enfant terrible* of the Wilson and Callaghan Administrations. It was equally exploited by the leading Tory 'Wets', such as Peter Walker and James Prior, during their surprisingly long Ministerial careers under Margaret Thatcher. In the 1990s, similar techniques were exploited by the so-called 'bastards' in the Major Cabinet (Michael Portillo, Peter Lilley and John Redwood) who occasionally made coded speeches undermining John Major's policy on Europe, but who were not sacked for their impertinence. In all such cases behaviour of this kind is only possible as long as the Prime Minister of the day feels unable or disinclined to punish it. Yet it is also worth noting that John Redwood eliminated himself from the Cabinet in June 1995 by resigning to fight John Major in the leadership election at that time.

Notwithstanding such drama and difficulty, the Cabinet is still the forum within which the most important decisions of Government in Britain are ratified, if not actually taken. It is the body in whose name the Government acts and its ostensible unity is vital to the continuation in office of any Administration. At times it can be a formidable brake on Prime Ministerial power and individual Ministerial initiative alike. Yet in modern British politics it has had a notably varied role, as illustrated by the contrast in its fortunes and behaviour under Margaret Thatcher, John Major and Tony Blair respectively.

Review of key problems

Another vital role of the Cabinet is the review of key problems which can affect the future of the Government and the country. To the outside observer this would appear to be an activity on which any Cabinet worth its salt ought to be engaged. After all, where else but around the Cabinet table should there be serious and timely discussion of such vital subjects as the concept of sustainable development, the continuing task of defeating inflation, or the difficulties of pursuing radical welfare reform? Yet sadly the truth seems to be that this aspect of the work of the Cabinet has often been neglected in favour of dealing with more urgent political issues.

In recent years the agenda of every regular Cabinet meeting has included an item on the following week's Parliamentary business (when Parliament is sitting), an item which permits the Prime Minister or Foreign Secretary to give a brief report on current international developments or recent international conferences with implications for Britain, and often an item which allows the Chancellor of the Exchequer to report on the state of the economy as indicated by the latest official statistics. Of course, any member of the Cabinet may apply to the Cabinet Secretary to have a particular item included on the agenda of a future meeting, but it is not uncommon for such requests to be turned down or for the matter to be referred to the appropriate Cabinet committee at the behest of the Prime Minister who is in effective control of the Cabinet agenda. On most occasions when Prime Ministers do this, they are merely acting as good chairmen by seeking to get decisions taken at the appropriate level consistent with the political importance of the issue. However, in the case of a real emergency or if a Cabinet Minister is not prepared to accept the decision of a Cabinet committee, the Prime Minister will normally ensure that the matter is put immediately on the agenda of the full Cabinet. Any other response would lead to a deterioration in the general atmosphere of mutual trust in the Cabinet and this would not be in the interest of any Prime Minister, however powerful. In general, therefore, the preparation and timing of Cabinet decisions is very much in the hands of the Prime Minister, which gives the holder of that office a real advantage over the rest of the Cabinet.

The fact that successive Prime Ministers and senior officials in the Cabinet Office have not always encouraged the Cabinet as a whole to discharge its responsibility for strategic policy review of this kind can be explained in a number of ways. First, it is doubtful whether regular Cabinet meetings are the appropriate occasions on which to attempt this task, since senior Ministers are always very busy and short of time – they have their own Departmental business to manage, the demands of Parliament to which to respond, and a variety of public engagements in Britain and abroad to fulfil. Secondly, the Cabinet exists mainly to settle or endorse the big decisions which have already been carefully prepared in Whitehall and which may even have been taken (in effect at any rate) by the Prime Minister and a few senior colleagues in advance of regular Cabinet meetings. In these circumstances it is not surprising that the Cabinet has an unimpressive record in this respect.

Just occasionally, of course, the Cabinet does engage in intensive and extensive discussions of this kind. This happened, for example, with the discussions in the Churchill Cabinet about British withdrawal from Egypt in 1954, in the Macmillan Cabinet about Britain's relationship with the rest of Western Europe in the late 1950s, in the Heath Cabinet about policy towards Northern Ireland in 1972–73, and in the Callaghan Cabinet in 1976 when it was necessary to agree on a package of public expenditure cuts to satisfy the conditions of the IMF loan to Britain. Reflective discussions also take place from time to time in the more informal setting of Chequers (the Prime Minister's official country residence), but these are usually focused on a single theme (for example, the protection of the global environment under Margaret Thatcher in the late 1980s) and do not necessarily involve the entire Cabinet. In general, most regular Cabinet discussions are largely pre-ordained and even a little ritualistic. The Cabinet remains the supreme decision-making body in the British political system, but it has often been a disappointment to those who have looked to it for deep or original discussion of the key political issues of the time.

Under John Major's leadership Cabinet government in Britain seemed to stage something of a revival, at any rate as compared with his immediate predecessor. He appeared to believe in genuine discussion before important decisions were taken and he was not in the habit of stating his desired conclusion at the outset of every important agenda item, as was all too often the practice of his predecessor. However, at the same time there were some issues which he felt the need to control more closely – such as the future of Northern Ireland, and Britain's relations with the rest of the European Union – because of political sensitivities and internal party disagreements of a potentially acute kind.

Soon after Tony Blair became Prime Minister in 1997 it was noted that the Cabinet had largely ceased to function as a forum for meaningful decision-making,[15] and that, with the Prime Minister standing 'at an unparalleled apex of power' Britain was, consequently, ' as close to having a presidential system as is possible.[16] On the other hand it was also noted that Tony Blair's style was to appear above party politics – as he did at the time of the death of Diana, Princess of Wales and during the Northern Ireland peace talks – while happy to leave many important matters to key Ministers, such as Gordon Brown, Lord Irvine and Jack Straw, and remain apparently detached on many key policy issues.[17] Such a technique has proved a clever way of keeping the Prime Minister 'in reserve' on issues which are controversial, thus enabling Tony Blair publicly to come out on the most popular side of the argument once the results of consulting the focus groups have pointed the way forward.

Inter-Departmental co-ordination

The third important role of the Cabinet is to ensure inter-Departmental co-ordination in the development of Government policy. In the opinion of many well-informed observers this has long been the most notable role of the Cabinet in Britain. It is obviously a vital aspect of Cabinet activity, since it helps to impart a degree of coherence and unity to Government policy and so reinforces the doctrine of *collective responsibility*. Indeed, it could not really be otherwise, since senior Ministers cannot be expected to be bound by Cabinet decisions affecting their spheres of responsibility if their Departmental interests and political points of view have not been adequately taken into account. Such inter-Departmental co-ordination helps to guard against the taking of political decisions by one Department which may have unintended or adverse consequences for other Departments. It is also meant to contribute to the administrative efficiency of any Government, in that it can help to avoid both unnecessary duplication in Whitehall and the creation of awkward or damaging gaps in the scope of official action.

Since individual Cabinet Ministers are not always good 'team players' by temperament or calculation, it is necessary to bolster the unity and collegiality of the Cabinet with a number of institutional devices. For example, the Permanent Secretaries of all the various Whitehall Departments speak to each other from time to time and have regular weekly meetings under the chairmanship of the Cabinet Secretary. The Press Officers in all the various Departments are also in frequent contact and work collectively under the overall guidance of the Press Secretary at 10

Downing Street. The Private Offices of all Cabinet Ministers keep in touch and include an increasingly significant sub-network of Political Advisers, each of whom works directly for a Cabinet Minister and is paid from party rather than public funds. The Policy Unit at 10 Downing Street works exclusively for the Prime Minister of the day and occupies itself principally with political trouble-shooting, speech-writing and party political initiatives. It has sometimes tried to provide long-term or synoptic ideas on policy for the Government as a whole, but more often it works as a sort of policy clearing-house and political 'thought police' at the heart of central Government. All these various Whitehall networks are there to reinforce the coherence of Government policy and the unity of the Government as a whole.

Indeed, it was in order to achieve these twin objectives that, on taking office in 1997, Tony Blair and his key advisers sought to apply in Government the strict and highly centralised controls over policy and its presentation that they had operated so successfully in Opposition. As part of this approach they stipulated that 'all major interviews and media appearances (by Ministers), both print and broadcast, should be agreed with the No. 10 Press Office before any commitments were entered into. The policy content of all major speeches, press releases, and new policy initiatives should be cleared in good time with the No. 10 Private Office; the timing and form of announcements should be cleared with the No. 10 Press Office.[18] These arrangements led one commentator to write of 'the biggest centralisation of power seen in Whitehall in peacetime',[19] and this approach was intensified in 1998 following the appointment of Jack Cunningham as Minister for the Cabinet Office with a seat in the Cabinet, a place on all key Cabinet committees, direct access to the Prime Minister, and with key responsibility for ensuring coherence and central control over all important Government policy and its presentation, achieving what Tony Blair likes to refer to as 'joined-up Government'.

It is clear that single party Government in Britain needs to be united Government if the political system is to work satisfactorily. The Cabinet is the main institutional expression of this unity and it is therefore vital that its decision-making procedures should contribute to rather than detract from the essentially collegiate nature of central Government in Britain. Whenever a Cabinet is seriously split on policy – as the Callaghan Cabinet was in 1976 over the IMF demand for public expenditure cuts, or the Thatcher Cabinet was in 1979–81 over the general thrust of economic policy, or the Major Cabinet was in 1992–97 on Britain's approach to further development of the European Union – the morale and effectiveness of the whole Government suffers. It can also lead to reduced levels of public support for the Government when the media and the general public perceive that the Cabinet is divided on important issues of policy or personality. It is therefore not surprising that all Prime Ministers strive mightily to avoid such splits and try to deal promptly with them when they occur.

12.5 Conclusion

Considerable controversy continues to surround the issues raised by the respective roles of the Prime Minister and Cabinet in modern British politics. There is no consensus of opinion among academic observers or practising politicians, although in

Margaret Thatcher's time at 10 Downing Street most people were persuaded that British central Government was becoming increasingly presidential, whereas during John Major's time as Prime Minister very different conclusions were drawn. In this respect the jury is still out on the Blair premiership, although it seems that he is emulating Margaret Thatcher's leadership style rather than John Major's more collegiate approach.

In view of the contradictory evidence, some observers agree with John Mackintosh, who wrote that 'the weight of evidence does suggest that British Prime Ministers are in a position of great strength as against their colleagues and within the whole framework of British Government'.[20] Others agree with George Jones who wrote that 'the Prime Minister is the leading figure in the Cabinet whose voice carries most weight, but he is not the all-powerful individual which many have claimed him to be'.[21] In the light of the evidence these would seem to be well-judged cautionary words. However, Robert Blake probably came to the most timeless conclusion when he wrote that 'the powers of the Prime Minister have varied with the personality of the Prime Minister or with the particular political circumstances of his tenure'.[22]

On the whole this judgement seems to accord most closely with the evidence over the centuries. It allows for the fact that there have been times when Prime Ministers have carried all before them – for example, in the immediate aftermath of General Election victories or other personal political triumphs – and times when powerful Ministers or the Cabinet collectively have asserted their authority over weak, lazy, sick, politically damaged or discredited Prime Ministers. Indeed, Prime Ministerial power is like a fortress built on sand: it can look impregnable, yet can be washed away by a turn in the tide.

Although we have been looking in this chapter at two distinct components of the British political system, the fortunes of the Prime Minister and Cabinet are always inextricably linked. Whatever their respective roles and capabilities, neither can function satisfactorily without the consent and co-operation of the other. In so far as each is limited in the exercise of political power, the constraints are essentially political rather than constitutional, practical rather than theoretical. It is the other actors in the political process – the political parties, pressure groups, the Civil Service, the media, the markets, Britain's European partners and public opinion – which keep both Prime Minister and Cabinet in check. Moreover, in the modern world it is the passage of events, very often in other countries, and the verdict of the British electorate which usually determine their fate.

Suggested questions

1 Describe the structure and problems of Cabinet government in Britain.
2 How powerful is the Prime Minister in modern Britain?
3 Does collective responsibility raise or lower the quality of decision making in British central Government?

Notes

1. In total, some 580 civil servants work in the Cabinet Office, but this includes a whole host of other officials (often at low level) who are not actually serving the Cabinet and its Committees.

2. See Andrew Marr, 'Blair Places his Bet on the Thin Controller, *Independent,* 6 May 1997.
3. For a description of the role of the press secretary – in this case Bernhard Ingham – see R. Harris, *'Good and Faithful Servant'* (London: Faber, 1990).
4. H. Wilson, *The Governance of Britain* (London: Weidenfeld & Nicolson, 1976), p. 8.
5. Quoted in R. Blake, *The Office of Prime Minister* (Oxford: Oxford University Press, 1975), p. 50.
6. A. Eden, *Full Circle* (London: Cassell, 1960), p. 269.
7. H.H. Asquith, *Fifty Years of Parliament, Vol. II* (London: Cassell, 1926), p. 185.
8. *Observer*, 25 February 1979.
9. This last condition of Prime Ministerial power is critical, as was made clear by the circumstances which led to Michael Heseltine's challenge to Margaret Thatcher for the leadership of the Conservative Party in November 1990 and hence the office of Prime Minister. This challenge to a very powerful Prime Minister and her subsequent downfall was the culmination of consistently low opinion poll ratings since July 1989 and a growing belief within both the Cabinet and the rest of the Conservative Parliamentary party that it would be impossible to win another General Election under her leadership.
10. On the other hand, it has been argued that Clement Attlee did not really have an effective choice, since his most senior Cabinet colleagues had either died (for example, Ernest Bevin and Stafford Cripps) or were exhausted after 11 continuous years both in war and in peace (for example, Herbert Morrison and Hugh Dalton), and since he was under pressure for some of his other Cabinet colleagues to hold a General Election at that time in any case.
11. Walter Bagehot, *The English Constitution* (London: Fontana/Collins, 1975), p. 68.
12. J.P.Mackintosh, *The British Cabinet*, 3rd edn (London: Stevens, 1977), p. 414.
13. These two prominent examples of high-level Ministerial resignation underlined how important it is for all Prime Ministers to stay on good working terms with their Chancellors of the Exchequer and how dangerous it can be if an occupant of 11 Downing Street, or a former occupant, becomes completely disaffected.
14. See Tony Benn's Diaries – 76, pp. 661–690; Denis Healey's Memoirs, *The Time of My Life*, pp. 426–35 and Kenneth O. Morgan's *Callaghan: A Life*, pp. 545–9. For more detailed accounts of this critical period in the life of the 1974–79 Labour Government.
15. See Andrew Rawnsley, *Observer*, 26 April 1998.
16. See editorial, 'President Blair', *The Sunday Times,* 26 April 1998.
17. See Peter Riddell, 'We're Missing You, Mr. Blair', *The Times*, 8 June 1998.
18. See *The Ministerial Code: A Code of Conduct and Guidance on Procedures for Ministers* (Cabinet Office, July 1997).
19. Peter Riddell, *The Times*, 1 August 1997.
20. In A. King (ed.), *The British Prime Minister* (London: Macmillan, 1969), p. 198.
21. In A. King (ed.), *The British Prime Minister*, 2nd edn.(London: Macmillan, 1985), p. 216.
22. R. Blake, *The Office of Prime Minister*, p. 51.

Further reading

Benn, A., *Diaries, Vols. I–IV* (London: Hutchinson, 1987–90).
Blake, R., *The Office of Prime Minister* (Oxford: Oxford University Press, 1975).
Burch, M. and Holliday, I., *The British Cabinet System* (Hemel Hempstead: Prentice-Hall, 1996).
Callaghan, L.J., *Time and Chance* (London: Collins, 1987).
Hennessy, P., *Cabinet* (Oxford: Blackwell, 1986).
Hogg, S. and Hill, J., *Too Close to Call: Power and Politics – John Major in No. 10* (London: Little Brown, 1995).

Howe, G., *Conflicts of Loyalty* (London: Macmillan, 1994).
James, S., *British Cabinet Government* (London: Routledge, 1992).
Kavanagh, D., *Thatcherism and British Politics* (Oxford: Oxford University Press, 1987).
Lawson, N., *The View from Number 11* (London: Bantam Press, 1992).
Morgan, K.O., *Callaghan: A Life*, (Oxford: Oxford University Press, 1977).
Seldon, A., *Major: A Political Life*, (London: Weidenfeld & Nicolson, 1997).
Shell, D. and Hodder-Williams, R. (eds), *Churchill to Major: The British Prime Ministership Since 1945* (London: Hurst and Company, 1995).
Thatcher, M., *The Downing Street Years* (London: HarperCollins, 1993).
Watkins, A., *The Road to Number 10: From Bonar Law to Tony Blair* (London: Duckworth, 1998).
Young, H., *One of Us*, rev. edn (London: Pan Books, 1990).

Website

No 10 Downing Street   http:/www.number–10.gov.uk.v

13 Ministers and Departments

Britain is a country with a long tradition of centralised Government. Some of the public offices of central Government have been in existence for centuries. For example, the first Lord Chancellor pre-dates the Norman Conquest of 1066 having been appointed by Edward the Confessor, the Exchequer developed in the twelfth century, and the office of Lord President of the Council dates from 1497. Some of the Departments of central Government are now over 200 years old, with two of the most prestigious Departments having been established in 1782 under George III when both a Department for Foreign Affairs and a Department for Home and Colonial Affairs (now the Home Office) were created.

Since the mid-nineteenth century Departments of central Government have been created, reorganised and dissolved. For example, the Board (Department) of Education was established in 1870 with a Minister directly responsible to Parliament for the whole area of public education. The Board of Agriculture and Fisheries was converted into a Ministry in 1919 after the struggle to feed the nation during the First World War. The Air Ministry was created in 1937 to organise what at the time was a relatively new arm of warfare. More recent examples include the Department of the Environment (now known as the Department of the Environment, Transport and the Regions), which was established in 1970 as one of a number of super-Departments designed to secure better co-ordination in Whitehall; the Department of Energy, which was established in 1974 as a partial response to the energy crisis at that time (and re-absorbed into the Department of Trade and Industry in 1992); and the Department of National Heritage (re-named in 1997 The Department for Culture, Media and Sport), which was created in 1992 to bring together in one Department the Government's responsibilities for the arts, sport and the media.

The organisation of Departments has often been changed in response to changes in Government functions and in political priorities. The 1974–79 Labour Government split the super-Departments into several smaller Departments – for example, the Department of Transport was re-established as a separate Department outside the Department of the Environment and the Department of Trade and Industry was split into a Department of Industry, a Department of Trade, and a new Department of Prices and Consumer Affairs. Equally, the 1979–83 Conservative Government abolished the Civil Service Department and redistributed its functions between the Treasury and the

Cabinet Office; the 1983–87 Conservative Government recreated the Department of Trade and Industry, but transferred some of its functions to an enlarged Department of Transport; the 1987–92 Conservative Government split the Department of Health and Social Security into separate Departments of Health and Social Security respectively; the Conservative Government elected in 1992 did away with the Department of Energy, redistributing its functions to the Department of Trade and Industry, and in 1995 merged the Department of Employment with the Department for Education. In 1997 the new Labour Government created a large Department of the Environment, Transport and the Regions. Thus it is apparent that there has been both change and continuity in the organisation of British central Government.

13.1 The structure and work of Departments

Throughout the entire period of Departmental government in Britain there has been only one fundamental examination of the overall structure of central Government. This was carried out by a committee chaired by Lord Haldane which reported to Lloyd George's Government in 1918.[1] The two main recommendations of the report were that Departmental boundaries should be based upon functional criteria (such as health, agriculture or defence), and that the Cabinet should be kept as a compact policy-making body at the apex of central Government. Neither recommendation has been fully implemented over subsequent years. Thus it has been quite common for Departments based on function (such as the Department of Health) to coexist with some based on responsibility for a mixture of subjects and functions (such as the Home Office) and others based on geography (such as the Scottish Office, the Welsh Office and the Northern Ireland Office). Furthermore, Cabinets have had as few as five members (Winston Churchill's War Cabinet in 1940) or as many as 24 members (Harold Wilson's Cabinet in 1975 and James Callaghan's Cabinet in 1977).

Departmental structure

The Departmental structure in Whitehall today consists of 21 Departments, including the co-ordinating offices and the three legal Departments. See Figure 13.1 for a diagram of the overall structure of central Government. In political terms the most important are the Treasury, the Foreign Office and the Home Office. Yet in terms of the public spending for which they are responsible, the Department of Social Security, the Department of Health, and the Department for Education and Employment are the most significant. In formal terms there is no Prime Minister's Department, although the staff at 10 Downing Street and in the Cabinet Office provide effective Civil Service support for the Prime Minister of the day. Having said this, however, it should be noted that the Cabinet Office, and indeed the Cabinet Secretary, advise the Cabinet as a whole, not just the Prime Minister. (Although this is a balance that is perhaps shifting – certainly the appointment by Tony Blair of Jack Cunningham as Minister for the Cabinet Office 'to ensure the Prime Minister's objectives were delivered' would indicate so.) See Figure 13.2 for a diagram of the Cabinet Office and Office of Public Service.

Figure 13.1 The structure of central government (1998)

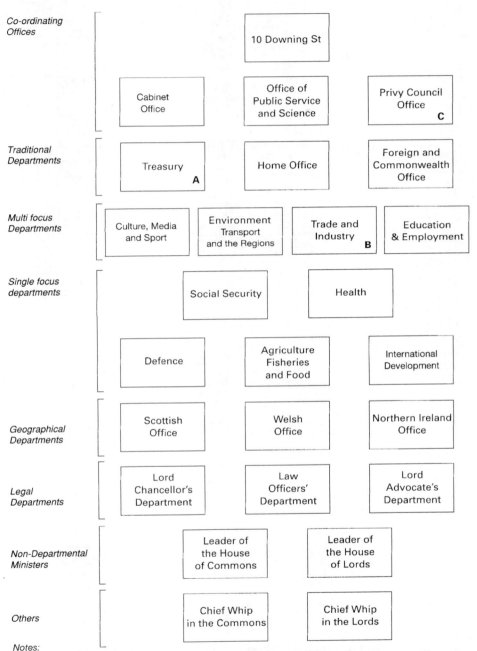

Notes:
A. Includes the Board of Customs and Excise, the Board of Inland Revenue and the Paymaster General
B. Includes Energy and the Export Credits Guarantee Department
C. Includes the Lord President of the Council and the Lord Privy Seal
D. Includes the Office of Public Service and Duchy of Lancaster

Figure 13.2 Cabinet Office and Office of Public Service organisation chart

Source: Adapted from *The Civil Service Yearbook* (London: The Stationery Office, 1998).

Apart from the Prime Minister, there are other non-Departmental Ministers. For example, there are the Lord President of the Council and the Lord Privy Seal, usually the titles taken by those appointed to lead the House of Commons and the House of Lords respectively.[2] In addition it is possible to appoint a Minister 'without portfolio', a convenient way for the Prime Minister of the day to include close political colleagues in the Government without burdening them with specific Departmental responsibilities, as was the case with John Major's appointment of the Chairman of the Conservative Party, Dr Brian Mawhinney, in July 1995 and with Tony Blair's appointment of Peter Mandelson as Minister in the Cabinet Office in May 1997.

Within each significant Department the normal pattern is for there to be a Secretary of State or Minister of equivalent Cabinet rank as Departmental head, supported by at least one Minister of State at the second level and perhaps two or more Under-Secretaries at the third level. There are, however, variations in this pattern which flow mainly from the nature and scope of each Department's responsibilities. For example, in 1998 the Department of Trade and Industry had one Cabinet Minister, four Ministers of State – two in the House of Commons and two in the House of Lords – and two Parliamentary Under-Secretaries of State; whereas the Welsh Office had only a Cabinet Minister and two Parliamentary Under-Secretaries. The Treasury is distinctive in many ways, not least in having two Cabinet Ministers – the Chancellor of the Exchequer and the Chief Secretary – and normally the backing of the Prime Minister as well (who is known formally as the First Lord of the Treasury). Nonetheless, there have been occasions when other Departments have been represented by more than one Minister in the Cabinet at the same time. This was the case in the first Cabinet formed by Tony Blair in 1997 when the Deputy Prime Minister, John Prescott, was appointed Secretary of State for the Environment, Transport and the Regions and Gavin Strang was appointed Minister for Transport with a seat in the Cabinet.

Just as the number and importance of Ministers varies from one Department to another, so the number of civil servants working in each Department also varies considerably. For example, in 1997 the Ministry of Defence employed 77,949 non-industrial civil servants and the Department of Social Security employed 93,030 non-industrial civil servants, whereas the Treasury only employed 888 (although this figure did not include those employed by the Inland Revenue (54,029) or Customs and Excise (23,071)), the Department for Education and Employment employed 33,662, the Department for Culture, Media and Sport employed 960 and the Northern Ireland office employed only 204. The explanation for these wide differences is that in the former category are to be found Departments whose functions cover a wide range of policy functions and the provision of extensive public services, whereas in the latter category are to be found Departments whose functions are limited to policy advice and supervisory responsibilities. Despite varying considerably in size and function, there is nevertheless a recognisably standard structure for each Department in Whitehall. This is shown in Figure 13.3.

Central Government functions

It is difficult to generalise about the way in which central Government works in Britain. So much depends on the personality, outlook and experience of the senior Ministers concerned and also on the calibre and performance of the senior civil servants involved as well as the various Departmental habits and traditions. According to the traditional view propounded by Sir Ivor Jennings, the essential features of British central Government are 'the clear division between politicians and public servants and the close relationship between policy and administration'.[3] This emphasises one of

Figure 13.3 *Government Department: standard structure*

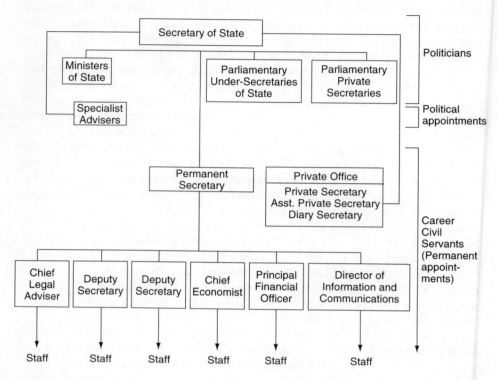

the key paradoxes of British central Government. On the one hand, there is a clear theoretical distinction between the role of Ministers, who are supposed to determine the policy and take all the decisions, and that of civil servants, who are supposed to advise Ministers and see that the business of Government is conducted in conformity with the policy laid down by Ministers. On the other hand, there is the practical impossibility in modern British Government of sustaining such a clear distinction. In short, it has become increasingly apparent that the theory that Ministers take the political decisions and civil servants carry them out has long since been overtaken by reality. This fact was certainly made apparent as far as the Foreign and Commonwealth Office was concerned by the findings of the Legg Report into the Arms to Sierra Leone affair, published in 1998.[4] Hence we find yet another example of the inherent contradictions in the British political system.

Most Ministers have to work very hard, often for between 12 and 18 hours a day. There are policy discussions to conduct, official papers to be considered and, where possible, approved, Ministerial correspondence to be dealt with, frequent meetings both within their own Departments and bilaterally with other Departments or 10 Downing Street, meetings of the Cabinet or Cabinet Committees to attend, meetings to be held with outside bodies and the representatives of various pressure or interest groups, Parliamentary committees to attend, Parliamentary Questions to be answered, Parliamentary debates in which to take part, official visits to be made to various parts of the country and abroad, foreign visitors to be welcomed and entertained, journalists and others in the media to be briefed, interviews to be given, meetings of the European Union and other international organisations to attend, constituents and party activists to be kept content as well as constituency work to attend to.

A graphic illustration of the demands of Ministerial life was given by Tony Benn, when describing how he allocated his time in 1977 when he was Secretary of State for Energy.[5] Although now more than twenty years ago, it is still valid:

1. Fulfilled 50 public engagements in the constituency, made 12 general speeches in Bristol, held 16 constituency surgeries, and handled more than 1000 personal cases.
2. Attended 4 General Management Committee meetings of the Bristol South East Labour Party; attended 20 ward meetings, and 5 Labour Group meetings to discuss policy.
3. Attended 12 meetings of the Parliamentary Labour Party, and made 14 speeches to various sub-group meetings of MPs.
4. Dealt in Parliament with three Energy Bills, produced 54 Statutory Instruments; presented 33 explanatory memoranda to the House on European Community energy matters; answered 51 oral questions and 171 written questions; had 154 meetings with non-Governmental groups; produced 1821 Ministerial minutes on papers taken home in the official red box; made 133 public appointments to various bodies.
5. Attended 42 Cabinet meetings and 106 Cabinet Committee meetings; submitted four Cabinet papers and 45 Cabinet Committee papers; received 1750 Cabinet papers covering the whole range of Government policies.
6. Made 19 visits abroad, and received 32 Ministers and Ambassadors from foreign countries.
7. In the first half of 1977, presided over the Energy Council of the European Community, which involved taking the chair at six Council meetings and having sundry other official meetings on European energy questions.
8. Attended 15 meetings of the Labour Party National Executive Committee and 62 other Labour meetings.
9. Made 80 speeches up and down the country, gave 83 radio interviews, 57 television interviews and 34 press conferences, wrote 16 articles, had 30 interviews with individual journalists, and received or answered 1000 letters which did not involve constituency casework or Ministerial responsibilities.

This is a considerable amount of work by any standards, but it is by no means untypical of Ministerial life today. However, any inventory can only provide a superficial and incomplete sketch of the full range of Ministerial activities, since it is impossible to give a definitive description of a working life which is inherently so varied and unpredictable.

In addition to the problems which can be caused by what can be termed 'Ministerial musical chairs'[6] whenever the Prime Minister has a reshuffle, incoming Ministers usually get no time to prepare for their jobs and little or no advice from their predecessors. New Ministers seldom have anything more than superficial knowledge or understanding of their new responsibilities unless they have been promoted from within or are returning to a Department which they already know. The normal assumption is that they will learn on the job with the assistance of their Ministerial colleagues and Civil Service advisers. Indeed, the ability to get to grips with a complex brief in a short period of time is considered to be one of the main qualifications for Ministerial office in British central Government.

Civil servants for their part, and notably those in the senior administrative grades who advise Ministers, do their best to ensure that Ministers are adequately briefed on all matters with which they have to deal. Yet at the same time they try to see that Ministers are not over-burdened with unnecessary paperwork or matters which can be handled by officials. This means that one of the key roles of senior civil servants, and especially those who work in Ministerial Private Offices, is that of 'gate-keeper' in the information-gathering and decision-making process of central Government. Every day such civil servants have to decide whether to refer matters to Ministers for information or decision or whether to deal with issues themselves within the confines of established Government policy. Although there is a natural tendency for civil servants to err on the side of caution by referring all politically sensitive matters to Ministers, their 'gate-keeper' role gives them considerable influence within central Government and the veil of official secrecy behind which they work makes it hard for the outside observer – and sometimes even Ministers – to evaluate just how satisfactorily they perform their tasks.

Perhaps the most characteristic aspect of activity in Whitehall is the work which is done in the extensive network of *inter-Departmental committees* both at political level in Cabinet Committees and bilateral Ministerial meetings and at official level in the inter-Departmental Committees made up of officials from the Departments concerned. Since many of the issues with which central Government has to deal are too broad and complex to be handled within the sphere of a single Department, the process of inter-Departmental co-ordination by officials, prior to collective Ministerial decisions, is vital to much of the policy and decision-making process. It puts a considerable burden on officials in the Cabinet Office, who have to see that the various strands of policy are pulled together. The process of government would not work so smoothly without such inter-Departmental co-ordination by officials.

Another important aspect of the work of British central Government is the frequent and extensive consultation which takes place between officials and various client or pressure groups. Nowadays nearly every Department finds it useful to consult widely with such groups, not so much about which policy to adopt as about the detailed effects and implications of policy already determined by Ministers. For example, the Ministry of Agriculture has worked very closely (some would say too closely) with the National Farmers' Union in accordance with the statutory duties of consultation laid down in the 1947 and 1957 Agriculture Acts. Equally, the Department of Trade and Industry has kept in contact with the Confederation of British Industry and the wide range of Chambers of Commerce and Trade Associations. In short, nearly all Departments make it their business to keep in touch with the various interest and cause groups which have a stake in their spheres of Departmental responsibility. Certainly any Government which totally spurned or neglected such contacts would not only find its tasks made more difficult, but also lay itself open to serious criticism in Parliament and in the media. As a consequence, political prudence dictates that Ministers and officials at least go through the motions of consultation, and usually much more than that.

13.2 The role of Ministers

The role of Ministers in British central Government can be simply defined as taking the lead in, and making decisions on, matters of policy; and the defence and promotion of that policy in Whitehall, Westminster, Brussels and the world at large. Within their Departments Ministers act essentially as political jurymen who take decisions on the basis of advice supplied to them by their civil servants and others. Of course, Ministers are always free to question, ignore or discard such advice, but this can be unwise. Civil servants do not usually recommend courses of action or inaction which they know would be politically unacceptable to Ministers at the time. Ministers for their part sometimes may not have the time or the inclination to question or reject the policy advice which is put to them. Usually only strong, self-confident and experienced Ministers, or those who are engaged on implementing clearly established party policy, manage to dominate all policy work in their Departments.

Every Government since the war has contained a few senior Ministers who have been able, more often than not, to get their way with officials, with their Ministerial colleagues and with Parliament. Of course this has applied particularly to strong and determined Prime Ministers, such as Clement Attlee and Margaret Thatcher. Yet it has also applied very clearly to some other leading figures who have not been Prime Minister. One obvious example of such a Ministerial heavyweight would be *Ernest Bevin*, who was Minister of Labour in the wartime Coalition Government and Foreign Secretary in the postwar Labour Government. Another example would be *Duncan Sandys*, who was successively Commonwealth Secretary and Defence Secretary in Conservative Governments in the 1950s. Yet another would be *Denis Healey*, who was Labour Defence Secretary, 1964–70, and Labour Chancellor of the Exchequer, 1974–79. More recently one could cite *Viscount Whitelaw*, who was successively Leader of the House of Commons and Northern Ireland Secretary in the 1970–74 Heath Government, and Home Secretary and then Leader of the House of Lords in Margaret Thatcher's first two Administrations (1979–83 and 1983–87); and *Nigel Lawson*, who was Chancellor of the Exchequer in Margaret Thatcher's Government from 1983 to 1989.

During the 1990s examples can be cited of *Kenneth Clarke*, who served as a Cabinet Minister at the Departments of Trade and Industry, Health, and Education under Margaret Thatcher, and as Home Secretary and then Chancellor of the Exchequer under John Major; *Michael Heseltine*, who first entered the Cabinet in 1979, serving as Environment Secretary and Defence Secretary under Margaret Thatcher before resigning in 1986 over the Westland Affair and subsequently rejoining John Major's Cabinet in 1990 again as Environment Secretary and later as President of the Board of Trade and then First Secretary of State and Deputy Prime Minister; *Douglas Hurd* who was successively Northern Ireland Secretary, Home Secretary and then Foreign Secretary under the leadership of Margaret Thatcher and John Major; and *Gordon Brown* who was Chancellor of the Exchequer under Tony Blair in the Labour Government which came into office in 1997.

It is not easy to define what qualities such Ministers have had which have earned them the accolade of 'political heavyweights'. Yet politicians and pundits alike know one when they see one. Force of character and political judgement undoubtedly play an important part, but so do Ministerial competence and Prime Ministerial backing.

It is evident that the balance of experience and ability can often determine the balance of power between Ministers and senior civil servants. In the final analysis it is apparent that a variety of factors are involved, including:

- popular support for a policy (certainly the absence of popular dissent);
- a Manifesto commitment to a policy (described by Richard Crossman as 'the battering ram of change');
- Prime Ministerial support for a policy (or, as a minimum, Prime Ministerial acquiescence);
- Cabinet commitment to and support for a policy (certainly the absence of hostility from among the Cabinet 'heavyweights');
- the availability of sufficient time in which to carry through a policy to fruition;
- favourable circumstances and conditions (namely the absence of other overriding policy priorities and time-consuming emergencies and crises);
- acceptance of and support for a policy amongst the senior Civil Service (certainly the absence of hostility towards a policy);
- support for a policy among Parliamentary colleagues (and the avoidance if possible of intra-party dissent);
- support for a policy amongst the party activists and members (certainly the absence of anything approaching organised opposition);
- an informed, competent, determined and politically astute Minister who is effective in the House of Commons.

Ministerial responsibility

Ministerial responsibility is both individual and collective. It is still one of the key concepts in British central Government. It has endured since the nineteenth century because it has advantages for Ministers and civil servants alike. Ministers have benefited from the fact that it puts them in a privileged position in which they are the main recipients of official information and advice. Traditionally, civil servants have also benefited from the fact that it has give them considerable influence over Government policy and decision making without the formal need to accept public responsibility for the outcome.[7] However, these traditional characteristics have been changed significantly in recent years not least by the growth of so-called 'Next Steps Executive Agencies' which have had the effect of putting responsibility for the *administration* of public policy fairly and squarely on the shoulders of the much more visible Chief Executives who lead them and who can, occasionally, be sacked if their performance does not come up to expectations.[8]

With regard to *individual responsibility*, the senior Minister in a Department is theoretically responsible for everything which happens or fails to happen within the Department and can be held to account by Parliament and the media for acts of omission as well as commission. The classic view holds that Ministers are responsible for every act of their civil servants, regardless of whether or not they are properly aware of what is happening in their Departments. The most often cited example of this doctrine was the resignation of the Minister of Agriculture, *Sir Thomas Dugdale*, in the 1954 Crichel Down Affair.[9] More recent examples cited usually include the resignation of *Lord Carrington* and most of his Ministerial colleagues at the Foreign Office in April 1982 in recognition of his Department's failure to foresee and prevent the Argentinian invasion of the Falkland Islands.[10]

On the other hand, there are a large number of examples of senior Ministers *not* resigning, even when their policies and personal reputations were in tatters. For example, *John Davies* did not resign as Secretary of State for Trade and Industry in 1971 in the wake of the Court Line collapse, or in 1972 after the failure of Vehicle and General. Equally, *Norman Lamont* did not resign as Chancellor of the Exchequer in September 1992 following the collapse of the Fixed Exchange Rate policy and the forced withdrawal of sterling from the Exchange Rate Mechanism of the European Monetary System. Similarly *Michael Howard* did not resign as Home Secretary in April 1995 when the Courts threw out his cost-cutting Crime Injuries Scheme, even though he was accused of abusing power and flouting the will of Parliament. Neither did either *William Waldegrave* or *Sir Nicholas Lyell* resign following criticisms in the Scott Report into the Arms to Iraq affair in 1996. Nor did *Robin Cook* resign as Foreign Secretary despite damning criticisms of his Department contained in a House of Commons Select Committee report into the arms to Sierra Leone affair in 1999. Indeed, Prime Ministers have often challenged the whole concept of Ministerial responsibility. For example, Margaret Thatcher refused to accept the resignation of William Whitelaw as Home Secretary following a widely publicised breach of security at Buckingham Palace in 1982, or James Prior as Secretary of State for Northern Ireland following a mass escape from the Maze prison in September 1983.[11]

It is apparent, therefore, that there are no hard and fast rules which determine the nature of Ministerial responsibility in all cases and the outcome depends on an unpredictable mixture of precedents and political circumstances. In contemporary conditions the factors which determine whether or not Ministers resign from office seem to depend more on the extent to which they still command the confidence of the Prime Minister, the Chief Whip and their own back benchers than on any objective assessment of the incompetence or impropriety of the action or inaction for which they may be criticised. In other words, holding on to Ministerial office seems to have taken precedence over principled resignation in the majority of cases.

The chain of responsibility in a Department is hierarchical, which means that civil servants and junior Ministers alike report to senior Ministers at the head of their Departments and it is the latter who have to take the ultimate responsibility for their action or inaction. Of course, there have been times when junior Ministers have been so out of sympathy with a particular policy of their Department or the Government as a whole that they have felt bound to resign. This was the case, for example, with *Ian Gow* who resigned as Minister of State at the Treasury in 1985 in protest against the Anglo-Irish Agreement.[12] Others have resigned in order to be free to criticise Government policy more generally – as was the case over policies towards Europe and the resignation of *David Heathcoat-Amory* as Paymaster-General in 1996. Yet on the whole junior Ministers stay at their posts and only tender their resignations if they are obliged to do so in the course of a Ministerial 'reshuffle' organised by the Prime Minister of the day or as a result of political pressure arising from some scandal publicised by the media.

Indeed, it seems that *individual Ministerial responsibility* has been blurred and eroded in modern times by the size and complexity of modern Government. This means that it has been effectively impossible for senior Ministers to be aware of, let alone control, everything which happens or fails to happen in their Departments. For example, thousands of planning appeals have to be decided every year by the Secretary of State for the Environment, Transport and the Regions, many of them important and nearly all of them complicated and contentious. Yet no Minister in that position can possibly hope to consider all of them personally, so junior Ministers and civil servants effectively take the decisions in the senior Minister's name in all but a few outstanding cases. Thus in most cases individual Ministerial responsibility has become little more than a constitutional 'cloak', a convenient fiction for Parliamentary and Civil Service purposes, but a convention which is put strictly into practice on very few occasions.

On the other hand, *collective Ministerial responsibility* is more of a reality in modern political conditions, because it reflects the collegiate and usually cohesive nature of single party Government in Britain. It is really a way of expressing the fact that all Ministers and Whips – and, indeed, Parliamentary Private Secretaries – are bound by Government policy and are expected to stand by it and to speak and vote for it. While politicians cannot really be expected to believe totally in everything which they have to support in public for reasons of party loyalty, those whose activities are covered by collective Ministerial responsibility are expected nevertheless to support the Government on all occasions. If they feel unable or unwilling to do so, they are supposed to resign or can expect to be dismissed as was the case in 1981, for example, when Keith Speed, the junior Navy Minister, was sacked for speaking out publicly against planned cuts in the Royal Navy budget, or in 1989 when Nicholas Ridley, then Environment Secretary, was sacked for speaking out against the Germans.

It should come as no surprise, however, that the convention of collective responsibility has not always been observed. Indeed, on those, admittedly rare, occasions when Governments have been so split that enforcement has been effectively impossible, temporary suspension has become the only effective course. For example, in 1931 there was an open 'agreement to differ' in the National Government on the issue of tariff reform, and in 1975 during the European Referendum campaign Labour Cabinet Ministers were allowed to argue against each other on public platforms. It is unwise, however, for those covered by collective responsibility to test the boundaries of the permissible too obviously or too often, since in doing so they are quite likely to invite dismissal by the Prime Minister of the day. On the whole, therefore, collective Ministerial responsibility is a reality in modern British government, but it is no longer the effective mechanism of Parliamentary accountability which it was originally meant to be.

Parliamentary accountability

In theory, the proper constitutional check on the power of the Executive in Britain is to be found in Ministerial accountability to Parliament. This is supposed to be achieved in three ways. None of these is adequate on its own, but taken together there are some safeguards for the public interest.

First, there are the opportunities for MPs to hold Ministers to account during proceedings in the Chamber of the House of Commons (and, to a lesser extent, for peers to do so in the House of Lords) – that is, at Question Time, following Ministerial statements and during debates. Yet the scope for effective Parliamentary influence in such proceedings – through challenge, criticism and attack – is limited by the ability of most competent Ministers to answer points in the House without revealing any new or substantial information if they do not want to do so. Experience also shows that such proceedings are often rather an empty ritual, since any attempt at a strong Parliamentary challenge usually gives way to mere party-political point-scoring. Also, invariably the media have discovered (or been briefed about) the points at issue long before Parliament gets its chance, in effect reducing the impact of Parliament.

Secondly, there are the opportunities for MPs and peers to probe Ministerial thinking and Government policy during Select Committee investigations and during the committee stage of Government Bills. These have proved to be somewhat more effective mechanisms for Parliamentary influence. Yet, in the former case, the usefulness of such investigations is limited by an unwillingness often shown by Governments to act on the findings of Select Committees and occasionally even to allow key Ministerial or official witnesses to appear before the Committee at all.[13] In the latter case, legislative scrutiny by the Opposition in Standing Committees has to be set against the normal voting power of the Government majority, both in the Committees and subsequently on the floor of the House at Report and Third Reading. Such proceedings provide a form of Parliamentary accountability and influence, but not effective Parliamentary control, unless, of course, the Government of the day has a relatively small or no majority in the Commons or a large enough number of its own backbenchers feel inclined to rebel.

Thirdly, there are the various opportunities for MPs and peers to use their power of publicity to dramatise the errors of Ministers or the shortcomings of Government policy. The principal effect of this form of Parliamentary accountability has been to encourage an attitude of defensiveness on the part of civil servants and to reinforce the tendency for Whitehall Departments to play safe in the conduct of Government business. Indeed, it is the capricious and unpredictable quality of such Parliamentary accountability which has led both Ministers and officials to treat it with wary respect. This has had a marked influence on attitudes and working practices in Whitehall and has sometimes discouraged bold or imaginative decision making by Ministers. It may, therefore, have lowered the quality of decision making in British central Government.

Thus, if we examine the various forms of Parliamentary accountability, we discover that none of them has proved to be a guarantee of representative and responsible Government. The lack of proper accountability has been most marked in the detailed areas of policy covered by Statutory Instruments, the secondary legislation which is drafted by civil servants in the name of Ministers and lawfully implemented under the authority of existing statutes. In effect, legislation of this type is no longer within the realm of effective Parliamentary control. Although there is a Joint Committee of the Lords and Commons which has the task of overseeing the spate of secondary legislation which pours out of Whitehall, the problem has really become unmanageable now that there are more than 2000 Statutory Instruments issued each year. The volume of such secondary legislation and the shortcomings of existing Parliamentary procedures for dealing with it are such that genuine Parliamentary accountability is really unattainable.

The other notable area in which Parliamentary accountability is clearly defective is that of *European Legislation*. Under the 1972 European Communities Act the

British Government is obliged to implement automatically the *Regulations* issued by the European Commission, notably in the spheres of agriculture, trade and competition policy, and to find appropriate national means of carrying out the *Directives* which flow from decisions taken by the Council of Ministers. In 1974 both the House of Commons and the House of Lords established special Select Committees to sift draft European legislation and to make recommendations as to whether or not the various items contained therein were sufficiently important to merit a debate on the floor of their respective Chambers. As things have turned out, such debates (in the House of Commons at any rate) are normally brief and late at night, if and when the 'usual channels' find time for them at all. In some cases it has not even proved possible to find time to debate a particular draft European proposal before it is considered by the Council of Ministers or before it is promulgated by the Commission as directly applicable European legislation. This means that it may well become law in Britain before there has been any consideration of its merits or otherwise by MPs on the floor of the House of Commons or by peers on the floor of the House of Lords.

One answer to the problem of insufficient Parliamentary accountability in this area of Executive action is for the tasks of scrutiny to be performed by the directly elected European Parliament which does have some enlarged rights of 'co-decision' with the other European institutions in specific areas of European Union activity. Yet this is not a complete answer, and in any case many of the national Parliaments remain jealous of their historic rights to legislate and to hold Ministers to account. The result is that there is what has been called a 'democratic deficit' in the European Union which could be closed either by a great leap forward towards fuller political integration in Europe with much greater powers for the European Parliament, or by a dramatic reassertion of democratic control by national Parliaments which seems both unlikely and possibly unattainable.[14] Other possible solutions would be to make at least some British Members of the European Parliament also members of the House of Lords; or for the member states to create a second Chamber of the European Parliament, made up of members drawn proportionately from the national Parliaments.

In reflecting generally upon the history of Parliamentary accountability in Britain since the Second World War, we must conclude that it has been notable more for the tendency of Ministers to escape the shackles of real accountability than for the ability of Parliament to impose its will and control on Ministers.[15] While there were the celebrated cases of the Crichel Down affair in 1954 and the Argentinian invasion of the Falkland Islands in 1982, each of which led to the resignation of the Cabinet Minister considered most culpable, in modern times such cases have seemed to be exceptions to the general rule that Ministers and civil servants can make grievous mistakes without ever really being subjected to full and effective Parliamentary accountability. They may get sacked later on when the heat has died down and the public attention has turned elsewhere, yet at the relevant time when they ought to be held strictly to account in Parliament, Ministers are often able to get away with suffering no more than Parliamentary and media censure because their own party colleagues rally to their support. On the other hand, if they lose such collective support – and particularly the backing of the Prime Minister – they have to go, as witnessed by a number of high profile resignations in the period 1997–99.

13.3 The problems of Government

The problems of Government vary from Department to Department and from time to time. The key question which has to be faced by all Governments is whether or not Ministers are really in full control of their Departments and therefore able to give the necessary political impetus to the Government as a whole. In this section we shall examine some of the problems which make it hard to give a convincing, affirmative answer to this basic question.

Ministerial workload

As touched upon previously, one major problem of British central Government is the heavy workload which Ministers have to bear, especially Cabinet Ministers in charge of large Departments such as Defence, Social Security or Environment, Transport and the Regions. The very size, scope and complexity of such Departments militate against the idea that senior Ministers can readily dominate or control every aspect of their Department's activities. Yet this is what they are expected to do, notwithstanding the extra requirements imposed by the insatiable demands of the modern media and the growing obligations of European Union membership. Indeed, in view of the collegiate nature of Cabinet government in Britain, it is a problem with which all senior Ministers have to cope to a greater or lesser extent.

One way of lightening the burden on Ministers has been to reduce the size of the public sector. This occurred from 1979 as a result of the policy of privatisation pursued by successive Conservative Governments. By 1997 this had reduced the state industrial sector by about two-thirds compared with its size when the Conservatives came to office. Thus the areas of activity for which Ministers are held directly responsible has diminished, even if the extent to which the general public seems to blame Ministers for things which go wrong has increased with the growing politicisation of daily life in Britain largely as a result of the relentless activity of the media.

Another possibility would be to reduce the range of tasks which Ministers are expected to perform – for example, by relieving them of their constituency duties as in France, or their responsibilities for the administration of policy as in Sweden. While the former idea may seem unthinkable in Britain, because back-benchers like to ensure that Ministers have to encounter and deal with the same constituency problems as themselves, considerable progress has been made towards implementation of the latter idea with the establishment of so many Departmental Agencies to do the run-of-the-mill administrative tasks previously done by Departments.

Of course, the problems of Ministerial workload are exacerbated by some of the conventions of central Government in Britain, notably the assumption that Ministers will consult widely and systematically before taking major decisions or introducing important new legislation. Admittedly, many of these consultations with interest groups and relevant experts are conducted by civil servants on behalf of Ministers. Yet Ministers still have to lay down the political guidelines for such discussions and in the most important cases often have to take a leading part in them as well. A balanced solution to the problem would take account of all these factors. Yet no matter which solutions are adopted, Ministers will always require great personal energy and strong political will in order to perform all their tasks successfully.

Departmental policy

Another major problem of central Government is the continuously powerful influence of established Departmental policy. This may not make itself felt very much during the first year or two of a Government's term of office, but it can assume considerable importance as time goes by if the political momentum of the party in office begins to falter. This phenomenon was particularly noticeable during the period of the postwar consensus from 1945 to 1973 and especially in the well-established Departments with long traditions and considerable self-confidence, such as the Foreign Office or the Home Office. Yet the outcome of disputes between Ministers and civil servants has never been a foregone conclusion. Much depends upon whether Ministers individually – and notably the Prime Minister – are determined to carry out their policies and to impose their authority on the Government. If they are so determined, both the realities of political power and the conventions of Whitehall enable them to get their own way whatever the personal preferences or reservations of senior civil servants. If they are not so determined, then the underlying strength of Departmental policy may triumph in the end.

The strength of Departmental policy, or at least the influence of senior civil servants, is enhanced by the habits of Ministerial life. This is because it has been customary for Prime Ministers to shift Ministers and move them from post to post quite frequently, sometimes simply to assert Prime Ministerial authority, but usually to broaden the experience of their most promising Ministerial colleagues. Typically, a Cabinet Minister holds office for about two and a half years and most Secretaries of State last only two years in a particular post.[16] However, these figures mask the fact that there are considerable differences between Departments. For example, between 1964 and 1998 there were only seven Lords Chancellor, but 22 Secretaries of State at the Department of Trade and Industry. Hence many Ministers are precluded from making anything more than a temporary or marginal impact upon the political issues with which their Departments have to deal.

The strength of Departmental policy is also enhanced by the habits of Civil Service life. This is because it has been customary to move civil servants in the higher administrative grades frequently from one job to another both within a single Department and sometimes between Departments. In many instances this means that key administrative staff may stay in post for only a year or two, with the result that they do not really have time to develop their own expertise in the policy area concerned. This happens mainly for reasons of career development and is largely for the benefit of those who have been identified as 'high flyers' early in their Civil Service careers. Although an able civil servant is very good at breaking into new policy areas – after all this is one of the professional skills which mark them out as 'high flyers' – nevertheless, the inevitable consequence is that even the best civil servants rely heavily upon their Departmental 'experts' and especially upon what is already in the Departmental filing cabinets – in other words the accumulated wisdom of established Departmental policy. Such tendencies can only be overcome by sustained political will on the part of Ministers and significant changes in Civil Service career development policy, changes which have already begun to come about.

The quality of advice

Another problem of central Government is the quality of official information and advice available to Ministers. While such material is a source of strength for Ministers in relation to the Opposition and all back-benchers, it does not necessarily strengthen their position within their own Departments. This is because it is not unusual for politicians who become Ministers to be posted to a Department about which they know little or nothing in advance and which deals with areas of policy of which they have had little or no previous experience.[17] Even when Ministers appoint expert personal advisers from outside the Civil Service, such outsiders are likely to be 'domesticated' by their Department and are unlikely, on their own, to be able to provide their Minister with sufficiently weighty countervailing advice to match or defeat the established Departmental view. The result is that, unless Ministers are engaged in the implementation of clear Manifesto commitments or are pushing through other forms of unambiguous party policy, they are seldom provided with a sufficiently compelling view of the available alternatives to existing policy and are therefore often obliged to rely on the advice from their Departmental civil servants, and will tend to do so provided they are convinced that it will persuade the Cabinet and Parliament.

This is an unfortunate state of affairs for two reasons. First, the best answers to many of the most difficult problems of central Government are not necessarily to be found either in the liturgy of party Manifestos or in the drawers of Departmental filing cabinets. Secondly, and often for partisan political reasons, the policy and decision-making process can be deprived of a good deal of high-quality information and advice from 'outsiders' who are both expert in their field and independent of Government. Some of this has changed with the tendency for Prime Ministers to hold all-day seminars and other 'brainstorming' sessions at Chequers or 10 Downing Street. It has also been modified by the growth in the number, although not necessarily the quality, of so-called 'special advisers' working directly for senior Ministers.[18] Yet there is undoubtedly still room for the quality and breadth of advice available to Ministers to be improved with task forces, special commissions and other devices.

13.4 Conclusion

Well-qualified observers of British politics and some distinguished practitioners have argued for years about whether Ministers are really in control of their Departments. As long ago as the 1850s Lord Palmerston wrote to Queen Victoria: 'Your Majesty will see how greatly such a system [of government] must place in the hands of the subordinate members of public Departments [civil servants] the power of directing the policy and the measures of the Government, because the value, tendency and consequence of a measure frequently depends as much upon the manner in which it was worked out [that is, administered] as the intention and spirit with which it was planned.'[19] This was one of the earliest and most perceptive statements of the now familiar argument that in the process of government the power to administer can be as important as the power to decide. In other words, civil servants can have nearly as much effective power as Ministers, even though the constitutional conventions do not admit it.

On the other hand, Herbert Morrison wrote in the 1950s that 'if the Minister in charge [of a Department] knows what he wants and is intelligent in going about it, he can command the understanding, co-operation and support of his civil servants'.[20] This statement from a senior Labour Minister with Departmental experience dating back to before the Second World War could be interpreted as an affirmation of Ministerial dominance in Whitehall. Yet it could also be interpreted as a back-handed compliment to the power of the civil service and a warning that Whitehall officials tend to fill any vacuum which may be left by Ministers. Clearly it is necessary to refine the conventional statement that Ministers decide the policy and civil servants simply carry it out. The contemporary realities are more subtle, and the traditional model takes insufficient account of the complexities of modern Government.

What we see is an *interdependent working relationship*. Civil servants look to Ministers to be clear about the policy objectives they wish to pursue, to heed advice on their likely consequences and methods of implementation, to be able to carry their Ministrial colleagues with them (including notably the Prime Minister and the Chancellor of the Exchequer), and to present a convincing case for the policy to Parliament, the media and the general public. Ministers look to senior civil servants to be responsive to their political directions, to provide prompt, accurate, candid, clear and constructive advice on policy, and to manage the administration of policy and the Department itself under overall Ministerial guidance.

A case can be made for radical changes in the positions of both Ministers and civil servants – and indeed the Major Government's reforms of the Civil Service had a significant impact on the traditional assumptions of central Government in Britain. However, the administrative continuity and the political impartiality which still characterise the British Civil Service provide a healthy antidote to the Ministerial system of party government which can involve at different times both partisan dogma and political indecision.

In modern political conditions it is, of course, possible for Ministers to exercise clear leadership, but this has usually become less likely as each General Election has receded further into the past. In this respect Margaret Thatcher and her senior Ministerial colleagues were distinctly unusual and might be regarded as one of the exceptions which prove the rule. Senior Ministers may believe that they are in complete charge of their Departments. Yet Civil Service control of official advice to Ministers, the long time-scale and great complexity of decision making in Government, and the limited scope for truly autonomous political action – especially if attempted purely at national level – all tend to reduce the impact and effect of Ministerial leadership. The broad conclusion must be that Ministers may be in charge of their Departments and of the Government as a whole, but usually within the limits set by established administrative procedures and the uncompromising political and economic realities in Britain and abroad.

Suggested questions

1   Describe the structure and work of British central Government.
2   The tradition that Ministers take the political decisions and civil servants carry them out has long been overtaken by reality. What factors give rise to such a view and how valid are they?

3   What are the problems of British central Government? Are they capable of solution within existing institutions and conventions?

Notes

1. See 'Report of the Committee on the Machinery of Government', Cd 9230 (London: HMSO, 1918).
2. The *Lord President of the Council* is formally responsible for the Privy Council Office and takes charge at the infrequent formal meetings of the Privy Council, while the only remaining formal task of the *Lord Privy Seal* is to arrange Royal Proclamations. The formal responsibilities of the *Chancellor of the Duchy of Lancaster* is for the general administration of the Duchy of Lancaster estates and revenues, but the real work is done by the professional staff concerned.
3. W.I. Jennings, *Cabinet Government,* 3rd edn (London: Cambridge University Press, 1959), p. 133.
4. See: 'The Report of the Sierra Leone Arms Investigation' (1016) (London: Stationary Office, 1998) (The Legg Report).
5. Cited in P. Kellner and Lord Crowther-Hunt, *The Civil Servants* (London: Macdonald, 1980), pp. 215–16.
6. See R. Rose, 'Too much Reshuffling of the Cabinet Pack?', *IEA Inquiry No. 27* (London: IEA, 1991).
7. The conventional wisdom on this matter has been significantly eroded in modern times by the fact that all recent Governments have, to some extent, abandoned the pure theory of Ministerial responsibility. The point was very well made by the late David Watt at the time of the 1986 Westland crisis when he wrote: 'if Ministers allow blame to rest with individual, identifiable civil servants, they must expect two consequences: critics of Government actions will hold officials publicly responsible; and the civil servant will claim, and deserve, the right to defend himself in public, if necessary by shifting blame back on the Minsters' (*The Times,* 7 February 1986).
8. See Chapter 14 pages 351–358.
9. See I.F. Nicolson, *The Mystery of Crichel Down* (Oxford: Oxford University Press, 1986) and J. Griffith, 'Crichel Down, The Most Famous Farm in British Constitutional History', Contemporary Record, Vol. 1, No. 1, Spring 1987 pp. 35–40.
10. See Lord Carrington, *Reflect on Things Past* (London: Collins, 1988), pp. 348–72.
11. See J. Prior, *A Balance of Power* (London: Hamish Hamilton, 1986), pp. 232–3, and W. Whitelaw, *The Whitelaw Memoirs* (London: Anrum Press, 1989), pp. 211–13.
12. See M. Thatcher, *The Downing Street Years* (London: HarperCollins, 1993), p. 403.
13. For example, when the Expenditure Select Committee sought to cross-examine Labour Ministers on public financial support for Chrysler UK in the 1970s, the then Prime Minister, James Callaghan, prevented any of his Cabinet colleagues from appearing before the Committee. Equally not all the key official witnesses were permitted by Margaret Thatcher when Prime Minister to testify before Select Committees in the wake of the 1986 Westland crisis.

    Select Committees have also been denied access to material. For example, during their 1995–96 investigation into whether the Conservative MP and BMARC Director Jonathan Aitken knew whether the company was selling naval cannon to Iraq, the DTI Select Committee was denied access to classified intelligence documents.
14. In 1989 the House of Commons began belatedly to address this problem when the Select Committee on Procedure considered the matter and issued a cautious report entitled 'Scrutiny of European Legislation', H.C. 622, 1988–89, Vols. I and II. See also the Government's response: 'Scrutiny of European Legislation', Cmnd 1081 (London: HMSO, 1990).

15. See A.H. Birch, *Representative and Responsible Government* (London: Allen & Unwin, 1964), pp. 141–8; J. Bruce-Gardyne and N. Lawson, *The Power Game* (London: Macmillan, 1976), pp. 10–37; and S. James, *British Cabinet Government* (London: Routledge, 1992), pp. 5–10.
16. See R. Rose, 'Too much Reshuffling of the Cabinet Pack?', *IEA Inquiry No. 27* (London: IEA, 1991).
17. As Harold Macmillan laconically observed in 1955 when moving – after only eight months – from the Foreign Office to the Treasury: 'After a few months learning geography I've got to learn arithmetic.' See N. Fisher, *Harold Macmillan* (London: Weidenfeld & Nicolson, 1982), p. 154.
18. In 1998 some 24 Ministers – excluding the Prime Minister – had a total of 51 special advisers.
19. Quoted in H. Parris, *Constitutional Bureaucracy* (London: Allen & Unwin, 1969), p. 114.
20. H. Morrison, *Government and Parliament* (London: Oxford University Press, 1959), p. 311.

Further reading

Birch, A.H., *Representative and Responsible Government* (London: Allen & Unwin, 1964).
Bruce-Gardyne, J., *Minsters and Mandarins* (London: Sidgwick & Jackson, 1986).
Drewry, G. and Butcher, T., *The Civil Service Today* (2nd edn), (Oxford: Basil Blackwell, 1991).
Hennessy, P., *Cabinet* (Oxford: Basil Blackwell, 1986).
Hennessy, P., *Whitehall* (2nd edn) (London: Fontana, 1990).
James, S., *British Cabinet Government* (London: Routledge, 1992).
Kaufman, G., *How to be a Minister* (London: Faber & Faber, 1997).
Kellner, P. and Crowther-Hunt, Lord, *The Civil Servants* (London: Macdonald, 1980).
Nairne, P., *The Civil Service: Ministers and Mandarins* (Barnstaple: Philip Charles Media, 1990).
Thompson, B. and Ridley, F.F. (eds), *Under The Scott-Light* (Oxford: Oxford University Press, 1997).
Young, H. and Sloman, A., *No Minister* (London: BBC, 1982).
Young, H. and Sloman A., *But, Chancellor* (London: BBC, 1984).

Websites

Cabinet Office   http://www.number–10.gov.uk
Treasury   http://www.hmt.gov.uk
Home Office   http://www.homeoffice.gov.uk
Department of Social Security   http://www.dss.gov.uk
Department of Trade and Industry   http://www.dti.gov.uk

⬡14 The Civil Service

In Britain the standard definition of a civil servant is still based on the one which was formulated by the Tomlin Commission in 1931, namely 'a servant of the Crown employed in a civil capacity who is paid wholly and directly from money voted by Parliament'.[1] In April 1997 this definition covered 475,339 permanent staff, (down from a high of more than 751,000 in 1976). Of this total 439,311 were non-industrial Civil Servants and 36,028 were industrial civil servants, 87 per cent of whom were employed by the Ministry of Defence. A total of 19,316 were casual staff. Some 48 per cent of the total were women (as opposed to 25 per cent in 1967), 5.4 per cent were from ethnic minorities and fewer than 20 per cent lived in London (contrasting with 50 per cent in 1967). By 1998 nearly 77 per cent of civil servants were working in executive agencies (see pp. 358–364), 159 of which had been created between 1988 and 1998, 139 of which were in existence in 1998.[2]

In this chapter we are concerned mainly with the civil servants who work directly for Ministers and more especially with those in the 'Senior Civil Service', a category created in 1996 and consisting of those at the old Grade 5 (Assistant Secretary) and above who are closely involved in policy work, some 3000 individuals. We are therefore considering the administrative elite at the heart of British central Government (popularly known as 'Whitehall' after the street in the centre of London in which a number of Government Departments have their headquarters).

14.1 Composition and functions

The 21 Departments in Whitehall vary greatly in size, mission and character. For example, the Treasury with 888 civil servants is the most powerful and prestigious Department in British central Government and has the endlessly difficult tasks of controlling public spending and advising the Chancellor of the Exchequer on economic policy; whereas the Ministry of Defence with 77,949 non-industrial civil servants has the tasks of ensuring civilian control of the nation's military effort and providing civilian support for the armed forces. Indeed, the three largest Departments in terms of personnel are Defence, Social Security (93,030) and the Inland Revenue (54,029), which together employ 52 per cent of the total number of civil servants. In terms of public expenditure the most significant Departments are Social Security, Health, Education and Employment, and Defence – with the last one now lower down the spending league following the end of the Cold War.

The variety of public bodies which exist today within the Whitehall orbit is wide and complex. Indeed, as has been pointed out: 'There are Departments of Government; Departments within Departments (such as the Department of Transport – which has its own Cabinet Minister); non-Ministerial Departments (such as the Charity Commission); Agencies (such as the Benefits Agency); Agencies within Agencies (such as the Government Property Lawyers); non-Departmental public bodies which call themselves "Agencies" (such as the Environment Agency); non-Departmental public bodies which don't call themselves "Agencies" (such as the Countryside Commission); there are advisory bodies (such as the Inland Waterways Amenity Advisory Committee); and there are regulatory bodies (such as OFTEL).'[3] By no means all of these structures are new, but the wide variety of structures which exists just serves to illustrate the complexity and intricacy of the structures within which civil servants work.

In a typical Department (if we can assume such a thing), perhaps half of the civil servants are involved in the administrative tasks of central Government, while the remainder perform a range of technical, scientific and support tasks. In central Government as a whole around 20,000 civil servants are involved in the policy and decision-making process at the centre of the various Departments, although of these only some 3000 at the most senior levels have close and frequent contacts with Ministers. It is this small elite which has set the conventions of Whitehall and determined much of the character of the Civil Service in Britain.

The personnel

In the higher administrative grades of the British Civil Service the traditional dominance of experienced 'generalists' still holds sway – that is, civil servants recruited largely in their twenties on the basis of their personal qualities and general academic attainments rather than any specialist skills (for example, as scientists, economists, or lawyers). This influences both the character and the quality of the service at every level and there are three traditional reasons for it: firstly, the Civil Service has not completely escaped from the long-lasting influence of the 1854 Northcote-Trevelyan Report which defined the role of civil servants as being 'to advise, assist, and to some extent influence those who are set over them from time to time'[4] (that is, Ministers). The legacy of this seminal view of the Civil Service is that in the Senior Civil Service no particular value has been placed upon the possession of specialist skills, except the skills of public administration and of working effectively with Ministers, which are considered to be best acquired mainly by experience in the job.

Second, there has traditionally been a disdain for technical expertise which was well expressed by Lord Bridges (Secretary to the Cabinet between 1938 and 1947) when he defined a good civil servant as someone 'who knows how and where to find reliable knowledge, can assess the expertise of others at its true worth, can spot the strong and weak points in any situation at short notice, and can advise on how to handle a complex situation'.[5] As the saying goes, the experts are supposed to be on tap but not on top. However, specialists now have considerable influence in a number of Departments and many generalist policy makers spend much of their career in a single Department, thus developing substantial expertise in its work.

Third, there has been a traditional tendency for the young recruits into the administrative grades to come disproportionately from middle-class family backgrounds and to have arts degrees from Oxford or Cambridge. Certainly this was true when the composition of the Civil Service was analysed for the Fulton Committee in 1967.[6] It appeared still to be true in the 1970s and 1980s when similar analyses were done.[7] However, in more recent times considerable effort has been made to recruit into the Senior Civil Service people from universities other than Oxford and Cambridge, more women, and more people from ethnic minorities. This has been facilitated in no small part by the introduction in the 1990s of open competition, with more and more vacancies to positions within the Senior Civil Service being advertised publicly and filled by open competition rather than by internal promotion as previously.[8] Nevertheless it is still true that those who are appointed to the most influential positions in the Civil Service are very much the product of the values and outlook of those who have such influence over their appointment. Consequently, the character of the top Civil Service is likely to change only slowly. Figure 14.1 provides information on Civil Service staffing levels.

Figure 14.1 Civil Service staffing levels

(a) *Civil Service staff in post at 1 April 1997 by full/part-time etc.*

| Head count | Permanent staff | | | Casual staff |
| | Total | of which | | Total |
		Agencies	All on next steps lines	
Non-industrial	439,311	262,736	341,366	17,944
Industrial	36,028	22,798	22,797	1,372
Total	475,339	285,534	364,163	19,316

(b) *Civil Service permanent staff in post at 1 April 1997 by gender*

Head count	Male	Female	Total
Non-industrial full-time	221,358	182,957	404,315
Non-industrial part-time	3,236	51,724	54,970
Non-industrial total	224,594	234,681	459,285
Industrial full-time	30,794	4,463	35,257
Industrial part-time	152	1,135	1,287
Industrial total	30,946	5,598	36,544
All full-time	252,152	187,420	439,572
All part-time	3,388	52,859	56,247
Total	255,540	240,279	495,819

Figure 14.1 continued

(c) *Civil Service staff in post at 1 April 1997 by responsibility level and gender*

Head count	Male	Female	Total
Senior Civil Service level	3,160	540	3,700
Level 6	4,000	800	4,800
Level 7	12,060	2,880	14,940
Senior Executive Officer level	18,190	4,480	22,660
Higher Executive Officer level	33,980	13,780	47,750
Executive Officer level	58,700	49,130	107,830
Administrative Officer level	68,120	98,960	167,080
Administrative Assistant level	25,210	45,330	70,540
Total (all non-industrial staff)	223,410	215,890	439,310

Source: Civil Service Yearbook, 1998

Main functions

The main functions of those within the Senior Civil Service can be summarised as:

- informing and advising Ministers;
- helping them to formulate policy and, if it involves legislation, to get it through Parliament;
- carrying out the ensuing administrative tasks;
- representing Ministers in meetings with and dealing with Ministers' correspondence from other Departments, interest groups and members of the public;
- managing the bureaucratic machine of central Government.

Civil servants are the main source of information and advice for Ministers. When Ministers need to know something or have to prepare for a meeting, make a speech, answer questions in Parliament or on the media, it is the civil servants in their own Departments (and sometimes in other Departments as well) who provide the necessary informmation and advice. Usually this is provided in writing in the form of background briefs or other internal memoranda. It is often supplemented (or even replaced) by oral information and advice given at internal Departmental meetings, since this can be quicker in an emergency and some Ministers prefer to be briefed in this way. On the whole, civil servants do not produce original work for these purposes, since they have neither the time nor the aptitude for the research upon which such work would have to be based. They therefore act essentially as filters and interpreters of existing information and advice which they derive mainly from Departmental sources and accessible outside experts whose discretion can be trusted.

Civil servants help Ministers to formulate policy and to make decisions by presenting them with option papers which usually encompass a range of possibilities and policy recommendations. They also provide most of the information and advice against which Ministers can test the soundness or otherwise of their own ideas and their party political commitments. The complex role of civil servants in the policy and decision making process is described more fully in Chapter 19.

Civil servants carry out the administrative tasks of central Government in accordance with the political guidelines laid down in Ministerial decisions. If this is not possible in certain cases when new situations arise, reference is usually made to the appropriate Minister or Ministers for further policy instructions. Although the administration of policy can be as important as the actual decisions made by Ministers, civil servants (and now the staff of Executive Agencies as well) are supposed to avoid action or inaction which embarrasses Ministers or prejudices Ministerial decisions. On the whole they seek faithfully to carry out the policies and decisions which they have helped Ministers to produce.

Civil servants have an important role as representatives of Ministers at meetings in Whitehall and elsewhere. These may be meetings with officials from other Departments, with the spokesmen of various pressure groups or with members of the general public. On occasions civil servants may speak on behalf of Ministers within the carefully defined limits of established policy – for example, when giving evidence to a Select Committee or taking part in an inter-Departmental committee – and they write numerous letters, memoranda and circulars on behalf of the Ministers for whom they work. On some occasions civil servants may state their Department's position in somewhat speculative terms if they are involved in exercises of 'kite-flying' or devil's advocacy in order to test some aspect of the conventional wisdom or the likely media response to a particular policy idea. Normally there is a clear distinction between the latitude allowed to them in the privacy of internal Whitehall meetings with Ministers and other civil servants, and the orthodox and cautious way in which they are supposed to reflect Government policy in meetings or written communications with outsiders.

Finally, there is the very important function of senior civil servants, namely that of *seeing that the machinery of central Government is managed in an efficient and cost-effective way*. This has long been one of the principal functions of those at the very top of the Civil Service (at Permanent Secretary and Deputy Secretary levels), but it assumed greater prominence during the years of Conservative Government between 1979 and 1997 because Ministers attached greater importance to it. Indeed, the spread of Executive Agencies since 1988 (see pp. 358–364 for more details) has been one of the most significant manifestations of the drive for greater efficiency and cost-effectiveness in the delivery of public services. As of April 1998 there were 139 such bodies in existence charged with the delivery of services to the public and in general they have proved to be a more businesslike, if sometimes controversial, way of meeting the objectives of Government policy.

Ever since the implementation of the Northcote-Trevelyan reforms in the second half of the nineteenth century, the Permanent Secretary of each Department has had to take personal responsibility as the senior official for the management of the Department and to act as its Accounting Officer. Each Accounting Officer is responsible for the complete activity and expenditure of the Department concerned within financial limits agreed each year by the Cabinet and central guidance provided by the Treasury and the Office of Public Service on financial management and personnel matters. Indeed, the efficient management of the Civil Service was regarded by the Thatcher Administration (1979–90) as being of such importance that at one time all senior Ministers were urged by the Prime Minister (often without much success, it must be said) to play a direct and continuous part in the management of their

Departments alongside their Permanent Secretaries. On the whole this rather revolutionary idea did not appeal to busy Ministers preoccupied with their political responsibilities or to the most senior officials who felt that it was an invasion of their territory. It was, therefore, not very surprising that by 1990 the emphasis of Government policy was switched towards implementing the Agency principle which has devolved both management and public accountability to a much greater extent than before onto the shoulders of Permanent Secretaries and Agency Chief Executives.

To summarise: the Civil Service in Britain today has at least five distinct but interconnected functions to perform. These are the analysis of policy issues, the formulation of policy under Ministerial direction, the implementation of decisions once taken by Ministers, the delivery of services to the general public, and the management of public resources.[9] Whereas traditionally the higher administrative grades were involved almost exclusively in the first three functions, they were drawn more deeply into the last two by successive Conservative Administrations during the period 1979–97.

Figure 14.2   The Civil Service – important dates

1853	The Northcote–Trevelyon Report on The Organisation of the Permanent Civil Service
1931	The Tomlin Commission Report on The Civil Service
1955	The Priestley Commission Report on The Civil Service
1961	The Plowden Committee Report on the control of public expenditure
1968	The Fulton Committee Report on The Civil Service
1968	Civil Service Department (CSD) established
1970	White Paper, 'The Reorganisation of Central Government'
1971	The Central Policy Review Staff (CPRS) set up within the Cabinet Office
1975	Policy Unit established
1979	Efficiency Unit established under Sir Derek – later Lord – Rayner
1980	The Pliatzky Report on non-Departmental public bodies
1981	Civil Service Department abolished
1982	White Paper, 'Efficiency and Effectiveness' and the launch of the Financial Management Initiative (FMI)
1983	The Central Policy Review Staff abolished
1987	Office of the Minister for the Civil Service established
1988	Publication of the Ibbs Report 'Improving Management in Government: The Next Steps' and the beginning of the process of 'agencification'
1994	White Paper, 'The Civil Service: Continuity and Change'
1995	White Paper, 'The Civil Service: Taking Forward Continuity and Change'
1998	White Paper, 'Better Government'

14.2 Key issues

There are several key issues in the continuing debate about the Civil Service in Britain today. In this section we shall concentrate on those which have had a significant effect upon the development of the British political system. Accordingly, we shall begin by considering some of the most influential Whitehall conventions and ways of working, and then go on to review the strengths and weaknesses of the service, including the issues raised by the nature and limits of civil servants' loyalty to Ministers. In nearly all cases we shall discover that it is not sensible to generalise about the role of civil servants, since they perform very different functions in relation to Ministers and the general public respectively.

Whitehall conventions

The Civil Service in Britain works within established conventions which have shaped its practices for many years.[10] Foremost among these are:

- support of Ministers both individually and collectively;
- accountability through Ministers to Parliament;
- integrity and objectivity in advice and service delivery;
- political impartiality at all times;
- equitable treatment of citizens under the law;
- selection and promotion on merit without political patronage or interference.

Senior civil servants tend to see their main role and duty as the support of Ministers in those areas of Departmental business to which Ministers attach import-ance. This means that in the past they have tended to give a higher priority to servicing the needs of their Ministers on matters of policy and assisting them in their dealings with Parliament, the media and the public than to meeting the managerial require-ments of running their Departments.[11] The tasks of bureaucratic management and control have tended to be seen as rather tedious and unattractive chores by most of the talented officials who have reached the top of the Civil Service over the years. Both the Thatcher and the Major Administrations set out to change this rather grand attitude with the result that senior civil servants were obliged to adopt more of the so-called 'new managerialism' both within their Departments and in dealings with the general public under the rubric of the *Citizen's Charter* originally set out by John Major in July 1991.[12] However, notwithstanding the significance of these developments, policy advice for Ministers still has to come first when it is really needed, especially if Ministers are faced with urgent demands from Parliament or the media.

Another well-established convention is that civil servants should take their instructions only from their superiors in their own Departments or sometimes directly from Ministers, but not from anyone else. This means that the lines of authority and reporting are strictly vertical and that to get anything new done in a Department of central Government it is usually necessary for Ministers, either directly or through officials, to give the initial policy instructions, or at least to indicate to civil servants that a possible alternative policy can be examined. This tends to put considerable burdens on the Ministers themselves and on the officials working most closely with them in their Private Offices. It means that if the Minister concerned is not an innova-tor or is very cautious, quite senior officials elsewhere in the Department may be quite lightly employed for considerable periods. It also underlines the fact that without a clear and decisive lead from Ministers, Departments are not usually very good at shaping a new agenda or responding to events speedily or with imagination.

Another well-established convention is that the administration of policy should be carried out according to the highest standards of probity and equity, while at the same time avoiding any form of political embarrassment for Ministers. This last consideration has often put a premium on a rather defensive and cautious approach to policy and decision making with particular emphasis being laid on avoiding risk and trying to see that neither Parliament nor the media get too many opportunities to identify short-comings or failures in Government policy which could turn the public against the party in office.

Another fundamental convention in Whitehall, which might better be defined as an aspiration, is that the Government of the day should at all times have a coherent and defensible position on every policy issue with which it has to deal. This is regarded as a minimum requirement for satisfactory Cabinet government, which has to be based on the principle of collective responsibility. It means that a great deal of Civil Service time and effort is spent on producing agreed positions with which all Departments can concur, even if such positions may represent little more than a lowest common denomi-nator within Whitehall. Notwithstanding the sometimes Herculean efforts of the most influential civil servants to formulate agreed policy positions to which all Ministers can adhere, there are times when the pressure of events becomes too great for coherence and unity to be maintained – as was evident, for example, in some aspects of the Conservative Government's European policy in the 1990s, and has been evident with regard to certain aspects of welfare reform under the Labour Government since 1997.

Another insight into the problems which can arise when Departments struggle to agree policy between them and seek to keep these problems from the public gaze was provided by the controversy over arms-related exports to Iraq. Media revelations of the Matrix-Churchill affair in 1992 led the then Prime Minister, John Major, to estab-lish a public inquiry under Sir Richard Scott. Right from the beginning, the evidence given to the inquiry highlighted the way in which the highest standards in public life can be compromised when Ministers and senior civil servants assume that their definition of 'the public interest' should override all other considerations, including in this case the legal right of certain British businessmen involved in international trade with Iraq to conduct a full and effective defence against the arms-trading offences with which they were charged.[13]

Essentially, all these Whitehall conventions flow from traditional adherence to the twin principles of Ministerial responsibility and Parliamentary accountability. The former has always meant that senior civil servants regard the support of Ministers as their principal and overriding duty. The latter means that civil servants can be cau-tious, even unimaginative, in the way they perform their tasks. In both cases these conventions derive from assumptions long held by politicians and officials alike, and from the political imperatives of Parliamentary government.

Strengths and weaknesses

The British Civil Service has both strengths and weaknesses which stem mainly from the nature of British Parliamentary government and the people involved in it. In many cases the weaknesses are merely the counterparts of the strengths which have been widely recognised for many years. Since the position can be regarded from at least two contrasting angles, it is unwise to be dogmatic when making an assessment. In any case, the situation changed quite fast and significantly during the 1980s and 1990s, so judgements should be tentative and provisional rather than dogmatic and definitive because it could change again in future.

One obvious strength is *the intellectual and administrative ability of those in the higher grades of the Civil Service.* This reflects the high entry and selection standards for this group, and the continuing attractions of such a career for many of the ablest students from the universities. It also reflects the fact that the elite group of 'fast stream' graduate entrants (known as Trainees in Policy Management) quickly benefit from accelerated promotion to positions of responsibility in the Service. In general, the result of this recruitment policy has been the formation and continuing renewal of a small cadre of clever and competent people who become skilled practitioners in the art of public administration and whose main strengths are their ability to advise Ministers on policy and to carry out Ministerial decisions effectively.

On the other hand, it has been argued that this elite group has smooth and generalist qualities which are not necessarily the most appropriate for tackling the challenges of Government in the modern world. Unfavourable contrasts have been drawn with their opposite numbers in the higher grades of the French Civil Service, for example, who are seen by some to have the dual advantage of intellectual distinction and a more specialised technical training in the arts of public administration before they enter the public service.[14] Other criticisms have been levelled at Britain's bureaucratic elite by those on the Left of British politics who have complained about the socially and educationally unrepresentative composition of the group and have argued that the situation will not be satisfactory until such cadres are recruited from a much wider background.[15] However, the situation is changing and recent figures show a steady move towards a less exclusive profile among those who enter the Senior Civil Service.[16]

Another strength of the British Civil Service has been *the tradition of political impartiality and the ability to work satisfactorily for Ministers of very different political persuasions.* Although individual civil servants retain their own private political views, in their professional lives they have to carry out the policies of the Government of the day without complaint or obstruction (as long as Ministers act lawfully). Resignations from the Civil Service on policy or political grounds are therefore very rare, although a number of civil servants do leave the public service every year for the different challenges and often higher financial rewards of the private sector – for example, the Inland Revenue Inspectors who leave to join private accountancy firms.

On the other hand, there have been critics of the British Civil Service who have interpreted this acknowledged political impartiality as tantamount to patient and practised obstruction of the more radical purposes of democratically elected Governments. Complaints of this kind have been expressed on both the Left and the Right of British politics. On the Left, Tony Benn and others have made the point in speeches, articles and memoirs reflecting upon the experience of the 1974–79 Labour Government.[17] On the Right, Sir John Hoskyns (a businessman who was for a time Head of the Policy Unit under Margaret Thatcher) criticised civil servants for withholding the last five per cent of commitment to the policies of any Government in order to preserve their credentials for serving a future Government of a different political persuasion.[18] It would seem from such matching complaints that the Civil Service is at least even-handed in its instinct for political impartiality and against excessive enthusiasm. Yet we should also note that by the mid1990s after what was at the time more than 16 years of continuous Conservative Government, very different concerns were expressed to the effect that some civil servants might have allowed their impartiality to be compromised by becoming too accustomed to doing the bidding of one political party.[19] It should however be pointed out that the return of a Labour Government to office in 1997 after 18 years of Conservative Government did not suggest any such difficulty.

As for *the almost complete absence of corruption in the British Civil Service* (at any rate in the financial sense), this must obviously be regarded as a virtue by any measurement. With very few exceptions British civil servants have demonstrated over the years that they are people of the highest personal integrity who do not succumb to the temptations of bribery and corruption which damage the reputation of Governments in a number of other countries. It is local government in Britain which has been more vulnerable to such venality, mainly because it offers more opportunities for officials to do favours in return for personal financial gain.

Obviously no one would claim that the almost total absence of corruption in the British Civil Service is anything other than a great strength of the system. However, during the 1990s doubts were raised about whether more insidious forms of political corruption might have afflicted at least some senior civil servants and heads of Executive Agencies because of the unusually long period of government by one political party. Prior to 1997 critics in the Labour Party, as well as in academia and the media, were disturbed by what they saw as inappropriately zealous commitment to some of the more controversial Conservative policies, such as market testing or occasional privatisation of public services traditionally delivered only by public servants. Evidently such people would have been happier if civil servants had withheld at least the last few ounces of commitment to the policies of a Government which such critics strongly opposed. Having said this, however, they do not appear to have retained this view following the return of their own party to power in 1997.

Loyalty issues

The British Civil Service has long been admired for its sense of dedication and commitment to public duty. This is based on the traditional Civil Service ethic which holds that civil servants must be scrupulously correct in their dealings with Parliament and public alike. It reflects what has sometimes been described as the 'mandarin culture' of Whitehall which has been transmitted from the centre and the top to all parts and layers of the Service with varying degrees of success. In its most theoretical form it is based upon the belief that there is something which can be called 'the public interest' which is supposed to be defined by Ministers in the Government of the day, but which occasionally has to be defined and defended by senior civil servants (notably the Cabinet Secretary) when it seems to come under unreasonable political threat or when there is a tricky constitutional point on which it may be impossible for Ministers to take an objective view. In this respect very senior civil servants can find themselves obliged to perform delicate acts of constitutional arbitration – such as ruling on questions of proper conduct and procedure for Ministers – in a way which could be considered analogous to the duty of the Monarch and her advisers to define and defend the public interest against the possibility of reckless action by Ministers – for example, if the Prime Minister of the day were ever unreasonably to ask for a premature dissolution of Parliament at a time when there was no constitutional justification for it (see Chapter 9, pp. 217–19).

There are at least two different views of this aspect of the Civil Service ethos in Britain. One view is held by those who really do not trust any politicians in office – seemingly an increasingly widespread view in Britain – and who therefore welcome the existence of what might be described as bureaucratic stabilisers in the political system. In the eyes of such people, who include notably the managers of large companies and other modern technocrats, it is always preferable to have a high degree of continuity and predictability in Government policy and regulatory arrangements laid down by law. In so far as British politics is thought by such people and their sympathisers to have suffered from a surfeit of political ideology and polarisation in the 1970s and 1980s, they have often looked to the Civil Service to provide the stability and moderation which was thought to have been missing. It is the argument for what might be described as the gyroscopic role of the Civil Service – that is, its presumed ability to draw most policy and nearly all Governments back to the middle ground of British politics before too much damage can be done by radical extremists.[20]

Another view, which is held with equal vehemence by so-called 'conviction politicians' of the Left and the Right, is that the British political system must be based upon the principle of 'winner takes all' and that this means that whatever the shortcomings and foolishness of Ministers, they have an absolute democratic right to define the public interest at any time. Consequently, according to this view, it is the duty of civil servants simply to carry out their Ministers' wishes in the most effective way unless and until the latter are dismissed by the Prime Minister or the whole crew is sent packing by the voters at a General Election.

For most of the time this controversy does not arise in acute form, since civil servants are usually very adept at steering an appropriate middle course between these two points of view. However, there have been some notable occasions when Civil Service power within powerful Whitehall Departments has been very much in evidence. Possibly the most vivid and recurrent examples have been associated with the power and influence of the Home Office bureaucratic Establishment. In the 1950s at least two Conservative Home Secretaries were persuaded by their civil servants of the need to retain capital punishment for murder, notwithstanding the publicly declared abolitionist views of the Ministers concerned when they first took charge of the Department. Equally, in the late 1980s and early 1990s Home Office Ministers were persuaded by their civil servants of the case against custodial sentences for young offenders, notwithstanding the perennial commitment of nearly all Conservatives to greater emphasis upon retributive forms of justice. These two examples are made all the more telling by the fact that during the intervening period the 'penal policy Establishment' completely changed its bias from a retributive to a permissive position, and yet was able apparently to get its way on each occasion.

The idea of civil servants seeking to set their own definitions of the public interest above that of Ministers was best illustrated perhaps by the case of Clive Ponting, a senior civil servant in the Ministry of Defence, who in 1984 deliberately passed two classified documents concerning the sinking of the Argentinian cruiser *Belgrano* during the Falklands conflict to Tam Dalyell, a Labour back-bencher who had been hounding Ministers on the issue since 1982.[21] When this was discovered after a rigorous internal investigation in Whitehall, Clive Ponting was charged with a criminal offence under Section 2 (1) of the 1911 Official Secrets Act and taken to Court where he pleaded not guilty. The principal grounds of his defence were that it had been his duty 'in the interests of the state' to inform Parliament (in the person of Tam Dalyell), since Ministers had misled the House of Commons and the Select Committee investigating the matter was in danger of being misled as well. Although the trial judge said in his guidance to the jury that 'the interests of the state' were synonymous with the policies of the Government of the day, the jury evidently thought otherwise, as it found Clive Ponting not guilty.

For our purposes two main issues were highlighted by this interesting case. First, it had to be established whether civil servants have a legal right to communicate classified information against the wishes of Ministers on the grounds that they have a higher duty to see that Parliament and the public are not misled. Secondly, there was the question of whether civil servants have a professional duty to their own conceptions of 'the public interest' and if so, whether this can ever be regarded as superior to their duty to serve Ministers. In his summing up in the Ponting case, the judge argued against both these propositions, but the jury – and much of the media and public opinion – were more inclined to sympathise with the defendant's point of view. The outcome was a technical victory for Clive Ponting and a moral victory for all those who believe that the Government of the day has no monopoly right to define the public interest. Yet Ministers and the Government's supporters in the country were entitled to argue in reply that if a civil servant really feels unable on grounds of principle or conscience to accept a Ministerial decision, then the correct course of action is for the civil servant to resign rather than break the terms and conditions of employment.

In 1985 in the wake of the Ponting case the then Head of the Home Civil Service, Sir Robert Armstrong, drew up a guide for civil servants on their conduct in relation to Ministers. Entitled 'The Duties and Responsibilities of Civil Servants in Relation to Ministers', it became known as the Armstrong Memorandum. This was revised in 1987 and in 1993 incorporated into 'The Civil Service Management Code'. In 1996 a new Civil Service Code was introduced along lines suggested by the Treasury and Civil Service Select Committee in its influential report on the role of the Civil Service. This Code is outlined in Figure 14.3.

The public interest

It has always been difficult to define 'the public interest' in an objective and enduring way. As has already been pointed out, the traditional view in Britain is that it is for Ministers, who are accountable to Parliament, to define. It is rare for civil servants, such as Clive Ponting, who have been in direct and frequent contact with Ministers, to press their objections to the extent of knowingly breaking the law, because they know that their prime and overriding duty is to Ministers, provided the latter do not actually break the law.

In modern political conditions more frequent dilemmas arise in those cases in which the arguments for confidentiality and transparency clash. This was illustrated most vividly during the course of the Scott Inquiry into the so-called Matrix-Churchill affair.[22] In this case a few Ministers and civil servants were involved in secret efforts to circumvent the Government's own ban on arms sales to Iraq. This involved providing information both to Parliament and to the public which was misleading, and the use of so-called Public Interest Immunity Certificates, the effect of which was to prevent certain British businesspeople accused of breaking the law from using official

Figure 14.3 Civil Service Code, 1996

1   The constitutional and practical role of the Civil Service is, with integrity, honesty, impartiality and objectivity, to assist the duly constituted Government, of whatever political complexion, in formulating policies of the Government, carrying out decisions of the Government and in administering public services for which the Government is responsible.

2   Civil servants are servants of the Crown. Constitutionally, the Crown acts on the advice of Ministers and, subject to the provisions of this Code, civil servants owe their loyalty to the duly constituted Government.

3   This Code should be seen in the context of the duties and responsibilities of Ministers set out in *Questions of Procedure for Ministers* which include:

- accountability to Parliament;
- the duty to give Parliament and the public as full information as possible about the policies, decisions and actions of the Government, and not to deceive or knowingly mislead Parliament and the public;
- the duty not to use public resources for party political purposes, to uphold the political impartiality of the Civil Service, and not to ask civil servants to act in any way which would conflict with the Civil Service Code;
- the duty to give fair consideration and due weight to informed and impartial advice from civil servants, as well as to other considerations and advice, in reaching decisions; and
- the duty to comply with the law, including international law and treaty obligations, and to uphold the administration of justice;

together with the duty to familiarise themselves with the contents of this Code.

4   Civil servants should serve the duly constituted Government in accordance with the principles set out in this Code and recognising:

- the accountability of civil servants to Ministers or, as the case may be, the office holder in charge of their Department;
- the duty of all public officers to discharge public functions reasonably and according to the law;
- the duty to comply with the law, including international law and treaty obligations, and to uphold the administration of justice; and
- ethical standards governing particular professions.

5   Civil servants should conduct themselves with integrity, impartiality and honesty. They should give honest and impartial advice to Ministers, without fear or favour, and make all information relevant to a decision available to Ministers. They should not deceive or knowingly mislead Ministers, Parliament or the public.

6   Civil servants should endeavour to deal with the affairs of the public sympathetically, efficiently, promptly and without bias or maladministration.

7   Civil servants should endeavour to ensure the proper, effective and efficient use of public money.

8   Civil servants should not misuse their official position or information acquired in the course of their official duties to further their private interests or those of others. They should not receive benefits of any kind from a third party which might reasonably be seen to compromise their personal judgement or integrity.

Figure 14.3 continued

9   Civil servants should conduct themselves in such a way as to deserve and retain the confidence of Ministers and to be able to establish the same relationship with those whom they may be required to serve in some future Administration. They should comply with restrictions on their political activities. The conduct of civil servants should be such that Ministers and potential future Ministers can be sure that confidence can be freely given, and that the Civil Service will conscientiously fulfil its duties and obligations to, and impartially assist, advise and carry out the policies of the duly constituted Government.

10   Civil servants should not without authority disclose official information which has been communicated in confidence within Government, or received in confidence from others. Nothing in the Code should be taken as overriding existing statutory or common law obligations to keep confidential, or to disclose, certain information. They should not seek to frustrate or influence the policies, decisions or actions of Government by the unauthorised, improper or premature disclosure outside the Government of any information to which they have had access as civil servants.

11   Where a civil servant believes he or she is being required to act in a way which:

   ● is illegal, improper, or unethical;
   ● is in breach of constitutional convention or a professional code;
   ● may involve possible maladministration; or
   ● is otherwise inconsistent with this Code;

   he or she should report the matter in accordance with procedures laid down in departmental guidance or rules of conduct. A civil servant should also report to the appropriate authorities evidence of criminal or unlawful activity by others and may also report in accordance with departmental procedures if he or she becomes aware of other breaches of this Code or is required to act in a way which, for him or her, raises a fundamental issue of conscience.

12   Where a civil servant has reported a matter covered in paragraph 11 in accordance with procedures laid down in departmental guidance or rules of conduct and believes that the response does not represent a reasonable response to the grounds of his or her concern, he or she may report the matter in writing to the Civil Service Commissioners.

13   Civil servants should not seek to frustrate the policies, decisions or actions of Government by declining to take, or abstaining from, action which flows from ministerial decisions. Where a matter cannot be resolved by the procedures set out in paragraphs 11 and 12 above, on a basis which the civil servant concerned is able to accept, he or she should either carry out his or her instructions, or resign from the Civil Service. Civil servants should continue to observe their duties of confidentiality after they have left Crown employment.

documents in their own defence when the case came to Court. In other words, it was alleged that Ministers and civil servants, after guidance from the Attorney-General, were ultimately prepared to see innocent British citizens convicted and sent to jail simply to safeguard what they had defined as 'the public interest' – which in this case involved *not* telling the media and the public the truth about the Matrix-Churchill affair.

Other current concerns

There are several other current concerns about the British Civil Service which need to be mentioned at this stage. *First*, it is often alleged that civil servants are disinclined to approach the problems of Government in the round and in a sufficiently long-term perspective. According to this view, there is too much focus in Whitehall upon immediate political issues within the sphere of each Department. In so far as this can be true, it stems from a natural bureaucratic instinct to play safe and working habits in Whitehall which have long attached importance to the orderly division of labour between the various Departments. Furthermore, in a system of government which is so heavily influenced by the political requirements of Ministers, it is naive to expect civil servants to pursue a broader or more long-term strategy than that of the Ministers whom they serve. Indeed, bearing in mind the sensitive issues discussed in the previous section, it would not be well received by Ministers if civil servants deliberately set out to do this.

Secondly, there is the familiar refrain in some political quarters that civil servants seem unwilling or unable fully to embrace radical policies (when set out by Ministers) or even radical departures from existing policy. It is argued that civil servants demonstrate this tendency by filtering or diluting many of the new and challenging ideas which do not fit the conventional wisdom in Whitehall. Yet nearly everything depends on the derivation of radical new ideas. If these come from the Prime Minister and other senior Ministers, it is almost certain that they will be accepted and implemented, albeit sometimes with private misgivings. On the other hand, if new ideas come from other less impeccable sources (such as back-benchers or unfashionable intellectuals), civil servants are rather unlikely to take them on board and will tend to regard them as political heresy until given the green light by senior Ministers.

Thirdly, in the mid-1990s perhaps the most notable element of informed concern about the Civil Service stemmed from the fact that one party (the Conservatives) had been in office for so long (in the end a total of 18 years) and had allegedly changed or destroyed the traditional ethos of public service in Britain. Such concerns were based on dislike of market-testing (that is, putting Civil Service activities out to tender to see if the private sector can perform them more cost-effectively) and, in some cases, outright privatisation of certain traditional state functions – such as low-security prisons. Initially, this concern also included misgivings about the spread of Executive Agencies, but gradually these came to be accepted as a valid and cost-effective way of delivering services directly to the public – for example, social security benefits or advice and help for job-seekers.

Finally, the critics of the Conservative policy of Civil Service reform carried out in the 1980s and 1990s expressed a general anxiety about the growth of 'the unelected state' and the infiltration of the Civil Service with what they viewed as the undesirable standards and practices more usually associated with activity in the private sector.[23] Certainly the traditional homogeneity of the public service was reduced by the creation of a large number of 'extra-governmental organisations' which are beholden to Ministers and within the orbit of central Government, but no longer an integral part of it or influenced to the same extent as Whitehall Departments by the traditional Civil Service codes of behaviour. Such developments were criticised by the House of Commons Public Accounts Committee when it drew attention to certain tendencies for some Health Authorities and Development Agencies to cut corners in relation to the usual Civil Service standards of probity and financial accountability.[24] They were also fiercely attacked by local politicians who resented the fact that the power and financial responsibilities of Local Authorities had been steadily eroded during the period of

Conservative Government from 1979 to 1997, leading to what they saw as the usurpation of democratic power by the 'unelected state'.

According to the Conservative point of view, however, much of this criticism came predictably from politicians who did not like the then Conservative Government's policy and from public sector trade unions which saw their members' job security threatened by such reforms. Under various charters since the *Citizen's Charter* of 1991, Conservatives had argued that traditional notions of public accountability needed to be changed and up-dated, so that accountability to the *users* of public services was set alongside the traditional forms of accountability to Members of Parliament and local Councillors, who are the democratically elected guardians of the public interest. Until the 1990s the sphere of central Government was one of the few areas of institutional activity which had not felt the full effects of Conservative determination to diminish the role of the state. With civil servants themselves becoming directly affected by the process of reform, it was not surprising that they and their allies became strongly concerned for their own future. However, the process of change focusing on greater efficiency and accountability continued – indeed was developed further – under the Labour Government which came into office in 1997.

14.3 Methods of control

Over the years in Britain politicians in office have developed a number of different methods for controlling the Civil Service and seeing that it does what elected Ministers want it to do. Each of the methods has been used to a certain extent, but none has proved sufficient. It has therefore proved necessary to use all of them in combination in a continuing effort to achieve real and lasting political control.

Ministerial responsibility

The classic method of controlling the Civil Service in Britain is based on the traditional doctrine of Ministerial responsibility. This may have been effective during the second half of the nineteenth century when the scope and complexity of central Government was very much smaller than it is today. In modern conditions, however, its effectiveness is much more dubious, as a number of well-placed witnesses have pointed out and as recent experience has shown.[25]

In theory, Ministerial responsibility is supposed to mean that Ministers are held to account and take responsibility for everything which happens or fails to happen within the allotted spheres of their Departmental responsibility. It is also supposed to mean that Ministers will offer their resignation or be sacked when things go seriously wrong in areas of policy and administration over which they are supposed to be in charge.

In practice, modern central Government and its Agencies have become so large and complex that Ministers, however dutiful and energetic, cannot possibly be aware of, let alone determine, everything which happens or fails to happen within their allotted spheres of 'responsibility'. Consequently, the best that sensible Ministers can do is to insist that their civil servants draw to their attention in a timely way (that is, at a stage when Ministerial intervention could make a difference) all the important or politically sensitive issues which arise within their allotted spheres of responsibility. This means that civil servants who work closely with Ministers should be able to distinguish between sensitive political issues and run-of-the-mill administration. If such assumptions cannot safely be made (as seems to have been the case with Ministerial 'responsibility' for the prison service when Michael Howard was Home Secretary, 1993–97), then the whole idea of Ministerial responsibility is revealed to be fatally flawed and out of date.

An earlier attempt to make more of a reality of the doctrine, at any rate in relation to the costs of central Government, was launched by Margaret Thatcher in the early 1980s under the heading of a new Management Information System for Ministers (MINIS). This was supposed to make it possible throughout Whitehall for senior Ministers to know the costs and benefits of every aspect of their Departments' activities, so that waste and duplication could be rooted out and efficiency and effectiveness could be enhanced.[26] In the event this systematic approach did not appeal to all senior Ministers, many of whom did not believe that such managerial activity constituted the best use of their own limited time and energy. Furthermore, it still did not address the fundamental problem that there are only 24 hours in a day and most senior Ministers have neither the time nor the inclination nor, realistically, the possibility of supervising everything which happens or fails to happen within their Departmental spheres – especially now that there are some 139 Executive Agencies in which the Chief Executives are supposed to take 'operational responsibility'. The net result of all this is that senior Ministers rarely resign on grounds of policy failure and virtually never on grounds of defective public administration.

Bureaucratic hierarchy

Partly because of the shortcomings of Ministerial responsibility, bureaucratic hierarchy has become the orthodox method of trying to control the machinery of central Government in Britain. Once again in origin it dates from the nineteenth century and the reforms of Whitehall which flowed from the 1854 Northcote-Trevelyan Report. It has always presupposed a simple and clear division between the responsibility of Ministers for policy and the responsibility of senior civil servants for the public administration which carries out the policy.

In theory, such a simple division of labour appears to be well established in Whitehall. After all, as mentioned earlier, every Permanent Secretary and every head of an Executive Agency is responsible for the money spent by the Department or Agency as the case may be. Procedurally, the executive heads of the Agencies report to the Permanent Secretaries of their parent Departments and thence to the Public Accounts Committee of the House of Commons for the public money which they spend. Yet in an era of greater functional accountability at lower levels of the Civil Service than before, this procedure has had to be modified to take account of the new 'managerial ethos' at nearly every level of the bureaucracy.

In practice, the very senior civil servants at the top of the various Departments (and increasingly some of the Agency Chief Executives) can be so preoccupied with their role as leading policy advisers to senior Ministers that they have little time to spend on the rather detailed tasks of managing their Departments (or Agencies). Thus much of the load of day-to-day management has to be delegated to more junior officials in the hierarchy. In fact, far from being a problem, this natural response to the realities of the situation may be part of a more effective solution in that it obliges more civil servants at lower levels to take charge of (and responsibility for) their own activities. Notwithstanding this necessary devolution and delegation of responsibility down the bureaucratic hierarchies of central Government, Permanent Secretaries have striven to respond positively to the various 'managerial' initiatives, and they now see effective staff leadership and management as key parts of their jobs.

Administrative efficiency

Another method of controlling the Civil Service is based on the principle of administrative efficiency. This assumes that it is possible to apply to the Civil Service some of the business and management techniques used in the private sector. As long ago as 1968 this idea was one of the main thrusts of the Fulton Report and it has been promoted intermittently by Governments in Britain ever since. For example, this approach attaches special importance to the achievement of a given level of output with less financial and other inputs, to the comparison of different methods to achieve a given objective, and to the use of cost–benefit analysis in the process of decision making.

It is fair to say that such techniques imported from the private sector have not always proved to be easily transferable to the public service where the goals, constraints and criteria of success or failure have tended to be rather different. In the private sector, the main goal is usually profit, the constraints are largely imposed by the market, and the criteria of success or failure include assessments made by investors and notably the rate of return on capital. In the public service, on the other hand, the goals tend to be more open-ended and changeable, the constraints include considerations of equity and 'the public interest' – not to mention the problems of Parliamentary and public accountability – and the criteria of success or failure depend very much upon the changing priorities and prejudices of senior Ministers.

In spite of the inherent problems of applying this approach to public administration in the Civil Service, the Thatcher Government (1979–90) demonstrated that it was possible to make progress in this direction. The so-called 'Rayner scrutinies' (named after Lord Rayner who was a managing director of Marks & Spencer before becoming Margaret Thatcher's first adviser on the efficiency of Government) identified potential financial savings in some of the routine support services in Whitehall – for example, typing pools, messenger services and Ministerial transport. Subsequently his scrutiny of Government research and development establishments revealed potential financial savings of at least 15 per cent, while a review of the non-office activities of central Government – such as HM Coastguards or the Property Services Agency – indicated further areas of possible savings. Indeed, in the first six years of the Efficiency Unit's existence, 266 'scrutinies' were completed, identifying annual savings of £600 million, and additional one-off savings totalling £67 million.[27]

On the other hand, not all the Rayner scrutinies were a success, especially when the proposals seemed politically unacceptable to Government back-benchers. For example, in 1981 it was suggested in one such scrutiny that certain payments made to pensioners through Sub-Post Offices should be made every other week rather than weekly or, in some cases, no longer made at all. This was anathema to millions of elderly people living on fixed incomes who raised such a storm of protest with MPs that Ministers soon decided to drop the idea. Notwithstanding such early setbacks, the general idea of seeking the maximum administrative efficiency within the public service has now become commonplace in Britain.

Judicial scrutiny

A final method of controlling the Civil Service in Britain is that of judicial scrutiny by the Courts and quasi-judicial bodies, such as Administrative Tribunals. The attraction of this method is that it can provide a framework of standards for good administrative practice without usually becoming too legalistic.[28] Yet so far it is doubtful whether the system of administrative law in Britain is sufficiently well developed really to achieve its purposes in this respect. This is because the Courts have remained fairly cautious in the face of the continuing doctrine of Ministerial responsibility, and have tended to confine their interventions to cases based upon the *ultra vires* doctrine when Government Departments or local authorities are alleged to have gone beyond the proper limits of their competence.[29] Nonetheless, judicial review has increasingly been used to challenge administrative decisions. In 1974 there were 160 applications in England for leave to seek judicial review; in 1987 there were 1529, and in 1993 there were 2886 – an increase of nearly twenty times in under twenty years.[30] Consequently, civil servants have had to take full account of the significance of judicial review and, as a result, its very existence can have a considerable impact upon Departmental legal advisers and hence indirectly upon Ministers and civil servants.

In the more legalistic atmosphere engendered by the incursion of European law into more and more areas of British national life, the Courts in Britain may become bolder in their political interventions if they choose to follow the European example.[31] In any case litigants in Britain now appeal more often to the European Court of Justice in Luxembourg on issues within the legal competence of the European Union and to the European Court of Human Rights in Strasbourg. Indeed, this tendency is likely to grow with the passage of the Human Rights Act 1998, which incorporates the European Convention into UK statute law.

Before concluding this section, mention should also be made of the decision taken by Parliament as long ago as 1967 to establish a Parliamentary Commissioner for Administration (popularly known as *The Ombudsman*) with statutory authority to investigate public complaints of maladministration in central Government Departments and, later, in the National Health Service as well.[32] Although the Ombudsman has so far been limited by the fact that the office has no powers of initiative or legal enforcement and can only respond to complaints referred (usually by MPs), the office has been successful over the years in rectifying faulty procedures in the Civil Service and occasionally in persuading Whitehall Departments to make *ex gratia* payments by way of compensation to people with clear and justifiable grievances. The powers of publicity and persuasion, backed by the House of Commons Select Committee which monitors its work, have proved to be valuable and significant additions to the range of methods available for imposing some control upon the Civil Service in Britain.

Figure 14.4 Executive Agencies in 1998

ARMED FORCES PERSONNEL ADMINISTRATION AGENCY (AFPAA)
Department: Defence
Launched: 1/4/97
Provides, on a tri-Service basis, the data and systems for the payment of military personnel (including pensions), and supports the Armed Forces personnel management function.

ARMY BASE REPAIR ORGANISATION (ABRO)
Department: Defence
Launched: 1/4/93
Provides a repair and refurbishment service for the Army.

ARMY BASE STORAGE AND DISTRIBUTION AGENCY (ABSDA)
Department: Defence
Launched: 5/4/95
The role of ABSDA is the storage, maintenance, distribution and issue of ammunition, vehicles, fuel, operational ration packs, stores and equipment on behalf of the Army and other customers (who include the Royal Navy, RAF and other government departments) to sustain the Army is peace, crisis annd war. ABSDA's mission statement is: "To operate efficiently the storage and distribution agency for the Services in peace and war."

ARMY PERSONNEL CENTRE
Department: Defence
Launched: 2/12/96
The Agency's task is to man the Army, manage the careers of Army personnel (including both officers and soldiers) and to provide Army pay, personnel and pensions administration.

ARMY TECHNICAL SUPPORT AGENCY (ATSA)
Department: Defence
Launched: 16/10/95
Primarily involved with providing technical and engineering advice and services to Armed Forces users and managers of military equipment.

ARMY TRAINING AND RECRUITING AGENCY
Department: Defence
Launched: 1/4/97
Re-launched as an enlarged agency: 1/7/97
Provides manpower trained in the individual skills required to sustain the Army's military effectiveness.

BENEFITS AGENCY
Department: Social Security
Launched: 2/4/91
Review completed: March 1995 (agency status confirmed)
The Benefits Agency is responsible for administering claims and payments of social security benefits.

BUSINESS DEVELOPMENT SERVICE (BDS)
Department: Northern Ireland – Finance and Personnel
Launched: 1/10/96
Provides business support services to Northern Ireland departments, their executive agencies and the wider public sector.

BUYING AGENCY (TBA), THE
Department: OPS
Launched: 31/10/91
TBA provides a high quality, professional procurement service to government and other public sector bodies.

CADW WELSH HISTORIC MONUMENTS
Responsible Minister: Secretary of State for Wales
Launched: 2/4/91
Review completed: July 1995 (agency status confirmed)
Maintains and preserves the built heritage of Wales and presents those monuments in the care of the Secretary of State to the public.

CENTRAL COMPUTER AND TELECOMMUNICATIONS AGENCY (CCTA)
Department: OPS
Launched: 1/4/96
Provides information technology expertise to public sector organisations.

CENTRAL OFFICE OF INFORMATION (COI)
Department: Chancellor of the Duchy of Lancaster/Cabinet Office
Launched: 5/4/90
Provides consultancy, procurement and project management services to central government for publicity and provides specialist services in certain areas.

CENTRAL SCIENCE LABORATORY (CSL)
Department: Agriculture, Fisheries and Food
Launched: 1/4/92
Re-launched as an enlarged CSL Agency following the merger with the MAFF Food Science Laboratories: 1/4/94
Review completed: December 1996 (agency status confirmed)
Provides a wide range of scientific services.

CENTRE FOR ENVIRONMENT, FISHERIES AND AQUA-CULTURE SCIENCE (CEFAS)
Department: Agriculture, Fisheries and Food
Launched: 1/4/97
Provides scientific research, assessment and advice in fisheries management, environmental ptotection, and fish health, hygiene and aquaculture, in order to enhance the protection of the public, the conservation of the aquatic environment and the rational management of natural resources.

CHILD SUPPORT AGENCY (CSA)
Department: Social Security
Launched: 5/4/93
Operates the new system under the guidelines of the Child Support Act, 1991 for assessing, collecting and, where necessary, enforcing Child Support maintenance.

CIVIL SERVICE COLLEGE
Department: OPS
Launched: 6/6/89
Review completed: June 1995 (agency status confirmed); additional review completed: April 1996
Provides a wide range of training and development opportunities for civil servants and others plus international consultancy services.

COMPANIES HOUSE
Department: Trade and Industry
Launched: 3/10/88
Registers companies and collects statutory documents and returns and makes information available to the public.

COMPENSATION AGENCY, THE
Department: Northern Ireland Office
Launched: 1/4/92
Review completed: October 1995 (agency status confirmed)
Administers the criminal injuries and criminal damage compensation schemes and pays compensation under the emergency provisions legislation.

CONSTRUCTION SERVICE
Department: Northern Ireland – Department of the Environment
Launched: 1/4/96
Provides a professional design, maintenance and advisory service to Government departments, agencies and other public bodies covering a wide range of construction industry disciplines.

CONTRIBUTIONS AGENCY (CA), THE
Department: Social Security
Launched: 2/4/91
Review completed: November 1994 (agency status confirmed)
Responsible for managing the National Insurance scheme. The Agency collects and records contributions and provides an information and advisory service to employers, the self-employed and contributors.

COURT SERVICE, THE
Department: Lord Chancellor's
Launched: 3/4/95

Figure 14.4 Continued

DEBT MANAGEMENT OFFICE
Department: HM Treasury
Launched: 1/4/98

DEFENCE ANALYTICAL SERVICES AGENCY (DASA)
Department: Defence
Launched: 1/7/92
Provides services including compilation of manpower, financial and logistical statistics, a manpower planning and forecasting service to the Armed Services.

DEFENCE ANIMAL CENTRE
Department: Defence
Launched: 1/4/93
Provision and training of animals for the Armed Forces and other government customers, the training of personnel in their handling, veterinary care and management and the provision of the UK Services Veterinary Hospital.

DEFENCE BILLS AGENCY
Department: Defence
Launched: 1/1/96
Provides bill payment, debt collection and associated management information services for MoD.

DEFENCE CLOTHING AND TEXTILES AGENCY
Department: Defence
Launched: 22/11/94
Supplies uniforms, clothing and some specialist equipment required by the Armed Forces.

DEFENCE CODIFICATION AGENCY (DCA)
Department: Defence
Launched: 8/7/96
Manages the UK codification system, ensuring it is consistent with NATO policy and promotes the benefits of codification throughout the MoD.

DEFENCE COMMUNICATIONS SERVICES AGENCY
Department: Defence
Launched: 1/4/98

DEFENCE DENTAL AGENCY
Department: Defence
Launched: 1/3/96
Provides dental personnel and other resources to supply dental treatment for Servicemen and dependants.

DEFENCE ESTATE ORGANISATION (DEO)
Department: Defence
Launched: 19/3/97
The role of DEO is to assist MoD in managing the optimum estate of land, buildings and installations to meet the operational needs of the Department, paying attention to its conservation, heritage, contractural and statutory obligations.

DEFENCE EVALUATION AND RESEARCH AGENCY (DERA)
Department: Defence
Launched: 1/4/95
Provides non-clear research for the MoD, Government Departments and other customers.

DEFENCE INTELLIGENCE AND SECURITY CENTRE
Department: Defence
Launched: 1/10/96
Trains the Armed Forces and other intelligence organisations in security, psychological and intelligence operations whilst contributing to effective and timely advice on appropriate intelligence and security policy matters and maintaining operational capability.

DEFENCE MEDICAL TRAINING ORGANISATION
Department: Defence
Launched: 1/4/97
Trains specialist defence medical personnel and provides medical services training for other service personnel to meet the operational requirements of all three services.

DEFENCE POSTAL AND COURIER SERVICES (DPCSA)
Department: Defence
Launched: 1/7/92
The mission of the DPCSA is to provide the highest quality of postal services to its customers whilst maintaining best value for money and sufficient military capability to meet Government's defence requirements in peace and war.

DEFENCE SECONDARY CARE AGENCY (DSCA)
Department: Defence
Launched: 30/4/96
Provides deployable, trained Service medical staff to supply medical care and support to the Armed Forces.

DEFENCE TRANSPORT AND MOVEMENTS EXECUTIVE (DTMX)
Department: Defence
Launched: 4/4/95
To provide surface transport and movements service for the world-wide support of HM Armed Force.

DEFENCE VETTING AGENCY (DVA)
Department: Defence
Launched: 1/4/97
The Defence Vetting Agency grants and maintains security clearances for Armed Forces Personnel, MoD Staff, Defence Industry employees and undertakes investigation work for other Government Departments.

DISPOSAL SALES AGENCY (DSA)
Department: Defence
Launched: 1/10/94
Sells surplus capital equipment on a Government-to-Government basis and acts as an intelligent contracting organisation for all other surplus items to secure the best return to the Ministry of Defence.

DRIVER AND VEHICLE LICENSING AGENCY (DVLA)
Department: Environment, Transport and the Regions
Launched: 2/4/90
Review completed: April 1995 (agency status confirmed)
(a) The registration and licensing of drivers in Great Britain.
(b) The registration and licensing of vehicles, together with the collection and enforcement of vehicle excise duty in the UK.

DRIVER AND VEHICLE LICENSING NORTHERN IRELAND
Department: Northern Ireland – Environment
Launched: 2/8/93

DRIVER AND VEHICLE TESTING AGENCY
Department: Northern Ireland – Environment
Trading Fund status
Launched: 1/4/92
Promotes and improves road safety in Northern Ireland by testing drivers and vehicles as required by legislation.

DRIVING STANDARDS AGENCY
Department: Environment, Transport and the Regions
Launched: 2/4/90
Review completed: April 1995 (agency status confirmed)
Driver testing for cars, motorcycles, lorries and buses and supervision of car and lorry driving instructors and approved training bodies for motorcyclists in Great Britain.

DUKE OF YORK'S ROYAL MILITARY SCHOOL
Department: Defence
Launched: 1/4/92
Provides boarding school education for the children, aged between 11 and 18 years, of Service personnel.

EMPLOYMENT SERVICE
Department: Education and Employment
Launched: 2/4/90
Review completed: October 1996 (agency status confirmed)
The Employment Service aims to provide a competitive and flexible labour market by helping into work unemployed people, while ensuring they understand and fulfil the conditions for receipt of the Jobseeker's Allowance.

EMPLOYMENT TRIBUNALS SERVICE (ETS)
Department: Trade and Industry
Launched: 1/4/97
Provides administrative support to the industrial tribunals and to the Employment Appeals Tribunal.

ENVIRONMENT AND HERITAGE SERVICE
Department: Northern Ireland – Department of the Environment
Launched: 1/4/96
Protects and conserves the natural and built environment and promotes its appreciation for the benefit of present and future generations.

Figure 14.4 Continued

FARMING AND RURAL CONSERVATION AGENCY (FRCA)
Department: Agriculture, Fisheries and Food and Welsh Office
Launched: 1/4/97
Assists government in the design, development and implementation of policies on the integration of farming and conservation, environmental protection and the rural economy.

FIRE SERVICE COLLEGE, THE
Department: Home Office
Launched: 1/4/92
Provides a wide range of specialist fire related and management and finance training for fire officers. It also provides training for commerce and industry, and for students from overseas fire brigades.

FISHERIES RESEARCH SERVICES
Department: Scottish Office
Launched: 1/4/97
Provides expert scientific and technical advice and information on marine and freshwater fisheries, on aquaculture, and on the protection of the aquatic environment and its wildlife.

FORENSIC SCIENCE AGENCY OF NORTHERN IRELAND
Department: Northern Ireland Office
Launched: 1/9/95
The provision of effective scientific advice and support principally to enhance the delivery of justice.

FORENSIC SCIENCE SERVICE (FSS), THE
Department: Home Office
Launched: 1/4/91
The purpose of the FSS is to serve the administration of justice principally by providing scientific support in the investigation of crime and expert evidence to the courts. It aims to do so with efficiency, effectiveness and economy.

FOREST ENTERPRISE
Department: Forestry Commission
Launched: 1/4/96
Manages the national forest to produce the environmental, financial, social and other outputs sought by Ministers and the Forestry Commissioners.

FOREST RESEARCH
Department: Forestry Commission
Launched: 1/4/97
Provides research, development, surveys and associated services to the industry and provides authoritative advice in support of development and implementation of the Government's forest policies.

FOREST SERVICE OF NORTHERN IRELAND
Department: Northern Ireland
Launched: 1/4/98

GOVERNMENT CAR AND DESPATCH AGENCY (GCDA)
Department: OPS
Launched: 1/4/97
Provides secure transport and mail services to central government.

GOVERNMENT PROPERTY LAWYERS, THE
Department: Treasury Solicitor
Launched: 1/4/93
Provides conveyancing and lands advisory services to government departments and other publicly funded bodies in England and Wales.

GOVERNMENT PURCHASING AGENCY
Department: Northern Ireland – Department of Finance and Personnel
Launched: 1/4/96
Establishes on behalf of customers effective contracts for the procurement of goods and services and provides advice and support to enable them to achieve value for money improvements in procurement.

HEALTH ESTATES
Department: Northern Ireland – Health & Social Services
Launched: 2/10/95
Provides policy, advice, guidance and support on estate matters at strategic and operational levels to the various

bodies charged with responsibility for the Health and Social Services in Northern Ireland.

HIGHWAYS AGENCY
Department: Environment, Transport and the Regions
Launched: 1/4/94
Responsible for managing safe, efficient, reliable and environmentally acceptable trunk road network throughout England.

HISTORIC SCOTLAND
Responsible Minister: Secretary of State for Scotland
Launched: 2/4/91
Review completed: November 1994 (agency status confirmed)
Protects and promotes public understanding and enjoyment of Scotland's ancient monuments and archaeological sites and landscapes; historic buildings, parks, gardens and designed landscapes.

HM LAND REGISTRY
Department: The Land Registry is a separate Government reporting directly to the Lord Chancellor
Launched: 2/7/90
Review completed: January 1996 (agency status confirmed)
Maintains and develops a unified and reliable system of land registration in England and Wales.

HM PRISON SERVICE
Department: Home Office
Launched: 1/4/93
Provides prison services in England and Wales, both directly and through contractors.

INDUSTRIAL RESEARCH AND TECHNOLOGY UNIT (IRTU)
Department: Northern Ireland – Department of Economic Development
Launched: 3/4/95
Promotes industrially relevant research, development and technology transfer in Northern Ireland.

INFORMATION TECHNOLOGY SERVICES AGENCY (ITSA)
Department: Social Security
Launched: 2/4/90
Review completed: February 1997 (agency status comfirmed)
Sets the Information Systems and Information Technology (IS/IT) strategic direction for the DSS.

INSOLVENCY SERVICE, THE
Department: Trade & Industry
Launched: 21/3/90
Administers and investigates the affairs of bankrupts and companies in compulsory liquidation, deals with the disqualification of directors in all corporate failures, regulates insolvency practitioners and their professional bodies, provides banking and investment services for bankruptcy and liquidation estates, and advises ministers on insolvency policy issues.

INTERVENTION BOARD
Department: Members of the Board are appointed by and are responsible to the Minister of Agriculture, Fisheries and Food and the Secretaries of State for Scotland, Wales and Northern Ireland.
Launched: 2/4/90
Review completed: June 1995 (agency status confirmed)
Responsible for the implementation of EC regulations covering the market support arrangements of the Common Agriculture Policy.

JOINT AIR RECONNAISSANCE INTELLIGENCE CENTRE (JARIC)
Department: Defence
Launched: 19/4/96
JARIC's mission is to exploit and analyse imagery from all available sources and produce intelligence products and services to meet MoD and operational command requirements.

LAND REGISTERS OF NORTHERN IRELAND
Department: Northern Ireland – Department of the Environment
Launched: 1/4/96
Supports the conveyancing and property markets in Northern Ireland.

Figure 14.4 Continued

LOGISTIC INFORMATION SYSTEMS AGENCY (LISA)
Department: Defence
Launched: 21/11/94
LISA's mission is to enhance the logistic effectiveness of the Army in peace and war by providing information systems, services and support.

MARITIME AND COASTGUARD AGENCY (MCA)
Department: Environment, Transport and the Regions
Launched: 1/4/98
The Agency was created by the merger of the Coastguard Agency (TCA) and the Marine Safety Agency (MSA) and is responsible for carrying out the functions of both organisations.

MEAT HYGIENE SERVICE (MHS)
Department: Agriculture, Fisheries and Food
Launched: 1/4/95
Protects public health and animal welfare through veterinary supervision and meat inspection in licensed fresh meat establishments.

MEDICAL DEVICES AGENCY
Department: Health
Launched: 27/9/94
Protects the public health and safeguards the interests of patients and users by ensuring thatbmedical devices and equipment meet appropriate standards of safety, quality and performance and that they comply with relevant Directives of the EU.

MEDICAL SUPPLIES AGENCY
Department: Defence
Launched: 1/3/96
Provides medical, dental and veterinary material, blood and blood products, trained personnel and technical and logistic support to the armed forces.

MEDICINES CONTROL AGENCY
Department: Health
Launched: 1/7/91
Review completed: July 1997 (agency status confirmed)
Safeguards public health by controlling medicines through a system of licensing, monitoring, inspection, and enforcement of standards which ensure that medicines marketed in the UK meet rigorous standards of safety, quality and efficacy.

METEOROLOGICAL OFFICE
Department: Defence
Launched: 2/4/90
Review completed: May 1996 (agency status confirmed)
The Meteorological Office is the State Meteorological Service, with responsibility for provision of meterological services to the Armed Forces and civil aviation, shipping, emergency services, media, commerce, industry and the public, and for undertaking research related to meteorology and climate.

MILITARY SURVEY DEFENCE AGENCY
Department: Defence
Launched: 2/4/91
To ensure the provision of geographic support to defence operations, planning and training.

MINISTRY OF DEFENCE POLICE AGENCY (MDP)
Department: Defence
Launched: 1/4/96
Primary role is the prevention, detection and investigation of crime within the MoD and Crown Estate.

NATIONAL SAVINGS
Department: National Savings reports directly to the Chancellor of the Exchequer
Launched: 1/7/96
Supports the Government's management of its debt and its policies for personal savings by attracting and retaining investments from the retail market efficiently and cost effectively.

NATIONAL STATISTICS, OFFICE FOR (ONS)
Department: Chancellor of the Exchequer
Launched: 1/4/96
Provides government at all levels with a statistical service to support the formulation and monitoring of economic and social policies.

NATIONAL WEIGHTS AND MEASURES LABORATORY (NWML)
Department: Trade & Industry
Launched: 18/4/89
Review completed: July 1995 (agency status confirmed)
Administers weights and measures legislation; regulation and certification of equipment in use for trade; EC Directives on measuring instruments; equipment testing, calibration and training services.

NAVAL AIRCRAFT REPAIR ORGANISATION (NARO)
Department: Defence
Launched: 1/4/92
The largest helicopter repair facility in Europe, the NARO provides a full range of repair, overhaul, modification and storage services for helicopters, aero engines and mechanical and avionic components for the United Kingdom's Armed Forces. It is also a repair centre for marine gas turbines for the Royal Navy.

NAVAL BASES AND SUPPLY AGENCY
Department: Defence
Launched: 11/12/96
Provides the Royal Navy, the Royal Fleet Auxiliary and other authorised customers with increasingly effective and efficient engineering, supply and naval personnel services to agreed standards in war, crisis and peace.

NAVAL MANNING AGENCY
Department: Defence
Launched: 1/7/96
Ensures that sufficient naval manpower is available in trained strength and effectively deployed at all times.

NAVAL RECRUITING AND TRAINING AGENCY
Department: Defence
Launched: 1/4/95
Primarily involved in providing and maintaining a pool of suitably trained manpower for deployment in the Naval Service.

NHS ESTATES
Department: Health
Launched: 1/4/91
Review completed: October 1995 (agency status confirmed)
Property advisers and consultants for the management and development of the National Health Service estate. Aim to encourage effective, efficient and economical management of property and to promote excellence of design, with value for money, in new buildings.

NHS PENSIONS AGENCY
Department: Health
Launched: 20/11/92
Administers the NHS Occupational Pension Scheme. It also provides information and advice on NHS pension matters.

NORTHERN IRELAND CHILD SUPPORT AGENCY
Department: Northern Ireland – Health & Social Services
Launched: 5/4/93
Operates the system created by the Child Support (Northern Ireland) Order 1991 in Northern Ireland.

NORTHERN IRELAND PRISON SERVICE
Department: Northern Ireland Office
Launched: 3/4/95

NORTHERN IRELAND STATISTICS AND RESEARCH AGENCY (NISRA)
Department: Northern Ireland – Department of Finance and Personnel
Launched: 1/4/96

ORDNANCE SURVEY
Department: Ordnance Survey is a separate Government Department, funded by Parliamentary vote, reporting directly to the Secretary of State for the Environment, Transport and the Regions
Launched: 1/5/90
Review completed: April 1995 (agency status confirmed)
Carries out official topographic surveying and mapping of Great Britain. From its databases, Ordnance Survey provides a wide range of maps and computer data products for Government, business, administrative, educational and leisure use.

Figure 14.4 Continued

ORDNANCE SURVEY OF NORTHERN IRELAND
Department: Northern Ireland – Environment
Launched: 1/4/92

PATENT OFFICE
Department: Trade & Industry
Launched: 1/3/90
Review completed: August 1996 (agency status confirmed)
Grants patents and trade marks, registers designs, and formulates policy on intellectual property.

PAY AND PERSONNEL AGENCY (PPA)
Department: Defence
Launched: 1/2/96
Provides a central payroll service to MoD and other departments.

PESTICIDES SAFETY DIRECTORATE
Department: Agriculture, Fisheries and Food
Launched: 1/4/93
Protects the health of human beings, creatures and plants, safeguards the environment and secures safe, efficient and humane methods of pest control, by controlling the sale, supply and use of pesticides.

PLANNING INSPECTORATE
Department: Environment and the Welsh Office
Launched: 1/4/92
Appeals and other casework under Planning, Housing, Environment, Highways, Transport and Works Legislation. Also provision of Inspectors to hold local inquiries into objections to local authority plans, and administration of the Lord Chancellor's Panel of Independent Inspectors.

PLANNING SERVICE, THE
Department: Northern Ireland – Department of the Environment
Launched: 1/4/96
Implements the Government's policies and strategy for town and country planning in Northern Ireland.

PROPERTY ADVISERS TO THE CIVIL ESTATE (PACE)
Department: OPS
Launched: 1/4/96
Responsible for promoting co-operation between Departments to enable them to obtain best value for money in the management of their property assets.

PUBLIC RECORD OFFICE
Department: The Public Record Office is a separate Government Department reporting directly to the Lord Chancellor
Launched: 1/4/92
The Public Record Office houses the national archives of England and Wales and the UK, that is records created by the actions of central government and the courts of law. Its responsibilities include ensuring the selection of records which should be permanently preserved, their preservation and their use by the public.

PUBLIC RECORD OFFICE OF NORTHERN IRELAND (PRONI)
Department: Northern Ireland – Department of Environment
Launched: 3/4/95

PUBLUC TRUST OFFICE (PTO)
Department: Lord Chancellor's
Launched: 1/7/94
Look after the private assets and financial affairs of members of the public who are suffering form mental disorder, those involved with trusts where the Public Trustee is executor of trust, those involved in civil actions in the courts and those interested in some institutional funds.

QUEEN ELIZABETH II CONFERENCE CENTRE, THE
Department: Environment, Transport and the Regions
Launched: 6/7/86
Provides conference and banqueting facilities for government and commercial use on a national and international scale.

QUEEN VICTORIA SCHOOL
Department: Defence
Launched: 1/4/92
An MoD-funded boarding school for the children of Scottish Sailors, Soldiers and Airmen, educating pupils from the age of 11 to 18 years.

RADIOCOMMUNICATIONS AGENCY (RA)
Department: Trade & Industry
Launched: 2/4/90
Review completed: August 1996 (agency status confirmed)
Responsible for the management of the civilian radio spectrum in the UK. It also represents UK radio interests internationally.

RAF LOGISTICS SUPPORT SERVICES
Department: Defence
Launched: 10/12/96
To strengthen and enhance RAF and Ministry of Defence operational capability by provision of effective and efficient specialist military aerospace logistics support and logistics consultancy services.

RAF MAINTENANCE GROUP DEFENCE AGENCY (RAFMGDA)
Department: Defence
Launched: 1/4/91
Review completed: October 1994 (agency status confirmed)
To provide aerosystems engineering, and spares and materials storage and distribution.

RAF PERSONNEL MANAGEMENT AGENCY (RAFPMA)
Department: Defence
Launched: 2/2/97
Provides personnel to meet the RAF's world-wide manpower commitments.

RAF SIGNALS ENGINEERING ESTABLISHMENT (RAFSEE)
Department: Defence
Launched: 22/11/94
Provide communications, information systems and electronic support to the Armed Forces.

RAF TRAINING GROUP DEFENCE AGENCY (RAFTGDA)
Department: Defence
Launched: 1/4/94
Re-launched as an enlarged agency: 1/4/97
Provides trained Service personnel and civillians to meet the operational requirements of the RAF.

RATE COLLECTION AGENCY
Department: Northern Ireland – Environment
Launched: 1/4/91
Review completed: February 1996 (agency status confirmed)
Collects rates and administers the Housing Benefit Scheme for owner-occupiers.

REGISTERS OF SCOTLAND
Responsible Minister: Secretary of State for Scotland
Launched: 6/4/90
Review completed: April 1994 (agency status confirmed)
Maintains registers of land etc. in Scotland.

RIVERS AGENCY
Department: Northern Ireland – Agriculture
Launched: 1/10/96
Maintains watercourses, flood and sea defences and provides water recreation facilities in Northern Ireland.

ROAD SERVICE
Department: Northern Ireland – Department of the Environment
Launched: 1/4/96
The aim of Roads Service is to ensure the provision of a safe and effective road network throughout Northern Ireland, recognising the need to protect the quality of the environmen.

ROYAL MINT
Department: Chancellor of the Exchequer
Launched: 2/4/90
Review completed: March 1997 (agency status confirmed)
The manufacture and distribution of UK and overseas coins (circulating and commemorative); medals and seals.

Figure 14.4 Continued

ROYAL PARKS, THE
Department: Culture, Media and Sport
Launched: 1/4/93
Manages and policies the Royal Parks in London.

SCOTTISH AGRICULTURAL SCIENCE AGENCY (SASA)
Department: Scottish Office
Launched: 1/4/92
Provides Government, primarily the Scottish Office, with expert scientific information and advice on agricultural and horticultural crops and aspects of the environment. Also performs stautory and regulatory work consistent with national and European legislation on topics such as plant health, crop improvement and protection of crops, food and the environment.

SCOTTISH COURT SERVICE
Department: Scottish Courts Administration
Launched: 3/4/95
Responsible for the provision and maintenance of Court Houses, and for ensuring the supply of trained staff and of administrative and organisational services, to support the judiciary, in the Supreme and Sheriff Courts in Scotland.

SCOTTISH FISHERIES PROTECTION AGENCY
Department: Scottish Office
Launched: 12/4/91
Review completed: June 1996 (agency status confirmed)
Enforces UK, EC and international fisheries law and regulations in Scottish waters and ports.

SCOTTISH OFFICE PENSIONS AGENCY
Department: Scottish Office
Launched: 1/4/93
Responsible of the person arrangements of some 330,000 people, mainly employees of the NHS and teaching service, including pensioners and former employees with preserved rights.

SCOTTISH PRISON SERVICE (SPS)
Department: Scottish Office
Launched: 1/4/93
Provides prison services in Scotland.

SCOTTISH RECORD OFFICE
Department: Scottish Office
Launched: 1/4/93
Responsible for preserving the public records of Scotland and other records which have been transmitted to it, and for making them available for public inspection. Also promotes the growth and maintenance of proper archive provision.

SECURITY FACILITIES EXECUTIVE (SAFE)
Department: OPS
Launched: 15/10/93
Provides a range of security support services, products and systems.

SERVICE CHILDREN'S EDUCATION
Department: Defence
Launched: 1/4/96
Provides an education service for the dependent children of service personnel and UK based civilian support staff residing overseas, and advice and support to service parents in the UK on the provision of schooling.

SHIPS SUPPORT AGENCY
Department: Defence
Launched: 11/12/96
Defines and directs the material support of the Royal Navy's ships and submarines.

SOCIAL SECURITY AGENCY (NORTHERN IRELAND)
Department: Northern Ireland – Health & Social Services
Launched: 1/7/91
Review completed: February 1997 (agency status confirmed)

SPECIALIST PROCUREMENT SERVICES
Department: Defence
Launched: 2/6/97
To provide specialist professional support and advice to all areas of the MoD involved in the procurement of defence material. Its four main service areas are pricing, quality assurance surveillance, cost forecasting and equipment accounting.

STUDENT AWARDS AGENCY FOR SCOTLAND (SAAS)
Department: Scottish Office
Launched: 5/4/94
Administers student awards and other related services for Scottish domiciled students in full-time higher education.

TRAINING AND EMPLOYMENT AGENCY
Department: Northern Ireland – Economic Development
Launched: 2/4/90
Review completed: February 1996 (agency status confirmed)
Administrations of employment and training services in Northern Ireland.

TREASURY SOLICITOR'S DEPARTMENT
Responsible Minister: The Attorney General
Launched: 1/4/96
Provides litigation and advisory services to government departments and other publicly funded bodies in England and Wales. Also administers estates of people who die intestate with no known kin.

UK PASSPORT AGENCY
Department: Home Office
Launched: 2/4/91
Review completed: November 1994 (agency status confirmed)
Issues passports and provides other related services for British nationals in the UK.

UNITED KINGDOM HYDROGRAPHIC OFFICE, THE
Department: Defence
Launched: 6/4/90
Review completed: January 1996 (agency status confirmed)
A Defence Agency. Produces charts and navigational publications for the Royal Navy and other customers at home and abroad.

VALUATION AND LANDS AGENCY
Department: Northern Ireland – Finance & Personnel
Launched: 1/4/93

VALUATION OFFICE
Department: Inland Revenue
Launched: 30/9/91
Review completed: July 1995 (agency status confirmed)
Provides land and buildings valuation service to government departments, other public bodies and a number of local authorities throughout Great Britain.

VEHICLE CERTIFICATION AGENCY (VCA)
Department: Environment, Transport and the Regions
Launched: 2/4/90
Review completed: September 1994 (agency status confirmed)
Tests and certificates vehicles and their components to UK and international standards.

VEHICLE INSPECTORATE
Department: Environment, Transport and the Regions
Launched: 1/8/88
Review completed: August 1996 (agency status confirmed)
The Vehicle Inspectorate carries out the Secretary of State for Environment, Transport and the Regions' statutory responsibilities for ensuring the roadworthiness of the vehicle fleet. It contributes to the maintenance and improvement of road safety and environmental protection by the enforcement of relevant legislation.

VETERINARY LABORATORIES AGENCY (VLA)
Department: Agriculture, Fisheries and Food
Launched: 1/10/95
Provides specialist veterinary advice.

VETERINARY MEDICINES DIRECTORATE (VMD)
Department: Agriculture, Fisheries and Food
Launched: 2/4/90
Review completed: April 1994 (agency status confirmed)
Assesses applications for veterinary medicines, issues authorisations and monitors suspected adverse reactions and the presence of residues of veterinary medicines. Advises Ministers on policy for veterinary medicines.

Figure 14.4 *Continued*

WAR PENSIONS AGENCY
Department: Social Security
Launched: 1/4/94
Responsible for the assessment and payment of war
pensions, the War Pensions Welfare Officers and the Ilford
Park Polish Home in Devon.

WATER SERVICE
**Department: Northern Ireland – Department of the
Environment**
Launched: 1/4/96
Provides water and sewerage services.

WILTON PARK
Department: Foreign & Commonwealth Office
Launched: 1/9/91

Review completed: March 1997 (agency status confirmed)
Arranges and runs conferences on international affairs for
politicians, officials, academics and others from around the
world. Also hosts conferences for public and private sector
customers.

HM CUSTOMS AND EXCISE
24 EXECUTIVE UNITS
Launched: 1/4/91
Review completed: 23/1/96

INLAND REVENUE
27 EXECUTIVE OFFICERS
Launched: 1/4/92
Review completed: 8/1/96

Under Consideration
(13 as of 30th April 1998)

Agricultural Colleges and Development Service (Northern
   Ireland)
Army Equipment Support
Criminal Records Agency
Crown Solicitor's Office (Northern Ireland)
Government Hospitality Fund/Lancaster House
Health Service Information Systems (Northern Ireland)

RAF Support Management Group
Recruitment (Northern Ireland)
Rent Officer Service
Science Service (Northern Ireland)
Superannuation (Northern Ireland)
Veterinary Service (Northern Ireland)
Youth Treatment Service

Privatised Agencies
The following former Executive Agencies have been privatised or contractualised. The date of privatisation is shown in brackets:

Accounts Services Agency (1/4/95)
ADAS (1/4/97)
Building Research Establishment (19/3/97)
Chessington Computer Centre (1/8/96)
DVOIT (17/12/93)
HMSO (30/9/96)
Laboratory of the Government Chemist (31/3/96)
National Environmental Technology Centre – formerly Warren
   Spring Laboratory and UKAEA (1/4/95)

National Physical Laboratory (1/10/95)
Natural Resources Institute (1/5/96)
NEL (1/11/95)
Occupational Health & Safety Agency (18/9/96)
Paymaster (1/4/97)
Recruitment and Assessment Services Agency (30/9/96)
Teachers' Pensions Agency (1/10/96)
Transport Reasearch Laboratory (31/3/96)

Source: Vacher's Parliamentary Companion, June 1998.

14.4 Executive Agencies and other developments

There have been a number of further developments in the nature and tasks of the Civil
Service in Britain in recent years, especially in relation to Executive Agencies which
have became very significant since their inception in 1988. Some have been logical
extensions of reforms initiated by the Thatcher Administration. Others were carried
forward more purposefully during John Major's time at 10 Downing Street. Still
others emanate from developments carried out under the Labour Government which
came into office in 1997. Cumulatively they have had far-reaching implications. See
Figure 14.4 for a list of all the Executive Agencies in 1998.

Tighter financial management

The initial thrust of Civil Service reform under the Conservatives between 1979 and
1997 was in favour of tighter financial management and this tendency was evident
throughout the period. It all began with the so-called Rayner Scrutinies, mentioned
above. These are estimated to have saved £600 million annually in the first six years

and to have produced additional one-off savings totalling £67 million. Lord Rayner originally suggested that each Department should conduct an annual scrutiny of some aspect of its activities. His successor, Sir Peter Levene, placed greater emphasis on trans-Departmental scrutinies and no longer expected each Department to undertake a scrutiny every year. The result of this shift of emphasis was that the 1993 programme, for example, included ten scrutinies from eight Departments, since most of the obvious candidates for scrutiny had already been scrutinised.

The *Financial Management Initiative* launched in 1982 was the next attempt by the then Conservative Government to get better value for money in the Civil Service. It sought to do this partly by giving Ministers greater personal responsibility for the management of their Departments, but mainly by introducing a more managerial and cost-conscious attitude into the procedures and practices of senior civil servants. This involved increasing the responsibilities of line managers, securing better management information, ensuring that Departments pay the real price of common services, putting greater emphasis on managerial skills in Civil Service training, and looking for increased efficiency at all levels of the bureaucracy. For a number of reasons it proved difficult to get this new managerial ethos established and accepted in the Civil Service, not least because most of the senior civil servants tended to find policy work more interesting than financial management. In an attempt to counteract this, posts in charge of executive operations were openly advertised and people with managerial skills brought into the Civil Service. Following the 1994 Civil Service White Paper, this process of open competition for senior posts was further extended.

Another thrust towards tighter financial management came from the *Competing for Quality* programme launched in November 1991 as part of the *Citizen's Charter* policy. At the beginning the market-testing and contracting-out which this involved was expected to produce 25 per cent savings which could then be ploughed back into Departmental programmes. It involved requiring in-house Civil Service teams to bid for specific tasks against competition from the private sector and in this competitive tendering process civil servants won the contracts in more than half the cases (measured by the value of the work to be performed). The Government estimated that in the first two years of the new approach total savings of £135 million had been achieved representing an average saving of 22 per cent. However, the 1991 White Paper also made it clear that there would be circumstances in which the Government might make strategic decisions *not* to continue as a direct provider of certain public services and that there should be a general presumption that all new public services would be contracted out to the private sector without going through the procedures of competitive tendering at all.[33]

Information subsequently provided by the Conservative Government in 1994 made it clear that 113 activities previously valued at £768 million had been contracted out with no opportunity for an in-house Civil Service bid over the period from November 1991 to the end of December 1993.[34] The rationale given by Ministers for this more radical approach involving the private provision of public services was that so-called 'strategic contracting-out' was justifiable when in-house provision might detract from a Department's ability to concentrate on its core functions or when the private sector was better equipped to provide a particular public service.

This tighter financial management has continued under the Labour Government which came into office in 1997. Pledged not just to devolve power but to improve the way public services were delivered, the Government took steps to pool Departmental budgets so that Departments could work together to spend money tackling problems which crossed Departmental lines. In addition it introduced a modernising fund designed to back innovation in the delivery of services with a view to ensuring that by 2002 one-quarter of all dealings with Government could be carried out by the public electronically, through television, telephone or computer. It also promoted joint working between local agencies to reduce overhead costs and the creation of 'one-stop shops' giving the public access to more than one service in a single visit. In short, the Government sought a combination of decentralisation and tough performance management to achieve its delivery targets.

Clearer distinction between policy and administration

Another objective has been the achievement of a clearer distinction between policy and administration in central Government. In Britain some of the earliest steps in this direction were taken by the Heath Government in the early 1970s when it experimented with the idea of 'hiving off' sections of Whitehall Departments in quasi-autonomous Agencies, such as the Civil Aviation Authority in 1971 or the Manpower Services Commission in 1973. The principle was taken a good deal further by the Thatcher Government following an influential report in 1988 by Sir Robin Ibbs, head of the so-called Efficiency Unit.[35] This recommended that to the greatest possible extent the executive (that is, administrative) functions of central Government should be carried out not by traditional Departments but by specially designed Agencies within the orbit of Whitehall's influence – the so-called Next Steps Agencies. The idea immediately appealed to the Conservative Ministers of the time and since then it has spread rapidly to nearly every sphere of central Government administration, so much so that by 1998 there were some 139 such Agencies in existence with nearly three quarters of the total number of civil servants working in them or similar executive structures.

Each Agency works within the terms of a Framework Agreement laid down by Ministers in the relevant Department and on the basis of an annual business plan seeks to meet a range of targets set by Ministers. The staff continue to be civil servants under the direction in each case of a Chief Executive who is in turn accountable to the relevant Minister for the Agency's performance in relation to its objectives and targets. Increasingly, the Chief Executives of Agencies respond directly to Parliamentary representations and complaints on behalf of constituents, although Ministers have argued that the traditional channels of political accountability also remain, since if an MP is dissatisfied with a direct response from an Agency Chief Executive, the matter can still be taken up directly with the Minister concerned.

Among the first Executive Agencies to be established were the Stationery Office, the Meteorological Office, and the Employment Services within the then Department of Employment. Since then the model has been applied throughout Whitehall to include such large bureaucracies as the Inland Revenue, the Customs and Excise, and the Benefits Agency. In every case the main goals have been to clarify and increase accountability, while enhancing through greater delegation the freedom to manage resources in the most effective ways. In pursuit of these objectives, at least one-third of all Agencies are operating as trading funds or under the discipline of net running cost controls. These mechanisms are designed to enable them to have the flexibility to meet the changing needs of their customers or users, while remaining under constant

pressure to increase efficiency. With the further backing of *Citizen's Charter* principles, serious and successful attempts have also been made to improve the quality and
reliability of all public services.

These aspects of Civil Service reform attracted all-party political support at
Westminister.[36] However, the progress of reform has thrown into sharper focus the
various definitions of public accountability put forward by the different parties. While
Ministers in the then Major Government spoke and acted increasingly in terms of
direct accountability to the users or customers of public service (whether taxpayers,
social security claimants or NHS patients, for example); the spokesmen for the then
Opposition parties tended to think of public accountability in terms of the duty of
everyone in the public service to respond to the inquiries and complaints of elected
politicians – in other words, *indirect* accountability via the people's elected representatives, whether in local authorities or the national Parliament. Furthermore, strong
opposition to the development of these Agency principles came from the Civil Service
and public service trade unions which were naturally worried about the apparent fragmentation of what used to be a unified Civil Service, and about the perceived threat to
the job security, pay and conditions of their members.

Given the obvious success of the Agency principle in these reforms, Conservative
Ministers evidently believed that it could be extended beyond the sphere of routine public
administration to the core Civil Service functions of policy advice and public sector regulation. This argument was powerfully put in the so-called Trosa Report written by a
senior French civil servant who was invited to review progress in 1993. Ministers then
drew upon this independent advice to extend the Agency principle still further when they
published a long-awaited White Paper on the Civil Service in July 1994.[37]

The 1994 White Paper proposed that the core Departments in Whitehall should
benefit from the Agency principle in at least three important ways. *First*, greater
freedom to manage was to be delegated to other Whitehall Departments by the
Treasury and the Office of Public Service, albeit within overall financial limits set by
controls on Departmental running costs. *Secondly*, the quality of management information within Departments was to be further improved by switching from current cost
accounting to resource-based or accruals accounting similar to that normally used in
the private sector. *Thirdly*, and more generally, Ministers were to continue to change
the overall culture of the Civil Service by reducing the layers of senior management
wherever possible and by consciously moving all Departments towards a more limited
policy role which would leave virtually all the routine work of public administration to
Executive Agencies.

The erosion of the state

When Margaret Thatcher launched the idea of Executive Agencies in February 1988,
she assured the House of Commons that the new institutions would be 'generally'
within the Civil Service and their staff would therefore continue to be civil servants.
Yet since that time it has become ever more apparent that Executive Agency status can
be something of a half-way house on the way to full-scale privatisation of activities
which traditionally have been regarded in Britain as part of the apparatus of the State.
The effect of this process has been gradually to shift the boundaries of central
Government and to erode the sphere of the Nation State.

This process started from modest beginnings with the privatisation of Forward, the Civil Service catering organisation, and the Driver, Vehicles and Operators Information Technology Agency. It has since spread to encompass the Crown Agents, the Transport Research Laboratory, the National Engineering Laboratory and a number of other technical Agencies within the Civil Service. In all cases the thinking behind the policy was based on the belief that many, if not most, of the support functions for central Government Departments would benefit from the greater managerial and financial freedom of the private sector.

The pursuit of this policy, however, has proved to be something of a mixed blessing in that while the threat (or promise) of privatisation may be said to keep the staff of the Executive Agencies on their toes, it has also served to demoralise at least some of the more traditionally minded staff who did not join the Civil Service in the first place in order to work in insecure conditions analogous to those in the private sector. The policy has therefore given rise to strong opposition from the Civil Service trade unions and has raised serious doubts about the chances of maintaining a unified Civil Service which upholds a common ethos of public service values and traditions.

The net numerical effect of all the changes and reforms covered in this section has been to reduce the overall size of the Civil Service in Britain by previously improbable proportions. In 1976 there were more than 751,000 civil servants. In May 1979 – when the Conservatives under Margaret Thatcher came to office for the first time – there were some 735,000 civil servants. Since then, this number has been steadily reduced to a total of 463,300 in April 1998, a decrease of 38 per cent in 22 years and the lowest since 1945.

From trust to contract

When considering the nature of the Civil Service in Britain, it is instructive to reflect upon the extent to which relationships within the Civil Service and between civil servants and Ministers have moved gradually from trust to contract. Put simply, this means that civil servants have increasingly been obliged to master the new language and assumptions of contractual relations with their superiors and with Ministers instead of the more traditional relations based upon the principles of trust and hierarchy. The 1994 White Paper on the future of the Civil Service proposed the establishment of a new Senior Civil Service at Grade 5 and above – roughly the top 3000 or so policy advising civil servants, a proposal which was implemented.[38] It also embraced the idea, previously suggested by the Efficiency Unit, of explicit written employment contracts for civil servants designed to promote a new culture in the Senior Civil Service. Although this did not go as far as the reforms in New Zealand – where a network of fixed-term contracts was introduced for all senior officials within a legislative framework provided by the 1988 State Sector Act – its adoption did, however, seem to have been informed by New Zealand experience.

This radical approach appears to have worked rather well when applied to the Chief Executives of the Executive Agencies which, in most cases, are charged with delivering specific services to the general public of a largely uniform and routine character. It is less certain how useful it is when applied to the more unpredictable activity of policy advice and the close, sometimes capricious, relationship between Ministers and civil servants.

The influence of the European Union

There is also the strong possibility that the Civil Service, like some other national institutions in Britain, will be increasingly affected by the influence of administrative practices on the Continent as the development of the European Union becomes more significant for many aspects of the British polity. If this turns out to be the case, the British will have to get used to living under a more highly developed system of administrative law, some of it derived directly from new European law binding upon Britain and some of it derived from British law increasingly influenced by Continental experience. Such developments would probably entail a more explicit separation of powers between the Executive, the Legislature and the Judiciary in Britain which, in its turn, would only be realistic if Parliament at Westminster legislated for a new codified constitution and a new structure of administrative Courts capped by a constitutional Supreme Court on the lines of the Conseil d'Etat (Council of State) in France or the Bundesverfassungsgericht (Federal Constitutional Court) in Germany.

Needless to say, such far-reaching legal and constitutional changes in Britain would transform the context within which the Civil Service and all other institutions of Government operate. At present such an outcome seems rather unlikely and remote, but it cannot completely be discounted. After all, the realities of Britain's membership of the European Union and the dynamic aspects of the continuing process of European integration have already affected much of the context and many of the assumptions of Civil Service work in Britain and may do so to an even greater extent in future.

14.5 Conclusion

On the basis of the evidence highlighted in this chapter, it is reasonable to conclude that civil servants wield considerable power and influence within British central Government, especially in Executive Agencies, and that they can have considerable influence over policy. Nevertheless the realities of British politics mean that Ministers remain in charge and their political rights are seldom questioned even by the most independent-minded or awkward civil servants. Officials are there to guide, assist and advise Ministers, not to control them. If the relationship between Ministers and officials works as it is supposed to, there need be no problems caused by over-mighty or manipulative officials.

On the other hand, the traditional ethos and conventions of Whitehall have been known to frustrate the intentions of Ministers (especially junior Ministers) and these factors may sometimes have lowered the quality or reduced the vitality of policy and decision making in British central Government. In this chapter we have noted the extent to which it is civil servants more than Ministers who tend to feel that some of their basic assumptions are under threat from the process of radical change. Yet at the same time we should not forget that well-established institutions – such as the most powerful Whitehall Departments – have traditions of their own which outlast even the most determined and long-serving Ministers.

At the outset of this chapter we made it clear that we would focus mainly on the Senior Civil Service, since these are the people who are most closely involved with Ministers in the process of policy and decision making. However, under the cumulative influence of Conservative reforms over the 1979–97 period, we should also note that the executive and regulatory functions of the Civil Service have become relatively more important, the significance of which is underlined by the fact that the vast majority of civil servants are involved either in routine administrative tasks or in delivering largely standardised public services to the general public. It is, therefore, the great mass of officials who have felt most threatened by the process of change since 1979.

Suggested questions

1 Describe the structure of the Civil Service in Britain both in general and within a 'typical' Department.
2 What are the functions of the Civil Service, and to what extent do they reveal strengths and/or weaknesses?
3 What is the traditional role of the Civil Service in Britain and how was this affected by the Conservative reforms of 1979–97?

Notes

1. Report of the Tomlin Commission, Cmnd 3909 (London: HMSO, 1931).
2. Of this number, 20 were subsequently privatised, merged or had their functions contracted out or abolished. In addition many functions previously undertaken by civil servants have been privatised or contracted out.
3. Report, 'House of Lords Select Committee on the Public Service, 1997–98' (HL Paper 55), (London: Stationery Office, 1998), Para. 110, p. 36.
4. Quoted in the Fifth Report of the Treasury and Civil Service Select Committee, 'The Role of the Civil Service', Vol. I, HC 27-I, 1993–94 (London: HMSO, November 1994), para. 65.
5. E. Bridges, *Portrait of a Profession* (London: Cambridge University Press, 1950), p. 25.
6. See the 'Report of the Fulton Committee', Cmnd 3628 (London: HMSO, 1968).
7. See B. Sedgemore, *The Secret Constitution* (London: Hodder & Stoughton, 1980), pp. 148–53; also, P. Kellner and N. Crowther-Hunt, *The Civil Servants* (London: Macdonald, 1980), pp. 121–3.
8. See Report, 'House of Lords Select Committee on the Public Service' (HL Paper 55), (London: Stationery Office, 1998), pp. 32–4.
9. See the Interim Report of the Treasury and Civil Service Select Committee on 'The Role of the Civil Service', HC 390-I, 1992–93, para. 6 (London: HMSO, July 1993) from which this definition of functions is drawn.
10. The authors are grateful to Richard Mottram, Permanent Secretary at the Office of Public Service and Science in 1994, for his expert guidance on the established conventions of the Civil Service.
11. See D. Howells, 'Marks and Spencer and the Civil Service, A Comparison of Culture and Methods', *Public Administration*, Autumn 1981.
12. See the *Citizens' Charters*, Cmnd 1599 (London: HMSO, July 1991).
13. See 'Report of the Inquiry into the Export of Defence Equipment and Dual-Use Goods to Iraq and Related Prosecutions', vols. 1–5 + index (HC Paper 115, 1996), (London: HMSO 1996).

14. For example, in a 'Report on the Civil Service by the House of Commons Select Committee on Expenditure', HC 535, 1977.
15. See B. Sedgemore, *The Secret Constitution*, pp. 11–48.
16. See 'Civil Service Commissioners' Report, 1993–94', and the '1997–98 Report of the House of Lords Select Committee on the Public Service', pages 93 and 97–98, for evidence of this trend.
17. See T. Benn, 'Manifestos and Mandarins', in W. Rodgers *et al.*, *Policy and Practise the Experience of Government* (London: RIPA, 1980), pp. 57–78.
18. See J. Hoskyns, 'Whitehall and Westminster, An Outsider's View', *Fiscal Studies*, November 1982.
19. See in particular evidence given to the Treasury and Civil Service Select Committee in May 1993 by Lord Carrington, Interim Report on 'The Role of Civil Service', HC 390II, pp. 138–9.
20. Of course, the so-called 'middle group' of British politics is an elusive and changing concept, as can be illustrated by the apparent policy convergence between the Conservative Party of first John Major and then William Hague and Tony Blair's 'New Labour' Party.
21. For a fuller analysis of the 'public interest' defence used in the Courts, see R. Thomas, 'The British Official Secrets Act, 1911–39 and the Ponting Case', in R.A. Chapman and M. Hunt (eds), *Open Government* (London: Routledge, 1989), pp. 95–122.
22. See 'Report of the Inquiry into the Export of Defence Equipment and Dual-Use Goods to Iraq and Related Prosecutions', vols. 1–5 + Index (HC Paper 115, 196), (London: HMSO, 1996).
23. See especially the evidence given to the Treasury and Civil Service Select Committee in 1933–94 by the Civil Service unions in 'The Role of the Civil Service', HC 27-11, pp. 132–52.
24. See the Eighth Report of the House of Commons Public Accounts Committee, 1993–94, on 'The Proper Conduct of Public Business' (London: HMSO, 1994) for further elaboration of this argument.
25. A good example was the non-resignation of Norman Lamont as Chancellor of the Exchequer in September 1992 immediately after 'Black Wednesday' when the British Government suffered the humiliation of having Sterling forced out of the European Exchange Rate Mechanism by huge financial movements in the markets.
26. MINIS is well described in paras 23–26 of the Third Report of the Treasury and Civil Service Select Committee, HC 236-I, 1981–82.
27. Report, 'House of Lords Select Committee on the Public Service, 1997–98' (HL Paper 55) (London: The Stationery Office, 1998), p. 25.
28. See G. Drewry, *Law, Justice and Politics* (London: Longman, 1975), pp. 75–6.
29. For example, in the 1981 case of *Bromley Council v. Greater London Council*, in which the Law Lords ruled that the GLC had acted *ultra vires* by subsidising London Transport fares to an excess extent via precepts upon the rates of the London Boroughs.
30. Report, 'House of Lords Select Committee on the Public Service, 1997–98' (HL Paper 55) (London: The Stationery Office, 1998), p. 29.
31. See Chapter 18, section 18.2, for discussion of the legal and constitutional implications of Britain's membership of the European Union.
32. See Chapter 17, section 17.6, for a fuller description of the role and statutory limits upon the activities of the Ombudsman.
33. See the White Paper 'Competing for Quality', Cmnd 1930 (London: HMSO, November 1991).
34. See the White Paper on 'The Civil Service, Continuity and Change', Cmnd 2627, July 1994, p. 93.

35. See 'The Financing and Accountability of Next Steps Agencies', Cmnd 914 (London: HMSO, 1989) for a fuller explanation of Conservative Government thinking on the Executive Agencies.
36. This point is best illustrated by successive reports of the all-party Treasury and Civil Service Select Committee in the late 1980s and early 1990s, culminating in the November 1994 Report on 'The Role of the Civil Service'.
37. See Sylvie Trosa, 'Next Steps – Moving On: A Progress Report to Government' (London: Office of Public Service and Science, February 1994).
38. See the White Paper 'The Civil Service, Continuity and Change', Cmnd 2627, paras 4, 13–4, 22.

Further reading

Barberis, P. (ed.), *The Whitehall Reader: The UK's Administrative Machine in Action*, (Buckingham: Open University Press, 1996).
Bruce-Gardyne, J., *Ministers and Mandarins* (London: Sidgwick & Jackson, 1986).
Drewry, G. and Butcher, T., *The Civil Service Today* (Oxford: Blackwell, 1988).
Dyness, M. and Walker, D., *The Times Guide to the New British State: The Government Machine in the 1990s* (London: Times Books, 1995).
Giddings, P., *Parliamentary Accountability: A Study of Parliament and Executive Agencies* (London: Macmillan, 1995).
Henderson, N., *Mandarin* (London: Weidenfeld & Nicolson, 1994).
Hennessy, P., *Whitehall* (London: Secker & Warburg, 1989).
James, S., *British Government: A Reader in Policy Making* (London: Routledge, 1997).
Metcalfe, L. and Richards, S., *Improving Public Management* (London: Sage, 1989).
Pyper, R., *The British Civil Service* (Hemel Hempstead: Prentice Hall/Harvester Wheatsheaf, 1995).
Report, House of Lords Select Committee on the Public Service, 1997–98 (HL Paper 55) (London: Stationery Office, 1998).
Report of the Inquiry into the Export of Defence Equipment and Dual-Use Goods to Iraq and Related Prosecutions, vols 1–5 + index (HC Paper 115, 1996), (London: HMSO, 1996).
Treasury and Civil Service Select Committee Report on 'The Role of the Civil Service', HC 27 I-III (London: November 1994).
White Paper on The Civil Service, Continuity and Change', Cmnd 2627 (London: HMSO, July 1994).
White Paper on 'The Civil Service, Taking Forward Continuity and Change', Cmnd 2748 (London: HMSO, January 1995).
Williams, W., *Washington, Westminster and Whitehall* (London: Cambridge University Press, 1988).

Websites

The Civil Service   http://www.civil-service.co.uk

PART 5

The Wider Public Sector

The changing role of the state

In this chapter the term 'public sector' is taken to include non-Departmental public bodies, extra-Governmental organisations, other public bodies and public corporations. It does not include the Departments of Central Government which we dealt with in Chapters 13 and 14 or the institutions of devolved and local government which we shall deal with in Chapter 16. In this chapter we shall begin by looking at those bodies of a semi-autonomous nature which operate to a greater or lesser extent at arm's length from Ministers and Departments but which effectively act as agencies for central Government and which carry out Government policies. We will then move on to consider a variety of other public bodies before turning to review the problems which were posed by the public corporations over the years. Finally, we shall go on to examine the issues raised by privatisation, which have included the need for new forms of regulation to deal with those sectors where there has been insufficient competition to protect the consumer interest. The various types of institution to be found in the British public sector are shown diagrammatically in Figure 15.1.

15.1 The orbit of Central Government

Semi-autonomous Governmental bodies

There has been a significant growth of public sector bodies which are neither an integral part of Central Government nor an integral part of local government, but which nevertheless are clearly located within the public sector. These bodies have been variously described at different times as 'non-departmental public bodies' (NDPBs), 'quasi-autonomous non-governmental organisations' (Quangos), or simply 'extra-governmental organisations' (EGOs). No matter what the subtle differences in nomenclature, it is possible to recognise these institutions when one sees them. Furthermore, they require investigation and analysis, because they have become a matter of considerable media interest and political controversy under both Labour and Conservative Governments in Britain.

In one of the earliest official surveys of this part of the public sector, Geoffrey Bowen identified 252 non-Departmental public bodies which he defined as 'organisations which have been set up or adopted by Departments and provided with public funds to perform some function which the Government wishes to have performed, but

Figure 15.1   The composition of the public sector

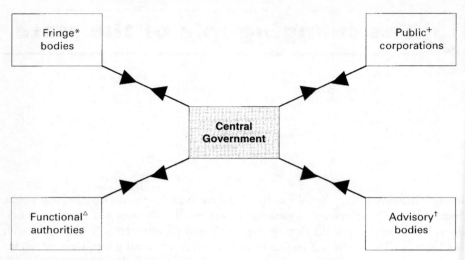

* Notably several hundred Quangos
+ Nationalised industries
△ Notably the health authorities
† Notably Advisory and Departmental Committees and Task Forces

which it does not wish to be the direct responsibility of a Minister or a Department'.[1] They were generally divided into three categories: executive bodies, advisory bodies, and administrative Tribunals. They therefore included a wide range of very different institutions exemplified by the British Library, the Equal Opportunities Commission, the Gaming Board, Trinity House, the Wales Tourist Board, the White Fish Authority, and the Supplementary Benefits Appeals Tribunals.

When this varied part of the public sector was reviewed again in the 1980 Pliatzky Report, it appeared that the number of such institutions had grown to 2167, they employed about 217,000 people and were responsible for a range of activities costing about £6.1 billion in all.[2] By 1993, following a deliberate cull of such institutions by Ministers, the total number had – according to official statistics – fallen to 1389, with Ministers being responsible for some 42,600 appointments.[3] However, according to a study published in 1994 by Democratic Audit and Charter 88 Trust, there were 5521 'extra-governmental organisations' responsible for £46.7 billion of public spending in 1992–93 and providing at least 70,000 jobs directly or indirectly in the gift of Ministers.[4] As Figure 15.2 shows, this provides extensive Ministerial patronage.

Clearly the number of such bodies depends on definition. An *exclusive* or limited definition – namely, bodies which have a role in the process of national Government but which are neither a Government Department nor a part of one and which operate at arm's length from Ministers – would omit NHS trusts, Training and Enterprise Councils (TECS), police authorities, incorporated colleges of further education and grant-maintained schools; an *inclusive* or broad definition – namely, bodies of a semi-autonomous nature which in practice act as agencies for central Government and which carry out Government policies – would include a much larger number of very diverse public bodies. In this chapter we are using the latter definition.

Figure 15.2 The network of Ministerial patronage

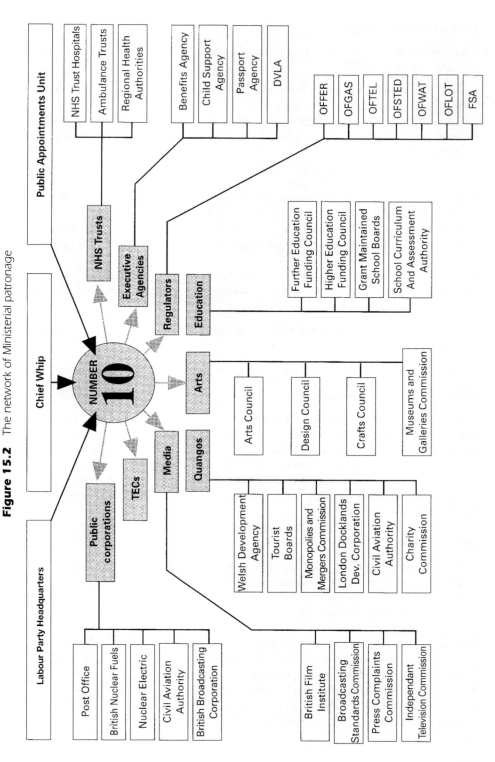

Common characteristics

On closer inspection it becomes clear that these various public bodies have a number of common characteristics:

1. They derive their existence from Ministerial decisions and can be answerable to Ministers for what they do or fail to do.
2. Their creation normally requires legislative approval by Parliament and most of them produce annual reports which have to be laid before Parliament and can be debated there.
3. They are usually financed by Exchequer grants, but may sometimes be given the power to raise their own statutory levies.
4. Each Chairman and Board are appointed by a Minister for a fixed term of office and can be reappointed – or not – by a Minister at the end of such a term.
5. Such bodies recruit their own staff (who do not usually have the status of civil servants), although their pay and conditions are often comparable with those of the Civil Service.
6. The annual accounts of such bodies are audited either commercially or by the National Audit Commission, which means that high standards of financial accountability can be achieved.

In short, they represent an identifiable and growing sub-species of public administration in Britain.

Advantages and disadvantages

Those who have investigated this opaque area of the public sector have identified a number of advantages and disadvantages in the existence of such bodies. At the outset it must be said that the advantages usually seem more obvious to the supporters of the Government of the day, whilst the disadvantages usually seem more obvious to its opponents. This is mainly because the public appointments concerned are made by the party in office for what are usually considered by its supporters to be good reasons.

On the *positive side*, the following points can be made for non-Departmental public bodies:

1. They permit certain activities of importance to the state to be conducted outside the confines of Government Departments, yet within the Whitehall sphere of influence.
2. They permit such activities to be conducted free from direct or frequent oversight by Parliament and therefore to some extent insulated from the party battle at Westminster.
3. They enable Parliament to pass what is essentially framework legislation in some areas of public administration with the confidence that any problems which may arise can be solved in a practical manner.
4. They make it easier to achieve a broad continuity of policy in a largely apolitical way.
5. They relieve civil servants of many tiresome administrative chores and so enable the Departments of central Government to concentrate more on policy advice and financial control.

6. They provide useful opportunities for the dispensing of political patronage by the party in office.

On the negative side, the following points can be made against non-Departmental public bodies:

1. There has been a lack of clarity or agreement about just how many such bodies there really are at any time and whether all those which have been identified by some as being in this category have been correctly categorised.
2. The growth of such bodies has produced an institutional proliferation which has proved expensive to administer and difficult to supervise and control.
3. The large number of appointments to such bodies has provided too much scope for political patronage on a scale which has been politically and ethically undesirable.
4. There has been a lack of effective democratic control over these bodies and a parallel lack of financial control over the public funds which are spent by them.

In short, they have been seen by their critics as a 'new magistracy' which has involved the steady replacement of elected local government with appointed administration.

In January 1988 Margaret Thatcher announced to Parliament the results of a comprehensive review of NDPBs and made it clear that such bodies would be subjected to further review at least every five years.[5] She told the House of Commons that such reviews would consider whether or not there was a need for each and every body, how well or badly it was fulfilling its objectives, and whether or not its financial and other management systems were adequate. Since that time this category of public administration has grown considerably. Grant Maintained Schools, NHS Trusts, Further Education Colleges, Training and Enterprise Councils, Urban Development Corporations, Regional Development Agencies – all these and many more institutions could be said to have joined the category.

The main criticism of these developments in the academic and political worlds has been that such bodies are not subject to the control of locally elected politicians (or indeed Members of Parliament) and that what they spend is not adequately audited at national level (only one-third of all NDPBs have their financial affairs scrutinised by the Audit Commission or the National Audit Office). On the other hand, Ministers in the Major Government argued the merits of direct accountability to those whom they described as 'the customers' of NDPBs. As William Waldegrave put it when he was the Minister responsible for the public service, the issue is 'not whether those who run our public services are elected, but whether they are ... consumer responsive'.[6] This definition of 'public accountability' stemmed from two strong feelings held by the Conservatives under both Margaret Thatcher and John Major: the desire to by-pass what they saw as the unreasonably obstructive attitudes of many Labour and Liberal Democrat controlled local authorities, and the wish to improve the performance of the public sector by setting higher standards for the public services under the rubric of the *Citizen's Charter*.

In short, the political parties in Britain came to espouse contrasting definitions of public accountability. The Labour Party put the accent on the traditional definition in Britain which stresses *upward* accountability to the elected representatives of the people at national and local level, whereas the Conservatives put the accent on their new definition which stresses the *downward* accountability directly to the people themselves in their various roles as consumers, users, customers or beneficiaries of the goods and services delivered at the behest of the state.

Royal Commissions, Committees of Inquiry, Reviews and Task Forces

The appointment of a Royal Commission, Committee of Inquiry, Review or Task Force is an act of the Executive which requires no prior Parliamentary approval, although it is often a Ministerial response to political pressures. As Lord Benson and Lord Rothschild put it, the purposes of such bodies are 'first to ascertain all the relevant facts, next to assemble them fairly and impartially, and finally to form balanced conclusions'.[7] Once established, bodies of this kind usually invite written and oral evidence from all interested parties both inside and outside the web of central Government. They may also undertake or sponsor research of their own in order to get a clearer understanding of the issues which they have to investigate. When their work is complete, they normally publish both their reports and records of the evidence submitted to them as a contribution to subsequent debate in Parliament and in public. Only when dealing with matters of national security or commercial confidentiality are such reports published with certain omissions and, very occasionally, a decision may be taken by Ministers not to publish at all.

Over the period 1954–69 which was reviewed by Lord Benson and Lord Rothschild, 24 Royal Commissions and more than 600 Committees of Inquiry were established. Most of them were disbanded when their tasks were complete, although a few were allowed to continue as Standing Commissions or Committees on a permanent basis – for example, the Royal Commission on Environmental Pollution or the Law Commission. Among the most significant Royal Commissions or Committees of Inquiry in more recent times have been the Kilbrandon Commission on the Constitution (1969–73), the Bullock Committee on Industrial Democracy (1975–77), the Wilson Committee on Financial Institutions (1977–80), the Scarman Committee on the Brixton Disorders (1981), and the Banham Commission on Local Government Boundaries (1991–94).

When such bodies have reported, it has been for Ministers to decide what to do about their recommendations. Sometimes this has led to administrative action, sometimes to new legislation. In many cases, however, it has been used as little more than a convenient device for deflecting criticism, defusing controversy or simply putting off difficult decisions on issues about which there may be little or no political agreement. Sometimes it has been used as a way of burying issues altogether, which is why Margaret Thatcher and other self-styled 'conviction politicians' usually eschewed this institutional device. However, the more pragmatic John Major was better disposed than his predecessor to the use of such bodies and, although only one Royal Commission was set up,[8] more than 60 Committees of Inquiry were established during his time at 10 Downing Street, including the Scott Inquiry into the Matrix-Churchill 'Arms to Iraq' Affair which reported in 1996, and the Nolan Committee on Standards in Public Life which reported in 1994.

Tony Blair in his first year as Prime Minister presided over the establishment of a remarkable 146 Commissions, Inquiries, Reviews and Task Forces, including a Royal Commission on Long-term Care, a Commission on the voting system chaired by Lord

Jenkins of Hillhead and an Inquiry into the causes of BSE[9]. This was done mainly to demonstrate how inclusive and open to ideas from non-traditional sources the Labour Government could be. It also gave an impression of purposeful activity without the need to take immediate tough decisions.

Departmental Advisory Committees

As for the many advisory committees which assist Whitehall Departments in the course of day-to-day public administration, these provide a clear illustration of the extent to which regular consultations with acknowledged experts and interested groups, whether formal or informal, have become a notable characteristic of British central Government. As we saw in Chapter 6, such advisory committees can meet the needs of Whitehall Departments for expert information and advice, while satisfying the claims of sectional interest groups for access to central Government and influence on policy making. They also provide one more means by which any Government can seek to gain and retain the consent of the governed – at any rate those who may be most directly affected by the consequences of a given Government policy.

Such advisory committees are particularly useful to Whitehall Departments in the detailed preparation of secondary legislation and technical Statutory Instruments. The need for this advice arises because many Acts of Parliament put statutory responsibilities on Ministers to consult certain specified advisory bodies when drawing up subsequent secondary legislation. For example, under the 1964 Police Act the Home Secretary was obliged to consult the Police Council which had been set up specifically to advise on regulations concerning the administration and conditions of service in police forces throughout the country. Equally, under the 1975 Social Security Act the Secretary of State for Social Security was obliged to consult the National Insurance Advisory Committee on all regulations issued in relation to National Insurance. More recently, the 1992 Social Security Amendment Act stipulated that the Secretary of State for Social Security was to be advised by the Industrial Injuries Advisory Council on proposals for regulations and other matters relating to industrial injuries benefits payable under the 1992 Social Securities Contributions and Benefits Act, and in particular on the Schedule of Prescribed Diseases.

There have also been examples of such detailed consultations which have taken place on a *non-statutory basis* over the years – for example, within the framework of the National Economic Development Council (NEDC) from its inception in 1962 to its abolition in 1992. During its heyday this provided a useful forum for regular meetings between the Government of the day (represented mainly by Ministers) and what were known at the time as 'the two sides of industry', namely employers and trade unions. However, with the considerable change in the political climate on industrial policy during the Thatcherite years, Ministers saw less and less need for the NEDC and associated it increasingly in their minds with the corporalist politics of the 1960s and 1970s. Another example, and one still in existence, would be the Women's National Commission, an independent advisory body formed in 1969. Its terms of reference are to ensure that the informed opinion of women are given their due weight in the deliberations of Government. Its members represent major national organisations of women across the United Kingdom.

Special Purpose Authorities

Until the privatisation of the water industry in the late 1980s, there were 10 *Water Authorities* in England and Wales (and separate ones in Scotland and Northern Ireland) responsible in the public sector for about three quarters of the water supply, water treatment and sewerage services. The remaining water services were provided by smaller private water companies which had been in existence for a long time in some parts of the country. The Water Authorities provided a good example of special purpose authorities in the public sector, since they had been established in 1974 by Act of Parliament with clear statutory duties to provide comprehensive water services within hydrologically determined geographical areas.

For many years *Health Authorities* provided another good example of special purpose Authorities. Their institutional structure was originally determined by the postwar Labour Government under the terms of the 1948 National Health Service Act. They were essentially unchanged for a quarter of a century, but then reorganised in 1974, 1982 and again in 1993 following the Conservative Government's far-reaching Health Service reforms in the early 1990s. The outcome of this period of institutional upheaval was that in England the structure of the National Health Service was capped by the National Management Board led by a Chief Executive responsible to the Secretary of State for Health. Below the National Board there were 100 Health Authorities which were the main bodies responsible for managing and purchasing health care at the local level. Unlike the situation before the 1990 Health Service reform, health care was provided (largely under contracts) by GPs working in primary practice, hospitals organised as NHS Trusts, and some other specialist facilities (including a few private ones). Together with the so-called NHS Outposts of the Department of Health in the various parts of the country and the few remaining special purpose Authorities (such as the Health Education Authority), these institutions made up the managerial, purchasing and regulatory structure of the National Health Service in England. Separate, but similar arrangements were made in Wales and Scotland, while Northern Ireland remained an exception with Health Boards answerable directly to a Minister in the Northern Ireland Office.

Under the aegis of the 1990 Health Service Reform Act the organisation of the NHS was therefore radically transformed for the first time since its creation in the late 1940s. A clear distinction was drawn between those responsible for *purchasing* health services on behalf of their local communities – that is, the Health Authorities and Family Health Service Authorities (which oversaw the primary health care provided by GPs) – and those responsible for *providing* the services – for example, the NHS Trusts (over 400), private hospitals and other specialist facilities. In primary care, a controversial distinction was drawn between the large number of GPs who became so-called 'fund holders' – around 3500 (representing half of GP practices – with the freedom to use their practice budgets to purchase specialist, acute or primary health care for their patients from wherever they deemed most appropriate, and all the others who remained tied to the services provided within their areas according to the priorities set by their Health Authorities and Family Health Service Authorities. The critics of this reform claimed that it has produced an excessively bureaucratic and more inequitable Health Service.[10] The proponents of the reform argued that the system delivered better value for money and hence a lower burden upon taxpayers than would otherwise have been the case.

The Labour Government which came into office in 1997 accepted the purchaser–provider split and left this principle of the Conservative health reforms broadly intact. However, it declared that it would end competition and, subject to Parliamentary approval, replace it with a new statutory duty for NHS Trusts to work in partnership with other NHS organisations. In addition it sought to reduce the number of Health Authorities, abolish GP fundholding and replace by Primary Care Groups – with single, unified budgets – in each area, and short-term contracts – stipulating instead that NHS Trusts would come to long-term agreements with Primary Care Groups, introduce National Service and Performance Frameworks which would set national standards of performance, efficiency and patient care, establish a National Institute for Clinical Excellence to promote clinical and cost effectiveness and set up an independent Commission for Health Improvement to oversee the quality of clinical services.

15.2 Public corporations

In Britain public ownership and control have traditionally been associated with the model of the public corporation. Yet there have been many different forms of public ownership and control which have been tried over the years. In the second half of the nineteenth century, the early Socialists advocated *municipal ownership* and control of key industries. Those who pressed for this 'gas and water Socialism' considered local authorities to be the best institutional mechanism for providing these essential public services. Before the Second World War more than two-thirds of electricity supply and about one-third of gas supply were under municipal ownership and control, as is still the case in some continental countries (for example, Denmark). Over the years a number of municipal authorities also provided passenger transport services, civic amenities and other local services through their direct labour departments.

After 1945 the focus of public ownership and control shifted to *nationalisation,* since the postwar Labour Government gave priority to considerations of national planning, economies of scale, and distributional equity. This model of centrally administered nationalised industries remained the archetypal public sector institution until 1979 when the alternative policy of privatisation began to be brought to the fore in Britain.

Notwithstanding the dominance of nationalisation as the model for the public sector in Britain from 1945 to 1979, other forms of public ownership and control were attempted with varying degrees of enthusiasm for shorter or longer periods during that time. These alternatives included *administrative control by Whitehall Departments* with Ministers directly accountable to Parliament for the running of nationalised industries, as with the Post Office until 1969; *financial control by state holding companies,* such as the Industrial Reorganisation Corporation in the late 1960s or the National Enterprise Board in the late 1970s; and the establishment of *state-owned financial institutions*, such as the Post Office Giro Bank in 1969.

In spite of these variations, the dominant model continued to be *public corporations*, more usually known as nationalised industries. At their peak in 1982 such institutions employed about 1,759,000 people (about 7 per cent of those in work at the time), they created about 11 per cent of Gross Domestic Product (GDP), and accounted for about 17 per cent of total fixed investment in the British economy.[11] They had come to dominate four vital sectors of the economy: energy, transport, steel, and communications. They included long-established institutions, such as British Rail and British Coal, as well as some relatively new institutions, such as British Telecom and the British National Oil Corporation. In their heyday they were important customers and suppliers of the private sector, and they had a profound and pervasive effect on the health of the British economy and the course of British politics.[12]

Common characteristics

Public corporations had a number of common characteristics which set them apart from other industrial and commercial undertakings in Britain.[13]

1. They were established by Acts of Parliament as statutory bodies responsible for the production of goods or the provision of services specified in the legislation.
2. They were publicly owned in the sense that any securities which they issued carry no private risk and usually paid fixed rates of interest, although in some successful cases they paid public dividends to the Exchequer.
3. They were subject to Government control via the indirect mechanisms of required rates of return on capital, external financial limits on investment and borrowing, and periodic Ministerial appointments of their Chairmen and Board members.
4. In return for meeting these politically determined obligations, they enjoyed varying degrees of day-to-day managerial autonomy, their employees were not civil servants (unlike in France or Germany, for example), and they enjoyed some limited financial freedoms from Treasury control (although this lessened as the years went by).

Essential problems

There were a number of essential problems which beset public corporations in Britain over the years. To a considerable extent these problems stemmed from the conflicting pressures which gave rise to the establishment of public corporations in the first place.

First, the theory of public ownership assumed that the major issues of macroeconomic policy could be kept separate from the day-to-day matters faced by the management of public corporations, and that Ministers and nationalised industry Boards could play distinct and complementary roles which would not clash. In practice, these were soon shown to be heroic or naive assumptions, since in a modern mixed economy Ministers were inevitably involved in the biggest decisions of public corporations. This was partly because of their economic weight and political importance in the British economy, which meant that their corporate decisions were bound to have a significant effect on the success or failure of Government policy. It was also because, whereas the Socialist ideal had been that the state should own the most vital industrial sectors on behalf of the people, all too often the reality was characterised by trade union demands for the state to rescue backward or uncompetitive undertakings (for example, the railways or ship-building) largely for the sake of keeping the employees in work.

Secondly, the problems of dealing with the public corporations were not made any easier by their great diversity which was reflected in their widely differing economic fortunes. For example, at various stages during public ownership, British Airways, British Gas, British Telecom and the Post Office each generated impressive profits which were returned in large part to the Exchequer in the form of public dividends, whereas British Rail, British Coal, British Shipbuilders and London Transport each had economic difficulties and were seldom able to generate an overall profit for the nation. The former group provided examples of successful industries (often with monopoly profits) which were capable of generating good returns on their capital and labour employed, whereas the latter group provided examples of strife-torn industries with economically debilitating social and regional obligations.

Thirdly, the public corporations suffered over the years from the fact that their very existence was the subject of bitter and long-lasting political conflict both between and, occasionally, within the two main parties. In many respects they were treated as a political football to be kicked back and forth between two entrenched ideological positions on the Left and the Right of British politics. The hard Left of the Labour Party invariably pressed for an enlarged public sector and the nationalisation (or renationalisation) of key economic sectors. The free market wing of the Conservative Party consistently sought to reduce the size of the public sector and, from the early 1980s in particular, to privatise as many public corporations as possible. Indeed, the extent of this determined drive to privatise is demonstrated by the fact that between 1979 and 1997 there were at least 50 significant acts of privatisation in Britain which reduced the remaining nationalised industries to under 2 per cent of GDP employing only approximately 1 per cent of the total workforce.[14]

Lastly, and most crucially, the central problem of the public corporations in Britain was the difficulty of establishing a satisfactory arm's-length relationship between the Boards of the nationalised industries and Ministers in the Government of the day. In so far as this was ever achieved, it involved reconciling managerial freedom for the Boards with the constant political temptation for Ministers to interfere with the managerial ground-rules of the public sector. Traditionally the public corporations were charged in their founding Statutes with twin duties: to break even financially taking one year with another, and to operate in the public interest. Needless to say, these duties were often incompatible and when they were, it was usually the latter (as defined by Ministers) which prevailed. This might have been all right if there had been a clear and lasting consensus between the two main political parties about what constituted 'the public interest' at any given time. Yet such a consensus never really existed, since there was an inherent conflict of interest between the interests of the employees of public corporations who wished to maintain their jobs and improve their rewards (backed by Labour) and the interests of taxpayers and others in the wider community who wished to contain the levels of financial support for the public corporations and who were invariably backed by the Conservatives.

In short, experience over at least five decades in Britain demonstrated the great difficulties in maintaining a satisfactory arm's-length relationship between public corporations and the Government of the day. All too often the former were required by the Treasury to reduce or defer their investment programmes for the sake of wider objectives of national policy, notably Government determination to limit or reduce the level of public sector borrowing. On other occasions they were obliged to subordinate their commercial judgement to the political priorities of Ministers. For example, there were occasions when British Coal wanted to close uneconomic pits, but the Government of the day insisted that these be kept open for social or political reasons. There were other occasions such as when British Steel was required to invest heavily in new plant and equipment at the behest of Ministers (notably by the Conservatives in 1972–73) only to find, when the new plant came on stream, that the forecast expansion of the market to justify it did not materialise. Even the rhetorically non-interventionist Conservative Government in the early 1980s instructed the nationalised gas and electricity industries to raise their prices by more than their commercial judgement suggested was wise simply to increase the flow of revenue from these public corporations to the Exchequer. In all such cases it could be argued that the nation as a whole suffered the effects of policies which combined the worst of both worlds.

In the face of this massive and sustained onslaught upon the public sector in Britain by the Conservatives in office, the Labour Party felt obliged in the 1990s to revise its traditional policy favouring nationalisation and renationalisation. At the 1994 Labour Party Conference Tony Blair declared his intention to re-write the 1918 Labour constitution and especially the party's long-standing commitment to public ownership of the means of production, distribution and exchange enshrined in Clause IV – something which the party did in 1995. During the 1997 General Election campaign Tony Blair went further, declaring that: 'Where there is no overriding reason for preferring the public provision of goods and services, particularly where those services operate in a competitive market, then the presumption should be that economic activity is best left to the private sector, with market forces being fully encouraged to operate'.[15] This has been the approach taken by the Labour Government in office since 1997. Thus it would appear that the long struggle over nationalisation and de-nationalisation may have come to an end, or at any rate it may have been transformed into a more subtle debate about regulation and control in the public interest.

15.3 Privatisation

The broad definition of privatisation includes everything from the sale of state owned enterprises to private investors (previously known in Britain as de-nationalisation), to the sale of public assets (such as public land or Council housing), to the contracting out of public services (such as cleaning or rubbish collection), to radical ideas for providing education or health services via individual vouchers cashable at public or private institutions. It can also be said to include aggressive liberalisation of many sectors of the economy, such as bus and coach services, cable television and telecommunications. Nor should we fail to note in this broad context the sustained Conservative policy in the 1980s and 1990s of reducing the size of the Civil Service, and the policy of eliminating some of the tiers of local government – such as the Greater London Council and the other Metropolitan County Councils. In all these various ways successive Conservative Administrations during the 1979–97 period sought to curtail and redefine the role of the state and its agencies, while simultaneously encouraging market forces in the areas of the economy from which public sector institutions were withdrawn.

The Labour Party which came to power in 1997 had in many respects come to accept this general approach – indeed, this was one of the factors that led to its 'rehabilitation' as a party of Government. Pursuing a so-called 'Third Way' between old Socialism and unrestrained free-market capitalism, believing that markets will ultimately deliver public benefits and that intervention, although necessary, is best kept to a minimum; the Labour Government under Tony Blair continued to privatise and roll back the frontiers of the state. This approach was evident from plans to sell 49 per cent of Air Traffic Control and to involve private enterprise in Education Action Zones.

Let us look first at the *sale of state-owned enterprises*. Intractable problems were caused for all British Governments after 1945 by the constant attempts to maintain a satisfactory arm's-length relationship between Ministers and public corporations. By 1979 the lesson of experience was that the public corporations were bound to pose serious problems for any Government, at any rate in so far as their commercial performance was so frequently disappointing and their impact upon taxpayers and the rest of the economy invariably unwelcome.

Against this background it was not surprising that some senior figures in the Conservative Government which came to power in 1979 wanted to embark upon a policy of radical and extensive privatisation. However, at that time many of their colleagues were still inhibited by the long-lasting influence of the postwar settlement which had led the nationalised industries to be regarded by both main parties as an inevitable, if not necessarily desirable, part of the British national economy.

As things turned out, the 1979–83 Conservative Government returned six large public corporations to the private sector, although only two (British Aerospace and Amersham International) were sold to investors in one go. We should also notice, however, that this period of Conservative Government was marked by the 1980 Housing Act, the most significant feature of which was the introduction of a statutory right for all Council tenants to buy (at generous discounts in most cases) the properties in which they lived as Council tenants. This triggered an enormous shift of wealth and power from the public to the private sectors and did a good deal to popularise the wider cause of privatisation. By the end of the 1980s it had resulted in the creation of more than one million extra people in owner-occupation and the raising of about £10,000 million in asset sales.

Following their victory at the 1983 General Election, Margaret Thatcher and her senior colleagues felt more confident about applying the principle of privatisation to more parts of the public sector. Accordingly, the Conservatives legislated in the 1983–87 Parliament for the return to the private sector of a larger number of state-owned industries, including two giant public utilities – British Telecom and British Gas. The gross proceeds of these two sales in 1984 and 1986 amounted to nearly £9,000 million and in each case the shares were bought extensively (at a discount to the real market price) by first-time shareholders and employees of the industries concerned. The cumulative result was that more than 50 significant privatisations took place under the Conservatives between 1979 and 1997 which yielded accumulated proceeds for the Exchequer of more than £80 billion at 1997–98 prices. Surprisingly perhaps, the policy of privatisation was pursued further by the Labour Government which came into office in 1997. For example, in 1998 the Government announced that a majority stake in the Air Traffic control system was to be sold and that an examina-

Figure 15.3 Privatisations since 1979

Privatisation proceeds, 1979–80 to 1996–97 £ million

	1979–80 to 1982–83	1983–84	1984–85	1985–86	1986–87	1987–88	1988–89	1989–90	1990–91	1991–92	1992–93	1993–94	1994–95	1995–96	1996–97
Amersham International	64														
Associated British Ports Holdings plc	46		51												
Atomic Energy Authority Holdings plc														−2	215
BAA plc						534	689								
Belfast International Airport													47		
British Aerospace plc	43			347											
British Airways plc					435	419									
British Coal												811		3	111
British Gas plc															
– sale of shares					1820	1758	1555	4	150						
– redemption of debt					750	250		800	350		350		350		
British Petroleum plc	284	543				863	3000	1363							
British Steel plc							1138	1287							
British Sugar Corporation	44														
British Telecommunications															
– sale of shares			1358	1246	1081					1666	3544	3773	1519		
– loan stock			44	61	53	23				106	113	124	130		
– redemption of preference shares					250	250	85	92	100						
Britoil plc	334	293		426											
BTG										25					
Cable and Wireless plc	181	263		577											
Chessington Computer Centre															11
DTELs												5			
DVOIT												12			
Electricity industries															
– sale of shares (England and Wales)									3134	2329	1465	13	1724	1029	796
– sale of shares (Scotland)										1112	907	703	2		
– redemption of debt										1106	110	654	390		
Enterprise Oil plc			384												
Forestry Commission	14	21	28	15	16	13	12	15	11	16	10	17	11		
Forward												4			
General Practice Finance Corporation						67									
Harland and Wolff							8								
Insurance Services Group										12					
Land Settlement		2	12	5	2										
National Enterprise Board Holdings	122	168	30		34										
National Freight Consortium	5														

Figure 15.3 continued

Privatisation proceeds, 1979–80 to 1996–97 £ million

	1979–80 to 1982–83	1983–84	1984–85	1985–86	1986–87	1987–88	1988–89	1989–90	1990–91	1991–92	1992–93	1993–94	1994–95	1995–96	1996–97
National Seed Development Organisation					65										
National Transcommunications Ltd											70				
Northern Ireland Electricity															
– sale of shares											350	148	187	2	9
– redemption of debt												70			
Nuclear Power industry															
– sale of shares														–8	528
– redemption of debt															160
Privatised companies' debt											1337		1617	517	734
PSA (Building management)														15	9
Professional and Executive Recruitment							5								
Railtrack															
– sale of shares														–10	839
– redemption of debt															282
Recruitment and Assessment Srv															7
Residual Share Sales														750	559
Rolls-Royce plc						1029			3						
Rover Group plc									150						
Royal Ordnance						186									
Short Brothers								30							
Transport Research Laboratories														–1	
Water companies															
– sale of shares								423	1487	1485					
– redemption of debt								73	130						
Wytch Farm					18										
Miscellaneous	394	16	5	–1	–3	–1	15	–22	–12	–12	–1	–70	–9	14	4
Total	1535	1139	2050	2706	4458	5140	7069	4225	5347	7925	8184	5453	6429	2493	4404

Source: Her Majesty's Treasury: Information on Privatisation in the UK (February 1998)

389

tion of both the Royal Mint and horse racing's Tote would be undertaken to see whether greater private sector participation would be appropriate. In addition, the Government's Private Finance Initiative (PFI) is designed to bring the private sector more directly into the provision of public services. By October 1998 PFI projects with a capital value of around £11,000 million had been signed and included the Channel Tunnel rail link, six new prisons, a number of hospitals, several road projects, a new National Insurance records system and a 'smart card' system for the Benefits Agency. See Figure 15.3 for a list of privatisations since 1979.

Meaning and extent of

It should be apparent that the full meaning and significance of privatisation is really to be found in the withdrawal of the State from the production of goods and the provision of services into the more limited, but necessary roles of purchaser and regulator of goods and services now provided mostly by the private sector.[16] Seen in this light it is not an exaggeration to say that privatisation has had the effect of redefining the national consensus about the appropriate role and extent of the state and its agencies in contemporary Britain.

This assertion is corroborated by the fact that the Labour Party no longer argues a case for renationalisation of the undertakings which were privatised by the Conservatives. Indeed, Tony Blair has made it clear that, unless there is an overriding reason for the public provision of goods and services, such provision should be left to the private sector and market forces. Consequently, political attention has shifted to focus on ways of achieving better regulation of what has been privatised and a degree of reliable accountability.

15.4 Regulation and control

Since 1976 there have been some significant developments in the ways in which successive Governments in Britain have sought to regulate and control the public sector. We take 1976 as our starting point, since it was then that the Labour Government was obliged by the International Monetary Fund (IMF) to introduce a system of rigorous cash limits on all forms of public spending, which included tighter financial controls on the public corporations. This system was refined and extended by the Conservative Government in the 1980s with the result that most public corporations were adversely affected both by the tight financial limits set by Ministers and (in the early 1980s at any rate) by the financial consequences of the economic recession at that time.

Two of the most unfortunate consequences of these developments for the public corporations were that they had to put up their prices by more than the rate of inflation (which they did not then wish to do) and that their capital investment programmes had to be cut back. Although in theory the Boards had the freedom to operate at arm's length from the Government of the day, in practice the political constraints on them severely reduced their capacity to do so. In such conditions the methods of external control fell into at least one of three main categories: Ministerial oversight, Parliamentary control, and other regulatory mechanisms. We shall now examine each of these in turn.

Ministerial oversight

Ministerial oversight has been the most common method of controlling the public sector. It is really a short-hand for supervision by Ministers and senior civil servants. As far as the public corporations were concerned, this usually took the form of frequent conversations between Ministers and the Boards of the public corporations on significant issues of policy, such as plans for large-scale corporate investment, key pricing decisions, important pay negotiations, and significant matters to do with the impact of corporate activity upon the wider environment – for example, an airport runway extension or the siting of a new power station. In these relationships Ministers sought to preserve the fundamental distinction between day-to-day management decisions (usually matters for the Boards) and long-term strategic decisions with a high political content in which they felt obliged to take a close interest. In such contacts Ministers were sometimes tempted to blur or ignore this vital distinction – indeed it was not always apparent that there was such a distinction – although in the event they usually shied away from directly usurping the role of senior management.

On those occasions when Ministers decided to intervene, they usually exercised their statutory right to do so by issuing a directive to the Board concerned. They were also tempted to influence Board decisions in more informal ways known as 'lunch-time directives' of which no written record was kept. This technique may well have been used to put pressure on British Rail to keep open certain uneconomic branch lines, on the Post Office to buy British rather than foreign equipment, and on British Coal in connection with the pace and scale of pit closures. However, since 1979 the sustained policy of privatisation left fewer and fewer public sector issues to be resolved in these ways.

When there was serious conflict between Ministers and the Boards of public corporations, it was often because the latter chose to interpret their statutory duties more narrowly (and commercially) than the sponsoring Departments wished. This then faced the Minister concerned with an invidious choice between doing nothing about an unpopular Board decision and so risking public and political criticism for apparent inactivity, and intervening in a particular Board decision and so perhaps jeopardising the commercial prospects of the public corporation. On the whole Ministers chose the latter course more often than the former, which was a reflection of the fact that the general public and Parliament had more political clout than the Board of any public corporation.

Parliamentary control

Another method of control, which was really the counterpart of Ministerial oversight, was achieved by making the public sector directly or indirectly accountable to Parliament at Westminster. When this was exercised indirectly via a Minister, it was not very satisfactory, since Ministers tended simply to tell MPs that they would draw the issues of concern to the attention of the relevant Chairman and Board. A greater degree of Parliamentary accountability was achieved via the mechanism of Select Committees in which the decisions and practices of bodies within the public sector were scutinised and criticised.

However, perhaps the most powerful and effective way of exercising political control and Parliamentary accountability was the straightforward practice of MPs writing to those concerned – for example the senior management of public corporations – whenever and wherever they had cause to do so on behalf of their constituents. Such written representations could be supplemented by the use of meetings and delegations, as well as backed up by the implied threat that the MPs concerned would raise the issue on the floor of the House if suitable steps were not taken to meet the point. Since ultimately all public bodies depend for their continued existence upon the support and approval of Parliament, and since most of them require support from public funds, MPs have had both the ability and the right to be quite demanding of public bodies when they needed to be.

Other regulatory mechanisms

From time to time other regulatory mechanisms were used in attempts to exercise some additional political control over institutions in the public sector. For example, the *Monopolies and Mergers Commission* conducted efficiency audits of public corporations under the powers provided for it in the 1980 Competition Act, audits which undoubtedly served to sharpen up the performance of the public corporations concerned.[17]

Occasionally, Ministers decided to establish a *Royal Commission* or *Committee of Inquiry* to conduct a full-scale review of a public corporation when its activities or prospects caused an unusual degree of public interest or concern. For example, in 1985 the Thatcher Government established the Peacock Committee to look into the future financing of the BBC.[18] Its controversial report, which was nevertheless a disappointment to the more radical elements in the Thatcher Government, subsequently triggered the far-reaching 1990 Broadcasting Act which set the legislative framework for British broadcasting in the 1990s, but was soon overtaken by the dynamism of financial markets and media technology. In general, however, Conservative Administrations in the 1980s and 1990s seemed rather allergic to the use of Royal Commissions, largely because of their traditional reputation as Civil-Service-inspired devices for gathering the opinion of 'the great and the good' and then recycling this back to Ministers in elegant prose.

Lastly, some of the public corporations were provided from the outset with statutory *Consumer Councils* to monitor their activities from a consumer point of view. The Electricity Consumers' Committees and the Post Office Users' National Council were two examples of this institutional device which invariably turned out to be a disappointment to campaigning bodies such as the Consumers' Association. Moreover, as is sometimes the case in arrangements of this kind, the practice of regular monitoring was often vulnerable to 'agency-capture' – in other words, a situation in which the watch-dog was tamed and rendered ineffective by the very institution which it was supposed to watch.

Problems and consequences of privatisation

We have seen how privatisation in Britain was regarded in the 1980s and 1990s both as a blessing and as a curse, depending on the political point of view of the observer. Even in the eyes of its most enthusiastic proponents, however, real problems have been posed which have made privatisation as controversial as the various forms of public ownership which it replaced.

Perhaps the key problem posed by privatisation is the paradox that the transfer of activities from the public to the private sectors has actually necessitated more elaborate forms of regulation than was the case before. In other words, the liberalisation implicit in the policy of privatisation has required *re-regulation*, not de-regulation, in a more explicit and legalistic form. Whereas in dealing with public corporations it was often necessary for Ministers to intervene in order to protect the interests of taxpayers against the commercial inefficiencies of nationalised industries; in dealing with privatised undertakings, it has been necessary for the independent regulators – such as OFTEL, OFGAS or OFWAT (see Figure 15.4) – to protect the interests of consumers against any exploitation of disproportionate market power by the privatised utilities.

For example, without such regulatory intervention (and many have argued that the initial approach by the regulators was too lenient towards the newly privatised undertakings), it would have been possible for British Telecom to charge very high prices for services of which it was the dominant supplier during the early years after privatisation (such as domestic phone calls) and thus cross-subsidise its attractively low charges for long distance and commercial phone calls where it faced more direct competition from Mercury and others. It is for this reason that the independent regulators set complicated formulae to control the prices which the utilities may charge in an attempt to ensure that regulation acts as a proxy for competition in areas of activity where there is not a fully liberalised market. Although the utilities have complained and the stock market has reacted against the degree of regulatory uncertainty, spokesmen for consumer groups and the general public have still complained of exploitation at the hands of monopoly or near-monopoly private corporations.

A more general problem caused by the regulatory consequences of privatisation has been the difficulty in achieving forms of regulation which are both fair to the

Figure 15.4 The regulatory framework

Establishment date	Body		Statutory basis
1984	OFTEL	Office of Telecommunications	Telecommunications Act 1984
1986		Securities & Investments Board[A]	Financial Services Act 1986
1986	OFGAS	Office of Gas Supply[B]	Gas Act 1986
1989	OFFER	Office of Electricity Regulation[B]	Electricity Act 1989
1989	OFWAT	Office of Water Services	Water Act 1989
1991		Radio Authority	Broadcasting Act 1990
1992	ITC	Independent Television Commission	Broadcasting Act 1990
1992	OFSTED	Office for Standards in Education	Education (School) Act 1992
1993	ORR	Office of the Rail Regulator	Railways Act 1993
1993	OPRAF	Office of Passenger Rail Franchising[C]	Railways Act 1993
1994	OFLOT	Office of the National Lottery	National Lottery Act 1993
1997	FSA	Financial Services Authority	
1998		– replaced the Securities & Investments Board – assumed responsibility for banking supervision	Bank of England Act 1998
1999		financial services regulatory system fully operational	Regulatory Reform Act 1998

Notes
A. See under Financial Services Authority.
B. The Labour Government which came into office in 1997 announced the intention of merging OFGAS and OFFER to form a single regulatory authority for gas and electricity (in 1998/99).
C. In its Transport White Paper published in July 1998 the Labour Government announced plans to abolish OPRAF and replace it by a new railway regulator: SRA – the Strategic Rail Authority, which was to have more powers than OPRAF, including the imposition of 'instant' and unlimited fines for companies failing to meet performance levels.

In July 1998 as part of plans announced to boost public sector house building the Labour Government announced plans for a new housing inspectorate with powers over housing similar to the powers of OFSTED in supervising schools.

privatised undertakings and acceptable to the general public. This has been a difficult balance to achieve, not least because the action of the regulators has often seemed to be both arbitrary and capricious. However, one principle is already clear: the more genuine competition there is in a particular sector, the less need there ought to be for elaborate regulation. This is because real competition should ensure that most customer requirements are met at the lowest cost consistent with the need to make sufficient profit to pay the employees, reward the shareholders and finance future investment. However, as long as explicit regulatory arrangements are necessary, it is desirable that there should be the following characteristics in such regulation:

1. It should be cost-effective and not too burdensome for the undertakings concerned.
2. It should involve the least and simplest restrictions upon the commercial freedom of the industries consistent with adequate protection of the consumer and public interest.
3. It should bring benefits to consumers which outweigh the compliance costs upon the industries, since these costs will tend to be passed on in prices especially in monopolistic markets.
4. As far as possible, it should be imposed in ways which do not make it vulnerable to 'agency capture' – that is, the situation which exists when the regulator becomes the servant rather than the master of the undertakings which are regulated.

A final and politically significant consequence of the drive to privatisation in Britain in the 1980s and 1990s was the development of *a more legalistic and contractual relationship between the private sector and the state*. This was brought about by a combination of market-led developments (notably in the financial services sector) and political necessity resulting from the fact that the Conservative Government of the time – intent on privatisation and liberalisation – was damaged by the behaviour of some of its friends and supporters who appeared to benefit disproportionately from the process at the expense of employees, consumers and the wider public. Ministers responded by strengthening the established regulatory bodies, such as the Office of Fair Trading and the Monopolies and Mergers Commission; and by creating new regulatory bodies, such as the Office of Telecommunications and the Securities and Investments Board (later the Financial Services Authority). What this has amounted to over the past decade and a half is that the state and its agencies have largely withdrawn from their previous combined roles as producers, purchasers and regulators to a more limited position of informed purchasing and independent regulation. In short, there has been a purchaser–provider split and a shift from trust to contract.

15.5 Prospects for the public sector

None of the familiar problems of the public sector in Britain has been made any easier to understand or solve by the various myths which have permeated the political debate over the years. There has been the myth that in dealing with public corporations it was possible to draw a clear and convincing distinction between political and commercial issues. There has been the myth that these hybrid institutions could act both in the public interest and as profit-maximising commercial undertakings. There has been the myth that there can be either full Ministerial control or complete managerial autonomy for institutions in the public sector. All of these mythical ideas, and many more, damaged both the image and the performance of the public corporations, and contributed to the demise of many of them.

The reality, of course, has been rather different. It is that all British Governments since the war were doomed to relations of inherent ambiguity with public corporations and, to a lesser extent, with all the other institutions in the public sector as well. This was certainly true during the period before 1979 when Ministers in all Governments felt inhibited from moving decisively either towards tighter political control or towards extensive privatisation of the public sector institutions. In so far as many of the problems of dealing with the public sector have diminished since the mid-1980s, this is because since then the policy of privatisation has been taken about as far as it can go in a modern mixed economy. Yet this very radicalism has produced other problems of regulation, equity and accountability which are proving almost as difficult to deal with.

Signposts to the future

Against this background it is difficult to be sure and unwise to be dogmatic about the future of the public sector in Britain. With the outlook of the two main parties tending to converge towards a new middle ground, it is possible only to suggest a few signposts to the future.

Firstly, it would seem that in the mixed economy of modern Britain there are certain goods and services which may be more suitably provided by public sector institutions if they are to be provided at all, such as loss-making postal services for outlying areas of the country or uneconomic commuter and rural rail services. For example, the new Labour Government decided to give the Post Office more commercial freedom within the public sector and to enable it to raise funds on the capital markets, but balked at the idea of real privatisation.

Secondly, there will usually be compelling considerations of national policy and national interest which make it virtually essential that the public sector should take charge of certain large and risky high technology projects, such as civil nuclear power, since it is difficult or impossible for the private sector to raise the necessary capital or secure the necessary insurance cover for its public liabilities.

Thirdly, there will continue to be a good deal of political argument about how far it may be possible to apply private sector managerial techniques and accounting conventions to the core state activities which seem almost certain to remain within the public sector. Such issues have already arisen via the processes of compulsory competitive tendering, market testing and resource accounting – all of which have been substantially piloted in the Civil Service. Yet the debate will continue about whether public goods and services really ought to be provided by the residual public sector as a point of political principle, or whether even this shibboleth can be safely discarded as long as public goods and services can be more cost-effectively and satisfactorily provided by the private sector within a framework of rigorous public sector regulation.

When public services are inherently more of a gift relationship than a commercial transaction – for example, in the case of state education or the National Health Service – then they will almost certainly have to remain within the public sector as public goods. In such cases the services concerned are likely to remain largely free at the point of use, although there will be continuing political and public debate about how much of these 'free goods' can be afforded at any time. Core public services and the drive for a more commercial approach within the public sector have been difficult to reconcile in the past, but there is some reason to suppose that this dilemma may be easier to deal with now that a cross-party consensus appears to have emerged in support of something like the current mix.

15.6 Conclusion

In this chapter we have seen that the most notable characteristics of the public sector in Britain have been its remarkable size and diversity, as well as the fierce political arguments which have raged over its scope and obligations. Such problems have been seen in sharpest relief in the chequered history of public corporations, but the rest of the public sector has not proved much easier to manage or control.

In political and constitutional terms, the public sector has posed problems for Governments of the Left and the Right alike. For example, the original Morrisonian model of the public corporation did not in the long run prove to be a satisfactory means of delivering public goods and services in both a cost-effective and a democratically accountable way. In the end few people derived much real benefit from such hybrid institutions, except perhaps the unionised employees of the nationalised industries in their heyday and the civil servants in the sponsoring Departments. Everyone else seems to have been frustrated or thwarted by public corporations, including notably their private sector competitors and the Ministers who were supposedly held to account for their actions. There was seldom sufficient trust between Ministers and the managers of public corporations; continuity of policy was prejudiced by the incessant party political conflict over the scope and the ground-rules of the public sector; and the holy grail of real public accountability seems to have eluded every attempt to achieve it.

It is not surprising, therefore, that from 1979 the Conservatives were determined to reduce the size and burdens of the public sector through their policy of privatisation, and that the Labour Party under Tony Blair abandoned its previous commitment to nationalisation and public ownership in favour of a much more positive attitude towards the private sector. In fluid political conditions it is not possible to forecast how things will develop in future. Yet it seems distinctly possible that the main political parties may indeed have converged upon a new zone of political consensus which supports the idea of a smaller but more effective public sector in Britain.

Suggested questions

1   To what extent should we be concerned by the 'new magistracy' of unelected Government in Britain?
2   Assess the contribution of public corporations in Britain since 1945.
3   Are there parts of the public sector which should never be privatised?

Notes

1. G. Bowen, *Survey of Fringe Bodies* (London: Civil Service Department, 1978).
2. See L. Pliatzky, 'Report on Non-Departmental Public Bodies', Cmnd 7797 (London: HMSO, 1980).

3. 'The Cabinet Office', *The Economist*, 6 August 1994.
4. See S. Weir and W. Hall (eds), *Extra-Governmental Organisations in the United Kingdom* (London: Charter 88 Trust, 1994); also *Independent on Sunday,* 30 January 1994, on the subject of Quangos.
5. *Hansard*, 28 January 1988, Cols. 313–314.
6. Quoted in *Independent on Sunday,* 22 May 1994.
7. Lord Benson and Lord Rothschild, 'Royal Commissions, a Memorial', *Public Administration,* Autumn 1982.
8. The single Royal Commission was on Criminal Justice and was chaired by Lord Runciman.
9. For an example of the scope and scale of Government reviews see *House of Lords Hansard*, 12 February 1998, Vol. 585, No. 102, cols WA231–WA244.
10. Over the period 1990–93 the Conservative reforms of the NHS produced a 10 per cent increase in the number of clerical and administrative staff, but more than a doubling in the number of general and senior managers, from 9700 to 20,000.
11. See *National Income and Expenditure* 1983, Tables 1.10 and 10.3; and *Economic Trends,* February 1983, Appendix 1, Table 1.
12. For example, in 1982 public sector purchases from the private sector amounted to about £9000 million, while public sector sales to the private sector amounted to about £11,000 million.
13. These generalisations refer essentially to the nationalised industries and not to all public corporations, some of which – such as the BBC created by Royal Charter in 1926 – were established for very different purposes.
14. The remaining major nationalised industries are the Post Office, London Transport and the Civil Aviation Authority.
15. Tony Blair, *Guardian*, 8 April 1997.
16. See C. Veljanovsky, *Selling the State* (London: Weidenfeld & Nicolson, 1987), for further elaboration of this argument.
17. Examples included efficiency audits of the London letter post, the Severn-Trent Water Authority, the Central Electricity Generating Board, and British Rail commuter services in London and the South East.
18. See the 'Report of the Committee on the Financing of the BBC', Cmnd 9824 (London: HMSO, 1986).

Further reading

Asher, K., *The Politics of Privatisation* (London: Macmillan Education, 1987).
Flynn, N., *Public Sector Management* (3rd edn), (London: Harvester Wheatsheaf, 1997).
Glynn, J., *Public Sector Financial Control and Accounting* (Oxford: Blackwell, 1987).
Pirie, M., *Privatisation – Theory, Practise and Choice* (London: Wildwood, 1988).
Plummer, J., *The Governance Gap – QUANGOs and Accountability* (London: Demos, 1994).
Prosser, T., *Nationalised Industries and Public Control* (Oxford: Blackwell, 1986).
Pryke, R., *The Nationalised Industries – policies and performance since 1968* (Oxford: Martin Robertson, 1981).
Redwood, J., *Popular Capitalism* (London: Routledge, 1988).
Ridley, F.F. and Wilson, D. (eds), *The Quango Debate* (London: Oxford University Press, 1995).
Velijanovsky, C. (ed.), *Regulators and the Market: An Assessment of the Growth of Regulation in the UK* (London: Institute of Economic Affairs, 1991).
Veljanovsky, C., *Selling the State* (London: Weidenfeld & Nicolson, 1987).
Weir, S. and Hallfield, W., *Ego Trip – Extra Governmental Organisations in the UK* (London: Charter 88, 1994). White paper on 'The Citizen's Charter', Cmnd 1599 (London: HMSO, July 1991).

16 Devolved and local government

The United Kingdom is a unitary, multi-national state. Consequently, all political authority is ultimately centralised. Constituencies in all the component parts of the United Kingdom – England, Scotland, Wales, and Northern Ireland – send representatives to the national Parliament at Westminster. However, following the election of a Labour Government in 1997, a Scottish Parliament with devolved powers, including primary law-making and tax-varying powers, was introduced and is to become fully operational in 2000. Similarly, a Welsh Assembly was introduced, also to be fully operational in 2000, while an Assembly for Northern Ireland came into being as a consequence of the so-called 'peace process'.

Within the nations and regions of the United Kingdom, the words 'local government' are a somewhat misleading term used to describe what has been largely the implementation and delivery of national policies under the guidance of locally elected Councillors. Local authorities (another term for the units of local government in the United Kingdom) do not have any real autonomy and are constitutionally subordinate to Parliament at Westminster. What they can and cannot do is specified in Acts of Parliament (as interpreted by the Courts), which means that Parliament at Westminster can both create and abolish local authority powers and, indeed, local authorities themselves.

It is, therefore, important to distinguish at the outset between *devolved and local government,* which can be defined simply as directly elected Parliaments, Assemblies and Local Authorities; and *devolved and local administration*, which includes the regional and local offices of central Government and its Agencies (see Chapter 14) and the local administration of justice (see Chapter 17). The focus in this chapter is on directly elected Parliaments, Assemblies and local authorities – in other words, primary devolved and local government.

16.1 Devolved government

In the 1960s and the 1970s the issue of governance in the various component nations of the United Kingdom came to the fore of political debate to an extent not seen – save for the Irish question – for almost two hundred years. It was in 1966 that Plaid Cymru, the Welsh Nationalist Party, although formed in 1925, won its first Parliamentary representation. Similarly, the Scottish National party, originally dating from 1928, won a by-election in 1967. Both Nationalist parties obtained considerable prominence and as a result the question of the 'break-up' of the United Kingdom moved onto the political agenda. At the very least it had to be recognised that the United Kingdom was a multinational and multicultural state and that its governmental and administrative structures should be fashioned accordingly. In 1969 a Royal Commission on the constitution was established under the chairmanship of first Lord Crowther and then Lord Kilbrandon. It reported in 1973, rejected separation or federation but approved devolution in general and unanimously came out in favour of a directly elected Scottish Assembly.[1]

In the October 1974 General Election – when the Scottish National Party received 30.4 per cent of the popular vote in Scotland and eleven MPs and Plaid Cymru received 10.8 per cent of the vote in Wales and three MPs – devolution came to the very centre of political debate. The Labour Government of 1974–79 then legislated on the issue, securing Parliamentary approval for both a Scotland Bill and a Wales Bill to establish directly elected Assemblies in both nations. However, in the ensuing referenda the proposals were rejected by the people of Wales – only 12 per cent of the Welsh electorate voting in favour of the proposals – while in Scotland although a majority of those who voted supported the proposals, this represented only 33 per cet of the Scottish electorate, a figure which fell short of the 40 per cent threshold which had been stipulated in the legislation. Consequently, neither Assembly was brought into being.

At the 1979 General Election the Scottish National Party vote fell back to 17.3 per cent and they lost nine of their eleven MPs; in Wales support for Plaid Cymru also declined, to 8.1 per cent and two MPs. The Conservative Government which came into office secured the passage of resolutions nullifying both the Scotland Act 1978 and the Wales Act 1978; devolution no longer appeared to be an option. Indeed, it was not until the 1990s that the matter again came to the forefront of the national political agenda.

Consequently, at the 1997 General Election the Labour Party declared that in Government it would meet the demand for devolution of power to Scotland and Wales, once this was approved in referenda.[2] True to its word, the new Labour Government published White Papers outlining proposals for both Scotland and Wales,[3] and enacted legislation providing for referenda to be held. The referendum in Scotland took place a week later, on 18 September. The results were as follows:

Scotland

: I agree that there should be a Scottish Parliament	74.29%
: I do not agree that there should be a Scottish Parliament	25.71%
: I agree that a Scottish Parliament should have tax-varying powers	63.48%
: I do not agree that a Scottish Parliament should have tax-varying powers	36.52%
Turnout	60.16%

Wales
: I agree that there should be a Welsh Assembly   50.3%
: I do not agree that there should be a Welsh Assembly   49.7%

Turnout   51.3%

These referenda produced a clear, even emphatic, result in Scotland, but the closest of results in Wales. Nevertheless, both electorates had voted in favour of the proposals on offer, so the Government moved ahead with the necessary legislation. As a result, the Scotland Bill and the Government of wales Bill both received Royal Assent towards the end of the 1997–98 Session.

Scotland

The *Scotland Act 1998* provided for a unicameral Parliament with 129 members (MSPs), of which 73 constituency members would be elected by first-past-the-post and 56 members from a party list system of proportional representation in which seven candidates are chosen from each of the eight Scottish European Parliamentary constituencies. Each elector therefore has two votes: one for a constituency MSP and one for a party list. The Parliament sits for a four-year term and is headed by a First Minister – a leading individual who can command majority support within the Parliament and who selects a Cabinet from amongst the membership.

The Parliament has tax-varying powers – the power to vary the basic rate of income tax by 3p – and autonomy over the spending of an assigned budget (£14 billion in 1998). It has the right to pass primary legislation and responsibility for health, education and training, local government, social work and housing, law and order, civil and criminal law, economic development, air and sea transport, the environment, food standards, agriculture, sport and the arts.

The Scottish Parliament and its Executive have an important role in scrutinising regulations emanating from the European Union which impact upon their devolved responsibilities, and in legislating on the implementation of European directives. The Executive also has responsibility over all public bodies whose functions and services have been devolved. The Parliament does not have jurisdiction over the United Kingdom constitution, foreign policy, defence and national security, protection of borders, macro-economic and monetary policy, employment legislation, social security policy, the regulation of professions (including doctors), United Kingdom transport, abortion, human fertilisation and embryology, nuclear safety and the licensing of cinemas.

The Scotland Act confirmed the overall supremacy of the Westminster Parliament and underlined the sovereignty of the Crown by stipulating that all legislation approved by the Scottish Parliament would have to receive Royal Assent prior to becoming law. The first elections to the Scottish Parliament are scheduled to take place in 1999, with the Parliament itself meeting for the first time in 2000.

Wales

The *Government of Wales Act 1998* provided for a 60-Member Assembly, with 40 members being elected every four years by the first-past-the-post system from

Parliamentary constituencies and 20 members being elected from a party list system of proportional representation in which four candidates are chosen from each of the five Welsh European Parliamentary Constituencies. Each elector has two votes: one for a constituency member and one for a party list. There is a ten-member Executive, the leader of which is elected by Assembly members.

Although the Assembly has neither tax-varying powers nor the power to pass primary legislation, it does have responsibility for the distribution of a large part of the budget assigned to Wales (£7 billion in 1998), and takes over the responsibilities previously exercised by the Secretary of State for Wales in such areas as industry and economic development, agriculture, forestry, fisheries and food; education and training; health and personal social services; housing, planning, local government and the environment; transport; arts, culture, heritage and the Welsh language; and sport and recreation. The Assembly also has control over non-departmental public bodies in Wales.

Among the functions which have remained the sole responsibility of the Westminster Parliament and the British Government are foreign affairs, defence, economic and monetary policy, taxation, social security and broadcasting. The first election to the Welsh Assembly is scheduled for 1999, with the Assembly taking up its responsibilities in 2000.

Northern Ireland

Under the terms of the *Belfast Agreement*,[4] subsequently supported by a public referendum, a Northern Ireland Assembly has been established and the first elections took place in June 1998. The Assembly comprises 108 members, with six being elected by proportional representation (STV) from each of the 18 Parliamentary constituencies. It exercises full legislative and executive authority – under a 12-member Executive Committee, including a First Minister – in those matters previously under the remit of the Northern Ireland Office, namely, health, education, the environment, economic development, agriculture and finance. Decisions are made by a system of weighted majority voting to ensure that no section of the community can dominate.

The Belfast Agreement also provided for the establishment of a North–South Ministerial Council as a forum for Ministers from both Belfast and Dublin to promote by agreement joint policies on matters of mutual interest. The Council meets in different forms: in plenary form three times a year, in specific sectoral form on a 'regular and frequent basis', and in an 'appropriate' form to consider institutional or cross-sectoral matters.

In addition, and again under the terms of the Belfast Agreement, a Council of the Isles has been created to promote the harmonious and mutually beneficial development of relationships among all the peoples involved. The Council consists of representatives of the British and Irish Governments, devolved institutions in Northern Ireland, Scotland and Wales; and, if appropriate, elsewhere in the United Kingdom, together with representatives of the Isle of Man and the Channel Islands. The Council meets in different forms: at summit level twice a year, in specific sectoral form on a regular basis with each participant being represented by the appropriate Minister, and in an 'appropriate' form to consider cross-sectoral matters.

England

When in Opposition during the 1990s, the Labour Party brought forward plans for elected Regional Assemblies in England, a proposal that had been Liberal Democrat policy for some years. But it was the Conservative Government under John Major which gave English regionalism its largest boost when in 1994 it integrated the regional administration of central Government functions. It did this by creating a number of Government Offices for the Regions (GORs). These GOR's, each under a Director responsible to the Secretaries of State of the Departments concerned – namely Environment, Transport and the Regions, Trade and Industry and Education and Employment – had a combined budget of £4.6 billion in 1997–98 and were given responsibility for administering and co-ordinating the various regional programmes of Government within their designated regional boundaries. See Figure 16.1 for a map of the boundaries.

In its 1997 election Manifesto the Labour Party held back from repeating its earlier pledge to legislate for elected Regional Assemblies, but instead committed itself to establishing Regional Chambers to co-ordinate transport, planning, economic development, bids for European funding and land use planning. It declared that in time it would introduce legislation to allow people, region by region, to decide by referenda whether they wanted directly elected regional government. Only where clear popular consent had been established would such arrangements be made, and then only where this would not mean adding a new tier of government (namely in those areas with a predominately unitary system of local government) and providing that it did not increase overall public expenditure.

In office the Labour Government legislated for the establishment of Regional Development Agencies (RDAs) which, working closely with GORs and sharing for the most part the same boundaries, were given the tasks of producing and implementing strategic economic plans for their respective regions, to attract inward investment to their regions, and administer grants and funding available to their regions. Each RDA is under the direction of a Chief Executive responsible to a 12-strong Board. In 1998 the Government launched the first Regional Chamber in Yorkshire, a 35-member body of local Councillors drawn from the region with the task of advising the RDA, and with the RDA being required to consult the Chamber on a regular basis and to submit itself to an annual hearing before the Chamber.

In January 1999 the Leader of the House of Commons, Margaret Beckett, announced a plan to revive a Commons Committee for the English regions so as to give the English regions a distinct voice in Parliament following Scottish and Welsh devolution.

Whither the nation state?

The creation of a Parliament for Scotland, an Assembly for Wales, an Assembly for Northern Ireland and a regional structure for the governance of England – against the back-drop of the increasing 'Europeanisation' of government and politics in the UK – inaugurated nothing short of a constitutional revolution in the United Kingdom. Consequently, whether by design or by default, a new quasi-federal system of government has come into being. In order to connect these devolved bodies together and to central Government it has been announced that – once the Assemblies are up and running and provided that they agree – a Joint Ministerial Committee will be established, the task of which will be to discuss and co-ordinate the treatment of devolved matters in different parts of Britain. Ministers would attend depending on the subject under discussion, Health Ministers to discuss health matters, Education Ministers to discuss education, and so on. A quasi-federal system of government by its very nature poses significant challenges to the traditional British nation state.

Devolution is a deliberate loosening of control by the centre which undoubtedly carries risks. However, as has been pointed out by the independent think-tank, the

Figure 16.1 *England Government Regions*

Source: Office for National Statistics

Constitution Unit, 'breaking the central monopoly on the design of public policy could bring overall benefits through the encouragement of competition, diversity, and wider participation in the political process all round'.[5] This could be one of the prizes for this adventurous policy.

16.2 Local government – structure and personnel

As might be expected, the system of local government that exists in Britain today is, in its fundamentals, rooted deeply in the past. Indeed, it is possible to trace its origins back to Saxon times.[6] Nonetheless, the first comprehensive system of local Councils was established in the latter part of the nineteenth century[7] and for the purposes of this chapter we can begin in the 1970s. See Figure 16.2 for a chronology of change in English local government.

England

The structure of local government in England was reformed by the 1972 Local Government Act which came into effect in 1974. It reduced the previous mosaic of about 1300 local authorities to six large Metropolitan Councils (outside Greater London, which had been created as a single Authority by the 1963 Greater London Act), 39 County Councils (for example, Devon, Kent, Norfolk), 36 Metropolitan District Councils (of which the largest was Birmingham with a population of more than one million), and 296 County District Councils (representing areas with local populations ranging from 60,000 to 100,000 in most cases). Thus a total of 377 Local Authorities replaced the previous 1300 or so, and the interdependence of town and country became the guiding principle of the structure of local government in England.

At the most local level, the former Parish Councils were retained and their powers were increased, although only to a limited extent. About 300 former Urban Districts and small Boroughs became Parish Councils. Parishes of more than 200 inhabitants were required to elect a Council, whereas those with fewer inhabitants than this were encouraged to practise the direct democracy of parish meetings.

The Greater London Council and the six other Metropolitan Counties – namely Greater Manchester, Merseyside, South Yorkshire, Tyne and Wear, West Midlands, and West Yorkshire – were abolished by Acts of Parliament in 1984 and 1985 which came into effect on 1 April 1986. This meant that the large conurbations no longer had any democratic representation at that level of local government. The functions of the Metropolitan Counties were reallocated to the Borough and District Councils, statutory Joint Boards and other unelected public bodies. The abolition of these upper-tier authorities was intended to remove a source of bitter conflict with central Government, save money after incurring some transitional costs, and provide a simpler and more accountable structure of local government in the large Metropolitan areas.

The Local Government Act of 1992 created a new Local Government Commission to review local government structures and boundaries in England. Its task

Figure 16.2 The chronology of change: key dates in English local government history

1834	**Poor Law Amendment Act**
	begins succession of legislation changing the shape and structure of local administration by setting up Boards of Guardians as special purpose parish authorities.
1835	**Municipal Corporations Act**
	establishes directly elected corporate boroughs in place of the self-electing medieval corporations which had become widely discredited and often corrupt.
1888	**Local Government Act**
	establishes 62 Elected County Councils, including the London County Council, and 61 all-purpose County Borough Councils in England and Wales.
1894	**Local Government Act**
	revives parish councils and establishes 535 Urban District Councils, 472 Rural District Councils and 270 non-county Borough Councils.
1899	**London Government Act**
	sets up 28 Metropolitan Borough Councils in London and the Corporation of London.
1925	**Royal Commission on Local Government**
	reports for the first time, under the chairmanship of the Earl of Onslow, with a further report published in 1929.
1929	**Local Government Act**
	abolishes the Poor Law Guardians Boards and transfers functions to local government.
1963	**London Government Act**
	creates 32 London Boroughs and a Greater London Council (GLC).
1966	**Royal Commission on Local Government in England**
	is established under the chairmanship of Lord Redcliffe-Maud, reports in 1969.
1970	**Reform of Local Government in England White Paper**
	supports most of the findings of the Royal Commission, particularly in respect of unitary local government.
1971	**Local Government in England White Paper**
	rejects unitary authorities and supports two-tier local government throughout England and Wales.
1972	**Local Government Act**
	removes County Borough Councils, reduces the number of County Councils in England and Wales to 47, establishes 6 Metropolitan County Councils and 36 Metropolitan District Councils.
1980	**Local Government Planning and Land Act**
	establishes Compulsory Competitive Tendering and Urban Development Corporations.
1983	**Streamlining the Cities White Paper**
	proposes to abolish the GLC and 6 Metropolitan County Councils and replace them with joint boards and ad hoc agencies.
1984	**Rates Act**
	establishes system of rate-capping.
1985	**Local Government Act**
	abolishes the GLC and the 6 Metropolitan County Councils and establishes a directly-elected Inner London Education Authority (ILEA), 24 centrally appointed bodies and 16 London-wide local government bodies.
1986	**Committee of Inquiry into the Conduct of Local Authority Business**
	chaired by David Widdecombe, reports on political organisation of local government.

Figure 16.2 continued

1988	**Local Government Finance Act** replaces domestic rates with the Community Charge or "Poll Tax".
1988	**Education Reform Act** abolishes the Inner London Education Authority.
1989	**Local Government and Housing Act** implements the Widdecombe report on political organisation and establishes basis of present capital finance system.
1992	**Local Government Finance Act** replaces "Poll Tax" with Council Tax.
1992	**Local Government Act** supports further structural reorganisation to create some new unitary councils.
1996	**Select Committee on Relations Between Central and Local Government** chaired by Lord Hunt of Tanworth, publishes its report, "Rebuilding Trust", supporting change and experimentation in political organisation.
1997	**Local Government and Rating Act** supports new opportunities for parish council formation and protection for village shops.
1997	**Local Government Finance (Supplementary Credit Approvals) Act** provides basis for release of capital receipts.
1997	**Local Government (Contracts) Act** confirms authorities' powers to enter into contracts.
1998	**A Mayor and Assembly for London White Paper** proposed establishment of Greater London Assembly with a separate directly-elected mayor for London, subsequently receives overwhelming support in referendum.
1998	**Modern Local Government: In Touch with the People White Paper**

Source: White Paper: 'Modern Local Government: In Touch with the People'
(Cm 4014) (London: Stationery Office, 1998).

was to tour the country examining the structures of local government in the different localities. The intention was that its resulting recommendations would lead to Parliamentary legislation designed to make a wide variety of structural changes (or no changes at all) according to the strength and direction of local representations. In this process there was to be no single model of local government reform for England, although Ministerial guidance in Circulars from the Department of the Environment indicated a general preference for the abolition of the Counties and the introduction of sizeable unitary authorities based on enlarged Districts. For the most part the Commission recommended the retention of two-tier local government, but did suggest unitary authorities in a number of areas. As a result 14 Unitary Authorities were introduced in time for the May 1995 Local Government Elections – for example, Bristol, the Isle of Wight, Middlesborough and Hull – and these took over their responsibilities in April 1996. By April 1998 a total of 46 Unitary Authorities were in place. See Figure 16.3 for a map of the English counties and unitary authorities.

In 1998 the Labour Government published proposals for modernising the governance of London.[8] Advocating an elected Mayor and a 25-member Assembly – collectively to be known as the Greater London Authority – the Mayor, scrutinised by

Figure 16.3 England: Counties and Unitary Authorities, 1 April 1998

	Counties
	Unitary Authorities

D   Darlington
H   Hartlepool
M   Middlesbrough
RC   Redcar and Cleveland
ST   Stockton-on-Tees

Bn   Blackburn
Bpl   Blackpool
H   Halton
W   Warrington
S   Stoke-on-Trent

De   Derby
KH   Kingston upon Hull
Lr   Leicester
NEL   North East Lincolnshire
Nt   Nottingham
Pe   Peterborough
R   Rutland

L   Luton
MK   Milton Keynes
Mtn   Medway Towns
SS   Southend-on-Sea
Tk   Thurrock

BF   Bracknell Forest
BH   Brighton and Hove
Po   Portsmouth
Re   Reading
Sl   Slough
So   Southampton
W   Wokingham
WM   Windsor and Maidenhead

Bo   Bournemouth
Pl   Poole
Py   Plymouth
Ty   Torbay

and accountable to the Assembly, was to be given responsibility over policy for transport, planning, economic development and regeneration, the environment, policing, fire and emergency planning, health, and culture, media and sport, and accountable for a budget of £3.3 billion. In short, what was proposed was a substantial transfer of powers from both central government and non-elected Quangos to a new tier of elected, accountable, local government.

The proposals were put to the people of London in a referendum in May 1998, which saw 72 per cent of those voting – on a turnout of only 34.13 per cent – vote in favour of what was being offered. The legislation required to establish the Mayor and the Assembly was introduced during the 1998–99 Session with a view to the GLA taking over its responsibilities in 2000.

Wales

As was the case for England, so the structure of local government in Wales was also reformed by the 1972 Local Government Act which came into effect in 1974, creating a system in which there were eight County Councils and some 37 District Councils.

In Wales, the Secretary of State took direct responsibility for the reorganisation of local government and in March 1993 a White Paper was issued which proposed 21 unitary authorities. In fact 22 single-tier Authorities were created in time for elections in May 1995, with the resulting Councils taking over their responsibilities in April 1996. See Figure 16.4 for a map of the boundaries in Wales.

Scotland

Until 1995 the structure of local government in Scotland was determined by the 1973 Local Government (Scotland) Act which came into effect in 1975. This involved the creation of nine Regional Councils (with populations ranging from about 2,500,000 in Strathclyde to fewer than 100,000 in The Borders) and 53 District Councils within the regions. The division of functions between the two levels of local government was in many ways similar to that in England and Wales. The structure was also similar, except that the three island areas (Orkney, Shetland and Western Isles) each became single, all-purpose local authorities.

The Secretary of State for Scotland had direct responsibility for the reorganisation of local government. In July 1993 a White Paper proposed reorganisation into single-tier Councils. These proposals – which were heavily criticised at the time because of what was said to be their arbitrary and politically inspired nature – were given statutory effect in the 1994 Local Government (Scotland) Act which created 29 single-tier Councils to go along with the three unitary Island Councils. See Figure 16.5 for a map of the boundaries in Scotland.

Northern Ireland

The present structure of local government in Northern Ireland was largely determined by the 1972 Local Government (Northern Ireland) Act which came into force in 1973. It created a single level of local government by establishing 26 District Councils based on the main population centres in the Province. The Districts vary considerably in area and resources, with populations ranging from about 13,000 to about 350,000. Under a subsequent reorganisation of local government in 1977, which was precipitated by the way in which the Protestant majority had abused its position of local power, the District Councils were stripped of all but some minimal functions, such as

Figure 16.4 *Wales: Unitary Authorities, 1 April 1998*

Bd   Bridgend
BG   Blaenau Gwent
Ca   Cardiff
Cy   Caerphilly
Mon   Monmouthshire
MT   Merthyr Tydfil
N   Newport
NPT   Neath Port Talbot
RCT   Rhondda, Cynon, Taff
T   Torfaen
VG   The Vale of Glamorgan

Source: Office for National Statistics

street cleaning and sanitation, markets and abattoirs, and recreational facilities. See Figure 16.6 for a map of the boundaries in Northern Ireland.

Prior to the creation of the Northern Ireland Assembly in 1998, all the more important functions of local government in the Province were carried out either by central Boards under the Northern Ireland Office (dealing, for example, with housing, police, fire services and electricity supply) or by area Boards (dealing, for example, with health, personal social services, education and libraries) or directly by the Northern Ireland Office (town and country planning, water and sewerage services, roads and car parks, vehicle registration and licensing, for example). Although the local Councillors in Northern Ireland had severely circumscribed direct functions, they had some indirect influence when they sat as nominees on the various area Boards and some consultative influence when they held formal discussions with Ministers and officials in the Northern Ireland Office.

The Northern Ireland Assembly, which came into being in 1998, was given full legislative and executive authority in respect of those matters previously the responsibility of the six Northern Ireland Government Departments, namely Agriculture,

Figure 16.5 Scotland: Council Areas, 1 April 1998

1	Inverclyde
2	West Dunbartonshire
3	Renfrewshire
4	East Renfrewshire
5	Glasgow City
6	East Dunbartonshire
7	North Lanarkshire
8	Falkirk
9	West Lothian
10	Edinburgh, City of
11	Clackmannanshire
12	Dundee City
13	Aberdeen City

Source: Office for National Statistics

Economic Development, Education, Environment, Finance and Personnel, and Health and Social Services.

Overall it can be seen that the structure of local government is different in the different parts of the United Kingdom. This is likely to militate against the development of neat or symmetrical solutions to local government organisation throughout the United Kingdom. However, the present position is represented diagrammatically in Figure 16.7.

Councillors and officials

The composition of local authorities in England and Wales can be summarised by saying that each Unitary Council has between 40 and 70 elected Councillors, each County Council has between 60 and 100 elected Councillors and each District Council

Figure 16.6 Northern Ireland: Districts, 1 April 1998

Cf	Carrickfergus
Cr	Castlereagh
ND	North Down
Nta	Newtownabbey

Source: Office for National Statistics

has between 30 and 80 elected Councillors. In each case, Councillors are elected for fixed terms. At present those elected to the London Borough Councils, the Unitary Councils, the County Councils and some of the non-Metropolitan District Councils are elected every four years, whereas in some others of the non-Metropolitan District Councils and in the Metropolitan District Councils outside London one-third of the Councillors are elected every third year. For electoral purposes some of the Unitary Councils and all of the County Councils are divided into single-member constituencies, whereas the District and London Boroughs and some Unitary Councils are divided into wards, each represented by between one and three Councillors, depending on geographical area and population.

At every level of local government the Chairman of the Council is elected annually by fellow Councillors. In those Councils which are predominantly urban, the Chairman takes the honorary title of Mayor and presides in that capacity over the Council proceedings. However, the real power in all Councils is wielded by the leader of the majority party and, to a lesser extent, by the political chairmen of the key committees – for example, education, finance, environment and social services. Most Councils have a Policy and Resources Committee (or its equivalent) which normally includes the chairmen of all the main committees and acts as a sort of 'Cabinet' for the local authority. Councillors of all political persuasions usually serve on more than one committee and the membership of committees reflects the relative strengths of the

Figure 16.7 The structure of Government in the United Kingdom

	England	Wales	Scotland	Northern Ireland
Supranational		The European Union		
	71 MEPs	5 MEPs	8 MEPs	3 MEPs
		Council of the Isles		
				North–South Ministerial Council
National		The Government of the United Kingdom		
		The House of Commons		
	529 MPs	40 MPs	72 MPs	18 MPs
Devolved	9 Government Offices of the Regions 9 Regional Development Agencies Regional Chambers	Assembly Leader Executive 60 Members	Parliament First Minister Cabinet 129 Members	Assembly First Minister Deputy Minister Executive Committee 108 Members
Local	England (Excluding London) 34 County Councils 46 Unitary Councils 36 Metropolitan District Councils 238 Non-Metropolitan District Councils 8000 (Approx) Parish Councils London Greater London Authority Mayor 25 Member Assembly 32 Borough Councils The Corporation of the City of London	22 Single-tier Authorities 750 Community Councils	29 Single-tier Authorities 3 Unitary Island Councils 1200 (approx) Community Councils	26 District Councils

political parties in the local authority concerned. Since many local authorities are politically dominated by one particular party, this usually means that the key committees are controlled by the majority party in the locality and are run in conformity with that party's political ideas and interests. However, in so-called 'hung Councils' in which no single party has an overall majority, political power – for example, the key committee chairmanships – is usually shared between two, or indeed more, parties.

Councillors are not much more representative of the general public than are Members of Parliament. To be eligible for election, however, they must live or work in the local authority area concerned. There is not a great deal of statistical evidence about their make-up and socio-economic characteristics. A survey conducted in 1964 revealed that only 12 per cent of Councillors were women, only 19 per cent were blue-collar workers, and the average age was 55 years.[9] In 1977 the Robinson Report confirmed that the general characteristics of Councillors had not changed very much, since at that time they were still predominantly male, middle-aged and middle-class, although the proportion of women had risen slightly to 17 per cent.[10]

Research into the characteristics and attitudes of Councillors carried out for the Widdicombe Committee in 1985 showed that fewer than one in five Councillors were women and that the majority of Councillors were still aged 55 or more.[11] However, with the exception of the English Shires and the Welsh local Authorities, all local Authorities showed an increase in the number of Councillors aged 45 or younger, with the most marked increases in London and Scotland. In general, Metropolitan Councillors have been getting younger on average, while Shire Councillors have retained their older age profile. Councillors had higher educational qualifications than the public as a whole and were more likely to have stayed on at school beyond the age of 16. Almost a quarter of the Councillors who took part in the survey had obtained a degree or higher qualification, compared with only 5 per cent of the general population and 12 per cent of the population aged 25–69 by 1995.

The Widdicombe Report also showed that in the period since the Robinson Report there had been an appreciable fall in the proportion of Councillors in paid employment – 60 per cent in 1985 compared with 72 per cent in 1976. This fall was matched not by an increase in the number declaring themselves to be unemployed, but rather by an increase in the number defined as retired. Councillors were drawn from a much narrower range of occupational backgrounds than would be found in the population as a whole, with 41 per cent coming from professional or managerial backgrounds and only 5 per cent from semi-skilled or unskilled manual occupations. Of those Councillors in paid employment at the the time of the survey, 36 per cent were employed in the public sector (exactly the same as the population as a whole at the time) and of those almost half were employed in local government, notably as teachers, lecturers, social workers or administrators. The practice of people being Councillors in one local authority while being employed as officials in another local authority caused some controversy and even hostility, especially among Conservatives in their attitude towards Labour-controlled local government in the 1980s. It was one of the things which the Widdicombe Committee was asked to examine and it led to the inclusion of a measure in the 1989 Local Government and Housing Act which enabled the Government to prohibit Council officials on salaries of more than £19,500 a year from standing for election in local government.

In 1994 a new study showed that there had been a steady increase in the proportion of women Councillors since Widdicombe, with women making up 25 per cent of Councillors. The study also showed that there had been a marked improvement in women Councillors' representation in leadership positions, with the proportion being virtually identical with those of men. Changes had also occurred in the educational background of Councillors, with a growth in graduates (to 28 per cent) and a decline in the proportion of Councillors with no educational qualifications (to 18 per cent). With regard to employment, the study found that 58 per cent of Councillors were in paid employment (32 per cent in full-time work, 7 per cent in part-time work and 19 per cent self-employed), while 4 per cent were unemployed, 31 per cent were retired and 8 per cent were not working for other reasons. In common with the Widdicombe findings, the 1994 study found that the majority of Councillors were employed in the private sector (63 per cent) with only 37 per cent in public sector employment. With regard to Councillor turnover, little had changed: 38 per cent of the Councillors who took part in the survey had served for more than ten years, compared with 35 per cent reported by Widdicombe, while it found that Councillors spent on average 74 hours a month on Council business, exactly the same figure recorded by the Widdicombe survey.[12] See Figure 16.8 for the figures on this.

In 1998 a census conducted by the Local Government Management Board and based on returns from almost 15,500 Councillors – two-thirds of the total – and covering 98 per cent of authorities in England and Wales showed that women, ethnic minorities and the young were seriously under-represented in the Councils of England and Wales: almost 75 per cent – nearly 80 per cent in Wales – were male; almost 97 per cent were white (88 per cent in London but 99.3 per cent in the North and Wales). The survey showed that the 'typical' Councillor was a 55 year old white male

Figure 16.8 Average hours per month Councillors spent on Council duties

Source: Guardian, 3 May 1994

with a degree or professional qualification who had been a Councillor for almost nine years and who was also a school governor or on the board of another public body.[13]

Local authority officials are the other vital element in local government. In general, they assist Councillors in much the same way as civil servants assist Ministers, but there are some significant contrasts with the Civil Service, especially the fact that the key officials in local government are normally well-qualified professionals in the particular sphere of local government activity in which they are engaged. Thus Chief Education Officers and their senior colleagues are often former teachers, Directors of Social Services and their senior staff are often former social workers, and Chief Planning Officers and others within the Planning Department are often qualified planners, surveyors or architects. The key point is that Departments of local government are staffed by professionals and, as such, have a considerable influence on the policy of their local authorities.

The main similarity between local government officials and civil servants in central Government is that both are expected to remain politically neutral and faithfully to carry out the policies of their political masters. In local government the principal effect of such political neutrality is that most policy decisions are heavily influenced by the technical and expert advice of the officials concerned. Of course, the decisions are always taken by the Councillors, but there can be occasions when they appear to be acting as little more than political spokesmen for the officials. On the other hand, there has also been some concern – especially in the Conservative Party – that some local government officials appear to be uncomfortably 'political' in their motivation and their actions, notably in Labour-controlled local authorities in inner city areas. Doubtless similar perceptions are held in the other direction by some of those strongly committed to the Labour Party when they look at the behaviour of local government officials in Conservative-controlled local areas. A balanced conclusion would seem to suggest that these things are largely in the eye of the beholder, although it should be added that both local and central Government do seem to have gone through a particularly polarised 'political' phase in the 1980s.

16.3 Local government – powers and functions

The powers and functions of local government in England and Wales are set out in the relevant statutes, notably the 1972 Local Government Act. Such legislation specified the powers which are to be exercised by the various levels of local government, and there is a clear understanding that all powers which are not statutorily designated for local authorities remain the preserve of either devolved Assemblies or ultimately central Government – assuming that Parliament has provided the necessary statutory powers in the first place. Indeed Parliament is able to create, modify or even abolish aspects of local government in the United Kingdom, as was witnessed in 1972 when the Northern Ireland Stormont Parliament was suspended and its powers transferred to Parliament at Westminster, or in 1984–85 when legislation was put through Parliament to abolish the GLC and the other Metropolitan County Councils, or in 1997–99 when legislation was passed to create a Scottish Parliament, a Welsh Assembly and a Greater London Authority.

Statutory duties

Local authorities are given statutory duties in Acts of Parliament. The Westminster legislation sets out what the statutory duties shall be in each case. This means that local authorities *have* to perform certain functions which Parliament has assigned to them and they carry out their duties in accordance with the terms of the legislation.

For example, the 1944 Education Act stipulated that local Authorities should be responsible for providing public education for all children in their areas who are within the statutory age range for school education. Equally, the 1972 Chronically Sick and Disabled Persons Act laid statutory duties on local authorities to provide care for all such people within their areas in the various ways prescribed in the legislation. Or again the 1977 Homeless Persons Act which imposed a statutory duty on local authorities to house the homeless, provided the latter satisfy certain prescribed conditions and have not made themselves deliberately homeless. Similarly, the 1992 Community Care Act obliged all local Authorities to take the lead in organising suitable care and support for all those who need care in the community, including the chronically sick and those with physical or mental handicaps. However, such statutes are sometimes vague, while Circulars from central Government are not binding. So even when performing statutory duties, there can be variations in the actual outcomes in local authorities. Consequently the professionals involved in the implementation of national standards can have an important effect upon what is or is not achieved.

Discretionary powers

Local authorities are also given discretionary powers in Acts of Parliament. Once again the Westminster legislation sets out in each case the areas and the extent to which such powers may be exercised. This means that local Authorities are endowed with discretionary powers to provide certain services, *if they wish to do so and assuming they can raise the necessary finance.*

For example, the 1969 Children and Young Persons Act gave local authorities the discretionary powers to do all sorts of caring and compassionate things for young people in trouble, but failed to make available the extra money without which it proved difficult to implement large sections of the Act. During the period of public expenditure restraint imposed by the Conservative Government after 1979, many local authorities pressed for discretionary rather than mandatory powers whenever they were affected by new legislation, so that they might have a better chance of living within the tight financial limits set by central Government. Thus the discretionary powers, which used to be seen as a way of extending local provision of national services, came to be regarded by many local authorities as a way of saving money, since this allowed them to reduce or withdraw such services without incurring legislative or judicial penalties.

Division of functions

The division of functions between the various levels of local government is fiendishly complicated and has been subject to a number of changes over the years.

Figure 16.9 Responsibility for some major services in English local authorities

| | Metropolitan areas | | Shire areas | | | London area | | | |
	Joint Authorities	District Councils	County Councils *or* Unitary Authorities	District Councils	Police Authorities	City of London	London Boroughs	London Fire & Civil Def	Met Police
Education		*	*			*	*		
Housing		*		*		*	*		
Planning Applications		*		*		*	*		
Strategic planning		*	*			*	*		
Transport planning		*	*			*	*		
Passenger transport (a)	*		*						
Highways		*	*			*	*		
Police (b)	*		*		*	*			*
Fire (c)	*		*					*	
Social services		*	*			*	*		
Libraries		*	*			*	*		
Leisure and recreation		*		*		*	*		
Waste collection		*		*		*	*		
Waste disposal (d)	*		*			*	*		
Environmental health		*		*		*	*		
Local taxation		*		*		*	*		

(a) Passenger transport in London is provided by London Regional Transport, which is outside the local authority sector.
(b) Before the setting up of new police authorities on 1 April 1995, county councils had responsibilities for police services, some on a combined basis.
(c) Combined Fire authorities are responsible for Fire services in the shire areas affected by reorganisation from April 1996 onwards.
(d) Waste disposal for some areas of London is carried out by separate waste disposal authorities. Waste regulation became the responsibility of the Environment Agency on 1 April 1996.

At present, the *County Councils* have statutory responsibilities for transport, highways, police, fire service, Court administration, overspill housing, strategic planning, consumer protection, refuse disposal, education, public libraries and personal social services.

The *non-Metropolitan District Councils* have statutory responsibilities for housing, local planning, environmental health, minor roads, licensing of public houses and places of entertainment, and the registration of births, marriages and deaths.

The *Metropolitan District Councils* have the same statutory responsibilities as the non-Metropolitan District Councils, with the addition of education, public libraries and personal social services. The upper and lower levels of Metropolitan local government used to share statutory responsibility for museums and art galleries, parks and open spaces, municipal swimming baths, regional airports and land acquired for development. However, since the abolition of the Metropolitan Counties in 1986, these tasks have been taken on by the Metropolitan Districts. Only police, fire services, and public transport were transferred to statutory joint boards, while a few residual functions (such as land drainage, flood protection and some arts sponsorship) were transferred to other public bodies.[14]

The *single-tier Unitary Authorities* introduced in England, Wales and Scotland in 1995/96 took over all aspects of local government within their geographical area. The distribution of responsibilities between the various different kinds of local authority and the vesting of functions in special purpose bodies by-passing local government are shown in tabular form in Figure 16.9.

Under the pressure of successive phases of Westminster legislation passed at the behest of the Conservative Government in the 1980s and 1990s, elected local government was required to 'market test' many of its own services, to introduce compulsory competitive tendering (CCT), and to cede to the growing category of 'special purpose bodies' or QUANGOs many of the duties, powers and functions which it previously performed within the legislative framework set by statute.[15] This gradual erosion of the role of local government as a *provider* (as distinct from purchaser or regulator) of local services was commended by its proponents as a drive towards the creation of 'enabling' local authorities.

The Labour Government which came into office in 1997 announced its intention to replace CCT with a new duty for local Councils to ensure 'best value' for the public. The criteria included increased efficency, reduced costs to the taxpayer, and improved quality of service.

16.4 Local government – financial arrangements

The financing of local government has long been both complicated and controversial in Britain. From the early 1950s local authority spending grew steadily and usually at a faster rate than the economy as a whole. This growth was bearable in the 1950s and 1960s when the British economy was growing at about 3 per cent a year and there was general public and political support for constantly increasing public expenditure. However, since the 1976 financial crisis, when the then Labour Government had to call in the IMF, successive Governments of both main parties have felt it necessary to

Figure 16.10 Local government expenditure and income

Expenditure

Total spending by service 1996/97
Revenue expenditure: £69,012 million

Capital expenditure: £6420 million

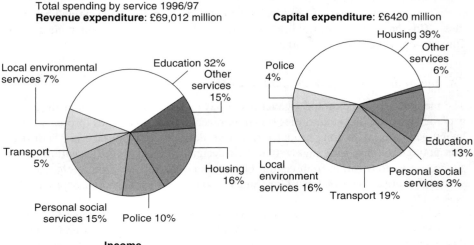

Income

Income by source 1996/97
Total £75,596 million

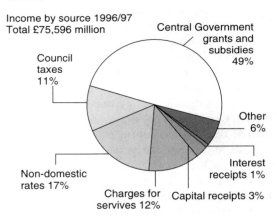

control all forms of public spending. Local authority spending, which has accounted for about one-quarter of the total, has been no exception to this rule. In such circumstances relations between local and central Government became strained and in the 1980s and 1990s struggles over local government finance and local government spending were exacerbated by sharp differerences of party politics between Conservative central Government and Labour and Liberal Democrat-controlled local authorities.

The financial problems of local government have not been made any easier by the fact that so much new legislation proposed by central Government and passed by Parliament has had financial implications for local Authorities for which they have not always been sufficiently compensated by the Exchequer. Many new statutory duties were placed on local authorities over the years in fields such as housing, education, social services and community care. Yet under Conservative Governments between 1979 and 1997, local authorities did not receive all the financial support from the centre which they felt they needed, while at the same time they were prevented by law from raising extra finance from local sources – traditionally domestic and business rates. This has been a continuing complaint of local authorities under the Labour Government which came into office in 1997.

The methods of local government finance

The methods of financing local government have varied over the years in Britain. In general, however, local authorities relied on revenue from local rates (property taxes) levied according to a complicated formula on domestic, commercial and industrial (but not agricultural) buildings within their designated areas; together with financial support in various forms from central Government and income from rents, fees and charges. A breakdown of local Government expenditure and income is provided in Figure 16.10.

Rates, which traditionally raised nearly half of the revenue needed to finance local services, were assessed on the rateable value of the land or buildings concerned. In theory they represented the rent at which the property could be let (if there were a market for such lettings), minus the notional cost of repairs, insurance and other maintenance expenses. They were paid every year (normally in two or more instalments) and the abstruse calculations on which they were based were reviewed about every ten years by the Inland Revenue in periodic revaluations which took account of inflation and any improvements to the property over the intervening period. Although rates were an unpopular form of taxation, it was never easy to identify a simpler or more cost-effective way of raising large sums of revenue from local sources.[16]

The rest of the money needed for local government revenue support came traditonally from a system of central Government grants to local authorities. These took two main forms. *First*, there were specific grants in aid of particular local purposes – for example, 50 per cent of local police expenditure or 90 per cent of mandatory student grants, or specific housing subsidies for poorer tenants. *Secondly*, there were general grants to the rate funds of individual local authorities in order to increase their overall income, notably in those parts of the country with a poor rateable base.

The total amount of *Rate Support Grant* (RSG) was fixed every year by the Department of the Environment in co-operation with the Treasury and after consultation with the local authority Associations and the Consultative Council on Local Government Finance. The RSG was composed of a *needs element* assessed for each local authority mainly on the basis of demographic factors, a *resources element* paid to those authorities where the rateable base was below the national average, and a *domestic element* designed to bring some relief to all domestic ratepayers. The most notable characteristics of the system were a bias in favour of income redistribution from the richer to the poorer parts of the country, and considerable power for central Government in its ability to switch or withhold grants from individual local authorities.

The fierce and seemingly endless tussle over local government finance in the 1980s made the then Conservative Government deeply unpopular, divided the Cabinet, and contributed to the downfall of Margaret Thatcher as Prime Minister in

November 1990.[17] The new Prime Minister, John Major, made it one of his first tasks to sort out these problems. He had little difficulty in persuading Parliament to legislate to abolish the highly controversial Community Charge (Poll Tax) and to replace it with the *Council Tax*, which came into effect on 1 April 1993.[18] This tax, which is levied on each and every residential household, is calculated largely on the basis of property values as reflected in broad valuation bands based on prices in April 1991. However, it also takes account of the number of people living in each dwelling by allowing a 25 per cent discount for those living alone. It was introduced at relatively low levels thanks to a considerable Exchequer subsidy paid for by increasing the standard rate of Value-Added Tax from 15 to 17.5 per cent, and its early impact was also mitigated by transitional relief phased over a number of years. For commercial and industrial premises the Uniform Business Rate was retained, although efforts were made to ameliorate its impact, especially on new business premises in the South-East of England, by adjusting the transitional reliefs. Agricultural land remained unrated. As for the system of Exchequer support to local authorities, this was retained in its new simplified form and paid to each local authority as a block grant.

16.5 Central–local relations

The relations between local and central Government have seldom been easy or unambiguously defined. In the nineteenth century there was a lengthy search for a system of local government which would be both efficient and democratic, although not necessarily for a relationship with central Government that was designed to be mutually beneficial. Throughout the twentieth century there have been notable occasions when the usual habits of co-operation between local and central Government have broken down and thus given rise to serious misunderstanding and conflict. In general, however, local authorities have sought faithfully to perform their statutory duties and have acted within the statutory constraints laid upon them by Parliament.[19]

Constitutional relations

The constitutional relations between local and central Government have varied greatly over the centuries in Britain. Between 1688 and 1835 the effective independence of local government could hardly have been greater, since there was virtually no interference from central Government and only minimal control. However, since the 1835 Municipal Corporations Act, the powers and influence of central Government have grown steadily and there has been an apparently remorseless tendency towards the centralisation of political power. This should not be thought particularly surprising in a unitary state, such as Britain, in which all the legal power and authority of local government has always derived from Acts of Parliament and in which local government has been able to rely only on local elections and local pride to buttress its sense of legitimacy in dealings with central Government.

Today the constitutional relationship between local and central Government is invariably described by Ministers as a partnership, but by Councillors in much less flattering terms and, occasionally, as a central dictatorship. In Whitehall and

Westminster not much more than lip-service is paid to the idea of partnership with local government, although relations have undoubtedly improved since. Labour came to power at Westminster in 1997.

It might have been more logical to have clear-cut statements and constitutional rules about the division of powers and responsibilities between local and central Government, and then to have entrenched such arrangements in a new constitutional settlement. Yet the principle of Parliamentary supremacy did not permit such an outcome and it seems rather unlikely that it ever will, unless such a move is brought about by Britain's membership of the European Union. Consequently the compromise which has been reached gives local government a clearly *subordinate* constitutional position, while allowing it a more *co-ordinate* relationship with central Government when dealing with a wide variety of practical issues which arise on a day-to-day basis.

Political relations

Political relations between local and central Government have not been easy in modern times, since they are often characterised by inherent conflict of interest and incompatible political objectives. This was especially true in the 1980s when an ideological Conservative Government in Whitehall had a long-running battle with several local authorities led by left-wing Labour politicians of a campaigning disposition. Of course, there is bound to be tension or worse in a relationship which depends on mutual understanding and co-operation between inherently unequal partners. Furthermore, the relationship is bound to become rather bitter when central Government seeks to impose tighter financial constraints on local authorities and when many local authorities are run by politically motivated men and women with principles and objectives which are entirely at odds with those of Ministers.

During the period of Conservative Government between 1979 and 1997 the Labour Party was particularly strong in urban local government, especially in the inner city areas and the great conurbations of the Midlands and the North. Equally, the Liberal Democrats steadily gained political control of more local authorities, notably in the West Country and the suburbs of London, where disgruntled voters who previously supported one or other of the main parties responded positively to the appeal of Liberal Democrat community politics. Consequently, mutual suspicion and resentment came to characterise the relationship between local and central Government, much to the detriment of the traditional conventions which previously facilitated comparatively civilised relations between the two levels of elected Government in Britain.

Even in difficult economic circumstances, and with fraught political relations, the partnership between local and central Government is supposed to involve some sharing of decision-making powers. Yet most people in local government would probably agree with N.P. Hepworth when he wrote that 'local government does not share in the decision making of central Government; it makes representations, but that is not the same thing'.[20] On the other hand, from the point of view of central Government, the partnership can seem quite real, in that many aspects of Government policy depend for their success on the active and willing co-operation of local government. For example, overall public expenditure restraint is dependent on local government co-operation – at a time when local authorities account for one-quarter of total public spending, even if the planning total was at one time redefined to exclude those categories of local spending which are financed exclusively from local revenue. Similarly many of the statutory obligations placed on local government by Parliament are couched in broad terms of principle which leave the precise methods of implementation very much in the hands of local authorities, not to mention the discretionary powers whose use or non-use depends entirely on local government decisions. Furthermore the local authorities have learned to combine in order to maximise their influence on central Government. They do this through their representative bodies – the Association of Metropolitan Authorities, the Association of County Councils and the Association of District Councils, and in strictly financial matters through the Consultative Council on Local Government Finance.

While the relationship between local and central Government is reasonably clear-cut in constitutional terms, it has often been ambiguous and even hostile in political terms. Neither level of government can really afford to alienate the other and neither can achieve all its objectives without the co-operation of the other. Local government now depends more heavily than before on central Government grants and the Uniform Business Rate whose level in any year is determined by central Government. On the other hand, central Government depends heavily on local government for the local administration of national services.

16.6 Methods of central control

There are four principal methods by which central Government seeks to control local government: namely, legislative control, policy control, administrative control and financial control. Of these, financial control is the most important, but we shall consider each of them in turn.

Legislative control

It is the legislative control in Acts of Parliament which establishes the nature and extent of the subordinate powers conferred on local government. As J.A.G. Griffith has explained, 'within the terms on which these powers are bestowed, local authorities are autonomous bodies and a Department [of central Government] which proposes to control the way in which or the extent to which local authorities exercise their powers must be able to point to statutory provisions authorising this intervention'.[21] Thus legislative control provides legal safeguards for local government as well as a means of control for central Government.

One of the most widespread criticisms of central control of local authorities, however, has stemmed from the excessive frequency of new Westminster legislation designed to limit, if not remove, what little is left of local government's legal discretion. It has been calculated that at least 150 Acts of Parliament were put on the Statute Book in the years between 1979 and 1997 which were designed in one way or another to diminish the powers of local authorities, and it has been forcefully argued that this did more than anything else to disable and demoralise both Councillors and officials in local government.

Such legislative control can take various forms. In many cases the original legislation confers on Ministers the power to make detailed regulations which are binding on local government. For example, it is customary for Whitehall to issue Statutory Instruments which set out the building regulations to be observed in the construction of buildings and the planning regulations to be observed in carrying out local property or transport developments. In some cases local authorities are given power to make by-laws about public footpaths and other very local matters. Yet it is always made clear in the original Westminster legislation that these by-laws must be confirmed by the relevant Minister. Of course, this legislative control involves two-way influence and communication, since the representative bodies of local government are often consulted in the preparation and always consulted on the implementation of Westminster legislation which affects local Authorities.

Policy control

Another form of central control is provided by the power and influence of Government policy. This can take various forms, depending on the priorities of the party in office and the legal basis of the relationship between local authorities and the different Departments of central Government. For example, the 1948 Children Act and the 1969 Children and Young Persons Act each stipulated that local authorities should exercise statutory functions in this area of policy under the guidance of the relevant Ministers, which has meant in effect the policy pursued by the Government of the day. Similarly the Secretary of State for Education has a supervisory and promotional role in relation to the organisation of schools and the supply of teachers in all the Local Education Authorities in England and Wales. This power derives from the 1944 Education Act, as amended by the 1988 Education Reform Act, and it has been exercised by successive Governments in accordance with their own particular education policies and with increasing force and frequency in relation to the implementation of the national curriculum in all state-funded schools since its introduction in 1988.

Other examples of policy control by Ministers and their civil servants in Whitehall can be found in the sphere of housing and other local services. Successive Conservative Governments in the 1980s and 1990s promoted policies of home ownership and home improvement, while previous Labour Governments had promoted policies of public sector house building and rent control. In these ways the policy of the Government of the day has had a considerable influence on the behaviour of local authorities. Sometimes it has led to bitter conflict between the two levels of Government, with local authorities vainly seeking to resist the policy favoured by central Government – for example, resistance to the right-to-buy provisions of the 1980 Housing Act by Labour-controlled Norwich, or general resistance from both Labour and Liberal Democrat-controlled local authorities to the Conservative policy of compulsory contracting out and competitive tendering for local services. Yet in the end central Government has the whip hand, since, if the existing statutory position is not sufficiently compelling, the party in office can always use its Parliamentary majority to put through further Westminster legislation to curb or eliminate what it may see as intolerable resistance by local government.

Administrative control

Administrative control is another form of central control which derives from central Government's responsibility for setting national standards and promoting the efficiency of local government. Ever since the nineteenth century it has been accepted that many functions of government in Britain should be national services locally administered.This has always implied the need for administrative control via national standards drawn up by Whitehall civil servants and enforced in many cases by powerful, independent Inspectorates. For example, in the case of education Her Majesty's Chief Inspector of Schools monitors – through the Office of Standards in Education (OFSTED) – levels of quality in schools and regulates the work of the independent registered inspectors. In the case of the police, the payment of central Government grants to police authorities is conditional on there being satisfactory reports from Her Majesty's Inspectorate of Constabulary about policing in the different areas of the country covered by different police forces.

Although the range and power of administrative controls exercised by central Government over local authorities has become increasingly formidable over the years, there have been instances when a countervailing tendency has been evident. For example, the 1979–83 Conservative Government sought to reduce the number and scope of certain controls on local government in the hope of thereby reducing the burden of compliance costs on the private sector. It is also believed that, by freeing local authorities from many forms of detailed supervision and administrative control, it would be possible for them to perform their statutory duties in a more cost-effective way. Some provisions in the 1980 Local Government Planning and Land Act were designed for precisely this purpose. Equally, the 1994 Deregulation Act sought to reduce the scope and quantity of detailed regulations which bear so heavily on local authorities, private firms and other public bodies alike, and which in consequence add to costs and create unnecessary delays. Indeed, there is a constant need to deregulate in modern government simply to prevent the inexorable tendency towards more and more regulation, whether driven from London or Brussels, from getting out of hand. Nonetheless, the general tendency has been rather the other way, with central Government seeking to control the activities of local government ever more closely.

Financial control

Certainly, the most powerful forms of central control has always been the financial control exercised by central Government. This can be traced back at least to the 1929 Local Government Act in which the earlier system of assigned revenues was abolished and replaced with a system of specific grants, together with a block grant from central Government to each local authority. In 1948 this system of financial control was supplemented by a system of deficiency payments to those local authorities with rateable values below the average, and in 1958 the whole system was rationalised to enable a new block grant (the Rate Support Grant) to replace the wide variety of specific grants which had grown up over the years. At every stage from then until the present day financial support from central Government has been synonymous with financial control by central Government, especially as the proportion of total local government spending financed by central Government grants or locally raised taxation entirely under the control of central Government has now risen to about 85 per cent. Little more than lip-service has been paid by central Government to the idea of encouraging real financial independence for local Authorities, because the Treasury has traditionally been determined not to relax its control over any significant category of public spending nor to relinquish the right to tax to subnational (or supranational) levels of government.

This stance has, however, changed to a limited extent with regard to the arrangements for Scotland as a consequence of the policy of devolution. The Scottish Parliament was given tax-varying powers, the ability to increase or decrease the basic rate of income tax (as set by the United Kingdom Parliament) by up to 3p in the pound, around £450 million – a figure that was both indexed linked and preserved in the eventuality of changes in UK income tax structures. In addition, the control of local authority expenditure and non-domestic rates along with other local taxation within Scotland were devolved to the Scottish Parliament.

Today the financial control of central Government over local government takes essentially four forms. *First,* central Government in essence sets a spending limit for each Council via the Standard Spending Assessment. *Secondly,* local government revenue-expenditure is supported – that is, controlled – to the tune of about 57 per cent on a national average basis by the Aggregate Exchequer Grant paid to each local authority according to its needs and its population. *Thirdly,* about 24 per cent of all local authority spending is financed by the proceeds of the Uniform Business Rate which is set by central Government at a level which should not rise by more than the rate of inflation and which might be held below that. *Fourthly,* local authority capital expenditure is tightly controlled by the Treasury, since local authorities are not encouraged to borrow directly (and more expensively) from the markets and have not been allowed by the Treasury to spend more than 25 per cent of their receipts from the sale of housing and 50 per cent of receipts from other sources in any one year.

The Conservative Government elected in 1979 was as keen to control local government capital expenditure as it was to control local government current expenditure. Initially this was part of its campaign to reduce and then eliminate public borrowing. By the early 1990s, however, when the length and depth of the recession produced an unparalleled public sector deficit, it was motivated principally by a desire to curb the current expenditure implications of all capital projects. Although this stance continued under the Labour Government which came into office in 1997, in 1998 the Government announced plans to boost public sector house building and modernisation by almost £4 billion from the release of Councils' capital receipts. It was a move that was to go hand-in-hand with the tough new powers to penalise under-performing Councils, including powers to remove functions from an offending Council and hand them over to a neighbouring authority or an Agency.

A final point which relates to central Government financial controls over local government is that between 1979 and 1997 a total of more than £25 billion of annual expenditure was transferred from local authorities to special purpose bodies created by central Government. This transfer greatly reduced the amount of public spending over which elected Councillors had some influence and further enhanced the degree of central financial control from Whitehall.

16.7 Whither local government?

With common sense and goodwill on both sides it should be possible to achieve fruitful co-operation between local and central Government. There appear to be three basic conditions for this.

1. It must be generally accepted that there are certain minimum nationwide standards for national services which are provided locally.
2. It must be accepted that local authorities are best placed to co-ordinate, if not necessarily provide, many of the public services which people expect.
3. It must be accepted that the relationship between local and central Government can only work satisfactorily on the basis of trust and mutual respect.

Unfortunately, the second and third of these conditions have proved difficult, if not impossible, to fulfil, because in the period between 1979 and 1997 the Conservatives at Westminster conducted something close to unending warfare against Labour and Liberal Democrat controlled local government, and politicians in local government were continuously opposed to many aspects of Conservative national policy. However, it seems possible that central–local relations can improve under the new Labour Government, assuming there is more give and take on both sides.

The politicisation of local government

The Conservative Government re-elected in 1992 carried through another restructuring of local government and continued the pressure towards centralisation and the marginalisation of elected local government with greater emphasis on special purpose bodies and the regional outposts of central Government. On the other hand, Labour and the Liberal Democrats, as well as the Nationalist parties in both Scotland and Wales, were committed to varying degrees of decentralisation and devolution of power to the localities.

The Labour Government which came into office in 1997 pursued the broad theme of 'inclusion' and this led Labour Ministers to be less overtly party-political than their Conservative predecessors in dealings with local government. This relatively benign attiitude may, of course, change if and when the Conservatives – or indeed other parties – make significant gains at local government elections in the future. However, it is possible that the Labour Government will take legislative steps to establish a number of Regional Assemblies in England (if these are wanted in the regions) to which will be allocated some of the strategic planning responsibilities of the Counties as well as the regional responsibilities of central Government Departments. This means that the Labour Government may perhaps abolish the existing County and District Councils and pass their most significant responsibilities – for example, education and social services – to enlarged and strengthened unitary Councils.[22]

As far as finance is concerned, the end of 'crude and universal' Whitehall capping of Council budgets has been proposed – though with the central Government retaining intervention powers – while although national Business Rates are to be retained it is possible that Councils could be given a measure of discretion over local Business

Rates. It is estimated, however, that the system of financial support from central Government will continue much as before.

Above all, Labour has felt offended by the enormous growth of extra-governmental organisations which took place under the Conservatives – in other words, Quangos and other public bodies based on Ministerial appointments and political patronage. It is therefore likely to return many of these functions – for example, those of Urban Development Corporations, the Funding Agency for Schools and NHS Trusts – to the democratic control of Regional Assemblies and elected local government.

In addition, under the Labour Government Scotland has been given a directly elected Parliament with substantial legislative and tax-varying powers, so that most decisions affecting Scotland are taken in Scotland. The Parliament will have a substantial budget of its own comparable in size to all the money previously allocated to Scotland under the auspices of the Scottish Office. In Wales the Labour Government has introduced an elected Assembly responsible for Welsh Office functions and the work of nominated bodies in the Principality. In Northern Ireland, a new 108-member Assembly has been set up, along with other institutions, as part of the peace process.

As for the positions of the other parties on devolved and local government, the Liberal Democrats advocate the introduction of a Local Income Tax related to the ability to pay and collected by the Inland Revenue, to replace the Council Tax; and the replacement of the Uniform Business Rate with Site Value Rating, locally administered and based on the taxation of land values with exemption for agricultural land and domestic properties. The Liberal Democrat approach is to take power away from Westminster and Whitehall and give it to stronger, more independent and more democratic local bodies. The party therefore advocates not only the transformation of local Councils into unitary authorities based on 'natural communities' and 'local wishes'; but also home rule for Scotland, home rule for Wales, and the creation of fully democratic regional governments in England.

William Hague for the Conservatives has pledged that the party will be committed to effective local government, declaring that this was not some radical departure for Conservatives, more a matter of 'coming home'. As part of this new approach, he has suggested that spending powers be returned to Town Halls and that local audit committees be set up to monitor individual Councils.[23]

The *Scottish National Party* is committed to an independent Scotland within the European Union, while *Plaid Cymru* advocates a 'self-governing Wales within a democratic European confederation'. Thus *all* the smaller Opposition parties are, to a greater or lesser extent, well disposed towards greater power and autonomy for sub-national government, and only the Conservatives seem to cling to the image of the United Kingdom as the most unitary state in the European Union.

Local autonomy or further centralisation?

The relationship between devolved or local and central government in Britain has to be considered in the light of broader arguments for greater local autonomy on the one hand or further centralisation on the other. We shall summarise each side of this important debate.

The *arguments in favour of greater local autonomy* include:

1. the need to diminish the remoteness of Government from its citizens;
2. the desirability of enhancing democratic accountability at local level;
3. the opportunities which could be created for greater public participation;
4. the improved efficiency of smaller units in public administration;
5. the reduced financial burden on the Exchequer.

The *arguments in favour of further centralisation* include:

1. the need for common national standards of public provision;
2. the uniformity of public expectations as to what Government should provide;
3. the attractions for Ministers and civil servants of a more direct and reliable form of control over local authorities.

With many tendencies in British society moving in the direction of greater homogeneity and even uniformity (see Chapter 1) there is obviously a strong countervailing case for more local autonomy. As Professors Jones and Stewart have argued, greater autonomy should be encouraged 'not to let loose rampant and uncontrolled localism and the sharpening of geographical inequalities, but to maintain a more balanced array of pressures in public policy making'.[24] In other words, there is strength in diversity and value in variety, not least as a way of minimising the risk of replicating mistakes on a large scale.

With the increasing politicisation of local government, central Government has been drawn to interfere more and more with the activities of local authorities. In the period 1979–1997 successive Conservative Governments took this tendency almost to its limit. Indeed the ultimate Conservative objective for local authorities would seem to have been the transformation of this layer of government into 'enabling authorities' which would have duties of service specification, purchase and regulation, but which would only rarely be involved in the actual provision or delivery of public services at local level.[25]

The Labour Party fought the 1997 General Election declaring that the basic framework, but not every detail, of local service provision must be for central Government to decide, but that Councils should *not be forced* to put their services out to tender. Equally, however, it argued that services should not be delivered directly by local authorities if other more efficient means of delivery were available.

In short, Conservative politicians at national level tried to increase central Government control over local government and to by-pass elected local government altogether whenever it was seen as an obstacle to the attainment of their national objectives. On the other hand, Labour and Liberal Democrat politicians have remained faithful to the cause of devolution, whether to national Parliaments in Scotland and Wales or to Regional Assemblies and strengthened unitary authorities in England.

16.8 Conclusion

It should be clear from this chapter that the position of devolved and local government in the United Kingdom is neither immutable nor easy to describe. However it can be assessed in terms of its efficiency, vitality, adaptability and capacity for genuine partnership with central Government. Let us conclude by touching upon each of these aspects in turn.

With regard to *efficiency*, it seems clear that the present division of responsibilities and functions is a fairly defensible one and does not put such a high premium on the interests of local democracy that the interests of efficiency are unduly compromised. For example, the emphasis on techniques of corporate management within local authorities and the discipline of tough financial limits set by central Government appear to have had a positive effect on the efficiency of local government – certainly that is what their advocates argue. On the other hand, the morale of those in local government has undoubtedly suffered in the relentless drive for greater efficiency, not least because many of the traditional functions and financial resources of local government steadily taken away from them by central Government under the Conservatives.

With regard to *vitality*, the available evidence is somewhat contradictory. On the one hand, the normal turn-out at local elections is seldom more than about 40 to 50 per cent of those entitled to vote, and at local by-elections it sometimes falls below 30 per cent. Equally, turn-out in the most recent devolution referendum in Scotland was only 60 per cent, while in Wales it was only 51 per cent; and the referendum on local government reform in London saw a turnout of only 34 per cent. This suggests rather scant public interest in the democratic process of devolved and local government. On the other hand, even a cursory glance at the columns of the local press in any part of the country reveals considerable public interest in the actual decisions of local government. For example, Council Tax payers are very interested in seeing that value for money is secured in local authority spending, while beneficiary groups usually favour the expansion of existing services or the creation of new ones.

With regard to *adaptability*, the record over the years has been quite good. Throughout the 1980s and 1990s, when many social needs increased, the financial resources made available by central Government to local government were consistently squeezed, so that the Aggregate Exchequer Grant came to cover less than half of total local authority spending compared with nearly two-thirds during the 1970s. The response of local authorities was one of angry criticism, especially from those local authorities in inner city areas where the social problems were often greatest. It is clear that local Councillors of all parties resented the financial restrictions which were imposed by central Government and would like to have had a system of local authority finance which enabled them to perform all their statutory duties in a more satisfactory way.

As for the capacity of local government to maintain a *genuine partnership* with central Government, this has been determined partly by the diminishing extent to which local government has retained sole responsibility for providing local services. Successive Conservative Governments in the 1980s and 1990s made determined attempts to encourage the privatisation of local services and to separate the idea of local government *provision* from local government *responsibility* – for example, in the field of Community Care. However, the main explanation for the rather lopsided partnership between local and central government in recent years has been the failure of the former to secure any significant degree of real financial autonomy. Indeed, with the switch from local business rates to the Uniform Business Rate and the use of central Government financial capping, the extent of local government financial autonomy decreased still further. It is, therefore, hard to demonstrate that local government has anything like a genuine or equal partnership with central Government. Whether or not the Scottish Parliament and the Welsh Assembly develop a genuine partnership with central Government, only time will show.

Even allowing for all these problems and shortcomings, devolved and local government in Britain still have several points in their favour. Their diversity contributes to political pluralism in the United Kingdom. Their institutions offer an important sphere of political activity to a considerable number of elected representatives. The process stimulates public interest in the local provision of national services. Apart from Parliament at Westminster and the European Parliament, they provide the only levels of elected representation in British democracy. Such positive attributes should not be underestimated or ignored.

Suggested questions

1   'The United Kingdom is a unitary state with all political authority ultimately centralised.' Discuss.
2   'Local government can do only what central Government wants it to do, so local autonomy is a farce.' Is such a view justified?
3   How and why has the structure of local government changed in the United Kingdom in the 1990s?

Notes

1. Lord Kilbrandon, *The Constitution* (CMND 5460), (London: HMSO, 1973).
2. See 1997 Labour Manifesto, *New Labour, Because Britain Deserves Better* (London: Labour Party, 1997), pp. 33–4.
3. See *Scotland's Parliament* (CM 3658), (London: Stationery Office, 1997) and *A View for Wales* (CM 3718), (London: Stationery Office, 1997).
4. See *The Belfast Agreement: An Agreement Reached at the Multi-Party Talks on Northern Ireland* (CM 3883), (London: Stationery Office, 1998).
5. The Constitution Unit Briefing – *Devolution in the Round*, (June 1996).
6. See Adams, G.B., *Constitutional History of England* (2nd edn), (London: Jonathon Case, 1941).
7. Of particular note in this context are the Local Government Act of 1888 and the District and Parish Councils Act of 1894. See Lord Redcliffe-Mand & Bruce Ward, *English Local Government Reformed* (Oxford: Oxford University Press, 1974).
8. See *A Mayor and Assembly for London* (CM 3897) (London: Stationery Office, 1998).
9. 'Report of the Maud Committee on Local Government Management' (London: HMSO, 1967).
10. Report of the Committee of Inquiry into the system of remuneration of members of local authorities, Vol. 2 CMND 7010 (London: HMSO, 1977).
11. See 'The Conduct of Local Authority Business' (CMND 9797), (London: HMSO, 1986), paras 2.23–2.31 for more information on the socioeconomic profile of modern councillors.
12. See K. Young and N. Rao, *Coming to Terms with Change? The Local Government Councillor in 1993* (London: Joseph Rowntree Foundation, 1994).
13. 'Local Government Management Board census, March 1998' *Guardian*, 20 March 1998.
14. The functions transferred to the Borough and District Councils included: planning, highways and traffic management; waste regulation and disposal; housing; trading standards and related functions; support for the arts, sport and historic buildings; civil defence and emergencies; funding for Magistrates' Courts and the probation service; Coroners; school

crossing patrols; building control; tourism and the licensing of places of entertainment; archives and libraries; recreation, parks and Green Belt land; safety of sports grounds; registration of common land and town or village greens; public rights of way and the registration of gypsy sites.

15. See S. Weir and W. Hall, *Ego Trip: Extra-governmental Organisation in the UK* (London: Charter 88 Trust, 1990).
16. See 'Local Government Finance' (the Layfield Report), Cmnd 6453 (London: HMSO, 1976). The Labour Government's response to the Longfield Report, Cmnd 6813 (London: HMSO, 1977); and 'Alternatives to Domestic Rates', Cmnd 8449 (London: HMSO, 1981), for a fuller discussion of these issues.
17. See N.D.J. Baldwin, *The Conservative Party: An Instinct to Survive* (Barnstaple: Phillip Charles Media, 1990).
18. See 'A New Tax for Local Government', Department of the Environment Consultation Paper, April 1991.
19. See K.B. Smellie, *History of Local Government* (London: Allen & Unwin, 1968), for a more detailed account.
20. N.P. Hepworth, *The Finance of Local Government*, 4th edn (London: Allen & Unwin, 1978) p. 255.
21. J.A.G. Griffith, *Central Departments and Local Authorities* (London: Allen & Unwin, 1966), p. 49.
22. See 1997 Labour Party Manifesto, *New Labour: Because Britain Deserves Better,* for a succinct and authoritative statement of Labour's approach to devolved and local government reform.
23. William Hague, address to the Local Government Association, 9 July, 1998.
24. *The Times*, 14 August 1981.
25. See M. Forsyth, *Re-Servicing Britain* (London: Adam Smith Institute, 1980), N. Ridley, *The Local Right: Enabling not Providing* (London: Centre for Policy Studies, 1988), and A. Seldon, *The State is Rolling Back* (London: E & L Brooks/Institute for Economic Affairs, 1994), for a fuller discussion of the approach.

Further reading

Alexander, A., *Local Government in the 1990s* (Barnstaple: Phillip Charles Media, 1990).
The Belfast Agreement (CM 3883), (London: Stationery Office, 1998).
Butcher, H. et al., *Local Government and Thatcherism* (London: Routledge, 1990).
Butler, D., Adonis, A. and Travers, T., *Failure in the British Government: The Politics of the Poll Tax* (Oxford: OUP, 1994).
Coulson, A., *Devolving Power: The Case For Regional Government* (Fabian Tract 537), (London: Fabian Society, January 1990).
Elcock. H., *Remarking the Union: Devolution and British Politics in the 1990s* (London: Frank Cass, 1998).
Gray, C., *Government beyond the Centre* (London: Macmillan, 1993).
Hampton, W., *Local Government and Urban Politics*, 2nd edn (London: Longman, 1991).
Hogwood, B.W. and Keating, M. (eds) *Regional Government in England* (Oxford: Clarendon Press, 1982).
Leach, S. et al., *The Changing Organisation and Management of Local Government* (London: Macmillan, 1994).
Rhodes, R.A.W., *Beyond Westminster and Whitehall* (London: Routledge, 1992).
Ridley, N., *The Local Right: Enabling not Providing* (Policy Study no. 92), (London: Centre for Policy Studies, 1988).

Stewart, J. and Stoker, G. (eds), *Local Government in the 1990s*, (Fabian Tract 537), (London: Macmillan, 1995).

Stoker, G., *The Politics of Local Government*, 2nd edn (London: Macmillan, 1991).

White paper 'A Mayor and Assembly for London'. (CM 3897), (London: Stationery Office, 1998).

White paper 'A Voice for Wales' (CM 3718), (London: Stationery Office, 1997).

White paper 'Scotlands' Parliament' (CM 3658), (London: Stationery Office, 1997).

White Paper 'Modern Local Government: In Touch with the People' (CM 4014), (London: Stationery Office, 1998).

Wilson, D., Game, C., et al., *Local Government in the UK* (London: Macmillan, 1994).

Young, K. and Rao, N., *Coming to Terms with Change? The Local Government Councillor in 1993* (London: Joseph Rowntree Foundation).

Website

Local government   http://www.local.detr.gov.uk

17 The legal system

There are five main aspects of the legal system in the United Kingdom.[1] All of them are significantly affected by the peculiar nature of the British constitution, which is uncodified and which vests supreme legal power and authority in Parliament rather than in any Court. They are:

1. The sphere of *criminal justice,* which involves the application of the criminal law to cases brought to Court by the prosecuting authorities and others.
2. The sphere of *civil justice,* which involves the application of the civil law to cases brought by various plaintiffs, including individuals, corporate bodies and the Law Officers of the Crown.
3. The process of *judicial appeal,* which allows those who are dissatisfied with the verdicts of lower Courts or Tribunals to seek redress or reversal of judgement in the higher Courts of Appeal.
4. The important sphere of *civil rights and duties,* which determines the complex legal relationship between citizens and the state.
5. The sphere of *administrative law,* which enables the Courts to review the actions of Ministers, local authorities and other public bodies.

This chapter reviews each of these aspects in turn. It does so against a contemporary backdrop which reveals declining public confidence in the police and the judicial system, an increasingly relevant European context, and mounting pressure for significant reform.

For our purposes in this chapter, the most important single feature of the British constitution is *Parliamentary supremacy* which in most circumstances permits the Executive to dominate the political sphere through Parliament. There is no formal separation of powers; rather, the Executive and the Legislature are intertwined and together are able to override the Judiciary. This position is derived from the traditional idea (dating from the seventeenth century) that Parliament can do anything it wishes: it can make, amend or repeal any law, with the consequence that primary legislation passed by Parliament can override any decisions made by the Courts and not even the Law Lords (the highest Court in the land) can rule that an Act of Parliament is unlawful or unconstitutional.[2] As a result Britain has traditionally been a country with a comparatively weak judiciary – certainly when compared with the United States or other constitutional systems based on codified constitutions. This has shaped and influenced much of the legal system in Britain, and made even very senior judges cautious about explicitly challenging the authority of Parliament.

From the start it should also be noted that Common Law and Statute Law are two distinct sources of law, and the power given to judges through the doctrine of precedent and the use of Common Law as a basis for judgement are of some constitutional significance. Similarly, it should be noted that judges are appointed from the ranks of legal professionals with experience in advocacy, that there is an independent body of barristers or advocates and that Court procedures are based for the most part on a preference for adversarial rather than inquisitorial proceedings.

17.1 Criminal justice

Machinery and procedure

The majority of criminal cases are disposed of in *Magistrates' Courts* and only a minority are tried in the higher Courts. Trial in a Magistrates' Court is summary (that is, without a jury) and takes place before a bench of two or more Justices of the Peace or one legally qualified Stipendiary Magistrate. Most cases are brought by the Crown Prosecution Service which prefers charges against defendants on the basis of police evidence and legal advice.

In the minority of cases which go to *Crown Courts* the procedure is one of trial by jury before a High Court Judge, a Circuit Judge or a Recorder (that is, a practising barrister or solicitor sitting in a judicial capacity). Most of the more serious cases are transferred automatically to the Crown Courts, although even in less serious cases the defendant can opt for trial by jury in a Crown Court rather than summary trial in a Magistrates' Court and many do in the hope and expectation that they will stand a better chance of acquittal in front of a jury.

The most serious cases (for example, murder, rape, or armed robbery) must be tried in the *High Court*. Other serious cases (for example, manslaughter or serious assault) are usually tried by a High Court Judge, but sometimes released to a Circuit Judge or a Recorder. Cases which involve lesser indictable offences or those in which the defendant has opted for trial by jury are usually tried by Circuit Judges or Recorders. In all these cases the most important role of the judge is directing the jury on matters of law.

Yet the passing of sentence on convicted defendants has become increasingly significant, at any rate in very serious cases, since judges have tended increasingly to make specific recommendations about the length of prison sentence which should be served, largely to pacify public opinion which has become increasingly vexed not only over what is widely regarded as insufficient or too lenient sentencing, but also by the practice of granting parole or remission of sentence sometimes when as little as a third or a half of a sentence has been served. It was for this reason that in the 1988 Criminal Justice Act the Attorney General was given the power to refer certain cases to the Court of Appeal if it was thought that the sentence imposed by a Crown Court Judge was unduly lenient. This power was extended by the Labour Government's 1998 Law and Disorder Act. See Figure 17.1 for a diagram of the system of criminal Courts.

Figure 17.1   The Court system

Controversial issues

There are many controversial issues in the criminal law. Most of them were considered by the *Royal Commission on Criminal Justice*, set up under the chairmanship of Lord Runciman in March 1991 which published its report in July 1993.[3] Previous to this there had been a similar investigation by the *Royal Commission on Criminal Procedure* which had been set up in 1977 and which reported in 1981.[4] Under the chairmanship of Sir Cyril Philips it had touched on the right of silence for criminal suspects, the exclusion of evidence which had been improperly obtained, the definition of arrestable offences, the extent of police powers to stop and search, the limits on detention in police custody, and the use of tape-recordings in interviews of criminal suspects. The result was the *1984 Police and Criminal Evidence Act*. Nonetheless, there has continued to be considerable controversy, not least because there are always considerable tensions between the rather reactionary views and prejudices of the general public – often eagerly nurtured by the tabloid press which does little to dispel public ignorance of the principles and procedures involved – and the more enlightened, often pragmatic, views of judges, magistrates, police and prison service.

The Runciman Commission was established in the wake of a number of prominent miscarriages of justice, not least the case of the 'Birmingham Six' who had each served more than 16 years in prison for a terrorist crime they did not commit. The 1993 Report included a total of 352 recommendations on virtually every aspect of the criminal justice system, including a defendant's right to silence, the use of DNA profiles, the issue of confessions, continuous tape-recording in custody suites in police stations, police disciplinary action, greater supervision of police investigations, the training of police, lawyers and judges, the ending of a defendant's right in certain cases to opt for trial by jury, discounts on sentences to encourage defendants to plead guilty, the abolition (where possible) of pre-trial committal hearings, time limits on the preparation of cases, and the establishment of an independent body to carry out investigations into alleged miscarriages of justice. By way of response the Conservative Government of the time brought forward two pieces of legislation, both of which attracted considerable criticism from the judiciary, lawyers, the police, pressure groups and Opposition parties. Nevertheless the Government's legislative proposals became law in the shape of the *1994 Criminal Justice and Public Order Act* and the *1994 Police and Magistrates' Courts Act*.

The Labour Government which came into office in 1997 was pledged to be 'tough on crime and tough on the causes of crime'. Consequently, it pledged to tackle youth crime by introducing a new 'fast-track' system for persistent young offenders, by replacing repeat cautions with a single final warning, by streamlining the system of youth Courts, and by introducing parental responsibility orders. In addition it promised to decentralise the work of the Crown Prosecution Service, to introduce stricter punishment for serious repeat offenders, to operate a 'zero tolerance' approach to tackle both anti-social behaviour leading to harassment, alarm or distress, and to create a new offence of racial harassment and a new crime of racially motivated violence and to introduce sex offender orders to protect the public from the serious harm caused by sex offenders. Its proposals to these ends were enacted in the *1998 Law and Disorder Act*.

One of the difficulties in reaching balanced and lasting conclusions in this sphere of the law is that many of the issues raise important questions to do with the relationship between the police and the public, especially in some inner city areas where the relationship can be very strained between police officers and individuals from the ethnic minority communities.[5] Problems have arisen particularly in the area of police powers to stop and search people for offensive weapons, such as knives and other sharp instruments. There have also been intermittent complaints from suspects that they have not been able to consult a solicitor before being charged or that they have been 'fitted up' by the police with fabricated evidence and induced to make false confessions. Such problems are likely to persist as long as there are shortcomings in police practice, great media and public pressures upon the police to catch and charge someone for offences of a particularly heinous character, and a deep and lasting mistrust of all law-enforcement agencies among some disaffected individuals and groups.

A more general problem is caused by the constant need to strike a fair and effective balance between the interests of the law-abiding majority, which wants the police and the Courts to maintain law and order in a strong, even draconian way, and those of certain vociferous minorities who are often more concerned with the protection of civil liberties and the maintenance of civil rights. Since it is always difficult to strike an appropriate balance between such strongly conflicting interests, the solution has typically involved attempts to balance increased powers for the police and the Courts with more effective legal safeguards for the law-abiding community. This was the intended approach behind both the 1984 Police and Criminal Evidence Act and the 1994 Criminal Justice and Public Order Act, although there was far from universal agreement that this was in fact the result. The passage in 1998 of the Labour Government's Law and Disorder Act and the incorporation of the European Convention on Human Rights into British law as the 1998 Human Rights Act – covering such matters as ill-treatment in custody – ought to be seen in this context as well.

Those who are strongly committed to the maintenance of law and order have invariably argued for changes in the criminal law – for example, the return of capital punishment – which they believe would enable the police and the Courts to deal more effectively with the current levels of crime and lawlessness. Indeed, very few people have argued for a more permissive attitude towards crime – except those who wish to decriminalise the purchase and use of soft drugs or legalise and regulate prostitution – or more lenient procedures for dealing with convicted criminals. However, growing concern has been expressed, not only by liberal-minded opinion-formers, about the large and growing number of people sent to prison in Britain[6] and about the smaller (but highly publicised) number of incidents of wrongful conviction, such as the Guildford Four, the Birmingham Six, the Maguire family, the Tottenham Three, the Bridgewater Four and the individual cases of Stefan Kiszko, Andrew Evans, John Roberts and Paddy Nicholls. Others have argued the need for improved procedures to deal with complaints against the police, since a growing number of people believe that there should be a genuinely independent element in any body established to investigate claims of police malpractice.

Finally, there is a section of largely intellectual, Left-wing opinion which is disturbed by what it sees as alarming tendencies for British society to develop in an authoritarian direction wholly at variance with British liberal traditions. Such people usually cite as evidence for their concern the occasional tendency for the police, the security services and the para-military units of the modern state to overstep the traditional bounds in a few highly publicised instances of brutality, excessive surveillance and democratically unacceptable uses of force. They cite examples such as the actions of the South Yorkshire Police against miners at the Orgreave Coke Plant during the 1984–85 strike (for which they were obliged to pay £500,000 compensation); the death in 1993 of Joyce Gardner, a Jamaican woman living in London, who collapsed during a struggle with police officers from the deportation squad; and some of the actions of the police during the protests by Animal Rights campaigners outside the Essex port of Brightlingsea in 1995.

17.2 Civil justice

Machinery and procedure

Most civil cases are heard initially either in County Courts by Circuit Judges or in one of the three civil Divisions of the High Court by High Court Judges. Magistrates' Courts have original jurisdiction in some cases involving the summary recovery of certain kinds of debt and some domestic proceedings, such as separation and maintenance, guardianship or adoption.

In the *County Courts* the jurisdiction is both local and limited. Such Courts deal with actions founded on the law of contract and tort where the claim of the plaintiff does not exceed the sum of £20,000, equity cases up to a value of £30,000 which affect trusts, mortgages and the dissolution of partnerships – both figures set in 1995 – and actions concerning the recovery of land. They also deal with matters arising from social legislation, such as the adoption of children, the validity of hire purchase agreements, and disputes arising from the various Rent Acts. Since 1977 undefended divorce cases have been dealt with under a 'special procedure' at a Divorce County Court. The procedure is administrative – there are no formal hearings – while complaints of racial discrimination are heard in Tribunals specially designated for the purpose in which procedures are intended to be less formal than in Court – While both barristers and solicitors may appear on behalf of those who come before these Courts and Tribunals, the judge often has to hear the case on the basis of submissions made without the benefit of lawyers.[7] In none of these cases is there call for a jury.

In the High Court, the *Queen's Bench Division* deals principally with actions founded on the law of contract and tort.[8] It also deals with actions on bills of exchange, insurance claims, shipping actions and some landlord and tenant actions. Only a small proportion of the actions actually come to Court and few are fought to a conclusion, since those involved are usually keen to avoid the high legal costs associated with fighting such cases. Either party may request a trial by jury in cases involving defamation of character, malicious prosecution, false imprisonment, fraud or seduction. The final decision as to whether or not a jury shall try such a case rests with the judge concerned. Another important function performed by this Division is the supervision of the lower Courts and Tribunals. This is done on an application for Judicial Review by issuing prerogative orders, such as *prohibition, mandamus* or *certiorari*, as well as an order of *habeas corpus*.[9] Whereas in former times these rights were available only to the Monarch, they can now be issued by the High Court upon application from an ordinary plaintiff.

The *Chancery Division* of the High Court, which was established in London in 1873, has effective jurisdiction over the estates of deceased persons, the execution of trusts, the dissolution of partnerships, disputes in private companies and the redemption or foreclosure of mortgages. In 1921 bankruptcy jurisdiction was added to its various responsibilities and breach of contract can be investigated here or in the Queen's Bench Division.

The Family Division of the High Court dates from 1971, when cases to do with wills and divorce were separated from those to do with shipwrecks with which they had been incongruously lumped since 1873 when the Probate, Divorce, and Admiralty Division was established.[10] Today the Family Division deals with all domestic and matrimonial cases, guardianship and probate. Most of its work is concerned with divorce proceedings in an age when one in three of all marriages end this way.

Following recommendations put forward in the 1996 Woolf Report, the Goverment brought forward a number of proposals designed to reduced the cost, delay and complexity of civil litigation.[11] The intention was to ensure that common sense prevailed in more disputes and to reduce the claims upon the public purse of fruitless litigation.

Controversial issues

The main controversial issues in the civil law today are connected with the public image of the law and lawyers, and with the costs and delays in the processes of the law. We shall, therefore, look briefly at each of these issues in turn.

It is a widely held belief among the general public that the attitudes of lawyers and judges – indeed, the whole paraphernalia of the law – are distinctly old-fashioned and middle class. Indeed, ever since the notorious Taff Vale case in 1901,[12] many have believed that the judiciary has been biased against trade unions, and the development of judge-made case law over the years has not done much to dispel that belief. As Gavin Drewry pointed out in 1975, 'most of the really telling criticism of lawyers centres upon their failure to win the confidence of working-class people and their inability to achieve an image of independence from the Establishment'.[13] It is a view many would continue to express today.

When hearing cases, judges are supposed to be strictly impartial. This means not only that they must not show any personal bias or prejudice, but also that they must exclude from their judgements any political or moral views which they may hold as individuals. Naturally, this is difficult if not impossible for anyone to achieve, so there have been times when judges have appeared to be far from impartial in the eyes of those who come before them. There is at least circumstantial evidence for these misgivings.

First, judges have tended to be drawn disproportionately from the ranks of the upper and middle classes; they are usually white, male and inevitably tend to be quite elderly by the time that they reach the bench. As J.A.G. Griffith has argued, 'they have by their education and training and the pursuit of their profession as barristers acquired a strikingly homogenous collection of attitudes, beliefs and principles which to them represents the public interest.'[14] In the 1990s both Conservative and Labour Lord Chancellors sought to open up the system of judicial appointments, at least at the lower level, with posts being advertised and the process being subjected to a slightly higher degree of public scrutiny.

Secondly, Griffith and others have argued that the judicial conception of the public interest has invariably been based upon the interests of the state, notably the preservation of law and order, the protection of property and the promotion of certain other political views normally associated with the Conservative Party. In so far as this may be so (and in some ways it would be surprising if it were not), it is almost inevitable that there are some people, especially among ethnic minority groups and embattled sections of the community, who believe that judges are inherently biased against them and their interests. Nonetheless, any investigation into cases of Judicial Review during the 1979–97 period of Conservative Government would fail to show a judiciary wholly supportive of the actions of Conservative Ministers.

Thirdly, there is a widely held view that access to the law, for those who want to have it, is not equally available to people from all classes and walks of life. Indeed, it is commonly said that only the very rich (who can afford it) and the very poor (who qualify for legal aid from the state) can now afford to go to law. In the latter category, the extent of legal aid available to any litigant has been limited by two tests: whether a solicitor, apart from the consideration of costs, would advise going to Court in the particular case; and whether the applicant falls within the prescribed means-tested limits for legal aid.[15] Over the years the effect of these two provisions has been to exclude quite a large number of fairly poor people from qualifying for legal aid, to penalise those who might otherwise want legal representation when appearing before administrative Tribunals, and to put at a disadvantage litigants with a strong case who are not legally aided when their opponents are. Of course, there are other forms of free legal advice available to people, for example, from Citizens' Advice Bureaux, Neighbourhood Law Centres and even Members of Parliament. Yet there still remains a large potential demand for legally aided litigation which probably goes unsatisfied, largely because of Treasury opposition to the mounting public expenditure cost.[16] In 1998 the Government announced that legal aid was to be abolished for 60 per cent of civil disputes and 'no win, no fee' litigation introduced in its place.

Fourthly, there is the deterrent effect of delays in the legal system. It is not just in Dickens' novels that characters sometimes die before their legal case is over. In Britain the problems of delay can be ascribed to the rising demand for litigation, the relative shortage of judges to hear cases, the time taken in amassing all the relevant evidence for use in Court, and the traditional commitment to an adversary procededure which involves the very time-consuming business of hearing and cross-examining witnesses testifying on oath. Some of the problems have been mitigated by improvements in the procedure of Small Claims Courts, which have served to speed up that particular kind of justice. Yet further progress could undoubtedly be made if more judges could be appointed and if more use could be made of written evidence, at any rate in all those cases where the facts of the matter are not seriously contested by the opposing parties.

Lastly, some have argued that the very nature of the legal system and the middle-class image of the law and lawyers deter many poor or inarticulate people from seeking the benefit of legal advice or legal services. To many people traditional legal procedures seem very off-putting, not to say alarming, with all the wigs and processions and general mumbo-jumbo. Indeed, this is exactly why some of the procedures have been simplified and made more 'user-friendly' in recent years, notably in cases involving families and children.

17.3 Judicial appeal

Machinery and procedure

The process of judicial appeal in Britain can be applied equally to cases of criminal and civil law. Most of the *criminal appeals* are heard by the criminal Division of the Court of Appeal. This is presided over by the Lord Chief Justice or a Lord Justice of Appeal. Queen's Bench judges sit with Appeal Court judges and there are usually three judges on the bench for any hearing. When a case raises an issue of general public importance, a further appeal may be made to the House of Lords, but in criminal cases such appeals are rare.

Most of the *civil appeals* are heard by the Master of the Rolls and the Lord Justices of Appeal, although the Lord Chancellor, the Lord Chief Justice and a few other very senior legal figures may sit *ex officio* (by virtue of their offices) in exceptional circumstances. An odd number of judges (usually three) hears such appeals and decisions of the Court are taken by majority.

On important points of law with wider legal application there is the possibility of further appeal to the House of Lords. Such appeals are made to the *Appellate Committee*, which is the final Court of Appeal and which can only be overruled by Parliament as a whole passing new legislation. The work of the Appellate Committee is done by the Law Lords – the Lord Chancellor, 12 Lords of Appeal in Ordinary and a few other very senior legal figures who may sit by virtue of having previously held high judicial office.[17] The Appellate Committee is usually made up of five Law Lords and their judgements take the form of motions, with each judge expressing a judicial opinion on the matter in question. Prior to 1966 the House of Lords had always been bound by its previous judicial decisions; since 1966 it has been able to overrule them.

Mention should also be made of the *Judicial Committee of the Privy Council,* which was established by statute in 1833. This adjudicates on disputes between the Scottish Executive and the UK Government and hears appeals on cases authorised by the Courts in the Isle of Man and the Channel Islands, in Britain's remaining colonial Dependencies (for example, the Falkland Islands or Gibraltar) and in those member states of the Commonwealth which have chosen to retain the right of legal appeal to it.[18] It also hears appeals from Admiralty Courts, ecclesiastical Courts, and the disciplinary committees of the General Medical Council and General Dental Council. The Lord Chancellor is nominally its president, but in practice nearly all the work is done by Lords of Appeal. In 1996 it heard 85 appeals and 99 petitions for special leave to appeal. It is the final arbiter of constitutional issues in the various territories and jurisdictions concerned.[19]

Since Britain's accession in 1973 to the European Community – now known officially as the European Union – Britain has been subject to the jurisdiction of the *European Court of Justice* in all those areas of national life covered by European law. This has meant that in an increasingly significant area of legal competence the European Court has provided a final level of judicial appeal higher even than the House of Lords, indeed even Parliament itself. Under Section 2 of the 1972 European Communities Act and subsequent legislation the Westminster Parliament is under a self-imposed legal duty at all times not to pass legislation which would conflict with any European legislation. Thus it can be said that in the areas of European competence, as defined by European Treaty obligations, European law takes precedence over national law and an appeal to the European Court of Justice trumps any appeal to a national Court. Following on from this, and as a direct consequence of the *Factortame Ltd* judgment in 1990 (see Chapter 18), it is quite clear that if an Act of Parliament is inconsistent with European Law, a domestic Court in Britain would have to refuse to give it effect. In this context it is worth noting that the *European Court of Human Rights* also has compulsory jurisdiction in Britain, but it is part of a separate jurisdiction derived from the 1950 European Convention on Human Rights. In 1998 this was incorporated into UK domestic law in the Human Rights Act, which should eliminate any future disputes about the legal status of the European Convention in the United Kingdom.

Controversial issues

The process of judicial appeal does not normally give rise to great political controversy, except on those rare occasions when issues of wider political importance are raised in particularly contentious cases. When this happens, judgements in the House of Lords are normally final, except when they trigger the Government of the day to introduce fresh legislation to overturn or confirm the previous legal position or when the British legal system is overruled by the European Court of Justice or, very occasionally, when an issue is considered for a second time as it was in the case of General Pinochet's possible extradition to Spain in 1998–99 for alleged crimes against humanity in Chile in the 1970s and 1980s.

Early examples of the first of these alternatives were provided by the 1906 Trade Disputes Act, which overturned the House of Lords' judgment in the 1901 Taff Vale case, and the 1913 Trade Union Act, which overturned the House of Lords' judgment in the 1910 Osborne case. A later well known example was the 1965 War Damage Act, which overturned the 1965 House of Lords' judgment in the case of Burmah Oil. A notable example in more recent times was the 1983 Transport Act, which took account of the 1982 House of Lords judgment in the case of *Bromley Borough Council v. the Greater London Council* on the politically contentious issue of passenger transport subsidies in Greater London on the bus and underground services. In all such cases, when matters of political importance have been involved, the Government of the day has felt obliged to introduce legislation either to overturn or to ratify the legal position as defined by the House of Lords.

Over the years there have been periods of judicial activism and creativity, and periods when the behaviour of the judiciary has been characterised by conservatism and a determination to defend the established legal order. On the whole, judicial conservatism has been the more prevalent. This is partly a reflection of the inherently conservative background and outlook of the judiciary in Britain, to which reference has already been made. Yet is also reflects the well-established constitutional attitude held by the judiciary over many years and most succinctly expressed by Lord Reid on several occasions. In 1961, in *Shaw v. the Director of Public Prosecutions,* he observed that 'where Parliament fears to tread, it is not for the Courts to rush in', and in 1972 he maintained that cases which raised political issues should be decided 'on the preponderance of existing authority'.[20]

A challenge to Parliament's constitutional right to ratify the 1992 Maastricht Treaty was rejected by the High Court on 30 July 1993, a decision which was undoubtedly influenced by the Speaker of the House of Commons who reminded the Courts in no uncertain terms of the supremacy of Parliament as established by the Bill of Rights in 1689. In rejecting the challenge, the Court declared that ratification involved an exercise of the Royal Prerogative, not a transfer of that Prerogative without Parliamentary approval.[21]

In these matters much has depended on whether the judiciary construes the law passed by Parliament literally and narrowly or contextually and broadly. For example, Lord Denning in his many years as Master of the Rolls and Chairman of the Court of

Appeal (1962–82) was usually inclined to interpret the law in a way which was well disposed towards whichever litigant he considered to be the underdog. Naturally, this did not endear him to those organisations which he deemed oppressive (for example, trade unions) or indeed to the Law Lords, who often had to review his judgments on further appeal. Much has also depended on the extent to which the judiciary has thought it proper or prudent to flex its muscles in defiance of the Government of the day. It has been said that on the whole Labour Governments have found themselves in conflict with the judiciary more often than their Conservative counterparts. However, in the 1980s the judiciary was something of a brake upon the radical intentions of the Thatcher Government and in the early-to-mid 1990s the judges were not only some of the sharpest critics of the Major Government's proposals to reform the criminal justice system, but also not infrequently ruled against Government Ministers in the Courts. Indeed, it could be argued that such facts demonstrate not so much judicial hostility to any particular Government, Left or Right, as the simple reality that there is always likely to be a conflict between the judiciary, with its invariable commitment to the preservation of the existing legal order, and any Government which tries to make radical changes or oversteps the limits of Ministerial discretion.

Since the bitter debates in Parliament and elsewhere over the application of the 1992 Maastricht Treaty to Britain, perhaps the most controversial legal issues have arisen from the clash of jurisdictions between British legal institutions and those of the European Union. In essence this has meant a *political* struggle between, on the one hand, those politicians and others who wish to preserve the legal sovereignty of Britain's national Courts and, ultimately, of Parliament itself; and, on the other hand, those politicians, officials, interest groups and others who see sectional and national advantage in Britain being prepared to subordinate its legal arrangements to those of the European Union, certainly in those policy areas where, by freely concluded Treaty commitments between the Governments of all the member states, it has been agreed that the matters concerned shall be justiciable not only in the national Courts but also, ultimately, in the European Court which has the supreme authority in all legal disputes involving European law. This fundamental clash of competences and jurisdictions – which some see as an inevitable but acceptable aspect of Britain's membership of the European Union, and others see increasingly as a reason to transform the terms and conditions of the entire project into an international rather than a supranational adventure – seems likely to become more acute and difficult to resolve as European integration becomes deeper and more extensive in future.

17.4 Citizens and the state

In the modern world the complex relationship between citizens and the state raises political and legal issues of great importance. Citizens expect to enjoy certain inalienable rights, including freedoms of both a positive and negative kind. There are the freedoms *to* do certain things, and the freedoms *from* having certain things done to you. Each category of freedom is equally valuable. Yet in every case the rights concerned have to be qualified or counterbalanced by certain rights of the state or its agencies to act on behalf of the community as a whole. It is in holding this balance between the rights of citizens and the interests of the state that the legal system in Britain has had to try to resolve some of the most difficult problems of modern society. Furthermore, the basis of civil rights in Britain is to some extent precarious, since there is neither a codified constitution nor an entrenched Bill of Rights. Notwithstanding the incorporation into domestic law of the European Convention on Human Rights in the form of the *1998 Human Rights Act*, the Courts have not been given the power to set aside primary legislation, past or future, on the ground of incompatibility with the Convention. It is therefore as well to be circumspect when pronouncing upon the important issues which are raised in this section.

International Conventions

There are issues which arise from the wide range of civil rights declared in international Conventions and in many cases subsequently embodied in British law by Parliament at Westminster. For example, the principle that all citizens should be equal before the law is a worthy aspiration in Britain as in other countries, but in Britain's constitutional arrangements it is not enshrined in a codified constitution. From the mid-1960s Parliament has legislated against racial discrimination (in 1965, 1968 and 1976) and against sexual discrimination (in 1975), although its stance on discrimination against the disabled or the aged or gay people has not been so clear-cut. Attempts have been made to counter and eventually eradicate both racial and sexual discrimination from all public behaviour, with public sector institutions (such as the Civil Service) often required to set an example to the private sector. Many of the initiatives in these spheres have been taken by the Commission for Racial Equality and the Equal Opportunities Commission, both of which were established by Labour Governments to act as watch-dogs and agenda-setters in these areas of policy. Thus, if individual citizens feel aggrieved on racial or sexual grounds, they can use the law, often with the help of these bodies, to take cases to Court in order to seek redress or reinstatement.

The protection of civil rights is a matter of wide international concern. Indeed pressure groups, such as Amnesty International, have been established, often with bases in Britain, to draw attention to human rights abuses and to campaign world-wide against such practices. National Governments have been prepared to make purposeful moves in this direction at least since the 1948 UN Declaration of Human Rights and the 1950 European Convention on Human Rights. The latter, which was ratified by the British Parliament in 1951, provides judicial procedures by which alleged infringements of civil rights in Britain may be examined at international level. The European Convention provides an overt constraint upon the legislative supremacy of Parliament in that successive British Governments have not wished to be found in breach of its provisions. However, the Convention was not originally incorporated within British national law on the somewhat complacent grounds that civil rights in Britain were adequately protected by British law and that such incorporation would be inconsistent with the traditional British claim to legal supremacy for Parliament at Westminster. Indeed, it was not until 1966 that the United Kingdom formally recognised the right of individual petition to the European Commission on Human Rights or the compulsory jurisdiction in Britain of the European Court of Human Rights. Since then various proceedings under the Convention helped to bring about changes in British law and legal practice, for example the introduction of immigration appeal

Tribunals, revised rules on access to lawyers for prisoners, press freedom and restrictions on the use of corporal punishment. See Figure 17.2 for a list of key British defeats before the European Court of Human Rights.

Figure 17.2 Key British defeats before the European Court of Human Rights

Date	Issue
1997	The Court ruled that the court martial system was unfair and in breach of human rights
1996	The Court ruled that the Home Secretary should no longer have the power to detain child killers indefinitely
1995	The Court ruled that the shooting dead of three IRA bombers by the SAS in Gibraltar was a violation of their human rights
1990	Three sex offenders won a ruling forcing a review of the way life-sentence prisoners were released on licence and then recalled
1988	The convicted killer Jimmy Boyle won a claim that letters were unlawfully interfered with in jail
1985	Three women from Malawi, the Philippines and Sri Lanka successfully challenged immigration laws that denied their husbands automatic entry into Britain
1982	The Court ruled against corporal punishment in state schools
1979	The Court ruled that it had been wrong to block publication in *The Sunday Times* of reports about children whose mothers had taken the thalidomide drug during pregnancy
1978	The Court ruled against birching as a punishment in the Isle of Man

Source: Adapted (and updated) from *The Times*, 25 October 1997.

In 1998 the Convention was finally incorporated into domestic law with the passage into law of the Human Rights Act. It is also necessary to recall the European Union aspect of the matter. For example, the 1992 Maastricht Treaty created a range of positive citizens' rights and established a European 'Ombudsman' to which all citizens of the Union have the right to appeal if they feel in need of redress.[22]

Citizenship and free movement

There are issues which arise from rights of citizenship and free movement. Under the 1981 British Nationality Act all British citizens have the same legal rights and status, although this applies only to those with full British citizenship. The position of others resident in Britain is limited by the various legal provisions governing the control of immigration. The position is qualified to some extent by the free movement provisions in European law by which British citizens are also bound, since once individuals have gained the right of abode in one of the other member states of the European Union, they then have the right to come to Britain in search of work.

Under the 1981 British Nationality Act those who are legally British citizens have the right of abode in Britain, and hence the right to enter the United Kingdom and to remain in the United Kingdom as long as they like. Such people cannot legally be deported. On the other hand, the right to leave Britain can be vitiated if people are without British passports (or at any rate temporary British visitors' documents) if they wish to take up legal residence outside the United Kingdom. Of course, under the provisions of European law, all citizens of the member states have the right to take up residence in any part of the European Union under the free movement provisions of the

European Treaties. In practice, this 'right' is not yet used by many people and there are considerable linguistic, cultural and administrative obstacles to its extensive realisation. Indeed, official figures have suggested that only a small number of people from the other member states of the European Union have settled in Britain, and an even smaller number of British have moved to settle in other parts of the European Union.[23]

The 1992 Maastricht Treaty altered the character of the European Community, turning it into a European Union and making every citizen of each member state into a citizen of the European Union with rights to live, work and vote (although not in national Parliamentary elections) anywhere in the Union. In addition, citizens of the Union have been given a 'European Charter of Citizens' Rights' and have the right to take national Governments to the European Court, to petition the European Parliament, and to appeal directly to a European Ombudsman.

Emergency powers and state security

There are issues which arise from the use of emergency powers by the Government and its agencies, together with the related problems of state security. In most serious emergencies the police, fire and ambulance services can cope with any problems which arise. Yet there are some occasions when the military has to be called in to assist the civilian power or to deal with particularly serious threats to the life and well-being of the community. In recent times the most notable example has been the need to keep thousands of British troops in Northern Ireland in order to help the civil authorities preserve peace and public order. Other examples have included the need to counter the action of terrorists by calling in the Special Air Service (SAS) and other special military units to assist the police and security services. The legal position on all such occasions is that military personnel have a duty to support the civil power when requested by the latter to do so. Since such emergencies usually involve sensitive and difficult issues of public safety, they require Ministerial supervision and control at the highest level.

During peace-time a state of emergency may be declared under the authority of the 1920 and 1964 *Emergency Powers Acts*. These statutes permit the Government of the day to make use of wide-ranging temporary powers designed to ensure the maintenance of essential services, subject to Parliamentary approval at least every seven days. During wartime even more far-reaching powers were available to the Government of the day in the shape of the 1914 and 1915 *Defence of the Realm Acts* and the 1939 and 1940 *Emergency Powers Acts*. These statutes, which were later repealed, gave the Government of the day almost unlimited powers, including detention without trial for indefinite periods and the seizure of private property without compensation. This legislation was subject to Parliamentary approval at least every 28 days.

In the case of special measures to deal with terrorism, Parliament passed some draconian statutes in 1973 and 1975 to deal with the threat in Northern Ireland from the IRA and other terrorist organisations, and in 1974 and 1976 to deal with terrorist offences anywhere in the United Kingdom. This legislation conferred very extensive powers upon the Government of the day, which enabled it to take almost any measures deemed necessary to counter such dire threats to national security, including detention without charge for up to seven days (subsequently reduced to three days with the endorsement of a Court in more recent legislation) and the power to exclude undesirable people from the country. In view of the political sensitivity of the terrorist threat from Northern Ireland over the years, the *Prevention of Terrorism (Temporary Provisions) Act* and the *Northern Ireland (Emergency Provisions) Act* have been re-enacted on many occasions and been put to Parliament for renewal on an annual basis. The 1998 *Criminal Justice (Terrorism and Conspiracy) Act*, enacted following the Omagh bombing which killed 29 people in August of that year, can be seen in the same light.

The interests of state security have also been invoked to justify the passage of the *1989 Official Secrets Act*, the retention of the D Notice system and the interception of private communications by telephone-tapping and other techniques of electronic surveillance. These practices have continued on the basis of rather tenuous legal authority, subject to no more than indirect control by Ministers (notably by a Cabinet Committee on the Intelligence Services chaired by the Prime Minister) and virtually no control by Parliament. Traditionally security matters of this kind have been kept under review by the Security Commission, a small supervisory body of Privy Councillors chaired by a Law Lord, which reports regularly to the Prime Minister and occasionally to Parliament. Although the whole process has been shrouded in mystery, since the early 1990s a little more information has been made available about MI5 and MI6; the Security Service has been put on a statutory footing and a special committee of senior Privy Councillors has been established to oversee this area of state activity.[24]

In these circumstances it is not surprising that there has been continuing pressure for reform and the replacement of the existing law with new legislation which would put more emphasis on the rights of ordinary citizens and less on the needs of national security (which are sometimes a cover for Ministerial convenience). There has been an active, all-party campaign for freedom of information throughout the sphere of Government and the public sector, which had some success at least in relation to local government and the release of environmental information. The problems of striking an appropriate balance between the needs of official secrecy (and commercial confidentiality) on the one hand and the rights of the citizen on the other have been very great. Indeed, the difficulties have been exacerbated by the growing use of computers throughout the public sector and by the development of what is known as the Government Data Network. Public concern about the possible misuse of personal information kept on official files led to the 1984 Data Protection Act, which provided some safeguards against malpractice in relation to nearly all official information which is mechanically processed and stored – but not simple card index systems.

In 1994 a new Code of Practice came into effect obliging Government Departments to respond to 'reasonable' requests for information. The Code stipulated that information would be provided 'as soon as practicable', with a target of 20 working days for 'simple requests for information'. Where information cannot be provided, Departments are obliged to provide an explanation. Breaches of the Code were to be monitored by the Parliamentary Ombudsman. There were, however, a wide range of exemptions, including all 'policy advice' to Ministers unless the Government considered it 'relevant and important'; 'original documents', with Ministers being obliged to disclose only information in digest form; and information harmful to national security, defence or international relations. The *1998 Data Protection Act* extended the access rights for individuals to structured sets of manual records (such as card indexes and microfiches), but did not create a general 'right of access' by individuals to all their personal files.

The Major Government (1990–97) was pledged to the concept of the *Citizen's Charter* – which it described as ' the most far-reaching programme ever devised to improve quality in public services' – and this needs to be seen in this context also. It was an attempt to improve standards of public service by treating citizens more as customers or clients. The main themes were quality, choice, standards and value for money. These formed the basis for a number of key principles including the setting, monitoring and publication of explicit standards for public services; the provision of full, accurate and easily understandable information on public services; an emphasis on greater responsiveness to the public and greater accessibility for the public; and the creation of effective procedures for complaints and redress of grievances.[25] These initiatives did not, however, defuse the pressures for freedom of information, not least from groups such as the 'Campaign for Freedom of Information' and 'Liberty'. Indeed, by the mid-1990s both the Labour Party and the Liberal Democrats were pledged to introduce legislation providing for freedom of information, a pledge which the Labour Government intends to act upon during the current Parliament.

In December 1997 the Government published a White Paper entitled 'Your Right To Know,'[26] in which it proposed to give the public a statutory right of access to official records and information not only held by Government Departments, local authorities, organisations such as the National Health Service and bodies like the Atomic Energy Authority, but also privatised utilities. Certain bodies were to be excluded, such as the Intelligence Services; and a number of areas protected, such as national security, personal privacy and commercial confidentiality. It was proposed that an Information Commissioner be appointed to adjudicate and enforce rights of access, and that a new criminal offence for wilful or reckless destruction, alteration or withholding of records from the Commissioner be introduced. Draft legislation was to be published in 1999, with legislation itself proposed for inclusion in the 1999–2000 Parliamentary Session.

Personal liberty and property

There are issues which arise from rights of personal liberty and property. Magna Carta in 1215 stipulated that 'no free man shall be taken or imprisoned or dispossessed or outlawed or in any way destroyed [...] unless by the lawful judgement of his peers or the law of the land'. This was an early expression of what became known as the 'rule of law' – in essence a belief that all are equal before the law and that no one can be punished without due process of law.

Although British citizens are free people, in certain circumstances they can lawfully be detained – for example, after arrest and pending trial on a criminal charge (assuming bail is refused by a Magistrates' Court), or when a local authority decides within its statutory rights to take a child into care. Any such departure from the principle of personal liberty can raise issues of considerable controversy and has sometimes led to investigations by a Royal Commission or the passage of new legislation. Powers of arrest, which are normally exercised by the police (but are legally available to any citizen) are regulated principally by the 1984 Police and Criminal Evidence Act. However, a number of other Acts, such as the latest version of the 1981 Prevention of

Terrorism (Temporary Provisions) Act, have an important bearing on these matters as well.

As for property rights in Britain, these have never been regarded as absolute or sacrosanct. Parliament has legislated on many occasions to limit such rights when they have conflicted with what is deemed by Ministers to be in the public interest – for example in the spheres of public health, nationalisation or compulsory purchase. As a general rule in modern times there has not been as much determination to use the law to defend economic or property rights as there has been to defend rights of personal liberty. This is in accordance with the European Convention on Human Rights which has a similar bias. Having said this, however, it should be noted that some certainly regarded the employment legislation of the 1980s as giving more weight to economic or property rights than rights of personal liberty.

Wrongful interference with the rights of personal liberty and property can be countered by the use of various legal remedies. These include civil action for damages, prosecution for assault, exercise of the right of self-defence, use of the police complaints procedure, and even the invocation of *habeas corpus*.[27] Yet there are no final or definitive solutions to these problems, since the law governing these aspects of civil rights can be changed from time to time by Act of Parliament – for example, the 1998 Crime and Disorder Act, or the 1994 Criminal Justice and Public Order Act, or the 1991 Child Support Act which created the Child Support Agency – and in any case all these issues have to be seen increasingly within a European context.

Freedom of expression

There are issues which arise from rights of free expression and their necessary limitation. In this sphere British law has usually relied upon the principle that anything which is not prohibited is permitted. Yet the extent to which restrictions have been imposed in civil or criminal law has varied from time to time. For example, the law of defamation protects individuals from slander and libel, or rather it provides a form of legal redress if the person concerned can afford to fight a case. Substantial damages may be awarded for injury to a person's reputation, and in some cases even the threat of such legal action can be sufficient to secure a retraction or to get a newspaper to publish a (usually inadequate) note of correction. In some cases those accused of defamation can plead absolute privilege (typically in fair and accurate reports of such proceedings). The defence of 'fair comment' can also protect expressions of opinion on matters of public interest, even if someone thinks what has been said is defamatory.

In the criminal law there are the offences of sedition, blasphemy, obscenity and criminal libel which theoretically protect society from some of the excesses of free expression. Yet in practice actions are rare and of dubious utility, since it is difficult to get juries to convict on the basis of such ancient laws. Furthermore, as was seen in the much publicised instance of Salman Rushdie's *Satanic Verses*,[28] the law (in this case the law of blasphemy) does not always apply. In this instance an alleged blasphemy against the prophet Mohammed fell outside the terms of the statute, which concerns itself only with blasphemy in a Christian context. However, it certainly focused public attention on the utility of such a law in a modern, multi-cultural society.

Freedom of expression in the media has traditionally been controlled to some extent by a combination of self-discipline on the part of the more responsible media and the intervention of certain statutory bodies whose task it has been to maintain what are regarded as 'proper' standards. In the case of newspapers, the Press Complaints Commission has had an unimpressive record in preventing and an even less impressive record in punishing severe lapses of taste or decency, or unacceptable invasions of privacy. The same can be said in the case of broadcasting with regard to first the Broadcasting Complaints Commission and more recently the Broadcasting Standards Commission. However, in this area the BBC Board of Governors, the Independent Television Commission (ITC) and the Radio Authority have great powers over the broadcasters in radio and television, although they have taken few opportunities to use their powers, especially if urged to do so by the Government of the day. In the sensitive areas of sex and violence on television the Broadcasting Standards Council and, since April 1997, the Broadcasting Standards Commission has wielded its statutory powers with apparent enthusiasm, causing some observers to comment upon what they regard as the creation of a general climate in which legitimate artistic expression may be inhibited.

In the world of cinema and video the British Board of Film Classification has the task of certifying films for public release and can prohibit exhibition on the grounds that it 'would offend against good taste or decency or would be likely to encourage or incite to crime or to lead to disorder or to be offensive to public feeling'. As far as advertising is concerned, standards of public taste and decency are monitored by the Advertising Standards Authority, although again with rather little obvious effect. In certain respects the media have become much more unrestrained with the liberalisation of the airwaves in the 1990s and increasingly intense competition between tabloid newspapers. It will also be difficult to regulate the electronic media as the new technologies become cheaper, more competitive and potentially global in their reach.[29]

Finally, it should be noted that it is not unknown for Governments to attempt to exert pressure on broadcasters in relation to particular programmes. For example, in 1985 the Conservative Government of the time leaned heavily on the BBC to withdraw the *Real Lives* programme which focused on a prominent member of the IRA (the programme was withdrawn, although shown at a later date following minor changes); while in December 1987 the Government took out an injunction to prevent the broadcast of a Radio 4 series *My Country Right or Wrong*. Nonetheless, those who work in the media jealously guard their freedom and seek vigorously to resist such Government interference. This was evident in the strength of the media reaction to the *Real Lives* controversy and to similar Government attempts in 1988 to ensure that a *This Week* programme, 'Death on the Rock', was not broadcast because of its portrayal of an SAS killing of three IRA terrorists in Gibraltar. Government can, however, use the law to curtail freedom of expression, as happened between 1984 and 1994 when the media were not allowed to broadcast the actual voices of members of the IRA and Sinn Fein, even though their pictures could be shown on television and their words could be spoken by an actor.

Meetings, procession and protest

There are issues which arise from rights to meet, process and protest freely, subject only to various necessary restraints in the interest of public order. In modern times, however, this has been a particularly difficult balance to strike, since it is bound to involve constant adjustment and compromise between conflicting interests. In principle, such freedom is not extended to senior civil servants, the armed services, the police, or registered charities. However, the Civil Service is heavily unionised at all levels and the police of lower ranks have powerful representation from the Police Federation. There is also undoubtedly a grey area covering registered charities and their ability apparently to circumvent some of the legal limitations of their charitable status. The provisions of the1986 Public Order Act and the 1994 Criminal Justice and Public Order Act curtailed what may lawfully be done on the streets and in public places by providing the police with stronger powers to avert public disorder. For example, the 1986 Act introduced a new offence of disorderly conduct to deal with some forms of modern hooliganism and the 1994 Act created new offences concerning various forms of trespass and causing intentional harassment, alarm or distress, which were designed to deal with racial violence and other forms of harassment.

Public and private meetings for any purpose are constrained not so much by the law as by the need to secure prior permission from the owners of suitable halls or open spaces. However, the 1994 Criminal Justice and Public Order Act contained powers to ban certain 'trespassory assemblies' altogether, while public meetings may not lawfully be held on the public highway and any such obstruction is an offence under the 1959 Highways Act. This has special relevance to the right to picket, which is supposed to be confined under the 1980 Employment Act to peaceful persuasion in contemplation or furtherance of a trade dispute by people attending either at their own place of work or that of so-called 'first customers' and 'first suppliers'.[30] Legal protection against disorderly conduct at a public meeting is still provided by the 1908 Public Meetings Act, as amended by the 1936 Public Order Act; although in modern conditions this has little practical bearing upon such matters.

In general, the preservation of public order in processions and public meetings depends on the police, who can exercise considerable discretion. Among the powers available to Chief Officers of Police under the 1986 Public Order Act are the power to specify routes for marches and demonstrations and to impose conditions on public meetings. The 1994 Criminal Justice and Public Order Act gave Chief Officers additional powers to apply to the relevant District Council for a ban on public meetings for up to four days within a specified area, and for a ban lasting not more than three months on any category of public procession and occasionally on all public processions.

17.5 The role of the police

For much of their contemporary history the police in Britain have been held in high regard, placed on a pedestal by public opinion as exemplifying an ideal model of behaviour and character. In short, the 'British Bobby' came to be seen as representing all that was 'right and proper' in British society. One survey in the early 1960s showed that no less than 83 per cent of those interviewed professed great respect for the police.[31] This level of public support had been the result principally of four particular features of policing in Britain. *First*, with certain exceptions such as the Diplomatic Protection Group and the police in Northern Ireland, the police do not normally carry firearms. Indeed, only 5.3 per cent of police personnel are trained in the use of firearms and no untrained personnel would ever be issued with a firearm. Between 1987 and 1997–98 British police personnel fired a total of 57 shots, an average of fewer than six shots a year. *Secondly,* individual police forces are locally based and locally controlled. There is no 'national' police force, but rather 52 local police forces in the United Kingdom – 43 in England and Wales, eight in Scotland and one in Northern Ireland. Outside London each force is under the direction of a Chief Constable who, in turn, is responsible to a local Police Authority. In London – with the exception of the City of London – the Metropolitan Police Force is under the command of the Commissioner who, in turn, is responsible to the Home Secretary. *Thirdly,* there is the belief, indeed the knowledge, that there is only one category of police officer whether uniformed or plain-clothed, rather than a range of special police forces answerable to different parts of Government as is the case in many other countries. *Lastly,* there is the perception that the police are non-political, non-partisan and impartial. Indeed, it is to preserve this position that the police are kept at arm's length from direct Government control and there are a number of local forces rather than a single national force. These features combined to produce an image of the police as local, disciplined, unarmed, and free from political bias. Thus, traditionally, the police in Britain enjoyed an enviable reputation – at any rate by international standards.

However, since the late 1960s not only has violence become a more apparent feature of British society, but also the reputation of the police has increasingly been tarnished in the eyes of the media and the public – at any rate those elements in society which come most frequently into contact with the police. For example, although a survey in 1990 showed that 77 per cent of those questioned felt that the police did either a 'very good' or a 'fairly good' job as against 21 per cent who felt that they did a 'poor' or 'very poor' job; the same survey showed that 31 per cent of respondents under the age of 25 said that the police did a poor job.[32] A survey published at the end of 1992 showed that while 76 per cent of white respondents said that the police did a 'very good' or 'fairly good' job, this figure was 62 per cent among Asian respondents and 52 per cent among Afro-Caribbean respondents.[33] Another survey carried out in 1994 showed that only 36 per cent of the public were satisfied with the way their own area was policed – down from 51 per cent in 1992, 67 per cent in 1985 and 75 per cent in 1981 – while only 41 per cent thought the police 'wonderful' – down from 62 per cent in 1983.[34] This movement of public opinion has been the cumulative consequence of five developments, namely: police corruption and other scandals, changes in policing methods, police malpractice in certain areas, problems of police powers and accountability, and rising levels of crime. We shall comment upon each of these points in turn.

With regard to *police corruption and other scandals,* public confidence in the police received a severe jolt in 1969 when The *Sunday Times* revealed the existence of institutionalised corruption in the Metropolitan Police, a situation made worse when it became apparent that members of the police force were covering up for each other. More revelations concerning corruption came to the fore, resulting in a massive internal police investigation known as 'Operation Countryman'. This was reported in 1978 and although it failed to substantiate most of the allegations, the damage had clearly been done. The public perception was that there had been a police cover-up, whether or not there had been any substance to the allegations. Since then a number of cases have come to light in which innocent people were convicted on the basis of falsified or distorted testimony in which police officers were implicated. There were the notorious cases of the Guildford Four, the Birmingham Six, the Maguire family, and the Tottenham Three. If these had been the only examples, they could perhaps have been explained away as special cases involving terrorism in the first three instances and the brutal murder of a police constable in the fourth. Yet there have been other cases involving serious police malpractice, for example in the West Midlands Serious Crime Squad in the 1980s and in the case of Stefan Kiszko who spent 16 years in prison because irrefutable evidence, which showed that he could not possibly have committed the crime for which he had been sentenced, was withheld from the Court by the police. The cumulative result of all such cases has been to damage the image and standing of the police in the eyes of large sections of the British public.

Turning to *changes in police methods,* the main factors have been the reorganisation of the foot patrol system into a motorised unit system in the late 1960s and the growing use of new police equipment. The unintended consequence of the first development was to make the police seem more remote and less reassuring to the law-abiding public. The consequence of the second development – the escalating use of new police equipment, such as helmets with vizors, riot shields, long truncheons, CS gas, pepper sprays, and the increasing use of firearms – was to disturb and alienate many members of the general public. Such high pressure policing may have become inevitable in certain violent circumstances – for example, the direct action by the miners in 1984–85 or the Poll Tax Riots in the late 1980s – but it has done nothing to enhance the traditional British doctrine of policing by consent.

With regard to *police malpractice in certain areas*, the police have increasingly been accused of bias in their dealings with certain minority groups, essentially ethnic minorities. For many, this is a view substantiated by the failure of the police to bring the racist killers of Stephen Lawrence to justice. Allegations of police racism have grown, with the police being accused of taking a heavy-handed approach especially towards members of the Afro-Caribbean community. One survey showed that Afro-Caribbeans were 50 per cent more likely to be stopped in their vehicles than white people and nearly four times more likely to be stopped on foot.[35] Indeed, one of the reasons given for the riots which took place in a number of inner city areas in the early 1980s and again in the early 1990s was the aggressive attitude of the police towards the black community. Similarly, the police have been accused of taking a provocative stance when dealing with public demonstrations and have been blamed – at any rate by extremist elements – for outbreaks of violence on occasions such as the Trafalgar Square Poll Tax riot of 1990 or the Hyde Park riot against what is now the 1994 Criminal Justice and Public Order Act in October 1994. In short, some have come to see police misconduct as widespread – evidenced by almost £2.5 million paid in court and out-of-court settlements to victims of misconduct by the Metropolitan Police in 1997–98.

As for *problems of police powers and accountability,* these have also become more salient since the 1980s. As previously pointed out, traditional policing in Britain was usually kept distinct from the Party political fray. However, with the breakdown of the postwar consensus in the late 1960s and early 1970s, and with rising levels of public concern about crime and lawlessness, issues of law and order and especially the role of the police inevitably became more controversial. At the same time a number of senior police officers – for example John Alderson in Devon and Cornwall and James Anderton in Greater Manchester – became prominent public figures in their own right.

The adequacy of the powers of the police and the effectiveness of legal safeguards against police abuse became highly controversial topics, with civil liberties groups demanding additional safeguards and the 'law and order' lobby demanding greater police powers. At the time those on the Left of the political spectrum were associated with the former view and those on the Right with the latter. In all this the need to address the apparent lack of police accountability became ever more evident and an increasing cause for public concern.[36]

Lastly, there has been the *rising level of crime and lawlessness.* In the early years of the twentieth century the British police recorded fewer than 100,000 offences each year. This figure rose gradually to reach 500,000 by 1950. Since then – and even taking account of the fact that there are today more offences on the statute book – recorded crime rates have risen dramatically – reaching a figure of 5.4 million offences recorded by the police in the 12 months to the end of June 1994. In 1996 there were a total of 4,865,689 recorded crimes in England and Wales. The proportion of crimes cleared up declined from 41 per cent in 1979 to 27 per cent in 1996. Despite the obvious difficulties associated with such statistics,[37] they have provided the focus for much of the debate in the 1990s, because little public benefit appears to have been gained from more than 70 items of law and order legislation passed by Parliament in the period 1979–98, or from the more than 15 per cent increase in police numbers and the 70 per cent real increase in spending on the police during the same period. These trends have undoubtedly eroded public confidence in the police, created a climate of cynicism and even paranoia in some sections of the public, and fostered a sense of anxiety bordering almost on despair among politicians and public alike.

Profound social factors underlie the issues which have generated controversy about the police. Since the late 1960s the social conditions which must underpin what can be termed 'policing by consent' have been eroded; economic and social inequality has increased; British society has become less homogeneous and less deferential than before. Consequently, as was pointed out by Lord Scarman in his Report into the 1981 Brixton disorders, it is no good blaming the police for rising crime and declining respect for the law. Indeed, it is difficult to escape the conclusion that all sections of society must take responsibility for what has happened and act constructively together to deal with both the causes and the consequences of crime and public disorder.

17.6 Administrative law

From a political point of view it is administrative law which is probably the most important aspect of the legal system in Britain. H.W.R. Wade defined this area of the law as 'the body of general principles which govern the exercise of powers and duties by public authorities.'[38] Since the end of the nineteenth century there has been a great expansion of Parliamentary legislation and hence a notable multiplication of administrative bodies created by statute. This has led to growing judicial and quasi-judicial intervention in the field of public administration. Members of the general public have felt the need to appeal to Tribunals and ultimately to the Courts on many points of administrative law. For its part the judiciary has attempted to compensate for the failure of Parliament adequately to protect citizens from the shortcomings or injustices which can be perpetrated by the public administration.

Administrative Tribunals

In the modern British political system there is a bewildering array of administrative Tribunals which have been created by Acts of Parliament. Some, such as the National Insurance Tribunals which decide disputed claims to benefits, were established as a function of the Welfare State. Some, such as the Industrial Tribunals which adjudicate on claims of industrial injury, unfair dismissal, and other employment disputes, are related to the problems of industrial relations. Some deal with housing disputes, some with pensions or unemployment, some with immigration, some with the National Health Service, and some with education disputes. All exist in order to provide simpler, cheaper, quicker and more accessible forms of justice than are available in the Courts. Certainly these are the intentions underpinning this approach.

The *main characteristics of Administrative Tribunals* are as follows:

- They are normally established by Act of Parliament.
- Their decisions are quasi-judicial in the sense that they investigate the facts of the case and then apply certain legal principles in an impartial manner.
- They are independent in the sense that their decisions are in no way subject to political or administrative interference.
- Their membership varies, but they usually consist of a legally qualified chairman and two lay members representing relevant interests.
- They are assisted by clerks who are usually civil servants from the relevant Department.
- Appeals against their decisions can be made in various ways, since Parliament has laid down no consistent procedures.
- Appeals may lie to a Minister, a superior Tribunal, a superior Court, or there may be no provision for appeal, as is the case with the Social Security Appeal Tribunal or the National Health Service Tribunal.

The *main advantages of Administrative Tribunals* are that they offer relatively quick, cheap and accessible procedures which are essential, for example, in the administration of welfare schemes involving large numbers of small claims, and that they are well suited to deal expertly with highly technical matters, such as those referred to the Income Tax Commissioners or the Medical Appeal Tribunals.

On the other hand, the *main disadvantages* of Administrative Tribunals are their institutional proliferation and jurisdictional complexity. Over the years the growth of these bodies has produced over 50 different types of Tribunal, all of which fall within the definition laid down in the 1971 Tribunals and Inquiries Act. They range from those which are very active, for example Supplementary Benefit or Rent Tribunals, to those which have heard no cases at all, such as the Mines and Quarries Tribunals.

In such a complex structure there are inevitable problems of overlapping and competing jurisdictions, and little has been done so far to amalgamate or group Tribunals according to their various functions. Considerable attention has also been paid to the search for effective ways of controlling and supervising this part of the legal system. None of the existing methods has proved wholly satisfactory, which is why some have looked to practice on the Continent and others to overall constitutional reform for appropriate answers. Consequently, it is necessary to consider each of the various solutions in turn.

Ministerial control

The traditional view of the problems of administrative law is that the public interest can best be safeguarded by Ministers responsible to Parliament. Yet this idea has been something of a constitutional fiction ever since its mythical properties were first revealed by Lord Hewart and Professor Robson more than 60 years ago.[39] The criticism then, and even more so today, is that Ministers cannot possibly be well informed about, still less truly accountable for everything which happens (or fails to happen) within all the various administrative Tribunals and other quasi-judicial bodies for which they may be nominally responsible.

Even before the Second World War, it was recognised that Parliamentary control of Ministers was vitiated by the growth of delegated legislation, just as the purity of judge-made laws was threatened by the growth of quasi-judicial powers exercised by civil servants in the name of Ministers and by administrative Tribunals. Yet for many years little was done to tackle these problems, since the pressing challenges of war and reconstruction had to be given a higher priority. It was not until after the notorious Crichel Down affair in the early 1950s that some effective action began to be taken.[40] A committee chaired by Sir Oliver Franks was established to look at all these matters and in 1957 it produced a report which was broadly acceptable to the Conservative Government of the day. This led to the 1957 Tribunals and Inquiries Act which provided for the creation of the Council on Tribunals to oversee the whole sphere of administrative law. Subsequently the legislation was consolidated and brought up to date in the 1992 Tribunals and Inquiries Act.

In general, Ministerial control has not been an adequate response to the problems of overseeing and reviewing this type of law. In effect, it has sought to deny the significance of the problems by assuming that public administration is bound to reflect the public interest as long as in each Departmental area it is headed by a Minister responsible to Parliament. Such an idea is obviously defective in contemporary conditions, now that the whole process of Government has become so large and complex. In circumstances in which few Ministers achieve complete control over their Departments and Parliament has even less effective control over Ministers, it is naive to pretend that the Ministerial principle provides a satisfactory answer.

The Ombudsman

Another approach to solving the problem has been the creation of an independent institution specifically designed to limit serious abuses of administrative power and to deal firmly with any which arise. In Britain, as in other countries – for example, New Zealand and Scandinavia – this has been achieved by the Parliamentary Commissioner for Administration, commonly known as the Ombudsman.[41] The institution was created by Act of Parliament in 1967 in a further attempt to ensure that the administrative procedures of central Government and its agencies are correctly followed and that any allegations of maladministration are investigated and, if possible, rectified.

The Ombudsman, who is usually a former lawyer or civil servant, is appointed by the Crown on the advice of the Lord Chancellor. The constitutional status of the position is similar to that of a High Court judge, namely completely independent of Governnment. As is the case for a judge, the salary is fixed by statute and charged automatically to the Consolidated Fund. The Ombudsman can only be removed from office by the Crown after addresses by both Houses of Parliament; in other words the incumbent is effectively unsackable during a five-year term of office. The staff of the Ombudsman are usually drawn from the ranks of the Civil Service. The jurisdiction of the Ombudsman is confined to the Departments of central Government and certain non-Departmental public bodies. However, in addition to the Parliamentary Ombudsman, there are *Health Service Ombudsmen* in England, Scotland and Wales whose job it is to investigate complaints about the National Health Service including NHS Trusts; *Local Government Ombudsmen* in England (where there are in fact three), Scotland and Wales whose job it is to investigate complaints made against local government bodies; an *Ombudsman for Northern Ireland* whose job it is to investigate complaints made against Government Departments and other public bodies in the Province; a *Housing Ombudsman*; and a *Prisons Ombudsman*, established in 1994 to investigate complaints from prisoners. There have also been *six financial services Ombudsmen* – for banking, building societies, insurance, investments, pensions and personal investments – which were amalgamated in 1998–99 by the new super-regulator, the Financial Services Authority, into a new single Ombudsman. There are also Ombudsmen for the Legal Services, Estate Agents and Funeral Services.

The jurisdiction of the Ombudsman does not cover either the police – this is the responsibility of the Police Complaints Authority – or public corporations. Similarly, although the Ombudsman can investigate complaints about the way in which Departments have discharged their functions, the jurisdiction does not extend to international relations, Court proceedings, employment issues, or the commercial transactions of central Government. Furthermore, there is no right to investigate cases where the complainant has a right of recourse to an Administrative Tribunal or a remedy in the Courts. Nor can complaints be investigated if made more than one year after the date when the complainant first had notice of the matter. In short, Parliament did not exactly give the institution *carte blanche,* largely because at the outset it was seen by many MPs as an interloper in their territory and some areas of administration are thought to pose special problems not amenable to these means of redress.

It is essentially for this reason that to this day most complaints are made to the Ombudsman via a Member of Parliament. Once the complaint has been officially received, it is first for the Ombudsman to decide whether or not it properly falls within his jurisdiction. In fact, fewer than half the complaints received fall within the Ombudsman's jurisdiction and can therefore be investigated. All official documents, except Cabinet papers, have to be produced for inspection at the request of the Ombudsman who has the same powers as a High Court judge to compel any witness to give evidence. When an investigation is complete, a report is normally sent to the MP concerned, who then sends it on to the complainant.

The Ombudsman has no executive powers, but the reports concerned often suggest appropriate remedies upon which the Department involved normally takes action. The remedies may include financial compensation from public funds, remission of taxation, administrative review of earlier decisions, or revised administrative procedures. For example, in the 1989 Barlow Clowes report the Ombudsman recommended that the private investors who had lost all their money to two investment funds which were not properly supervised by the Department of Trade and Industry should receive substantial financial compensation for their losses on a diminishing scale as the amounts increased. This reflected implied culpability on the part of the supervisory Department and, following a lengthy Parliamentary campaign by back-benchers for recompense for their constituents, led Ministers to offer taxpayers' money for the purpose. MPs work quite happily in partnership with the Ombudsman in joint efforts to secure redress for their constituents. In formal terms this relationship has been cemented by the work of a Select Committee of the House of Commons which supervises the work of the Ombudsman and takes evidence, where appropriate, from Departments which are the subject of such investigations. This all helps to ensure that the recommendations are carried out.

Since its inception in 1967 the trend has been for steadily increasing numbers of complaints to be received by the Ombudsman. By the early 1990s this amounted to some 800–900 cases, of which approximately 200 were taken to full investigation. In 1995 a total of 1706 cases were received and a total of 62 per cent of cases taken to full investigation were upheld. In 1996 a total of 1920 cases were received – a record number – almost half of which were complaints against the Department of Social Security. A total of 260 investigations were completed of which 246 (94 per cent) were found to be wholly or partly justified.

On the European front, under the terms of the Maastricht Treaty a European Ombudsman has been appointed to consider complaints of maladministration levelled against the institutions of the European Union.

Judicial review

Another way of dealing with injustices or abuses which are perpetrated by the public administration is judicial review. The basic leverage for the judiciary is provided by the doctrine of *ultra vires*, which holds that acts of public administration can be unlawful if they offend against the rules of natural justice or otherwise go beyond the bounds of statutory powers. It is this doctrine which enables the High Court to set aside administrative decisions which, although perhaps within the literal scope of the statutes, are plainly unreasonable. The issues involved are inevitably controversial, since the nub of the argument is usually the degree of discretionary power which can properly be exercised by a public body. The judiciary has the difficult responsibility of interpreting the meaning of statutes on the basis of what reasonable people would reasonably decide. This can be approached in a narrow and literal sense or a broad and contextual sense, and the outcome of such cases will often depend upon which of the two approaches is adopted.

When a complaint against the public administration is brought before the High Court, several legal remedies are available to the plaintiff. There are the traditional pre-rogative remedies which were originally vested in the Monarch, but which are now available to ordinary citizens. These are *certiorari* to quash an administrative decision already made; *prohibition* to prevent a public authority from considering a matter which it has no statutory right to consider; and *mandamus* to compel a public body to perform a public duty. Then there are the two non-prerogative remedies which are often more useful nowadays. These are an *injunction* to prohibit a public body from doing something and a *declaration* which is simply a statement by the Court clarifying the legal position, so that the powers and duties of a public body can be defined more precisely.[42]

Judicial review is impartial in the sense that it is in no way influenced by the position of the complainant or the power of the public body about which the complaint has been made. Yet there are weaknesses in such procedures. For example, the Courts can only intervene if a plaintiff starts legal proceedings; it can only deal with the case before it; it usually lacks the detailed expertise of the public administration which it seeks to control; it cannot oversee the way in which its remedial orders are carried out; and it proceeds so slowly and expensively that many would-be plaintiffs are deterred from going to law in the first place.

In conducting the process of judicial review, the judges tend to be guided essentially by the principles of natural justice. These are the right of the complainant to be heard before the relevant decision is taken and the absence of prejudice on the part of the Court or other public body charged with the duty of adjudication. Clearly, there is a difficult balance which has to be struck by the Courts between the interests of the plaintiff and those of the general public as represented by the decisions of public bodies. The balance has shifted back and forth over the years. Yet as Hartley and Griffith have pointed out, the Courts have tended to be guided 'more by policy than by precedent, more by what they think is fair and reasonable than by rigid rules.[43] Judicial review is therefore a more than usually political form of justice.

Since about the mid-1960s the judiciary in Britain has been prepared to play a more active part in arguments of political principle.[44] This has been evident especially in cases which bear upon the definition of individual rights, such as personal property, liberty, freedom of movement, retention of office and access to employment. It could also be argued that over these years the tide of judicial opinion turned against some unpopular groups of which others in society tended to disapprove, such as trade unionists or students. Notwithstanding the fluctuations in both judicial and public opinion on these and other questions, the judiciary has shown a growing willingness to use the process of judicial review to deal definitively with disputes which can arise in the sphere of public administration.

The number of applications for judicial review has risen sharply over recent years from 160 in 1974 to 1529 in 1987 to 2886 in 1993 and successive Governments have fallen foul of Court rulings. For example:

- In 1976 the Courts struck down a direction by the then Secretary of State for Education, Shirley Williams, to Tameside Council to implement a scheme to convert a number of grammar schools to comprehensive schools.
- In 1981 the High Court ruled that the then Secretary of State for the Environment, Michael Heseltine, had acted improperly in refusing to listen to representations from various London Boroughs concerning his decision to reduce their rate support grant.
- In 1990 the High Court overruled Government guidelines on the administration of the Social Fund introduced in 1988.
- In 1993 the Law Lords ruled that the then Home Secretary, Kenneth Baker, had been in contempt of Court when deporting a Zairean refugee in May 1991.

- In 1994 the High Court found that the Foreign Secretary, Douglas Hurd, had acted illegally in authorising aid worth £234m for the Pergau Dam in Malaysia.
- In 1995 the Law Lords ruled that the Home Secretary, Michael Howard, had abused his powers and flouted the will of Parliament when he introduced a cheaper, fixed rate Criminal Injuries Compensation Scheme.
- In 1997 the Law Lords noted that the Home Secretary, Michael Howard, had acted illegally when he raised the term of imprisonment imposed on the two boys convicted of murdering James Bulger from ten years to 15 years.

Although not all cases involve the action of Ministers, and notwithstanding the fact that in those that do, not all result in the action of the Minister being struck out, the apparently greater willingness of the Courts to play an active role in this respect has undoubtedly shifted the balance of power somewhat against the Government of the day and in favour of ordinary citizens.

Continental solutions

There are some who argue that Britain should look further afield to find the most effective ways of supervising and controlling the public administration. Specifically, they maintain that the best solution would be to establish in Britain a new Administrative Division of the High Court (similar to that which exists in France) or a new Administrative Appeals Tribunal (along the lines of that which exists in Sweden). Such approaches have been advocated by those members of the judiciary who would like to see the process of judicial review extended into all corners of the public administration.

Such solutions would almost certainly be opposed by those who already harbour a deep suspicion of the judiciary and hence a strong unwillingness to allow them a more influential political role. Certainly many of those on the Left of British politics would oppose any extension of the powers and competence of the judiciary unless and until they could feel satisfied that the judiciary had ceased to be drawn from such a deeply conservative section of the population. At the same time many of those on the Right would resist it on the grounds that it is undesirable to import foreign judicial practices into Britain.

Yet, as Britain becomes more deeply drawn into the process of European integration, it seems almost certain that the impact of European law and especially the influence of the European Court will be increasingly felt in both the public and private sectors.[45] Indeed, much of the acrimonious debate between the so-called 'Eurosceptics' and the so-called 'Europhiles' has centred on the growing concern of the former about the intrusion of the European Court into more and more areas of British national life.

Constitutional reform

Finally, some eminent legal figures, such as Lord Scarman and Lord Hailsham, have at times argued the case for comprehensive constitutional reform entailing a new Bill of Rights and the introduction of an entrenched and codified constitution which would be interpreted and protected by a newly established and completely independent Supreme

Court.[46] Those who favour this way of dealing with the problems of administrative law have to contend with the traditional British response that civil rights and political liberties are most secure if founded upon the established custom and practice of common law. Of course, they would probably reply in their turn that the traditional approach has become obsolete in view of the scope and complexity of public administration in contemporary political circumstances. This would then lead them to the conclusion that a new Bill of Rights should include a formal statement of civil rights and public duties.

Whatever the attractions of this idea, there would be several considerable difficulties with such an approach in Britain. There would need to be a codified constitution which anyone could invoke in the event of a dispute with the public authorities. There would need to be a wholly new Supreme Court quite independent of the political considerations which are sometimes seen as influencing the judgements of the Law Lords. There would need to be public acceptance of a very different and more distinctive role for the senior members of the judiciary. Above all, Members of Parliament would have to be willing to acknowledge that Parliament itself could no longer claim its traditional political and constitutional supremacy.

Here it is interesting to note that the 1998 Human Rights Act – incorporating the European Convention on Human Rights into domestic British law – actually stipulated that the British Courts did *not* have the power to set aside Acts of the United Kingdom Parliament even if they considered that such legislation conflicted with the rights enshrined in this statute. Of course, the irony is that the idea of Parliamentary supremacy is already rather dated, being challenged by Britain's membership of the European Union, and it is likely to be further eroded if more national sovereignty is pooled in the process of shared decision making in the Council of Ministers and democratic power sharing between Westminster and the European Parliament.

Among those who favour such all-embracing changes, Nevil Johnson has argued that 'the challenge is to construct a different relationship between law and politics and in so doing to give law [...] a new and wider part in the regulation of the affairs of society'.[47] We have seen in Chapter 15 how this has already happened in response to the challenges of privatisation. It may yet be taken further if politicians in all parties can accept the idea of playing second fiddle to judges in the determination of some of the really big legal and constitutional issues in British society.

17.7 Conclusion

It remains to be seen whether the legal system in Britain will develop in a more creative and independent direction, or whether it will remain fundamentally conservative and obedient to the idea – however mythical – of Parliamentary supremacy. There are clearly major implications for the traditional doctrines of Ministerial responsibility and Parliamentary accountability if the judiciary does develop more independent and creative powers. Yet it must be said that such a development is likely to depend essentially on the Government of the day voluntarily agreeing to be limited by the Courts rather than on any inclination of the judges to strike more heroic postures. Such a condition seems unlikely to be met in the future irrespective of the political complexion of the Government of the day.

Prior to taking up office in 1997 the Labour Party had put forward proposals for a 'Charter of Rights', backed up by statute, in order to establish in law the specific rights of every citizen. It also advocated additional anti-discrimination legislation, Freedom of Information, a Right to Privacy and a Security Services Act; proposed to create a Department of Legal Administration, to improve access to legal aid and to extend its availability to Tribunal hearings; and proposed to diminish Ministerial patronage in the sphere of Quangos and to create elected Police Authorities. If implemented, all of this – together with proposals for reform of the House of Lords and the establishment of new Assemblies in Scotland and Wales as well as the option of regional assemblies in England – will undoubtedly add up to the greatest package of legal and constitutional reform in the twentieth century.

However, competition for legislative time in Parliament is invariably fierce and consequently not all of these constitutional proposals were allocated time during the first two sessions. At the time of writing it would be wise to suspend judgement not only on the practicality but also possibly on the determination of the Labour Government to carry through such a large agenda of reform, since students of these matters can recall their disappointment on previous occasions when politicians in office appeared to lose sight of their impressive commitments in Opposition, or failed to deliver because of insufficient appreciation of the complexities of what was involved.

One of the reasons why Labour's proposals have fallen some way short of delivering a constitutionally guaranteed Bill of Rights is that the Labour Party (and indeed many politicians in other parties as well) have not overcome their traditional antipathy towards the judiciary. As H.W.R. Wade rightly pointed out, 'if they [the judges] fly too high, Parliament may clip their wings'.[48] In other words, constitutional reform of this kind is unlikely to come about unless the Judiciary *and* the Legislature make common cause against the Executive, and that is unrealistic in the British political system where the Executive and the Legislature are fused.

It is well to remember that there never has been a truly effective separation of powers in Britain. Such a triangular balance nearly came about in the eighteenth century, when central Government was at its weakest. Yet in more modern times the politicians in Government have definitively asserted their position and the judiciary has been careful not to step too far out of line with the Government of the day. This is because in the last resort the politicians in office can always use their whipped majority in the House of Commons to trump any judicial challenge.

Of course, relations between the Judiciary, the Executive and the Legislature may change in future in response to more demanding public attitudes or different constitutional arrangements. For example, the public may come to expect more from the Courts by way of judicial protection and redress against an over-mighty or unrepresentative Government. The incorporation into British law of certain fundamental constitutional principles enshrined in the European Convention on Human Rights – effected in the 1998 Human Rights Act – may well alter entrenched attitudes as time goes by. Equally, the supremacy of European law over British law, at least in the areas of expanding European competence, may hasten the day when the traditional doctrine of Parliamentary supremacy can no longer be sustained as the cornerstone of the British constitution.

Suggested questions

1 What is the nature of the legal relationship between the state and its citizens in Britain today?
2 Describe the structure and problems of either the criminal justice or the civil justice system in contemporary Britain.
3 How appropriate and effective are the arrangements for applying and reviewing administrative law in Britain?

Notes

1. There is no single legal system – either in terms of judicial organisation or body of law – which is applicable throughout the United Kingdom. Rather, there is one set of arrangements in England and Wales, one in Scotland, and one in Northern Ireland. In the detailed descriptions of civil and criminal courts and proceedings which follow, the focus is on the system as applicable to England and Wales. Nevertheless, these five points are essentially applicable throughout.
2. This concept has, however, been modified in significant respects by Britain's membership of the European Union. See Chapter 18 for more on this.
3. See 'Report of the Royal Commission on Criminal Justice', Cmnd 2263 (London: HMSO, 1993).
4. See 'Report of the Royal Commission on Criminal Procedure', Cmnd 8092 (London: HMSO, 1981).
5. For a fuller discussion of these issues see the Scarman 'Report on the Brixton Disorders', Cmnd 8487 (London: HMSO, 1981).
6. In 1996 the average prison population was 55,280 in England and Wales and 5900 in Scotland; an increase of more than 175% in 40 years.
7. Solicitors are the branch of the legal profession chiefly concerned with advising clients and preparing their cases, while Barristers who have been 'called to the Bar' (qualified) are entitled to practise as advocates in superior Courts.
8. These are breaches of duty leading to liability for damages, but non-contractual in the case of tort.
9. *Prohibition* prevents a public authority from considering a matter which it has no statutory right to consider. *Mandamus* enables the High Court to compel a public body to perform a public duty which it is statutorily obliged to perform. *Certiorari* enables the High Court to quash an administrative decision already made by a public body. A writ of *habeas corpus* is supposed to prevent the police from detaining without charge for more than 24 hours those suspected of non-serious offences, although in the case of suspected terrorists there is statutory provision for this time limit to be extended to three days inland and seven days at a port of entry.
10. The reason for this incongruous grouping was simply that all jurisdictions had a common basis in Roman law.
11. See 'Access to Justice – Final Report', The Rt. Hon. the Lord Woolf (London: HMSO, 1996).
12. See Keith Laybourn, *A History of British Trade Unionism C. 1770–1990* (Stroud: Alan Sutton, 1992, pp. 88–86).
13. G. Drewry, *Law, Justice and Politics* (London: Longman, 1975), p.128.
14. J.A.G. Griffith, *The Politics of the Judiciary* (London: Fontana, 1977), p. 193.
15. In 1992–93 eligibility for legal aid was reduced to those with disposable incomes of less than £2213 per annum. Consequently whereas it was estimated that 79 per cent of households were eligible for legal aid in 1979, by 1992–93 this had declined to 48 per cent.

16. Legal aid has, however, grown dramatically over the years. For the first 20 years of the scheme the total cost of aid did not exceed £10m a year. By 1980 the cost had risen to £100m, by 1990–91 it had reached £682 million; in 1996–97 it reached £1477 million. In 1989 2.3 million people obtained legal aid. By 1993 this figure had risen to 3.5 million. At the same time the average cost of each individual action had also risen: in 1989 the average cost was £204; in 1994 it stood at £350. (See R. Rice, 'Trapped in a time warp', *Financial Times*, 4 October 1994.)

Legal aid supply expenditure and volume trends 1993–94 to 1998–99

(£ million)	1993–94 Outturn	1994–95 Outturn	1995–96 Outturn	1996–97 Outturn	1997–98 Forecast outturn	1998–99 Plans
Total Expenditure (£m cash)	1210	1299	1391	1476	1487	1602
Increase (%) of which:		7	7	6	1	8
Civil Legal Aid (£m)	544	602	643	671	635	657
Criminal Legal Aid (£m)	428	464	498	539	621	621
Advice and assistance (£m)	238	233	250	266	306	324
Total number of bills paid (thousands)	3459	3447	3452	3481	3591	3705
Increase (%) of which:	0	0	1	3	3	
Civil Legal Aid (000 bills)	359	358	373	359	335	306
Criminal Legal Aid (000 bills)	689	750	766	770	799	805
Advice and assistance (000 bills)	2410	2340	2314	2351	2457	2595

Source: Lord Chancellor's Department, September 1998.

17. Formerly there was no restriction on the participation of lay peers in the judicial proceedings of the House of Lords. However, after the O'Connell case in 1844 (see Norman Gash, Sir Robert Peel (London: Longman, 1972) pp. 424–5), in which their intervention would have had the effect of overturning the decision of the Law Lords (that is, the Lord Chancellor, the Lords of Appeal and such peers as held or had high judicial office in a superior Court), it became an established convention that they should not take part in the judicial office. The 1876 Appellate Jurisdiction Act provided for the appointment of two Lords of Appeal and declared that appeals to the Lords should not be heard unless at least three Law Lords were present. In 1948 the Lords authorised (on a temporary basis at first) the hearing of appeals by an Appellate Committee drawn from amongst the appointed Lords of Appeal (including the Lord Chancellor) and the other senior legal figures already mentioned. After a time this innovation became permanent, so that nearly all appeals to the House of Lords are now heard by the Law Lords sitting as either one or two Appellate Committees, depending on the number of cases to be heard.
18. These are Trinidad and Tobago, Singapore, Dominica, Kiribata, and The Gambia.
19. The Judicial Committee has been available as a source of advisory opinion for the Crown on matters of public concern or legal difficulty which cannot otherwise be brought conveniently before the Courts, for example cases relating to disqualification from the House of Commons or those to do with Parliamentary privilege. It had a role under Section 5 of the 1920 Government of Ireland Act in that, until Stormont was dissolved in 1972, the Government in London was enpowered to refer to it questions relating to the interpretation of the Act, notably issues of legislative competence. As things turned out, this provision was used only once, in 1936. It would also have had a similar role of constitutional arbitra-

tion if the devolution legislation of the 1974–79 Labour Government had been brought into effect; it has however been given a similar role under the 1998 Scotland Act.

20. Both quoted in J.A.G. Griffith, *The Politics of the Judiciary*, p. 179 and p. 183. see also *Journal of the Society of Public Teachers of Law* (1972), vol. 12, p. 22.

21. Queen's Bench Divisional Court, *Regina v. Secretary of State for Foreign and Commonwealth Affairs*, ex parte Rees-Mogg, 30 July 1993, see Law Report, *The Times*, 31 July 1993.

22. See: Part 2, Articles 8–8d, Treaty on European Union (Luxembourg: EUR OP, 1992).

23. In 1992 800,500 EU citizens had settled in Britain; in the five years to 1992 an average of 58,300 British citizens per year had left Britain to settle in other parts of the EU. (See Eurostat, University of London (The *Guardian*, 16 February 1995) and *The Times*, 26 January 1995). Official figures for 1995 show that 71,000 EU citizens migrated to Britain while 55,000 British Citizens migrated to other parts of the EU (Office for National Statistics,1998).

24. For example, see *Central Intelligence Machinery* (London: HMSO, 1993).

25. See 'The *Citizen's Charter*', Cmnd 1599 (London: HMSO, 1991).

26. See 'Your Right To Know' (CM 3818), (London: Stationery Office, 1997).

27. This is the name given to a writ addressed to an individual who holds another in custody, directing them to produce the individual held and show cause for their detention. Where a writ is granted the individual held must be released at once. Failure to do so amounts to contempt of court. See note 9 for more information.

28. Salman Rushdie's book *Satanic Verses* was seen by some Muslims as blasphemous and, as a result, Ayatollah Khomeni of Iran issued a *fatwa* (a decree of death) against the author in February 1989. This was perceived, almost throughout the world, as an attack on the fundamental freedom of expression, religious tolerance and rule of law.

29. This problem has been addressed in attempts to reach agreement between the nations in both the European Union and the Council of Europe. However, no international broadcasting agreement is likely to be completely effective in an increasingly deregulated, global media market.

30. This restricted legal immunity from civil action in the Courts to the employees of the firm in dispute or the employees of a direct supplier or customer of the firm in dispute, thus theoretically limiting the scope for 'blacking' or sympathy strikes.

31. See 'Report of the Royal Commission on the Police', Cmnd 1728 (London: HMSO, 1962).

32. See 'Operational Policy Review' (Police Federation, 1990).

33. See 'Public Satisfaction with Police Services', Home Office Research and Planning Unit, Paper 73, December 1992.

34. See MORI survey carried out 20–24 January 1994 on behalf of *Reader's Digest* magazine, and published in the April 1994 issue.

35. See 'Public Satisfaction with Police Services', Home Office Research and Planning Unit, Paper 73, December 1992.

36. See T. Jones, T. Newbury, and D. Smith, *Democracy and Policing* (London: Policies Studies Institute, 1994).

37. Many offences are never reported to the police, and some of those that are do not get recorded. For example, the *British Crime Survey* published in November 1993 showed that only about one in three offences was recorded in official statistics.

38. H.W.R. Wade, *Administrative Law*, 4th edn (Oxford: Clarendon Press, 1979), pp. 5–6.

39. See Lord Hewart, *The New Despotism*, 2nd edn (West Point: Greenwood, 1945), and W. Robson, *Justice and Administrative Law*, 3rd edn (London: Stevens, 1951).

40. The Crichel Down affair involved an area of farmland in Dorset about which misleading replies and false assurances were given by a junior civil servant in the Ministry of Agriculture. Subsequent inquiries established that there had been muddle, bias, inefficency and bad faith on the part of a few officials, as well as weak organsation in the Department. This led eventually to the resignation of the Minister, Sir Thomas Dugdale.
41. See C.M. Clothier, *Ombudsman: Jurisdiction, Powers and Practise* (Manchester: Manchester Statistical Society, 1981), for a fuller description of the role of the Ombudsman in Britain.
42. An *injunction* and *declaration* are two of the legal remedies generally available to litigants and they are not confined to cases in which citizens seek to challenge public authorities.
43. T.C. Harley and J.A.G. Griffith, *Government and Law* (London: Weidenfeld & Nicolson, 1975), p. 230.
44. Notably in the Court of Appeal where Lord Denning had a long and active period as Master of the Rolls from 1962 to 1982.
45. See Chapter 18 for more on the European Court of Justice and its role in European integration.
46. See Lord Scarman, *English Law, the New Dimension* (London: Stevens, 1974), and Lord Hailsham, *The Dilemma of Democracy* (London: Collins, 1978).
47. N. Johnson, *In Search of the Constitution* (London: Methuen, 1980), p. 149.
48. H.W.R. Wade, *Administrative Law*, p. 30.

Further reading

Bradley, R., *Public Expectations and Perceptions of Policing*, Police Research Series Paper 96 (London: Home Office Research, Development and Statistics Directorate, 1998).
Clothier, C.M., *Ombudsman: Jurisdiction, Powers and Practise* (Manchester: Manchester Statistical Society, 1981).
de Smith, S. and Brazier, R., *Constitutional and Administrative Law*, 6th edn (London: Penguin, 1990).
Dickson, B., *The Legal System of Northern Ireland*, 2nd edn (1989).
Griffith, J.A.G., *The Politics of the Judiciary*, 5th edn (London: Fontana, 1997).
Ingleton, R., *Arming the British Police* (London: Frank Cass, 1997).
Jackson, R.M., et al., *The Machinery of Justice in England*, 8th edn (London: CUP, 1989).
Morris, T., *Crime and Criminal Justice since 1945* (Oxford: Blackwell, 1989).
'Police Reform', Cmnd 2281 (London: HMSO, 1993).
Reiner, R., *The Politics of the Police*, 2nd edn (London: Harvester Wheatsheaf, 1992).
'Rights Brought Home: The Human Rights Bill' (CM 3782), (London: Stationery Office, 1997).
Robertson, G., *Street's Freedom: The Individual and the Law*, 6th edn (London: Penguin, 1989).
'Report of the Inquiry into Police Responsibilities and Rewards', Vols I and II, CM2280- T/CM 2280-II, 30 June 1993.
Stainsby, P., *Tribunal Practise and Procedure* (London: Law Society, 1988).
Wade, H.W.R., *Administrative Law*, 6th edn (Oxford: Clarendon Press, 1988).
Walker D.M., *The Scottish Legal System*, 6th edn (1992).
Wright, A., *Citizens and Subjects* (London: Routledge, 1993).

Websites

Amnesty International   http://www.amnesty.org.uk
Home Office   http://www.homeoffice.gov.uk
Justice   http://www.justice.org.uk
Lord Chancellor's Department   http://www.open.gov.uk/LCD

PART 6

Democracy in Britain

(18) Britain in Europe

No modern textbook on the British political system can afford to ignore Britain's membership of the European Union and still be an accurate and complete reflection of contemporary political realities. The vast network of economic and political relationships which this involves and especially the legal and constitutional issues which it raises, are essential to a proper understanding of contemporary British politics. Things have not been the same for Britain ever since it joined the European Community (as the European Union was then called) in January 1973. Even more significant changes took place under the aegis of the 1986 Single European Act which made possible the European Single Market, the 1992 Treaty of Maastricht which set the course for Economic and Monetary Union, and the 1997 Treaty of Amsterdam which sought to improve the efficiency of the European Institutions and extend the concept of European citizenship.

18.1 Historical background

The origin of postwar European integration can be found in the decision of six states – France, West Germany (as it was then), Italy, Holland, Belgium and Luxembourg – to establish the European Coal and Steel Community in 1950. This experiment in supranationalism, from which Britain decided to stand aside, involved the pooling of national economic sovereignty in the two vital sectors of coal mining and steel making which were then regarded as 'the sinews of war'. The founding fathers – Jean Monnet and Robert Schuman (both Frenchmen), Konrad Adenauer (a German), Alcide de Gasperi (an Italian), and Paul-Henri Spaak (a Belgian) – chose these two sectors quite deliberately because they had been at the heart of national war-making capacities for the previous century or so. By pooling these national resources irrevocably and then allowing them to be managed and controlled by a new supranational 'High Authority', it was confidently expected that war in Europe between European nations would thus be rendered impossible once and for all.

Although Britain had participated in all the *international* organisations which had been established after the Second World War – such as the Brussels Treaty Organization in 1948 (which in 1955 became the Western European Union), the Council of Europe and the North Atlantic Treaty Organization in 1949 – the political leaders in Britain at that time could not bring themselves to participate in *supra-national* organisations of which the European Coal and Steel Community was the prominent example. There were various reasons for this, but the principal explanation was that the realities of Britain's weakened position in the postwar world had been masked by its war-time achievements and postwar preoccupations with its Empire and embryonic Commonwealth. After all, Britain had stood alone against the might of Hitler's Germany in 1940, had been acknowledged as one of the three victorious Powers in 1945 (along with the United States and the Soviet Union), and British politicians and people alike tended to look to Britain's relations with the United States and with the British Empire and emerging Commonwealth before they considered relations with the nations on the shattered Continent of Europe. Of the famous 'three circles' of British influence in the world – the special relationship with the Americans, the imperial responsibilities in the Empire and Commonwealth, and the various aspects of European entanglements – of which Winston Churchill spoke so eloquently at the time, there was little doubt in British minds about the order of priorities. Relations with the other European nations generally came third in the British world-view. In Churchill's words, Britain was 'with them, but not of them'.

However, during the 1950s Britain was drawn into closer involvement with Continental Europe as our so-called 'special relationship' with the United States suffered a series of blows and disappointments, notably at the time of the ill-fated British and French invasion of the Suez Canal Zone in 1956 and as the process of British de-colonisation produced a Commonwealth which came to be seen by some in Britain as much as a liability as an asset. With the collapse of the attempt to form a European Defence Community in 1954, Britain moved swiftly to sign the 1955 Paris Accords which established the Western European Union, brought West Germany into conventional (but not nuclear) defence arrangements with its European partners, and committed Britain to keep more than 50,000 troops on the mainland of Europe for 50 years. However, when the Six took the process of European integration one stage further by signing in 1957 the Rome Treaties, which established the European Economic Community (EEC) and Euratom in the following year, Britain once again stood aside after having sent only observers to the seminal conference at Messina in 1956. The British Conservative Government then made a futile attempt to negotiate a wider European Free Trade arrangement with the Six in 1957–58. When this was understandably rebuffed by the Six, Britain and the other excluded European nations (Austria, Denmark, Norway, Portugal, Sweden and Switzerland) decided to establish the European Free Trade Association (EFTA) as a partial counterweight to their exclusion from the mainstream of European economic and political integration.

It was not long before the Conservative Government, then led by Harold Macmillan, realised the error of its ways in having stood aside from the mainstream of European integration. Accordingly, in July 1961 the Government initiated negotiations with the European Communities (as they were then called) to see whether a basis existed for future British membership which would be consistent with the interests of Britain, the Commonwealth and EFTA. The subsequent formal statement introducing the application declared that the Government's decision had been reached 'not on any narrow or short-term grounds, but as a result of a thorough assessment over a considerable period of the needs of our own country, Europe and the free world as a whole'.[1] It is interesting to note in passing the clear implication in this statement that 'Europe' was somewhere other than Britain or conversely that Britain was not in Europe. By this stage Britain seemed at last to be set on a course to bring it into full membership of the European Community. Yet in spite of the considerable progress which was later made in resolving many of the technical problems, the negotiations between Britain and the Six had to be broken off following President De Gaulle's veto delivered at a famous press conference in Paris on 29 January 1963.[2]

Throughout the 1960s successive British Governments, both Conservative and Labour, sought to keep alive the possibility of Britain's membership of the European Community. In May 1967 the Wilson Administration made another formal application for Britain to join the European Community, but once again this was rebuffed by French opposition. However, two years later in April 1969 President De Gaulle staked his political fortune on the result of a constitutional referendum in France and lost, thus leaving himself with no choice but to resign. This had the effect of opening the way for Britain to renew its application to join the European Community, which was duly done by the Heath Administration immediately after the Conservatives came to power in June 1970.

The detailed negotiations with the Six took little more than one year and were brought to a satisfactory conclusion. Both Houses of Parliament debated and voted on the principle of British entry in October 1971. The House of Commons voted in favour by 356 to 244, a majority of 112, in which 69 Labour MPs defied a three-line whip in order to vote for the Government motion; and on the same day the House of Lords approved the same motion by a larger majority of 393. On 22 January 1972 Edward Heath, as Prime Minister, signed the Treaty of Accession in Brussels on behalf of Britain. Parliament was then required to legislate to bring British law into line with European law and the resulting Westminster statute was the all-important 1972 European Communities Act. The passage of this legislation was fraught with difficulties. It was opposed by a determined minority of Conservative 'anti-Marketeers' (as they were then called) and on occasions the Government only survived because some Labour MPs were prepared to abstain in key votes. Eventually, however, the way was cleared for full British membership of the European Community from 1 January 1973, when Denmark and Ireland also joined (although Norway had earlier decided not to join in a public referendum decision which rejected the view of the Norwegian Government).

Because the Labour Party had been split on the European issue at least since the vote of principle in October 1971, Labour fought the two General Elections in 1974 pledged to a policy of renegotiating what it described as the unacceptable terms of entry. The process of renegotiation which followed was backed by the implicit threat that the renegotiated terms would be put to the British people in a consultative referendum and, if continued membership on such terms were rejected, then the Government would take the necessary steps for British withdrawal. When the referendum was held in 1975, the British people voted by a two-to-one majority in favour of Britain remaining in the European Community and this verdict was accepted (however reluctantly in some cases) by the Government and by Parliament.

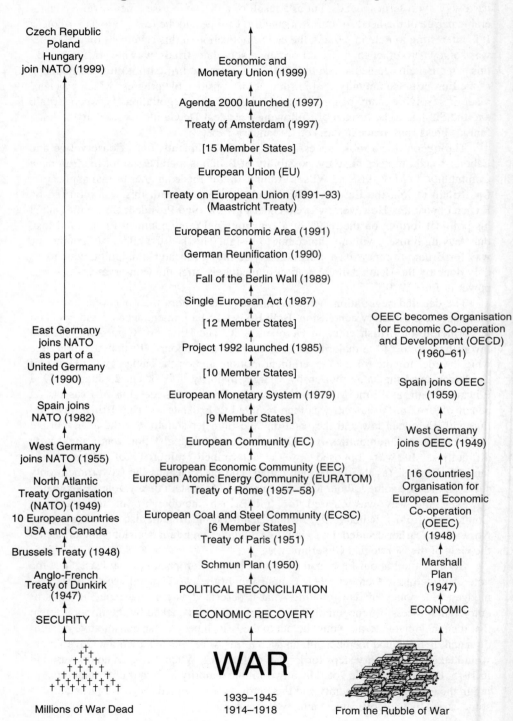

Figure 18.1 The development of European integration

Czech Republic
Poland
Hungary
join NATO (1999)

Economic and
Monetary Union (1999)

Agenda 2000 launched (1997)

Treaty of Amsterdam (1997)

[15 Member States]

European Union (EU)

Treaty on European Union (1991–93)
(Maastricht Treaty)

European Economic Area (1991)

German Reunification (1990)

Fall of the Berlin Wall (1989)

Single European Act (1987)

[12 Member States]

OEEC becomes Organisation
for Economic Co-operation
and Development (OECD)
(1960–61)

East Germany
joins NATO
as part of a
United Germany
(1990)

Project 1992 launched (1985)

[10 Member States]

European Monetary System (1979)

Spain joins OEEC
(1959)

Spain joins
NATO (1982)

[9 Member States]

European Community (EC)

West Germany
joins OEEC (1949)

West Germany
joins NATO (1955)

European Economic Community (EEC)
European Atomic Energy Community (EURATOM)
Treaty of Rome (1957–58)

[16 Countries]
Organisation for
European Economic
Co-operation
(OEEC)
(1948)

North Atlantic
Treaty Organisation
(NATO) (1949)
10 European countries
USA and Canada

European Coal and Steel Community (ECSC)
[6 Member States]
Treaty of Paris (1951)

Brussels Treaty (1948)

Schmun Plan (1950)

Marshall
Plan
(1947)

Anglo-French
Treaty of Dunkirk
(1947)

POLITICAL RECONCILIATION

SECURITY

ECONOMIC RECOVERY

ECONOMIC

WAR

Millions of War Dead

1939–1945
1914–1918

From the Rubble of War

Figure 18.2 European integration: a chronology

1945	End of the Second World War
1947	Marshall Plan launched by USA to aid European reconstruction
1948	Creation of the Organisation for Economic Co-operation (OEEC) to co-ordinate Marshall Plan aid
1949	North Atlantic Treaty establishes NATO
1950	Schuman plan put forward
1951	The Six sign the Treaty of Paris establishing the European Coal and Steel Community (ECSC)
1955	Messina negotiations for the creation of a European Common Market
1957	The Six sign the two Treaties of Rome establishing the European Economic Community (EEC) and the European Atomic Energy Community (EURATOM)
1961	UK, Ireland and Denmark apply for membership of the EEC
1962	Norway applies for membership of the EEC
1963	France (President de Gaulle) vetoes UK membership; other applicant states suspend applications
1964	Common Agricultural Policy (CAP) comes into effect
1967	UK, Ireland, Denmark and Norway apply for membership of the EEC – but meet continued hostility from France (President de Gaulle)
	The EEC is merged with the ECSC and EURATOM to form a single European Community (EC)
1970	EC membership negotiations open with UK, Ireland, Denmark and Norway
1972	Treaties of Accession signed between the EC and the four applicant countries
	The people of Norway reject membership in a referendum
1973	The Six became Nine as the UK, Ireland and Denmark become members of the EC
1974	UK seeks 'renegotiation' of terms of entry
1975	Referendum in the UK votes in favour of continued EC membership
	Greece applies for membership
1977	Portugal and Spain apply for membership
1979	European Monetary System (EMS) established
	First direct elections to the European Parliament
	Dublin summit: Margaret Thatcher demands 'our money back'
1980	Provisional solution found to the problem of the UK's budgetary contribution as terms for a rebate are agreed
1981	The Nine became Ten as Greece joins the EC
1984	Second direct elections to the European Parliament
	Agreement reached on the UK's budgetary contribution
1985	Jacques Delors becomes President of the European Commission
1985	'Project 1992' – a plan to remove some 300 barriers to the creation of an internal market – is agreed. The required Treaty amendments become known as the Single European Act
1986	The Ten become Twelve as Spain and Portugal join the EC
1987	Turkey applies for membership
	The Single European Act (SEA) comes into force
1989	Third direct election to the European Parliament
	Austria applies for membership
	Fall of the Berlin Wall – collapse of Communism in Eastern Europe
1990	Madrid summit approves principle of three-stage move to economic and monetary union (EMU)
	Cyprus and Malta apply for membership
	East Germany becomes part of the EC as consequence of German reunification
1991	Sweden applies for membership
	Agreement reached on the future establishment of the European Economic Area (EEA)
	Maastricht summit – agreement reached on a Treaty on European Union including arrangements for EMU with a single currency 'by 1999'
1992	Finland applies for membership
	Switzerland applies for membership
	Denmark rejects Maastricht Treaty in a referendum
	Switzerland rejects the EEA in a referendum
1993	Denmark accepts Maastricht Treaty in a second referendum
	Maastricht Treaty comes into force – the EC becomes the European Union (EU)
1994	The EEA comes into being
	Fourth direct elections to the European Parliament
	Norway rejects membership of the EU in a national referendum

Figure 18.2 *continued*

1995	The Twelve become Fifteen as Austria, Finland and Sweden join the EU
	Jacques Santer becomes President of the European Commission
	EUROPOL established
	First EU Ombudsman (Jacob Söderman) appointed
	Bulgaria, Estonia, Latvia, Lithuania, Romania and Slovakia apply for membership
1996	Czech Republic applies for membership
	Slovenia applies for membership
1997	Treaty of Amsterdam agreed
	European Commission launches 'Agenda 2000' including plans to take in six applicant countries and make key spending reforms
1998	Brussels summit determines founding members of the single currency (all but UK, Denmark, Sweden and Greece)
	Win Dusenberg named as the first President of the European Central Bank (ECB)
1999	EMU launched
	Fifth direct elections to the European Parliament
2002	Euro notes and coins scheduled to enter circulation. Old currencies of participating countries disappear

Since that time Britain's membership of the European Union has not been seriously in doubt in the sense that British withdrawal is not considered to be a serious option any longer, even by those who have remained or become hostile to the current arrangements. However, there have been long-lasting battles by the British Government – especially during Margaret Thatcher's first Administration from 1979 to 1983 – further to improve the terms of membership, notably in relation to the working of the Common Agricultural Policy (CAP) and the size of Britain's net contribution to the European Budget. By the mid-1980s the 'British Question' seemed to have been more or less resolved, although Margaret Thatcher was always prepared to fight Britain's corner in the process of European decision making. Nevertheless it was also Margaret Thatcher who agreed to an extensive revision of the European Treaties which resulted in the 1986 Single European Act .

Things changed yet again in a number of significant ways from the late 1980s. *First*, the development and destiny of the European Union was greatly influenced by the disintegration of the Soviet Union (1989–91), the end of the Cold War and the reunification of Germany (1990). These great events helped to trigger the further enlargement of the European Union to the north and the east to include Austria, Finland and Sweden (but not Norway which once again rejected entry in a referendum in 1994). It also opened the way for the European Union to be enlarged beyond the year 2000 to include the more developed of the former Communist states in Eastern Europe, namely Poland, Hungary, the Czech Republic, and Slovenia (see Figure 18.3).

Secondly, the member states of the European Union (with the notable exception at the time of Britain and possibly Denmark) came to accept the need to 'deepen' the process of economic and political integration before, or at any rate in parallel with, the next phase in the process of enlargement. This European vocation was enshrined in the 1992 Treaty of Maastricht, especially those sections of it which provided for the creation of Economic and Monetary Union by 1999 at the latest, and in the 1997 Treaty of Amsterdam.

Thirdly, the peoples of the various member states (and indeed some of the applicant states) clearly became more cynical and disenchanted with the whole 'European project'. This meant that the political elite on the Continent (but not necessarily in Britain) became

Figure 18.3 The European Union prospects of enlargement

INTO THE NEW MILLENIUM (c 2000)

16 Cyprus† (1990)
17 Czech Republic† (1996)
18 Estonia† (1995)
19 Hungary† (1994)
20 Poland† (1994)
21 Slovenia† (1996)

AND ON FROM THERE

22 Bulgaria† (1995)
23 Latvia† (1995)
24 Lithuania† (1995)
25 Romania† (1995)
26 Slovakia† (1995)

OTHER POTENTIAL MEMBERS

27 Albania
28 Iceland
29 Malta (1990)²
30 Norway† (1962–63, 1967–72, 1993–94)
31 Switzerland† (1992)³
32 Turkey† (1987)

† Have formally applied to join (Date of application)
1 East Germany entered the EU as part of a united
  Germany in 1990
2 Not currently (1997) being proceeded with
3 Not currently (1997) being proceeded with

dangerously detached from the views and feelings of the various peoples whom they presumed to lead. However, the younger generation of political leaders in Europe appeared not so sentimental about the unalloyed value of closer and deeper European unity and strong campaigns were fought – for example in France (a key country in the whole issue) – against the conventional wisdom. In Britain, whereas the Conservative Party became markedly more 'Euro-sceptic', the Labour Party adopted an increasingly pro-European posture – although elements within the party were undoubtedly hostile to such an approach; only the Liberal Democrats remained consistently federalist and pro-European.

During the 1997 General Election campaign the Conservative Party appeared increasingly divided over the issue of Britain's position within the European Union and notably on the issue of British participation in a Single European currency. These divisions contributed, along with other factors, to the rout of the Conservative Party at the polls and the election of a Labour Government. From the outset the Labour Government has been committed to playing a 'leading role' in Europe, and has been positive about British participation in economic and monetary union at some time in the new century, once the idea has the clear approval of the British people.

18.2 Legal and constitutional implications

Britain's membership of the European Union has profound legal and constitutional implications which have become increasingly apparent as the member states have continued to enhance the degree of integration with one another. Yet it is fair to say that the problems posed by the incursion of European law into Britain should have been clear from the very beginning when Parliament debated Britain's entry into the European Community in 1971–72. The fact that many MPs and others may not have fully realised what they were letting themselves and subsequent generations in for owed a good deal to the fact that the then Conservative Government, in its understandable wish to secure the approval of Parliament for Britain's entry, was less than completely honest (or significantly underestimated) the longer term legal and constitutional implications of this great European adventure.[3]

Section 2 (1) of the 1972 European Communities Act made provision for European law to take direct effect in the United Kingdom.[4] It provided for the European Treaties and European legislation under the Treaties to take direct effect in Britain. It also included *future* European law and it made clear that European, rather than British, law would determine whether or not a particular provision was directly effective in Britain. Section 2 (2) of the Act made provision for the implementation of European law by means of subordinate British legislation at Westminster. However, in section 2 (1) it had been made clear that such Statutory Instruments could *not* be used in four specific areas which would require primary legislation: the imposition of new or increased taxation, the creation of new serious criminal offences, retrospective legislation, and sub-delegated legislation. Section 2 (4) determined that both past and future Acts of Parliament should be subordinate to European law in those areas where a conflict might arise. This was reinforced by Section 3 (1) which declared that any question about the effect of European law in Britain should be decided in accordance with the principles of any relevant ruling of the European Court of Justice (ECJ), the most notable of which is the supremacy of European law over national law in all the member states. Thus all these interlocking and mutually reinforcing sections of the 1972 European Communities Act served to establish the supremacy of European law over national law, although it was an Act of Parliament at Westminster which made this possible in Britain.

Over the years rulings of the European Court of Justice (ECJ) have impacted on Britain in a variety of areas including, for example, fishing rights, compensation to victims of breaches of EU law, anti-terrorism laws, pension age and employment rights and the sale by supermarkets and discount stores of designer goods imported into Europe without the brand owners' consent. These are all examples of rulings which have been seen as having gone against the wishes of the British Government, and as a consequence the Court has been criticised by Euro-sceptics as seeking to extend the jurisdiction of the European Union without the explicit authority of the member states. It should, however, be noted that the Government of the United Kingdom has in fact had only a small number of direct actions brought against it, just 41 by 1998 (2.82 per cent of all direct actions brought against member states; 1.1 per cent of all direct actions), and the United Kingdom has sought a ruling in 245 cases (6.73 per cent of all references for a preliminary ruling). It is also not the case that the Court's rulings always go against the British. For example, it was following a ruling of the Court that Italy was obliged to reduce taxes imposed on luxury cars, taxes which were estimated to have been costing Britain some £80 million annually in lost exports. Similarly, it was following a ruling of the Court that Spain was obliged to change its rules on food additives which opened a market in Spain for British chewing gum. A balanced interpretation of the role of the ECJ should take account of all these factors.

Important features

The most important features of the relationship between European law and national law in Britain are the direct effect of European law in the British Courts, the supremacy of European law over national law if and when the two conflict, and the procedures by which European law is enforced in Britain and the other member states. It is important to be clear about the meaning and implications of these features and we shall deal with each one in turn.

The *concept of direct effect* means that a provision of European law grants individual rights to citizens in Britain and the other member states which must be upheld by the national Courts. This principle was clarified for the first time in the *1962 Van Gend en Loos case*, when it was established that the European Court may legitimately determine that a given provision of European law is directly effective.[5] This principle may sound relatively simple, but, as enunciated by the European Court ever since 1962, it has not accorded very easily with the traditional view of such matters in Britain. In the leading case just mentioned the European Court held that the European institutions are 'endowed with sovereign rights, the exercise of which affects member states and their citizens'. It also declared that Member States had 'limited their sovereign rights, albeit within limited fields' and that European law can confer rights on individuals 'which become part of their legal heritage'. These were bold assertions on the part of the European Court which the passage of time has since done nothing to dispel. Yet they are some way removed from the theoretical principle of British law which holds that European legislation is applicable in Britain only because the 1972 European Communities Act delegated powers to the European Union to legislate for the United Kingdom in certain designated areas covered by the European Treaties.

The *supremacy of European law* means that a directly effective provision of European law always prevails over a provision of national law, irrespective of whether the former was agreed before or after the latter. The *1977 Simmenthal case* provided a good example of this.[6] In this leading case the Italian authorities had argued that Italian national law should prevail, because it had been passed *after* the two relevant European regulations, and that Italian law should stand until such time as its conflict with European law had been declared unconstitutional by the Italian Constitutional Court. When the matter was referred to the European Court, the latter held that the national Court had a duty to give full effect to European law and not to apply any conflicting national provisions, even if these were adopted subsequently. It also held that there should be no question of waiting for national law to be set aside by a national constitutional Court or a national Legislature before accepting the supremacy of European law. However, the European Court ruling was limited to Treaty provisions and the directly applicable measures of the European institutions. It did not state that conflicting national provisions were void, merely that they were inapplicable. Moreover, its ruling was concerned not only with conflicting national law, but also with all national laws which 'encroach upon the field within which the Community exercises its legislative power'.

It can be seen from this and other judgements of the European Court that European law prevails over national law in all cases where the former has direct effect, as long as the legal right contained in a given European instrument is invoked against the recalcitrant member state. Indeed, the *1973 French Merchant Seamen case* demonstrated that there is a positive obligation upon member states to repeal national legislation which conflicts with European law, even if the latter is considered inapplicable by the national authorities.[7] Experience in the European Union has also shown that the powers of the member states can be limited or removed even where the conflict with European law is only indirect or potential. For example, under Articles 113 and 238 of the 1957 Rome Treaty the member states have lost the power to enter into commercial or association agreements with third countries, since these powers are explicitly reserved to the European Commission acting on behalf of the European Union as a whole. Equally, the *1978 Pigs Marketing Board case* demonstrated that in the field of the Common Agricultural Policy, if the European Commission has introduced a common market regime for a given farm product, the member states are precluded from adopting any national measures which might undermine or create exceptions to it.[8] The most significant confirmation of this principle was the *1991 Factortame case* when the European Court ruled that the 1988 Merchant Shipping Act was in breach of European law by preventing Spanish owned trawler companies from registering in Britain to take advantage of the British fishing quota under the terms of the Common Fisheries Policy. As a result of this decision, the British Government repealed the offending portions of the Act.

The *enforcement procedures for European law* are the third important feature of the relationship between European law and national law. There are two ways in which European law can be enforced against national Governments in the member states.

The first is through legal action taken by private individuals or firms in the national Courts which seeks to apply the doctrine of direct effect. For example, when the Irish Government imposed restrictions on fishing in Irish waters which were contrary to European law under the Common Fisheries Policy, a Dutch fisherman was able to invoke European law as a defence to a charge of illegal fishing.[9] Equally, when in 1977 the Ministry of Agriculture in Britain imposed a ban on the import of main crop potatoes, this was challenged by a Dutch potato exporter as contrary to European law.[10] In both cases the European Court upheld the position of the Dutch who had challenged national restrictions which were found to be contrary to European law.

The other way in which European law can be enforced against national Governments is by direct legal proceedings against the member state concerned. This can be done under Article 88 of the Paris Treaty (ECSC Treaty), Articles 169–171 of the Rome Treaty (EEC Treaty), and Articles 141–143 of the Euratom Treaty. The procedure is divided into two stages. In the first stage, the European Commission either delivers a 'Decision' under the ECSC Treaty which is binding and conclusive (unless the member state concerned wishes to challenge it in proceedings before the European Court) or it merely delivers a 'reasoned opinion' under the EEC and Euratom Treaties which is not binding. This means that if the member state concerned fails to comply, the European Commission can bring the matter before the European Court for definitive determination.

In the second stage, the European Court proceedings are not a review of the European Commission decision or reasoned opinion, but rather a fresh consideration of the case to establish whether or not a violation of the Treaties has occurred. If the European Court finds that the allegations are proved, it will give judgment against the offending member state. Under the ECSC Treaty this has the effect of confirming the European Commission decision which is binding and it opens the way for the imposition of sanctions against the offender if that proves to be necessary. Under the EEC and Euratom Treaties this takes the form of a declaration setting out how and why the offending member state has failed to fulfil its obligations under the relevant European Treaty. Although the European Court has no power to order a member state either to take or not to take a particular course of action and it cannot declare invalid any national legislation, the member state is obliged to terminate the violation found by the European Court.

Such enforcement procedures have been effective in most cases, even when member states have indulged in deliberate delaying tactics. This is largely because in the leading *Pig Producers case* in 1978, the European Court upheld the European Commission's application for an interim injunction to terminate a British subsidy scheme which had been designed by the British Government to help British pig producers compete against imports which were subsidised at European level. Together with a similar case at about the same time which was brought by the European Commission against Ireland for introducing fisheries conservation measures which were regarded as being contrary to European Treaty obligations, this meant that the principle of using interim measures against offending member states became established.[11] Such developments are evidence of the political nature of European jurisdiction. When deciding whether to grant an interim injunction to the European Commission, the European Court takes into account: (1) the chances of the proceedings being successful; (2) the extent to which the matter is urgent; and (3) such evidence as there may be of irreparable damage being done to the European Union if no judicial action is taken. In those rare cases when a Member State has deliberately sought to break European law and to defy the European Court, the issues have only been capable of resolution on a political basis, because it is upon *the continuing will to co-operate* that the satisfactory functioning of the European Union finally depends.

Principal problems

When Britain joined the European Community in 1973, it laid itself open to three principal legal and constitutional problems. The essential dilemma was vividly described by Lord Denning in 1979 when he referred to the threat from 'the flowing tide of Community law' and warned that 'we have to learn to become amphibious if we wish to keep our heads above water'.[12] In other words, as long as successive British Governments and Parliaments take the view that Britain's membership of the European Union is *on balance* beneficial to the interests of the country, the British will find themselves increasingly woven into the fabric of evolving European law. As this body of law is extended by agreement in the Council of Ministers into more areas of European activity, the real scope for autonomous action by Britain (or any other member state) will gradually diminish. Only a determined attempt to halt (and then perhaps to reverse) this secular trend in Europe will be able to make any real difference.

The first problem is that legal provision for Britain's membership of the European Community (now called the European Union) could not be made by means of a constitutional amendment – as happened in the case of Ireland for example – but had to be made by passing an Act of Parliament, in this case the 1972 European Communities Act. The reason for this was, of course, the well-rehearsed fact that Britain did not have, and still does not have, a codified constitution. We should therefore note the paradox that in Britain's case the legal means of providing for permanent membership of the European Community was the decidedly impermanent mechanism of an Act of Parliament which, by its very nature, can be amended or repealed at any time.

The second problem is that the British attitude towards international law is essentially dualist, which means that in Britain national and international law are regarded as being quite distinct. There never has been a general rule of law in Britain which allows Treaties to take effect within the British legal system without the essential enabling mechanism of an Act of Parliament. By contrast, in other European countries which have codified constitutions, such as France or Germany, international Treaties signed by their Governments take precedence over national law and have direct effect in their national jurisdictions without any requirement for enabling legislation as in Britain.

The third and most fundamental problem (which really underpins the first two) is the hallowed British constitutional principle of Parliamentary supremacy. This means that there is no legal authority superior to Parliament in the United Kingdom and that any Parliament can overturn the laws of its predecessors – in other words, no Parliament can bind it successors. *In theory,* this peculiarity of the British constitution means that Parliamentary supremacy and the primacy of European law in the areas covered by the European Treaties are fundamentally incompatible. *In practice*, the circle has been squared by the doctrine contained in the 1972 European Communities Act which holds – in Section 2 (1) in particular – that Parliament evidently *intended* that all Acts of Parliament, whether before or after that Act, *should* be subordinate to European law in those areas of jurisdiction covered by the European Treaties and subsequently interpreted by the European Court.

On the face of things, this resolution of the problem seems to be inconsistent with the rule that no British Parliament can bind its successors and the possibility that a future British Parliament might pass an Act which defied European law. Yet in reality such an acute constitutional difficulty is unlikely to arise for two important reasons. *First*, if a future Parliament at Westminster were determined to pass a new law which flouted established European law, it would probably do so only in circumstances in which a British Government was actively considering British withdrawal from part or all of Britain's legal obligations to the European Union – a situation which does not seem very likely to materialise unless a very different view is taken of fundamental British national interests in future. *Second*, as long as the Government of the day with the support of a majority in the House of Commons values continued British membership more than partial or complete withdrawal, then the situation will not arise in the first place and Britain will continue to comply with its obligations under European law. Indeed, Section 2 (4) of the 1972 European Communities Act makes it clear that Parliament at Westminster is presumed *not* to intend any future statute to conflict with, still less override, any provisions of European law. In other words, as long as successive British Governments, backed by the British Parliament, *choose* to remain in the European Union, European law will be recognised as superior to national law in Britain in the areas covered by the European Treaties.

Since the 1992 Treaty of Maastricht and the debates in Parliament and elsewhere about its legal and constitutional implications, and on through the negotiation and subsequent ratification of the 1997 Treaty of Amsterdam, there has been deep and continuing disagreement in Britain and, to a lesser extent, in the other member states of the European Union about the pace and direction of European integration. All pro-Europeans on the Continent and in Britain have appeared to be comfortable with Article A of the Common Provisions of the Maastricht Treaty which stated that 'this Treaty marks a new stage in the process of creating an ever closer union among the peoples of Europe in which decisions are taken as closely as possible to the citizen'. The clear implication of this majority point of view is that the doctrine of *subsidiarity*, which is spelt out in Article 3 (b) of the Treaty, should prevail. This made it clear that new competences should be allocated to the supranational level in the European Union 'only if and in so far as the objectives of the proposed action cannot be sufficiently achieved by the member states and can therefore, by reason of the scale or effects of the proposed action, be better achieved by the Community'. In practice, the application of this doctrine has already led to the repatriation to the member states of a number of competences previously claimed or exercised by the European institutions and has proved attractive to Germany and other member states where national constitutions are explicitly federal in character.

On the other hand, the so-called 'Euro-sceptics' in Britain and, to a lesser extent, in some other member states such as France and Denmark, regard these words in the Treaty as little more than window-dressing designed to reassure those people within the European Union who feel uncomfortable with the integrationist methods and potentially federalist destiny of the European project. Such people have pointed out that, in the event of constitutional dispute on these matters, it is ultimately the

European Court which will arbitrate, and they argue that its record over many years shows a clear institutional and philosophical bias in favour of defending the *acquis communautaire* (the body of European law already established) and advancing the interests of the other supranational institutions of the European Union – notably the European Commission and the European Parliament. For these reasons they argue that cumulative European case law is likely to favour the cause of even closer European integration and all who put their faith in the doctrine of subsidiarity as the best way of limiting the ambitions of those who seek 'an ever-closer union' are likely to be bitterly disappointed.

18.3 Political and institutional impact

The political and institutional impact of Britain's membership of the European Union has already been significant and seems likely to become more significant in future. Ever since Britain's entry into the European Community (as it was then called) in 1973, the country has been involved to an increasing extent in the process of European integration. This process has been well described by Sir Michael Butler, a former UK Permanent Representative at the European institutions in Brussels, as 'primarily about solving detailed, complicated and usually technical problems by consensus in a political framework which makes it extremely difficult for the national Governments to do other than agree in the end'.[13] It is this apparent irreversibility of European integration which has been both the secret of its success so far and the main cause for concern among those in Britain and some other member states who wish to limit, or even reverse, the process in future. Certainly the drive towards 'an ever closer union of the European peoples' (in the words of the Treaty of Rome) seems to have posed greater political and institutional problems for Britain than for the other member states. See Figure 18.4 for an outline of the decision-making process within the European Union.

Impact on Ministers

The impact of Britain's membership of the European Union has been felt first and foremost in the sphere of central Government. This is because Ministers in all British Governments have had to play an active part in the process of European decision making. From the beginning this has involved Departmental Ministers representing Britain and defending British national interests in the Council of Ministers, whether the General Affairs Council composed of Foreign Ministers or the specific 'subject' Councils, such as Agriculture, Finance, Transport or the Environment, depending upon the particular policy area under discussion. Since 1974 it has also involved the Prime Minister of the day participating in what has come to be known as 'the European Council' with the other heads of Government and the President of the European Commission. Such 'summit meetings' are now held twice a year under the chairmanship of whichever member state holds the Presidency of the European Union for the relevant six-month period. The purpose of these meetings has been to provide renewed impetus for the development of the European Union and on a number of occasions this is what has been achieved.

Figure 18.4 The European decision-making process

COURT OF JUSTICE

15 JUDGES
9 ADVOCATES-GENERAL

COURT OF
FIRST INSTANCE

15 MEMBERS
Ensures that EU law
is interpreted and
applied correctly

COURT OF AUDITORS

15 MEMBERS
Checks accounts
against authorised
budget

THE EUROPEAN COUNCIL
Heads of Government
Foreign ministers
President of the commission
Vice president of the commission

COUNCIL OF MINISTERS

Ⓑ

3
7
10
ⱯENDS: 11   4

62 votes
constitute
a majority

7   4A   6A

THE COMMISSION

Ⓐ

BEGINS 1

3

▼ 2
26 Directorates General

4D   6D

COMMITTEE OF
PERMANENT
REPRESENTATIVES
(COREPER)

Ambassadors of each
member state and national
civil servants

4B   6B

▼ 4C   Working   ▼ 6C
groups

ECONOMIC AND
SOCIAL COMMITTEE
(ESC)

5   Ⓓ   5

COMMITTEE OF
THE REGIONS
(COR)

Ⓔ   5
5

EUROPEAN
PARLIAMENT

5 and 9 Ⓒ   5

8A   4A

▼ 8B   Committees   ▼ 4B

NATIONAL
GOVERNMENTS   Appoints

NATIONAL
PARLIAMENTS

Elects

Elects

Figure 18.4 continued

(A) THE COMMISSION

Jacques Santer	**Luxembourg**	President
Martin Bangemann	**Germany**	Industrial policy
Ritt Bjerregaard	**Denmark**	Environment
Emma Bonino	**Italy**	Fish, consumers
Sir Leon Brittan	**UK**	Trade, Asia, US
Hans van der Broek	**Netherlands**	Foreign policy, Eastern Europe
Edith Cresson	**France**	Research, training
Joao de Deus Pinherio	**Portugal**	Africa, Caribbean, Pacific
Franz Fischler	**Austria**	Agriculture
Padraig Flynn	**Ireland**	Social policy
Antita Gradin	**Sweden**	Immigration, interior policy
Neil Kinnock	**UK**	Transport
Erkki Liikanen	**Finland**	Budget
Manuel Marin	**Spain**	Mediterranean, Latin America
Mario Monti	**Italy**	Internal market
Marcelino Oreja	**Spain**	Institutional affairs
Christos Papoutsis	**Greece**	Energy
Yves-Thibault de Silguy	**France**	Economic and Monetary affairs
Karel van Miert	**Belgium**	Competition policy
Monika Wulf-Mathies	**German**y	Regional policy

(B) THE COUNCIL OF MINISTERS

Germany/France/Italy/ United Kingdom	Each have 10 votes
Spain	Has 8 votes
Belgium/Greece/ Netherlands/Portugal	Each have 5 votes
Austria/Sweden	Each have 4 votes
Denmark/Finland/Ireland	Each have 3 votes
Luxembourg	Has 2 votes
Total	87 votes

(C) THE EUROPEAN PARLIAMENT

Germany	99
France/Italy/United Kingdom	87 each
Spain	65
Netherlands	31
Belgium/Greece/Portugal	25 each
Sweden	22
Austria	21
Denmark/Finland	16 each
Ireland	15
Luxembourg	6
Total MEPs	626

(D) ECONOMIC AND SOCIAL COMMITTEE

France/Germany/Italy/ United Kingdom	24 members each
Spain	21 members
Austria/Belgium/Greece/ Netherlands/Portugal/ Sweden	12 members each
Denmark/Finland/Ireland	9 members each
Luxembourg	6 members
TOTAL MEMBERSHIP	222

(E) COMMITTEE OF THE REGIONS

France/Germany/Italy/ United Kingdom	24 members each
Spain	21 members
Austria/Belgium/Greece/ Netherlands/Portugal/ Sweden	12 members each
Denmark/Finland/Ireland	9 members each
Luxembourg	6 members
TOTAL MEMBERSHIP	222

The most obvious consequence for Ministers of all these meetings has been the growing amount of time which they have had to devote to them as the sphere of European competence has been extended by agreement into more areas of policy. For example, there was no mention of environmental policy in the 1957 Treaty of Rome, since at that time there was no general recognition of the importance of acting at European level to deal with environmental problems, whereas nowadays these matters are considered to be significant European concerns. Equally, the 1992 Treaty of Maastricht enshrined an agreement by all the member states (except Britain and Denmark which reserved their national positions) to proceed in stages towards Economic and Monetary Union based upon a single European currency administered and safeguarded by a European Central Bank by 1999 at the latest.

The traditional method of decision making in the Council of Ministers has been to continue the discussion of difficult issues, such as the reform of the Common Agricultural Policy or the level of each country's net contribution to the European Budget, until the combined effects of physical exhaustion and the spirit of compromise emerge and combine to make a European decision possible. This so-called 'Community method' has not only contributed to the number and duration of meetings, and as a result the length of time Ministers are obliged to devote to European business, but also has imposed great strains upon Ministers themselves.

It is also important to note that there have been significant changes in the rules of the game since 1986 when the Single European Act became law in all the member states. This important advance in European decision-making procedures involved the introduction of qualified majority voting in the Council of Ministers on all issues to do with realising the Single European Market – with the exception of taxation, immigration, and workers' employment rights, which were reserved for decision making by unanimity. This means that British Ministers – like Ministers from other member states – can find themselves outvoted when the Council of Ministers takes decisions by qualified majority, unless a blocking minority can be assembled – namely 26 votes out of a total of 87 votes.[14]

On the other hand, it is well to remember that qualified majority voting can, and often has, worked in Britain's favour, so the rules of the game cut both ways. For example, it would have been much more difficult to make speedy progress with implementing the Single European Act if the policy had remained subject to decision making by consensus or unanimity. Although there is nearly always considerable pressure to find a compromise even in the most intractable disputes in the Council of Ministers, national Governments sometimes find it quite convenient to be outvoted if they have significant problems with public opinion in their own countries, but nevertheless recognise privately that the decision taken is the right one in the interests of Europe as a whole.

Impact on civil servants

The impact upon civil servants has probably been even greater than the impact upon Ministers. This is because Britain's membership of the European Union has spawned a vast network of bureaucratic relationships between Whitehall and the European institutions in Brussels, Luxembourg, and Strasbourg – as well as complicated bilateral relations between the various national capitals. Within Whitehall itself it has been necessary for the Foreign Office and the Cabinet Office to co-ordinate the work of all the various Departments involved in the European decision-making process. Those civil servants, who are involved in actual or potential issues of European policy, spend a good deal of their time commuting to and from Brussels for meetings with their counterparts from the other national capitals. Some of them are also stationed at the UK Permanent Delegation in Brussels (UKREP for short) where they have an essential role to play in liaising with the European institutions and the other national delegations. They are also involved in preparing the British Government's position at meetings of the Council of Ministers and in assisting their sponsoring Departments in Whitehall. In this way they carry forward the process of permanent dialogue between the European institutions and the British and other Governments of the member states.

In view of the growing volume of European legislation emanating from the institutions in Brussels, civil servants in those Departments particularly involved in European policy have had to spend an increasing amount of their time upon the negotiation and subsequent implementation of European law. For example, the Ministry of Agriculture spends probably three-quarters of its official time on the negotiation and enforcement of the Common Agricultural Policy in Britain, while the Departments of Trade and Industry, Environment, Transport and the Regions, and Education and Employment are also among those busiest with European regulations and directives. Even such proud and traditionally independent Departments as the Treasury and the Home Office have been increasingly drawn into the process of European policy making and law enforcement.

In addition, a growing proportion of the issues considered by the Cabinet and its committees has a European dimension of one kind or another, while Whitehall preparation for the meetings of the European Council every six months often involves strenuous work in 10 Downing Street, the Cabinet Office, the Foreign Office and many other Departments. This is, of course, particularly so when it is the turn for the British Presidency – as was the position during the first six months of 1998. Consequently, it can be argued that the administrative process of the European Union has affected the Civil Service more than any other component of the British political system. This characteristic is one of the principal reasons for the continuing 'democratic deficit' in what is still a rather bureaucratic European Union.

Impact on Parliament

The impact on Parliament of Britain's membership of the European Union has been emphasised by the anti-Europeans and the 'Euro-sceptics' as perhaps the most serious and adverse of all the negative consequences flowing from the original decision to enter the European Community taken by Parliament in October 1971. This argument was put with great conviction at Westminster in 1992–93 when the legislation designed to give legal effect to the Maastricht Treaty in Britain was fought by the Euro-sceptics every inch of the way. Yet the suspicion remains that the doom-laden forecast that Parliament at Westminster (and the other national Parliaments) will be reduced to the status of County Councils has been exaggerated for propaganda effect. Indeed, some recent political developments in the European Union have foreshadowed a revived role for national Parliaments. For example, the 1997 Treaty of Amsterdam encouraged national Parliaments to take a closer interest in European Union matters by introducing a minimum period of six weeks within which national Parliaments are able to make their views known on proposals before the Council of Ministers. Another aspect of this is the idea that a European Second Chamber, comprising members from each national Parliament, should be created, although it is by no means certain that this idea will have appeal in many other member states.

Nevertheless both the proponents and the opponents of further political integration within the European Union have recognised that there are a number of real problems, both procedural and substantial, which face the national Parliaments as they endeavour to come to terms with institutional developments at European level. The fundamental difficulties were well expressed in a 1989 Procedure Committee Report which reminded the House of Commons that 'European legislation is initiated almost exclusively by an executive organisation (the European Commission) with which the UK Parliament has no formal relationship and over which it has no direct control'.[15] This means, as the Report went on to explain, that 'while the House may, by changes in its own internal procedures, find ways of bringing to bear more efficiently such authority as it retains over European legislation, it cannot by such means increase its authority or seek to claw back powers which have been ceded by Treaty'. The report concluded that 'the House has never realistically expected to exercise total accountability in relation to Ministers' prospective actions in the Council of Ministers, although it has always demanded explanations and justifications after the event'. In other words, Members of the House of Commons realise that they can no longer exercise much democratic control over political developments in the European Union *before* the event, although they can retain some influence on British Ministers and insist upon Parliamentary accountability *after* the event. This means that in circumstances of qualified majority voting, in particular, it is the European Parliament, rather than any national Parliament, which is better equipped under European law to exercise at least some effective democratic control.

When considering these rather bleak prospects for Parliament at Westminster and the other national Parliaments in the European Union, it is as well to remember that Ministers in Britain have long been able to conclude Treaties without prior Parliamentary approval by exercising the powers of the Royal prerogative on behalf of the Crown – hence the formal appellation 'Her Majesty's Government'. Thus the largely retrospective nature of Parliamentary control in Britain in relation to developments in the European Union is no different to the limited and retrospective power which MPs are able to exert over Ministers acting within national jurisdiction. However, whereas Parliament at Westminster has long claimed to have supreme jurisdiction over British national laws, it has already had to share jurisdiction with the European Parliament (and to some extent with the other national Parliaments) in the sphere of European legislation introduced under the European Treaties. Indeed, in many respects Parliament at Westminster has no effective role in those areas of legislation where European law takes direct effect (for example, the Common Agricultural Policy), and only a subordinate role in those areas where following the 1997 Treaty of Amsterdam the European Parliament has acquired powers of co-decision with the Council of Ministers at certain stages of the European legislative process.[16]

In these circumstances there are a number of procedural and other problems for Parliament at Westminster which have been identified by observers and practitioners alike. *First,* there is the volume of European legislation which is hard for the House of Commons to deal with properly within the constraints of an already congested legislative timetable. Attempts have been made to address this problem via the European Legislation Select Committee which sifts draft European proposals for legislation and recommends some for debate by the House as a whole, and more recently via two European Standing Committees to which many European proposals are now referred in order to relieve pressure on the chamber itself. In many ways the House of Commons seems to have taken some procedural lessons from the House of Lords where these matters have been handled better via a powerful European Communities Committee and its various sub-committees.[17] The size of the problem has been growing with the increasing scope of European legislation. However, with the determination to repatriate some European competences to the member states – as expressed in both the 1992 Maastricht Treaty and the 1997 Treaty of Amsterdam – it may be that this problem of European legislative overload on national Parliaments will ease in the future. Within the United Kingdom the process of devolution may help in this regard as the Scottish Parliament has been given the power to scrutinise legislative proposals eminating from the European Union.

Secondly, there has been the problem of the *attitude* of a large number of British MPs towards European legislation from Brussels. Many MPs, especially in the Conservative Party, bemoan the fact that Westminster is not equipped to deal with this extra legislation, but are equally not prepared to countenance further increases in the powers of the European Parliament which would be the most logical way to close the so-called 'democratic deficit'. The result is that when Westminster does get a chance to debate European legislation, the discussion takes place in clouds of resentment and recrimination often during ill-attended debates after 10.00 p.m. This attitudinal problem will not really be alleviated until more constructive relationships evolve between the two main levels of democratic representation in Europe, although the two European Standing Committees which meet to discuss European proposals on Wednesday mornings at Westminster may assist in resolving some of the problems.

The third and most serious problem for Parliament, which has arisen since the 1986 Single European Act – extended in the 1997 Treaty of Amsterdam – is that the use of qualified majority voting in the Council of Ministers has reduced the areas in which any member state can veto decisions at European level. This development has been particularly disturbing for the 'Euro-sceptics', but it has not exactly delighted the great ballast of Parliamentary opinion at Westminster either. There is now widespread concern among MPs in all parties at Westminster that European developments will continue to erode the power and position of national Parliaments, unless the latter exert themselves in a concerted campaign to regain some of the ground which has been lost. However, there have been only limited signs that this view held by many British MPs is shared by their counterparts in the other member states.

Whereas the power of Parliament at Westminster in relation to European legislation has been relatively weak and in decline, the European Parliament has come to wield more power than before in the European legislative process. Originally, the Treaty of Rome gave the Parliament only a consultative role, allowing the Commission to propose and the Council of Ministers to decide legislation. Subsequent Treaties – the 1986 Single European Act, the 1992 Treaty of Maastricht and the 1997 Treaty of Amsterdam – have extended Parliament's influence via both the 'co-operation precedure' and the 'co-decision procedure' so that the Parliament and the Council now share the power of decision in a large number of areas. In short, once the Council of Ministers has reached a common position by qualified majority, the European Parliament has the power to reject this common position or propose amendments to it which, if then adopted by the European Commission (which made the original proposal for legislation), can only be amended subsequently by the Council of Ministers on a basis of unanimity. The general effect of this procedure so far has been to cause the European Commission to modify its original proposals in perhaps one-third of all cases when the European Parliament has used this power.

Impact on the political system

It is clear that Britain's membership of the European Union has had a significant impact on the British political system in a number of other ways. This has been manifest in nearly all areas of political activity to a greater or lesser extent, although it has obviously been concentrated in the areas of European legal competence – such as agriculture and external trade. Figure 18.5 shows the areas and extent of European involvement and legal competence. In these circumstances it is fair to say that the evolving European Union provides the economic, political and institutional context within which many of the decisions of British national life are taken. Unless a future British Government backed by a future British Parliament (and probably with the backing of another referendum) were to take Britain out of the European Union, Britain's membership of it (even on a modified basis) is likely to play an increasingly influential part in the lives and well-being of the British people.

In the first place, British political parties are now considerably affected by the need to conduct politics not just at a local and national level, but also at a European level in the European Parliament and the various trans-national political groupings in which they play a part. For example, following the 1994 Elections to the European Parliament, the Labour Party became the largest national component in its transnational grouping (the Socialist International), whereas the Conservative Party is only loosely associated with the Christian Democratic Group in the European Parliament and plays only a limited role in its trans-national political grouping (the European People's Party). For these and other reasons the Labour Party came to appear more 'European' than the Conservative Party, although the Liberal Democrats can justifiably claim to represent the most consistently pro-European tendency in British politics.

Secondly, the development of the European Union is having a powerful influence on pressure groups in Britain and other member states and increasingly on the private sector in general. As more key decisions of interest to the private sector are taken by European institutions rather than national Governments and national Parliaments, more power has levitated to the European level. For example, British farmers are now at least as keen to lobby the European Commission and the European Parliament via their transnational European organisation COPA (Comité d'Organisations de Producteurs Agricoles) as they are to lobby the Ministry of Agriculture and Parliament at Westminster via the National Farmers' Union and other national pressure groups. This is because they know that most of the key decisions which affect their livelihood – for example, on BSE, guaranteed farm prices and agricultural levies – are taken at European level rather than national level. Similar conclusions have also been drawn in the manufacturing and industrial sectors as substantial progress has been made towards the completion of the Single European Market with its common rules and obligations for the entire European Union, and in the financial sector as most of the European Union moves towards a Single Currency.

Figure 18.5 Areas and extent of European involvement and legal competence

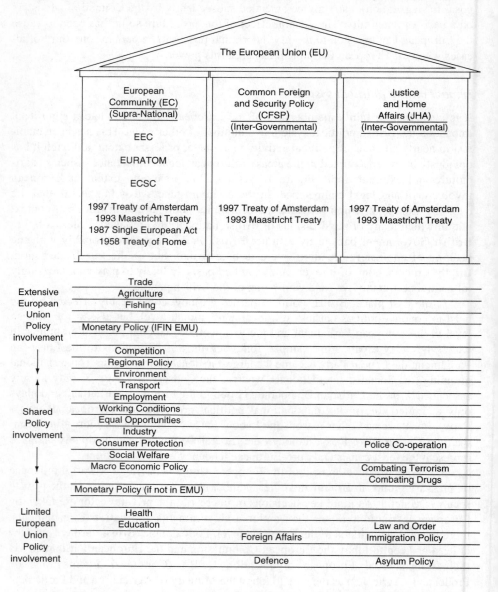

Thirdly, the working of the European Union is having a growing impact on local and sub-national Government in Britain and all the other member states. Increasingly, local Authorities in Britain are looking to the European institutions for financial assistance and political support. For example, the large conurbations and outlying regions of the United Kingdom are now very interested in the fruits of the European Social and Regional Funds within the European Budget. They have therefore lobbied persistently and effectively to get their share of European transfer payments under these headings.

Equally, the nationalist parties in Scotland, Wales and Northern Ireland see action at European level as one of their best chances of developing political counterweights to the influence of English central Government and Parliamentarians in London whom they regard as mainly unsympathetic to their claims for 'national' independence. It is not surprising that the Scottish Nationalists have adopted the idea of an independent Scotland within Europe as their party's slogan.[18]

Fourthly, it is becoming increasingly true that the media, and hence public opinion, in Britain are affected by Britain's membership of the European Union. Of course, the extent of this influence fluctuates according to the turn of events. Sometimes there is intense media interest in European issues, as there has been when the British Government has been strongly at odds with its European partners over 'mad-cow disease' or fishing for example, or when 'the European issue' has caused deep and bitter divisions within the political parties – as happened with the Conservative Euro-rebels when they had the party whip withdrawn from them between December 1994 and April 1995. At other times European issues have taken second place to apparently more pressing national or local preoccupations. Yet as the world has come to seem smaller and as decisions taken in a European framework or by European institutions have come to affect people's lives more and more, public awareness of the costs and benefits of being in the European Union seems to have risen and the whole context of British politics seems to have been enlarged.

Obviously, this raised European consciousness in Britain has affected some sections of society more than others. For example, those who travel on behalf of British companies, those with professional contacts on the Continent and most of the internationally mobile younger generation seem to take Britain's membership of the European Union very much for granted and see themselves as much as 'Europeans' as English, Welsh, Scottish, or Northern Irish. On the other hand, it must be admitted that many of the older sections of the British population are still suspicious or resentful of 'Europe' and will take a great deal of persuading that anything good can come out of the European institutions. It will still take a considerable time before British people can go anywhere else in Europe and, in Churchill's words, say with conviction: 'here I feel at home'.

18.4 Possible future developments

It is difficult to foresee how the European Union will develop in the years ahead and almost as difficult to predict how Britain and its political institutions will respond to the challenges involved. Yet there are a few developments already discernible which seem likely to be among the main driving forces of European integration into the new century and beyond, while there are also some divisive issues which could be factors for disintegration.

Main driving forces

The *first* and most obvious driving force in the European Union both now and in the future is the determination of firms and individuals in the private sector to take advantage of the economic and commercial opportunities offered by the increasingly unified European Single Market of, currently, some 370 million people. In this sense it is the private sector which is likely to lead the member states in further moves towards European integration. National authorities and public sector organisations which depend on them are more likely to be relatively unenthusiastic and to lag behind, usually seeking to validate but sometimes trying to obstruct further developments in a supranational direction.

The best examples of this process of private sector integration are to be found in the activities of large companies, whether based within the European Union or outside, which exert pressure in their own corporate interests upon the member states and the European institutions to reach agreement on a growing web of common rules, standards and obligations which will enable them to exploit the full potential of the European Single Market. The real pace-setters will continue to be the likes of IBM and General Motors, Siemens and GEC, Nomura and Nissan, Deutschebank and Rhone Poulenc, Phillips and Fiat – to name but a few of the most prominent examples. However, such large companies are increasingly joined by a myriad of small and medium sized companies which are finding that they too can exploit valuable niches and opportunities in the large single market. By pursuing their own corporate interests, they are driving forward the whole process of European integration.

A *second* and equally significant driving force is likely to be the power of the trans-national trade union confederations once they begin to act effectively to advance the interests of organised labour at European level. Powerful national trade unions, such as IG Metal in Germany or UNISON in Britain, will forge alliances with their counterparts in other member states and create supranational representative bodies in order to increase their influence on the decisions of employers and national Governments. Sometimes they will do this through the mechanisms of collective bargaining with national or multinational employers. At other times they will put pressure on the European institutions, especially the European Commission and European Parliament, in attempts to encourage the growth of what is described as 'European solidarity'.

The most obvious examples of such trade union pressure are the campaigns which have been waged throughout the European Union for a shorter working week and a statutory minimum wage. Of course, such campaigns will tend to be resisted by many employers and by some national Governments (as was the case with John Major's Conservative Government between 1990 and 1997) which are opposed to measures which they believe would add to industrial costs. They also resent what they regard as interference by European institutions in the free play of market forces. Yet it is equally clear that at the level of general principles such initiatives will continue to find favour in the European institutions and in most member states – as was exemplified by the Social Chapter of the 1992 Treaty of Maastricht which was strongly supported by eleven of the twelve member states with only the British Conservative Government in strong opposition to the whole idea. Subsequently, the Labour Government which came into office in 1997 signed up to the Social Chapter.

A *third* main driving force will continue to be the power of highly mobile finance capital. We have already seen the emergence of London and Frankfurt as centres of financial operations in the European time zone, filling the gap between Tokyo and New York in global financial markets. Such developments are likely to grow and accelerate in future as capital, currencies and other financial instruments circulate and are exchanged with dramatic ease and rapidity around the globe. The enormous weight of these financial flows (which are effectively beyond the control of any national authorities) can be illustrated by the fact that in 1989 the daily turn-over of financial transactions on the New York financial markets was the equivalent of three times the total gold and foreign-exchange reserves of Britain, and the total value of currency flows in the world (that is, the buying and selling of currencies for speculative, hedging or other financial purposes) has been estimated to be at least 20 times the total value of all currency transactions used to finance the business of world trade in goods and services.

Such developments have already had an awesome influence on the claimed economic 'sovereignty' of each member state in the European Union and they have been influential, even decisive, factors in leading eleven of the member states to form a single currency area – in other words, Economic and Monetary Union. This is happening because these member states regard it as both a vital corollary of the European Single Market and the best available way of exercising, albeit in common, at least some real economic sovereignty in the face of global market forces. This provides one of the most powerful examples of a supranational imperative in Europe which is driving most of the member states of the European Union to pool even more of their national sovereignties in an attempt to regain some real power jointly to control their common economic and political destiny.

A *final* driving force for the future, which we have already discussed earlier in this chapter, is the incremental development of European law. Britain and the other member states have been and will be affected by the incursion of European law into more areas of activity which were previously subject only to national competence and jurisdiction. This happens every time that the member states resolve to make a further move towards closer integration, as they did in the 1986 Single European Act or the 1992 Treaty of Maastricht or the 1997 Treaty of Amsterdam. In future, the further development of European law is likely to be driven at least as much by the evolving case law of the European Court as by the political decisions of national Governments to break fresh European legal ground. Indeed, the doctrine of subsidiarity and the stated determination of some member states – including Britain and Germany – to repatriate to the member states some of the powers and competences exercised by the European institutions at European level suggests that the integrationist forces within the European Union will not have things all their own way.

Main divisive issues

Since the very beginning of the drive towards European unity in 1950, there have been a number of divisive issues which have caused difficulty and sometimes crisis for the Member States of the European Union. Yet whenever the member states have been plunged into crisis, they have usually emerged with their fundamental unity intact and sometimes even strengthened by the experience. Indeed this has continued to be the pattern with every enlargement. The almost theological dispute between those who wish to 'deepen' the process of European integration as a corollary of enlargement and those who wish to halt or even reverse the process of integration seems likely to continue, although apparently with less acrimony in Britain under a Labour Government than was the case under its Conservative predecessor.

The essential problem arises from the debate about 'sovereignty' in Europe and people disagree fundamentally about what the term means. Indeed, the word has different meanings and elicits different reactions in the various member states and national traditions. Virtually everywhere on the Continent, except perhaps in Denmark and in some sections of French opinion, the idea of pooling national sovereignties for the common good of Europe as a whole does not really cause any difficulties for politicians and constitutional lawyers alike. This is partly because in many cases on the Continent the nation state has had a chequered and even discredited history, whereas in Britain it still largely symbolises the pride of the British (more exactly the English) in their own nationality. It is also because the so-called 'Community method' holds few fears for the Continental Governments and peoples, since they have been committed to working pragmatically towards 'an ever closer union of the European peoples' (in the words of the 1957 Treaty of Rome) for several decades and have become quite used to the habits and compromises of integration; whereas successive British Governments and the British people have been much more alarmed by the prospect of an apparently irreversible loss of national sovereignty every time member states commit themselves to a new phase of European integration. For British 'Euro-sceptics' the implied erosion of Parliamentary supremacy and the perceived threat to national identity have been the most potent bogies.

With regard to the supremacy of Parliament at Westminster, we have already noted in earlier sections of this chapter that those who have been consistently hostile to Britain's membership of the European Union, especially its supranational aspects, have deeply resented the way in which all the key UK Statutes dealing with Britain's membership (notably the 1972 European Communities Act, the 1986 European Communities Amendment Act, the legislation implementing the 1992 Treaty of Maastricht and the 1997 Treaty of Amsterdam) effectively provided for the supremacy of European law over national law in those areas of policy covered by the European Treaties. However, Ministers in the Conservative Government of John Major argued that the Treaty of Maastricht represented the high-water mark of the traditional approach towards European integration, since its 'architecture' included at least two *international* rather than supranational 'pillars' (foreign policy and internal security policy) and since the doctrine of 'subsidiarity' provided for the repatriation of at least some European competences to the national level of decision making. This latter view appeared to gain some support at the 1996 Inter-Governmental Conference and in the resulting 1997 Treaty of Amsterdam.

As for the preservation of British and other national identities, there are those in Britain who worry that as the member states and societies become more closely integrated within the European Union, the British people and others will in some way lose their distinctive national identities in a sort of multi-national *minestrone*. Such misgivings and fears cannot be dismissed or disproved, because they are essentially subjective and affective in character. Yet at the same time it is wise to observe that the French do not seem any less French, the Germans any less German or the Italians any less Italian as a result of their longer involvement in the process of European integration. The real problem for the British in this regard seems to be that their sense of identity is unusually bound up with their proud and apparently independent history (symbolised by the folk memory of 1940–41 when Britain stood alone against Hitler's

Germany) and with their long-established institutions of Parliamentary government which sit rather uneasily with the habits and assumptions of Continental law.

The substantial aspect of the debate about national sovereignty within the European Union concerns issues of political and institutional *competence*. It raises important questions about whether or not the member states have a *legal right* to act unilaterally in the spheres covered by the European Treaties (which in Britain's case would appear to have been retained at least in theory under the doctrine of inalienable Parliamentary sovereignty) and more subtle questions about whether or not they have *the capacity to act* effectively in certain areas of policy on their own – a proposition which seems much more dubious in the modern global economy.

On the former point, no one really denies that each member state retains the right to act in defiance of European law (at the risk of being disciplined by the European Court) and the ultimate right to adopt an 'empty chair' policy or even to leave the European Union altogether.[19] Yet in contemporary circumstances this is a somewhat theoretical definition of national sovereignty, since its implementation would probably leave the member state that tried it less rather than more able to protect its national interests. On the latter point, we come to the heart of the argument for membership of the European Union and all the previous forms of European integration which preceded it namely that by freely pooling national sovereignties in certain agreed areas of policy, the member states have discovered that collectively they have a capacity to act which is superior to anything which they could have achieved on their own. Indeed, this is the very *raison d'être* of European integration.

Since a part of political and public opinion in Britain has not been prepared to accept this argument, an arcane and rather obscure discussion has developed about Governmental functions and the most appropriate and effective levels at which these should be exercised in particular cases. This is the debate under the heading of *subsidarity*, a notion widely canvassed by Jacques Delors when President of the European Commission (1985–95) and apparently supported by the British and German Governments in particular.[20] The doctrine is based on the contention that the loss of national power to the European level of government can be limited by the fact that the member states and the European institutions are said to agree (under Article 3(b) of the Maastricht Treaty) that no functions should be exercised at supranational level which could more appropriately and effectively be exercised at national level and, it should be added, no functions should be exercised at national level which could more appropriately and effectively be exercised at sub-national level – that is, regional or local government.

So far this apparently reassuring doctrine has not made much difference to the way in which the European Union functions and it seems likely that in the majority of cases the member states and national political institutions will continue to lose effective power and real autonomy in the face of real-world developments (for example, in global capital markets), quite apart from the growing power and influence of European institutions above them and of regional and local institutions below them. In any case the role of the European Court will be crucial, since at present it alone has the legal competence to define and interpret what is 'appropriate' and 'effective' whenever there is a constitutional dispute between a national Government and the European Institutions.

Assuming that national powers and functions levitate upwards to the European level and gravitate downwards to the institutions of sub-national government, many political theorists and practitioners believe that the current 'democratic deficit' in the European Union could get worse unless and until the powers of the European Parliament are increased and extended, and the powers of democratically elected local authorities are enhanced and even put on a newly entrenched constitutional footing. If measures of this kind are not taken, there is a real danger that national Parliaments in the European Union will continue to lose power to European judges and civil servants on the one hand and to unaccountable public bodies and local administration on the other. After all, national Parliaments have found themselves increasingly less able to monitor and control national Governments, so it is not surprising that policy making and public administration at European level have almost completely escaped their democratic grasp.

As far as the future of Parliament at Westminster is concerned, we dealt with the issues of democratic accountability in the European Union in earlier sections of this chapter. Suffice it to say at this point that the 'Europhiles' in British politics are relatively relaxed about the idea of sharing the responsibilities of democratic control with the members of the European Parliament, whereas the 'Euro-sceptics' wish to emasculate what they see as a rival institution. They also insist that the Council of Ministers should take all the important decisions by unanimity and preferably only with the prior consent of national Parliaments. In the longer term, however, it seems likely that the European Parliament (often in alliance with the European Commission and the European Court) will continue to press for increased powers of democratic control at the expense of national Parliaments and that in this it will be successful.

18.5 Conclusion

We have seen in this chapter how Britain excluded herself from full participation in the early stages of European integration after the Second World War and how the country paid an economic and political price for this self-imposed exclusion. However, since joining the European Community in 1973, Britain has played a full part in nearly all European developments, even if she has invariably been ranged on the side of those trying to slow down the pace and limit the scope of European integration. This was especially the case when Margaret Thatcher saw in the end of the Cold War and the disintegration of the Soviet bloc in Eastern Europe a chance to enlarge the European Union and in the process dilute the strength of European integration. It also seemed to be the case with John Major who, although trying very hard to hold his party together on the European issue, was probably more of a 'Euro-sceptic' than was immediately apparent when he took over from Margaret Thatcher in 1990 and said that he wanted Britain to be 'at the heart of Europe'.

The Labour Government of Tony Blair declared from the outset in May 1997 that it was opposed to the concept of a European federal superstate and sought a Europe of independent nation states choosing to co-operate to achieve together what they could not achieve alone. Under New Labour Britain has pursued the completion of the Single Market, placed a high priority on enlargement, sought continuing reform of both the Common Agricultural Policy and the Common Fisheries Policy, urged greater openess and democracy in the institutions of the European Union – including greater powers of scrutiny for the European Parliament – been willing to accept some extensions of qualified majority voting while seeking to retain the national veto over key matters of national interest (including taxation, the budget, security and defence, immigration and Treaty changes), and signed up to the Social Chapter. On the issue of Economic and Monetary Union, it has been positive about future British participation – on the twin assumptions that the economic conditions for British participation are right and the British people give their clear approval in a referendum.

The reasons for the traditionally cautious approach towards the European ideal have been the widely held British suspicion of supranationalism in all its forms (except perhaps in NATO) and the marked preference for an international approach towards co-operation with the rest of Europe based on the sovereign rights of nation states. There is also considerable hostility at Westminster to the prospect that European law will increasingly encroach upon, and perhaps eventually dominate, British national law, and widespread resentment at the erosion of real national autonomy – even though this is much more the consequence of real-world economic and technological developments than any decisions taken by the European Union. In short, many of the misgivings felt in Britain about membership of the European Union stem from a nostalgic yearning for the era when Britain was truly a Great Power strong enough to be able to steer clear of binding or permanent entanglements on the Continent and to throw her weight from time to time decisively into the European balance of power.

No one can tell how the European Union will develop over the years ahead or exactly what part Britain will play in it. The Labour Government of Tony Blair seems to be somewhat more *Communautaire* than its Conservative predecessor. The Conservative Party remains strongly committed to the creation of a genuine Single European Market, but is increasingly sceptical about any other moves towards deeper European integration, and under William Hague is committed to opposing British participation in Economic and Monetary Union for ten years or two Parliaments. In the political spectrum the Liberal Democrats and the nationalist parties (SNP and Plaid Cymru) remain the most 'European' of all the political formations in Britain. Whatever else happens in British politics over the years ahead, Britain is surely in the European Union to stay and her destiny will be heavily influenced by this fact, for good or ill.

Suggested questions

1   Explain why it was that Britain did not join the Six original member states of the European Union, but nevertheless did so subsequently.
2   How profound and far-reaching are the legal and constitutional implications of Britain's membership of the European Union?
3   What seem likely to be the main driving forces and divisive issues in the European Union in the future, and in what ways are these likely to affect the course of British politics?

Notes

1. See White Paper on 'The United Kingdom and the European Community', Cmnd 1565 (London: HMSO, 1961), para. 3.
2. President De Gaulle's verdict was that: England in effect is insular, she is maritime, she is linked through her exchanges, her markets, her supply lines to the most diverse and often the most distant countries; she pursues essentially industrial and commercial activities and only slight agricultural ones. She has in all her doings very marked and very original habits and traditions. In short, the nature, the structure, the very situation that are England's differ profoundly from those of the Continentals.
3. The key paragraphs in the 1971 White Paper 'The United Kingdom and the European Communities', Cmnd 4715 (London: HMSO, July 1971) baldly stated: there is no question of any erosion of essential national sovereignty; what is proposed is a sharing and enlargement of individual national sovereignties in the general interest (para. 29) [and] at present the Communities' institutions are purely economic – but if the development of European policies in non-economic fields calls for new institutions, then as a member Britain will play a full and equal part in devising whatever additions to the institutional framework are required (para. 30).
4. Section 2 (1) of the 1972 European Communities Act clearly states: all such rights, powers, liabilities, obligations and restrictions from time to time created or arising by or under the Treaties, and all such remedies and procedures from time to time provided for by or under the Treaties, as in accordance with the Treaties are without further enactment to be given legal effect or used in the United Kingdom, shall be recognised and available in law, and be enforced, allowed and followed accordingly; and the expression 'enforceable Community rights' and similar expressions shall be read as referring to one which this subsection applies.
5. See Case 26/62 (1963) ECR1.
6. See Case 10/77 (1978) ECR 629.
7. See *Commission v. France*, Case 167/73 (1974) ECR 359.
8. See *Pigs Marketing Board v. Redmond*, Case 83/78 (1978) ECR 2347.
9. See *Minister for Fisheries v. Schoenenberg*, Case 88/77 (1978) ECR 473.
10. See *Major v. Department of Trade*, Case 118/78 (1979) ECR 1387.
11. See *Commission v. Ireland*, Case 61/77 (1978) ECR 417.
12. See *Shields v. E. Coomes (Holdings) Ltd* (1979), 1 All ER 456, 461-2.
13. See M. Butler, *Europe, More than a Continent* (London: Heineman, 1986), p. 169.
14. Qualified majority voting was originally defined in Article 148(2) of the 1957 Rome Treaty. Under this procedure today the votes of each of the 15 member states are weighted as follows: Belgium 5, Denmark 3, Germany 10, Greece 5, Spain 8, France 10, Ireland 3, Italy 10, Luxembourg 2, Netherlands 5, Portugal 6, United Kingdom 10, Austria 4, Sweden 4, Finland 3. To attain a qualified majority, it is necessary to secure 62 votes in favour out of a total of 87 on a proposal from the European Commission or 62 in favour cast by at least ten member states on any other proposal.
15. See Fourth Report from the Select Committee on Procedure, 1988–89, 'The Scrutiny of European Legislation', Vol. 1, 622–1, 8 November 1989.
16. The originally limited legislative powers of the European Parliament have been significantly strengthened by the 1986 Single European Act (which came into effect in 1987), the 1992 Maastricht Treaty (which came into effect in 1993), and the 1997 Treaty of Amsterdam (which came into effect in 1998). Despite these changes, however, the Parliament is still inferior to the Council of Ministers in the legislative process. Nonetheless, the power of co-decision means that once the Council of Ministers has adopted a 'common position' by qualified majority, the European Parliament has three months in which to approve, reject or amend it. If the Parliament approves or fails to act, the Council simply adopts the decision.

If the Parliament rejects the 'common position', then the Council can act only by unanimity. If the Parliament amends the proposal, the Council can either accept the Commission's revised proposal by qualified majority or it can reject or amend it in the light of the Parliament's opinion, but only by unanimity.

17. The European Communities Committee of the House of Lords divides itself into six sub-committees, namely, A. Economic and Financial Affairs, Trade and External Relations; B. Energy, Industry and Transport; C. Environment, Public Health and Consumer Protection; D. Agriculture, Fisheries and Food; E. Law and Institutions; and F. Social Affairs, Education, and Home Affairs.

18. In the devolution arrangements made for Scotland in the 1998 Scotland Act it was stipulated that although relations with the European Union would remain the responsibility of the Government of the United Kingdom, the Scottish Executive would be involved as closely as possible in United Kingdom decision-making on Europe. Indeed, Ministers of the Scottish Executive are expected to participate in relevant meetings of the Council of Ministers and the Scottish Parliament has the authority to scrutinise legislative proposals emanating from the European Union.

19. Under the terms of a Protocol to the 1992 Treaty of Maastricht it was recognised that 'the United Kingdom shall not be obliged or committed to move to the third stage of Economic and Monetary Union without a separate decision to do so by its Government and Parliament'. The Conservative Government of the time also secured an 'opt-out' from the social Protocol attached to the Maastricht Treaty under which eleven out of the then twelve member states declared their intention to introduce binding measures to implement the provision of the 1989 Social Charter which the UK did not sign. However, the pre-existing Social Action Programme, based on earlier Treaty commitments, was not affected by the UK 'opt-out' and the UK continued to participate in negotiations on Commission proposals in this area of policy. Subsequently, the Labour Government elected in 1997 ended this Social Charter opt-out. The 1997 Treaty of Amsterdam recognised the overall flexibility of the European Union by introducing ground rules allowing some member states to go faster than others in particular areas of policy.

20. The doctrine of 'subsidarity' has its intellectual origin in a pronouncement by Pope Pius XI in 1931 in his *Rundschreiben uber die gesellschaftliche Ordnung* (Encyclical in Social order).

Further reading

Barnes, I. and Barnes, P.M., *The Enlarged European Union* (London: Longman, 1995).

Buchan, D., *Europe, the Strange Super-Power* (Aldershot: Dartmouth, 1993).

Business, Britain and Europe: The First 25 Years (London: Anderson Consulting, 1998).

Butler, M., *Europe, More than a Continent* (London: Heinemann, 1986).

Dinan, D. (Ed.), *Encyclopedia of the European Union* (London: Macmillan, 1998).

Fraser, M. (Ed.), *Britain in Europe* (London: Strategems, 1998).

George, S., *An Awkward Partner, Britain in the European Community*, 2nd edn (Oxford: Oxford University Press, 1994).

Hartley, T.C., *The Foundations of European Community Law*, 2nd edn (Oxford: Clarendon Press, 1988).

Holland, M., *European Integration – from Community to Union* (London: Pinter, 1993).

Leonard, D., *Guide to the European Union*, 5th edn (London: The Economist/ Profile Books 1997).

Limon, D. and McKay, W.R. (eds) (22nd edition), *Erskine May's Treatise on the Law, Privileges, Proceedings and Usage of Parliament* (London: Butterworth, 1997).

Neville Brown, L. and Jacobs, F.G., *The Court of Justice of the European Communities*, 3rd edn (London: Sweet & Maxwell, 1989).

Pinder, J., *European Community, the Building of a Union*, 2nd edn (London: Oxford University Press, 1995).

Story, C., *Europe in Britain* (London: World Reports, 1993).

The Treaty of Amsterdam in Perspective: Consolidated Treaty on European Union (Stroud: British Management Data Foundation, 1998).

Treaty on European Union, Maastricht, 7 February 1992, Cmnd 1934 (London: HMSO, 1992).

Urwin, D.W., *The Community of Europe*, 2nd edn (London: Longman, 1997).

Wallace, H., *Budgetary Politics, the Finances of the European Communities* (London: Allen & Unwin, 1980).

Young, H., *This Blessed Plot: Britain and Europe from Churchill to Blair* (London: Macmillan, 1998).

Websites

European Central Bank   http://www.eub.int/
European Court of Justice   http://www.curia.eu.int
European Commission   http://www.cec.cu/
European Commission's Representative in the UK   http://www.cec.org.uk
European Council   http://www.ue.eu.int
European Movement   http://www.euromove.org.uk
European Parliament   http://www.europarl@eu.int
European Union   http://www.europa.eu.int
The Eurosceptics   http://www.euro.sceptic.org/
Foreign and Commonwealth Office   http://www.flo.gov.uk
NATO   http://www.nato.int

19 Policy and decision making

In this chapter we are concerned with the policy and decision-making process of British national politics, but only with the two main parties since none of the other parties has actually been in office since the Second World War. We may define *policy* as a deliberate course of action or inaction worked out by the leading figures of either of the two main parties with the help of others in order to define their political purposes and, to some extent, the methods by which they intend to achieve them. We may define *decision making* as an act by a Minister or Ministers collectively (and sometimes by civil servants in the name of Ministers) to select a particular course of action or inaction on a matter of public policy. Such definitions may seem rather abstract and general, but if they are to reflect the realities of modern British Government and politics, this is bound to be the case.

At the outset it is worth heeding Richard Neustadt's observation that 'in Britain governing is meant to be a mystery'.[1] This can be attributed to a number of different factors. *First*, there is the tradition of official secrecy in British central Government, which can be traced back at least to the 1911 Official Secrets Act and which was long established as one of the ruling conventions of conduct in Whitehall. *Second*, there is the tendency for all Ministers and civil servants to exploit the fact that their privileged access to official information is a form of real power in any political system. *Third*, there are the limitations imposed on all investigations in this area by the fact that those politicians and others who might be able to shed real light on what happens are usually unreliable or self-serving witnesses trying to re-write history to their own advantage, while those academics and others who might be more reliable and objective analysts are not usually given sufficient access to the evidence until many years after the event under the so-called 30 year rule.[2]

For these and other reasons it is wise not to be dogmatic about the policy and decision making process in Britain. It is certainly not easy either to lay down hard and fast rules which apply in all circumstances or to draw all the right conclusions about what actually happens.

In many ways it is somewhat artificial to divide the policy and decision-making process into a number of discrete stages, since in reality there is always a good deal more overlap and confusion than any neat presentation would suggest. However, Figure 19.1 is a useful means of clarifying the way the process works and identifying the key participants and procedures.

Figure 19.1   The policy and decision-making process

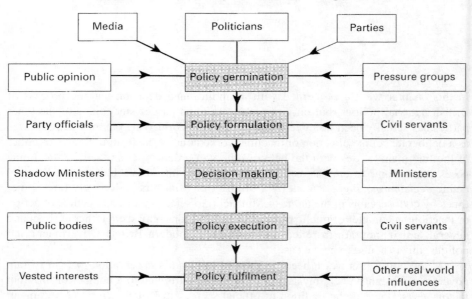

Policy germination

The process begins with the stage of policy germination. This usually takes place when a party is in Opposition, although it also has to take place when a party is in Government if the party concerned wishes to win successive General Elections.

In the *Labour Party*, policy germinates in a way which reflects the organisational and ideological traditions of the party. Political power and influence over policy has traditionally been diffused within the entire Labour movement. Thus ideas and pressure for the germination of policy come from a wide range of sources – such as constituency activists, internal party pressure groups and affiliated trade unions, as well as many friendly academics, intellectuals and experts in mass communications. The role of the Parliamentary leadership has often been to act as something of a brake on the wilder policy ideas which can emerge, especially at those times in the party's history when the hard Left has been strong in the constituency parties.

The approach to policy making changed following Labour's third electoral defeat in a row in 1987 when Neil Kinnock and his closest colleagues recognised the need for a thorough policy review. In organisational terms, the conclusion drawn was the absolute necessity to keep the policy and decision-making process firmly within the control of the Party Leader and a few trusted collaborators. In policy terms, Neil Kinnock came to the conclusion that only a revisionist and modernising approach to Labour policy would suffice if the party were to stand a chance of making a winning appeal to the voters in the 1990s. This new approach was broadly followed by John Smith as Leader of the party from 1992 to 1994, although with some caution about the danger of offending key trade union Leaders on sensitive policy issues such as public ownership and industrial relations. Since Tony Blair became Leader in July 1994, the drive for policy modernisation has been taken much further – notably with the reformulation of Clause IV of the party's constitution in modern language and in many other ways.

In the *Conservative Party*, what usually happens is that the Leadership identifies a problem or a set of problems arising from its previous experience in office or its observation of the current economic and political scene, and then decides on the need for a new policy or the reconsideration of an existing policy. It has then to see whether there are the necessary sources of information and advice within the party fold to enable it to embark on the formulation of policy proposals. If it seems that there are, the Leadership will probably press ahead by setting up a policy group (or policy groups) to look into it. On the other hand, if it is clear that there are not sufficient sources of information and advice within the party and its orbit, efforts are made to enlist the assistance of sympathetic and expert outsiders who can be trusted to keep a confidence and who have both the time and the inclination to help the party in such policy work.

When Margaret Thatcher was Leader of the party (1975–90), the more ideological thrust of Conservative policy was somewhat influenced by self-styled 'think tanks', such as the Institute of Economic Affairs (IEA) and the Centre for Policy Studies (CPS) – the latter having been established by Sir Keith Joseph and Margaret Thatcher in 1975 to help them chart a new course for the Conservatives. The IEA, which had been founded by Ralph Harris and Arthur Seldon in the 1950s, had been an unrelenting campaigner for a free-market approach not only in economic policy but also in social policy and other spheres as well. Throughout the Thatcherite period such bodies had some influence in helping to create an intellectual climate which made Thatcherite policies more acceptable than they might otherwise have been.

Under John Major's Leadership (1990–97), the influence of such 'think tanks' diminished, while the influence of the Policy Unit at 10 Downing Street and of senior civil servants increased as the process of policy and decision making became more short term and reactive to events. John Major usually listened closely to the Chief Whip and was fond of a more collegiate style of political Leadership. Consequently the influence of the Cabinet and indeed of troublesome back-benchers like the so-called 'Euro-rebels' increased as compared with the position during Margaret Thatcher's time as Prime Minister.

Under the Leadership of William Hague (1997–) and with the party back in Opposition, one of the key principles underpinning the reforms initiated to 'renew' the party has been wider 'involvement'. Consequently, the party membership has been promised greater involvement in the development of policy – through the Conservative Policy Forum (a reformed Conservative Political Centre) as well as through ballots of the entire party membership on issues such as participation in the euro and eventual approval of the party Manifesto before the next General Election.

In the case of each main party the mechanisms just described may be referred to as the pure models of policy germination. In practice this stage of the process is often more hit-or-miss, since it is influenced by developments in the real world which require a greater or lesser degree of pragmatism depending on the political correlation of forces at any time. The Labour Policy Review of 1987–89 was a good example of the reactive model of policy germination in that the Labour Leadership felt obliged to take full account of the so-called 'new realism' engendered by about ten years of Thatcherism in action. Equally, the almost revolutionary change in Conservative policy from 1975 to 1979 had exemplified another kind of reactive model in that the party Leadership was consciously responding to the perceived failures of the second half of Edward Heath's term as Prime Minister. Similarly the Hague reforms after 1997 were a response to the huge success of the Blair approach in modernising the Labour Party.

At this early stage in the policy and decision-making process, the key questions are:

1. who defines the problems to be addressed;
2. who sets the priorities of the policy work to be undertaken;
3. what are the ideological objectives of the various policy groups which are established?

When a party is in Opposition, it is invariably the party Leadership which takes charge of the agonising reappraisal that is normally thought to be necessary following a decisive defeat at the polls. When a party is in Government, somewhat different motives and considerations usually apply, since the school of experience and the lure of ideas tend to coexist in the process of turning political thought into action.

Policy formulation

The next stage in the process is that of policy formulation. By this we mean the translation into coherent policy proposals of the political ideas which have germinated in the ways already described. This is also a stage which takes place more systematically when a party is in Opposition that when it is in Government, although each situation needs to be examined carefully if we are to get a complete and accurate picture of this stage of the process.

In the *Labour Party*, the work of policy formulation is done by party officials employed by the party's Research Department. They work under the direction and control of the leading politicians in charge of the various policy groups, which in turn are located within the formal structure of policy committees under the auspices of the National Executive Committee (NEC). Except for the drafting of some of the most important policy documents (for example, some of those produced for the 1987–89 Policy Review), this work is done by party officials who remain employees of Labour headquarters in Millbank Tower when the party is in Government.

In Government, however, the policy formulation stage tends to be rather different, since the leading politicians concerned are Ministers and can benefit at least from the factual information and advice supplied by civil servants. In these circumstances the real work of drafting and re-drafting policy proposals, which may or may not find their way into the party Manifestos, is done mainly by Ministers and their political advisers, since it would be constitutionally improper for civil servants to be closely involved in such party political tasks.

In the Labour Party the structure of policy groups tends to be as elaborate when the party is in Government as when it is in Opposition, since the NEC provides the framework for the policy-making process at any rate in formal terms. Informally, however, the situation has tended to be rather different in that Labour Party Leaders in Government have usually been able to impose their authority on the party's policy-making process. Even in the 1970s when this proved to be more difficult for Harold Wilson and James Callaghan, Labour Ministers and Shadow Ministers remained free to decide which of the many policy proposals put forward by the policy groups within the NEC structure they would accept and which they would reject for the purposes of official party policy. When in Government, Labour Ministers have retained considerable flexibility and discretion in deciding on the methods and the timing of policy implementation, and this is likely to be even more true in current circumstances with Tony Blair and Gordon Brown dominant within the Labour Government.

In the *Conservative Party,* policy formulation is usually the work of party officials and others who draft the papers in which the policy proposals are contained. Of course, such people work under the careful direction and control of the chairmen of the policy groups concerned and indirectly of the Party Leader and other senior figures in the party. Over many years this drafting work was usually done by officials of the Conservative Research Department (CRD), which had been a relatively small but rather competent back-room organisation staffed mainly by bright young graduates with personal political ambitions. However, the role of the CRD became less prominent after Margaret Thatcher decided to amalgamate it with Conservative Central Office in 1980 and, in any case, it never seemed so essential when the party was in Government, since Ministers were able to rely on civil servants for factual briefing and support.

In the Conservative Party the structure of policy groups has tended to be less elaborate when the party is in Government than when it is in Opposition. This is because there has been no equivalent of Labour's National Executive Committee and because the party Leader and other senior figures had retained almost complete control of the policy formulation stage of the process. This has changed somewhat under the Hague reforms, although the full extent of the change is still not clear. Policy groups are established at the behest of the Leader of the party and these are normally chaired by senior Ministers when the party is in office and by equivalent leading politicians when the party is in Opposition. The actual drafting of policy proposals is usually done by party officials who support the various policy groups. The various policy formulations are considered and reconsidered by the policy groups which will normally be made up of a fairly broad spectrum of interested party opinion from both within and outside Parliament. Under the Hague reforms policy discussion is encouraged throughout the party via the Conservative Policy Forum (CPF) and through regional policy congresses. Once the proposals have been refined and finalised by the policy groups and endorsed by the CPF, they are submitted to the Party Leader and senior colleagues for crucial decisions about inclusion or exclusion from the party Manifesto. Finally, the whole membership is now asked to approve the outline of the Manifesto.

It must be added, however, that in both main parties there is some cynicism and even resentment at the way in which the germination and formulation stages of the process seem to have been captured by the party Leaders and a few close colleagues. There is evidence for this view which can be drawn particularly from the Thatcher period for the Conservatives and from the Blair period for Labour. In Labour's case the problem was mitigated somewhat when the party was in Opposition by the work of the Social Justice Commission under the chairmanship of Sir Gordon Borrie, and when in Government by the Jenkins Commission on Electoral Reform and the Wakeham Commission on Lords reform since these bodies included people drawn from outside the mainstream of Labour politics. In the case of the Conservative Party, the problem may be mitigated at least in part by the Hague reforms. However, it is back-bench MPs in both main parties who have the fewest opportunities for real influence on the deliberations of policy groups and the eventual policy decisions. Even when invited to serve on such groups, there remains the suspicion among back-benchers that they have been co-opted into what is largely a placebo exercise with all the big decisions predictably remaining in the hands of the party Leaders and their most senior colleagues.

Decision making

The next stage in the process is that of decision making. On all important and politically sensitive issues this is unavoidably the work of party Leaders and their most senior political colleagues.

In Opposition, the requirements and procedures are quite simple. Usually all that is necessary is that the Shadow Cabinet should meet to accept or reject the policy proposals which have been formulated and refined in the ways already described. Of course, there are some issues which require lengthy discussion even at this stage and which cannot be resolved at a single meeting. Yet in most cases, by the time that a policy formulation reaches this stage, the actual decisions can be taken quite quickly, not least because the Leader of the party and close colleagues will have taken care to prepare the ground for agreement before the meeting.

In Government this stage in the process is both more varied and more complex. Some Government decisions can be taken quite quickly by individual Ministers acting within their allotted spheres of responsibility. Some are taken by groups of Ministers within a particular Department. Yet nearly all important Government decisions affect a variety of Departmental interests and therefore have to be taken at least by a Cabinet committee and often by the Prime Minister and a few very senior colleagues. It is difficult to make any definitive generalisations about decision making at meetings of the Cabinet and its committees. It would appear that in full Cabinet most decisions are taken quite expeditiously and it is only when the Cabinet has to deal with the most difficult and contentious political issues – for example, the public expenditure cuts imposed by the IMF on the 1974–79 Labour Government – that it has had to return to the same issues on several occasions in order to secure agreement. This really underlines the lengths to which Whitehall officials will go to prepare the ground for difficult Cabinet decisions and the efforts which all Prime Ministers make to facilitate smooth Cabinet decision making.

When a Cabinet committee has to make a decision on a particular subject, the terms of reference are usually supplied to the chairman by the Prime Minister or, occasionally, by the Cabinet as a whole. It is then for the chairman of the committee to hold as many meetings as necessary in order to reach a decision which can be recommended to the Cabinet, often within an agreed period of time. In the later stages of the 1964–70 Labour Government, it became conventional that any member of the Cabinet who was not on a particular Cabinet committee would not challenge the decisions of the committee in full Cabinet without the prior approval of the Prime Minister or the chairman of the committee concerned. Indeed, the whole rationale of Cabinet committees is that they should be able to take decisions on behalf of the Cabinet without normally having to submit them to a further stage of discussion in full Cabinet. Only if they function in this way can they truly be said to save the time and energy of the Cabinet.

Yet it remains true that the conventions of collective responsibility and the traditions of Cabinet government in Britain entitle all Cabinet Ministers, if they are sufficiently determined, to pursue a particularly sensitive or important political issue in full Cabinet, and they can insist (sometimes backed by a threat of possible resignation) on having it put on the agenda of a future meeting. To cope with the wide variety of such situations which can arise, some Prime Ministers (such as Harold Wilson) have found it necessary to lay down strict ground-rules for Cabinet decision making, especially if some members of the Cabinet are not sufficiently amenable to Prime Ministerial Leadership. Others (most notably Margaret Thatcher) have not found it necessary to act in this way, because for various reasons they have usually been able to dominate and control their Cabinet colleagues. Others (such as John Major) have developed a more collegiate approach to decision making which encourages the expression of all points of view in Cabinet before collective and binding decisions are reached. Still others (for example Tony Blair) surround themselves with a small group of colleagues not necessarily members of the Cabinet. In the case of Tony Blair the inner circle has included his Press Officer Alastair Campbell, his Chief of Staff Jonathon Powell, the Lord Chancellor 'Derry' Irvine, his old friend from legal days, Lord Falconer, and Philip Gould, his private pollster and organiser of focus groups.

Notwithstanding all of this, three factors should be borne in mind. *First*, that there is an important distinction between the appearance of prime ministerial dominance in decision making and the reality which makes it impossible in practice for any Prime Minister to control all the levers of power. *Second,* although the Cabinet has long since ceased to be a real decision-making body and even its committees matter only occasionally, it does still provide what can be essential political insurance and it has to be managed by any successful Prime Minister. Consequently Prime Ministers 'take the voices' around the Cabinet table before important decisions are reached because it is clearly in their own interest to carry their senior colleagues with them and to bind them together on the issues which really matter. *Third*, it should always be remembered that all Prime Ministers need a measure of good fortune during their time in office, because even if they are 'control freaks' they cannot actually determine every aspect of the course of events whatever their power and authority on the political stage.

Policy execution

Next comes the stage of policy execution. This is the stage at which civil servants excel, provided decisions have been clearly taken by Ministers and clearly communicated by officials to those who need to know about them. The greatest difficulties tend to occur later in the process, since the law of unintended consequences seems to apply to policy and decision making as much as any other sphere of human activity.

Policy execution normally follows immediately after the previous stages already described. As far as civil servants are concerned, its roots can be traced back to an earlier stage of the process. Once the broad objectives of a party's policy have been set and a General Election campaign has begun, it is normal for civil servants in all Whitehall Departments to prepare position papers designed to assist incoming Ministers to implement their policies, no matter which party wins a mandate from the electorate to form the Government. Thus incoming Labour Ministers in 1997 had advice on their desks on how to phase out the Assisted Places Scheme in schools and to provide nursery places for all four-year-olds; whereas – had the Conservative Government of John Major been re-elected – Conservative Ministers would have had comparable advice on how to implement their pledges to set up a Grammar School in every major town and to extend the scheme for Nursery Vouchers. The advice is neither sanguine nor cautious, but merely intended to suggest the most effective ways of executing the policies of the incoming (or returning) Government, while emphasising the practical consequences.

From then on the initiative is with Ministers and their behaviour varies according to their personal drive and ambition, and the extent to which the party commitments in their own Departmental sphere are given priority by the Government as a whole. If a Minister is charged with the execution of a policy which is given a high political priority and if the commitment is clearly expressed in the party Manifesto or other formal statements by the party Leadership, then it will usually be a straightforward matter of taking the appropriate Ministerial decisions for the initiation of administrative action or new legislation, whichever is more appropriate. On the other hand, if a Minister has to execute a policy which has been given only a low priority by the party in office, then there will probably be little alternative to preparing the ground with suitable administrative action and Ministerial speeches, while putting in a Departmental bid for a place in the future legislative timetable. In anticipation of such progress, a Minister can try to improve the Department's prospects by stimulating interest in Parliament and the media, and by mobilising the support of the relevant interest groups and among the general public. If all this can be done successfully, it will increase the chances of a Minister making a mark at a later stage of the Parliament.

Assuming that the appropriate Ministerial decision has been taken, the stage of policy execution is initially the responsibility of the Cabinet Office if the decision was taken by the Cabinet or one of its committees. It therefore communicates the decision to all Departments and other agencies which need to know about it. For example, if a decision concerns the operation of the railways, it will be communicated first to the sponsoring Department which will in its turn see that the decision is conveyed to those responsible for running the railways, including those in the regulatory framework. However, this does not necessarily mean that the decision will be faithfully implemented in strict accordance with Ministerial wishes; for this, specific legislation may be required. A decision affecting the Royal Mail would be communicated via the Department of Trade and Industry, a decision on the role and status of the Bank of England would be communicated via the Treasury and so on. If the decision involves a matter of local government responsibility (such as local planning, housing or

Community Care), it will be communicated to the Department of the Environment, Transport and the Regions for onward transmission to the local authorities in England, and similarly to the Welsh, Scottish, and Northern Ireland Offices for decisions affecting people who live in those parts of the United Kingdom. All such Civil Service communication is carried out between the Cabinet Office and the appropriate Ministerial Private Offices which are then responsible for onward transmission within the respective Departments. These Civil Service channels therefore complement and support the direct communications between Ministers which take place in Cabinet committees and on many other more informal occasions in Whitehall, Westminster and elsewhere.

If a decision requires legislation for its implementation, it becomes the responsibility of the Minister or Ministers who will have to pilot the legislation through Parliament. The Department or Departments concerned have to work closely with legal experts from the Office of Parliamentary Counsel who act as the legislative draftsmen for the entire Government. The role of these Parliamentary draftsmen can be of considerable significance, since the precise wording of Bills can sometimes be almost as important as the fundamental principles involved – notably, in the annual Finance Bill which gives legislative expression to every Budget.

If the execution of a Government decision requires new primary legislation, the process begins with an important pre-Parliamentary stage within the confidential confines of Whitehall. This often involves extensive consultations between civil servants in the Departments concerned and relevant experts and other interested groups both within and outside the web of central Government. Such detailed discussions may continue for weeks or even months on the basis of draft legislative proposals and it is not unknown for the results of this work to be rejected by the Legislation Committee of the Cabinet if the timetable is too tight or the legislative programme too full or the likely political outcome too dubious. By the time that a proposed Bill is ready for inclusion in the Queen's Speech at the beginning of a Parliamentary session, it can usually be assumed that its content has been fully discussed in this way. On the other hand, there are a few occasions when Ministerial decisions or even draft Bills are introduced at the eleventh hour on the basis of only minimal or perfunctory discussion even within the Government, let alone with relevant outside interests. Examples of this phenomenon include:

- the decision to abolish the Greater London Council and the Metropolitan County Councils which was taken by Margaret Thatcher and a very small circle of Ministerial colleagues just before the 1983 General Election;
- the decision to hold a fundamental review of the National Health Service which seems to have been sprung on most of the Government by Margaret Thatcher during a television interview on *Panorama* in January 1988;
- the decision taken in 1997 by the then Social Security Secretary, Harriet Harman, to cut the state benefits paid to single parents as part of the Governments 'welfare-to-work' approach;
- the decision to amend the Crime and Disorder Bill in 1998 to equalise the gay and heterosexual age of consent at 16.

In other instances the execution of a Government decision may require only the introduction of Secondary Legislation, in other words a Statutory Instrument issued under the authority of an existing Act of Parliament. Once again there are usually detailed consultations within Whitehall with a wide range of relevant experts and interested groups. Indeed such consultations are particularly important in such cases, since the subsequent procedures for Parliamentary scrutiny of Statutory Instruments are widely regarded as cursory and inadequate.

If the decision falls within the sphere of lawful administrative discretion for Ministers derived from legislation which is already on the Statute Book, the Minister concerned normally acts in an executive capacity and communicates directly with the persons or bodies concerned via Departmental Circular or by ordinary letter or memorandum. In some cases the decision may entail the delegation of executive responsibility to statutory bodies which already have lawful powers in certain specified areas, such as local authorities or increasingly the Executive Agencies of central Government. Yet in many cases it is still a matter of Departmental action carried out directly on behalf of the Ministers by the civil servants in the Department.

Policy fulfilment

The final and most problematic stage in the process is policy fulfilment. Recent British history suggests that this is the stage at which the failures of successive Governments have been most marked. Among the reasons for this may be that Governments have tried to do too much, pursued often mutually contradictory objectives, had to share power with formidable interest groups, found themselves constrained by expected or revealed public opinion, and been obliged to work within the limiting framework of established social assumptions and the uncompromising realities of the modern world. Faced with such difficulties, successive Governments have sought to ensure the fulfilment of their policies by using one or more of the following political techniques.

First, there is the *technique of accommodation*. This is a standard political ploy whereby a Government seeks to neutralise any threats to its policies by the simple expedient of accommodating critical points of view and absorbing critical people. It may take the form of co-opting troublesome or obstructive individuals onto official consultative committees, or appointing them to positions of responsibility on public bodies, or simply holding privileged discussions with powerful groups with a view to incorporating at least some of their ideas or concerns into Government policy. It is certainly one of the most effective and well-tried methods, since it can turn critics or adversaries of Government policy into compliant or at least semi-pacified partners. Yet it is usually not enough to ensure the fulfilment of policy.

A second technique is that of *manipulation*. This is really little more than a sinister term for the well-tried art of political persuasion and it subsumes such often practised skills as news management – that is, attempting to influence public opinion via careful and deliberate guidance of the media. This technique has been used for years with varying degrees of success and it is a normal part of the process of government. Efforts have also been made from time to time to use fiscal policy in an attempt to buy political popularity in the run-up to a General Election by cutting taxes or increasing public expenditure more than would otherwise have been the case. This technique seems to have worked in 1959 for Harold Macmillan and 1992 for John Major. Yet it has become an increasingly uncertain and risky practice, inviting swift retribution from the financial markets if badly misjudged in terms of timing or amount. Unexpectedly, John Major led the Conservative Party to victory at the 1992 General

Election at the depth of a long recession. This outcome probably owed more to the doubts about Neil Kinnock as an alternative Prime Minister in the eyes of floating voters than to any of John Major's positive attributes or to the record of his party in office. Equally, the Conservatives lost office in 1997 despite the evident strength of the economy, as their position in this regard was undermined by their general unpopularity in the eyes of the British people who were more than ready for a change of Government.

A third technique is that of *public opinion mobilisation*. This is really a matter of seeking the support of the 'silent majority' in order to redress the political balance against the excessive influence of vociferous and articulate minorities. As an exercise in political Leadership, it is usually no easier than the other techniques already mentioned, and it can often be more difficult in view of the problems involved in trying to hold public opinion constantly to one particular line and then translating it into actual voting behaviour at either a referendum or an election when necessary. Such difficulties are illustrated by the familiar tendency for many people to give strong support in answering public opinion polls to increased expenditure on certain desirable public services, but then to vote in the subsequent General Election for the party which most obviously stands for lower taxation and public borrowing and hence a less indulgent attitude towards public spending. Nevertheless, there are various ways in which this technique can be applied. These may involve the use of powerful rhetoric, constant repetition of simple messages, persuasive argument designed to appeal to the general public, symbolic gestures designed to evoke a favourable public response, and specially commissioned political advertising or opinion polls. None of these methods on its own is decisively effective, but they can all help at the margin. Sensible politicians usually fall back on the more traditional methods of rational argument and emotional appeal as well.

Then there is the technique of *political shock treatment*. This involves confronting the public with the full implications of failing to support Government policy. In a sense this is a technique which was used by the Thatcher Government in its efforts to change public attitudes radically and permanently in the vital areas of economic productivity and industrial performance. It is certainly a technique which has been successful in the past at times of clear and present danger – as in 1940 when Winston Churchill appealed so successfully to the British people when they stood alone against Nazi Germany – and it may also have worked for the Conservative Government during the 1982 Falklands conflict when public opinion rallied strongly behind the British armed forces and the Government. Yet there can be no certainty that it will work in normal circumstances during times of peace and relative prosperity, so Governments are wise not to try it too often or count on it too much.

19.2 Key aspects

The postwar consensus and its legacy

It should be clear from the foregoing description of the policy and decision-making process in Britain that it is essentially a continuous phenomenon which proceeds from week to week, month to month, year to year and even Government to Government. This is mainly because the problems of central Government in Britain have remained broadly the same over the decades since the Second World War, almost regardless of which party has been in office. Every Government has been faced with the need to maintain and improve the competitiveness of the economy, every Government has wrestled with the problems of securing adequate resources for the Welfare State without imposing an intolerable burden on the wealth creators; every Government since 1973 has had to cope with the implications of Britain's relationship with her partners in the European Union. It is also because the Civil Service has a natural preference for orderly and continuous government, something which is to be expected from a permanent and politically impartial bureaucracy. In view of the institutional inertia in the system, once a policy consensus becomes established, it requires a prolonged period of disappointment with its consequences – even when exploited by radical political Leadership fully prepared to embark in new directions – for the broad thrust of policy to change and a new consensus to emerge.

As we have already noted in Chapter 8, for about 25 years after the Second World War the continuity of Government policy in Britain stemmed from the high degree of policy consensus which had been established within the Coalition Government during the war. This was extended and carried forward with conviction by the postwar Labour Government, widely recognised as one of the great reforming Administrations of the twentieth century in Britain. The consensus continued to apply under both Conservative and Labour Governments in the 1950s and 1960s – hence the term 'Butskellism' which was used to describe the policy approach followed by R.A. Butler (Conservative) and Hugh Gaitskell (Labour) when they were each prominent policy makers within their respective political parties.

It was not until the early 1970s – at the time of the Yom Kippur war between Israel and Egypt and the ensuing oil crisis in 1974–75 – that the postwar consensus in Britain began to crumble, although there had been harbingers of this development in some of the more radical free-market policies attempted at the outset of the Heath Government. By 1979, when the Conservatives were returned to office under Margaret Thatcher, the era of the postwar consensus was effectively over, having been destroyed in the 1970s by the hammer blows of unreliable economic performance and disappointed public expectations. This created the conditions in which each of the two main parties felt it right to adopt a more ideological approach to politics.

Of course, there were also *discontinuities* during the period from 1945 to 1979, but these were usually the result of Governments having to respond to great events or other developments over which they had little or no control. This was true, for example, of the following decisions:

- The Attlee Government decision in 1947 to develop an independent nuclear weapons capability for Britain.
- The Eden Government decision in 1956 to send British forces to invade the Suez Canal Zone.
- The Macmillan Government decision in 1960 to open negotiations with the Six with a view to full British membership of the European Community.
- The Wilson Government decision in 1967 to devalue the pound.

- The Health Government decision in 1972 to impose direct rule from Westminster on Northern Ireland.

  Other more recent examples include the decisions taken:

- in 1976 by the Callaghan Government to apply for a massive loan from the International Monetary Fund;
- in 1982 by the Thatcher Government to send a Task Force to the South Atlantic to recapture the Falkland Islands;
- in 1992 by the Major Government for Britain to leave the Exchange Rate Mechanism of the European Monetary System.

These cases all provide examples of decisions which entailed notable discontinuities of policy but which could have been said to permit no other response from Goverment. In all cases they appeared aberrant in the context of the policy consensus prevailing at the time. Yet with the advantage of hindsight we can now see that they were virtually inevitable.

An era of polarised ideologies

After 1979 the British people experienced a new era of polarised ideologies, which had its roots in the bitter industrial disputes of the 1970s but which only came to fruition during Margaret Thatcher's time at 10 Downing Street and particularly in the early 1980s when her brand of radical Conservative ideology was opposed with equal vehemence by Michael Foot's Labour Party and by the so-called 'Wets' in her own party who represented the older 'One Nation' tradition of Conservatism. The foundations for the mould-breaking Conservative policies of the 1980s had been laid when the party was in Opposition in the late 1970s at a time when it very largely succeeded in winning the intellectual argument against Socialism.

For its part the Labour Party had also become more ideological in the 1970s partly as a result of the disappointment felt by its activists with the minimal Socialist achievements of the 1964–70 and 1974–79 Labour Governments and partly as a response to the Thatcherite onslaught of the 1980s. The result of these parallel developments in the two main parties was ideological polarisation and the virtual destruction of the common ground which had been established in the postwar consensus. This shifted the centre of gravity of British politics and laid the foundations for a new neo-Thatcherite consensus which appears to have been largely accepted by Tony Blair and New Labour as well as by the Liberal Democrats.

This era of ideological polarisation stemmed from the tendency of each main party, when in Opposition, to return to ideological first principles in an attempt to bring forward purer and more radical policies in preparation for its return to Government. The overall effect of this kind of political response was to lead each of the main parties, when returned to office as a function of the failure of its opponent, to claim that it had a mandate for everything in its Manifesto, no matter how unrealistic or harmful such policy might prove to be in practice. This was one of the main causes of the sharp discontinuities of policy in the 1970s and it left a heavy mark on the more ideological attitudes of both main parties in the 1980s. Indeed, one of the most remarkable features of British politics in the 1980s was the extent to which the party in office became *more* rather than less ideological under the singular Leadership of Margaret Thatcher.

At the same time it should be made clear that an ideological approach to politics – although not really in the mainstream of the postwar tradition of mutual accommodation in Britain – can bring some real benefits to the country and can be justified as necessary and legitimate on certain important conditions. *First*, when a party is in Opposition, its Leadership should try to mobilise the maximum possible public understanding and support for its fundamental ideas and values. *Secondly*, during the political campaign running up to and during the General Election, it should make its policy intentions and commitments as clear as possible, so that it will be difficult or impossible for its defeated opponents (or indeed its internal critics) subsequently to argue that it does not have a mandate for what it does in office. *Thirdly*, once in Government, the party in office must constantly explain and justify its actions through the media at least for the benefit of the politically attentive public. If it manages to fulfil all these conditions, its policies will have a reasonable chance of commanding public acquiescence, even perhaps positive support.

Towards a new consensus?

In the 1990s, however, it seemed that the two main parties were converging towards a new policy consensus built on the post-Thatcherite central ground of British politics. This was partly because Tony Blair and his two predecessors as Labour Leader all concluded that it would not be possible for the Labour Party to return to power without first establishing credible credentials in the eyes of the English middle class. It was equally because first John Major and subsequently William Hague seemed to be much more cautious and pragmatic than Margaret Thatcher and appeared to travel with relatively little ideological baggage. Of course, it is possible that this observable policy convergence was more apparent than real and more temporary than permanent, in that it very largely reflected the fact that both main parties became very risk-averse. The Conservatives experienced such deep unpopularity from September 1992 to May 1997 that the Party appeared (temporarily at least) to have lost all its drive and initiative. Labour, for its part, could scarcely believe its luck not only in winning the 1997 General Election with such a large majority but enjoying such a long honeymoon period in the opinion polls. In Government it has followed a deliberate policy of seeking to keep its Manifesto commitments, no more and no less, aware of the fact that what the electorate gives the electorate can take away. Yet behind this cautious moderation in both main parties lurk other more radical and ideological figures who would eagerly seize either the Leadership or the policy initiative if given the chance.

It seems clear that most of the British people are looking for moderation and a sense of security from their leading politicians, not least after the ideological exhilaration in the 1970s and 1980s. To that extent it seems likely that Tony Blair and William Hague are more in tune with the spirit of the times than any of the more radical figures in their respective parties who might wish to succeed them. At the end of the 1990s the new form of politics based on warm and friendly concepts such as 'community', 'responsibility' and 'partnership' seem to resonate well with the British people.

Indeed, the Leaders of all three national Parties seem to have recognised and tried to respond to this public mood. Yet it is also worth remembering that in all parties future policy will have to be developed in conditions of considerable uncertainty about the global economy and technological innovation, and this is likely to have unpredictable social and political consequences in Britain as in other countries.

19.3 Strengths and weaknesses

There are both strengths and weaknesses in the policy and decision-making process in Britain. It is neither one of the best nor one of the worst of its kind in the liberal democracies of the world. It has some characteristics which are universal and some which are peculiar to Britain. In any event it ought to be assessed on its merits and within its own terms.

Strengths

(1) The most obvious strength is the ability of the process to translate party political commitments into Government action or legislation. This derives principally from the way in which the electoral system is capable of turning a plurality of the votes cast in the nation as a whole into a majority of the seats won in the House of Commons. Thus it enables a particular interpretation of the popular will to be transformed into executive or legislative action by the Government of the day, usually without encountering any insuperable obstacles, at any rate in Whitehall and Westminster. However, any Government can be vulnerable to a back-bench revolt on its own side – as was evident, for example, in the 1986 defeat of the Thatcher Government on its proposals to liberalise the Sunday trading laws or in the enormous difficulties posed for the Major Government in 1992–93 by the 'Euro-sceptics' on its own back-benches in their determined and sustained opposition to the legislation necessary to align British law with the requirements of the Maastricht Treaty.

(2) Another strength of the process is its efficiency in turning Ministerial decisions into administrative action or legislation. This is a tribute largely to the efficiency of the Civil Service in Whitehall Departments and Executive Agencies. It means that the writ of Ministers usually runs quite effectively throughout Whitehall and its satellite Agencies, but much less certainly in public corporations and local authorities, and only in the private sector when reinforced by the full power of the law and statutory regulation. For example, the Conservative Administrations between 1979 and 1997 had continuing difficulties in imposing public expenditure restraint on local authorities, even some of those under the control of Conservative Councillors. This was attested by the fact that at least 15 Bills were introduced by central Government during that time in repeated (but not wholly successful) attempts to curb local authority spending by legislative means.

(3) Yet another strength of the process is its ability to cope with abrupt and radical changes of policy. Any institutions of Government which have this ability to accommodate changes of political direction so quickly and completely must be very

robust. What is more, such changes are made without any significant change in the administrative personnel involved – something which contrasts sharply with what happens in other democracies such as the United States. Yet even this has changed somewhat in recent years and is reflected in concerns about the alleged politicisation of the highest grades of the Civil Service and the tendency for incoming Governments to employ more special advisers and other politically motivated people whose involvement in policy making is not subject to any familiar lines of public accountability.[3]

Weaknesses

There are equally some notable weaknesses in the process which might be considered to outweigh the strengths just enumerated. The conclusion to be drawn may depend upon the uses to which the policy process is put.

(1) It can be argued, that the robust flexibility of the process has permitted too many abrupt and often damaging discontinuities of policy. As has already been pointed out, these have usually stemmed from the determination of politicians in office to implement their Manifesto commitments regardless of the consequences and in the 1970s and 1980s from the polarisation of ideologies.

(2) Paradoxically, another weakness in the process is that there has been too much unimaginative continuity of thinking in Whitehall which has often stymied the prospect of radical policy initiatives. It used to be the case that this had the effect of bringing virtually all Governments back to the safe middle ground of British politics within about two or three years of every General Election. This reflected the gyroscopic influence of the senior policy advisers at the top of the Civil Service which Shirley Williams (after her time as a Cabinet Minister in the 1974–79 Labour Government) described as 'a beautifully designed and effective braking mechanism'.[4] However, this impression of the influence of the Civil Service was called into question during the heyday of the Thatcher Administration when contrary allegations were made that the higher grades of the Civil Service demonstrated excessive political zeal.

(3) Another weakness of the process (which is apparent in most democracies around the world) is that it encourages both Ministers and civil servants to pay too much attention to short-term political considerations at the expense of the quest for fundamental long-term solutions to the nation's most serious and intractable problems. While this is partly a function of the relatively short political timescale imposed by the five-year maximum span of a Parliament, it is mainly due to the congenital tendency of nearly all politicians in office to give priority to what appears to be urgent over what they know to be important (when the two categories conflict), largely because the media leave them with little alternative and because they know that most members of the public have impatient expectations.

(4) Another weakness of the process is that both Ministers and civil servants tend to rely too heavily on a rather narrow range of official information and advice. This is perhaps inevitable, since civil servants control the flow of people and ideas to Ministers and because their advice often reflects essentially the 'Departmental view'

supplemented by advice from a rather limited compass of expert opinion. In other words, because of the weight of Whitehall custom and practice and the habits of official secrecy, the policy making process in Britain has tended to be much less open than in other Western countries where the governing elites have been more receptive to ideas and information from a wide range of sources.

(5) Another weakness of the process has been described as 'Government overload'.[5] Essentially, this means that most Ministers and some senior civil servants working directly for them invariably have far too much to do in too little time. This can be attributed to a number of different causes, among which are the increase over the years in the scope and complexity of modern Government, the growth of the sub-national and supra-national dimensions of policy and decision making, and the impact of modern mass communications which has created a need for Ministers to be informed about and often to comment at short notice on a huge variety of developments, allegations and rumours revealed or sometimes created by the media. This is particularly true at the highest levels of Government where the Prime Minister and members of the Cabinet bear disproportionate burdens of paperwork, meetings and media performance.

(6) A final weakness of the process could be said to be the rather limited scope for Parliamentary or public participation. This is mainly because central Government in Britain is regarded as the exclusive and confidential preserve of a chosen few in the relevant 'policy communities'. Policy ideas, especially in their formative stages, are not very widely shared other than among those with a direct need to know or who can be relied on to give compatible and confidential advice. Perhaps the most notable group among the company of the excluded are back-benchers in the governing party who invariably learn of new policy developments not from their Ministerial colleagues but from the media. Although Parliament is supposed to be the first to be informed (when it is sitting), it is usually quite a long way behind the game as compared with privileged interest groups (who are consulted early on by Whitehall) and the media. This is yet another reflection of the habits of confidentiality which influence so much of the behaviour of British central Government.

19.4 Possible improvements

This is not the place to rehearse in any detail the wide range of possible changes which have been proposed from time to time in order to improve the policy and decision-making process in Britain. It is sufficient here to mention only a few of the more familiar suggestions in order to give a flavour of the reformist discussion which has taken place over the years.

Increased support for the Opposition

Some people have argued that there should be increased support for the Opposition parties, so that they can be better informed on the great issues of the day. To this end it has been suggested that there should be created a small but capable Department of the Opposition to enable Opposition politicians to scrutinise and argue with Ministers on a more equal basis. The covert purpose of such an innovation might be to keep the policy making of Opposition parties more closely in touch with the realities and constraints of Government and so reduce the risk that the policy of an incoming Government might reflect little more than the views and prejudices of unrepresentative political minorities. It is also argued that this would raise the quality and sophistication of policy making in Opposition and make it less likely that Parliament as a whole would be dominated by the resources of Government.

Another way of achieving the objective of 'educating' the Opposition would be to give all politicians not in Government much fuller and more frequent access to official information and advice. This happens to some extent in the case of Privy Councillors (former Ministers of senior rank and a few others) who are allowed to see restricted official information and advice on privileged terms. It also happens in a more routine way during the Standing Committee stage of some complicated Government Bills when the MPs concerned are supplied with Notes on Clauses (Civil Service explanatory briefing). It is thought that this principle could be extended more widely if Ministers felt sufficiently self-confident and indulgent towards the Opposition to do it.

Yet another way of achieving the objective would be to provide all political parties with substantially greater financial support from public funds – as happens in many other European countries – perhaps in proportion to the votes which each party received at the previous General Election. This would enable parties in Opposition to employ more of their own advisers and so enable at least their front bench spokesmen to be better informed and possibly more effective critics of the Government. However, it could not guarantee a higher overall standard of Opposition, since that is bound to depend most of all on the motivation and capabilities of the politicians concerned.

Wider advice for Ministers

Another proposal which has been put forward is that there should be a wider range of advice available to Ministers from a wider range of people.[6] This could be achieved by bringing into Whitehall a larger number of 'special advisers'. Yet it could as well be achieved by opening up the higher grades of the Civil Service to recruitment from a wider range of backgrounds in other parts of the public sector and from the private sector as well.[7] To some extent this is now happening under the aegis of open advertising of all senior posts and with the use in some cases of specific short-term contracts. As this more eclectic approach to Civil Service recruitment gathers momentum, it may well make quite a difference to the traditionally rather narrow and cautious attitudes of the senior mandarins in Whitehall.

Some of the business people who have had direct experience of working within British central Government, such as Sir John Hoskyns who headed Margaret Thatcher's Policy Unit at 10 Downing Street during her early years as Prime Minister, have argued that this idea should be taken a good deal further by opening up Civil Service procedures to permit the recruitment in each Department of perhaps 10 or 20 senior policy officials drawn from the private and voluntary sectors to serve in central Government on fixed-term contracts with market-related rates of pay.[8] The argument is that such temporary officials would be likely to offer Ministers support and advice which would be more completely in tune with the political purposes of the Government of the day than anything offered by career civil servants who are always likely to have an eye on the different views and interests of the official Opposition as the potential future Government.

In this context, it is interesting, and quite revolutionary for Labour, to see the extent to which Tony Blair, Gordon Brown and other senior Ministers in the Labour Government have been successful in persuading senior business people to take time off from their usual duties in the private sector in order to head special Government Task Forces on big policy issues, such as global competiveness or tax and benefit reforms. This is powerful evidence of the Prime Minister's determination to make the Government at least appear inclusive and in touch with the concerns of the business world.

Such approaches to the business of Government may be well suited to a hegemonic Administration which, for the present at least, appears to carry all before it. However, there is likely to come a time for the current Labour Government, as with all its predecessors, when it feels the need once again for the cautionary and more orthodox advice normally given by senior civil servants performing their traditional role.

Structural change in Whitehall

Another proposal which has been made by some is that there should be structural change in Whitehall in order to make the centre more powerful in relation to the various Departments. This has led people, such as Lord Hunt (a former Cabinet Secretary), to propose the creation of a new central Department – either a fully-fledged Prime Minister's Department or an enlarged and strengthened Cabinet Office.[9] Such changes have usually been suggested by those who feel a need to strengthen the hand of the Prime Minister in the policy and decision-making process and to encourage greater policy coherence throughout Whitehall.

This was certainly the approach adopted by the incoming Labour Government in 1997. From the outset under Tony Blair we saw the expansion of the Downing Street Policy Unit, the appointment of Peter Mandelson as a co-ordinating Minister in the Cabinet Office, the formation of a Strategic Communication Unit to aid the presentation of policy, and the creation of the Social Exclusion Unit. These developments were taken one stage further, following the Ministerial reshuffle in July 1998, when Jack Cunningham was appointed as the Cabinet Minister with special responsibility for the co-ordination of Labour policies throughout Whitehall and the enforcement of Tony Blair's political objectives throughout the Government. All these moves were intended to produce a decisive power shift in favour of the Prime Minister's political objectives by enhancing the reach and the capacity of 10 Downing Street.

However, it is by no means self-evident that the shortcomings in the British policy and decision-making process derive from insufficient Prime Ministerial power and influence. Indeed, it might seem unwise gratuitously to increase the power of 10 Downing Street when there is already a long-run tendency towards 'presidentialism' in British central Government which can become particularly marked when there is a strong personality at 10 Downing Street who enjoys a comfortable majority in the House of Commons. In so far as there can be a problem of excessive 'Departmentalism' in Whitehall, the most appropriate solution could well be the more effective and timely use of the Cabinet and its committees rather than any attempt to bolster the institutional power of the Prime Minister.

Greater role for Parliament

Some people have been attracted by the idea that Parliament should be given a greater role during the formative stages of the policy and decision-making process. Such a change would add a creative role to the main functions of Parliamentary activity which are those of scrutiny of the acts of Government and the mobilisation of public consent. To be successful, it would almost certainly require the further development of Select Committees in ways which would enable them to be more deeply involved in the formative stages of policy making. For example, it might mean giving Select Committees the power to consider legislative proposals at a pre-legislative stage or to influence the composition and balance of the public accounts *before* any final decisions are taken by the Chancellor of the Exchequer on the unified Budget.

Such an enhanced role for at least some back-benchers would probably require the strengthening of the sources of expert and independent advice available to Members of Parliament – perhaps through new institutions along the lines of the General Accounting Office or the Office of Technology Assessment which serve the US Congress. In fact, there is already a modest analogue of the latter which serves the House of Commons, although without the visibility and prestige of its larger American counterpart. Yet even with the benefit of such institutional strengthening of the resources available to Parliament, there would still be considerable obstacles to taking such ideas very far forward in a political system in which the essential role of Parliament is to scrutinise and criticise policy rather than to make it.

19.5 Conclusion

A balanced conclusion to the issues raised in this chapter would seem to be that the policy and decision-making process works rather well in Britain, but only if its performance is measured in terms of its relatively smooth operation in Whitehall and Westminster. Beyond the walls of these twin citadels the process is not so satisfactory or effective, especially since it is not very good at mobilising the understanding and consent of the general public. Even those interest groups and other privileged bodies which are consulted fairly fully by Ministers and civil servants cannot feel confident that they have much more than marginal influence on either the process or the outcome of policy making. While they may occasionally pull off a policy *coup*, it is invariably the most senior politicians and their closest political advisers who dominate the policy making discussions and monopolise the decisions. British politics is still very much party politics and this fact of life in Britain leaves little scope for outsiders. In contemporary circumstances only the increasingly influential media seem to be an exception to this rule, although under Tony Blair it may be that certain business people also fall within such a category.

In the future, the process may well change quite significantly as the world in which national policy making operates becomes more intrusive and more complicated and global events impinge to a greater extent than before on what national politicians can achieve. If Britain is to be 'a Leader in Europe', the process of policy and decision making will also be curtailed and complicated by the requirements of the evolving European Union. Moreover, as and when the general public becomes more aware of the realities of modern politics and wishes to participate directly in a growing variety of ways, politicians and civil servants could find it even more difficult than before to keep up with rising public expectations. In such demanding circumstances all the key participants would be wise to try to explain more fully the inherent limitations of a policy-making process based on sometimes puerile party competition and the clash of artificially polarised positions. They would also be wise to emphasise more often the severe limitations imposed by European and global influences which constrain the room for manoeuvre of any national Government. Britain is fortunate in having a robust and mature system of policy and decision making, but there are no grounds for complacency as long as the problems of Government remain so hard to solve.

Suggested questions

1 Describe the policy and decision-making process in British central Government.
2 Where does real power lie in the policy and decision-making process?
3 How could the process be improved in modern conditions which are so heavily influenced by external factors, such as the media and the markets?

Notes

1. Quoted in R. Rose (ed.), *Policy making in Britain* (London: Macmillan, 1969), p. 292.
2. Government records of historical value are selected for permanent preservation and, under the terms laid down in the 1967 Public Records Act which sets the statutory closure period after which records must be made available for public inspection as 30 years (except for certain defined reasons), they are made available to the public in the Public Records Office.
3. On the first point – the alleged politicisation of Civil Servants – specific examples would include both Charles Powell and Bernard Ingham under Margaret Thatcher and Jonathon Powell and Alastair Campbell under Tony Blair. On the second point – the influence of specific advisers – a specific example would be Sir Alan Walters, Margaret Thatcher's personal adviser on economic policy, who was a factor in the resignation of Nigel Lawson as Chancellor of the Exchequer in October 1989. This was because his public utterances (in themselves an unusual breach of normal Civil Service conventions) were an outward and visible sign of the growing differences of view on policy between Margaret Thatcher and her longest-serving Chancellor. However, it was the growing breach between the two neighbours in Downing Street on the conduct of monetary policy which was the real cause of Nigel Lawson's eventual resignation.
4. In W. Rodgers et al., *Policy and Practise: The Experience of Government* (London: RIPA, 1980), p. 81. Also see T. Benn, 'The Mandarins in Modern Britain', *Guardian*, 4 February 1980.
5. Lord Hunt of Tanworth, a former Cabinet Secretary who had served four different Administrations, elaborated this point in a lecture given to the Chartered Institute of Public Finance and Accountancy on 9 June 1983.
6. One of the foremost proponents of the idea of wider advice for Ministers from a more open and flexibly recruited Civil Service is Peter Hennessey in his magisterial book *Whitehall* (London: Secker & Warburg, 1989).

7. See the White Paper 'The Civil Service, Continuity and Change', Cmnd 2627 (London: HMSO, July 1994), paras 4.13–4.22 for more information on this subject.
8. See J. Hoskyns, 'Whitehall and Westminster, An Outsider's View', *Fiscal Studies*, November 1982.
9. Lord Hunt outlined four possible options, but expressed no clear preference: a fully developed Prime Minister's Department, a strengthened Cabinet Office, a recreated and strong Central Policy Review Staff, and an enlarged Prime Minister's Office.

Further reading

Ashford, D.E., *Policy and Politics in Britain* (Oxford: Blackwell, 1981).
Butler, D. et al., *Failure in British Government* (London: Oxford University Press, 1994).
Dynes, M. and Walker, D., *The Times Guide to the New British State: The Government Machine in the 1990s* (London, Times Books, 1995).
Healey, D., *The Time of my Life* (London: Michael Joseph, 1989).
Hennessy, P., *Whitehall* (London: Secker & Warburg, 1989).
James, S., *British Government: A Reader in Policy Making* (London: Routledge, 1997).
Kaufman, G., *How To Be A Minister* (London: Faber & Faber, 1997).
Lawson, N., *The View from Number 11* (London: Bantam Press, 1992).
Rose, R., *Ordinary People in Public Policy* (London: Sage, 1989).
Sanders, D., *Losing an Empire, Finding a Role – British Foreign Policy since 1945* (London: Macmillan, 1990).
Savage, S.P. et al., *Public Policy in Britain* (London: Macmillan, 1994).
Thompson, B. and Ridley, F.F. (eds), *Under The Scott-Light* (Oxford: Oxford University Press, 1997).

British Parliamentary democracy

British Parliamentary democracy has evolved over the centuries. From Simon de Montfort's Parliament in 1265 to the outbreak of the Civil War in 1642, it was based upon the changing relations between the Monarch and the various estates of the realm. By the time of the Bill of Rights in 1689 a more explicit constitutional contract had evolved between the Monarch's Government and the two Houses of Parliament. From then until the 1832 Reform Act Britain was essentially governed by the landed aristocracy. With successive extensions of the franchise from the 1867 Representation of the People Act to the 1969 Representation of the People Act, a recognisably modern democracy gradually emerged. The contemporary result of this long evolutionary process is that since the entry of the United Kingdom into the European Community in 1973, British politicians and people alike have lived in a Parliamentary democracy which is a constitutional Monarchy within the European Union.

20.1 The conditions of democracy

There are a number of conditions which have to be met if the system of Parliamentary democracy in Britain is to function satisfactorily. These are conditions which can be applied to any modern democracy and which Joseph Schumpeter described as 'conditions for the success of the democratic method'.[1]

The *first condition* is that the politicians active in the political system should be of a high calibre. It would obviously be invidious for the authors to comment in any detail upon this point, save to observe that quality is influenced by attitude in that politicians who adopt a positive and constructive approach to the problems which confront them are often more attractive and persuasive than those whose approach is negative and destructive. Clearly high quality in the political class is a necessary but not a sufficient condition for success in a democracy, while cynical or negative politicians are usually unattractive to the voters.

The *second condition* is that the range of political activity should be limited. This is obviously a salutary point to make in relation to contemporary politics, since the persistence of unrealistic public expectations – often encouraged by unscrupulous politicians at election time – leads people to suppose that Governments can find a solution to every problem. Unless leading politicians show themselves capable of preaching and practising the virtues of limited government, public disappointment is likely to increase with potentially dangerous consequences for democracy.

The *third condition* is that there should be a strong and impartial bureaucracy to advise the politicians in office and to administer the decisions of Government. The importance of this condition is perhaps best demonstrated by its absence – for example, in certain countries where the lack of a competent and incorrupt public administration can be a real barrier to political, economic and social development. It is therefore ironic that in Britain the nature and quality of the Civil Service has some-times been portrayed as an obstacle rather than an aid to national success, because of the perceived tendency for traditional British bureaucrats to prefer established ideas and procedures to anything new or untried – except when insisted upon by Ministers.

The *fourth condition* is that vanquished political minorities (notably the losing political parties at a General Election) should acquiesce in their electoral defeat and accept the consequences of the voters' verdict. This condition is fundamental to the satisfactory functioning of a democracy and in Britain the rule of the (Parliamentary) majority has invariably been accepted by all parties. Of course, a healthy democracy ought also to have safeguards for the defeated minorities against possible abuse of power by the majority. Yet in Britain this is difficult to achieve as long as the electoral system enables the victorious party (which normally gains no more than a plurality of the votes cast) to impose its political will upon Parliament and the country simply by dint of its overall majority in the House of Commons.

The *fifth condition* is that everyone involved in politics, especially those in the victorious party at a given time, should show tolerance and magnanimity towards the interests and concerns of all those on the losing side at the previous General Election. This is a condition which was broadly fulfilled in Britain during the first 25 years or so after the Second World War. It ought also to appeal to any party in Government which realises that its period in office cannot be indefinite and that sooner or later it will find itself licking its wounds in Opposition. There were however, signs of Conservative tri-umphalism in the 1980s which infected certain politicians and impacted upon the style of politics at the time, marking a clear contrast with the more modest behaviour of earlier generations in British politics and, incidentally, with the normal conventions of coalition politics on the Continent of Europe.

20.2 Essential characteristics

It can be said that there are a number of essential characteristics in British Parliamentary democracy which have been widely recognised over the years. We shall take a closer look at each of them in turn.

A representative and accountable system

The first essential characteristic of British Parliamentary democracy is that it is a rep-resentative system which is supposed to function in a democratically accountable way. This has some positive consequences for the political system. It endows the

Government of the day with democratic legitimacy, although a wise Government will not push its wishes too far or take its own authority for granted. It allows the electorate every four or five years to deliver a verdict on the party in office and on the competing attractions of the other parties. It provides institutional channels of communication between the Government and the governed, although by no means the only channels in a pluralist political system in which pressure groups and the media play such an important part. It can have the effect of magnifying or filtering the force of public opinion according to the nature of the various issues which emerge and the different imperatives for each political party.

Notwithstanding these positive characteristics, the British form of Parliamentary democracy has not always been held in high repute. This is partly because the main actors – the two leading political parties – have been in the habit of raising their party political conflict above all other considerations on many occasions. It is partly because public assumptions and expectations of Britain's much vaunted political system have been seriously disappointed on many occasions. It is also because the nature of the political debate as conveyed via the media so often seems to be related scarcely, if at all, to the concerns and aspirations of the general public. For example, the almost theological debate within and between the two main parties about the nature and extent of Britain's participation in the future evolution of the European Union can seem very remote from the more prosaic concerns and aspirations of most people. In these circumstances it is not surprising that some intellectuals and reformers in all parties and in none have been more attracted to the sort of political arrangements which pertain in other countries, notably on the Continent of Europe where coalition Governments based on broad economic and social consensus tend to be the order of the day and all political relations take place within the framework of a codified constitution.

Needless to say, there are some significant points to be made on each side of this argument. Those who defend the British system argue that the legitimacy of Government is largely based upon the fact that the party in office is usually the sole victor of the previous General Election and can therefore command the support of an overall majority in the House of Commons on virtually all occasions. Of course, this is necessarily a qualified legitimacy, since it is normally based upon no more than a plurality of the votes cast at the previous General Election – in other words, the largest single minority of the total national vote – and it is valid for no more than the duration of a single Parliament. This means that British representative democracy is really based upon an implicit contract between the Government and the people. Ministers accept that there are limits to the action which they can properly take if they are to remain within the bounds of constitutional convention and public tolerance. The general public accepts (sometimes with deep reservations) that the party in office should be allowed considerable latitude in its attempts to fulfil its election mandate and even more so in the day-to-day government of the country.

The limits of public tolerance and acceptability vary from time to time and from Government to Government. Much depends upon the extent to which policy runs counter to powerful opinion in the political parties and in pressure groups; the generally perceived gravity or urgency of the situation with which Government has to deal; the possibilities of making progress by stealth without attracting media or public attention – something which is now virtually impossible in view of the determination of the media to look under every stone. Some issues will turn on the likelihood of policy reversal in the event of the Opposition winning power at the ensuing General Election. In general, such limits are quite flexible and cannot really be determined in advance.

Those who criticise the British system argue that the power of the electorate is largely based upon the fact that, whatever the governing party may do or fail to do during its term of office, it is the voters (especially the floaters) who have the final say at every General Election and can therefore forgive or punish those who have been in power. Yet even this final power of the electorate needs to be qualified in a number of significant ways. *First*, the voters are able to exercise no more than intermittent democratic control in view of the relative infrequency of General Elections in Britain. At other times, in order to put pressure upon their elected representatives, they have to rely on stressing the vulnerability of all politicians to rejection in the ballot box if by the end of the Parliament the public's reasonable wishes are not met. *Secondly*, while the voters are able to exercise a democratic choice, they are only able to do so within the range of electable alternatives offered by the serious political parties. Thus Conservative voters who live in safe Labour seats and who support root and branch reform of the Welfare State are unlikely to be able to return an MP who shares and expresses their views. Equally, Labour voters who live in safe Conservative seats and who support expanded welfare provision are unlikely to be able to return an MP who shares and expresses their views. As for the supporters of minor parties, they seem doomed to cast wasted votes (unless their voting strength is locally concentrated) given the nature and characteristics of the British electoral system, unless or until the system is changed for Westminster elections. *Thirdly*, the ignorance and apathy of many voters is another limiting factor in British democracy, since people who vote with little or no real knowledge of the issues or who are too apathetic to vote at all cannot really be said to have a good claim to democratic authority.

The vital role of political parties

The second essential characteristic of British Parliamentary democracy is the vital role played by the political parties as the traditional channels of communication between the Government and the people and as the principal pool of talent from which members of the Government and the Opposition front bench are recruited. Of course, the political parties are by no means the only mechanism of contact, nor indeed the most significant, between Government and people and the figures show that active participation in them has been in secular decline for many years. However, they still manage to channel the energies of political activists in lawful and constitutional directions by representing real class and other interests in British society. As long as the parties are performing their traditional tasks satisfactorily, those who have political causes to advance should feel able to do so within one of the recognised political parties. Once this ceases to be the case on any significant scale – as many people would now argue that it has – there is real cause for concern about the future of Parliamentary democracy.

One of the main reasons for this concern in recent years has been the marked trend in British society away from this traditional form of political participation towards growing public support for and membership of a large number of very active and often influential pressure groups. These groups are very often focused upon a single overriding issue – such as animal welfare or single parents – and they have become all the more formidable because of the degree of personal commitment which they inspire in their members. The reasons for these developments are complicated, but they seem to have a great deal to do with the increased importance and influence of the media in virtually every sphere of modern politics. Indeed, as we saw in Chapter 6, the almost symbiotic relationship between many established pressure groups and the media is one of the main explanations for the growth of their power at the expense of Parliament and the political parties. In these circumstances the main forum for public debate has moved to a considerable extent away from the Palace of Westminster to the columns of the press and the studios of the electronic media.

The regulatory duties of Government

The third essential characteristic of British Parliamentary democracy is the way in which all Governments feel obliged to try to hold the ring between the various organised and competing interests in the country. This is, of course, a function of the legislative and regulatory role of Government and Parliament. Yet it is also evidence of the relative weakness of every Government in the face of competing power centres in the private sector both in Britain and increasingly abroad. In these increasingly difficult circumstances every Government strives to see that the general interest gets at least an equal hearing above the cacophony of special pleading from sectional interests. This task seems to have become more difficult over the years, not least because too many Ministers can themselves be portrayed as representing narrow sectional interests of an ideological or political variety. Indeed, one of the obvious disadvantages of one party being continuously in office for a very long time – as the Conservatives were between 1979 and 1997 – is that Ministers can plausibly be accused of equating their party political interests with those of the nation as a whole and so be seen as moving away from the Solomon-like role expected from all Governments. Clearly senior civil servants from the Cabinet Secretary downwards have been mindful of this danger and have sought from time to time to lean against it. Yet their 'constitutional' task is not made any easier by judges and others who have been in the habit of opining that the national interest is, by definition, what Her Majesty's Government says it is at any time.

In forming an objective assessment of this aspect of the political system, the real questions to ask are how far any Government seeks genuinely to represent and hold the ring for the general interest, and how far it demonstrates an ability to do so without simply equating the general interest with its own party political view of the world. Too great an influence for party political objectives lays any Government open to the charge that it is ignoring its wider responsibilities. Too great a willingness to endorse the demands of sectional interests can suggest a feebleness of purpose which can undermine the authority of Government. An unusually altruistic emphasis upon the longer term can earn plaudits perhaps in the history books, but guarantee defeat at a General Election. In short, governing has always been difficult, but it has probably become even more so in a modern democracy.

20.3 Other significant features

British Parliamentary democracy has some other significant features which need to be taken into consideration if we are to get a complete picture of it in modern conditions. Each of the following features has assumed particular importance at different times, but all have shaped the British political system over the years.

Political polarisation

The tendency towards political polarisation in Britain has deep historical roots in the eighteenth-century struggle between the Whigs and the Tories and the nineteenth-century struggle between the Liberals and the Conservatives. During most of the twentieth century it has been the Conservative and Labour parties which have slugged it out with each other, sometimes in a spirit of considerable bitterness and recrimination. For example, in the 1970s and 1980s the two main parties became particularly polarised, partly as a function of internal dissatisfaction within each of the parties with the way in which both Harold Wilson and Edward Heath had followed what were perceived by some fundamentalists in their own ranks to have been weak and vacillating policies, but mainly because it was clear by then that the policies of the postwar consensus had run their course. The result of these matching political developments in each of the main parties was that by the mid-1980s politics in Britain had become less consensual and more polarised than at any time since the 1930s.

This state of affairs was in marked contrast to the much more limited party political differences during the 1950s and 1960s when each of the main parties broadly accepted the political consensus which had emerged in Britain during and immediately after the Second World War. It can also be differentiated from the apparent political convergence in the 1990s between the pragmatic Conservatism of first John Major and then William Hague and the 'modernised' Socialism of Neil Kinnock and John Smith and the new Labour approach of Tony Blair. It would seem that both main parties – indeed the Liberal Democrats as well – are now camped on the post-Thatcherite central ground of British politics which accepts the role of market mechanisms and the need to regulate them, but which is also characterised by an acute awareness of what the media and the general public will tolerate at any time. The irony which was brought home to Conservative radicals by the defeat at the 1997 General Election was that their party had held office for so long that it had created the political conditions in which it had been possible for modern leaders of the Labour Party to make the policy and organisational changes required to make their party electable.

Institutional inertia

Institutional inertia is another significant feature of the British political system which is quite capable of coexisting with the political polarisation just described. Although a number of important institutional changes have been made in Britain over the past

35 years or so – for example, the reform and emasculation of local government, the transformation of the Civil Service, and the almost complete transfer of the nationalised industries to the private sector – few of these changes have proved to be an unqualified success and all have entailed considerable (often unforeseen) problems. This has led the opponents of institutional change to insist that such initiatives can do more harm than good and are not necessarily a complete remedy for political problems which may be attitudinal or psychological in origin. They have also argued very forcefully that the political upheaval which such institutional changes usually entail brings in its wake a level of cost and disruption which is inimical to the interests of good government.

On the other hand, all those who believe in the value or need for institutional change have tended to argue that it is impossible to entrench really significant policy changes without buttressing them with new, or at least radically reformed institutions. For many such people (especially those who signed up to Charter 88), the most vital institutional and procedural change which (at the time of writing) has *not* been made in Britain, but which in their eyes ought to be made to facilitate the rest of their agenda, is the introduction of proportional representation for elections to Parliament at Westminster. Unlike the defenders of the *status quo* in each of the two main parties, they argue that Britain's first-past-the-post electoral system is still the most significant obstacle to all the other institutional changes which they tend to favour – such as the introduction of a codified constitution, an entrenched Bill of Rights, and a completely new way of working in Parliament.

Naturally, the defenders of the institutional *status quo* cling to the principle of Parliamentary supremacy at Westminster and the uniquely powerful position which it gives to the party which happens to have been victorious at the previous General Election. Of course, there are strong arguments for retaining the existing electoral system in Britain (as we pointed out in Chapter 3), since it does at least give the voters a clear choice at General Elections and provides other opportunities (notably at local elections and Parliamentary by-elections) for the voters to register dramatic protest votes against the Government of the day. Moreover, it needs to be borne in mind that the present electoral system is capable of producing single party Governments which pursue not only consistent and sometimes radical policies, such as those pursued by the Thatcher Administrations between 1979 and 1990, but also cautious and pragmatic policies such as those pursued by the Major Administration in the mid-1990s.

In practice, nearly everything depends upon the needs of the times, the policies favoured by the politicians temporarily in office and the nature of the Parliamentary arithmetic at any time. Indeed, analysis of the constitutional agenda pursued by the Labour Government of Tony Blair since 1997 shows that the driving force for each of the individual changes lay not in some carefully thought out, coherent, overall constitutional settlement, but rather in *ad hoc* solutions to particular problems – such as how to deal with the seperatist 'threat' posed by the Nationalists in Scotland, and how to balance the conflicting cultural and religious traditions in Northern Ireland. Indeed, the Lord Chancellor, Derry Irvine, has described New Labour's approach to constitutional reform as 'principled pragmatism'.

Elective dictatorship

There have been those who have argued that in certain circumstances British Parliamentary democracy can be virtually an 'elective dictatorship'.[2] This is undoubtedly true in the sense that any British Government with an effective majority in the House of Commons can usually get its way in Parliament, at any rate on the issues which really matter. This fact of British political life was reflected in the ability of successive Labour Governments whether in the late 1940s or the late 1970s to impose relatively high rates of direct taxation, to nationalise parts of British industry and to increase the level of welfare benefits; and the ability of successive Conservative Governments whether in the 1950s or the 1980s to switch the burden of taxation relatively from direct to indirect taxation, to return to private ownership many of the nationalised industries, and to concentrate on means-tested rather than universal welfare. It has also been reflected in the whole series of policy initiatives designed to reduce the autonomy of local government under successive Conservative Administrations between 1979 and 1997, and in the constitutional measures introduced by the Labour Government of Tony Blair following the General Election of 1997. In each case a principled political agenda has been followed, often almost regardless of the criticism of the Opposition or the hostility from elements of the British public. Such action has been possible because of the relatively high level of political security enjoyed by most majority Governments since the Second World War, at any rate as long as they enjoyed a comfortable working majority in the Commons. Of course, at those times when this essential precondition was not met, talk of 'elective dictatorship' has seemed rather hysterical.

From another point of view it has been argued that an 'elective dictatorship' is an exaggerated description of one aspect of British Parliamentary democracy which tends to be voiced mainly by those who have lost a General Election and are predictably bemoaning the uses to which the governing party puts its power. The reality is that beyond the twin citadels of central Government – Whitehall and Westminster – powerful private sector interests and mighty external events have demonstrated the ability to frustrate or defeat even the best-laid plans of the most powerful democratic Governments.

Two examples drawn from the past two decades in Britain may serve to illustrate the point. In 1983 the Stock Exchange was able to persuade Ministers in the second Thatcher Administration not to submit it to statutory regulation, even though the liberalisation of financial services which was then beginning in Britain seemed already to require a degree of regulation by the state and the Conservatives had a commanding majority in the Commons which they could have used if they had felt so inclined to steamroller through such a reform. Equally, the teacher trade unions were able in the early 1990s to persuade Ministers in the Major Government extensively to modify the regime of standard tests in schools, even though this was a key component of Conservative education policy which was built on the introduction of the national curriculum.

Even more dramatic was the example of 'Black Wednesday' in September 1992 when the centrepiece of the then Government's counter-inflation policy – Britain's membership of the European Exchange Rate Mechanism – became impossible to sustain in the face of overwhelming pressures in the financial markets. In all these cases (and in many other examples which could be given) it was made clear that even the most powerful national Governments enjoy only limited and conditional power and that talk of 'elective dictatorship' can often be wide of the mark. In a pluralist, and increasingly global society, national Governments have to share power with the media, the markets and many other powerful actors in both the public and private sectors.

Diminished scope for national Governments

It may seem strange to argue in a book on the British political system that the diminished scope for national Governments and indeed all national authorities is now one of the most significant features of the modern world. Yet this has been borne out in Britain (and indeed in all other nation states) by the mounting evidence which emphasises that the writ of even the most powerful and determined Ministers does not always run unchallenged and can sometimes be defeated. There are several reasons for this diminished power and status of national institutions.

One reason is that in a modern pluralist society the successful implementation of policy often depends to a greater extent than members of the political class are prepared to admit upon at least the tacit acquiescence, if not the active support, of those most directly affected by the policy. It is only necessary to reflect upon the successful Parliamentary and public campaign against the Poll Tax in the late 1980s and early 1990s, or the power for example of the Ulster Unionists in talks within the framework of the so-called 'peace process' in Northern Ireland to see the force of this argument.

Another reason for the limited power of Governments is that so many problems in the world today are not really susceptible to solutions imposed by politicians and civil servants through legislative or administrative action, because they require action by individuals, families and private organisations beyond the effective sphere of any Government. The cautionary tale of Conservative attempts to formulate and implement a 'family policy' under the slogan of 'Back to Basics' in 1993–94 serves to illustrate the point. In another sphere, some forms of market activity in the financial services sector (such as derivatives) are so sophisticated and obscure to laymen that it is very difficult for national authorities fully to understand, let alone effectively to regulate and tax these activities. When they do succeed, the most notable effect may be to drive such activities 'off-shore' to more relaxed and welcoming jurisdictions.

The most significant reason, however, why all national Governments seem increasingly by-passed or even left behind by the swirl of events is that they no longer operate on the levels required to match the most significant developments in the global economy and in the noticeably dynamic interaction between local and global communities – as exemplified by the rapidly growing world of Internet and cyberspace. In these new circumstances the policies and aspirations of even the most powerful national authorities are vulnerable to developments and decisions elsewhere over which they may have little influence and even less control. For example, the free movement of capital around the world, the growing interaction between computer and television technologies, and the looming tendency for millions to migrate across national borders in search of a better life all pose threats to the ambitions and jurisdictions of national Governments. So far their response has usually been to seek ways of combining their power and influence through international organisations. Yet because of the fundamental diversity of national interests which has been revealed, the most successful responses have tended to include supranational elements – as we have seen in the leading postwar examples of NATO and the European Union.

The dilemma for any British Government, and indeed for all national Governments, is that if they stubbornly persist in making claims to exclusive competence and control within their national jurisdictions, they are likely to discredit themselves in the eyes of their electorates because of their almost inevitable inability to deliver all that they have promised. On the other hand, if they give up most of their traditional pretensions, more and more people in their electorates may begin to look elsewhere for satisfaction of their material needs and aspirations. In these circumstances both supra-national and sub-national levels of political authority could begin to come more into their own, while the appeal of self-help in the private and voluntary sectors is already growing fastest of all.

This growing gap between the ambitious objectives of nearly all modern Governments and their rather modest and often disappointing achievements at the end of their period in office has certainly harmed the reputation of Parliamentary democracy in the eyes of many people. In Britain, as in many other countries, it has undermined public faith in national political institutions from the Monarchy to the political parties to the judicial system. Appropriate remedies are likely to be difficult to find and even more difficult to put into practice. It seems that institutional reform will increasingly play a significant part in the remedies proposed and that broadly based campaigns for electoral reform and the more frequent use of referenda will figure prominently in the future.

20.4 Signposts to the future

With the arrival of the new millennium, it is likely that there will be a number of unresolved issues which will influence the shape and nature of British politics. Among the key questions are whether there is scope for significant change in a national political system which is characterised by such ingrained conservatism; and whether, against a background of disappointed expectations, it will be possible to gain and retain public consent for the actions of any Government.

The scope for change

It is a paradox that although successive Governments in Britain since 1945 have sought to make a radical mark upon national performance and public attitudes, there have been relatively few changes of lasting significance which have been brought about by Governments. This may be explained by the fact that Britain is a very conservative (with a small 'c') country and by the fact that any Government has only limited means at its disposal with which to reshape society. Essentially, Governments can seek to act in one or more of the following ways: they can introduce new policies; they can create, reform or abolish institutions; and they can seek to modify or transform public attitudes. As we have observed during the course of this book, successive Governments have used some or all of these instruments in their quest for achievement.

In the 1950s and early 1960s successive Governments relied mostly on fairly minor policy adjustments within a well-defined and broadly accepted political consensus which had been in place since the Second World War. In the later 1960s and the 1970s successive Governments concentrated more on trying to make institutional changes as the leading remedies for Britain's national problems. In the 1980s successive Thatcher Administrations attempted a radical programme of change which was akin to a cultural revolution of comparable ambition to that of the great radical Administrations of 1906 (Liberal) and 1945 (Labour). Great claims have been made for the positive impact of this Thatcherite crusade and indeed its ideological legacy is still very much in evidence in attenuated form in each of the three main parties. Yet a sober verdict upon the Thatcher years (1979–90) must be that while a sizeable minority of the British population learned to exploit the opportunities of the new economic liberalism unleashed by the Conservatives at that time, the vast majority of the British people seemed unwilling or unable to make the attitudinal step-changes that were expected of them. This conclusion was reinforced by the experience of John Major's time at 10 Downing Street when the most striking characteristics of Government policy were caution, nostalgia, and pragmatism, and the British people seem to have returned at least in part to attitudes of insularity, resentment and insecurity.

There are various plausible explanations for this assessment. First, the accumulated evidence seems to suggest that the radical instinct does not come naturally or remain very long with most British people who invariably prefer an approach to life which is less strenuous and more comforting. Secondly, when a determined political minority – such as the Thatcherite radicals – manages to establish a temporary ascendancy in Britain, it usually sows the seeds of its own destruction either by going unrealistically far in its chosen direction or by failing to recognise that the world has changed around it. When such developments occur, the conditions are created for the gradual acceptance of political alternatives which come to appear more attractive and more relevant to most people. Perhaps this is one of the reasons why the new Labour Government of Tony Blair has been so incredibly popular for so long in the eyes of the British people.

The importance of consent

Any modern British Government has to give a high priority to the gaining and retaining of public consent, if only because its absence or attenuation can fatally undermine the position of even the most powerful and determined Administration. Of course, in many cases the Government of the day can get by with no more than the tacit acquiescence of the general public. Yet for the assured fulfilment of policy, active consent is usually required and this implies satisfying a number of important conditions. *First*, it requires a well-informed and influential Parliament in which all MPs not in the Government can have real opportunities to influence policy and to scrutinise and control the Executive. *Secondly*, it requires genuine and extensive consultations with a wide range of interest groups representing the full gamut of sectional interests in modern British society. *Thirdly*, it requires a serious and responsible approach by the media to the discussion and interpretation of the political issues of the day –

something which seems almost impossible to achieve on a reliable and sustained basis. Even if all these conditions are met, the achievement of good government can still be vitiated by complicating factors in the private sector and in government at the European or global levels which increasingly constrain the actions of any national Government.

Thus if any British Government is to deal successfully with the leading problems of our time – for example, the endemic threat of inflation, the powerful effects of new technologies, or the far-reaching consequences of environmental pollution – there will always be a need for responsible and far-sighted leadership by politicians both in Government and in Opposition. In a world in which some things change very rapidly while other things seem to change hardly at all, such leadership will require policies which increase, rather than reduce, the chances of securing public consent. The general public, for its part, will need to recognise that many traditional attitudes and assumptions, which may be held very deeply, can obstruct rather than assist the emergence of new syntheses which are likely to be essential if appropriate and timely action is to be taken. Even on the charitable assumption that politicians and people manage to co-operate in such virtuous ways, it is not likely to be possible to avoid periodic bouts of public disappointment and distress in view of the intractable nature of the challenges which have to be faced.

20.5 Conclusion

It should be clear from this book that British Parliamentary democracy is neither easy to describe nor to explain. Although it is changing in certain respects all the time, in many other ways it remains the same. It is imbued with fascinating paradoxes and contradictions. While the political system allows for and even encourages strong Government, it is less good at legitimising the decisions which are actually taken. This is sometimes because the most controversial decisions are not founded upon a sufficiently broad basis of political consent at the time when they are taken. Yet more often it seems to have been a matter of willing the ends of policy, but not necessarily the means required to achieve them.

We can see that the political mould set during the Second World War was finally broken by Thatcherite radicalism in the 1980s. This in its turn helped to create the spirit of the late 1990s – now described as the 'Third Way' – which seems to be an interesting amalgam of Liberal market economics and Social collectivism. In the future, as in the past, politicians and public alike will need to strive for mutual understanding and accommodation without which political life is likely to disappoint nearly everyone. In such circumstances there can be no guarantee of success, but it should be possible for Parliamentary democracy not merely to survive but to prosper in a Britain which is more dependent than ever upon influences and events in the rest of Europe and the wider world.

Suggested questions

1   What is the essence of British Parliamentary democracy?
2   Is the British political system successful in gaining and retaining the consent of the people?

3 Have British politics been permanently altered by Britain's membership of the European Union?

Notes

1. See J.A. Schumpeter, *Capitalism, Socialism and Democracy*, 3rd edn (New York: Harper & Row, 1962), pp. 289–96.
2. See Q. Hailsham, *The Dilemma of Democracy* (London: Collins, 1978), pp. 280–1.

Further reading

Barker, R., *Political Legitimacy and the State* (Oxford: Clarendon Press, 1980).
Beetham, D., *The Legitimation of Power* (London: Macmillan, 1991).
Blair, T., *The Third Way: New Politics for the New Century* (London: Fabian Society, 1998).
Blundell, J. and Gosschalk, B., *Beyond Left and Right: The New Politics of Britain* (London: Institute of Economic Affairs, 1997).
Brittan, S., *The Role and Limits of Government* (London: Temple Smith, 1983).
Dahrendorf, R., *Life Chances* (London: Weidenfeld & Nicolson, 1979).
Giddens, A., 'After the Left's Paralysis', *New Statesman*, 1 May 1998, pp. 18–21.
Hailsham, Q., *The Dilemma of Democracy* (London: Collins, 1978).
Hirsch, F., *Social Limits to Growth* (London: Routledge & Kegan Paul, 1977).
Leadbeater, C., *Civic Spirit: The Big Idea For A New Political Era* (London: Demos, 1997).
Luard, E., *The Globalisation of Politics* (London: Macmillan, 1990).
Marquand, D., *The Unprincipled Society* (London: Fontana Press, 1988).
Marr, A., *Ruling Britannia: The Failure and Future of British Democracy* (London: Michael Joseph, 1995).
Miliband, R., *Capitalist Democracy in Britain* (London: Oxford University Press, 1984).
Schumpeter, J.A., *Capitalism, Socialism and* Democracy, 3rd edn (New York: Harper & Row, 1962).
Wright, T., *Who Wins Dares: New Labour – New Politics* (London: Fabian Society, 1997).

Names index

Subject index

civil service
administrative efficiency 356
advice/assistance for Ministers 339, 342
change in ethos 353
composition 339–41
contract relationships 365–6
control by bureaucratic hierarchy 355
control by Ministers 354–5
delaying power 146
Departmental staffing 322–3, 334
elitism 347
functions 342–4
integrity 347–8
judicial scrutiny 357
key dates 344
loyalty issues 348–50
need for new ideas 353
need for perspective 352
policy/administration 366–7
political impartiality 347
politicisation 513, 523 n3
pressure groups contacts 137–8
public interest 350
as representatives of Ministers 343
strengths and weaknesses 346–8
support for Cabinet 292, 295–300
support for central government 343
the unelected state 353
Whitehall conventions 345–6
see also Senior Civil Service
Civil Service Code 351
Civil Service Management Code 350
Civil Service White Paper (1994) 367, 368
Civil War (1642–49) 213
class distinctions, in British society 6
Classic *FM* (radio service) 156
Clean Air Act (1956) 143
Coal and Steel Community see European
Coal and Steel Community
Coalition Government 1940 233 n8
Code of Practice (information requests) 448
cohort theory 184
collective representation, value 129
colonial constitutions, royal prerogative 223
Comité d'Organisations de Producteurs
Agricoles (COPA) 491
Commission for Racial Equality 445
Commission on Urban Priority Areas 193
Committee on Public Corporation 392
Committee on Standards in Public Life see
Nolan Committee
Committee of Vice-Chancellors and
Principals (CVCP) 145
Committees of Inquiry 380–1
Common Agricultural Policy (CAP) 139,
476

Common Fisheries Policy 480
Common Law, as basis for judgement 435
Commonwealth, development 472
Communist Party of Great Britain 103
Community Care Act (1992) 416
Community Charge (Poll Tax) 30, 185,
189, 191, 421, 533
Community method 491
Competing for Quality programme 365
Competition Act (1980) 392
Competition Bill (1997) 251
compulsory competitive tendering (CCT)
418
Confederation of British Industry (CBI)
130, 132, 136, 139
consensus politics 9–13
post-Thatcherite 202
postwar 200–1, 513–15, 529
Conservation Society 143
Conservative Administrations 29–30
Conservative Party
1922 Committee 114
attitude to Europe 16, 472
Cabinet resignations 310–11
candidate selection 121, 123
class voting 81
comparison with Labour 115–16
Conservative Policy Forum (CPF) 112
current policies 96–7
fund-raising 106–8, 118
Hague reforms 112–13
House of Lords reform proposals 254–5
leadership 114–15
membership 106, 119
organisation 112–15
policy making 105–6, 504–8
traditional principles 96–7
Conservative Policy Forum 255
constitution
characteristics 20–22
classic liberal view/elitist 23
empirical view 25–6
governmental view 24
reform 12, 27–32, 461–2
Constitution Unit 30, 33 n13, 145
Constitutional Commission (on House of
Lords) 255
Consultative Council on Local Government
Finance 420
Consumer Councils 392
Consumers' Association 136, 388
continuity, historical 3–4
contracting-out policy 365–6
conventions, importance 22
copyright laws 164
Corn Laws, repeal 236

increase in   30, 355
see also Next Steps Agencies
experience, effect on voting behaviour   184
extra-governmental organisations (EGOs)
   375–6

Factortame case   442, 480
'fair comment' defence   450
Faith in the City (report)   193
Falklands conflict 1982   189, 223, 267, 309,
   311, 329, 332, 349, 513
Family Expenditure Survey   193
Family Health Service Authorities   382
family influence, on voting behaviour   184
Fancy Dress Party   104
Finance Bill, proposed procedure changes
   283
Finance Bill (1909)   237
Finance Bill (1994)   146
finance capital, importance   494
Financial Management Initiative   365
Financial Services Authority   394
financial transactions, effect of European
   Union   494–5
Firearms (Amendment) Bill (1997)   250
First Reading Stage, Bill procedure   276–7
first-past-the-post electoral system   43–5
floaters, voting pattern   62
focus groups   192
foreign donations, to political parties   108
fox-hunting, suggested ban   192
freedom of expression   450–1
   civil service   452
   police and armed services   452
   registered charities   452
freedom of information   164–5
freedoms, citizens rights   444
French Merchant Seamen case   480
Friends of the Earth   144, 147
front-benchers   261–2
fuel, VAT levy   195
fund holders, NHS   382
fund-raising, political parties   106
Funding Agency for Schools   428

GCHQ, union membership removal   223–4
gender differences, in voting behaviour   64
General Election (1983)   62, 63, 64, 65, 66,
   74
General Election (1987)   59, 62, 64, 65, 68,
   74
General Election (1992)   62, 63, 64, 65, 66,
   68, 74, 75
General Election (1997)
   age-related voting   65
   floating voters   62, 82

geographical variations   66–7
House of Commons composition
   259–60
party policies   59, 75, 76, 100–1
voting share by class   63, 69
General Elections   52, 187–8
   class voting   63–4, 80–1
   effect on public opinion   187
   mandate concept   187–8
   present system   39–40, 51–2
   timing   36
geographical variations, in voting behaviour
   65–6
Glasgow Media Group   169, 170
Glorious Revolution (1689)   214
Good Friday Agreement, Northern Ireland
   see Northern Ireland
Government
   central control   423–4
   diminished scope   533–4
   performance influence on voting behaviour
      72–3
   powers   265–6
   problems   333–5
   role   24–6
   structure   408
   see also central government; local
      government
Government Data Network   448
Government Departments
   functions   323–6
   inter-departmental co-ordination   314–15,
      326
   organisation changes   319–20
   policy   334
   Royal prerogative   223
   structure and work   320–3
Government of Ireland Act (1914)   243
Government Offices for the Regions (GORs)
   402
Government of Wales Act (1998)   400–1
Grant Maintained Schools   379
Great Reform Act (1832)   35
Greater London, referendum   28, 190,
   408
Greater London Authority   190, 406–7,
   415
Greater London Authority (Referendum) Bill
   (1997)   250
Greater London Council, abolition   30, 250,
   386, 404
Green Party   103
Greenpeace   144
group theory   129
'guillotine' procedural device   277
gun control legislation   195

National Freight Corporation   388
National Front   103
National Government
   economic crisis management   187
   tariff reform   216, 330
National Health Service Act (1946)   132
National Health Service Act (1948)   382
National Health Service (NHS)
   reform plans   136, 146, 382–3
   Trusts   376, 382, 428
National Insurance Advisory Committee
   381
National Insurance Tribunals   456
National Liberal Federation   91
National Party List System   48
National Referendum Campaign   141
National Society for Clean Air   143
National Trust   147
National Union of Conservative Associations
   91
National Union of Mineworkers (NUM)
   136, 186, 187, 196, 206 n37
National Union of Teachers (NUT)   146,
   196
nationalisation see public corporations
nationalist parties   102
Natural Law Party   104
Neighbourhood Law Centres   441
Neill Inquiry   126 n9
New Labour   9, 79, 81, 70, 186, 516
newspapers see press
Next Steps Agencies   328, 366
   Chief Executives   366
NHS Outposts   382
NHS Trusts   376, 379, 428
'Nimby' groups   131
Nolan Committee   31, 108, 264, 380
non-departmental public bodies (NDPBs)
   375–9
non-Metropolitan District Councils, functions
   418
Norman Conquest   212
North Atlantic Treaty Organization   472
North-South Ministerial Council, Northern
   Ireland   401
Northcote-Trevelyan Report   340, 343, 355
Northern Ireland
   Belfast Agreement   7, 103, 401
   constitution   30–1
   devolved government   401
   emergency powers   447–8
   Good Friday Agreement   31
   local government   408–9
   peace process   7, 31, 103, 308, 533
   political parties   102–3
   referendum   28, 190

Northern Ireland Assembly   61, 398, 401,
   409–10
Northern Ireland (Emergency Provisions) Act
   448
Northern Ireland Office   401, 409
Nuffield Election Studies   86 n9

Office of Fair Trading   394
Office of Public Service   322
Office of Standards in Education (OFSTED)
   425
Official Raving Loony Party   104
Official Secrets Act (1911)   163, 503
Official Secrets Act (1989)   163, 179 n14,
   448
'Ombudsman'   357, 448, 457–9
   1967 Act   457–8
   European   446, 459
   specific appointments   458
One Member One Vote (OMOV) principle
   94
Operation Countryman   453
opinion polls, effect on public opinion
   197
Opposition parties, increased support for
   519–20
Orgreave Coke Plant incident   438
Osborne case   443
Outer Circle Policy Unit   164

pardon, Royal prerogative   222
Paris Accords (1955)   472
Paris Treaty   481
Parliament
   accountability   330–2
   beginnings   213–15
   culture   268–9
   dissolution   217–19
   effectiveness   50–1
   hung   216–17, 218
   increased decision-making role   521–2
   reform   281–5
   role   25–6, 27
   supremacy principle   434, 443, 482
   see also Scottish Parliament
Parliament Act (1911)   21, 25, 36, 188, 219,
   220, 237, 238, 243, 252, 278
Parliament Act (1949)   238, 243, 278
Parliament (No.2) Bill (1968)   239, 252
Parliamentary Bills   270–3, 511
Parliamentary Boundary Commissions
   244
Parliamentary Commissioner for
   Administration see 'Ombudsman'
Parliamentary Commissioner for Standards
   264

voting system   40–3

Wales
  Assembly *see* Welsh Assembly
  bond with England   4
  devolution referendum   28, 190
  devolved government   400–1
  local government   408
Wales Act (1978)   399
War Crimes Act (1991)   243
War Damage Act (1965)   443
Water Authorities   382
Welsh Assembly   397–8, 400–1, 402
Welsh Church Act (1914)   243
Welsh Nationalist Party *see Plaid Cymru*
Western European Union   472
Westland Affair   185, 280, 311, 337 n7
Whig group   91
Whips
  role   261, 262
  typical papers   270–4

Whitehall
  administrative control   381
  departments composition   339
  issue of Statutory Instruments   424
  structural change   521
  support for Cabinet   295, 298–9
Widdicombe Committee (1985)   413, 414
Wilson Administrations   9, 252, 473
Wilson Committee   380
'Winter of Discontent'   81, 266, 307
Witan   212
Woolf Report   440
Workers' Revolutionary Party   103
working class, Conservative voting   81

young offenders, fast track system   437
'Your Right to Know' (White Paper)   165,
  449

zero tolerance approach   437
Zimbabwe Independence Act (1980)   223